Medical and
Social Aspects of
Alcohol Abuse

Medical and Social Aspects of Alcohol Abuse

Edited by

BORIS TABAKOFF

Alcohol Drug Abuse Research and Training Program
University of Illinois at the Medical Center and
Westside Veterans Administration Medical Center
Chicago, Illinois

PATRICIA B. SUTKER

Veterans Administration Medical Center and
Tulane University School of Medicine
New Orleans, Lousiana

and

CARRIE L. RANDALL

Veterans Administration Medical Center
Charleston, South Carolina

PLENUM PRESS • NEW YORK AND LONDON

Library of Congress Cataloging in Publication Data

Main entry under title:

Medical and social aspects of alcohol abuse.

Includes bibliographical references and index.
1. Alcoholism. 2. Alcohol — Physiological aspects. I. Tabakoff, Boris, date-
II. Sutker, Patricia B. III. Randall, Carrie L., date-   . [DNLM: 1. Alcohol,
Ethyl. 2. Alcoholism. WM 274 M4875]
RC565.M346 1983   616.86'1   83-4786
ISBN 0-306-41221-7

© 1983 Plenum Press, New York
A Division of Plenum Publishing Corporation
233 Spring Street, New York, N.Y. 10013

Printed in the United States of America

Contributors

ERNEST L. ABEL • Research Institute on Alcoholism, 1021 Main Street, Buffalo, New York

GLENN R. CADDY • Department of Psychology, Nova University, Fort Lauderdale, Florida

R. LORRAINE COLLINS • Department of Psychology, State University of New York at Stony Brook, Stony Brook, New York

RICHARD A. DEITRICH • Alcohol Research Center, Department of Pharmacology, University of Colorado Medical Center, Denver, Colorado

GERHARD FREUND • Veterans Administration Medical Center and Departments of Medicine and Neuroscience, College of Medicine, University of Florida, Gainesville, Florida

WALTER A. HUNT • Behavioral Sciences Department, Armed Forces Radiobiology Research Institute, Bethesda, Maryland

TING-KAI LI • Departments of Medicine and Biochemistry, Indiana University School of Medicine, and Veterans Administration Medical Center, Indianapolis, Indiana

G. ALAN MARLATT • Department of Psychology, University of Washington, Seattle, Washington

GARY McCLURE • Department of Psychology, Georgia Southern College, Statesboro, Georgia

BARBARA S. McCRADY • Brown University and Butler Hospital, Providence, Rhode Island

PETER M. MILLER • Sea Pines Behavioral Institute, Sea Pines Plantation, Hilton Head Island, South Carolina

TED D. NIRENBERG • Psychological Services, Veterans Administration Medical Center, Providence, Rhode Island

DENNIS R. PETERSEN • Alcohol Research Center, School of Pharmacy, University of Colorado, Boulder, Colorado

CARRIE L. RANDALL • Research Services, Veterans Administration Medical Center, 109 Bee Street, Charleston, South Carolina

EDWARD P. RILEY • Department of Psychology, State University of New York at Albany, Albany, New York

JEFFREY ROTHSTEIN • Department of Physiology and Biophysics, University of Illinois at the Medical Center, Chicago, Illinois

MARC A. SCHUCKIT • Alcohol Treatment Program, Veterans Administration Medical Center, 3350 La Jolla Village Drive, San Diego, California, and Department of Psychiatry, University of California, San Diego, California

KENNETH J. SHER • Department of Psychology, University of Missouri, Columbia, Missouri

BORIS TABAKOFF • Westside Veterans Administration Medical Center, Chicago, Illinois, and Alcohol and Drug Abuse Research and Training Program, Department of Physiology and Biophysics, University of Illinois at the Medical Center, Chicago, Illinois

DAVID H. VAN THIEL • Department of Medicine, Division of Gastroenterology, University of Pittsburgh School of Medicine, Pittsburgh, Pennsylvania

Preface

Alcohol use affects, either directly or indirectly, nearly all facets of Western civilization. Eastern cultures are also not exempt from the influence of alcohol, and the present decade has been a time of increased alcohol use in all parts of the world. The problems of alcohol abuse and alcoholism are of concern to a variety of professionals in the biomedical and psychosocial health sciences, and—although the alcohol research literature contains much information on the relationships between alcohol ingestion and physiological, neurochemical, pharmacologic, genetic, environmental, and psychological effects in humans and in subhuman species—there is at the present time no advanced textbook that integrates the available information for use by both students and professionals.

The writing of *Medical and Social Aspects of Alcohol Abuse* constitutes an attempt to create a scholarly reference and resource for students, researchers, practicing clinicians, and paraprofessionals who wish to understand the complex interplay of factors related to acute and chronic alcohol intoxication, the effects of alcohol on body functions, and treatment approaches to alcohol abusers and alcoholics.

The book includes an introductory section that summarizes the history of alcohol production and use and provides definitions of alcohol abuse, problem drinking, and alcoholism. The following chapters discuss the neurochemical and neuropharmacologic effects of acute and chronic alcohol intoxication and issues related to the genetic basis of alcoholism, alcohol metabolism, pathological consequences of alcohol abuse, the phenomena of alcohol tolerance and dependence, and the effects of prenatal alcohol exposure on the fetus. Problems arising from alcohol's interactions with other drugs and issues related to the prevention and treatment of alcoholism are extensively covered.

In summary, we hope that this book will represent an important component of the education and training of a variety of professionals in the basic and clinical sciences. The content should enable such individuals to better understand the factors leading to alcohol abuse and the consequences of such abuse, and it should stimulate thought regarding directions for continued research and clinical efforts.

Boris Tabakoff
Patricia B. Sutker
Carrie L. Randall

Contents

Chapter 3
**The Absorption, Distribution, and Metabolism of Ethanol and Its
Effects on Nutrition and Hepatic Function** 47
TING-KAI LI

Chapter 4
**Effects of Ethanol upon Organ Systems Other than the Central
Nervous System** 79
DAVID H. VAN THIEL

Chapter 5
Ethanol and the Central Nervous System 133
WALTER A. HUNT

Chapter 6
Neurologic Diseases Associated with Chronic Alcohol Abuse ....
GERHARD FREUND

Chapter 9
Interaction of Ethanol with Other Drugs 247
RICHARD A. DEITRICH and DENNIS R. PETERSEN

Chapter 10
**Psychological Correlates and Explantions of Alcohol
Use and Abuse** 273
R. LORRAINE COLLINS and G. ALAN MARLATT

Chapter 11
**Alcoholism Treatment Approaches: Patient Variables, Treatment
Variables** 309
Barbara S. McCrady and Kenneth J. Sher

Chapter 12
Prevention of Alcohol Abuse 375
Peter M. Miller, Ted D. Nirenberg, and Gary McClure

Alcohol Use and Abuse

Historical Perspective and Present Trends

GLENN R. CADDY

Those engaged in scientific pursuits only occasionally cast themselves in the role of social activists; yet, as Koestler (1968) so clearly articulated, the contributions made by scientists and thinkers on the leading edge of a conceptual development typically have profound social and political implications. The social context, however, must be ready to accept the emerging perspectives or social acceptance will not occur (see also Kuhn, 1970).

Our history is replete with so-called revolutions dealing with how we see ourselves and the world around us. Sometimes these revolutions truly represent advances in our thinking. Often though, particularly when empirical data are insufficient to permit the convincing acceptance of a specific conceptual perspective, the changes that occur appear little more than the recycling of ideas rather than the emergence of a new conceptual orientation. Perhaps nowhere is this point better illustrated than in the lore and literature on alcohol, where concepts of alcohol use and dependence have been recycled over the centuries and where scholars and lay people alike have defined alcohol-related problems in various ways, depending upon the time, the social customs, and their personal inclinations.

GLENN R. CADDY • Department of Psychology, Nova University, Fort Lauderdale, Florida 33314.

1. ALCOHOL USE IN HISTORICAL PERSPECTIVE

The use of psychoactive substances, alcohol especially, has been described in many societies since the beginning of recorded history (see the review by Austin, 1978). Forbes (1958) reviewed evidence indicating that wine had been used in Mesopotamia as early as 3000 B.C.; Keller (1958) has described a 4,000-year-old clay table found at Nippur, on which are written in Sumerian cuneiform the directions for making various remedies with beer as the solvent; and McKinlay (1948, 1949) has documented drinking practices among the ancient Greeks and Romans as well as other peoples of antiquity. The records from these ancient times were commonly filled with praise for the goodness and beneficence of the potions that were derived from the various wines and beers. Thus, Lönnrot (1963) recalled that the poet of the Finnish epic *Kalevala* sang of the "good beer" that "set women to laughing, put men in good humor, and the righteous of making merry," and Mandelbaum (1965) has noted that anthropological studies of cultural attitudes toward alcohol indicate a full range of meaning from sacred to profane. It has been used as an energizer, a tranquilizer, a superego solvent, a sacred symbol, a medicine, a food, a social leveler, a source of subjective feelings of power, and for a host of other social and symbolic functions (see also Heath, 1975).

Just as throughout recorded history alcohol has been praised, so too records attesting to its disabling effects and the existence of alcohol abuse have been available from early times: "Who hath woe? . . . who hath babbling? Who hath wounds, without cause? Who hath redness of eyes? They that tarry long at the wine" (Prov. 23:29–30). In fact, as early as 1700 B.C., the Code of Hammurabi detailed restrictions that were to be placed on the sale of wine and forbade riotous assembly in the houses of the wine merchants throughout Babylonia (Harper, 1904). By the end of the first century A.D., the Roman Emperor Domitian had ordered a decrease in vitriculture in order to promote temperance and stop the dedication of so much land to grape production (see Liebowitz, 1967; Blum & Associates, 1969).*

The customs and the consequences of alcohol use throughout antiquity and into classical times have been summarized by Keller (1976) in the following manner:

> There was social and integrative public drinking, and private drinking for pleasure which was moderate and not apparently harmful. There was ceremonial and religious and medicinal drinking. In short, drinking was widely practiced nearly everywhere in the world and drink was appreciated as a good, often as a particularly divine blessing, so recognized in the Old and New Testment of the religions that have powerfully influenced our culture. There was also harmful over drinking. It was common enough to attract the repeated condemnation of potentates and prophets, philosophers and physicians. It was alcoholism. (p. 9)

*Domitian's edict was repealed around A.D. 280 largely because it proved unenforceable (see Baird, 1943–1944).

There is little documentation of the drinking practices in western society during the Middle Ages. The evidence that is available, however, suggests that there may not have been all that much excessive alcohol use in Europe during the period because drunkenness was regarded as a common sin and, like gluttony, was condemned. The discovery of distillation in about the 10th century provided a technology that in future centuries would bring about a major change in the use of alcohol. Up to the end of the Middle Ages, however, distilled spirits were costly; they were used mainly for medicinal rather than recreational purposes. Indeed, the common name for spirits was *aqua vitae* ("water of life").

With the Renaissance, a more secular world emerged; to at least some degree, many of the previous social and religious controls on human conduct were loosening. In the later Renaissance period in England, for example, beer drinking began to be seen as one of the distinguishing virtues of the English and excessive drinking became commonplace. In fact, by 1606 the situation had deteriorated to such a degree that Parliament passed an Act to Repress the Odious and Loathsome Sin of Drunkenness. This act, which remained in effect until 1872, is a landmark in the history of liquor control in England, for it represented one of the first attempts to legislate moderation. The act had little effect, however, for after the Elizabethan period a dramatic increase in the rate of production and consumption of distilled spirits continued. This pattern did not alter until the "gin epidemics" of the mid-18th century (Coffey, 1966). It was only after these epidemics of drunkenness and crime that strong legislative action was taken to bolster retail controls, thereby bringing about at least some reform to the supply side of the demand–supply relationship.

While no such gin epidemic beset colonial America, nevertheless drinking practices in the colonies reflected their European origins. Thus, early New Englanders consumed ale and beer, fermented cider, perry, and cider brandy or applejack (Baron, 1962). Wines like canary, claret, sack, and sack-possett were enjoyed, and liquors such as brandy, rum, whiskey, creams and elixirs, ratafias, and spirituous waters were taken (Brown, 1966). Following English precedent, the colonists established taverns and inns to provide refreshment, accommodate travelers, and facilitate the transaction of business. The consumption of liquor was not only integrated into the pattern of family life but also figured prominently in colonial trade and in the local economy, especially revenue collection. Further, contrary to the stereotype, the Puritans in these colonies neither detested or prohibited alcohol use. To be sure, drunkards were reproached for errant drinking, for damaging themselves, for denying the power of godliness, and for wasting time, but they were seen as sinners to be redeemed rather than as people of little inherent worth. Even during the late 18th century—with the exception of men like John Wesley, who began in 1773 to call for a prohibition against distilling, and Benjamin Rush, who authored an "Inquiry into the Effects of Ardent Spirits on the Human Mind and Body" (1785)—there was no significant movement reflecting concern throughout the society about the consequences of drinking. In fact, between 1790 and 1830

Americans seemed to participate in a veritable alcoholic binge, with the per capita consumption of spirits rising to approximately 2.5 gal annually (Cherrington, 1920; see also Winkler, 1968). An additional perspective on the apparent (tax-based) consumption of all alcoholic beverages by the American population of the period is provided by Keller and Gurioli (1976) who report that between 1790 and 1830 the average per capita adult absolute alcohol consumption figure rose from 5.8 to 7.1 gal. Rorabaugh (1976) commented on the forces contributing to this binge in the following terms:

> At that time Americans retained a belief that liquor was healthful, nutritious, stim-ulating and relaxing. The predisposition to drink meshed with a rising abundance of cheap whiskey as settlers planted fertile grain lands in the midwest. Amid a grain glut, the price of whiskey fell to 25 cents a gallon, less than wine, beer, coffee, tea or milk. Then, too, the preference for strong drink reflected the need to wash down poorly cooked, greasy, salty and sometimes rancid food. Americans, however, also drank to enjoy the effect. Intoxication met certain psychological and social needs in a period of economic and social dislocation. (pp. 361–362)

There were very few social controls in the environment of the hard-drinking cowboy, miner, Indian fighter, or riverboating westerner. And in the east during the period that Bacon (1967) terms the preclassic temperance era, alcohol was seen as a problem to the extent that it could sometimes be used excessively. It was social irresponsibility and drunkenness that were frowned upon, not alcohol or its use. Further, since the society was founded in the "rational man" perspective, efforts to remediate excessive drinking were limited to the use of moral suasion designed to encourage socially responsible behavior. Reduction in the availability and visi-bility of the "heaviest drink," distilled spirits, was also considered to be of value.

[By the 1830s however, the American social perspective regarding alcohol and its use began to change. Groups like the New England Federalist elite and the Congregationalists and Presbyterians began to reflect grave concern about the spread of drunkenness and religious irreverence.] It was not long thereafter that a new kind of temperance movement began to emerge (Gusfield, 1963). In the clas-sic era of the American Temperance Movement (Bacon, 1967), alcohol came to be seen as a creation of Beelzebub, and a 1,500-year position of the Christian Church was subtly reversed. As this movement grew, so it left behind much of its earlier orientation regarding reform through persuasion and education; by 1880 it had become coercive and prohibitionistic.

By the turn of the century there was a strong and growing antialcohol sen-timent throughout much of the country. The consequences of chronic overindul-gence and the development of alcohol dependence had become widely understood as a moral failing. The elixir which Increase Mather had described in 1673 as "a creature of God" had become an agent of Satan, capable of destroying health and intellect and, in Lyman Beecher's terms, "bringing upon the souls of men ever-lasting destruction" (Winkler, 1972). Drinkers, it was asserted, needed the strong push of potentially punishing controls to facilitate their rationality, and government power was to be the tool employed to provide just such a push.* Interestingly, even by the time the temperance movement had established some of its early momentum, the consumption of alcohol in the United States had begun to wane. By 1840, for example, the apparent absolute alcohol consumption of the average drinker had dropped to 3.1 gal. By 1919 it had dropped further, to a mean of 1.9 gal (Keller & Gurioli, 1976).

Despite these data, prohibitionistic sentiment, shaped by strong, capable political leadership through the Anti-Saloon League, succeeded eventually in engineering the ratification of the Eighteenth Amendment to the Constitution, and, in 1919, prohibition became a reality. For Keller (1976), the "fantastic consequence of prohibition" was not that there was a temporary shortage of alcohol or that there was a temporary reduction in arrests for drunkenness. Rather, Keller's amazement came from his observations that "people acted as if there would be no more alcohol problems," a premise that totally disregarded all historic precedent.

1.1. Recent Trends in Alcohol Consumption

The noble experiment of prohibition was repealed in 1933 because it had failed and because it proved unenforceable. This repeal signaled a shift in the status of various groups in the American culture. As Willner (1975) has commented: "The new virtues were not hard work and self-mastery, but rather, the ability to get along with others, tolerance and expression of solidarity" (p. 133).

The drinking habits of the new emerging middle class were permissive and, in many instances, those who continued to view the drinking of alcohol in moral terms found themselves alienated from the mainstream of society and even became the objects of a degree of public scorn.

Within this new social climate Americans increased their drinking quite markedly. This increase was particularly great in the period 1950–1970, during which an increasing affluence and a relative decrease in the price of alcoholic beverages permitted people to divert more of their income to the purchase of luxuries than had been possible previously. In fact, the taxed per capita absolute alcohol consumption of American drinkers (age 14 and over) increased from 0.97 gal in 1934 to 2.0 gal in 1965 and to 2.68 gal in 1976 (Keller & Gurioli, 1976). Perhaps even more significant, however, is the trend indicated by the data showing that in 1940 there were 40 million drinkers in the United States out of a population of 135 million (30%), of whom an estimated 2.4 million (2%) were intemperate users (Haggard & Jellinek, 1942). By the early seventies, however, there were some

---

*Much of the political influence of the temperance movement came from the fact that the Women's Christian Temperance Movement, and other groups, managed to link the temperance (prohibition) movement to status-enhancing middle-class morality and issues of self-improvement. For these reasons these groups were particularly successful.

145 million drinkers out of a population of 210 million (68%), of which an estimated 9% exhibited serious drinking problems (Rosenberg, 1971).

As Straus (1976) commented regarding the period 1940–1970, it is abun-
dantly clear that prevalence statistics of users and misusers of alcohol were neither
decreasing nor standing still despite thirty years devoted to combating stigma,
modifying misconceptions, replacing fear tactics with "enlightened" education,
training personnel, developing numerous rehabilitation approaches, intensifying
research activity, and mobilizing significant community, state, and federal
programs.

It may be significant, however, that there appears to have been little, if any,
increase in per capita absolute alcohol consumption in the United States during
the seventies (Noble, 1978). Nevertheless, such an observation provides little perspective on the possibility of subcultural or age- or sex-related drinking differences
and developments in certain sectors of the society.* For example, there is some
evidence suggesting that alcohol use by women has continued to rise during the
early 1970s, and with this increase has come an increase in the extent of problem
drinking in women (Gomberg, 1976; United States Senate, 1976).

Turning now briefly to the international scene, the trends that have characterized the American experience have also been played out, to at least some degree,
in many other countries. Over the past century, for example, we have seen the
introduction of prohibition in both Finland and Sweden, with movements seeking
such an approach in large segments of other industrialized countries as well. Further, as the data compiled by Sulkunen (1976) indicate that, just as in the United
States, there has been a trough in the per capita alcohol consumption statistics for
the period 1920–1940 in many western countries, with an appreciable and consistent increase in apparent alcohol consumption thereafter. Indeed, the average
increase in the apparent alcohol consumption across 21 of the major industrialized
countries for the period 1955–1974 was 56% with only two countries, France and
Israel, not reflecting an increase in consumption (computed from the data compiled by Keller & Gurioli, 1976). Further, in recent years the rates of per capita
alcohol consumption of countries like Denmark, Finland, West Germany, Ireland,
Canada, and the Netherlands have shown average increases in excess of 2% per
annum (Keller, 1974).

Even more provocative is the rate of growth of alcohol consumption in the
countries that have not had a tradition of significant alcohol use. In Japan, for
example, between 1955 and 1974, alcohol consumption increased by 460%,
roughly paralleling the rate of growth of the per capita real national gross expenditure. While as little as 20 years ago alcoholism was virtually unknown in Japan,

---

*Cahalan (1970, 1978) and Cahalan and Room (1974) provide some particularly interesting data
regarding these matters, but a review of these issues is beyond the scope of this chapter.

today it is recognized as a serious, growing problem, with some 2.1 million Japanese being diagnosed as alcoholics. Although social and cultural constraints in Japan operate against what may be termed "loss of control" or disinhibited behavior, today approximately 67% of people in the Tokyo area drink at least occasionally. This figure is all the more important because of the heavy loading of western-style beverage preferences in the younger age groups and the increasing number of young women who now are beginning to drink alcohol (Leisure Development Center Report, 1977). Table 1 presents both the per capita consumption of alcoholic beverages and the rate of change of this statistic across a number of countries during the period 1950–1972.

Perhaps most disconcerting of all is the observation that the greatest rate of growth in world alcohol production and consumption has not yet occurred. There is disturbing evidence that the populations of the so-called third-world countries are now becoming increasingly involved with the consumption of alcohol as well as its attendant problems (WHO, 1978). These developing countries are particularly vulnerable to the consequences of increased alcohol consumption, for with rapid growth inevitably come changes in the society and the culture that, in turn, tend to loosen the traditional forms of control over the individual. Additionally, as these countries increasingly become markets, inevitably the highly efficient multinational alcohol manufacturers will seek to address these new markets, and as these corporations supplant the traditional local methods of brewing and distilling, the supply of alcohol to these countries will vastly increase. The likelihood of massive increases in both alcohol consumption and alcohol-related problems in third-world countries becomes all the more distressing when it is recognized that at present some 80% of the world's entire beverage alcohol supply is being consumed by slightly less than 25% of its population.

Sulkunen (1976) has summarized his observations regarding international trends in the level of alcohol consumption and in beverage structure in the following terms:

> A rise in the consumption level is a global phenomenon insofar as it can be judged in the light of available statistical data. The rise has been steepest in countries where the level of consumption was low to begin with and particularly in those countries in which hard liquor has accounted for a high proportion of the total consumption of alcohol. Differing rates of growth in consumption have brought the consumption levels closer together (quantitative homogenization). A tendency toward uniformity has taken place in the structure of consumption in the sense that spirits, beer, and wine-drinking nations are beginning to resemble each other more and more in their typical consumption behavior (qualitative homogenization). The qualitative homogenization of drinking patterns has resulted from the adoption of new consumption habits ... not at the expense of but in addition to traditional habits. In many cases, especially in wine and beer countries, the increase in the consumption of traditional types of beverages has had the greatest effect on the level of total consumption. (pp. 272–273)

Table 1. Changes in Consumption of 100% Alcohol (Liters per
Capita) between 1950 and 1977[a]

Country[b]	Period	Volume Changed	Percentage Changed
Afganistan	70–72	0.0–0.01	0
Argentina	50–77	9.0–11.1	+ 23.3
Australia	50–77	5.4–9.7	+ 51.6
Austria	50–77	5.4–11.2	+ 107.4
Belgium	50–77	6.6–10.2	+ 54.5
Brazil	54–72	0.2–0.7	+ 250.0
Bulgaria	54–77	1.1–6.7	+ 509.0
Canada	50–77	4.9–9.0	+ 83.7
Chile	55–77	8.3–7.0	− 15.7
Columbia	54–72	1.9–1.7	− 10.5
Cuba	50–77	2.0–2.5	+ 25.0
Cypress	50–77	3.1–3.8	+ 22.5
Czechoslovakia	50–77	4.9–9.2	+ 87.8
Denmark	50–77	4.0–8.9	+ 123.0
Egypt	63–72	0.0–0.1	0
Finland	50–77	2.2–6.4	+ 190.0
France	50–77	17.6–16.4	− 6.8
Gambia	58–72	0.2–0.2	0
German Dem. Rep.	50–77	1.9–12.4	+ 553.0
German Fed. Rep.	50–77	3.6–8.5	+ 136.0
Greece	54–77	0.2–5.7	+2750.0
Hungary	50–77	4.8–11.2	+ 133.0
Iceland	51–77	1.1–3.9	+ 225.0
Ireland	50–77	3.4–7.7	+ 126.0
Italy	50–77	9.2–12.1	+ 31.5

(continued)

2. ALCOHOL CONSUMPTION AND ALCOHOL PROBLEMS

There is little question but that there appears a close relationship between a country's per capita alcohol consumption and the proportion of its population using alcohol beverages. Of more significance, however, is the fact that the higher the per capita alcohol consumption in a country, the higher the proportion of its people who are exposed to the risk of developing alcohol-related problems and the higher the incidence of those problems (de Lint & Schmidt, 1971). It has been demonstrated for a variety of populations that the distribution of consumption levels closely approximates a logarithmic normal curve (Ledermann, 1956, 1964; de Lint & Schmidt, 1968; Skog, 1971). Such a curve shows a small percentage of the consuming public to be drinking the greatest amount of the alcohol consumed, regardless of the average level of consumption in the society. There is evidence throughout much of the world indicating that at least 10% of the population in

Table 1. (Continued)

Country[b]	Period	Volume Changed	Percentage Changed
Japan	56–77	0.3–5.1	+1600.0
Kuwait	69–72	0.0–0.0	0
Luxembourg	50–77	9.4–14.04	+ 53.2
Mexico	54–72	1.1–2.5	+ 127.0
Netherlands	50–77	1.9–8.8	+ 363.0
New Zealand	50–77	5.6–9.5	+ 69.6
Norway	50–77	2.1–4.4	+ 110.0
Poland	50–77	3.1–8.6	+ 177.0
Portugal	52–77	12.9–14.0	+ 8.5
Romania	54–77	4.7–7.4	+ 57.4
Saudi Arabia	70–72	0.0–0.0	0
Spain	50–77	8.1–13.1	+ 61.7
Sweden	50–77	4.0–5.8	+ 45.0
Switzerland	50–77	6.6–10.4	+ 57.6
U.S.S.R.	56–77	0.3–6.1	+1933.0
United Kingdom	50–77	4.9–8.2	+ 67.3
United States	50–77	5.0–8.3	+ 66.0
Yugoslavia	52–77	2.7–8.5	+ 215.0

[a]These data were collated from tables provided by Sulkunen (1976) and from the Swedish Council for Information on Alcohol and Other Drugs (Centralforbundet for alkohol-och narkotikaupplysining, Stockholm, 1978, 1979).
[b]Comparisons between countries must be treated with caution, especially when the time is not the same. Even a relatively short time (date) difference may alter substantially the apparent consumption figures. Also questionable is the use of the same population base (whether total population or over a particular age, etc.) for all countries, since the proportions of actual drinkers vary in different countries. Only the per capita consumption of actual drinkers would give a satisfactory comparison across countries, and typically this is not available.

most countries may be categorized as drinking heavily. Mäkelä (1971), for instance, observed that in 1968 some 10% of adult Finnish males drank 53% of all the alcohol consumed by their sex, while some 10% of the women drank as much as 72% of all the alcohol consumed by the female population. In similar vein, the first alcohol and health report (Rosenberg, 1971) indicated that some 12 % of people aged 21 and above in the United States (21% of the men and 5% of the women) could be characterized as drinking heavily (defined as drinking "nearly every day with five or more drinks per occasion at least once in awhile, or about once weekly with usually five or more drinks per occasion").

An interesting observation, and one of particular significance to our understanding of the relationship between per capita alcohol consumption and the identification of heavy drinkers in a country, has been made by Skog (1971). Following an analysis of survey material covering a number of different countries, Skog observed that the concentration of consumption in a country is all the greater the lower the average level of consumption. (Such an observation has intuitive appeal, of course, for the consumption of heavy drinkers must stay above some minimal level.) If, indeed, the concentration of alcohol consumption is great in those countries with relatively low overall consumption levels, the disparity between the "average consumer" and the regular drinker appears rather great, for the former drinks enough to become intoxicated only extremely rarely.

But what about alcohol problems? While it is reasonable to propose a relationship between drinking and alcohol-related problems, especially when the consumption statistics exceed some high value, at lower consumption levels the relationship is less clear. Nevertheless, drinking may still provoke significant difficulties. Plaut (1967) defines problem drinking as a repetitive use of beverage alcohol causing physical, psychological, or social harm to the drinker or to others; and Knupfer (1967) offers a similar though more general definition when she notes that "a problem—any problem—connected fairly closely with drinking constitutes a drinking problem" (p. 974). In most research examining drinking problems, many or all of the following problems have been considered: frequent intoxication, binge drinking, symptomatic drinking, psychological dependence, problems with spouse or relatives, problems with friends or neighbors, job problems, problems with police or accidents, health, financial problems, and belligerence associated with drinking (see, for example, Clark, 1966; Knupfer, 1967; Cahalan, 1970). In the United States, in particular, there have been a relatively large number of studies addressing the extent of problem drinking (see the review by Cahalan & Cisin, 1976). Data presented by Johnson, Armor, Polich, and Stambul (1977) are representative of these studies. These investigators reported the results of a survey conducted in June 1975 showing that of the males sampled, 57% reported no problems, 31% reported potential problems, and 13% regarded themselves as problem drinkers. The percentages for the females sampled were 73%, 21%, and 6% respectively. Combining both these subsamples, 63% of the drinkers reported no problems, 26% reported potential problems, and 10% regarded themselves as problem drinkers. Also, as in other studies, Johnson et al. reported the highest rates of problem drinking to have occurred in those men in their sample aged 18 to 20—a full 21%. This figure is appreciably lower than that provided by Cahalan and Room (1974), however, for these latter investigators found problem drinking rates as high as 40% in their male population aged 21 to 24.

Data revealing the highest rate of problem drinking in the under-25 age group are especially significant conceptually when juxtaposed against the well-known early-fortyish age range in which the average clinical alcoholic is first clearly identified. Of equal significance is the evidence from longitudinal studies indicating the statistics of turnover in problem drinking status over time (Cahalan & Roizen, 1974). These findings cast serious doubt on the usefulness of the common characterization of drinking concerns in terms of a relatively irreversible progressive deterioration, since a large proportion of those who show relatively severe signs of drinking problems at one time may be found, several years later, to show a material remission of such problems. Nevertheless, as the retrospective reports of heavy drinkers about their early drinking behavior have revealed (Cahalan, Cisin, & Crossley, 1969), many problem drinkers in their forties formed their drinking habits twenty or more years earlier. During these years the nature of this drinking and the consequences following from it led many of these ardent drinkers to the diagnosis of alcoholism.

3. DEVELOPMENT OF THE CONCEPT(S) OF ALCOHOLISM

Straus (1973) has stated that without some agreed upon behaviorally based definitions, terms such as "alcoholism" have little value. Yet both this term and others such as "excessive drinking" and "problem drinking" exist as societal designations of individuals' relationships with alcohol. These labels differ in connotation and denotation, yet all involve conceptions of alcohol abuse that have been instrumental in shaping popular, professional, and political opinion. Generally in this chapter I have avoided using the term "alcoholism," for although the word communicates meaning (given the extent to which the concept described by the term is seen differently by many of us), this meaning may not be transmitted clearly and with precision. There are a number of conceptual issues regarding alcohol use and abuse that deserve attention in this chapter, and I will broach these subsequently. I will not, however, become enmeshed in specific definitional issues related to what I regard as the inadequately validated construct of alcoholism. These definitional issues have been covered most adequately by Davies (1976). Rather, I will offer some global perspective on the conceptual issues associated with alcohol abuse and alcoholism.

Surely one of the earliest recorded attempts to distinguish the concept of alcoholism from the context of heavy drinking came from Seneca (4 BC–AD 65), who maintained that the word "drunken" could have two meanings. The first, he said, involved the man who is loaded with wine and has no control of himself. The second involved the man who is accustomed to getting drunk and is a slave to the habit (Seneca, 1942). In reviewing the history of the concept of alcoholism, Paredes (1976) has noted that the problems we label "alcoholism" have been conceptualized variously throughout history as an expression of the free will of individuals, the result of transcendental influences on the person, psychological responses to experiental stress, an epiphenomenon of disturbances in the social system, a disease, and a learned behavior.

Benjamin Rush regarded inebriety as an "odious" disease that appeared with an array of symptoms ranging from "capriciousness and disposition to quarrel" to "certain extravagant acts which indicate a temporary fit of madness." To this array of symptoms Rush added a description of the many physical signs characteristic of habitual drunkenness. He also provided an inventory of therapeutic measures, most of them rather drastic, that were to be used to restore the alcoholic to sobriety. While inebriety was in Rush's opinion a disease, he still appealed to the forces of religion to contain it. He asked ministers of the gospel to "Aid me with all the might that you possess in society, from the dignity and usefulness of your sacred office, to save our fellow men from being destroyed by the greater destroyer of their lives and souls" (Rush, 1943).

Later, in Europe, Esquirol (1838) wrote that the condition was best described as a "monomania of drunkenness"—a mental illness whose principal character is an "irresistible tendency toward fermented beverages." In this illness, the wish to drink is "instinctive and imperious . . . and persists during the whole duration of the paroxysm." But it was Magnus Huss (1852) who first coined the term "alcoholism." His designation encompassed not only the neurologic sequelae to habitual excessive drinking but certain behavioral manifestations as well. Huss also suggested that there was no definite boundary between the symptoms of alcoholism and mental disease in general. His coining of the term proved a felicitous discovery, for prior to his designation of the disorder physicians had often shown little interest in drunkenness and drunkards. With the rapid acceptance of the term, an increasingly large number of physicians came to acknowledge their scholarly and clinical interest in the disorder. (See also Kurtz & Kraepelin, 1901; Bleuler, 1924, and the review of the European perspectives offered by Marconi, 1959.)

For some medical professionals both in Europe and the United States, the early 20th century brought with it an image of man under the influence of liquor that was conceptualized in terms of disease, as had occurred previously (see Krout, 1925; Maxwell, 1950; Wilkerson, 1966). In the United States, in fact, a small group of physicians took on the task of lobbying for the proposition that alcoholism was a disease and should be treated as such (MacAndrew, 1969). This effort, however, met with considerable criticism and failure largely because it was incongruent with the ambient public images of man and drunkenness—the conventional wisdom of the period. By 1960, though, with the support of a paradigmatic change that had been building since before the founding of Alcoholics Anonymous in the 1930s, a similar movement influenced greatly by the thinking of Jellinek (1954, 1960) came to the fore in both lay and professional circles. Interestingly, as Caddy and Gottheil (1983) have asserted, the development and acceptance of the disease concept of alcoholism occurred within a scientific context that offered little additional data on which to base acceptance of the disease model than had existed fifty years previously.

Glock (1964) has observed that the general public image of the individual in western culture has been changing during this century from a free-will, moral image to a deterministic, nonmoral one. Examining this observation with regard to substance abuse generally, Pattison, Bishop, and Linsky (1968) measured public opinion from popular literature in the United States over the seven decades from 1900 to 1970. These investigators found that during the period 1900–1930 there was a steady decrease in the degree of moral blame ascribed to a user of drugs. By 1930, in fact, the public seemed to view the substance abuser as much more the product of impersonal, determined forces. Drug abuse had taken on more the image of a sickness. Examining also the locus of the public perception of the causal factors associated with substance abuse, Pattison *et al.* found that social etiology was regarded as most significant in 1900, with this trend continuing until about 1920. After 1920 there was a gradual change to a mixture of social and individual factors, a primary emphasis being placed on individual factors by the 1970s. Over these decades there seems to have been a change in the attribution of moral blame to the substance abuser. While the person is seen to be exercising free will in choosing to engage in substance abuse, the behavior has come to be seen generally as "sick." Rather than being held morally blameworthy for engaging in deviant behavior, the substance abuser of very recent times has come to be seen more as engaging in behavior that is the product of a sick mind. In keeping with the changing public images about the nature of substance abuse, Pattison *et al.* found that the conventional wisdom about the desired methods of intervention has also undergone a transformation. Whereas in 1900 the importance of legal control was implied in the popular literature by 1950 this picture had changed markedly, the emphasis now being on "medicalization." As Stoll (1968) has said:

> (1) to the extent that individuals believe non-conformity to be conscious defiance of rules, they will prefer to restrict and castigate deviants, and, (2) to the extent that individuals believe non-conformity to be the result of external forces ... they will prefer to treat or cure deviants without accompanying opprobrium. (p. 121)

These changes in public thinking about substance abuse have brought with them a number of important social implications. First, there has emerged, or perhaps persisted, a confusion between the issues associated with moral blame and moral responsibility. As Pattison (1980) notes, when the alcohol or drug abusing patient has been placed in the sick role, too often the accompanying reduction in moral blame brings with it a reduction or even abolition of moral responsibility. Second, a shift in the assumptions about the population at risk has occurred. Whereas in 1900 the substance abuser was portrayed, at least generally, as the hapless victim of social circumstances and the entire society was seen to be at risk of succumbing to evil social forces, by the 1960s the problem was believed to be located in the individual and the majority was no longer seen to be at risk. Only the socially and psychologically vulnerable and intrinsically sick person was seen as at risk of becoming drug-addicted. Thus, two populations could be presumed to exist: a majority who were not at risk and a "sick" minority at high risk. Moreover, in accordance with this view, recent social policy has been directed toward interventions aimed solely at this high-risk minority; public policy that would affect the nonrisk majority population was seen as irrelevant.

Turning now more specifically to contemporary perspectives of alcohol abuse, it is true that large segments of our society hold definite opinions about alcoholism (Albrecht, 1973); however, current conceptions regarding alcohol abuse and alcoholism are neither clear nor consistent (Marconi, 1967; Linsky, 1972).

Siegler, Osmond, and Newell (1968) have described eight separate models of alcoholism that exist concurrently (in varying degrees) in our society. More recently, Caddy, Goldman, and Huebner (1976a) have suggested that the multiple theoretical models of alcoholism that exist in the public consciousness can be conceptually clustered into the three general categories of "physical disease," "underlying psychological illness," and "learned pattern of behavior." These clusters, it was demonstrated, account for the vast amount of the public opinion about alcoholism. Interestingly, these investigators also reported that the same person could hold more than one conceptual model of alcoholism concurrently.

In a subsequent study, Caddy, Goldman, and Huebner (1976b) explored the relationships among various groups in their attitudes toward alcoholism. In this second study, the investigators compared concepts about alcohol use and alcoholism held by members of Alcoholics Anonymous, a college student group, and members of a religious sect that forbids the use of alcohol. The results indicated that the members of the three groups differed along two dimensions: (1) restriction versus freedom of alcohol use and (2) volitional control versus no control over drinking. Members of Alcoholics Anonymous and the religious sect were both rather similar on the first dimension—both favored restriction. Both groups seemed to endorse the idea that people should be discouraged from drinking—if not actually prevented—by means other than self-control. College students, on the other hand, tended to favor personal freedom of choice regarding alcohol use. The Alcoholics Anonymous and religious groups were most different on the second dimension. Members of Alcoholics Anonymous were found to believe that drinking behavior is not under the personal control of the alcoholic, whereas the members of the religious group tended to believe that alcohol abuse is not "compelled" by some external force but is caused by either inadequate self-control or an unwillingness to exert self-control. Thus, alcohol abuse is seen as a moral issue. College students were found to lie in between the other two groups on this dimension. This position might best be categorized as recommending the view that responsible drinking involves a degree of self-control and that even alcoholics should or could exert a greater degree of self-control.

Caddy et al. (1976b) also noted some interesting attitudinal differences separating men and women on the topic of alcoholism, though these were difficult to interpret. One aspect of these differences may be related to a contemporary definition of masculinity involving "the ability to hold one's liquor." Perhaps women perceive this societal norm more clearly than men, leading women to believe that society must change in order to reduce alcoholism. Women from all three groups also saw alcoholism to be more widespread than did men. This may be due partly to the personal control aspect of some definitions of alcoholism. Women, who are more apt to perceive frequent drinking as a compulsion, are also more likely to label it as alcoholism. Men, who are more likely to see personal control over drinking as the criterion of alcoholism, are less likely to label the behavior alcoholism. (See also Huebner, Slaughter, Goldman, & Caddy, 1976.)

From the viewpoint of both current knowledge and general influence, the symptomatic and disease concepts identified by Caddy *et al.* may be combined to form what Pattison, Sobell, and Sobell (1977) have termed the traditional approach—the "folk science" (Kalb & Propper, 1976) model of alcoholism. This position contrasts sharply with the "academic science" approach that appears to have moved, or is moving, from a social-learning behavioral model toward a behaviorally oriented multivariate account of alcoholism (Caddy, 1978).

3.1. The Traditional Approach

The beliefs, values, and ideologies comprising the traditional approach to alcohol dependence view it as an identifiable unitary disease process. Various disease conceptualizations of alcoholism have appeared in the literature over the past forty years (Alcoholics Anonymous, 1939, 1955, 1957; Jellinek, 1952, 1960; Ausubel, 1961; Keller, 1962; American Medical Association, 1968; Mann, 1968; Gitlow, 1973; among many others). While these authorities offer differing explanations of the nature of the disease, it is possible to draw together the themes they espouse to outline the elements of a "traditional" approach to alcoholism. These themes variously indicate the following: alcoholics are different from nonalcoholics; this "difference" either leads to or includes psychological/sociological and/or biochemical/physiological changes; these changes become part of a progressive and irreversible disease process; the disease is characterized by "an inability to abstain" and/or a "loss of control" over alcohol. It has been hypothesized that the supposed "difference" between alcoholics and nonalcoholics is based on a psychological predisposition (Wall, 1953; Shae, 1954; Rado, 1958), an allergic alcohol reaction (Silkworth, 1937; Alcoholics Anonymous, 1939, 1955, 1957; Randolph, 1956), or some nutritional deficit that may or may not be genetically influenced (Mardones, 1951; Sirnes, 1953; Williams, 1954; Madsen, 1974). The traditional approach dictates that treatment must emphasize the permanent nature of the alcoholic's "difference" and, in so doing, stresses that the disease can be arrested only by abstinence, which must be lifelong.

Just as the appropriateness of disease models for describing behavioral problems has been questioned recently (Szasz, 1961, 1970; Ullmann & Krasner, 1969), so too have the models and postulates of the traditional view of alcoholism received increasing criticism. The problem is that despite continued widespread acceptance in both professional and lay circles, especially within the fellowship of Alcoholics Anonymous, the traditional approach has failed to win empirical support. Keller (1972a), for example, has summarized the many studies examining "differences" between alcoholics and nonalcoholics and has noted that "alcoholics are different in so many ways that it makes no difference" (p. 1147). In a similar vein, research examining the construct of "craving," the "loss of control" hypothesis, and the "irreversibility" aspects inherent in most of the disease concepts of alcoholism has shown the traditional explanations severely lacking (see, for example, Merry, 1966; McNamee, Mello, & Mendelson, 1968; Cutter, Schwaab, & Nathan, 1970; Caddy, 1970; Cohen, Liebson, & Faillace, 1971; Engle & Williams, 1972; Keller, 1972b; Mello, 1972; Robinson, 1972; Sobell, Sobell & Christelman, 1972; Gottheil, Crawford, & Cornelison, 1973; Marlatt, Demming, & Reid, 1973; Wilson, Leaf, & Nathan, 1975; and Pattison, Sobell, & Sobell, 1977).

Further, there is now provocative evidence indicating that, for at least some alcoholics, abstinence does not represent the only possible treatment alternative (see, for example, Lovibond & Caddy, 1970; Sobell & Sobell, 1972, 1973, 1975, 1976; Hamburg, 1975; Lloyd & Salzberg, 1975; Armor, Polich, & Stambul, 1976; Caddy & Lovibond, 1976; and Miller & Caddy, 1977) and that abstinence does not necessarily indicate improvement in other areas of "life health" (Flaherty, McGuire, & Gatski, 1955; Gerard, Saenger, & Wile, 1962; and Pattison, 1966, 1968). Such evidence has led to the serious questioning of the validity of the traditional models of alcoholism by increasing numbers of scientists working in the field. Despite what may even be the continuing growth of the influence of the disease view generally, the essentially unidimensional perspective inherent in the current disease conceptualizations has proved incapable of adequately accounting for the complex behavioral and other phenomena generally associated with alcohol abuse and alcohol dependence. Some theorists, in fact, have asserted that the traditional approach may be hindering rather than helping our understanding of alcohol dependence (Maisto & Schefft, 1977).

3.2. The Social-Learning/Behavioral Models

These models involve an elaboration of the learning-theory-based drive/tension-reduction account (Dollard & Miller, 1950; Conger, 1956) to include the sociocultural factors that have also been indicated as important in the development of alcoholism (McCord & McCord, 1960; Chafetz & Demone, 1962; and Schmidt, Smart, & Moss, 1968). According to the social-learning/behavioral approach, alcoholism is fundamentally a manner of drinking alcohol. Drinking by the alcoholic, like drinking by the nonalcoholic, is initiated and maintained by its antecedent cues and consequent reinforcers (Ullmann & Krasner, 1965, 1969; Bandura, 1969; and Hunt & Azrin, 1973). Drinking is learned within a sociocultural context, with the term "alcoholic" being both a label applied to some aspects of that drinking (Goffman, 1963a, 1963b, Szasz, 1970) and a socially ascribed role taken on by some drinkers (Roman & Trice, 1968, 1970; Steiner, 1971). Social-learning models typically support abstinence as the treatment goal of choice for alcohol-dependent persons. However, acceptance of abstinence as the only treatment goal is not a necessary requirement for acceptance of the social-learning approach, as is the case with the traditional models.

Advocates for traditional approaches to alcoholism have typically accepted elements of the social-learning/behavioral models. For example, Alcoholics Anonymous (1957) has agreed that psychological and situational factors are important in the initiation of drinking by an alcoholic following long periods of abstinence, and Jellinek (1960) considered that Conger's (1956) learning approach at least partly complemented his disease model.

While the social-learning/behavioral approach has facilitated an impressive array of empirical research advancing our knowledge of alcoholism, it has nevertheless developed as a unitary-trait approach and so, again, is somewhat limited. This limitation is especially apparent when one examines the capacity of the approach to account for the importance of the cognitive features that recent research has indicated to be of major significance in alcoholism (see Marlatt, 1977).

3.3. The Multivariate Approach

The observations that (1) the most significant element common to persons diagnosed "alcoholic" is that they drink too much and (2) that the range of physiological, psychological, and sociocultural correlates of alcoholism is vast have led many to reject global etiological theorizing and univariate linear conceptualizations of alcoholism in favor of the development of a multivariate approach (see, for example, Goldstein & Linden, 1969; Horn & Wanberg, 1969, 1970; Partington & Johnson, 1969; Wanberg & Knapp, 1970; Edwards 1974, 1976; Pattison, 1974a, 1974b; Sobell & Sobell, 1975; Kissin, 1977; Caddy & Gottheil, 1983). The multivariate approach views alcohol dependence not as an entity represented by symptoms but as an array of behaviors and cognitions that collectively produce different types of problems which are subsequently labeled.

More specifically, this approach suggests that:

1. There are multiple patterns of use, misuse, and abuse that may be denoted as a pattern of alcohol addiction.
2. There are multiple interactive etiological variables that may combine in variable permutations to produce an alcohol-related problem.
3. All people are vulnerable to the development of different syndrome patterns of alcohol problems.
4. Treatment interventions must be multimodal to correspond to the particular syndrome pattern and the particular person.
5. Treatment outcomes will vary in accordance with the syndrome patterns, persons, and social contents.
6. Preventative interventions must be multiple and diverse to accommodate multiple etiologies.

To underline this perspective, Horn and Wanberg (1969) have recommended that terms like "alcoholism" and "alcoholic" not be used, for they argue that a specific attribute "alcoholism" does not exist in a unitary fashion (see Cahalan, 1970).

The disease models of alcoholism began to be undermined in some academic circles by the early reports of successful social drinking in a small number of alcoholic patients (Davies, 1962, 1963, Kendall, 1965; Bailey & Stewart, 1967). Within several years of Davies's now famous article, some clinicians and theorists like Chafetz (1966), Pattison (1966, 1968), and Scott (1968) were laying the foundations for a multivariate view of alcoholism. Chafetz (1966), for example, provocatively asserted that "we . . . must conclude that alcoholic excesses, alcoholic problems, alcoholism, or any label you care to affix, is produced by complex, multidimensional factors, and that, in fact, there is no such thing as an alcoholic" (p. 810).

The multivariate approach owes much of its conceptual development to the empirically based criticisms of the disease models which have been noted previously as well as other data addressing the epidemiology of alcohol misuse (see Cahalan, Cisin, & Crossley, 1969; Cahalan, 1970; and Cahalan & Room, 1974). The growing appreciation for the multivariate nature of alcohol problems has also been facilitated by the recent application of factor-analytic techniques to clinical data in the field. Horn and Wanberg (1969) undertook the factor analysis of drinking history data from 2,300 alcoholic patients and identified 13 independent primary factors of etiologic significance. These same investigators (Horn & Wanberg, 1970) have also identified a set of seven background factors (like youthful rebellion, parental drinking problems) and eight current status factors (like work status, social stress, and introversion) from the analyses of social history data also drawn from large patient populations.

Perhaps most significantly, however, the multivariate approach to alcoholism has been facilitated by the entry of a small number of behaviorally oriented clinical researchers into the alcoholism field (see, for example, Lovibond & Caddy, 1970; Sobell & Sobell, 1972, 1976). These and other clinical pragmatists have been less concerned with models of alcoholism and more concerned with broad-spectrum approaches (Lazarus, 1965, 1971) to the treatment of individuals for whom alcohol use has become a serious problem. The approach of these investigators to the treatment of alcohol dependence has been idiographic in character.

Until quite recently, the development of a multivariate approach to alcohol dependence may be characterized most accurately as a social systems approach (see Nathan, Lipson, Vettraino, & Solomon, 1968; Steinglass, Weiner, & Mendelson, 1971a, 1971b; and Holder & Stratas, 1972). One such systems approach, for example, that of Pattison (1974a, 1974b), suggests that there are several alcoholic populations that may be treated by several different methods leading to different patterns and outcome.

> It may be possible to match a certain type of patient with a certain type of facility and treatment method, to yield the most effective outcome.... treatment programs can maximize effectiveness by clearly specifying what population they propose to serve, what goals are feasible with that population, and what methods can be expected to best achieve those goals. (Pattison, 1974b, p. 59)

This and other systems approaches represent major advances over the still widely held view that there is essentially one population of alcoholics to be treated by one best method (often through the fellowship of Alcoholics Anonymous) with only one therapeutic outcome in mind. However, the multivariate systems approaches are limited at present because the technology by which patients could be matched to treatment techniques and outcomes is not yet available.

Pattison, Sobell, and Sobell (1977) have provided an excellent integration of the current clinical and laboratory research evidence in the alcoholism field. The most significant conclusions drawn by these investigators are as follows:

1. Alcohol dependence summarizes a variety of syndromes defined by drinking patterns and the adverse physical, psychological, and/or social consequences of such drinking. These syndromes are best considered as a serious health problem.
2. An individual's use of alcohol can be considered as a point on a continuum from nonuse to nonproblem drinking to various degrees of deleterious drinking.
3. The development of alcohol problems follows variable patterns over time and does not necessarily proceed inexorably to severe or fatal stages. A given set of alcohol problems may progress or be reversed through either naturalistic or treatment processes.
4. Psychological dependence and physical dependence on alcohol are separate and not necessarily related phenomena.
5. Continued drinking of large doses of alcohol over an extended period of time is likely to initiate a process of physical dependence.
6. The population of individuals with alcohol problems is multivariate; therefore, treatment intervention must be multivariate.
7. Alcohol problems typically are interrelated with other life problems, especially when alcohol dependence is long established.
8. Because of the documented strong relationship between drinking behavior and environmental influences, emphasis should be placed on treatment procedures that relate to the drinking environment of the person.
9. Treatment and rehabilitative services should be designed to provide for continuity of care over an extended period of time. This continuum of services should begin with effective identification, triage, and referral mechanisms, extend through acute and chronic phases of treatment, and provide follow-up aftercare (see also Pattison, 1980).

While Pattison and his colleagues cautiously avoid the hazards of model building, they do stress that the dynamic complexity of alcoholism cannot be assessed unless the disorder is conceptualized multidimensionally.

In an effort to extend the multivariate approach to the assessment and treatment of alcohol abusing and/or dependent individuals, Caddy (1978) offered a multivariate model in which he proposed that alcohol-related problems could be understood best as behavioral disorders that are established and maintained as a result of the unique direct and reciprocal interactions of behavioral, discriminative, incentive, and social elements, all of which function with varying degrees of cognitive mediation. Within the framework of this multivariate approach, it is assumed that each of these elements or dimensions is interactive and yet sufficiently discrete to preserve its own, albeit cognitively mediated, locus of control. Such a multivariate approach permits an assessment of both the nature and the extent of the involvement of each of the elements (behavioral, discriminative, incentive, and social) that are variously integrated within the overall cognitive functioning of the individual and account for that person's "alcoholic" behavior. An analysis of the numerous elements that may be implicated in the disorder also permits drinkers, their families, and their therapists to have a far clearer view of the complex we call alcoholism. From such a vantage point more specific treatment elements can be directed at specific difficulties, and specific research questions can be developed and tested.

Until quite recently, alcoholism treatment methods have been based on the supposition that there was essentially one population of alcoholics having only one major problem, alcoholism. The corollary of this is, of course, that alcoholics require one form of therapy that ultimately leads to one treatment outcome, abstinence. While some characteristics are shared by many people with alcohol problems and alcoholic subpopulations may be clustered according to attitudes, role ascriptions, degree of dysfunction, etc. (Hurwitz & Lelos, 1968), it is clear that different alcoholic populations have distinctly different characteristics (see Pattison, Coe, & Doerr, 1973; English & Curtin, 1975) and that the alcoholic population is a multivariate one.

3.4. Advantages of the Multivariate Approach

The multivariate approach to the issues of alcohol use and dependence, I submit, offers major advantages over the still dominant traditional perspectives of alcoholism. Despite the 93 or so diagnostic criteria for alcoholism proposed by the National Council on Alcoholism (1972), the conceptual chaos that was noted more than ten years ago (Christie & Brunn, 1969) still exists today. The "big fat words without very much content"—words like "alcoholism," "addiction," "dependence," and the like, which Christie and Brunn suggested serve to maintain the status quo and thereby allow the viability of inconsistencies in values—continue to be widely accepted. Despite continuing increases in inquiry about alcohol problems, the field still suffers from major difficulties of conceptualization and communication.

Contrast the conceptual complexity of the traditional disease perspective of alcoholism, with its recently proposed 93 diagnostic criteria, with the more straightforward, behaviorally based operational definition of responsible and excessive drinking proposed by Caddy (1972) and by Lovibond (1977) and the strength of the multivariate approach becomes obvious.

The diagnostic criteria of "alcoholism" proposed by the National Council on Alcoholism includes three major diagnostic levels: (1) classical definitive, obligatory symptoms clearly associated with the disorder (e.g., gross tremor, hallucinations, withdrawal seizures); (2) frequent or indicative symptoms that provide a basis for the strong suspicion of alcoholism (e.g., major alcohol-associated illness, alcoholic hepatitis, cirrhosis, etc.); and (3) possible or incidental symptoms that are common to alcoholism but do not by themselves give strong indication of its existence (e.g., choice of employment that facilitates drinking, frequent automobile accidents, major family disruptions, etc.).

The behavioral perspective, on the other hand, focuses on the act of drinking rather than its consequences and so permits an operational definition of excessive drinking to be established against a backdrop of limited, nonproblematic or responsible drinking in terms of peak blood alcohol concentrations (BACs) and absolute quantities of alcohol consumed per unit of time. The criterion suggested for *acceptable* or *responsible drinking* is use of alcohol which rarely results in BACs greater than 70 to 80 mg/100 mL. Thus, not more than six drinks will be consumed during a single drinking occasion and not more than eight drinks in any one day (one drink = 10 oz beer, 4 oz table wine, 2 oz fortified wine, or 1 oz spirits). The suggested criterion for *excessive drinking* is distinguished by two levels: *Level I excessive drinking* may be defined as that which results consistently in BACs approaching or exceeding 150 mg/100 mL. Often 10 or more drinks will be consumed on a single occasion, and daily intake is likely to average 10 drinks or more. Over the long term, this level is associated with a high risk of impairment of family and other social relations and decreased work performance. Moreover, deterioration of health is virtually certain. *Level II excessive drinking* involves drinking that results consistently in BACs of 200 to 300 mg/100 mL or higher. At this level drinking may occur so frequently that a BAC of zero is seldom attained, or periods of abstinence may alternate with binge type drinking. Physical dependence is likely to be present to some degree and tolerance is commonly developed to the point where a BAC of 150 mg/100 mL results in virtually no obvious signs of intoxication. When continued over a sufficient time period, this level of excessive drinking inevitably results in personality deterioration, destruction of family and other social relationships, and marked deterioration of health and work performance.

Such a behaviorally based operational approach to alcoholism permits one to focus squarely on the parameters of the individual's alcohol consumption patterns and the social context in which this drinking occurs. No longer, I suggest, do we need to seek definitions of alcoholism in terms of the consequences of alcohol-related patterns of consumption. The concept of alcoholism cannot be defined adequately. It is an abstraction—an ill-defined medical/social construct, sometimes a self-labeling process, frequently an appelation based on a heterogeneous array of medical, legal, and social considerations. Yet in one form or another, the concept is applied when the probable consequences of excessive drinking become realized. It is preferable, I believe, to view excessive drinking as the fundamental individual and social problem rather than to wait until such drinking has brought forth its inevitable negative consequences and then to create the construct "alcoholism" to describe the drinker and account for much of his or her life-style.

3.5. Implications for the Future

There is little question but that the traditional perspective of alcohol abuse and alcoholism continues in one form or another to dominate the public consciousness. Nevertheless, this conceptual paradigm is not congruent with our extant empirical scientific knowledge. Moreover, it brings with it some significant and negative social policy implications:

1. It averts attention from prevention strategies, for it ignores the data that all people are at risk to various degrees of alcohol misuse and abuse.
2. It promotes a nihilistic attitude of futility toward any social policy rather than encouraging the development of viable and valuable social policies.
3. It ignores and/or minimizes the extent to which treatment and rehabilitation are interdigitated with social attitudes, behaviors, sanctions, prescriptions, and proscriptions.

Despite thousands of years of experience with alcohol, we have learned more about it and its abuse in the past fifty or so years than we have conceptualized in all the preceeding centuries of our experience. Thus, we appear to be at a particularly fortunate point in our history to address the implications of our emergent perspectives regarding alcohol and alcoholism. It may be, in fact, that the accumulation of knowledge of the past several decades has prepared us for a paradigmatic shift regarding our concepts surrounding alcohol and its use.

From the prevention standpoint, both at the individual clinical and social policy levels, the emergent perspectives offer some profound and rather obvious implications. If the focus of prevention programming is placed on the act of drinking and those who engage in excessive drinking are considered to be at risk of developing the problems which we currently describe as alcoholism, then these individuals can be targeted for specific prevention programming. Further, with the focus on drinking, we can develop social policies to provide programs ranging from teaching people how to drink in a restricted manner (see for example, Caddy, 1977) to providing social and legal sanctions for those who engage in excessive drinking. We could also, given enough political integrity and cooperation, establish national and international guidelines for the production, distribution, and sale of alcoholic beverages. (Such activity would appear particularly significant given the recent evidence illustrating the risks of emergent alcohol-related problems in many of the developing nations.) Of course, many of these proposals do not seem to be very different from previous prevention efforts (see the review by Gusfield, 1976). They have the capacity, however, to be quite different, for if the zeitgeist within which alcohol problems are conceptualized is moved from a problems to a drinking perspective and if the disease orientation is replaced with a multivariate behavioral approach, the canvas upon which we sketch our prevention efforts will be very different indeed.

The change in perspective toward a behaviorally based multivariate account of alcohol use and abuse would also have profound treatment implications. The disclaiming of poorly validated concepts such as "loss of control" and "craving" and the rejection of the "sickness" view would encourage the acceptance of individual responsibility for the action and consequences of drinking. Yet, recognizing the complex dynamics of the learning basis of excessive drinking, we could attack these dynamics directly. Further, such a perspective would in no way require a return to a moral culpability approach to drinking and drunkenness. Perhaps most important of all, however, is the fact that the multivariate orientation would inevitably recommend that treatment services be truly individually oriented and that broad-spectrum programming would be essential to meet the diverse needs of the individual case.

4. REFERENCES

Albrecht, G. L. The alcoholism process: A social learning viewpoint. In P. G. Bourne & R. Fox (Eds.), *Alcoholism: Progress in research and treatment.* New York: Academic Press, 1973.

Alcoholics Anonymous. *The story of how more than 100 men have recovered from alcoholism.* New York: Works Publishing Company, 1939.

Alcoholics Anonymous. *The story of how many thousands of men and women have recovered from alcoholism.* New York: Alcoholics Anonymous Publishing, 1955.

Alcoholics Anonymous. *Alcoholics Anonymous comes of age.* New York: Harper, 1957.

American Medical Association. *Manual on Alcoholism.* American Medical Association, 1968, *9801,* 468-32E-25 M.O.P. 185.

Armor, D. J., Polich, J. M., & Stambul, H. B. *Alcoholism and treatment* (R-1739-NIAAA). Santa Monica, Calif.: Rand Corporation, 1976.

Austin, G. A. *Perspectives on the history of psychoactive substances* (Research Issue 24, National Institute on Drug Abuse, U.S. Department of Health, Education, and Welfare). Washington, D.C.: U.S. Government Printing Office, 1978.

Ausubel, D. P. Personality disorder is disease. *American Psychologist,* 1961, *61,* 69–74.

Bacon, S. D. The classic temperance movement of the U.S.A.: Impact today on attitudes, action and research. *British Journal of Addiction,* 1967, *62,* 5–18.

Bailey, M. B., & Stewart, J. Normal drinking by persons reporting previous problem drinking. *Quarterly Journal of Studies on Alcohol,* 1967, *28,* 305–315.

Baird, E. The alcohol problem and the law: I. The ancient laws and customs. *Quarterly Journal of Studies on Alcohol,* 1943–1944, *4,* 535–556.

Bandura, A. *Principles of behavior modification.* New York: Holt, 1969.

Baron, S. *Brewed in America: A history of beer and ale in the United States.* Boston: Little, Brown, 1962.

Bleuler, E. *Tratado de psiquiatriá.* (J. M. de Villaverde, Trans.) Madrid: Calpe, 1924.

Blum, R. H., & Associates. *Society and drugs.* San Francisco: Jossey-Bass, 1969.

Brown, J. H. *Early American beverages.* New York: Bonanza Books, 1966.

Caddy, G. R. *Abstinence or cure: A re-evaluation of the nature of alcoholism and implications for treatment.* Paper presented at the 29th International Congress on Alcoholism and Drug Dependence. Sydney, Australia, 1970.

Caddy, G. R. *Behavior modification in the management of alcoholism.* Unpublished doctoral dissertation, University of New South Wales, 1972.

Caddy, G. R. Blood alcohol concentration discrimination training: Development and current status. In G. A. Marlatt & P. E. Nathan (Eds.), *Behavioral approaches to the assessment and treatment of alcoholism.* New Brunswick, N.J.: Center for Alcohol Studies, 1977.

Caddy, G. R. Toward a multivariate analysis of alcohol abuse. In P. E. Nathan, G. A. Marlatt, & T. Loberg (Eds.), *Alcoholism: New directions in behavioral research and treatment.* New York: Plenum Press, 1978.

Caddy, G. R., & Gottheil, E., Contributions to behavioral treatment from studies on programmed access to alcohol. In M. Galanter (Ed.), *Recent advances in alcoholism* (Vol. 1). New York: Plenum Press, 1983.

Caddy, G. R., & Lovibond, S. H. Self-regulation and discriminated aversive conditioning in the modification of alcoholics' drinking behavior. *Behavior Therapy,* 1976, *7,* 223–230.

Caddy, G. R., Goldman, R. D., & Huebner, R. Relationships among different domains of attitudes toward alcoholism: Model, cost, and treatment. *Addictive Behaviors,* 1976, *1,* 159–167. (a)

Caddy, G. R., Goldman, R. D., & Huebner, R. Group differences in attitudes towards alcoholism. *Addicitve Behaviors,* 1976, *1,* 281–286. (b)

Cahalan, D. *Problem drinkers: A national survey.* San Francisco: Jossey-Bass, 1970.

Cahalan, D. Subcultural differences in drinking behavior in U.S. National surveys and selected European studies. In P. E. Nathan, G. A. Marlatt, & T. Loberg (Eds.), *Alcoholism: New directions in behavioral reserach and treatment.* New York: Plenum Press, 1978.

Cahalan, D., & Cisin, I. H. Epidemiological and social factors associated with drinking problems. In R. E. Tarter & A. A. Sugerman (Eds.), *Alcoholism: Interdisciplinary approaches to an enduring problem.* Reading, Mass.: Addison-Wesley, 1976.

Cahalan, D., & Roizen, R. *Changes in drinking problems in a national sample of men.* Paper presented in the North American Congress on Alcohol and Drug Problems. San Francisco, December 1974.

Cahalan, D., & Room, R. *Problem drinking among American men.* New Brunswick, N.J.: Rutgers Center of Alcohol Studies (Monograph No. 7), 1974.

Cahalan, D., Cisin, I. H., & Crossley, H. *American drinking practices: A national survey of behavior and attitudes.* New Brunswick, N.J.: Rutgers Center of Alcohol Studies (Monograph No. 6), 1969.

Chafetz, M. E. Alcohol excess. *Annals of the New York Academy of Sciences,* 1966, *133,* 808–813.

Chafetz, M. E., & Demone, H. W. *Alcoholism and society*. New York: Oxford University Press, 1962.

Cherrington, E. *The evolution of prohibition in the United States of America*. Montclair, N.J.: Patterson Smith, 1969. (Originally published, 1920.)

Christie, N., & Brunn, K. Alcohol problems: The conceptual framework. In M. Keller & T. G. Coffey (Eds.), *Proccedings of the 28th International Congress on Alcohol and Alcoholism* (Vol. 2). New Haven, Conn.: Hillhouse Press, 1969.

Clark, W. Operational definitions of drinking problems and associated prevalence rates. *Quarterly Journal of Studies on Alcohol*, 1966, *27*, 648–668.

Coffey, T. G. Beer street: Gin lane: Some views on 18th century drinking. *Quarterly Journal of Studies on Alcohol*, 1966, *27*, 669–692.

Cohen, M., Liebson, I. A., & Faillace, L. A. The modification of drinking in chronic alcoholics. In N. K. Mello & J. H. Mendelson (Eds.), *Recent advances in studies of alcoholism*. Washington, D.C.: U.S. Government Printing Office, 1971.

Conger, J. J. Reinforcement theory and the dynamics of alcoholism. *Quarterly Journal of Studies on Alcohol*, 1956, *17*, 296–305.

Cutter, H. S. G., Schwaab, E. L., Jr., & Nathan, P. E. Effects of alcohol on its utility for alcoholics and non-alcoholics. *Quarterly Journal of Studies on Alcohol*, 1970, *31*, 369–378.

Davies, D. L. Normal drinking in recovered alcohol addicts. *Quarterly Journal of Studies on Alcohol*, 1962, *23*, 94–104.

Davies, D. L. Normal drinking in recovered alcohol addicts (Comment by various correspondents). *Quarterly Journal of Studies on Alcohol*, 1963, *24*, 109–121, 321–332.

Davies, D. L. Definitional issues in alcoholism. In R. E. Tarter & A. A. Sugerman (Eds.), *Alcoholism: Interdisciplinary approaches to an enduring problem*. Reading, Mass.: Addison-Wesley, 1976.

de Lint, J., & Schmidt, W. The distribution of alcohol consumption in Ontario. *Quarterly Journal of Studies on Alcohol*, 1968, *29*, 968–973.

de Lint, J., & Schmidt, W. The epidemiology of alcoholism. In Y. Israel & J. Mardones (Eds.), *Biological basis of alcoholism*. New York: Wiley–Interscience, 1971.

Dollard, J., & Miller, N. E. *Personality and psychotherapy*. New York: McGraw-Hill, 1950.

Edwards, G. Drugs: Drug dependence and the concept of plasticity. *Quarterly Journal of Studies on Alcohol*, 1974, *35*, 176–195.

Edwards, G. The alcohol dependence syndrome: Usefulness of an idea. In G. Edwards & M. Grant (Eds.), *Alcoholism: New knowledge and new responses*. Baltimore: University Park Press, 1976.

Engle, K. B., & Williams, T. K. Effects of an ounce of vodka on alcoholics' desire for alcohol. *Quarterly Journal of Studies on Alcohol*, 1972, *33*, 1099–1105.

English, G. E., & Curtin, M. E. Personality differences in patients at three alcoholism treatment agencies. *Journal of Studies on Alcohol*, 1975, *36*, 52–61.

Esquirol, E. *Des maladies mentales*. Paris: Bailliere, 1838.

Flaherty, J. A., McGuire, H. T., & Gatski, R. L. The psychodynamics of the "dry drunk." *American Journal of Psychiatry*, 1955, *112*, 460–464.

Forbes, R. J. *Man the maker: A history of technology and engineering*. London: Abelard–Schuman, 1958.

Gerard, D. L., Saenger, G., & Wile, R. The abstinent alcoholic. *Archives of General Psychiatry*, 1962, *16*, 83–95.

Gitlow, S. E. Alcoholism: A disease. In P. G. Bourne & R. Fox (Eds.), *Alcoholism: Progress in research and treatment*. New York: Academic Press, 1973.

Glock, G. Y. Image of man and public opinion. *Public Opinion Quarterly*, 1964, *28*, 539–546.

Goffman, E. *Behavior in public places.* New York: Free Press, 1963. (a)

Goffman, E. *Stigma.* Englewood Cliffs, N.J.: Prentice-Hall, 1963. (b)

Goldstein, S. G., & Linden, J. D. Multivariate classification of alcoholics by means of the MMPI. *Journal of Abnormal Psychology,* 1969, *74,* 661–669.

Gomberg, E. The female alcoholic. In R. E. Tarter & A. A. Sugerman (Eds.), *Alcoholism: Interdisciplinary approaches to an enduring problem.* Reading, Mass.: Addison–Wesley, 1976.

Gottheil, E., Crawford, H. D., & Cornelison, F. S. The alcoholics' ability to resist available alcohol. *Disorders of the Nervous System,* 1973, *34,* 80–82.

Gusfield, J. R. Status conflicts and the changing ideologies of the American temperance movement. In D. J. Pittman & C. R. Synder (Eds.), *Society, culture and drinking practices.* New York: Wiley, 1963.

Gusfield, J. R. The prevention of drinking problems. In W. J. Filstead, J. J. Rossi, & M. Keller (Eds.), *Alcohol and alcohol problems: New thinking and new directions.* Cambridge, Mass.: Ballinger, 1976.

Haggard, H. W., & Jellinek, E. M. *Alcohol explored.* New York: Doubleday, 1942.

Hamburg, S. Behavior therapy in alcoholism: A critical review of broad-spectrum approaches. *Journal of Studies on Alcohol,* 1975, *36,* 69–87.

Harper, R. F. *The code of Hammurabi, King of Babylon.* Chicago: University of Chicago Press, 1904.

Heath, D. B. A critical review of ethnographic studies of alcohol use. In R. J. Gibbins, Y. Israel, H. Kalant, R. E. Popham, W. Schmidt, & R. G. Smart (Eds.), *Research advances in alcohol and drug problems* (Vol. 2). New York: Wiley, 1975.

Holder, H. D., & Stratas, N. E. A systems approach to alcoholism programming. *American Journal of Psychiatry,* 1972, *129,* 32–37.

Horn, J. L., & Wanberg, K. W. Symptom patterns related to the excessive use of alcohol. *Quarterly Journal of Studies on Alcohol,* 1969, *30,* 35–58.

Horn, J. L., & Wanberg, K. W. Dimensions of perception of background and current situation of alcoholic patients. *Quarterly Journal of Studies on Alcohol,* 1970, *31,* 633–658.

Huebner, R., Slaughter, R. E., Goldman, R. D., & Caddy, G. R. Attitudes toward alcohol as a predictor of self-estimated alcohol consumption in college students. *International Journal of the Addictions,* 1976, *11,* 377–388.

Hunt, G. M., & Azrin, N. H. A community-reinforcement approach to alcoholism. *Behaviour Research and Therapy,* 1973, *11,* 91–101.

Hurwitz, J. I., Lelos, D. A multilevel interpersonal profile of employed alcoholics. *Quarterly Journal of Studies on Alcohol,* 1968, *29,* 64–76.

Huss, M. *Chronische Alkoholskrankheit, oder Alcoholismum chronicus* (Van dem Busch, Trans.). Stockholm: C. E. Fritze, 1852.

Jellinek, E. M. The phases of alcohol addiction. *Quarterly Journal of Studies on Alcohol,* 1952, *13,* 673–684.

Jellinek, E. M. *International experience with the problem of alcoholism.* Paper presented to the Alcoholism Research Symposium, Fifth International Congress on Mental Health, Toronto, 1954.

Jellinek, E. M. *The disease concept of alcoholism.* Highland Park, N.J.: Hillhouse Press, 1960.

Johnson, P., Armor, D., Polich, S., & Stambul, H. *U.S. drinking practices: Time trends, social correlates, and sex roles.* Draft report prepared for the National Institute on Alcohol Abuse and Alcoholism (under contract no. ADM-281-76-0020). July, 1977.

Kalb, M., & Propper, M. The future of alcohology: Craft or science? *American Journal of Psychiatry,* 1976, *133,* 641–645.

Keller, M. Beer and wine in ancient medicine. *Quarterly Journal of Studies on Alcohol,* 1958, *19,* 153–154.

Keller, M. The definition of alcoholism and the estimation of its prevalence. In D. J. Pittman & C. R. Synder (Eds.), *Society, culture and drinking patterns.* New York: Wiley, 1962.

Keller, M. The oddities of alcoholics. *Quarterly Journal of Studies on Alcohol,* 1972, *33,* 1147–1148. (a)

Keller, M. On the loss-of-control phenomenon in alcoholism. *British Journal of Addiction,* 1972, *67,* 153–166. (b)

Keller, M. (Ed.). *Second special report to the U.S. Congress on alcohol and health: New knowledge.* (DHEW Publication No. (ADM) 75-212). Washington, D.C.: U.S. Government Printing Office, 1974.

Keller, M. Problems with alcohol: An historical perspective. In W. J. Filstead, J. J. Rossi, & M. Keller (Eds.), *Alcohol and alcohol problems: New thinking and new directions.* Cambridge, Mass.: Ballinger, 1976.

Keller, M., & Gurioli, C. *Statistics on consumption of alcohol and on alcoholism.* Unpublished manuscript, Rutgers University Center for Alcohol Studies, New Brunswick, N.J., 1976.

Kendall, R. E. Normal drinking by former alcoholic addicts. *Quarterly Journal of Studies on Alcohol,* 1965, *26,* 247–257.

Kissin, B. Theory and practice in the treatment of alcoholism. In B. Kissin & H. Begleiter (Eds.), *The biology of alcoholism* (Vol. 5): *Treatment and rehabilitation of the chronic alcoholic.* New York: Plenum Press, 1977.

Knupfer, G. The epidemiology of problem drinking. *American Journal of Public Health,* 1967, *57,* 974–986.

Koestler, A. *The sleep-walkers.* New York: Macmillan, 1968.

Krout, J. *The origins of prohibition.* New York: Knopf, 1925.

Kuhn, T. S. *The structure of scientific revolutions.* International Encyclopedia of Unified Science (Vol. 2, No. 2). Chicago: University of Chicago Press, 1970.

Kurtz, E., & Kraepelin, E. Über die Beeinflussung psychicher Vorgänge durch regelmässigen Alkoholgenuss. *Psychologische Arbeiten,* 1901, *3,* 417–457.

Lazarus, A. A. Toward the understanding and effective treatment of alcoholism. *South African Medical Journal,* 1965, *39,* 736–741.

Lazarus, A. A. *Behavior therapy and beyond.* New York: McGraw-Hill, 1971.

Ledermann, S. *Alcool-alcoolisme-alcoolisation. Données scientifiques de caractère physiologique. Économique et social.* Institute National d'Études Démographiques. Cahier No. 29, Presses Universitaires de France, 1956.

Ledermann, S. *Alcool-alcoolisme-alcoolisation: mortalité, morbidité, accidents du travail.* Institute National d'Études Démographiques. Cahier No. 41, Presses Universitaires de France, 1964.

Leibowitz, J. Studies in the history of alcoholism, 2: Acute alcoholism in ancient Greece and Roman medicine. *British Journal of Addiction,* 1967, *62,* 83–86.

Leisure Development Center. *Drinking habits of the Japanese: Actual drinking habits and problem drinking tendencies.* Report of the Leisure Development Center, Tokyo, 1977.

Linsky, A. S. Theories of behavior and social control of alcoholism. *Social Psychiatry,* 1972, *7,* 47–52.

Lloyd, R. W., Jr., & Salzberg, H. C. Controlled social drinking: An alternative to abstinence as a treatment goal for some alcohol abusers. *Psychological Bulletin,* 1975, *82,* 815–842.

Lönnrot, E. *The Kalevala* (F. P. Mogoun, Jr., trans.). Cambridge Mass.: Harvard University Press, 1963.

Lovibond, S. H. Behavioral control of excessive drinking. In M. Hersen, R. M. Eisler, & P. M. Miller (Eds.), *Progress in behavior modification* (Vol. 5). New York: Academic Press, 1977.

Lovibond, S. H., & Caddy, G. R. Discriminated aversive control in the moderation of alcoholics' drinking behavior. *Behavior Therapy,* 1970, *1,* 437–444.

MacAndrew, C. On the notion that certain persons who are given to frequency drunkenness suffer from a disease called alcoholism. In S. C. Plog & R. B. Edgerton (Eds.), *Changing perspectives in mental illness.* New York: Holt, 1969.

Madsen, W. *The American alcoholic.* Springfield, Ill.: Charles C Thomas, 1974.

Maisto, S. A., & Schefft, B. K. The constructs of craving for alcohol and loss of control drinking: Help or hindrance to research. *Addictive Behaviors,* 1977, *2,* 207–217.

Mäkelä, K. Concentration of alcohol consumption. *Scandinavian Studies in Criminology* (Vol. 3). Universitetsforlarget, Oslo, 1971.

Mandelbaum, D. C. Alcohol and culture. *Current Anthropology,* 1965, *6,* 281–293.

Mann, M. *New primer on alcoholism.* New York: Holt, 1968.

Marconi, J. The concept of alcoholism. *Quarterly Journal of Studies on Alcohol,* 1959, *20,* 216–235.

Marconi, J. Scientific theory and operational definitions in psychotherapy with special references to alcoholism. *Quarterly Journal of Studies on Alcohol,* 1967, *28,* 631–640.

Mardones, R. J. On the relationship between deficiency of B vitamins and alcohol intake in rats. *Quarterly Journal of Studies on Alcohol,* 1951, *12,* 563–575.

Marlatt, G. A. *Craving for alcohol, loss of control, and relapse: A cognitive-behavioral analysis* (Technical Report No. 77-05). Seattle: University of Washington, Alcoholism and Drug Abuse Institute, 1977.

Marlatt, G. A., Demming, B., & Reid, J. B. Loss of control drinking in alcoholics: An experimental analogue. *Journal of Abnormal Psychology,* 1973, *81,* 233–241.

Maxwell, M. The Washingtonian movement. *Quarterly Journal of Studies on Alcohol,* 1950, *11,* 410–451.

McCord, W., & McCord, J. *Origins of alcoholism.* Stanford: Stanford University Press, 1960.

McKinlay, A. P. Ancient experience with intoxicating drinks: Non-classical people. *Quarterly Journal of Studies on Alcohol,* 1948, *9,* 388–414.

McKinlay, A. P. Ancient experience with intoxicating drinks: Non-attic Greek states. *Quarterly Journal of Studies on Alcohol,* 1949, *10,* 289–315.

McNamee, H. B., Mello, N. K., & Mendelson, J. H. Experimental analysis of drinking patterns of alcoholics: Concurrent psychiatric observations. *American Journal of Psychiatry,* 1968, *124,* 1063–1069.

Mello, N. K. Behavioral studies of alcoholism. In B. Kissin & H. Begleiter (Eds.), *The biology of alcoholism* (Vol. 2): *Physiology and behavior.* New York: Plenum Press, 1972.

Merry, J. The "loss of control" myth. *Lancet,* 1966, *1,* 1257–1258.

Miller, W. R., & Caddy, G. R. Abstinence and controlled drinking in the treatment of problem drinkers. *Journal of Studies on Alcohol,* 1977, *38,* 986–1003.

Nathan, P. E., Lipson, A. G., Vettraino, A. P., & Solomon, P. The social ecology of an urban clinic for alcoholism. *International Journal of Addictions,* 1968, *3,* 55–64.

National Council on Alcoholism. Criteria for the diagnosis of alcoholism. *American Journal of Psychiatry,* 1972, *129,* 127–135.

Noble, E. P. (Ed.). *Third Special Report to the United States Congress on Alcohol and Health.* Washington, D.C.: U.S. Government Printing Office, 1978.

Paredes, A. The history of the concept of alcoholism. In R. Tarter & A. A. Sugerman (Eds.), *Alcoholism: Interdisciplinary approaches to an ending problem.* Reading, Mass.: Addison-Wesley, 1976.

Partington, J. T., & Johnson, F. G. Personality types among alcoholics. *Quarterly Journal of Studies on Alcohol,* 1969, *30,* 21–34.

Pattison, E. M. A critique of alcoholism treatment concepts with special reference to abstinence. *Quarterly Journal of Studies on Alcohol,* 1966, *27,* 49–71.

Pattison, E. M. Abstinence criteria: A critique of abstinence criteria in the treatment of alcoholism. *International Journal of Social Psychiatry,* 1968, *14,* 268–276.

Pattison, E. M. Drinking outcomes of alcoholism treatment. Abstinence, social, modified, controlled, and normal drinking. In N. Kessel, A. Hawker, & H. Chalke (Eds.), *Alcoholism: A medical profile*. London: B. Edsall and Company, 1974. (a)

Pattison, E. M. The rehabilitation of the chronic alcoholic. In B. Kissin & H. Begleiter (Eds.), *The biology of alcoholism* (Vol. 3). New York: Plenum Press, 1974. (b)

Pattison, E. M. *A bio-psycho-social analysis of alcohol and drug abuse: Implications for social policy*. Paper presented at the First Pan-Pacific Conference on Drugs and Alcohol, Canberra, Australia, 1980.

Pattison, E. M., Bishop, L. A., & Linsky, A. S. Changes in public attitudes on narcotic addiction. *American Journal of Psychiatry*, 1968, *125*, 160–167.

Pattison, E. M., Coe, R., & Doerr, H. D. Population variation between alcoholism treatment facilities. *International Journal of the Addictions*, 1973, *8*, 199–229.

Pattison, E. M., Sobell, M. B., & Sobell, L. C. (Eds.). *Emerging concepts of alcohol dependence*. New York: Springer, 1977.

Plaut, T. F. *Alcohol problems: A report to the nation by the cooperative commission on the study of alcoholism*. New York: Oxford University Press, 1967.

Rado, S. Narcotic bondage: A general theory of the dependence on narcotic drugs. In P. H. Hock & J. Zubin (Eds.), *Problems of addiction and habituation*. New York: Grune & Stratton, 1958.

Randolph, T. G. The descriptive features of food addiction. Addictive eating and drinking. *Quarterly Journal of Studies on Alcohol*, 1956, *17*, 198–224.

Robinson, D. The alcoholologist addiction: Some implications of having lost control over the disease concept of alcoholism. *Quarterly Journal of Studies on Alcohol*, 1972, *33*, 1028–1042.

Roman, P. M., & Trice, H. M. The sick role, labelling theory and the deviant drinker. *The International Journal of Social Psychiatry*, 1968, *14*, 245–251.

Roman, P. M., & Trice, H. M. The development of deviant drinking behavior. *Archives of Environmental Health*, 1970, *20*, 424–435.

Rorabaugh, W. J. Estimated U.S. alcoholic beverage consumption, 1790–1860. *Journal of Studies on Alcohol*, 1976, *37*, 357–364.

Rosenberg, S. (Ed.). *First special report to the U.S. Congress on alcohol and health*. Washington, D.C.: U.S. Government Printing Office, 1971.

Rush, B. *An inquiry into the effects of ardent spirts upon the human body and mind; with an account of the means of preventing and of the remedies for curing them* (8th ed.). Brookfield, Mass.: Merriam, 1814. Reprinted with introduction by M. Keller in *Quarterly Journal of Studies on Alcohol*, 1943, *4*, 321–341. (Originally published, 1785.)

Schmidt, W., Smart, R., & Moss, M. *Social class and the treatment of alcoholism*. Toronto: Addiction Research Foundation (Brookside Monograph No. 7), 1968.

Scott, P. D. Offenders, drunkenness and murder. *The British Journal of Addiction*, 1968, *63*, 221–226.

Seneca, E. On drunkenness. Classics of the alcohol literature. *Quarterly Journal of Studies on Alcohol*, 1942, *3*, 302–307.

Shae, J. E. Psychoanalytic therapy and alcoholism. *Quarterly Journal of Studies on Alcohol*, 1954, *15*, 595–605.

Siegler, M., Osmond, H., & Newell, S. Models of alcoholism. *Quarterly Journal of Studies on Alcohol*, 1968, *29*, 571–591.

Silkworth, W. D. Alcoholism as manifestation of allergy. *Medical Records*, 1937, *145*, 249–251.

Sirnes, T. B. Voluntary consumption of alcohol in rats with cirrhosis of the liver. A preliminary report. *Quarterly Journal of Studies on Alcohol*, 1953, *14*, 3–18.

Skog, O. J. *Alkoholkonsumets fordeling i befolkningen*. Statens Institutt for Alkoholforskning, Oslo, 1971 (Mimeograph).

Sobell, M. B., & Sobell, L. C. *Individualized behavior therapy for alcoholics*. Sacramento, Calif.: California Department of Mental Hygiene (Research Monograph No. 13), 1972.

Sobell, M. B., & Sobell, L. C. Individualized behavior therapy for alcoholics. *Behaviour Research and Therapy*, 1973, *4*, 49–72.

Sobell, M. B., & Sobell, L. C. The need for realism, relevance and operational assumptions in the study of substance dependence. In H. D. Cappell & A. E. LeBlanc (Eds.), *Biological and behavioral approaches to drug dependence*. Toronto: Addiction Research Foundation, 1975.

Sobell, M. B., & Sobell, L. C. Second year treatment outcome of alcoholics treated by individualized behavior therapy: Results. *Behaviour Research and Therapy*, 1976, *14*, 195–215.

Sobell, L. C., Sobell, M. B., & Christelman, W. C. The myth of "one drink." *Behaviour Research and Therapy*, 1972, *10*, 119–123.

Steiner, C. N. *Games alcoholics play: The analysis of self-scripts*. New York: Grove Press, 1971.

Steinglass, P., Weiner, S., & Mendelson, J. H. Interactional issues as determinants of alcoholism. *American Journal of Psychiatry*, 1971, *128*, 275–280. (a)

Steinglass, P., Weiner, S., & Mendelson, J. H. A systems approach to alcoholism. *Archives of General Psychiatry*, 1971, *24*, 401–408. (b)

Stoll, C. S. Images of man and social control. *Social Forces*, 1968, *47*, 119–127.

Straus, R. Alcohol and society. *Psychiatric Annals*, 1973, *3*, 107.

Straus, R. Problem drinking in the perspective of social change, 1940–1973. In W. J. Filstead, J. J. Rossi, & M. Keller (Eds.), *Alcohol and alcohol problems: New thinking and new directions*. Cambridge, Mass.: Ballinger, 1976.

Sulkunen, P. Drinking patterns and the level of alcohol consumption: An international overview. In R. J. Gibbins, Y. Israel, H. Kalant, R. E. Popham, W. Schmidt, & R. G. Smart (Eds.), *Advances in alcohol and drug problems* (Vol. 3). New York: Wiley, 1976.

Szasz, T. S. *The myth of mental illness: Foundations of a theory of personal conduct*. New York: Hoeber-Harper, 1961.

Szasz, T. S. *Ideology and insanity*. New York: Doubleday, 1970.

Ullmann, L. P., & Krasner, L. (Eds.). *Case studies in behavior modification*. New York: Holt, 1965.

Ullmann, L. P., & Krasner, L. *A psychological approach to abnormal behavior*. Englewood Cliffs, N.J.: Prentice-Hall, 1969.

United States Senate. Committee on labor and public welfare. Sub-committee on alcoholism and narcotics. *Alcohol abuse among women; Special problems and unmet needs*. Hearings, September 29, 1976. Washington, D.C.: U.S. Government Printing Office, 1976.

Wall, J. H. Alcoholism: A medical responsibility. *Medical Records*, 1953, *47*, 497–500.

Wanberg, K. W., & Knapp, J. A multidimensional model for the research and treatment of alcoholism. *The International Journal of the Addictions*, 1970, *5*, 69–98.

Wilkerson, A. E. *A history of the concept of alcoholism as a disease*. Unpublished doctoral dissertation, University of Pennsylvania, 1966.

Williams, R. J. The genetotrophic concept—nutritional deficiencies and alcoholism. *Annals of the New York Academy of Sciences*, 1954, *57*, 794–811.

Willner, W. F. Drinking in America—and how it grew. *Resident and Staff Physician*, 1975, *21*, 132–139, 142.

Wilson, G. T., Leaf, R., & Nathan, P. E. The aversive control of excessive drinking by chronic alcoholics in the laboratory setting. *Journal of Applied Behavior Analysis*, 1975, *8*, 13–26.

Winkler, A. M. Drinking on the American frontier. *Quarterly Journal of Studies on Alcohol*, 1968, *29*, 413–445.

Winkler, A. Lyman Beecher and the temperance crusade. *Quarterly Journal of Studies on Alcohol*, 1972, *33*, 939–957.

World Health Organization. *Alcohol-related problems: The need to develop further the WHO initiative*. Report by the Director-General to the Executive Board, November 27, 1978.

2

The Genetics of Alcoholism

MARC A. SCHUCKIT

The familial nature of alcoholism has been known for centuries. However, only in recent times have scientists seriously begun to address the possibility that this disorder might be genetically influenced.

Evidence has accumulated over the past fifty years that alcoholism, indeed, has a genetic basis, but what is inherited still remains to be elucidated. The first section of this chapter is an overview of the different types of studies supporting the heredity of alcoholism; the second section suggests some possible biological determinants of this disorder that lend themselves to scientific validation. Finally, the third section summarizes our own prospective research study comparing, on the biological parameters outlined in Section 2, males with a family history of alcoholism with a matched control group.

1. TYPES OF STUDIES SUPPORTING A GENETIC INFLUENCE IN ALCOHOLISM

For any behavioral disorder, it is rarely possible to demonstrate the importance of genetic factors in a way that leaves no room for doubt. This is especially

Parts of this chapter appeared in M. A. Schuckit, A prospective study of genetic markers in alcoholism. In I. Hanin & E. Usden (Eds.), *Biological markers in psychiatry and neurology*. Oxford, England: Pergamon Press, 1981.

MARC A. SCHUCKIT • Alcohol Treatment Program, Veterans Administration Medical Center, 3350 La Jolla Village Drive, San Diego, California 92161, and Department of Psychiatry, University of California, San Diego, California 92161. This work was supported in part by the Veterans Administration, NIAAA Grant PHSAA04353-02, and a grant from the Raleigh Hills Foundation.

true for a problem as prevalent as alcoholism, since it is unlikely that this disorder will follow simple Mendelian inheritance patterns (Cloninger, Christiansen, Reich, & Gottesman, 1978). Since human studies do not allow for complete control of diverse environmental factors, it is important to look at the pattern of results obtained from different types of studies and subject populations in order to evaluate a genetic influence (Robins, 1978). In this light, the genetics of alcoholism is supported by family studies, animal studies, genetic marker investigations, twin research, and adoption studies.

1.1. Family Studies

Without doubt, alcoholism is a familial disorder. The lifetime risk for alcoholism in children of alcoholics far exceeds that of the general population, and alcoholism in the offspring is more prevalent in families with alcoholics than in families with other psychiatric disorders (Cotton, 1979). When compared with alcoholics without a family history of alcoholism, those alcoholics who demonstrate a positive family history for this problem also appear to have a more severe course, as shown by lower levels of social functioning and greater involvement of alcohol-related physical pathology (Frances, Timm, & Bucky, 1980; Penick, Read, Crowley, & Powell, 1978). These findings point to the possibility that genetic factors may be responsible, at least in part, for the familial nature of alcoholism. In addition, genetics may influence the expression of the disorder.

1.2. Animal Studies

Animal studies, particularly in rodents, have demonstrated some genetic factors that may influence alcohol consumption (Eriksson, 1975; McClearn, 1979). These determinants in animals may be important clues to biological factors influencing alcohol consumption in humans. In turn, this may have potential relevance to the propensity of some individuals to develop alcoholism. It is well documented that mouse and rat strains differ in their voluntary consumption of dilute ethanol solutions when water is available as an alternative fluid. Some strains consume more than 80% of their total fluid intake per day as alcohol, while other strains prefer water. These strains are referred to as alcohol-preferring and alcohol-avoiding, respectively.

Alcohol preference is under strong genetic control in mice. When fertilized ova from the alcohol-preferring C57BL strain were transferred to the uterus of a timed-pregnant alcohol-avoiding DBA female, to be born to and raised by her, the offspring retained their strain-typical alcohol preference (Randall & Lester, 1975). These results strongly suggest that genetic variables are more potent determinants of alcohol preference than pre- and/or postnatal maternal variables. Selective breeding studies have also supported this notion. It has been possible to develop strains of animals with extremes in voluntary alcohol consumption by selectively breeding animals who demonstrate these extremes with phenotypically similar mates over several generations. Thus, both the inbred mouse strains and selectively bred rat strains offer a unique opportunity to search for the biochemical/physiological basis of alcohol preference and aversion. Because even the alcohol-preferring strains do not voluntarily consume enough alcohol in a choice situation to become physically dependent or to impair functioning, the generalization to alcoholism *per se* is limited. This raises the possibility that different genetic factors may be involved in alcohol ingestion than are involved in alcohol dependence. In any event, the existence of animals with well-known phenotypic extremes in alcohol consumption promises to be a useful tool for investigations of the biological determinants of alcohol intake.

1.3. Genetic Marker Studies

The third type of study addressing the possible importance of genetics in alcoholism is the genetic marker study. Using population surveys or family studies, this approach searches for an association or linkage of alcoholism to factors known to be genetically influenced, such as blood proteins. These genetic marker studies have yielded fairly inconsistent results. One possible explanation is that, for the most part, investigators looked for associations in large populations and rarely went on to the more sophisticated types of analyses that are required in order to establish actual linkage, on a specific gene, between alcoholism and other genetically controlled biological factors (Hill, Goodwin, Cadoret, Osterland, & Doner, 1975). Nevertheless, possible associations have been established between blood proteins and alcoholism, and brain proteins such as Pc1 Duarte have also been found to be more common in alcoholics than in the general population (Comings, 1979). Additionally, black male alcoholics have been reported to have elevated superoxide dismutase levels, which may increase their vulnerability to the toxic effects of heavy doses of ethanol (Del Villano, Miller, Schacter, & Tischfield, 1980). Genetic marker studies generally have been consistent with the possibility of genetic factors in alcoholism, but they have added only limited information.

1.4. Twin Studies

It is difficult to argue the nature–nurture question in relation to alcoholism because of the difficulty in separating heredity from environment. Twin studies attempt to do this by comparing monozygotic (Mz) twin pairs with same-sex dizygotic (Dz) or fraternal twin pairs. Twin pairs of both types share major childhood environmental events such as death of a parent or financial crises in the family. Thus, if alcoholism were a genetically influenced disorder and not dependent solely on environmental events, one would expect the Mz twin pairs (who share

100% of their genes) to be much more similar or concordant for alcoholism than the Dz twin pairs (who share only 50% of their genes). In fact, studies using samples of twins only a small number of whom are alcoholic have demonstrated a probable heritability for drinking versus abstention and also for drinking patterns (Partanen, Bruun, & Markkanen, 1966). Studies of large samples of alcoholics some of whom are twins similarly have shown a two- to threefold higher level of concordance for alcoholism in Mz than Dz pairs. It has been reported that if one member of a monozygotic twin pair was alcoholic, the other was an alcoholic in 54% of the cases; while if one member of a dizygotic twin pair was alcoholic, the other was an alcoholic in only 28% of the cases (Kaij, 1960). Other studies of twins have demonstrated not only that alcoholism appears to be genetically influenced but also a higher concordance for specific alcohol-related problems, such as cirrhosis or alcoholic psychosis, in Mz than in Dz pairs (Hrubec & Omenn, 1981). The twin studies are not conclusive, however; their shortcomings have been discussed in another manuscript (Schuckit, 1981b-c).

1.5. Adoption Studies

The final type of approach to studying the genetic basis of alcoholism in humans is the use of adoption studies. The premise is that if alcoholism is genetically influenced, children of alcoholics separated from their biological parents near birth and raised by unrelated foster parents would have higher rates of alcoholism than adopted away children of nonalcoholic biological parents. Indeed, studies approaching this problem through a half-sibling methodology or through actual adoption records in the United States and Scandinavia have routinely supported genetic factors in alcoholism (Bohman, 1978; Cadoret, Cain, & Grove, 1980; Goodwin, Schulsinger, Moller, Hermansen, Winokur, & Guze, 1974; Schuckit, Goodwin, & Winokur, 1972). In most of these investigations, the risk for alcoholism in sons of alcoholics adopted out shortly after birth is four to five times higher than for sons of nonalcoholics adopted out and reared under similar circumstances. Susceptibility to alcoholism in adopted daughters, on the other hand, is more often inherited if the biological maternal parent is an alcoholic, despite the fact that alcohol abuse is more common in the male parent (Bohman, Sigvardsson, & Cloninger, 1981). It is probable, however, that there are genetically different types of susceptibility to alcoholism that must be differentiated and elucidated with further research.

Taken together, all types of studies mentioned above are consistent with the probability that genetics explains at least some of the variance in whether an individual will develop alcoholism. As demonstrated by the lack of a 100% concordance in alcoholism in Mz twins, it is probable that environmental factors also contribute to this development. The relative influence of environmental variables may be more pronounced in some racial groups than others (Reich, Winokur, &

Mullaney, 1975) and in daughters more than sons (Cloninger *et al.*, 1978), although this latter point recently has been challenged (Bohman *et al.*, 1981). Assessment of environmental influence is also complicated by the fact that a nonalcoholic mother may have an affective disorder or that either parent, though nonalcoholic, might have an alcoholic parent (Stabenau & Hesselbrock, 1980).

Even in animal models, the possible importance of environment is demonstrated by the change in level of alcohol preference (although not the reversal of drinking practices) by cross-fostering offspring of low drinking strains to higher drinking mothers (Randall & Lester, 1975). However, in humans there are few clues as to what, if any, specific environmental factors might be involved. Alcoholism in the rearing parent appears to have little, if any, influence. Sons of alcoholics reared by alcoholics are not at greater risk for the development of alcoholism than if they were reared by nonalcoholics (Cadoret *et al.*, 1980; Goodwin *et al.*, 1974; Schuckit *et al.*, 1972). Socioeconomic stratum of upbringing, interruptions in continuity of mothering, premorbid psychological symptoms, or dependency on parents also do not appear to be important variables in the genesis of alcoholism (Cadoret *et al.*, 1980; Jones, 1968; McCord & McCord, 1960).

Despite some assertions to the contrary (Spalt, 1979), there is no strong evidence that a specific Mendelian type of inheritance is involved in alcoholism, nor would most data be consistent with linkage of alcoholism to a specific set of genes, such as the X chromosome, for example. It is most probable that the predisposition toward alcoholism rests with the influence of several genes. That is, alcoholism is probably a polygenic disorder that interacts with environmental events. Alternatively, alcoholism may be the phenotypic expression of several different genotypically distinct disorders.

In the final analysis, the genetic data are impressive. This is true even though clinical studies cannot adequately control for prenatal or intrauterine factors or the mode of parenting during the first six weeks of life, which may be of possible importance. The combined series of animal and clinical investigations, however, is strong enough to justify further speculation on inherited biological variables that predispose an individual to consume alcohol and to develop alcoholism.

2. POSSIBLE BIOLOGICAL MECHANISMS FOR A GENETIC INFLUENCE IN ALCOHOLISM

To be of benefit, speculations about what might be inherited as part of a predisposition toward alcoholism must follow a number of guidelines. While almost anything is possible, it seems best to limit speculation to things that "make sense," those that have some tentative data supporting them, and those that are testable. As we have noted before (Schuckit, 1980a), there are at least five and perhaps six possible mechanisms, as indicated in Table 1.

Table 1. Possible Biological Influences in
Alcoholism

1. Absorption/metabolism
2. Acute reaction
3. Subacute reaction
4. Chronic consequences
5. Personality
6. Linkage to other psychiatric disorders

2.1. Absorption/Metabolism

It is probable that the rate of absorption of ethanol may be at least in part under genetic control (Randlow & Conway, 1978). Also, the overall rate of ethanol metabolism may be genetically influenced. For example, ethanol elimination rate has been demonstrated to have a greater similarity in Mz than in Dz twin pairs (Vesell, 1975) and might differ among ethnic groups, although these latter results are inconsistent (Reed, 1978; Schaefer, 1978). A search for the explanation of metabolic differences logically begins with the enzymes and coenzymes involved in alcohol metabolism, such as alcohol and aldehyde dehydrogenase (Bosron & Li, 1981). These enzymes have been shown to be under genetic control in animals and to exhibit divergent isoenzyme forms in different ethnic groups. Whether the form and/or activity is unique in persons predisposed to alcoholism is worthy of investigation.

Not only the rate of alcohol metabolism but also the level of acetaldehyde accumulated following alcohol ingestion may be a critical factor in alcoholism. The accumulation of acetaldehyde appears to be higher in alcoholics than in controls, as measured by a variety of methods in different populations. Some of this differential may, however, relate to different drinking patterns (Freund & O'Hollaren, 1965; Korsten, Matsuzaki, Feinman, & Lieber, 1975; Lindros, Stowell, Pikkarainen, & Salaspuro, 1980; Truitt, 1971). The increased accumulation of acetaldehyde in alcoholics is difficult to interpret, since high levels are presumed to be toxic and are related to decreased voluntary consumption in some ethnic groups and in animals. For example, acetaldehyde levels have been reported to be higher in alcohol-avoiding inbred mouse strains following alcohol challenge than in alcohol-preferring strains, and the activity of aldehyde dehydrogenase has been shown to be correspondingly lower (Sheppard, Albersheim, & McClearn, 1968). These data have been offered as an explanation for alcohol aversion. On the other hand, rats will self-administer acetaldehyde into the cerebral ventricles and may show subsequent increased alcohol intake (Amit, Brown, Rockman, Smith, & Amir, 1980). Elevations in blood acetaldehyde can also increase the risk for organ damage. In any event, acetaldehyde accumulation remains a possible determinant of alcohol ingestion and alcoholism (Schuckit & Duby, 1982).

In summary, one possible mediator of a genetic propensity in alcoholism could rest with genetic control of absorption and/or metabolism of alcohol. This could relate to any single factor or the combination of several factors, such as the rate of absorption of alcohol, absolute rate of ethanol metabolism, rates of accumulation and disappearance of acetaldehyde, or the accumulation of any of a variety of other metabolites.

2.2. Acute Reaction

A second possible biological mediator or genetic influence in alcoholism may relate to an individual's reaction to the first few drinks (i.e., his or her acute reaction to ethanol). It is possible that individuals at higher risk for alcoholism demonstrate a more pleasant or intense "high," which might encourage them to continue drinking. On the other hand, they may continue to consume alcohol because they are insensitive to low doses and, therefore, do not experience or recognize the internal cues associated with intoxication.

There are a variety of factors consistent with the possibility that the acute sensitivity to ethanol could be under genetic control. Animal studies have demonstrated significant differences in duration of alcohol-induced anesthesia between inbred mouse strains when loss of righting reflex was the dependent variable. For example, alcohol-preferring C57BL mice regain their righting reflex twice as fast as alcohol-avoiding BALB mice in spite of the fact that they have higher waking brain alcohol levels than BALB mice (Randall & Lester, 1974). These results imply a marked difference in CNS sensitivity to alcohol in inbred mice. Similar strain differences in sensitivity to alcohol have been reported for other types of reflexes and motor tasks (Schneider, Trzil, & D'Andrea, 1974; Malila, 1978). It is tempting to speculate that these genetically mediated differences in sensitivity to acute ethanol administration are related to chronic ethanol intake, since alcohol-avoiding strains appear to be more sensitive to the pharmacological actions of alcohol than alcohol-preferring strains.

Differences in CNS sensitivity to alcohol may be related to genetically influenced variations in neurochemistry. Even though this hypothesis cannot be directly tested in clinical studies, indirect measures offer support for it. For example, platelet monoamine oxidase (MAO) levels, which presumably reflect brain activity, may be lower in alcoholics than in controls (Major & Murphy, 1978; Sullivan, Cavenar, Maltbie, Lister, & Zung, 1979). Low MAO may indicate an aberration in monoamine metabolism in alcoholics or individuals predisposed toward this disorder (Sullivan, Stanfield, Schanberg, & Cavenar, 1978; Schuckit, O'Connor, Duby, Moss, & Vega, 1981). In any event, altered neurochemistry may turn out to be an important genetically influenced biological marker for acute alcohol sensitivity and/or the development of alcohol tolerance and dependence.

2.3. Functional Tolerance

A possible biological mediator for a genetic influence in alcoholism could rest with differential levels of functional or behavioral tolerance. This, in turn, could result in increased voluntary alcohol consumption in order to obtain desired psychological benefits. Frequent use of large amounts of alcohol might be expected to alter the time course of physical dependence. For example, selectively bred mouse strains differing in their acute sensitivity to alcohol also differ in their rate of development of functional tolerance (Tabakoff, Ritzmann, Raju, & Deitrich, 1980). Also, mouse strains demonstrating decreased sensitivity to the behavioral actions of alcohol and acute CNS tolerance (Tabakoff & Ritzmann, 1979) showed a briefer and milder alcohol withdrawal syndrome. This raises the speculation that the genetically mediated ability of the CNS to adapt rapidly in the presence of, ethanol may actually be related to its ability to adapt rapidly to its removal (Grieve, Griffiths, & Littleton, 1979). Taken together, the animal studies suggest that genetic factors might underlie functional tolerance and that, in turn, functional tolerance is possibly related to physical dependence. These results have implications for predicting as well as understanding variations in the time course of alcohol addiction and functional recovery after detoxification.

2.4. Susceptibility to Chronic Consequences

The genetic influence in alcoholism could result in a diverse group of predispositions toward alcohol-related organ damage. For example, susceptibility to alcohol-related disorders such as the Wernicke–Korsakoff syndrome and cirrhosis may have a genetic basis. Indeed, Wernicke–Korsakoff syndrome has been reported to result from a genetically mediated transketolase deficiency in some alcoholics (Blass & Gibson, 1977). In addition, alcoholic cirrhosis is found to occur more frequently in Mz alcoholic twins than in Dz alcoholic twins (Hrubec & Omenn, 1981). It is possible, therefore, that vulnerabilities toward alcohol-related pathology may be related to inherited defects in alcohol metabolism. This would, for instance, result in elevated acetaldehyde levels or defects in other biochemical systems and would, in turn, increase the risk for organ pathology (e.g., Del Villano et al., 1980).

2.5. Personality

Another possible mechanism for increased susceptibility could rest with personality variables. While it is very unlikely that there is an "alcoholic personality" (Miller, 1976; Schuckit & Haglund, 1977), it is possible that individual personality attributes may be associated with an elevated risk for alcoholism. However, while some studies have reported increased anxiety levels and distinct Minnesota

Multiphasic Personality Inventory (MMPI) profiles in alcoholics, these effects have not been observed in young men at high risk for alcoholism (Saunders & Schuckit, 1981; Schuckit, 1982a).

2.6. Relationship to Other Psychiatric Disorders

Finally, it is possible that a predisposition toward alcoholism may be mediated through genetic factors related to other psychiatric disorders. For instance, individuals qualifying for the diagnosis of the antisocial personality (or sociopathy) report high rates of alcohol misuse (Robins, 1978). However, when the two disorders are carefully defined and primary alcoholics singled out (Schuckit, 1973), there is little evidence that the families of sociopaths show elevated risks for primary alcoholism (Cadoret, 1978). Moreover, adoption studies do not demonstrate a high level of crossover between alcoholism and non-alcohol-related criminality (Bohman, 1978). It appears as if alcoholism and the antisocial personality are distinct entities. Most sociopaths demonstrate secondary alcoholism, but primary alcoholics generally do not show pervasive antisocial problems in early life.

Another area of important speculation is the possible interaction between alcoholism and affective disorder, a problem also felt to be under genetic influence (Gershon, Baron, & Leckman, 1975). However, the adoption study of Goodwin, Schulsinger, Knop, Mednick, and Guze (1977), while demonstrating a higher risk for depression in daughters of alcoholics (but *only* if they were reared by alcoholics), did not demonstrate any close association for men (Goodwin *et al.*, 1974). Other authors have given evidence that bipolar affective disorder and alcoholism do not appear to have any significant level of genetic crossover (Dunner, Hensel, & Rieve, 1979). Interpretation of possible linkage between primary alcoholism and *bona fide* primary affective disorder is complicated by the probable increased prevalence of affective problems in the mothers of male alcoholics (Stabenau & Hesselbrock, 1980). Thus, the association between the two disorders might be through assortative mating between affectively impaired women and alcoholic men rather than by true genetic linkage.

It appears that once psychiatric syndromes are carefully defined, there is little evidence that the genetic factors for alcoholism interact closely with genetic predispositions toward other major psychiatric disorders. A similar case can be made regarding drug abuse, since elevated rates of heroin abuse in first-degree relatives of primary alcoholics have not been demonstrated (Schuckit, 1980a).

In summary, it is clear that the biological mediators of alcoholism are not known. The possibilities outlined above represent viable starting points in a search for the genetic basis of the disorder. Of course, the task of identifying the factor or factors predisposing an individual to alcoholism is complicated and requires a systematic approach to the problem.

Several approaches can be taken, each of which has its advantages and disadvantages. For example, one can choose to compare alcoholics to controls who are not alcoholics. However, any differences between the two groups could be attributed to chronic alcohol abuse rather than to an inherent biochemical or psychological imbalance. In order to circumvent this criticism, ideally one would like to study prealcoholics. By using the familial nature of alcoholism as a tool for selecting groups at elevated risk for the disorder, the likelihood of identifying future alcoholics among the general population is increased significantly (Schuckit, 1980c). It is this target group (i.e., children of alcoholics) that we have chosen to investigate systematically.

The remainder of this chapter will be devoted to a brief description and summary of our search for the genetic influence in alcoholism. Details of our procedure and results have been reported elsewhere (Schuckit, 1980a,b,c,d; 1981a).

3. A PROSPECTIVE SEARCH FOR THE BIOLOGICAL DETERMINANTS OF ALCOHOLISM

In selecting our target group, we have, for two reasons, chosen to limit ourselves to males. First, the actual risk for development of alcoholism is higher in males than in females (Haglund & Schuckit, 1977) and, second, in the study of male subjects it is not necessary to control for phase of the menstrual cycle and other endocrinologic variables unique to women (Jones, Jones, & Paredes, 1976). In order to select males at high risk for alcoholism who are old enough to consume alcoholic beverages legally but not likely to be alcoholics yet, we included men aged 21 to 25 in our sample. Comparisons of such men with suitable controls can yield important results, even if later follow-ups do not show that all of the individuals carrying the factor(s) actually develop alcoholism. The trait, even if not expressed, might lead to the identification of other genetic factors or environmental events that mediate the actual final development of alcoholism. Therefore, the groups now under study will be followed up in the future to determine the correlation between the factors attributed to alcoholism and the eventual development of the trait itself. Currently, within our study population we are also investigating multiple biological mediators believed to reflect the genetic influence in alcoholism. This is because, as mentioned previously, it is impossible to be sure which (if any) of the hypothesized elements might be critical and because multiple genetic factors may well interact to determine the final risk (Cloninger et al., 1978; Reich et al., 1975; Schuckit, 1980a).

Any studies of higher-risk individuals must, to be optimally effective, compare results with lower-risk controls. We have chosen to use family-history-positive (FHP) and family-history-negative (FHN) pairs of men matched on demography, height/weight ratio (as these may affect absorption or metabolism), and drinking history. FHP is operationally defined as a family history of alcoholism in either a parent or sibling. Regarding the drinking history variable, it is impossible to be certain that an accurate drinking history was given, but the self-reported drinking history is probably more valid than the information from relatives or friends and appears to generate higher estimated levels of consumption than do those ancillary sources (Adams, Grant, Carlin, & Reed, 1981; Sobell, Sobell, & Samuels, 1974). While no perfect validity check for drinking history is available, FHP/FHN pairs are also matched on a variety of blood markers known to increase with excessive drinking, including gamma-glutamyl-transferase (GGT), uric acid, and mean corpuscular volume (Schuckit, 1982b, Whitehead, Clarke, & Whitfield, 1978).

Over the past three years, our laboratory has generated results on selected aspects of personality, absorption/metabolism of ethanol, and several aspects of the acute reaction to alcohol ingestion in these two well-defined groups. For example, we have reported that alcohol absorption and elimination rates seem similar for FHP and FHN subjects. Acetaldehyde levels on the other hand, while much lower than those observed in a disulfiram reaction, were found to be twofold higher in the FHP groups. While the clinical importance of these findings has not been established, it is tempting to speculate that elevated acetaldehyde levels may enhance the quantity or quality of intoxication or increase the risk for alcoholism through other means. For instance, it is possible that heightened acetaldehyde levels interact with brain biogenic amines to produce morphinelike alkaloids which, in turn, produce a stronger drive to consume alcohol or mediate a heightened predisposition toward addiction (Myers, 1978; Davis & Walsh, 1970; Duncan & Deitrich, 1980). It is also possible, as stated previously, that increased acetaldehyde levels are toxic; therefore, the risk for organ damage would increase when alcohol is consumed chronically. Whether acetaldehyde mediates alcohol intake and/or alcoholism remains to be clarified.

Our studies of the acute reaction to ethanol have yielded some interesting results. FHP men report less intense intoxication than FHN men despite almost identical BACs (Schuckit, 1980b; Duby & Schuckit, 1981). This finding is consistent with our speculation that FHP individuals may require more alcohol than FHN men to feel intoxicated.

The personality tests that were administered to our subjects revealed no significant differences between the two groups on level of assertiveness or trait anxiety. Both FHP and FHN individuals scored within the "normal" range on all relevant MMPI subtests, although FHP men tended to score higher on the MacAndrew "alcoholism scale."

Taken together, these findings suggest that young men at risk for the development of alcoholism differ from matched controls on their subjective intoxication following alcohol consumption as well as their physiological response to the drug but not on the personality variables we have examined. Our unpublished preliminary results on blood cortisol levels and auditory evoked potential following alcohol ingestion offer additional support for the notion that FHP men have a different physiological reaction to alcohol than FHN individuals.

4. SUMMARY

That alcoholism runs in families is a well-documented fact. Although it is highly probable that environmental variables contribute to this, evidence from clinical and animal research strongly suggests that alcoholism is a genetically influenced disorder. Exactly what is inherited, however, is not certain. In a search for the genetic mediators of alcoholism, it makes sense to begin investigating determinants specific to alcohol metabolism as well as the individual's reaction, both physiological and psychological, to the drug.

Toward this end, we have begun a series of studies in young men with a family history of alcoholism (FHP) and a matched control group (FHN). Studies to date indicate no significant differences between the groups on absorption or disappearance of ethanol, but we have demonstrated elevated acetaldehyde levels following alcohol ingestion in FHP subjects. The two groups also have demonstrated differences in their subjective level of intoxication. That is, young FHP men appear to be less sensitive to the intoxicating effects of alcohol than FHN subjects. Of course, it is not possible to conclude from our present data whether any of these variables relate to the vulnerability toward alcoholism. This type of invaluable information will be obtained in follow-up studies of our cohorts. Ideally, these data will provide critical information on possible biological mediators of alcohol addiction and suggest avenues of investigation into inheritance patterns.

5. REFERENCES

Adams, K. M., Grant, I., Carlin, A. S., & Reed, R. Cross-study comparisons of self-reported alcohol consumption in four clinical groups. *American Journal of Psychiatry*, 1981, *134*, 445–449.

Blass, J. P., & Gibson, G. E. Abnormality of a thiamine-requiring enzyme in patients with Wernicke-Korsakoff syndrome. *New England Journal of Medicine*, 1977, *297*, 1367–1370.

Bohman, M. Some genetic aspects of alcoholism and criminality. *Archives of General Psychiatry*, 1978, *35*, 269–276.

Bohman, M., Sigvardsson, S., & Cloninger, C. R. Maternal inheritance of alcohol abuse. *Archives of General Psychiatry*, 1981, *38*, 965–969.

Bosron, W. F., & Li, T. K. Genetic determinants of alcohol and aldehyde dehydrogenases and alcohol metabolism. *Seminars in Liver Disease*, 1981, *1*, 179–188.

Cadoret, R. J. Psychopathology in adopted-away offspring of biologic parents with antisocial behavior. *Archives of General Psychiatry*, 1978, *35*, 176–184.

Cadoret, R. J., Cain, C. A., & Grove, W. M. Development of alcoholism in adoptees raised apart from alcoholic biologic relatives. *Archives of General Psychiatry*, 1980, *37*, 561–563.

Cloninger, C. R., Christiansen, K. O., Reich, T., & Gottesman, I. I. Implications of sex differences in the prevalences of antisocial personality, alcoholism, and criminality for familial transmission. *Archives of General Psychiatry*, 1978, *35*, 941–951.

Comings, D. E. Pc1 Duarte, a common polymorphism of a human brain protein, and its relationship to depressive disease and multiple sclerosis. *Nature*, 1979, *277*, 28–32.

Cotton, N. S. The familial incidence of alcoholism: A review. *Journal of Studies on Alcohol*, 1979, *40*, 89–116.

Davis, V. E., & Walsh, M. J. Alcohol, amines, and alkaloids: A possible biochemical basis for alcohol addiction. *Science*, 1970, *167*, 1005–1007.

Del Villano, B. C., Miller, S. I., Schacter, L. P., & Tischfield, J. A. Elevated superoxide dismutase in black alcoholics. *Science*, 1980, *207*, 991–993.

Duby, J., & Schuckit, M. A. *Subjective effects of alcohol intoxication in young men with alcoholic relatives.* Presented at the National Council on Alcoholism Annual Scientific Meeting, New Orleans, La., 1981.

Duncan, C., & Deitrich, R. A. A critical evaluation of tetrahydroisoquinoline induced ethanol preference in rats. *Pharmacology, Biochemistry, and Behavior*, 1980, *13*, 1–17.

Dunner, D. L., Hensel, B. M., & Rieve, R. R. Bipolar illness: Factors in drinking behavior. *American Journal of Psychiatry*, 1979, *136*, 583–585.

Eriksson, K. Alcohol imbibition and behavior: A comparative genetic approach. *Psychopharmacogenetics*. New York: Plenum Press, 1975.

Frances, R. J., Timm, S., & Bucky, S. Studies of familial and nonfamilial alcoholism. *Archives of General Psychiatry*, 1980, *37*, 564–566.

Freund, G., & O'Hollaren, P. Acetaldehyde concentrations in alveolar air following a standard dose of ethanol in man. *Journal of Lipid Research*, 1965, *6*, 471–477.

Gershon, E. S., Baron, M., & Leckman, J. F. Genetic models of the transmission of affective disorders. *Journal of Psychiatric Research*, 1975, *12*, 301–317.

Goodwin, D. W., Schulsinger, F., Moller, N., Hermansen, L., Winokur, G., & Guze, S. B. Drinking problems in adopted and nonadopted sons of alcoholics. *Archives of General Psychiatry*, 1974, *31*, 164–169.

Goodwin, D. W., Schulsinger, F., Knop, J., Mednick, S., & Guze, S. B. Psychopathology in adopted and nonadopted daughters of alcoholics. *Archives of General Psychiatry*, 1977, *34*, 1005–1009.

Grieve, J., Griffiths, P. J., & Littleton, J. M. Genetic influences on the rate of development of ethanol tolerance and the ethanol physical withdrawal syndrome in mice. *Drug and Alcohol Dependence*, 1979, *4*, 77–86.

Haglund, R. M. J., & Schuckit, M. A. The epidemiology of alcoholism. In N. Estes & E. Heinemann (Eds.), *Alcoholism: Development, consequences and intervention.* St. Louis: Mosby, 1977, 28–43.

Hill, S. Y., Goodwin, D. W., Cadoret, R., Osterland, C. K., & Doner, S. M. Association and linkage between alcoholism and eleven serological markers. *Journal of Studies on Alcohol*, 1975, *36*, 981–992.

Hrubec, Z., & Omenn, G. S. Evidence of genetic predisposition to alcoholic cirrhosis and psychosis: Twin concordances for alcoholism and its biologic end points by zygosity among male veterans. *Alcoholism: Clinical and Experimental Research*, 1981, *5*, 207–214.

Jones, B. M., Jones, M. K., & Paredes, A. Oral contraceptives and ethanol metabolism. *Alcohol Technical Reports*, 1976, *5*, 28–32.

Jones, M. C. Personality correlates and antecedents of drinking patterns in adult males. *Journal of Counseling and Clinical Psychology*, 1968, *32*, 2–12.

Kaij, L. *Studies on the etiology and sequels of abuse of alcohol.* Department of Psychiatry, University of Lund, Sweden, 1960.

Korsten, M. A., Matsuzaki, S., Feinman, L., & Lieber, C. S. High blood acetaldehyde levels after ethanol administration. *New England Journal of Medicine*, 1975, *292*, 386–389.

Lindros, K. O., Stowell, A., Pikkarainen, P., & Salaspuro, M. Elevated blood acetaldehyde in alcoholics with accelerated ethanol elimination. *Pharmacology, Biochemistry, and Behavior*, 1980, *13*, 119–124.

Major, L. F., & Murphy, D. L. Platelet and plasma amine oxidase activity in alcoholic individuals. *British Journal of Psychiatry*, 1978, *132*, 548–554.

Malila, A. Intoxicating effects of three aliphatic alcohols and barbital on two rat strains genetically selected for their ethanol intake. *Pharmacology, Biochemistry, and Behavior*, 1978, *8*, 197–201.

McClearn, G. E. Genetics and alcoholism simulacra. *Alcoholism: Clinical and Experimental Research*, 1979, *3*, 255–258.

McCord, W., & McCord, J. *Origins of alcoholism*. Stanford, Calif.: Stanford University Press, 1960.

Miller, W. R. Alcoholism scales and objective assessment methods: A review. *Psychological Bulletin*, 1976, *83*, 649–674.

Myers, R. D. Tetrahydroisoquinolines in the brain: The basis of an animal model of alcoholism. *Alcoholism: Clinical and Experimental Research*, 1978, *2*, 145–154.

Partanen, J., Bruun, K., & Markkanen, T., *Inheritance of drinking behavior*. Helsinki: Kekuskirjopoino-Centraltryckeriet, 1966.

Penick, E. C., Read, M. R., Crowley, P. A., & Powell, B. J. Differentiation of alcoholics by family history. *Journal of Studies on Alcohol*, 1978, *39*, 1944–1948.

Radlow, R., & Conway, T. L. *Consistency of alcohol absorption in human subjects*. Presented at The American Psychological Association Convention, Toronto, Canada, August 31, 1978.

Randall, C. L., & Lester, D. Differential effects of ethanol and pentobarbital on sleep time in C57BL and BALB mice. *Journal of Pharmacology and Experimental Therapeutics*, 1974, *188*, 27–33.

Randall, C. L., & Lester, D. Social modification of alcohol consumption in inbred mice. *Science*, 1975, *189*, 149–151.

Reed, T. E. Racial comparisons of alcohol metabolism: background, problems, and results. *Alcoholism: Clinical and Experimental Research*, 1978, *2*, 83–87.

Reich, T., Winokur, G., & Mullaney, J. The transmission of alcoholism. In R. R. Fieve, D. Rosenthal, & W. Brill (Eds.), *Genetic research in psychiatry*. Baltimore: Johns Hopkins University Press, 1975.

Robins, L. N. Sturdy childhood predictors of adult antisocial behaviour: replications from longitudinal studies. *Psychological Medicine*, 1978, *8*, 611–622.

Saunders, G. R., & Schuckit, M. A. MMPI scores in young men with alcoholic relatives and controls. *Journal of Nervous and Mental Disease*, 1981, *169*, 456–458.

Schaefer, J. M. Alcohol metabolism and sensitivity reactions among the Reddis of South India. *Alcoholism: Clinical and Experimental Research*, 1978, *2*, 61–69.

Schneider, C. W., Trzil, P., & D'Andrea, R. Neural tolerance in high and low ethanol. *Pharmacology, Biochemistry, and Behavior*, 1974, *2*, 549–551.

Schuckit, M. A. Alcoholism and sociopathy—diagnostic confusion. *Quarterly Journal on the Studies of Alcohol*, 1973, *34*, 157–164.

Schuckit, M. A. Alcoholism and genetics: possible biological mediators. *Biological Psychiatry*, 1980, *15*, 437–447. (a)

Schuckit, M. A. Self-rating of alcohol intoxication by young men with and without family histories of alcoholism. *Journal of Studies on Alcohol*, 1980, *41*, 242–249. (b)

Schuckit, M. A. A theory of alcohol and drug abuse: a genetic approach. In D. J. Lettieri, M. Sayers, & H. W. Pearson (Eds.), *Theories on Drug Abuse*. Washington, D.C.: NIDA Research Monograph 30, 1980, 297–302. (c)

Schuckit, M. A. Biological markers: Metabolism and acute reactions to alcohol in sons of alcoholics. *Pharmacology, Biochemistry, and Behavior*, 1980, *13*, 9–16. (d)

Schuckit, M. A. Peak blood alcohol levels in men at high risk for the future development of alcoholism. *Alcoholism: Clinical and Experimental Research*, 1981, *5*, 64–66. (a)

Schuckit, M. A. Twin studies on substance abuse: An overview. In L. Gedda, P. Parisi, & W. Nance, *Twin research 3.* New York: Alan R. Liss, 1981. (b)

Schuckit, M. A. Anxiety and assertiveness in relatives of alcoholics and controls. *Journal of Clinical Psychiatry,* 1982, *43,* 238-239. (a)

Schuckit, M. A. Gamma glutamyl-transferase values in nonalcoholic drinking men. *American Journal of Psychiatry,* 1982, *139,* 227-228. (b)

Schuckit, M. A., & Duby, J. Alcohol related flushing and the risk for alcoholism in sons of alcoholics. *Journal of Clinical Psychiatry,* 1982, *43,* 415-418.

Schuckit, M. A., & Haglund, R. M. J. An overview of the etiological theories on alcoholism. In N. J. Estes & M. E. Heinemann (Eds.), *Alcoholism: Development, consequences, and interventions.* St. Louis: Mosby, 1977.

Schuckit, M. A., Goodwin, D. A., & Winokur, G. A study of alcoholism in half siblings. *American Journal of Psychiatry,* 1972, *128,* 1132.

Schuckit, M. A., O'Connor, D., Duby, J., Moss, M., & Vega, R. DBH activity levels in men at high risk for alcoholism and controls. *Biological Psychiatry,* 1981, *16,* 1067-1075.

Sheppard, J. R., Albersheim, P., & McClearn, G., Enzyme activities and ethanol preference in mice. *Biochemistry and Genetics,* 1968, *2,* 205-212.

Sobell, M. B., Sobell, L. C., & Samuels, F. H. Validity of self-reports of alcohol-related arrests by alcoholics. *Quarterly Journal of Studies on Alcohol,* 1974, *35,* 276-280.

Spalt, L. Alcoholism: Evidence of an x-linked recessive genetic characteristic. *Journal of the American Medical Association,* 1979, *241,* 2543.

Stabenau, J. R., & Hesselbrock, V. Assortative mating, family pedigree, and alcoholism. *Substance and Alcohol Actions/Misuse,* 1980, *1,* 375-382.

Sullivan, J. L., Stanfield, C. N., Schanberg, S., & Cavenar, J. Platelet monoamine oxidase and serum dopamine-B-hydroxylase activity in chronic alcoholics. *Archives of General Psychiatry,* 1978, *35,* 1209-1212.

Sullivan, J. L., Cavenar, J. O., Maltbie, A. A., Lister, P., & Zung, W. K. Familial biochemical and clinical correlates of alcoholics with low platelet monoamine oxidase activity. *Biological Psychiatry,* 1979, *14,* 385-394.

Tabakoff, B., & Ritzmann, R. F. Acute tolerance in inbred and selected lines of mice. *Drug and Alcohol Dependence,* 1979, *4,* 87-90.

Tabakoff, B., Ritzmann, R. F., Raju, T. S., & Deitrich, R. A. Characterization of acute and chronic tolerance in mice selected for inherent differences in sensitivity to ethanol. *Alcoholism: Clinical and Experimental Research,* 1980, *4,* 70-73.

Truitt, E. B. Blood acetaldehyde levels after alcohol consumption by alcoholic and nonalcoholic subjects. *Biological Aspects of Alcohol,* 1971, *3,* 212-232.

Vesell, E. S. Ethanol metabolism: Regulation by genetic factors in normal volunteers under a controlled environment and the effect of chronic ethanol administration. *Annals New York Academy of Sciences,* 1975, *197,* 79-88.

Whitehead, T. P., Clarke, C. A., & Whitfield, A. G. W. Biochemical and haematological markers of alcohol intake. *Lancet,* 1978, *1,* 978-981.

5.1. Books and Reviews

Amit, Z., Brown, Z. W., Rockman, G. E., Smith, B., & Amir, S. Acetaldehyde: A positive reinforcer mediating alcohol consumption. In H. Begleiter (Ed.), *Biological Effects of Alcohol.* New York: Plenum Press, 1980, 413-423.

Goodwin, D. W. *Is alcoholism hereditary?* New York: Oxford University Press, 1976, 51-84.

Gottesman, I. I., & Shields, J. A critical review of recent adoption, twin, and family studies of schizophrenia: Behavioral genetics perspectives. *Schizophrenia Bulletin,* 1976, *2,* 360-401.

McClearn, G. E. The genetic aspects of alcoholism. In P. G. Bourne & R. Fox (Eds.), *Alcoholism: Progress in research and treatment*. New York: Academic Press, 1973, 337–358.

Schuckit, M. A. A theory of alcohol and drug abuse: A genetic approach. In D. J. Lettieri, M. Sayers, & H. W. Pearson (Eds.), *Theories on Drug Abuse*. Washington, D.C.: NIDA Research Monograph 30, 1980, 297–302.

Schuckit, M. A., & Haglund, R. M. J. An overview of the etiological theories on alcoholism. In N. J. Estes & M. E. Heinemann (Eds.), *Alcoholism: Development, consequences, and interventions*. St. Louis: C. V. Mosby, Co., 1977.

Warner, R. H., & Rosett, H. L. The effects of drinking on offspring. An historical survey of the American and British literature. *Journal of Studies on Alcohol*, 1975, *36*, 1395–1420.

The Absorption, Distribution, and Metabolism of Ethanol and Its Effects on Nutrition and Hepatic Function

TING-KAI LI

1. INTRODUCTION

The factors that govern blood and tissue concentrations of ethanol are the rate of absorption from the site of administration, the distribution space for ethanol in the body, and the rate of its elimination. Ethanol is neither accumulated to any extent by specific organs nor preferentially bound to cellular components. It is eliminated principally by oxidative metabolism in the liver. Consequently, after absorption and distribution in tissue and extracellular water, the primary determinant of the duration and extent of its pharmacologic action is the rate of its oxidation by the liver. For this reason, the enzymatic pathways of ethanol metabolism and their control by genetic and environmental factors have been important areas for detailed study. Furthermore, the oxidation of ethanol can produce profound abnormalities in the metabolic functions of the liver as well as nutrient imbalance. Knowledge of these interrelationships is fundamental to the understanding and treatment of many of the medical consequences of alcohol abuse and alcoholism,

TING-KAI LI • Departments of Medicine and Biochemistry, Indiana University School of Medicine, and Veterans Administration Medical Center, Indianapolis, Indiana 46223.

some of which may be life-threatening. These aspects of the biochemistry and pharmacology of ethanol are the principal focus of this chapter.

2. ABSORPTION AND DISTRIBUTION

Ethanol is infinitely soluble in water and slightly soluble in lipids. Like any dissolved substance, it changes the colligative properties of water; however, it lacks an osmotic effect in biologic systems because it is freely diffusible across cell membranes. After oral administration, ethanol is rapidly absorbed by diffusion from the small intestine. It is much less readily absorbed from the stomach. Accordingly, factors that delay gastric emptying and cause dilution will also slow absorption. For example, a concentrated solution of ethanol is absorbed more slowly than a dilute solution, because ethanol in concentrations greater than 10% tends to inhibit gastric motility. The ingestion of food prior to or concurrently with ethanol has similar effects, reducing both the rate and the efficiency of absorption of the latter.

Ethanol distributes itself in total body water. At equilibrium, extracellular and intracellular (adjusted for water content) concentrations are approximately equal. Establishment of equilibrium occurs more rapidly in well-vascularized organs that have high blood flow (e.g., liver, brain, lung, kidneys) than in poorly vascularized tissue with low blood flow (e.g., muscle). It has been shown that following the oral administration of ethanol and before equilibration among all tissue and extracellular compartments is reached, the concentrations of ethanol in the brain and arterial blood are substantially higher than those in muscle and peripheral veins. Accordingly, measurements of the ethanol content of expired air more accurately reflect the level of central nervous system exposure than similar measurements of venous blood during the ascending portion of the blood alcohol concentration curve. These conditions may prevail for as long as 1.5 hours in both human subjects and experimental animals (Forney, Hughes, Harger, & Richards, 1964).

Intravenous and intraperitoneal administration of ethanol obviates the variability associated with gastrointestinal absorption and results in more predictable blood alcohol levels than with oral administration. Equilibration also occurs more quickly. However, both these routes initially produce very high alcohol concentrations in the brain. Accordingly, the lethal dose administered parenterally is considerably lower than that given by mouth (Wallgren & Barry, 1970).

Because ethanol is distributed in total body water, conditions that change body water content (e.g., sex, age, obesity, edema, ascites, and retained fluid in the gastrointestinal tract) affect blood alcohol levels and rates of alcohol elimination from blood. For the same dose of ethanol, an increase in total body water decreases the peak height and elimination rate of ethanol in blood, whereas a decrease has the opposite effect.

3. PHARMACOKINETICS AND ALCOHOL ELIMINATION RATES

The alcohol elimination rate of human subjects and experimental animals can be estimated by the sequential measurement of alcohol concentrations in blood (Erickson, 1979) following the administration of ethanol either by mouth or parenterally. After absorption and equilibration are complete, the rate of decline in blood alcohol concentration is used to calculate elimination rate. The method most commonly employed for this purpose is a zero-order kinetics model. First proposed by Widmark (1933), the model assumes that, after the absorption–equilibration phase, blood ethanol concentration decreases linearly with time and the rate is constant, independent of ethanol concentration, down to about 20 mg/100 mL. A simplified equation for computation is:

$$R = \beta \times \frac{A}{C_0 \cdot W}$$

where R is the rate of ethanol elimination corrected for body weight; β is the rate of decay of blood ethanol concentration; A is the dose of ethanol administered; C_0 is the apparent concentration of ethanol at zero time, obtained by extrapolating the line for blood ethanol decay to the y axis; and W is the body weight. The apparent volume of distribution, V, for ethanol is calculated from the relationship:

$$V = \frac{A}{C_0}$$

The calculated R values, according to this model, would represent the maximal alcohol elimination capacities of the animals. By this method, the maximal elimination rate for normal human subjects has been determined by many investigators to be, on the average, about 100 mg/kg/h (2.2 mmol/kg/h) or 170 g ethanol/day for a 70-kg person. Most of these studies employed low to moderate loading doses of ethanol, which generally raised initial blood alcohol concentrations to 150 mg% or less. By use of the same method, studies in experimental animals have shown that those very much smaller in body size than humans exhibit higher rates (e.g., 300 mg/kg/h for rats and 550 mg/kg/h for mice), whereas those larger in body size exhibit lower rates (Wallgren & Barry, 1970).

The validity of the above model was challenged shortly after it was proposed by Widmark, because it was observed in both humans and experimental animals that the rate of ethanol elimination is not independent of the amount of ethanol in the body and that β may increase with an increase in dose. Therefore, alcohol elimination rates determined by means of a single ethanol dose in the manner described by Widmark would tend to underestimate the maximal capacity for clearance, because the dose chosen may not be saturating for the processes responsible. However, because of its simplicity and the impracticality of administering multiple ethanol doses to the same subject, most investigators have continued to use Widmark's method of analysis but employing single, identical doses (e.g., 1.0 g/kg body weight) for all subjects whose elimination rates are being compared.

More recent, detailed studies of the pharmacokinetics of ethanol have shown that the time course of ethanol elimination is best described not by zero-order but by Michaelis–Menten kinetics (Wilkinson, 1980). The equation describing the process is:

$$-\frac{dC}{dt} = \frac{V_{max} \cdot C}{Km + C}$$

where dC/dt is the instantaneous rate of change of concentration with time, C is the concentration at time t, V_{max} is the maximal velocity, and Km is the Michaelis constant (concentration of ethanol at which rate is one-half maximal). When the above equation is integrated between the limits $C = C_0$ at $t = 0$ and $C = C$ at $t = t$, the following equation is obtained:

$$C_0 - C + Km \ln (C_0/C) = V_{max} \cdot t$$

The equation is applicable to all blood concentrations of ethanol in the postabsorption–distribution phase.

The Michaelis–Menten model predicts that for all doses of ethanol administered, approximately the initial two-thirds of the decay curve is pseudolinear whereas the terminal portion is curved. However, the slope of the pseudolinear phase (comparable to β in Widmark's equation) is not constant but increases with dose, the amount of change being a function of the Km of the system. For example, if Km is 10 mg/100 mL (2.2 mM), the slope of the pseudolinear portion of the alcohol disappearance curve would be 91% of maximum at an initial concentration of 100 mg/100 mL (22 mM), 96% of maximum at 250 mg/100 mL (54 mM), and 98% of maximum at 500 mg/100 mL (108 mM). Thus, after administration of different doses of ethanol, the Km and V_{max} can be calculated from the reciprocal plot of the rate of pseudolinear decline of blood ethanol concentration versus C_0 or from the application of the integrated Michaelis–Menten equation when a single dose is employed. In a limited number of studies performed in this manner, the maximal elimination rate for normal, male, human subjects was found to be, on the average, about 130 mg/kg/h or 220 g/day for a 70-kg person. The average Km was 1.6 mmol.

Figure 1 is a schematic illustration of the Michaelis–Menten kinetics model. The progression of blood ethanol concentrations following the oral administration

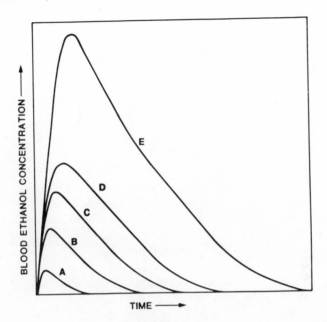

Figure 1. Illustration of Michaelis–Menten kinetics for ethanol elimination when increasing amounts of ethanol are ingested. Curves A through D show progressive saturation of a single (low) Km process. Curve E shows the additive effect of a second, high-Km process.

of increasing amounts of ethanol is plotted against time. It is assumed for curves A through D that the pathway or pathways of elimination have the same or similar Km values, whereas for curve E it is assumed that there are two pathways with substantially different Km values *(vide infra)*. The slopes of the initial pseudolinear portions of curves A–D increase in steepness with increasing ethanol dose to approach a maximum value at concentrations of ethanol greater than 25 times the value of Km.

The effect of food upon such blood ethanol concentration progression curves has also been studied. Food decreases the peak ethanol concentration, decreases the area under the curve, and increases the time required to attain peak concentration. These effects are attributable to delayed gastric emptying in combination with the action of the Michaelis–Menten kinetics for elimination during the absorption–equilibration phase (Sedman, Wilkinson, Sakmar, Weidler, & Wagner, 1976).

The studies that convincingly demonstrated the validity of Michaelis–Menten kinetics for ethanol elimination were performed in normal human subjects, also with the use of low to moderate doses of ethanol. Peak blood alcohol concentrations were almost always less than 100 mg/100 mL and the data were adequately described by a single Michaelis–Menten function (or an aggregate of functions with similar Km values). If elimination were mediated by multiple processes whose Km values differ substantially, nonlinearity would occur at both ends of the blood ethanol disappearance curve (Wilkinson, 1980). As illustrated by curve E in Figure 1 for two parallel Michaelis–Menten functions with different (greater than three- to fivefold) Km values, two separate pseudolinear segments of different slopes may become evident in the high and intermediate concentration ranges. It has now been established that human livers have enzymatic activity with substantially different Km values (e.g., less than 2 mM and 10 to 40 mM) for ethanol oxidation (Li, 1977). Moreover, there are observations that after the ingestion of large amounts of ethanol, tolerated usually by individuals exhibiting tolerance, the blood ethanol disappearance curve is entirely nonlinear (Hammond, Rumack, & Rodgerson, 1973) or similar to curve E of Figure 1 in the high concentration ranges (Feinman, Baraona, Matsuzaki, Korsten, & Lieber, 1978). Thus, while analysis of the pharmacokinetics of ethanol by means of a single Michaelis–Menten function is operationally useful at low to moderate ethanol consumption levels, the application of models with multiple Km values may be more appropriate when blood ethanol concentrations are high (e.g., greater than 150 mg/100 mL). It is evident that repeated, careful observations are still needed in this regard. The existence of pathways of elimination with high Km for ethanol can, in part, explain the increased elimination or metabolic rate for ethanol also reported to occur at high ethanol concentrations in experimental animals and isolated liver preparations, *in vitro*. Later sections discuss the various mechanisms by which ethanol elimination rate can be increased.

As discussed above, the average, maximal elimination rate of ethanol for normal, human subjects has been estimated to be about 220 g/day. There is evidence both in humans and in experimental animals that ethanol elimination rates can increase 75% or more with chronic alcohol ingestion. Therefore, it is conceivable that the average, maximal capacity for elimination can be 385 g/day or higher in the chronic alcoholic individual. The maximal intake tolerated by such subjects when measured under experimentally controlled conditions of drinking is in good agreement with this estimate (Isbell, Fraser, Wikler, Belleville, & Eisenman, 1955). Self-reports of intake in alcoholics have yielded average maximum consumptions of about 300 g/day. Expectedly, there is a wide range of variation.

3.1. Intra- and Interindividual Variations in Alcohol Elimination Rates

It is uncertain to what extent alcohol elimination rate under "basal" conditions varies from day to day and from one test period to another in the same individual. Some investigators have seen essentially no change, whereas others have reported variations three times larger than that of the method. In one recent study, a coefficient of variation of about 10% was found upon repeated testing in the same subjects (Kopun & Propping, 1977). It is unclear what environmental and physiologic factors or combination of factors may underlie small variations of this kind. Food ingestion, exercise, increased ventilatory rate, and changes in hormonal status have only trivial or negligible effects when each is examined separately as an independent variable. However, smoking and chronic ethanol use have been shown to accelerate ethanol elimination rate by 30% or more. A variety of drugs can accelerate or retard ethanol clearance, depending upon chronicity and proximity of use. There is also a limited amount of data suggesting that ethanol elimination rate exhibits circadian rhythmicity (Sturtevant, Sturtevant, Pauly, & Sheving, 1978); however, the magnitude of change has been difficult to establish owing to the repeat dose design and other features of studies of this nature.

While it would appear that within-individual variations are relatively small, the literature is in full agreement that between-individual variations in ethanol elimination rates are substantial. Almost all studies have found a range of 200% to 300% for values of both β and R when subjects are administered the same dose of ethanol per unit body weight and the data are analyzed by the Widmark equation (Bennion & Li, 1976). In the studies that have employed Michaelis–Menten kinetics for analysis, two- to threefold variation has also been observed in V_{max} (Wagner, Wilkinson, Sedman, Kay, & Weidler, 1976). Thus the extent of variation cannot be attributed to methodologic differences in the calculation of elimination rates. Interindividual differences in ethanol pharmacokinetics can result from genetic or environmental factors or both. Their contributions can be discerned through studies in identical and fraternal twins. It has been found that identical twins exhibit greater concordance than do fraternal twins in rates of absorption, rates of ethanol disappearance from blood, and rates of ethanol elimination per unit body weight. The estimate of heritability for these parameters is 0.57, 0.41, and 0.46, respectively. Therefore, roughly one-half of interindividual variability in ethanol elimination rate can be attributed to genetic factors (Kopun & Propping, 1977).

Differences in alcohol-metabolizing capacity between different racial groups have also been sought. It has been reported that the mean ethanol elimination rate of North American Indians is lower than, higher than, or the same as that for whites (Reed, 1978). The difference in results may be due to the different origins of the different groups of Indians studied or to environmental factors. Orientals residing in Hawaii and Canada have been found to exhibit higher average elimination rates than whites residing in the same area. However, it has also been reported that the mean ethanol elimination rate of Japanese living in Japan is the same as that of whites (Mizoi, Ijiri, Tatsuno, Kijima, Fujiwara, & Adachi, 1979).

It is notable that, with the exception of the Ojibwa American Indians, the differences in mean elimination rates between whites and Orientals and between whites and American Indians are rather small (10% to 28%) when compared to the wide range of individual differences (200% to 300%) within each of the racial groups. These findings are not surprising, since it has been shown through extensive biochemical studies that genetic variation within races is much greater than the mean difference between races.

4. PROCESSES AND ORGANS RESPONSIBLE FOR ETHANOL ELIMINATION

Most ethanol elimination takes place by oxidation, ultimately to carbon dioxide and water. The rate of ethanol metabolism correlates directly with the basal energy requirement of animals; those with high basal metabolic rates eliminate ethanol more rapidly than those with low basal metabolic rates. The metabolic basis for this phenomenon is discussed in a later section. Small quantities of ethanol are also excreted unchanged in breath and urine. Since ethanol is freely diffusible, the contribution of these routes of elimination is more significant at high blood concentrations of ethanol than at low concentrations. Pulmonary and renal excretion may account for 10% to 15% of the total in humans when blood ethanol concentration is 200 to 300 mg/100 mL. The amount excreted by these routes is also affected by respiratory rate and urine flow rate. The analysis of ethanol in expired air is a commonly employed method for estimating the alcohol content of blood. The accepted ratio for the distribution of ethanol between blood and expired air is 2,100:1 (Wallgren & Barry, 1970).

A number of studies in human subjects and in different species of experimental animals have shown that the liver is the principal organ responsible for the metabolic elimination of ethanol (Li, 1977). Quantification of the role of the liver in humans has been obtained directly by hepatic vein catheterization: hepatic metabolism accounted for about 75% of total elimination under the experimental conditions employed. In one study, the mean rate of extraction of ethanol by human livers was estimated to be 1.6 mmol ethanol/min, while in another, the average maximal hepatic metabolic capacity was determined to be about 2 mmol/min.

Organs and tissues other than liver also oxidize ethanol, although singly their contribution to total metabolic rate is small. Kidneys, stomach, intestines, lung, heart, and skeletal muscle all exhibit significant ethanol oxidizing ability. Very little, if any, ethanol is metabolized by the brain (Mukherji, Kashiki, Ohyanagi, & Sloviter, 1975). Extrahepatic ethanol metabolic rate in man has been estimated to be about 0.4 mmol/min.

5. SIGNIFICANT PATHWAYS OF ETHANOL METABOLISM

Ethanol is first oxidized to acetaldehyde and then to acetate (Li, 1977). Both these reactions occur primarily in the liver and most of the acetate thus formed is released into the circulation. Studies in humans and experimental animals have shown under a variety of conditions that only 15% or less is oxidized further within the liver or converted into other metabolic intermediates such as fatty acids and ketone bodies. In agreement with this conclusion, the acetate concentration in blood during ethanol elimination may be as high as 1 to 2 mM, whereas that of acetaldehyde is usually less than 20 μM.

After release from liver, acetate is readily taken up by other tissues and organs and rapidly oxidized to carbon dioxide and water by way of the tricarboxylic acid cycle. The rapidity with which this process occurs is indicated by observations that most of ethanol-derived acetate is converted to CO_2 before ethanol disappears completely from the circulation. In some tissues, acetate serves as the preferred substrate over other substrates, such as glucose and fatty acids. It has been estimated, for example, that acetate utilization by hearts of human subjects given a low dose of ethanol can account for 20% or more of the myocardial oxygen uptake. The reason that the liver does not metabolize acetate in the presence of ethanol is that the oxidation of ethanol and acetaldehyde creates a tremendous change in the redox potential ($NAD^+/NADH$ ratio) of the liver. The principal mechanism for regenerating NAD^+ from NADH is oxidative phosphorylation. This activity of the electron transport chain causes inhibition of the tricarboxylic acid cycle, necessary for acetate oxidation, in the liver.

Several minor pathways of ethanol metabolism have been described. These include conjugation reactions to form ethyl sulfate and ethyl glucuronide as well as formation of fatty acid esters and condensation of acetaldehyde with pyruvate and α-ketoglutarate. These reactions appear to be quantitatively insignificant under usual circumstances. However, it has been reported that 2,3-butanediol, presumably formed as a product of the condensation of pyruvate with acetaldehyde, is found in the blood and urine of alcoholic patients during ethanol elimination (Felver, Lakshmanan, Wolf, & Veech, 1980).

6. ENZYMES THAT OXIDIZE ETHANOL TO ACETALDEHYDE

Enzyme systems that can catalyze the oxidation of ethanol to acetaldehyde *in vitro* are alcohol dehydrogenase (ADH), catalase, and the microsomal ethanol-oxidizing system (MEOS). Since the product of all these reactions is acetaldehyde, the assessment of the functional significance of these pathways in ethanol oxidation *in vivo* has necessarily been indirect.

6.1. Alcohol Dehydrogenase

Alcohol dehydrogenase catalyzes the reaction:

$$CH_3CH_2OH + NAD^+ = CH_3CHO + NADH + H^+$$

The literature is in good agreement that this enzyme in liver is the principal enzyme responsible for ethanol elimination *in vivo,* particularly when the concentration of alcohol is less than 20 mM. The total activity of rat liver ADH measured at pH 7.4 *in vitro* exceeds, but not by much, the ethanol oxidizing capacity of isolated rat liver cells (Crow, Cornell, & Veech, 1977) and the ethanol elimination rate of the intact animal. Similarly, on the basis of the specific ADH activities of human liver biopsy specimens, measured at pH 7.4 *in vitro,* the highest estimated alcohol elimination rates in humans can be readily accommodated by the total activity of this enzyme. However, when the steady-state rate of ADH is calculated—from the rate equation for the ADH reaction; the kinetic constants of the enzyme; and the *in situ* concentrations of ethanol, acetaldehyde, free NAD$^+$, and NADH in liver cytosol—it would appear that the activity of the rat liver enzyme *in vivo* may be only about 60% of V_{max}. Accordingly, the activity of ADH at steady state may not account for all of the ethanol oxidation *in vivo*. For example, for rats given 2 g ethanol/kg body weight, such calculations indicate that ADH activity, corrected for the concentrations of substrates and products *in situ,* is 55% to 60% of V_{max} and 80% to 90% of the *in vivo* ethanol elimination rate (Lumeng, Bosron, & Li, 1980).

Another approach to evaluating the contribution of the ADH pathway relative to that of catalase and MEOS is to compare the fate of tritium from [1R-^{3}H]ethanol with that of tritium-labeled substrates of other NAD$^+$-dependent dehydrogenases having the same reaction stereospecificity. Since catalase and MEOS are not dependent upon NAD$^+$ for ethanol oxidation, the tritium is incorporated solely into water. By contrast, the NAD$^+$-dependent pathways cause labeling of water as well as other reaction products, such as lactate and glucose. Such studies in experimental animal preparations have led to the conclusion that the ADH pathway accounts for 70% to 90% or more of ethanol oxidation in liver (Rognstad & Grunnet, 1979).

A third approach for estimating the role of ADH in ethanol oxidation is the use of inhibitors. Pyrazole compounds are potent and relatively specific inhibitors of ADH. However, they are competitive with ethanol and their efficacy is dependent upon the ratio of the concentrations of inhibitor and ethanol in the test system (Rognstad & Grunnet, 1979). Pyrazole and 4-methylpyrazole have been used for this purpose in humans, rats, and isolated liver preparations of rats. Variable results have been obtained even in those experiments wherein ADH should have been more than 90% inhibited, with estimates ranging between 60% and 100% as the contribution of ADH to ethanol oxidation in liver. A lower percentage contribution by ADH appears to occur in studies that employ high concentrations of ethanol, suggesting that a high Km, pyrazole-insensitive enzyme system gains in importance at high ethanol concentrations. Collectively, the data indicate that ADH accounts for as much as 100%, certainly more than 80% of ethanol oxidation by liver at low to moderate ethanol concentrations, but that at high concentrations another pathway—such as MEOS, catalase, or π-ADH (in humans)—may become functionally more important.

6.2. Properties of Alcohol Dehydrogenase and Genetic Variation in Isoenzymes of Human Alcohol Dehydrogenase

Alcohol dehydrogenase activity has been detected in virtually every animal species studied thus far. Where organ specificity has been examined, about 85% to 90% of total activity has been found in the liver. Other organs exhibiting high ADH-specific activity are stomach, intestines, kidneys, and lung. Liver ADH from the horse, rat, rabbit, monkey, and human have been purified (Lange & Vallee, 1976), but only the horse and human enzymes have been studied to any degree of detail with regard to their molecular and kinetic properties. The enzyme is a dimeric molecule of approximately 80,000 daltons. It has two active enzymatic sites, one per subunit, and contains four firmly bound zinc atoms per molecule. In horse liver ADH, two of the zinc atoms are situated at the active sites and are essential for catalytic activity. The other two, positioned in another part of the molecule, serve to stabilize structure. In sharp contrast to yeast ADH, the mammalian enzyme exhibits broad substrate specificity. Substrates include a wide range of aliphatic alcohols, diols, sterols, hydroxylated fatty acids and their respective aldehydes (Pietruszko, 1979). The coenzyme requirement, however, is quite specific; NAD(H) is greatly preferred over NADP(H).

Most mammalian species appear to exhibit multiple molecular forms or isoenzymes of ADH which can be separated from one another by electrophoretic techniques. There are three major isoenzyme forms and as many as six minor ones in horse liver. The three major isoenzymes arise from the dimerization of two dissimilar polypeptide chains, E and S, yielding two homodimeric forms, EE and SS, and one heterodimeric form, ES. Interestingly, the EE and SS isoenzymes are different in substrate specificity. Human livers contain an even larger array of isoenzymes, most of which have also been shown to form by the dimerization of similar or dissimilar polypeptide chains (Bosron & Li, 1980). Importantly, the pattern and number of isoenzymes in human livers vary from individual to individual. Other tissues and organs also exhibit multiplicity and individual variation in ADH isoenzymes, but the number of enzyme forms are fewer than those present in liver.

In 1971, a systematic analysis of ADH isoenzyme patterns in the liver and other organs of a large number of subjects culminated in the proposal of a genetic model for human ADH isoenzyme formation that satisfactorily accounted for the most prevalent isoenzyme forms visualized in the study (Smith, Hopkinson, & Harris, 1971). It was proposed that there are three gene loci, ADH_1, ADH_2, and ADH_3, coding for three dissimilar polypeptide chains, α, β, and γ, respectively. Furthermore, it was deduced that genetic polymorphism is commonly present at the ADH_3 gene locus, with two different alleles, ADH_3^1 and ADH_3^2, coding for chains, γ_1 and γ_2, respectively. Since ADH is a dimer, the molecular forms would be either homodimeric, $\alpha\alpha$, $\beta\beta$, $\gamma_1\gamma_1$, and $\gamma_2\gamma_2$, or heterodimeric, $\alpha\beta$, $\alpha\gamma_1$, $\alpha\gamma_2$, $\beta\gamma_1$, $\beta\gamma_2$, and $\gamma_1\gamma_2$. Individuals would be homozygous or heterozygous for the ADH_3 gene locus. It was noted that isoenzymes containing γ chains exhibit higher activities with long-chain alcohols (e.g., n-amyl alcohol), whereas those composed of α and β chains exhibit higher activities with ethanol. These molecular forms have Km values for ethanol oxidation ranging from 0.2 mM or lower to 2 mM and pH-optima for ethanol oxidation at 10.5. It has been found that the frequency of occurrence of the ADH_3^1 and ADH_3^2 alleles in white populations (British, U.S., and German) is approximately 1:1; but it is 9:1 and 8:2 in Japanese and black American populations, respectively.

There are other isoenzymes of human liver ADH, either seen infrequently or not at all in that first population study of Smith et al. (1971). One of these is π-ADH, not detected initially because it is more unstable than the other isoenzymes. π-ADH is similar to the other forms in physical and chemical properties except for electrophoretic mobility. However, it differs strikingly from them in kinetic properties. Its Km for ethanol is high, 40 mM, and it is relatively insensitive to inhibition by pyrazole (Li, Bosron, Dafeldecker, Lange, & Vallee, 1977). These properties resemble those of MEOS. Hence differentiation of MEOS and ADH on the basis of differences in Km and pyrazole sensitivity alone cannot be used in the human. The high Km for ethanol of π-ADH indicates that it may serve an important function in ethanol elimination at concentrations that are highly intoxicating. In vitro estimates indicate that it may account for as much as 20% of ethanol oxidation at these concentrations of ethanol (Li et al., 1977).

Other isoenzymes forms not accounted for by the genetic model of Smith et al. are the so-called atypical ADH (von Wartburg & Schürch, 1968) and ADH$_{Indianapolis}$ (Bosron, Li, & Vallee, 1980). Livers containing such ADH isoenzymes exhibit activity bands migrating cathodic to $\beta\beta$ on electrophoresis. Furthermore, livers with atypical ADH have a pH-optimum for ethanol oxidation at 8.5 instead of at 10.5, while those containing ADH$_{Indianapolis}$ have dual pH-optima at 10.5 and 7.5. Atypical ADH is present in about 20% of the population of Switzerland, where it was first discovered, in 5% of the white population in Britain and the United States, but in more than 85% of Oriental populations. This enzyme form, therefore, may be more appropriately designated Oriental ADH. ADH$_{Indianapolis}$ thus far has been found to be most prevalent (20%) among black

Americans. It has been proposed that both atypical ADH and ADH$_{Indianapolis}$ arise from genetic polymorphism at the ADH_2 gene locus and the production of variant β chains with altered pH optima for ethanol oxidation. In accord with this hypothesis, the homodimeric form of ADH$_{Indianapolis}$, $\beta_{Indianapolis}$ $\beta_{Indianapolis}$, has been isolated and shown to exhibit a single pH-optimum at 7.5. The isolated heterodimeric forms, $\alpha\beta_{Indianapolis}$ and $\gamma\beta_{Indianapolis}$ exhibit dual pH optima at 7.5 and 10.5. Similar tests of the hypothesis for atypical ADH have not been possible owing to difficulties in separation of the individual atypical forms. Figure 2 illustrates the electrophoretic separation and identification of the different ADH isoenzyme forms.

In summary, the multiplicity of human liver ADH isoenzymes and their strikingly different Km values for ethanol and pH-optima for ethanol oxidation impart a high degree of flexibility in their roles as the major enzyme responsible for ethanol oxidation in humans. Furthermore, the individual variation in isoenzyme pattern may be, in part, the basis of the genetic variability in ethanol elimination in humans, since the isoenzymes differ in kinetic properties. π-ADH may function in concert with MEOS, both high in Km for ethanol, in increasing

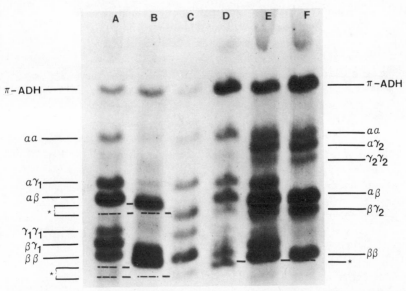

Figure 2. Starch-gel electrophoresis of human liver alcohol dehydrogenase isoenzymes, stained for ethanol oxidizing activity. Samples A, E, and F show the variations thought to be the result of genetic polymorphism at the ADH_3 (γ chain) gene locus. These specimens exhibit a pH-optimum for ethanol oxidation at 10.5. Sample B contains "atypical" ADH. Its pH-optimum for ethanol oxidation is 8.5. Samples C and D contain ADH$_{Indianapolis}$ enzyme forms. They exhibit dual pH-optima at 7.5 and 10.5. The activity bands marked by asterisks in samples B, C, and D are presumed to contain variant forms of the β chain.

ethanol elimination rates at high ethanol concentrations. Our current understanding of the pharmacokinetics of ethanol and future research in this area bear further scrutiny in the light of these findings.

6.3. Catalase and MEOS

The ADH- and NAD^+-independent pathways of ethanol oxidation are catalase and MEOS. Catalase catalyzes the decomposition of hydrogen peroxide by the reaction:

$$2H_2O_2 = 2H_2O + O_2$$

In the presence of a suitable hydrogen donor (e.g., ethanol), the following peroxidatic reaction occurs:

$$CH_3CH_2OH + H_2O_2 = CH_3CHO + 2H_2O$$

The rate of ethanol peroxidation is dependent upon the rate of H_2O_2 production, catalase concentration, and ethanol concentration. The peroxidation reaction is favored when the rate of H_2O_2 generation relative to catalase heme concentration is low. Under these conditions, the concentration of ethanol required to produce half-maximal activity of the peroxidation reaction appears to be 1 mM or less. At higher H_2O_2 generation rates, the ethanol concentration necessary to produce half-maximal activity increases (Oshino, Oshino, & Chance, 1973).

The liver exhibits very high catalase activity, much of which resides in peroxisomes. The principal rate-limiting factor of ethanol peroxidation *in vivo* appears to be the rate of H_2O_2 production. Estimates consistently show that this pathway normally is responsible for a small fraction, less than 10%, of hepatic ethanol oxidation (Rognstad & Grunnet, 1979). However, if experimental preparations are supplemented with substrates that stimulate H_2O_2 production (e.g., glycolate), the contribution by catalase can be increased to 30% or more, particularly at high ethanol concentrations (Oshino, Jamieson, Sugano, & Chance, 1975). The functional importance of catalase in human ethanol metabolism has not been investigated.

The MEOS is a membrane-associated electron transport system that, in the presence of NADPH and oxygen, oxidizes ethanol to acetaldehyde.

$$NADPH + H^+ + O_2 + CH_3CH_2OH = CH_3CHO + NADP^+ + 2H_2O$$

The terminal enzyme in this chain is cytochrome P-450. This microsomal monooxygenase system is involved in the oxidative metabolism of a wide variety of organic and xenobiotic compounds, including ethanol and other alcohols. It appears that one of the isoenzyme forms of cytochrome P-450 may be more specific for ethanol than for other substrates (Hasumura, Teschke, & Lieber, 1975). The MEOS activity of microsomes can be reconstituted from the purified components of the system, cytochrome P-450, NADPH-cytochrome c reductase, and lecithin (Ohnishi & Lieber, 1977). The Km for ethanol of MEOS is about 10 mM and the pH-optimum for ethanol oxidation is 7.4.

There has been controversy about the functional significance of MEOS *in vivo*. Some studies have claimed that MEOS can account for as much as 20% to 25% of the ethanol oxidation rate of liver, whereas others have found its contribution to be insignificant (Berry, Fanning, Grivell, & Wallace, 1980). In view of its high Km for ethanol, the role of MEOS would not be expected to be experimentally discernible or functionally significant until ethanol concentrations become very high. The most convincing demonstration of the *in vivo* action of MEOS in ethanol oxidation has come from a study of alcohol metabolism in a strain of the deermouse, *Peromyscus maniculatus,* that is genetically deficient in alcohol dehydrogenase (Burnett & Felder, 1980). These animals have no hepatic ADH activity and yet are able to eliminate ethanol at a rate approaching two-thirds that of normal animals when blood ethanol concentrations are greater than 200 mg/100 mL. Interestingly, the hepatic MEOS activity of the ADH-deficient deermouse is more than twice that of the normal animals, while catalase activity is the same in both strains. Although human livers exhibit MEOS activity, the functional significance of this pathway in humans has not been critically evaluated.

The hepatic microsomal enzymes are inducible and MEOS activity has been shown to increase with chronic ethanol ingestion and with the administration of certain drugs. Hence increased MEOS activity may be one of the contributing factors to the increased ethanol elimination rate seen after chronic ethanol ingestion in humans and experimental animals. Again, there is controversy about how quantitatively important MEOS is in this regard. Some studies have suggested that increased MEOS activity may account for at least a part, perhaps as much as 50%, of the increased metabolic rate, particularly at high alcohol concentrations. Others have suggested alternative mechanisms involving the ADH pathway and accelerated rates of NAD^+ regeneration from NADH. A later section discusses the factors that control ADH activity.

In summary, there is convincing evidence that by far the most important enzyme for the oxidation of ethanol to acetaldehyde is hepatic ADH. While catalase and MEOS are also capable of oxidizing ethanol, there remains disagreement about the quantitative significance of their function *in vivo*. Conditions that change the H_2O_2 generating capacity of liver, such as the provision of unique substrates and chronic ethanol ingestion, can perhaps increase the contribution of catalase. On the other hand, the inducibility of MEOS and its high Km for ethanol endow this pathway with the potential to increase its functional importance at high alcohol concentrations and also following chronic ethanol ingestion. The existence of multiple pathways clearly provides a degree of versatility in the elimination of ethanol that would not be possible were metabolism limited to a single enzyme.

7. ENZYMES THAT OXIDIZE ACETALDEHYDE TO ACETATE

The equilibrium constant for the alcohol dehydrogenase reaction is approximately 1×10^{-11} and, with the concentrations of free NAD^+ and NADH thought to exist in liver cytosol, the formation of ethanol from acetaldehyde is actually favored. Therefore, in order for ethanol oxidation to continue, there must exist very effective mechanisms for acetaldehyde removal. Indeed, it has been shown in isolated liver preparations that, when the ambient concentration of acetaldehyde is increased, ethanol oxidation rate decreases and increasing amounts of acetaldehyde are converted to ethanol (Lindros, 1978).

Most of the acetaldehyde formed from ethanol in the liver is also oxidized there to acetate. At steady state, a constant amount, less than 10%, of the acetaldehyde formed appears in the hepatic vein. Thus the rate of acetaldehyde oxidation by liver normally equals that of ethanol oxidation. The maximal capacity for hepatic acetaldehyde oxidation of isolated rat liver cells has been estimated to be 3 to 4 μmol/min/g wet weight of cells. It is notable that this rate does not greatly exceed the ethanol oxidation rate. During ethanol elimination, the concentration of acetaldehyde in the peripheral circulation is approximately a thousand times lower than that of ethanol, generally in the μM range. The concentration in liver and hepatic vein is somewhat higher. Therefore, extrahepatic tissue and erythrocytes also have substantial capacity for acetaldehyde oxidation. The measurement of acetaldehyde in biologic materials, blood in particular, has been fraught with methodologic problems. These have been overcome to a large extent only recently (Eriksson, 1980). Current estimates of the concentration of acetaldehyde in rat liver during ethanol metabolism is usually about 50 μM or less, while that in peripheral blood is 10 μM or less. Concentrations in human blood are also usually less than 10 μM, although it has been reported to be elevated in alcoholics (Korsten, Matsuzaki, Feinman, & Lieber, 1975). Other studies have not found elevated concentrations in alcoholics. The concentration in liver and blood, however, can be increased dramatically when acetaldehyde oxidation is impaired (e.g. with disulfiram administration or, perhaps, with liver injury). Acetaldehyde is much more toxic than ethanol and elevated concentrations produce a host of unpleasant and potentially lethal reactions.

The principal enzymes known to catalyze the oxidation of acetaldehyde to acetate are aldehyde dehydrogenases, aldehyde oxidase, and xanthine oxidase. The

Michaelis constants of the flavoprotein oxidases are considerably higher than that of most aldehyde dehydrogenases. Because the steady-state concentration of acetaldehyde can be effectively maintained in the micromolar range during ethanol oxidation, aldehyde dehydrogenases are likely to be the only functionally significant enzymes in acetaldehyde oxidation. It has been estimated that the activities of the flavoprotein oxidases can account for only less than 15% of acetaldehyde oxidation by rat liver, even when acetaldehyde concentration is as high as 40 mM. Moreover, studies with isolated rat liver preparations have shown that acetaldehyde oxidation occurs almost entirely in the mitochondrial compartment when acetaldehyde concentrations are below 0.4 mM. At concentrations between 0.4 and 10 mM, acetaldehyde uptake increases by as much as 60% and oxidation occurs also in cytosol. This subcellular distribution and concentration dependence are consistent with the subcellular distribution and properties of aldehyde dehydrogenase in rat liver (Lindros, 1978).

7.1. Aldehyde Dehydrogenase

Aldehyde dehydrogenase oxidizes acetaldehyde to acetate in the reaction:

$$CH_3CHO + NAD^+ + H_2O = CH_3COOH + NADH + H^+$$

The affinity of some molecular forms of the enzyme for acetaldehyde is exceedingly high and the redox potential of the reaction is such that oxidation of acetaldehyde is essentially an irreversible process. NAD^+-dependent aldehyde oxidizing activity is present not only in liver but also in a variety of tissues, such as kidneys, intestines, adrenals, brain, heart, and lung. The liver exhibits the highest specific activity.

Aldehyde dehydrogenase activity in liver is located in multiple subcellular compartments: mitochondria, cytosol, and microsomes. They appear to be similar in molecular weight, 200,000 to 250,000, and in subunit molecular weight, 50,000 to 60,000, but they differ in isoelectric point and substrate specificity (Weiner, 1979). Some forms have low Km values μM for acetaldehyde whereas others have high Km (mM). There appear also to be interspecies differences in the subcellular distribution and amounts of the high- and low-Km forms in liver. Thus, rat liver contains a low-Km form in mitochondria and multiple, high-Km forms in mitochondria, cytosol, and microsomes. Bovine and equine livers exhibit predominantly low-Km forms in both mitochondria and cytosol. Human livers have one high-Km form and two low-Km forms, one of which is apparently in the mitochondria. Whereas most of aldehyde dehydrogenase activity in rat liver is found in mitochondria and microsomes, most of the activity in horse liver is in cytosol. In human livers, about 50% of the activity is in mitochondria and 30% in cytosol. A wide range of Km values for NAD^+, 3 to 400 μM, has been described for aldehyde dehydrogenases from different species. As with alcohol dehydrogenase, aldehyde dehydrogenase has broad substrate specificity. A variety of aliphatic and aromatic aldehydes are oxidized by the enzyme to the corresponding acids. Substrates include acetaldehyde, formaldehyde, glyceraldehyde, and aldehydes derived from the metabolism of biogenic amines.

The subcellular location at which acetaldehyde oxidation occurs during ethanol metabolism can be expected to vary with the rate of acetaldehyde production and with animal species, owing to the differences in subcellular location of the high and low-Km forms in the different species. Because the steady-state concentrations of acetaldehyde are normally kept in the micromolar range during ethanol metabolism, the low-Km forms clearly play a major role. This has been shown in rats treated with either cyanamide or disulfiram, inhibitors of the mitochondrial low-Km form of the enzyme. Acetaldehyde levels in the liver and blood become abnormally elevated when the activity of this enzyme form is inhibited by as little as 25%. When methylpyrazole is given to these animals in order to lower ethanol oxidation rate by 20%, acetaldehyde levels are lowered concomitantly. These observations indicate that the acetaldehyde oxidizing capacity of rat liver is normally not much in excess of the capacity for ethanol oxidation and that the amount of the low-Km mitochondrial enzyme is an important determinant of this process. The high-Km forms are not expected to become functionally important until acetaldehyde concentrations rise toward the millimolar range, when the maximal oxidizing capacity of the low-Km enzyme is exceeded.

A response to ethanol commonly observed among certain Asian populations is the rapid onset of facial flushing, vasodilatation, and tachycardia even after the intake of relatively small amounts of ethanol. This alcohol sensitivity, the so-called flushing reaction, is similar to the alcohol–disulfiram (Antabuse) reaction, and has been shown to be associated with a conspicuous and rapid rise in blood acetaldehyde concentration (Mizoi *et al.*, 1979). Subjects who exhibit this reaction, however, have the same ethanol elimination rate as those who do not. It has been postulated that the phenomenon is the result of a genetic deficiency of one of the low-Km forms of aldehyde dehydrogenase (Goedde, Harada, & Agarwal, 1979). This hypothesis has preliminarily been confirmed (Agarwal, Harada, & Goedde, 1981).

8. CONTROL OF ETHANOL AND ACETALDEHYDE METABOLISM IN LIVER

The rate of ethanol metabolism is governed by: (1) the hepatic content of ADH, the enzyme that catalyzes the rate-limiting step in ethanol oxidation, (2) the activity per unit weight of ADH (i.e., specific activity), and (3) the activity of pathways independent of ADH (i.e., MEOS and catalase). The specific activity of ADH *in vivo* is determined by the kinetic and equilibrium constants of the enzyme and the concentrations of its substrates and products in cytosol at steady state. For example, it can be calculated from the hepatic concentrations of free NAD^+, NADH, ethanol, and acetaldehyde during ethanol metabolism *in situ* that the activity of rat liver ADH is limited to only 50% to 60% of its maximal velocity (Lumeng *et al.*, 1980). The steady-state concentrations of NAD^+, NADH, and acetaldehyde in cytosol are, in turn, governed by the rate of NAD^+ regeneration from NADH and by acetaldehyde oxidation. These processes, therefore, are important rate-controlling factors of the metabolic elimination of ethanol because in their absence ethanol oxidation would promptly diminish in rate and ultimately cease.

The amount of ADH in liver is an important factor in rate regulation because its total activity measured even under optimal conditions *in vitro* may not exceed by much the ethanol elimination rate *in vivo*. For example, the maximum total ADH activity in rat liver is but 150% to 170% of the hepatic metabolic rate and the *in vivo* elimination rate (Lumeng, Bosron, & Li, 1979). An increase or decrease in enzyme amount should produce a proportionate change in rate, regardless of whether the enzyme is operating at maximal or submaximal velocity, provided that the kinetic constraints imposed by the steady-state concentrations of substrates and products remain unchanged. However, the latter condition may not always prevail, thus forcing the enzyme to operate at a level of specific activity different from before. Accordingly, a change in ethanol oxidation rate may not always parallel the change in enzyme content. Nevertheless, it has been shown that fasting, the feeding of a weight-restricting diet, and the feeding of a protein-deficient diet decrease to about the same degree both ethanol elimination rate and ADH content, as measured by the total maximal ADH activity in liver (Lumeng *et al.*, 1979). Orchiectomy increases ADH content and elimination rates to about the same extent in certain strains of male rats (Mezey, Potter, Harmon, & Tsi-touras, 1980). It should be noted that these events require time to develop, because they involve protein synthesis and degradation, relatively slow processes. Changes in enzyme content, therefore, cannot be expected to underlie rapid or acute increases or decreases of metabolic rate. Rather, a change in the steady-state veloc-ity of the enzyme brought about by changes in rates of NAD^+ regeneration, acet-aldehyde disposal, or both should be sought. A doubling of rate is theoretically attainable in the rat, since the enzyme normally is operating at 50% to 60% of maximal velocity.

Most of the NADH generated by the ADH reaction in cytosol is reoxidized in mitochondria by way of the electron transport chain. Only a small part, perhaps 20%, is reoxidized in cytosol through linkage to reactions such as the reduction of pyruvate to lactate. The mitochondrial inner membrane, however, is impermeable to NADH, and the reducing equivalents of cytosolic NADH must be transported indirectly into the mitochondria by shuttle mechanisms. The two most important shuttles in liver are the malate-aspartate and the α-glycerophosphate cycles (Williamson & Tischler, 1979). The malate-aspartate shuttle transfers the reducing equivalents to NAD^+ within the mitochondria. The NADH thus formed is oxidized by the electron transport chain, yielding 3 moles of ATP/mole of NADH. The α-glycerophosphate shuttle produces only 2 moles of ATP/mole of NADH, because the reducing equivalents are transferred directly to the respiratory chain by way of a flavoprotein. In rat liver, the malate–aspartate shuttle may to be two to three times as active as the α-glycerophosphate shuttle.

During ethanol metabolism, the cytosolic free NAD^+/NADH ratio decreases from about 800 to 300. The inability to restore this ratio to 800 is presumably the consequence of a limitation in the rate of NAD^+ regeneration. In support of this conclusion, the rate of ethanol oxidation can be increased by supplying shuttle intermediates to liver cell preparations or by increasing the activity of the electron transport chain through accelerated ATP consumption. The latter can be accomplished by the provision of substrates such as fructose (Grunnet, Quistorff, & Thieden, 1973), by stimulation of gluconeogenesis, or by use of uncoupling agents (e.g., dinitrophenol). Therefore, the activity of both the shuttles and the respiratory chain can limit NAD^+ regeneration and alcohol oxidation rate. It is thought that, in the fed state, the primary rate-limiting factor both *in vitro* and *in vivo* is respiratory chain activity, whereas it is the depletion of shuttle intermediates in liver cells when they are prepared from starved animals. Starved rats exhibit a lesser degree of depletion of shuttle intermediates *in vivo* and the decrease in ethanol elimination rate *in vivo* brought about by starvation can be largely accounted for by decreased ADH content. As might be expected, efforts to stimulate ethanol oxidation rate by accelerating the rate of NAD^+ regeneration generally have not produced increases greater than 100%.

The rate-determining factors of hepatic acetaldehyde metabolism have not been studied as extensively as that of ethanol metabolism (Lindros, 1978). The affinity of the mitochondrial form of aldehyde dehydrogenase for acetaldehyde is high and the reaction it catalyzes is essentially irreversible. There is no product inhibition by acetate. However, its affinity for NAD^+ in some animal species is not as high as that for acetaldehyde, and the mitochondrial concentration of free NAD^+ and its availability may become a rate-limiting factor, especially when NADH reoxidation by the respiratory chain is suppressed. As already discussed, a second factor is the maximal activity of the mitochondrial low-Km form of aldehyde dehydrogenase, which is not much greater than the maximal hepatic ethanol oxidation rate. These features of acetaldehyde elimination may significantly affect ethanol oxidation rate. The aldehyde dehydrogenase reaction competes with the malate-aspartate shuttle (also essentially irreversible) one-to-one for the supply of mitochondrial NAD^+, and this relationship has the potential to reduce the capacity of the shuttle for regenerating cytosolic NAD^+. It is thus conceivable that an acceleration of acetaldehyde oxidation rate can result in a decrease in the activity of alcohol dehydrogenase. On the other hand, suppression of the mitochondrial aldehyde dehydrogenase activity can both increase and decrease alcohol dehydrogenase activity by lessening the competition for mitochondrial NAD^+ and raising acetaldehyde concentration, respectively. Clearly, the interplay between the factors that regulate ethanol and acetaldehyde oxidation is complex and the effects of interventions on hepatic ethanol metabolic rate need to be analyzed in the light of these interrelationships. They further emphasize the dependence of both ethanol and acetaldehyde oxidation upon the metabolic state of the liver cell.

The oxidation of ethanol by MEOS and catalase is not NAD^+-dependent and hence is not limited by the process of NAD^+ regeneration. It has been suggested that MEOS activity facilitates ethanol oxidation because it requires NADPH, which by transhydrogenation reactions can promote the regeneration of NAD^+ in cytosol. However, as already discussed, the contributions of MEOS and catalase to ethanol oxidation are probably minor, although with high ethanol concentration, microsomal proliferation, and increased H_2O_2 production, their activities can increase significantly. The postulated roles of these pathways of ethanol oxidation following chronic ethanol consumption are discussed in the following section.

9. EFFECT OF CHRONIC ETHANOL INGESTION ON ALCOHOL ELIMINATION RATE

Chronic ethanol ingestion is capable of accelerating alcohol elimination from the blood of experimental animals and man as much as 50% to 70%. There have been many studies of the underlying basis of this "metabolic tolerance," but no uniformity in viewpoint has emerged. The two mechanisms most frequently championed are MEOS induction and increased ADH activity as a result of increased rate of NAD^+ regeneration. Considerable data have been marshaled both in support of and against either mechanism.

Chronic ethanol administration produces proliferation of the hepatic smooth endoplasmic reticulum, increased drug-metabolizing enzyme activity and increased NADPH-dependent ethanol-oxidizing capacity in both man and experimental animals (Lieber, 1980a,b). Since MEOS has a high Km for ethanol, its action would be more apparent at high blood ethanol concentrations than in the lower ranges (Feinman et al., 1978). Indeed, it has been shown that after the chronic administration of ethanol to humans, baboons, and rats, an increase in ethanol elimination rate is more pronounced at high blood alcohol concentrations than in the low to moderate concentration ranges. The results of some studies with pyrazole compounds as inhibitors of ADH have been consistent with a role for MEOS in accelerating ethanol elimination rate, while others have not. It should noted that human π-ADH also exhibits high Km (40 mM) for ethanol and is insensitive to inhibition by pyrazole compounds. While *in vitro* results suggest that π-ADH can account for as much as 20% of ethanol oxidation at high alcohol concentrations, its role as a mediator of alcohol metabolic tolerance has not been examined. The microsomal NADPH-oxidase activity, inducible by chronic ethanol ingestion, also generates H_2O_2. To what extent this might increase the contribution of catalase to ethanol oxidation is unknown.

Since the activity of ADH is estimated normally to be only 50% to 60% of its maximal velocity, metabolic changes associated with chronic ethanol ingestion might be sufficient to alter the redox state of the cell through enhanced basal metabolic rate. It has been shown in some studies that chronic ethanol administration increases Na^+, K^+-ATPase activity, thereby increasing the need for ATP synthesis (Israel, Videla, MacDonald, & Bernstein, 1973). This increased energy demand or "hypermetabolic state" would accelerate the rate of NADH reoxidation which, in turn, allows ADH to function at a higher level of activity. In accord with this kind of mechanism, the cytosolic free NAD^+/NADH ratio does not fall after chronic ethanol administration to as low a level during ethanol metabolism as that characteristically seen in naive animals (Salaspuro, Shaw, Jayatilleke, Ross, & Lieber, 1981). The concept that a hypermetabolic state can accelerate ethanol oxidation rate is supported by findings that thyroxine and epinephrine administration also accelerates ethanol elimination rate. On the other hand, some studies have been unable to substantiate the appearance of increased oxygen consumption following chronic ethanol administration, although ethanol oxidation rate is increased.

The content of ADH in liver has been noted by some investigators to increase with chronic ethanol administration, while others have found no change or a decrease. In view of the responsiveness of ADH content to altered states of nutrition, such findings are not surprising (Li, 1977). The recent observations of the suppressive action of testosterone upon liver ADH content in certain strains of rats (Mezey *et al.*, 1980) suggest yet another mechanism: chronic ethanol ingestion inhibits testosterone production which, in turn, leads to increased hepatic ADH content.

It thus appears that, although the concept of metabolic tolerance is well supported by experimental evidence, agreement is lacking on the underlying biochemistry of the phenomenon. The disparity in results may be due to differences in experimental preparations, species and strain of animals, duration of ethanol exposure and dose, the nutritional state of the experimental animals, and the metabolic state and normality of the pair-fed control animals. Accordingly, there may not be a single, unique mechanism; rather, the predominant pathway varies with the metabolic state and experimental conditions under scrutiny, as has been discussed also in the preceding section.

10. CHRONIC ETHANOL INGESTION AND NUTRITION

The combustion of 1 g of ethanol yields 7.1 kcal of energy. Balance studies in intact animals have shown that about 25% of this energy is not physiologically available, presumably lost as heat. It has been suggested that MEOS, which actually consumes reducing equivalents (derived from NADPH) in ethanol oxidation, or that the activation of NA^+,K^+-ATPase is responsible for the wasting of this amount of ethanol-derived energy. Thus one-quarter of the ethanol-derived calories are "empty" and only three-quarters of them "count."

The consumption of ethanol can produce nutrient imbalance because alcoholic beverages are almost entirely devoid of essential nutrients other than calories and hence are also "empty" in nutrient value. Individuals with high alcohol intake are confronted with the need to stay in caloric balance, on the one hand, and nutritional balance, on the other. For example, assume that caloric and nutritional balance requires the ingestion of a 2,400-kcal diet containing 48% carbohydrates, 40% fats, 12% proteins, and all necessary vitamins and minerals. If eating habits are unaltered in order to ensure nutritional normality, the consumption of one pint of an 86-proof beverage or 10 to 12 standard-sized drinks would add an extra 1,200 kcal to intake, and rapid weight gain would ensue. Alternatively, if energy balance is to be maintained, food intake must be reduced sharply, resulting in a curtailment of the ingested amount of normal dietary nutrients as well as a severe imbalance in proportion. Nutrient deficiency resulting from lack of sufficient intake is termed a "primary" nutritional deficiency state.

In the past, frank malnutrition, protein–calorie malnutrition, deficiency states involving one or more of the water-soluble vitamins (thiamin, niacin, riboflavin, pyridoxine, folic acid and ascorbic acid) and deficiency of one or more minerals (magnesium, potassium, calcium, iron, and zinc) have been described as common occurrences in the alcoholic population. Deficiencies of fat-soluble vitamins (A, D, and K) have also been observed. More recently, the frequency and severity of these nutritional deficiencies may have diminished among alcoholics to some extent, owing to the general availability of nutrient supplements, the fortification of foods, and improved public awareness of health and nutrition in general. Nevertheless, although many alcoholics are now seemingly well nourished, there remain large numbers exhibiting marginal nutritional adequacy or overt deficiencies involving specific nutrients (Li, Schenker, & Lumeng, 1979; see also Chapter 4 of this volume).

It is now known that ethanol or its metabolic products can specifically impede the absorption, disrupt the metabolism and storage, or enhance the excretion of vitamins and other nutrients, thereby accelerating the development of deficiency, particularly when intake is marginal. Specific deficiencies occurring through these processes are termed "conditioned" or secondary deficiency states. For example, it has been shown in experimental animals, both *in vivo* and *in vitro,* that ethanol reduces the absorption of thiamin (Hoyumpa, 1980), impairs both the absorption and hepatic metabolism of folate (Halsted, 1980), and depletes the storage of pyridoxine (Veitch, Lumeng, & Li, 1975). The latter apparently is mediated by acetaldehyde, which accelerates the degradation of pyridoxal 5′-phosphate, the coenzyme and storage form of this vitamin. Perhaps because of the nature of the respective conditioning factors, folate deficiency and pyridoxine deficiency are still commonly found among alcoholics.

Nutritional derangement and conditioned deficiency can also result when the structure and function of the intestinal tract and associated organs have been damaged by chronic ethanol consumption. Gastritis, pancreatitis and dysfunction of intestinal motility can produce maldigestion and malabsorption. For example, steatorrhea resulting from chronic pancreatic insufficiency can lead to deficiency of fat soluble vitamins. Liver disease and cirrhosis can impair the metabolism and storage of many vitamins and nutrients critically dependent upon the function of this organ (e.g., folate, pyridoxine, vitamin B_{12}, vitamin K, and others). It should also be noted that folate deficiency *per se* can lead to malabsorption of other compounds, presumably owing to the megaloblastic changes induced in the intestinal epithelial cells (Halsted, 1980).

11. ETHANOL OXIDATION AND HEPATIC METABOLISM

The liver normally utilizes fatty acids as the preferred substrate for energy (ATP) production. However, when ethanol is present, its oxidation and the attendant need to regenerate NAD^+ via the electron transport chain become so dominant that the oxidative metabolism of other substrates is sharply curtailed (Williamson & Tishler, 1979). It has been estimated that ethanol can displace 75% to 90% of all other substrates in this regard. Furthermore, the lowering of $NAD^+/$ NADH ratio during ethanol metabolism produces a reducing environment that favors synthetic processes and the hydrogenation of substrate intermediates. A large number of the metabolic changes in liver produced by ethanol can be ascribed to this redox change. Figure 3 illustrates the impact of ethanol oxidation on hepatic metabolism. A description of the medical consequences of chronic ethanol ingestion on liver metabolism is contained in the chapter by van Thiel in this volume.

11.1. Effects on Carbohydrate and Fat Metabolism

A decrease of $NAD^+/NADH$ ratio in cytosol favors the conversion of pyruvate to lactate, fructose to sorbitol, oxaloacetate to malate, and dihydroxyacetone phosphate to glycerol-3-phosphate. Other NAD^+-dependent reactions are simi-

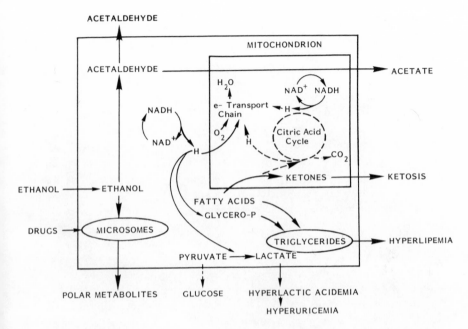

Figure 3. Metabolic effects of ethanol oxidation in liver. Broken lines indicate inhibition.

larly affected. Increased cytosolic NADH concentration also suppresses the oxidation of galactose, through inhibition of the enzyme, UDP-galactose epimerase. In mitochondria, the decrease in $NAD^+/NADH$ ratio brought about by the inward transport of reducing equivalents via the malate–aspartate shuttle and by acetaldehyde oxidation promotes the conversion of acetoacetate to β-hydroxybutyrate and of α-ketoglutarate to glutamate and inhibits the activity of the citric acid cycle, the β-oxidation of fatty acids, and the activation of acetate to acetyl CoA.

Inhibition of gluconeogenesis is a major sequela of hepatic ethanol oxidation. When chronic ethanol administration is superimposed upon a glycogen-depleted state, frank hypoglycemia can ensue in both humans and experimental animals. The basic abnormality appears to be the lack of substrates essential for glucose synthesis (e.g., pyruvate, oxaloacetate, and dihydroxyacetone phosphate), depleted as a result of the altered $NAD^+/NADH$ ratio. Additionally, inhibition of the citric acid cycle impairs the entry of amino acids into the cycle and the gluconeogenic pathway. Decreased activities of enzymes necessary for gluconeogenesis have also been observed. They include fructose 1,6-bisphosphatase, pyruvate kinase, glutamate dehydrogenase, and pyruvate carboxylase (Reitz, 1979).

Chronic ethanol consumption superimposed upon a starved or semistarvation state can produce severe ketoacidosis. This occurs usually after the cessation of ethanol intake. In the starved state, circulating insulin is decreased and glucagon is increased in concentration, resulting in enhanced lipolysis. The concentration of free fatty acids in the circulation rises, as does also the rate of fatty acid oxidation in liver. Fatty acids are converted by β-oxidation to acetyl CoA. The capacity of the liver to synthesize acetoacetate from acetyl CoA exceeds its capacity to oxidize acetyl-CoA further to CO_2 and H_2O (via the citric acid cycle). Thus acetoacetate and β-hydroxybutyrate, formed from acetoacetate, appear in the circulation in large amounts, producing ketoacidosis. Ethanol ingestion also stimulates lipolysis. Alcoholic ketoacidosis, therefore, appears to be an exaggerated form of starvation ketosis, brought about in large measure by the enhanced lipolytic response of adipose tissue to ethanol ingestion (McGarry & Foster, 1980).

The chronic ingestion of ethanol produces the accumulation of lipids in liver. There are multiple contributing factors, although the bulk of evidence indicates that the principal ones are increased esterification of fatty acids and decreased fatty acid oxidation (Baraona & Lieber, 1979). The lipids that accumulate in liver are esters of fatty acids and glycerol (triglycerides or triacylglycerols). Ethanol consumption increases hepatic fatty acid uptake by stimulating hepatic blood flow. The fatty acids may come from both adipose tissue and dietary sources. Ethanol oxidation increases glycerol-3-phosphate formation from dihydroxyacetone phosphate because of the change in $NAD^+/NADH$ ratio. Chronic ethanol administration also increases the activity of glycerophosphate acyltransferase, the microsomal enzyme responsible for the synthesis of triacylglycerols. Thus both increased availability of precursors and increased activity of the synthetic enzyme contribute to triglyceride accumulation in liver. Furthermore, ethanol metabolism inhibits the oxidation of fatty acids primarily because of suppression of citric acid cycle activity, through mechanisms already discussed. Finally, chronic ethanol consumption inhibits the secretion of lipoproteins by liver, thus decreasing the transport of lipids into the circulation, by mechanisms to be discussed in the following section. The hepatic content of phospholipids and cholesterol is also increased following ethanol administration. The accumulation of cholesterol is mainly in the form of cholesterol esters.

11.2. Effects on Protein and Amino Acid Metabolism

Experiments *in vitro* with perfused livers and isolated liver cells have shown that ethanol is capable of inhibiting protein synthesis, particularly if the preparations are derived from fasted animals. This effect can be overcome by the addition of amino acids, pyruvate, and various intermediates of the hydrogen translocation shuttles, suggesting that metabolite depletion in these preparations is in part responsible. Inhibition can also be prevented by lessening the redox change caused by ethanol oxidation and by stopping ethanol oxidation with 4-methylpyrazole.

Thus it appears that the change in $NAD^+/NADH$ ratio and/or acetaldehyde may be mechanistically implicated as well. The perfusion of isolated livers with acetaldehyde also produces inhibition of protein synthesis (Rothschild, Oratz, Schreiber, & Mongelli, 1980), although it cannot be clearly differentiated whether the effect is due to acetaldehyde itself or to its oxidation which also alters $NAD^+/NADH$ ratio in the cell. In contrast to the *in vitro* studies, the inhibitory effect of ethanol on hepatic protein synthesis is not consistently observed *in vivo*. Presumably, intact animals are more able to attenuate and reverse the abnormalities in protein synthesis produced by ethanol oxidation (Lieber, 1980a).

The effect of chronic ethanol administration on protein synthesis has also been studied. Results have been conflicting. Inhibition, no change and increased synthesis have all been reported. These differences may stem from differences in the metabolic or nutritional state of the animals, differences in duration of ethanol administration and dose, and/or differences in the strain and species of animals employed. For example, in some studies, the animals exhibited hepatomegaly, steatosis, and weight gain, whereas in others no such changes were observed (Lieber, 1980b). Collectively, the findings serve to further emphasize the importance of alcohol–nutrition interactions in the expression of the metabolic abnormalities produced by ethanol.

While studies on the effects of ethanol on protein synthesis have produced variable results, those examining hepatic secretory function have shown a distinct abnormality. Studies both *in vitro* and *in vivo* have demonstrated that ethanol oxidation impairs the secretion of albumin, lipoproteins, and glycoproteins. In the instance of glycoproteins, a defect in glycosylation has been identified (Sorrell & Tuma, 1980). Furthermore, it has been shown that ethanol oxidation impairs the polymerization of tubulin, necessary for the secretory process, through the binding of acetaldehyde to tubulin. The disruption of liver microtubules produced by ethanol oxidation is associated with engorgement of the secretory vesicles of the Golgi complex with protein, suggesting that this is the basis of impaired protein secretion (Lieber, 1980b).

The effect of ethanol oxidation on hepatic amino acid metabolism has not been studied extensively. Ethanol acutely decreases NH_4^+ and urea output of isolated hepatocytes and perfused liver, respectively. Concomitantly, the nitrogen and carbon from alanine are diverted to aspartate, glutamine, and glutamate. The basis for these abnormalities is unclear, but they are accompanied by a decrease in oxaloacetate concentration and an increase in glutamate concentration. These changes may be mediated by the change in $NAD^+/NADH$ ratio accompanying ethanol oxidation, since a decrease in this ratio favors the conversion of α-ketoglutarate to glutamate by glutamate dehydrogenase and these changes, in turn, favor the conversion of oxaloacetate to aspartate by aspartate aminotransferase. Actually, transamination involving glutamate and α-ketoglutarate and deamination via glutamate dehydrogenase are reactions common to the catabolism of most amino acids. Thus the mechanism stated above may pertain to potential effects of ethanol oxidation on other amino acids as well. Other specific abnormalities in amino acid metabolism produced by ethanol oxidation are an increased concentration of proline, brought about by the inhibition of the NAD^+-dependent proline dehydrogenase (Hakkinen & Kulonen, 1980) and the depletion of glutathione, a tripeptide made up of glutamate, cysteine, and glycine (Vina, Estrela, Guerri, & Romero, 1980). Glutathione protects the liver and other cells against oxidative and peroxidative damage. Chronic ethanol administration also produces an elevation in liver and serum of the concentration of α-amino-n-butyric acid, presumably the result of increased methionine degradation (Shaw & Lieber, 1980). This abnormality apparently occurs both in liver and in muscle with the chronic administration of ethanol.

12. REFERENCES

Agarwal, D. P., Harada, S., & Goedde, H. W. Racial differences in biological sensitivity to ethanol: The role of alcohol dehydrogenase and aldehyde dehydrogenase isoenzymes. *Alcoholism: Clinical and Experimental Research,* 1981, *5,* 12–16.

Bennion, L. J., & Li, T.-K. Alcohol metabolism in American Indians and whites. *New England Journal of Medicine,* 1976, *294,* 9–13.

Berry, M. N., Fanning, D. C., Grivell, A. R., & Wallace, P. G. Ethanol oxidation by isolated hepatocytes from fed and starved rats and from rats exposed to ethanol, phenobarbitone or 3-amino-triazole. *Biochemical Pharmacology,* 1980, *29,* 2161–2168.

Bosron, W. F., Li, T.-K., & Vallee, B. L. New molecular forms of human liver alcohol dehydrogenase: Isolation and characterization of ADH$_{Indianapolis}$. *Proceedings of the National Academy of Sciences (USA),* 1980, *77,* 5784–5788.

Burnett, K. G., & Felder, M. R. Ethanol metabolism in Peromyscus genetically deficient in alcohol dehydrogenase. *Biochemical Pharmacology,* 1980, *29,* 125–130.

Crow, K. E., Cornell, N. W., & Veech, R. L. The rate of ethanol metabolism in isolated rat hepatocytes. *Alcoholism: Clinical and Experimental Research,* 1977, *1,* 43–47.

Eriksson, C. J. P. Problems and pitfalls in acetaldehyde determinations. *Alcoholism: Clinical and Experimental Research,* 1980, *4,* 22–29.

Feinman, L., Baraona, E., Matsuzaki, S., Korsten, M., & Lieber, C. S. Concentration dependence of ethanol metabolism *in vivo* in rats and man. *Alcoholism: Clinical and Experimental Research,* 1978, *2,* 381–385.

Felver, M. E., Lakshmanan, M. R., Wolf, S., & Veech, R. L. The presence of 2,3-butanediol in the blood of chronic alcoholics admitted to an alcohol treatment center. In R. G. Thurman (Ed.), *Alcohol and Aldehyde Metabolizing Systems—IV.* New York: Plenum Press, 1980.

Forney, R. B., Hughes, F. W., Harger, R. N., & Richards, A. B. Alcohol distribution in the vascular system. *Quarterly Journal of Studies on Alcohol,* 1964, *25,* 205–217.

Goedde, H. W., Harada, S., & Agarwal, D. P. Racial differences in alcohol sensitivity: a new hypothesis. *Human Genetics,* 1979, *51,* 331–334.

Grunnet, N., Quistorff, B., & Thieden, H. I. D. Rate-limiting factors in ethanol oxidation by isolated rat liver parenchymal cells. *European Journal of Biochemistry,* 1973, *40,* 275–282.

Hakkinen, H., & Kulonen, E. Effect of ethanol administration on free proline and glutamate in the intact rat liver. *Biochemical Pharmacology*, 1980, *29*, 1435-1439.

Halsted, C. H. Folate deficiency in alcoholism. *The American Journal of Clinical Nutrition*, 1980, *33*, 2736-2740.

Hammond, K. B., Rumack, B. H., & Rodgerson, D. O. *Journal of the American Medical Association*, 1973, *226*, 63-64.

Hasumura, Y., Teschke, R., & Lieber, C. S. Hepatic microsomal ethanol-oxidizing system (MEOS): Dissociation from reduced nicotinamide adenine dinucleotide phosphate oxidase and possible role of form I of cytochrome P-450. *The Journal of Pharmacology and Experimental Therapeutics*, 1975, *194*, 469-474.

Hoyumpa, A. M. Mechanisms of thiamin deficiency in chronic alcoholism. *American Journal of Clinical Nutrition*, 1980, *33*, 2750-2761.

Isbell, H., Fraser, H. F., Wikler, A., Belleville, R. E., & Eisenman, A. J. An experimental study of the etiology of "rum fits" and delirium tremens. *Quarterly Journal of Studies on Alcohol*, 1955, *16*, 1-33.

Israel, Y., Videla, L., MacDonald, A., & Bernstein, J. Metabolic alterations produced in the liver by chronic ethanol administration. *Biochemical Journal*, 1973, *134*, 523-529.

Kopun, M., & Propping, P. The kinetics of ethanol absorption and elimination in twins and supplementary repetitive experiments in singleton subjects. *European Journal of Clinical Pharmacology*, 1977, *11*, 337-344.

Korsten, M. A., Matsuzaki, S., Feinman, L., & Lieber, C. S. High blood acetaldehyde levels after ethanol administration. *New England Journal of Medicine*, 1975, *292*, 386-389.

Lange, L. G., & Vallee, B. L. Double-ternary complex affinity chromatography: preparation of alcohol dehydrogenases. *Biochemistry*, 1976, *15*, 4681-4686.

Li, T.-K., Bosron, W. F., Dafeldecker, W. P., Lange, L. G., & Vallee, B. L. Isolation of π-alcohol dehydrogenase of human liver: Is it a determinant of alcoholism? *Proceedings of the National Academy of Sciences (USA)*, 1977, *74*, 4378-4381.

Lumeng, L., Bosron, W. F., & Li, T.-K. Quantitative correlation of ethanol elimination rates *in vivo* with liver alcohol dehydrogenase activities in fed, fasted and food-restricted rats. *Biochemical Pharmacology*, 1979, *28*, 1547-1551.

Lumeng, L., Bosron, W. F., & Li, T.-K. Rate-determining factors for ethanol metabolism *in vivo* during fasting. In R. G. Thurman (Ed.), *Alcohol and Aldehyde Metabolizing Systems—IV*. New York: Plenum Press, 1980.

McGarry, J. D., & Foster, D. W. Regulation of hepatic fatty acid oxidation and ketone body production. *Annual Review of Biochemistry*, 1980, *49*, 395-420.

Mezey, E., Potter, J. J., Harmon, S. M., & Tsitouras, P. D. Effects of castration and testosterone administration on rat liver alcohol dehydrogenase activity. *Biochemical Pharmacology*, 1980, *29*, 3175-3180.

Mizoi, Y., Ijiri, I., Tatsuno, Y., Kijima, T., Fujiwara, S., & Adachi, J. Relationship between facial flushing and blood acetaldehyde levels after alcohol intake. *Pharmacology Biochemistry and Behavior*, 1979, *10*, 303-311.

Mukherji, B., Kashiki, Y., Ohyanagi, H., & Sloviter, H. A. Metabolism of ethanol and acetaldehyde by the isolated perfused rat brain. *Journal of Neurochemistry*, 1975, *24*, 841-843.

Ohnishi, K., & Lieber, C. S. Reconstitution of the microsomal ethanol oxidizing system (MEOS): Qualitative and quantitative changes of cytochrome P-450 after chronic ethanol consumption. *Journal of Biological Chemistry*, 1977, *252*, 7124-7131.

Oshini, N., Oshino, R., & Chance, B. The characteristics of the "peroxidatic" reaction of catalase in ethanol oxidation. *Biochemical Journal*, 1973, *131*, 555-567.

Oshino, N., Jamieson, D., Sugano, T., & Chance, B. Optical measurement of the catalase-hydrogen peroxide intermediate (compound I) in the liver of anesthetized rats and its implication to hydrogen peroxide production *in situ. Biochemical Journal,* 1975, *146,* 67-77.

Pietruszko, R. Nonethanol substrates of alcohol dehydrogenase. In E. Majchrowicz & E. P. Noble (Eds.), *Biochemistry and pharmacology of ethanol* (Vol. 1). New York: Plenum Press, 1979.

Rothschild, M. A., Oratz, M., Schreiber, S. S., & Mongelli, J. The effects of acetaldehyde and disulfiram on albumin synthesis in the isolated perfused rabbit liver. *Alcoholism: Clinical and Experimental Research,* 1980, *4,* 30-33.

Salaspuro, M. P., Shaw, S., Jayatilleke, E., Ross, W. A., & Lieber, C. S. Attenuation of the ethanol-induced hepatic redox change after chronic alcohol consumption in baboons: Metabolic consequences *in vivo* and *in vitro. Hepatology,* 1981, *1,* 33-38.

Sedman, A. J., Wilkinson, P. K., Sakmar, E., Weidler, D. J., & Wagner, J. G. Food effects on absorption and metabolism of alcohol. *Journal of Studies on Alcohol,* 1976, *37,* 1197-1214.

Shaw, S., & Lieber, C. S. Increased hepatic production of alpha amino-n-butyric acid after chronic alcohol consumption in rats and baboons. *Gastroenterology,* 1980, *78,* 108-113.

Smith, M., Hopkinson, D. A., & Harris, H. Developmental changes and polymorphism in human alcohol dehydrogenase. *Annals of Human Genetics (London),* 1971, *34,* 251-271.

Sorrell, M. F., & Tuma, D. J. Selective impairment of glycoprotein metabolism by ethanol and acetaldehyde in rat liver slices. *Gastroenterology,* 1978, *75,* 200-205.

Sturtevant, R. P., Sturtevant, F. M., Pauly, J. E., & Sheving, L. E. Chronopharmacokinetics of ethanol III. Variation in rate of ethanolemia in human subjects. *International Journal of Clinical Pharmacology,* 1978, *16,* 594-599.

Veitch, R. L., Lumeng, L., & Li, T.-K. Vitamin B_6 metabolism in chronic alcohol abuse. The effect of ethanol oxidation on hepatic pyridoxal 5'-phosphate metabolism. *Journal of Clinical Investigation,* 1975, *55,* 1026-1032.

Vina, J., Estrela, J. M., Guerri, C., & Romero, F. J. Effect of ethanol on glutathione concentration in isolated hepatocytes. *Biochemical Journal,* 1980, *188,* 549-552.

von Wartburg, J.-P., & Schürch, P. M. Atypical human liver alcohol dehydrogenase. *Annals of the New York Academy of Sciences,* 1968, *151,* 936-946.

Wagner, J. G., Wilkinson, P. K., Sedman, A. J., Kay, D. R., & Weidler, D. J. Elimination of alcohol from human blood. *Journal of Pharmaceutical Sciences,* 1976, *65,* 152-154.

Widmark, E. M. P. Verteilung und Umwandlung des äthyl Alkohols in Organimus des Hundes. *Biochemische Zeitschrift,* 1933, *267,* 128-134.

12.1 Monographs and Reviews

Baraona, E., & Lieber, C. S. Effects of ethanol on lipid metabolism. *Journal of Lipid Research,* 1979, *20,* 289-315.

Bosron, W. F., & Li, T.-K. Alcohol Dehydrogenase. In W. B. Jacoby (Ed.), *Enzymatic basis of detoxification* (Vol. 1). New York: Academic Press, 1980, p. 231-248.

Erickson, C. K. Factors affecting the distribution and measurement of ethanol in the body. In E. Majchrowicz & E. P. Noble (Eds.), *Biochemistry and pharmacology of ethanol* (Vol. 1). New York: Plenum Press, 1979.

Li, T.-K. Enzymology of human alcohol metabolism. *Advances in Enzymology,* 1977, *45,* 427-483.

Li, T.-K, Schenker, S., & Lumeng, L. (Eds). *Alcohol and nutrition.* Research Monograph No. 2, National Institute on Alcohol Abuse and Alcoholism. Department of Health, Education and Welfare, Publication No. (ADM) 79-780, 1979.

Lieber, C. S. Alcohol, protein metabolism and liver injury. *Gastroenterology,* 1980, *79,* 373-390. (a)

Lieber, C. S. Metabolism and metabolic effects of alcohol. *Seminars in Hematology,* 1980, *17,* 85-99. (b)

Lindros, K. O. Acetaldehyde—its metabolism and role in the actions of alcohol. In Y. Israel, F. B. Glaser, H. Kalant, R. E. Popham, W Schmidt, & R. G. Smart (Eds.), *Research advances in alcohol and drug problems* (Vol. 4). New York: Plenum Press, 1978.

Reed, T. E. Racial comparisons of alcohol metabolism: Background, problems and results. *Alcoholism: Clinical and Experimental Research,* 1978, *2,* 83-87.

Reitz, R. C. Effects of ethanol on the intermediary metabolism of liver and brain. In E. Majchrowicz & E. P. Noble (Eds.), *Biochemistry and pharmacology of ethanol* (Vol. 1). New York: Plenum Press, 1979.

Rognstad, R., & Grunnet, N. Enzymatic pathways of ethanol metabolism. In E. Majchrowicz & E. P. Noble (Eds.), *Biochemistry and pharmacology of ethanol* (Vol. 1). New York: Plenum Press, 1979.

Wallgren, H., & Barry, H., III. *Actions of alcohol. Part I: Biochemical, physiological and psychological aspects.* Amsterdam: Elsevier Publishing Co., 1970.

Weiner, H. Aldehyde dehydrogenase: Mechanism of action and possible physiological roles. In E. Majchrowicz & E. P. Noble (Eds.), *Biochemistry and pharmacology of ethanol* (Vol. 1). New York: Plenum Press, 1979.

Wilkinson, P. K. Pharmacokinetics of ethanol: A review. *Alcoholism: Clinical and Experimental Research,* 1980, *4,* 6-21.

Williamson, J. R., & Tischler, M. Ethanol metabolism in perfused liver and isolated hepatocytes with associated methodologies. In E. Majchrowicz & E. P. Noble (Eds.), *Biochemistry and pharmacology of ethanol* (Vol. 1). New York: Plenum Press, 1979.

4

Effects of Ethanol upon Organ Systems Other than the Central Nervous System

DAVID H. VAN THIEL

1. INTRODUCTION

Chronic alcoholism is a multisystem disease that adversely affects all of the organs of the body. Adverse effects on organs such as the gastrointestinal tract can begin immediately following ingestion of alcohol and extend to the liver as well as other organs following absorption. The liver is particularly susceptible to alcohol-associated injury, as it is the site within the body where most of the metabolism of ethanol occurs (see Chapter 3). Until the liver has disposed of the ingested ethanol, however, alcohol is present in the bloodstream and can affect the function of the brain, heart, muscles, and gonads. Ethanol is not only toxic *per se* but its metabolism may produce toxic metabolites such as acetaldehyde and acetate. In addition, changes in cellular redox potential occurring as a result of ethanol metabolism can disturb cellular intermediary metabolism at multiple sites.

It is estimated that there are 9.3 to 10 million problem drinkers in the adult population of the United States (U.S. Dept. of HEW, 1978). This figure represents 7% of the total adult population age 18 and over. In addition to this massive adult problem-drinker population, there are an estimated 3.3 million problem drinkers among young people, which represents 19% of those in the 14- to 17-year age group.

As recent as 1975, cirrhosis deaths, 95% of which are alcohol-related, ranked sixth on the most common cause of death list in the United States (U.S. Dept. of

DAVID H. VAN THIEL • Department of Medicine, Division of Gastroenterology, University of Pittsburgh School of Medicine, Pittsburgh, Pennsylvania 15261.

HEW, 1975). Moreover, during fiscal year 1975, it was estimated that the cost of alcoholism in the United States was nearly $43 billion (U.S. Dept. of HEW, 1978). This estimated cost includes $12.7 billion spent directly on health and medical costs. As must be obvious from the preceding figures, chronic alcoholism is a major health problem within the United States.

2. ETHANOL AND THE GASTROINTESTINAL TRACT

2.1. Ethanol and the Oral Cavity

Ethanol is known to initially stimulate and later inhibit salivary flow. The effect on salivary flow would appear to be a local one, as it occurs in response to local application but not to intragastric administration. Parotid enlargement is common in alcoholics, but it is uncertain whether it occurs as a result of alcohol *per se* or is due to the associated protein-deficient diets that such individuals usually ingest.

Stomatitis and cheilitis are common in alcohol abusers. They are thought to occur as a result of poor nutrition, particularly vitamin B complex and iron deficiency. It also has been said that the prevalence of dental caries and periodontal disease is greater in alcoholics than in controls, but the mechanisms responsible and exact figures for such phenomena are lacking.

There is an association between chronic alcoholic use and the occurrence of cancer of the mouth, tongue, pharynx, and esophagus. Several authors have suggested that a synergistic effect between alcohol and tobacco use may be responsible (Wynder, 1975). Other factors that may contribute to such carcinogenesis include vitamin (both A and B vitamins) and zinc deficiencies that may be present in the alcoholic (Wynder & Chan, 1970).

Support for a relationship between vitamin deficiency and incidence of carcinoma comes from the observation that animals deficient in vitamin A are more susceptible to squamous cell carcinoma of the skin, mouth, and esophagus than are normal animals (Sporn, Dunlop, Newton, & Smith, 1976). Not only do vitamin and mineral deficiencies predispose animals to develop such cancers but ethanol has been shown to promote the conversion of procarcinogens to carcinogens.

2.2. Ethanol and the Esophagus

The occurrence of nonmalignant esophageal disease is common in the alcoholic. Esophagitis has been associated with chronic alcohol abuse (Krasner, 1977; Shirazi & Platz, 1978). In normal human volunteers, ethanol has been shown to reduce lower esophageal sphincter pressure and to interfere with acid clearing mechanisms of the esophagus (Mayer, Grabowski, & Fisher, 1978). In addition, ethanol has been shown to be a direct mucosal irritant.

Not only is alcohol probably directly toxic to the esophagus but retching associated with acute alcohol abuse can produce linear mucosal tears, termed Mallory–Weiss lesions, at the gastroesophageal junction (Watts, 1976). Other pathologic alterations of the esophagus indirectly related to excessive alcohol use include esophageal varices secondary to portal hypertension and Barrett's epithelium secondary to chronic acid reflux (Martini & Weinback, 1974; Axon & Clarke, 1975).

It is interesting to note that decompensated alcohol-induced cirrhosis characterized by ascites and portal hypertension is associated with an enhanced lower esophageal sphincter pressure. Such increased sphincter pressure would appear to protect against esophageal reflux, which might otherwise precipitate variceal bleeding (Van Thiel & Stremple, 1977a; Eckardt, Grace, & Kantrowitz, 1976).

2.3. Ethanol and the Stomach

Acute alcohol administration stimulates secretion of gastric juice. This effect is seen whether the ethanol is administered orally, intragastrically, or intravenously and appears to be maximal at ethanol concentrations between 8% and 16%, approximately the concentration found in wine (Davenport, 1967; Elwin, 1969). Moreover, there appears to be a linear relationship between gastric acidity and the dose of ethanol when the ethanol is given intravenously under experimental conditions (Weise, Schapiro, & Woodward, 1961; Hirschowitz, Pollard, Hartwell, & London, 1956). Such alcohol-induced acid secretion occurs independently of the extrinsic nerves to the stomach (Elwin, 1969; Saint-Blanquot & Deroche, 1972), independently of the histamine responses of the gastric mucosa (Davenport, 1967), and independently of gastrin release (Korman, Soveny, & Hansky, 1971). Chronic ethanol feeding (12 months) has been shown to enhance the daily and maximal acid secretion from Heidenhain pouches (Chey, 1972), and this has led to suggestions that ethanol increases the parietal cell mass as well as the ultrastructural secretory apparatus of the parietal cells (Lillibridge, Yoshimori, & Chey, 1973).

Presumed acid-induced gastric mucosal injury is a common event in clinical and experimental studies (Gottfried, Korsten, & Lieber, 1978) and has been characterized at both the histological and ultrastructural levels (Eastwood & Kirchner, 1974; Eastwood & Erdmann, 1978). Aspirin, commonly utilized by alcohol abusers to alleviate the discomfort associated with intemperate use of the drug, may also contribute to the gastric injury in such individuals (Robert, Nezamis, Hanchar, & Lancaster, 1980; Smith, Skillman, & Edwards, 1971).

Alcohol abuse as a cause of gastric ulcer remains controversial. One study using alcoholics found a greater incidence of gastric ulcer but not duodenal ulcer (Engeset, Lygren, & Idsoe, 1963). Two later studies of extremely large populations, however, failed to confirm the earlier report (Friedman, Siegelaub, & Seltzer, 1974; Pfoffenbarger, Wing, & Hyde, 1974). In patients with alcoholic liver disease, the incidence of peptic ulcer has been reported to be 20.6% (Bode, 1981), and an association between the two has been assumed although not proven.

The effects of alcohol on gastric motor function appear to be concentration dependent (Barboriak & Meade, 1969). Concentrations of alcohol as low as that found in wine (8 to 10 g/100 mL) have been reported to produce measurable alterations in gastric emptying (Gottfried, Korsten, & Lieber, 1976). At these concentrations both acceleration and delay in gastric emptying have been noted (Gottfried *et al.*, 1976; Baraona, Pirola, & Lieber, 1974). At high ethanol concentrations, gastric emptying is delayed (Gottfried *et al.*, 1976; Baraona *et al.*, 1974), presumably because of the hyperosmolarity of the ethanol solutions. Whether ethanol has a direct irritative effect upon gastric mucosa is uncertain.

There is conflicting evidence concerning the role of ethanol in the pathogenesis of gastric carcinoma. In the majority of reported series, there is no clearly defined association between the two (Krawitt, 1974; Rubin, Rybak, Lindenbaum, Gerson, Walker, & Lieber, 1972; Dinda & Beck, 1977). However, a limited number of studies have shown a positive correlation between ethanol use and the development of gastric cancer (Dinda, Beck, Beck, & McElligott, 1975). Whether alcohol-induced gastritis is a premalignant lesion, particularly if it occurs repeatedly, is an important question for which evidence is not yet available.

After the stomach, the small bowel is exposed to higher concentrations of ethanol than any other organ in the body. As might be expected, structural changes in the small bowel have been documented to occur following ethanol administration in both animal and human studies.

2.4. Ethanol and the Small Bowel

Hemorrhagic lesions in duodenal villus tips have been produced in alcoholic human volunteers after ingestion of alcohol at doses as small as 1 g/kg body weight at a concentration of 35 g/100 mL (Gottfried *et al.*, 1976). Such lesions heal rapidly, however, as duodenal biopsies obtained from the same volunteers 16 hours after ethanol administration failed to demonstrate the lesions. Acute administration of ethanol to rats and hamsters has been shown to produce hemorrhagic erosions in jejunal villi. Such lesions are more severe proximally and develop within 10 minutes. At one hour, they are well developed, but they diminish rapidly and frequently disappear by 4 to 16 hours after ethanol exposure. Interestingly, rats chronically fed ethanol do not demonstrate such erosions. Instead, they demonstrate shortened jejunal villi with decreased numbers of surface cells.

Ultrastructural changes in small bowel can be seen after chronic ethanol administration to alcoholic volunteers maintained on a nutritionally adequate diet (Baraona *et al.*, 1974). These include enlarged and bizarre mitochondria, dilatation of the endoplasmic reticulum and cisterns of the Golgi apparatus, and focal cytoplasmic degeneration.

In animals, ethanol has been shown to acutely inhibit glucose transport (Dinda & Beck, 1977). Such information is still lacking in humans. In contrast, decreased absorption of d-xylose has been shown repeatedly to occur in alcoholics (Krasner, Cochran, Russel, Carmichael, & Thompson, 1976).

Decreases in brush-border enzymes (lactase, sucrase, and alkaline phosphatase) are common in experimental animals and humans following ethanol administration (Baraona et al., 1974; Perlow, Baraona, & Lieber, 1975). The mechanisms responsible for such damage may be due to the hyperosmolarity of intestinal contents, as similar changes can be produced after intragastric administration of urea (Baraona et al., 1974).

Both in animal and human (Israel, Valenzuela, Salazar, & Ugarte, 1969) studies, amino acid active transport systems are inhibited by ethanol. Using the rat small bowel in vitro, moderate doses of ethanol have been shown to inhibit transport of L-phenylalanine, L-lysine, glycine, L-leucine, L-methionine, and L-valine. Moreover, the effect of alcohol on L-phenylalanine transport has been shown to be concentration dependent.

Although tissue damage secondary to high-dose ethanol exposure could contribute to inhibition of amino acid transport, the fact that it is reversible immediately suggests instead that a physiochemical change rather than toxic injury is responsible (Krawitt, Sampson, & Katagiri, 1975). Absorption of D-phenylalanine, an amino acid that is not actively transported, is not disturbed as a result of ethanol exposure (Israel, Salazar, & Rosemann, 1968). However, the absorption of its isomer, L-phenylalanine, is inhibited. This finding suggests that the abnormalities of amino acid transport seen after ethanol exposure are secondary to injury to specific active transport systems rather than to nonspecific tissue injury.

Vitamin absorption is affected by alcohol. At physiologic concentrations ($<$ 1 mM), folate uptake from the lumen of the small bowel is an energy-dependent, saturable process (Smith, Matty, & Blair, 1970; Dhar, Selhub, & Gay, 1977) that may function via the interaction of folate with a binding protein (Selhub & Rosenberg, 1976). Folate release from mucosal cells is also energy-dependent (Dhar et al., 1977). At high concentrations ($>$ 2 mM), folate can be absorbed by simple diffusion. Using an intestinal perfusion method, studies involving folate-deficient alcoholics have shown a significant reduction in jejunal uptake of folic acid when compared with folate uptake in control subjects (Halsted, Robles, & Mezey, 1973). However, after two weeks of nutritional supplementation, folic acid uptake improved despite continued ethanol administration. This suggests that under normal physiologic concentrations, impaired folate absorption may be a function of poor nutrition rather than being due to a direct toxic effect of ethanol upon the small bowel. In support of this contention, studies of acute ethanol administration to normal subjects have shown a decreased folate absorption in only 20% of the subjects studied (Halsted, Griggs, & Harris, 1967). Folate deficiency is the most common nutritional deficiency present in alcoholics (Leevy, Baker, & Ten Hove, 1965). It has been reported that alcohol interrupts the enterohepatic circulation of folate by impairing secretion of folate into bile (Steinbert, Campbell, & Hillman, 1980). When this occurs, there is a rapid decrease in serum folate, presumably because of reduced absorption of hepatically secreted folate. Alcohol use also promotes the hepatic synthesis of inactive polyglutamates that are stored in the liver despite functional folate deficiency (Steinbert et al., 1980). There also is evidence to suggest that there is a decreased tissue affinity for folate after acute alcohol administration to either normal (Lane, Goff, McGuffin, Eichner, & Hillman, 1976) or alcoholic (Cherrick, Baker, Frank, & Leevy, 1965) individuals.

As with folate, thiamine absorption is known to occur by way of a dual system. At low concentrations (< 1 mM), transport is active, sodium dependent and saturable (Hoyumpa, Middleton, & Wilson, 1975). At concentrations above 2 mM, transport appears to be passive and occurs by simple diffusion (Hoyumpa, Middleton, & Wilson, 1975). The active uptake of thiamine by mucosal epithelial cells is not affected by ethanol (Hoyumpa, Breen, & Schenker, 1975). However, movement across the serosal border and out of the cell is impaired (Hoyumpa, Breen, & Schenker, 1975). Once thiamine transport is inhibited, increasing the ethanol dose does not further inhibit thiamine transport (Selhub & Rosenberg, 1976). In contrast, ethanol has no affect on thiamine transport at concentrations above 2 mM when passive diffusion predominates (Hoyumpa, Breen, & Schenker, 1975; Hoyumpa, Middleton, Wilson, & Schenker, 1974). Available human studies generally support animal work, which suggests that ethanol inhibits thiamine absorption only at physiologic levels of thiamine (Tomasulo, Kater, & Iber, 1968; Thomson, Baker, & Leevy, 1970). It should be noted, however, that thiamine absorption may be impaired secondary to other ethanol-related nutritional deficiencies, including deficiencies of folate, B_6, or B_{12} (Howard, Wagner, & Schenker, 1974; Thompson, Frank, & DeAngelis, 1972; Nishimo & Itokawa, 1977).

Ethanol inhibits vitamin B_{12} absorption in the terminal ileum (Lindenbaum & Lieber, 1975). In a small group of alcoholics in whom a significant part of daily caloric intake was alcohol, 6 of 8 subjects demonstrated a measurable decrease in B_{12} absorption which was not corrected by intrinsic factor or pancreatic enzyme replacement (Lindenbaum & Lieber, 1975). When the investigators studied a small group of normal volunteers with Schilling tests (a measure of vitamin B_{12} absorption) both before and after ethanol administration, the average urinary excretion of ^{57}CO-labeled vitamin B_{12} after ethanol was decreased significantly (Lindenbaum & Lieber, 1969a). In rats, ethanol has been shown to impair B_{12} absorption at concentrations of B_{12}, which would indicate the involvement of an active transport mechanism, and to decrease intrinsic factor secretion as well as to impair the binding of the intrinsic factor–B_{12} (IF–B_{12}) complex to ileal receptors

(Lindenbaum, Saha, Shea, & Lieber, 1973). Other studies confirm a decreased absorption of B_{12} in ethanol-treated rats but do not confirm the finding that ethanol impairs ileal binding of $IF-B_{12}$ complex (Findlay, Sellers, & Forstner, 1976). In one study in which electron microscopy was used to examine ileal enterocytes obtained from human subjects after alcohol exposure, ultrastructural changes were found (Lindenbaum & Lieber, 1969b). These included dilatation of endoplasmic reticulum and focal cytoplasmic degeneration. It should be noted that these ultrastructural changes were observed when light-microscope examination of the tissue indicated no changes (Lindenbaum & Lieber, 1969b). This suggests that specific ultrastructural alterations in ileal enterocytes might account for at least some of the inhibitory effects of ethanol upon B_{12} absorption.

The effect of ethanol on iron absorption is unsettled. In one human study, it was found that a single dose of ethanol increased absorption of ferrous chloride but had no effect on the absorption of hemoglobin iron (Charlton, Jacobs, & Seffel, 1964). In contrast, others have found no effect of either acute or chronic ethanol administration on iron absorption (Murray & Stein, 1968). Adding further confusion to this issue are the studies that used isolated duodenal loops and showed that ferrous iron absorption was inhibited rather than enhanced by the presence of ethanol (Tapper, Bushi, & Ruppert, 1968).

Zinc is an essential cofactor for many key enzymes including those involved in gluconeogenesis, lipogenesis, amino acid metabolism, as well as DNA and RNA synthesis (Thompson, 1978). In animals, zinc is absorbed from the small bowel via an active transport system (Kowarski, Blair-Stanek, & Schachter, 1974). Available data examining the effect of ethanol on zinc absorption are quite variable. Although zincuria is common in alcoholics, no one has been able to show that ethanol produces zinc deficiency by increased urinary zinc losses either in normal human volunteers or in chronic alcoholics (Sullivan, 1962). In contrast, studies using rats chronically fed ethanol note a decreased ileal but not duodenal absorption of zinc (Antonson, Barak, & Vanderhoof, 1978). Moreover, although alcohol dehydrogenase is a zinc metalloenzyme, it has not been shown that zinc deficiency decreases ethanol metabolism (Whang & Pierson, 1975). One group has shown that in cirrhotics, a greater portion of plasma zinc is bound to an α 2 macroglobulin which sequesters zinc and makes it metabolically inert (Schachter, 1976). This effect would exaggerate zinc deficiency in such individuals.

The mechanisms involved in calcium transport by the small bowel have not been completely delineated. However, it is known that transport of calcium requires an active vitamin D-dependent process (Dowdle, Schachter, & Schenker, 1960) which involves a calcium ATPase (Kowarski & Schachter, 1973) and a soluble calcium-binding protein (Wasserman & Taylor, 1968). The few animal studies that have examined the effects of ethanol upon calcium transport suggest that ethanol inhibits calcium absorption (Krawitt, 1973; Krawitt, 1974). However, the mechanism of such inhibition is not entirely clear. Possibilities that have been eliminated include (1) the hyperosmolarity of the ethanol solutions used, (2) a depression of brush-border calcium or magnesium ATPase activity, (3) a depression of the activity of calcium binding protein, and (4) a lack of vitamin D or 1,25 dihydroxycholecalciferol (Krawitt, 1975). Administration of vitamin D preparations does not reverse the adverse effect of ethanol on calcium absorption. In contrast to animal studies, one human study performed in nonalcoholics given short-term ethanol showed no effect on calcium absorption (Verdy & Caron, 1973). However, others have reported a greater than twofold increase in fecal calcium in human volunteers after ethanol ingestion, suggesting reduced net calcium absorption.

Alcohol has multiple effects on lipid metabolism within the small bowel. In general, chronic ethanol administration has been shown to increase triglyceride synthesis (Carter, Drummery, & Isselbacher, 1971; Baraona, Pirola, & Lieber, 1975; Cohen & Raecht, 1980). Many investigators have reported that mucosal triglyceride synthesis is increased in rats given alcohol. Moreover, microsomes prepared from intestinal slices incubated for one hour in a medium containing 2.6 g/ 100 mL of ethanol have been shown to have an increased ability to convert C_{14}-labeled palmitate into triglyceride even when placed in a medium containing no ethanol (Carter et al., 1971). Similarly, direct addition of 2.6% ethanol to untreated, normal intestinal slices produced a 30% increase in the esterification of C_{14}-labeled palmitate to triglyceride (Carter et al., 1971). Ethanol administration also causes a decrease in fatty acid oxidation. Thus, after acute ethanol perfusion of the gut in rats, there is a 60% to 65% decrease in the conversion of C_{14} palmitate to water and other oxidative metabolites (Gangl & Ockner, 1975). In contrast, intestinal slices taken from rats fed a nutritionally adequate diet containing ethanol show an increase in fatty acid oxidation (Baraona et al., 1975). There is an increase in mucosal cholesterol synthesis after acute ethanol administration (Middleton, Carter, Drummery, & Isselbacher, 1971). Moreover, there is an increased activity of the jejunal and ileal lipid reesterifying enzymes acyl CoA monoglyceride acyltransferase and microsomal acyl CoA synthetase (Rodgers & O'Brien, 1975). Following ethanol administration, an increased intestinal lymph output of cholesterol and triglyceride has been demonstrated. This effect of increasing intestinal lymph cholesterol is seen only when ethanol is present within the intestinal lumen (Middleton et al., 1971). In addition, there is a redistribution of cholesterol among the various intestinal lymph lipoproteins following ethanol exposure. If ethanol is given subcutaneously, this redistribution does not occur. This suggests a local effect of ethanol on the small bowel mucosal enzymes involved in cholesterol synthesis. Chronic ethanol feeding abolishes or inhibits these acute effects of ethanol on lipid transport (Rodgers & O'Brien, 1975; Baraona & Leiber, 1975). Thus, the relationship of these findings to the clinical condition of alcohol-induced hyperlipidemia remains unclear (Mistilis & Ockner, 1972; Baraona, Pirola, & Leiber, 1973).

The effect of ethanol administration on the motility of different small bowel segments is variable, but the net effect is to shorten intestinal transit time. Initially, when intravenous ethanol is given to volunteers, there is an increase in motility, particularly in the second portion of the duodenum (Pirola & Davis, 1970). This increased motility is characterized by an increase in the intraluminal pressure and in the number of contractile waves generated. Later, there is a decrease in duodenal activity, with a gradual return toward normal. When either oral or intravenous ethanol is administered to experimental subjects, initially there is a decrease in Type I mixing waves in the jejunum and an increase in Type III propulsive waves in the ileum (Robles, Mezey, Halstead, & Schuster, 1974). Ethanol depresses nonpropulsive motility of the colon in dogs and humans. It should be noted that these changes in small and large intestinal motor activity may contribute to the diarrhea commonly seen following indiscriminate alcohol ingestion (Martin, Justus, & Mathias, 1980).

2.5. Ethanol and the Large Bowel

Essentially there are no data concerning the effects of ethanol upon the large bowel. It would not be surprising, however, if the effects were similar to those in the small bowel in terms of salt and water absorption and secretion as well as motility.

2.6. Ethanol and the Pancreas

Not until the 1960s was it shown that alcoholic pancreatitis is a distinct clinical and pathologic syndrome separate from gallstone pancreatitis (Howard & Ehrlich, 1960).

According to the Marseille Symposium held in 1962, gallstones may cause one or more episodes of acute pancreatitis between which the pancreas returns completely to normal (Sarles, 1963). Alcohol, on the other hand, causes chronic recurrent calcifying pancreatitis in which histologic lesions and functional insufficiency persist even after the offending agent has been removed (Sarles, 1974).

Alcoholism is present in over 75% of the cases of chronic pancreatitis seen within the United States. Moreover, pathologic changes and/or alterations in pancreatic function can be detected in half of the asymptomatic alcoholics seen on most general medical wards (Reber, 1978). It is estimated that a period of 6 to 12 years of steady alcohol consumption is necessary before pancreatic symptoms occur.

Despite strong evidence of the epidemiologic link between alcoholism and pancreatic disease, the mechanism responsible for such injury remains unclear. Early speculation about alcohol's effect on the pancreas was based mostly on circumstantial evidence. In 1936 Rich and Duff postulated that pancreatitis resulted from an excess of pancreatic flow against ductal resistance. The excess flow was allegedly due to alcohol and the resistance was due to alcohol-induced spasm of the sphincter of Oddi. Their theory was based upon the observation of Bayless and Starling that alcohol stimulated the release of secretin by a direct action on the duodenal mucosa. In addition, they were aware that other investigators had shown that the volume of pancreatic flow could be increased as a result of ethanol administration into the stomach, the duodenum, or an isolated loop of small bowel.

Recent studies have documented that intragastric administration of alcohol induces gastrin release and increases gastric acid secretion (Dreiling & Bordalo, 1973), which in turn stimulates release of secretin from the duodenal mucosa (Straus, Urbach, & Yalow, 1975). Brooks and Thomas reported in 1953 that in the dog, single doses of intravenous alcohol did not effect pancreatic secretion if gastric acid was not permitted to enter the intestine. More recent studies have shown that, under the same experimental conditions, ethanol inhibits both basal and secretin-stimulated pancreatic water, bicarbonate, and protein secretion. This inhibition is suppressed by atropine and partially blocked by vagotomy, suggesting that it is mediated by a vagal and extravagal cholinergic mechanism. Thus, the acute action of ethanol on pancreatic secretion is extremely complex and involves both simulatory and inhibitory mechanisms. The final result is a weak stimulation of water, bicarbonate, and protein output. This effect of ethanol is much less than that caused by a normal meal (Sarles, 1975). Thus, one would not expect it to be pathologically significant. In fact, no one has ever produced pancreatic lesions by the acute administration of ethanol. Furthermore, no known effect of ethanol can explain the chronic nature of alcohol pancreatitis.

In this regard, Strum and Spiro (1971) have pointed out that acute pancreatitis usually does not occur in the nonalcoholic who occasionally overindulges. On the other hand, symptoms of acute pancreatitis develop in the alcoholic only after functional and histologic changes of chronic pancreatitis are well established. Moreover, progressive destruction of the pancreas continues even after the patient stops drinking.

Chronic ethanol ingestion causes a progressive series of effects on the pancreas and duodenum (Sarles, 1975). After 14 months of alcohol consumption, gastroduodenal hormone release is greatly augmented by the usual stimuli. Thus, intraduodenal installation of oleic acid leads to pancreatic protein secretion six times greater than that seen during the prealcohol period, suggesting an increased cholecystokinin-pancreozymin release. Parenthetically, it should be noted that elevated cholecystokinin levels have been noted in individuals with chronic pancreatitis (Ederle & Vantini, 1978). Similarly, a standard meat meal causes a significantly greater and more prolonged gastrin release in chronic alcohol-fed dogs than in controls. This effect can be further augmented when ethanol is added to the meat meal.

The most surprising effect of chronic alcohol administration to the dog is a complete reversal of the inhibitory effect of alcohol administration on pancreatic secretion. This excitatory effect can be abolished by atropine and does not occur in previously vagotomized dogs. Again, alcohol seems to be acting through a cholinergic mechanism with an action opposite to that seen in nonalcoholic control animals. The reason why chronic alcoholism reverses this effect of ethanol on the pancreas is not known.

Regardless of the specific mechanism involved, the final consequence of chronic alcohol ingestion is the secretion of a juice more concentrated in protein as well as the production of protein precipitates. These plugs are rich in calcium carbonate and are identical to small pancreatic stones found in humans with chronic pancreatitis (Nakamura, Sarles, & Payan, 1972). In both dogs and humans, these plugs of precipitated protein obstruct the ducts, blocking secretion.

The ultrastructural changes that occur in the pancreas after alcohol ingestion are similar to those found in hepatic cells (Darle, Ekholm, & Edlund, 1979). There is a large number of lipid droplets in acinar cells which show swelling of their mitochondria and a loss of mitochondrial cristae. In addition, the endoplasmic reticulum is hypertrophied and dilated. Focal cytoplasmic degeneration occurs in both acinar and ductal cells. This last change may be a nonspecific, nonpathologic finding as it is seen also after cholecystokinin-pancreozymin stimulation. The ultrastructural changes seen in early human chronic pancreatitis are present only in acinar cells and are similar to those observed in animals chronically treated with gastrin or cholecystotokinin-pancreozymin.

The earliest pancreatic lesion seen with light microscopy is a ductular precipitate of protein (Sarles & Sahel, 1976). These precipitated protein plugs irritate the ductular epithelium, producing ductular atrophy and a proliferation of periductular connective tissue.

It has been suggested that the precipitation of hyperconcentrated protein in human chronic pancreatitis may be favored by the occurrence of a greatly increased concentration of the iron-binding bacteriostatic protein lactoferrin. This protein is normally present in very low concentrations in pancreatic juice. It is known to combine with other proteins to form large molecular complexes. The reason for its increase in pancreatic secretions seen in chronic pancreatitis is as yet unknown. Recent studies also have demonstrated the presence of acetaldehyde within pancreatic secretions of pigs chronically fed ethanol. Acetaldehyde, like lactoferrin, is a highly labile and reactive substance that readily forms macromolecular complexes with proteins. Thus, acetaldehyde may also contribute to ductal stone formation and obstruction.

An association between chronic alcoholism and carcinoma of the pancreas has been suggested. Burch and Ansari (1968) made such a suggestion based on a retrospective study in which 75% of the patients with pancreatic cancer also had a history of moderate to heavy alcohol intake. Additional support for this thesis was provided by Ishii (1968), who reported that the risk of pancreatic cancer was twice as great in males who consume alcohol daily as it is in nondrinkers.

It should be noted that studies relating pancreatic cancer to alcohol abuse may also reflect a close association between alcohol and tobacco use. This is important, as the latter has been definitely linked to pancreatic cancer. It is also possible that degradation products of tobacco smoke, excreted in bile, are carcinogenic and that chronic alcohol use allows bile regurgitation into pancreatic ducts, thus possibly contributing to pancreatic ductal neoplastic change. Interesting as these hypotheses are, it should be remembered that the association between chronic alcoholism and pancreatic cancer is at present controversial.

2.7. Ethanol and the Liver

Until recently it was unclear whether liver disease associated with alcohol ingestion was a direct effect of the alcohol or of the malnutrition which often accompanies alcoholism. Principally as a result of the landmark work of Lieber, Spritz, and DeCarli (1966) ethanol now can be incriminated as a direct hepatotoxin.

Alcohol is not effectively stored in tissues and little less than 10% of an ingested dose can be eliminated through the kidneys, lungs, and skin. For practical purposes, one can assume that the body rids itself of alcohol only by oxidizing it in the liver, the organ which contains the bulk of the enzymes required for ethanol oxidation. This organ-specificity of alcohol oxidation and the complexity of hepatic function each contribute to the multiplicity of deleterious effects of ethanol within the liver.

Three hepatic enzyme systems have been shown to catalyze the oxidation of ethanol to acetaldehyde *in vitro*. They are, in descending order of importance, alcohol dehydrogenase (ADH), microsomal ethanol-oxidizing system (MEOS), and catalase. The metabolism of ethanol by these enzymes is described in detail by Li in this volume.

The initial product of ethanol metabolism is acetaldehyde, and most of the acetaldehyde formed during ethanol oxidation is rapidly metabolized in the liver. Only small amounts of acetaldehyde leave the liver and enter the circulation. In the mitochondria, acetaldehyde is oxidized to acetate by an NAD^+-linked aldehyde oxidase which has a high affinity for acetaldehyde. *In vitro*, acetaldehyde has been found to have many adverse effects on mitochondria, one of which results in a reduced capacity of mitochondria to metabolize acetaldehyde. The alcoholic may therefore be a victim of a vicious circle: high acetaldehyde levels impair hepatic mitochondrial function; acetaldehyde metabolism is decreased; as more acetaldehyde accumulates, liver damage is enhanced.

Rates of ethanol oxidation are accelerated in chronic alcoholics after heavy ethanol ingestion, with such increases being in the order of 30% to 40%. Because such increases in the rate of ethanol oxidation are associated with increases in

MEOS but not with increases in the usual forms of ADH, MEOS induction has been proposed as the mechanism responsible for this phenomenon. Alternatively, the recent discovery of II-ADH suggests that the increased ethanol metabolism seen with high-dose alcohol could be the result of a progressively greater saturation of this low-affinity ADH isoenzyme (Li, Bosron, & Dafeldecker, 1977). Increased mitochondrial reoxidation of NADH is yet another potential mechanism for the increased rate of ethanol metabolism following ethanol ingestion. The rate-limiting factor in the metabolism of ethanol by ADH is the capacity of the liver to reoxidize the NADH produced from the reduction of NAD^+ by hydrogen derived from ethanol. Mitochondrial uncouplers, which increase the ability of mitochondria to oxidize NADH, have been shown to increase the rate of ethanol metabolism in vitro. However, the mechanism whereby chronic ethanol ingestion might stimulate the reoxidation of NADH is still a matter of controversy.

Ethanol alters amino acid metabolism in the liver and causes certain amino acids to accumulate in the liver (Krebs et al., 1973). Moreover, plasma amino acid abnormalities have been described in patients with alcoholic hepatitis (Ning, Lowenstein, & Davidson, 1967), cirrhosis (Fischer, Yoshimura, & Aguirre, 1974), and hepatic insufficiency (Rosen, Yoshimura, & Hodgman, 1977). However, the significance of these abnormalities has been difficult to interpret due to failure to control the three main variables which alter plasma amino acids; alcohol consumption, nutrition, and liver injury.

The role of protein deficiency in the pathogenesis of ethanol-associated hepatic injury is particularly relevant in the alcoholic. Protein deficiency is known to be associated with the genesis of fatty liver, and protein deficiency compounds ethanol-induced experimental liver injury (Shaw & Leiber, 1978).

The respective roles for alcohol, nutrition, and liver injury in producing plasma amino acid abnormalities were defined in a recent report (Shaw & Lieber, 1978). In addition, alcohol inhibits the synthesis of certain proteins, most notably albumin. Albumin plays a key role in osmotic regulation and nonpolar molecular transport. Alcohol also inhibits the synthesis of transferrin and complement, a deficiency of the latter contributing, at least in part, to the increased susceptibility of alcoholics to infection. Acute ethanol administration also inhibits the synthesis of constituent as well as export proteins of the liver. These effects have been attributed either to the redox changes generated by the oxidation of ethanol (Chambers & Piccrillo, 1973; Perin & Sessa, 1975; Sorrell, Tuma, & Schafer, 1977) or to a direct binding of acetaldehyde to amino acids or proteins (Perin & Sessa, 1975; Sorrell, Tuma, & Schafer, 1977; Sorrell, Tuma, & Barak, 1977) (for additional discussion, see the discussion by Li in Chapter 3). However, the precise mechanism whereby the metabolism of ethanol causes alteration in protein metabolism remains undefined. Relevant to this issue is the observation that increased levels of acetaldehyde have been noted in patients with liver disease secondary to chronic ethanol intake (Korsten, Matsuzaki, & Feinman, 1975); also, acetaldehyde, but not ethanol, has been shown to interfere with protein synthesis in cardiac muscle (Schriber, Briden, & Oratz, 1972).

Alcohol stimulates the synthesis of lipoproteins in the liver (Baraona & Lieber, 1970), particularly the synthesis of very-low-density and high-density lipoproteins.

Fatty infiltration of the liver following ethanol intake is due to an increased availability of fatty acids in the liver. The origin of the fatty acids that contribute to fatty liver depends upon the dose of ethanol ingested and the lipid content of the diet (Lieber & Spritz, 1966; Isselbacher, 1977). After an acute isolated ingestion of a large dose of ethanol, the liver's fatty acids are found to originate from adipose tissue, while following chronic ingestion there is an increased synthesis and decreased degradation of fatty acids in the liver. While the decreased degradation of fatty acids is related to the increase in $NADH/NAD^+$ ratio occurring during ethanol oxidation, the synthesis of fatty acids is stimulated by increases in NADPH produced when reduced equivalents from NADH are transferred to $NADP^+$.

An additional consequence of the decreased fatty acid oxidation resulting from ethanol ingestion is the formation of ketones and the development of ketoacidosis. Susceptibility to alcoholic ketoacidosis varies with the individual, appears to be more prevalent in women than in men, and is probably more common than thought. Its development may be unrelated either to the amount of alcohol ingested or to blood alcohol levels. The initial laboratory findings reveal increased serum ketones and mild hyperglycemia, though the blood sugar is usually not as high as it is in diabetic acidosis. The anion gap is great and probably results from increased β-hydroxybutyrate, with only a mild to moderate elevation in serum lactate. The ratio of serum β-hydroxybutyrate to lactate, which is normally 1:1, is characteristically increased to levels between 2:1 and 9:1 (Isselbacher, 1977).

The pathogenesis of alcoholic ketoacidosis is undefined, but hormonal factors and enhanced generation of NADH in the oxidation of ethanol to acetaldehyde are probably involved. Serum levels of insulin are low, while those of growth hormone, epinephrine, glucagon, and cortisol are high (Isselbacher, 1977). The increased release of these hormones most likely contributes to the mild hyperglycemia. Such hormones mobilize free fatty acids from adipose tissue and enhance fatty acid metabolism by the liver. Because of increased oxidation of fatty acids and the conversion of acetoacetate to β-hydroxybutyrate, induced by the high levels of NADH generated as ethanol is oxidized to acetaldehyde, the serum β-hydroxybutyrate levels are increased.

The clearance of steroid hormones, such as cortisol (Peterson, 1960), aldosterone (Coppage, Island, & Conner, 1962), and testosterone (Southren, Gordon, Olivo, Rafii, & Rosenthal, 1973), from the circulation is decreased in patients with cirrhosis due to alcoholism, and these effects are probably related to both an increase in plasma protein binding and decreased hepatic blood flow. Alcohol at moderately high concentrations increases hepatic blood flow (Stein, Lieber, & Leevy, 1963) but at lower concentrations decreases it. Also, large doses of alcohol can cause hypothermia, which in turn reduces both hepatic blood flow and the rate of alcohol metabolism. The more a given hormone is bound to protein, the less "free" or easily diffusable hormone there is for delivery to peripheral target tissues. For hormones such as aldosterone, which are weakly bound to protein, decreased hepatic blood flow or portosystemic shunting may be an important mechanism accounting for the reduction in clearance of the hormone from the circulation (Peterson, 1960; Coppage et al., 1962; Southren et al., 1973).

Reduction in the enzyme activity which catalyzes steroid A-ring reduction is an alternative mechanism which accounts for decreased hepatic extraction and metabolism of hormones (Gordon, Vittek, & Ho, 1979). This reaction is rate-limiting in the hepatic intracellular metabolism of cortisol, aldosterone, andro-stenedione, and testosterone and results in their metabolic inactivation. In a recent study, chronic alcohol feeding was associated with a decreased level of hepatic testosterone 5α-A-ring reductase (HTAR) activity in the baboon (Gordon, Vittek, & Ho, 1979). More pertinently, in humans with alcoholic liver disease, levels of this enzyme also have been shown to be decreased (Gordon, Vittek, & Ho, 1979). That HTAR levels in baboon are varied independently of changes in liver histology suggests that alcohol per se, rather than liver disease, alters the functional state of enzyme (Gordon, Vittek, & Ho, 1979).

Chronic alcohol ingestion is associated with a hypermetabolic state characterized by a high metabolic rate, increased oxygen consumption, inefficient use of calories, increased heat output, and weight loss (Israel, Videla, & Bernstein, 1975). This hypermetabolic state is thought to result, at least in part, from increased hepatic mitochondrial sodium–potassium–ATPase activity (Videla, Bernstein, & Israel, 1973), but the increased rate of oxygen consumption by the hypermetabolic liver tissue can be markedly depressed by surgically removing the thyroid in alcoholic rats (Bernstein, Videla, & Israel, 1975); the increased oxygen consumption can also be abolished by propylthiouracil (PTU) (Israel, Kalant, Orrego, Khanna, Videla, & Phillips, 1975). These observations suggest that PTU may be of potential value in alcoholic patients with liver disease. Indeed, in a recent study, PTU was shown to exert a beneficial short-term effect on both the magnitude and the rate of improvement in patients with alcoholic hepatitis. Moreover, the therapeutic value of PTU was greatest in those patients with the most severe liver disease (Orrego, Kalant, Israel, Blake, Medline, Rankin, Armstrong, & Kapur, 1979).

Chronic alcohol ingestion leads to proliferation in liver cells of the smooth endoplasmic reticulum which houses the enzymes involved in detoxification of many drugs. Therefore it is not surprising that enhanced metabolism of drugs can be demonstrated in alcoholic patients. The metabolism of meprobamate, pento-barbital, antipyrine, tolbutamide, warfarin, and diphenylhydantoin is enhanced in alcoholics after heavy alcohol intake and persists up to three weeks after alcohol is discontinued (Mezey, 1979). Alternatively, administration of some drugs while alcohol is still in the body results in a decrease in their metabolism because of competition between alcohol and these drugs for metabolism by hepatic microsomes. Clearance of pentobarbital and meprobamate is slow in the setting of acute alcohol administration (Mezey, 1979). (See further discussion of this subject in Chapter 9.)

There are three clinicopathologic expressions of alcoholic liver disease: alcoholic fatty liver, alcoholic hepatitis, and alcoholic cirrhosis. In its early stages, alcoholic liver disease is characterized by accumulation of excess fat in the liver (i.e., fatty liver). When liver cells die and necrosis occurs with inflammation, alcoholic hepatitis results. This more severe form of injury is associated with a mortality ranging from 10% to 30% of patients afflicted. Eventually scarring by fibrous tissue results, distorting the normal architecture and altering the function of the liver. Cirrhosis characterizes this later severe and irreversible form of alcohol-induced injury.

Alcoholic fatty liver is a completely reversible lesion, and there is no convincing evidence that it predisposes to cirrhosis. The majority of patients with alcoholic fatty liver are asymptomatic. However, attention may be drawn to them by the discovery of hepatomegaly. Liver function tests are usually normal in such individuals.

The criteria for the diagnosis of alcoholic hepatitis were set forth at the 1975 meeting at the Fogarty International Center (Nomenclature, diagnostic criteria, 1976). The proposed clinical criteria included jaundice, abdominal distress, fever, leukocytosis, and manifestations of portal hypertension. In the milder forms of alcoholic hepatitis, all of these may be absent. The SGOT (aspartate transaminase) level is slightly to moderately elevated, and is characteristically higher than that of the SGPT (alanine transaminase); an SGOT/SGPT ratio of >2.0 is considered to be highly suggestive of alcoholic hepatitis or cirrhosis. To investigate the mechanism for this characteristic SGOT/SGPT pattern in alcoholic liver disease, GOT and GPT activities were measured in human liver tissue and compared with serum values. Hepatic GPT activity was significantly decreased in liver tissue of patients with alcoholic liver disease compared with individuals with normal livers and other types of liver disease. The decreased liver GPT is specific for alcohol-associated liver disease and is not due to the chronicity of the disease or its severity. Hepatic GOT activity is decreased also but to a lesser extent, and it is not as specific for an alcoholic etiology.

The histologic features of alcoholic hepatitis help to explain its natural evolution into cirrhosis. Edmondson, Peters, and Telfer (1963) made the critical observations that hyaline sclerosis was located in the centrilobular liver cells (Zone 3 of Rappaport) in the precirrhotic state of the disease (Edmondson et al., 1963). Gerber & Popper (1972) expanded on this concept, noting that in acute alcoholic hepatitis, fibrosis first occurred in the centrilobular zone; only later did centrilobular–portal fibrous tract connections develop. As a result of this "bridging," cirrhosis ensued. Clinical studies have confirmed that although acute alcoholic hepatitis may be reversible, sclerosing hyaline necrosis is an obligatory step in the evolution of alcoholic liver disease into cirrhosis.

Swelling of hepatocytes is characteristic of alcoholic hepatitis, and the ballooned cells often contain alcoholic hyaline. A new concept to explain the balloonlike swelling suggests that it develops from the accumulation in the liver cell of lipid and protein which normally would have been secreted into plasma (French, Sims, & Franks, 1977). The retention of such export proteins results from degenerative effects of alcohol on subcellular structures called microtubules, which are important in the secretory activity of the liver. In this manner, alcohol may act in the same manner as antitubulin drugs—colchicine and griseofulvin—which bind to the protein tubulin and produce Mallory bodies in human liver cells.

It should be noted at this point that the severity of the lesions of the liver as seen by histologic examination correlates poorly with either the duration of drinking or the amount of alcohol consumed. Thus, the definitive diagnosis of alcoholic hepatitis must be based on liver biopsy.

Not all patients with alcoholic hepatitis develop cirrhosis (Galambos, 1975). The sex of the patient plays a role in this selection; in one study of 100 patients with alcoholic liver disease, alcoholic hepatitis was present with or without cirrhosis in 29% of male and 47% of female alcoholics (Morgan & Sherlock, 1977). Genetic factors also play a role, and cirrhosis is associated with the presence of specific histocompatibility antigens. Specifically, HLA-B8 was more prevalent in patients with cirrhosis than in controls. In contrast, patients with fatty liver had a normal prevalence of this antigen. This suggests that genetic factors determine, in part, an alcoholic's susceptibility to develop fibrosis and cirrhosis in response to alcohol abuse.

3. MUSCLE SYSTEMS

3.1. Heart Muscle

An association between alcoholism and heart disease has been suggested for over a hundred years. This association has not been considered etiologic until recently, when the effects of malnutrition, particularly thiamine deficiency, could be eliminated as an important contributing factor (Ferrans, Rios, Gooch, Wintter, DeVita, & Datlow, 1966).

The major symptoms of alcoholic cardiomyopathy are chronic shortness of breath and signs of congestive failure such as ankle edema, chest pain, fatigue, palpitations, and hemoptysis. Objective clinical signs include rales, cardiomegaly, reduced heart sounds, edema, and hepatomegaly. Cardiac output is decreased;

right atrial, wedged pulmonary artery, and right and left ventricular diastolic and systolic pressures are increased. The isometric phase of ventricular contraction is prolonged.

At present, alcoholic cardiomyopathy is believed to be caused by either the toxic effects of alcohol or acetaldehyde, with the general consensus being that the latter agent is more important than the former.

Alcoholic cardiomyopathy does not occur suddenly. It gradually progresses from a subclinical condition characterized by minimal cardiac findings and non-specific electrocardiographic abnormalities to overt congestive heart failure. The severity of the illness appears to be related directly to the duration of alcoholism. The prospect for recovery is reasonably good if the individual ceases to imbibe alcohol. Recovery is slow, however, and may require five to six years.

In contrast to the popular view that ethanol has a beneficial effect on the heart, ethanol at doses that are only mildly intoxicating has been shown to affect left ventricular function adversely (Ahmed, Levinson, & Regan, 1973). Larger doses actually impair contractility. Six ounces of scotch fed to normal individuals over a two-hour period have been shown to diminish the force of heart muscle contraction at ethanol concentrations as low as 75 mg/dl. This adverse effect progresses as blood ethanol levels rise (Ahmed et al., 1973).

Cardiac arrhythmias are common in individuals with alcohol-related disease and in particular during alcohol intoxication (Ettinger, Wu, de la Cruz, Weisse, & Regan, 1976; Ettinger, Wu, de la Cruz, Weisse, Ahmed, & Regan, 1978). Ventricular fibrillation caused by alcohol intoxication and palpitations following alcohol ingestion are common. In one study of 15 severely intoxicated men, 3 went into cardiac arrest, 11 showed disturbed heart rhythm, and 2 evidenced low blood pressure. Similar results have been reported in a Scandinavian study that identified a syndrome of rapid cardiac arrhythmia in patients with actual or impending delirium tremens. Finally, Gould and coworkers (1969) have reported that sudden death probably caused by cardiac arrhythmias may be relatively common among young adults who are found to have large fatty livers at autopsy. It is likely that alcohol-induced cardiac arrhythmias are due to the direct effects of alcohol and to the adverse effects of acetaldehyde on the heart's conduction system. Relevant to this issue, it has been shown that 2 ounces of whiskey administered to patients with organic heart disease can cause suppression of the sinoatrial node recovery time. Moreover, another study indicated that alcohol intoxication can affect the atrioventricular node so severely as to cause complete heart block, requiring pacemaker therapy.

Observations of chronic ethanol ingestion by young adult male dogs, fed 36% of their calories as ethanol, provide direct experimental evidence for ethanol-associated cardiac toxicity. Compared to their isocaloric controls, ethanol-fed animals have a significantly greater end diastolic pressure despite a lower end diastolic volume. Ejection fraction, mean heart rate, and aortic pressure were similar in both groups. However, QRS duration was prolonged with increasing alcohol use. Similarly, the conduction time from the His bundle to the onset of ventricular depolarization was prolonged (Ettinger, Lyons, Oldewurtel, & Regan, 1976).

In addition, several investigators using the isolated heart have shown that alcohol infusions cause a decline in cardiac contractility characterized by slowing of the rate of development of heart muscle tension, reduced ventricular systolic pressure, and lowered velocity of contraction (Horwitz & Atkins, 1974). Values for maximal velocity of muscle shortening at zero load also are reduced significantly.

It is generally believed that damage to the mitochondria of heart muscle is the major component of alcoholic cardiomyopathy. Electron-microscopic studies document degenerative changes of the mitochondria as a result of chronic alcohol consumption. Other subcellular structures may also be abnormal, as swelling and vesiculation of the endoplasmic reticulum and glycogen and lipid accumulation in liposomes are seen. Biochemical correlates of ultrastructural abnormalities of the mitochondria of heart muscle in response to ethanol exposure include depression of mitochondrial respiration, liberation of mitochondrial enzymes, and reduction of myocardial ATP levels. The effect of alcohol on mitochondrial function appears to be tied to hepatic alcohol metabolism, as the heart lacks alcohol dehydrogenase. Acetaldehyde, which adversely affects heart function, reaches the heart via the circulation from the liver. Such acetaldehyde has been shown to increase heart rate, systemic arterial pressure, and myocardial contractility, whereas ethanol is associated with myocardial depression. Moreover, acetaldehyde adversely influences myocardial metabolism by inhibiting mitochondrial electron transport, mitochondrial energy formation and use, and the shuttle mechanisms that transport reducing equivalents into and out of the mitochondria (Cederbaum, Lieber, & Rubin, 1973).

Finally, it would appear that alcoholics with at least one episode of heart failure may exhibit a greater sensitivity to the adverse myocardial effects of ethanol or acetaldehyde with a substantial elevation of left ventricular diastolic pressure as compared with alcoholic individuals not previously known to have had cardiac failure.

3.2. Skeletal Muscle

As was the case with myocardial disease, an association between alcohol abuse and disease of skeletal muscles has been known for about 120 years. Modern concepts of alcoholic myopathy originated, however, in 1955 with the studies of Ekbom, who first described a syndrome of insidious muscle weakness without evidence of myoglobinuria or other symptoms in alcoholics (Ekbom, Hed, Kirsten,

& Astrom, 1964). Eventually, a wide spectrum of alcoholic myopathy, from completely asymptomatic to near fatal, has come to be recognized (Hed, Lundmark, Fahlgren, & Orrel, 1962).

Subclinical myopathies are reported to occur in more than one-third of alcoholics. These are manifested by an elevation of the serum CPK level. Some individuals will have a history of muscle cramps, weakness, and occasional episodes of dark urine, which is thought to be due to myoglobinuria. Electromyographic changes are common in such individuals (Faris, Reyes, & Abrams, 1967). Acute alcoholic myopathy is suggested by the development of muscle weakness in an alcohol-abusing individual. In such individuals, there may be a sudden attack of pain in the involved skeletal muscle or a rapid progression of a previous chronic myopathy accompanied by the appearance of myoglobin in the urine. Such attacks can be fatal. Generally, the muscles are exquisitely tender. Weakness is usually centered in one group of muscles, although it can on occasion be diffuse. In such individuals, the blood level of lactic acid is reduced in response to ischemic exercise; the electromyogram is almost always abnormal. Fortunately, if alcohol use is discontinued, the disease and its symptoms disappear. Muscle biopsies in such patients demonstrate patchy damage to muscle cells and mitochondrial muscle cells appear swollen, myofibrils disordered, and organelles disarrayed. The endoplasmic reticulum is dilated and contains inclusions. In patients whose symptoms include rhabdomyolysis, hyperkalemia and renal failure can occur. Such hyperkalemia can induce additional electrocardiographic changes and enhance the risk of sudden death. Muscle fibers of patients with rhabdomyolysis are characterized by swelling, fragmentation, hyaline degeneration, and a loss of striation. Acute inflammation involving polymorphonuclear leukocytes is rare. Vacuolation of muscle fibers is common; basophilia of muscle fibers is increased and may be the primary manifestation of alcohol associated muscle injury. Chronic alcoholic myopathy is characterized by atrophy of muscle fibers, increasing interstitial fat, and proliferation of muscle fiber nuclei.

Alcohol ingestion by nonalcoholic volunteers has been shown to produce ultrastructural changes accompanied by increased activity of serum creatine phosphokinase, alterations in contractile proteins, and decreased calcium uptake by isolated sarcoplasmic reticulum of muscles.

In vitro alcohol has been shown to depress muscle excitability by depolarizing the membrane of muscle fibers. Others have demonstrated that ethanol depresses electrical transmission in muscles by interfering with impulse conduction in the terminal nerve branches. Both ethanol and acetaldehyde interfere with the functioning of isolated actinomyosin, the contractile protein in muscle, and inhibit its response to ATP (Puszkin & Rubin, 1975). Repeated administration of ethanol to volunteers produces a depression in ATP activity in isolated actinomyosin and a decrease in its sensitivity to calcium (Puszkin & Rubin, 1976).

4. THE HEMATOLOGIC SYSTEM

4.1. Bone Marrow

Alcohol has been implicated as a causal factor in the development of several hematologic abnormalities, including vacuolization of nucleated cells in the bone marrow, megaloblastic changes secondary to folic acid deficiency, the development of a sideroblastic marrow, iron deficiency from hemorrhage, the anemia of chronic disease, thrombocytopenia, granulocytopenia, and decreased leukocyte mobilization and adherence. Human experiments in which alcohol has been administered in significant doses while protein and vitamin intake has been maintained within normal limits have shown that the majority of these changes are not due to the direct actions of ethanol but to abnormal dietary habits, the quantity and duration of alcohol and vitamin intake, and the status of the individual's liver function.

One of the first signs to be observed following excess ethanol ingestion by humans is the vacuolization of the pronormoblast and, to a lesser extent, the promyelocyte. Moreover, the intensity of such vacuolization has been shown to be proportional to the quantity of ethanol consumed.

Vacuolization of red cell precursors was first described in association with early and usually reversible bone marrow depression caused by chloramphenicol. Although the morphological appearance of the vacuolated proerythroblasts in alcoholics is virtually identical to those occurring as a result of chloramphenicol exposure, there are differences between the two conditions. Chloramphenicol produces an almost complete disappearance of red cell precursors beyond the proerythroblast stage. In contrast, all stages of red cell maturation are present when alcohol has caused the vacuolization (McCurdy, Pierce, & Rath, 1962). Experimentally it has been shown that the ingestion of 0.5 to 1.0 quart of 86 proof whiskey or its equivalent daily for five to seven days usually results in red cell precursor vacuolization (Sullivan & Herbert, 1964; Sullivan, Adams, & Liu, 1977). Such vacuoles disappear within three to seven days after ethanol ingestion has ceased. Light- and electron-microscopic observations suggest that membrane damage is responsible for the vacuolization.

4.2. Iron Kinetics

The serum iron concentration has been shown to increase during ethanol ingestion and decrease below control values following withdrawal. This pattern probably reflects hepatocyte injury with release of iron and recovery following ethanol ingestion. Hemodilution is common in individuals with cirrhosis, particularly those with Laennec's cirrhosis. Thus, caution must be exercised in making a diagnosis of anemia based on red cell count, hemoglobin concentration, or packed red cell volume. Despite these experimental observations, anemia is common in individuals with chronic liver disease, particularly those with alcoholic liver disease (Laennec's cirrhosis), and can be due to blood loss, hemolysis, diminished production of red blood cells, or a combination of these factors. GI blood loss is a common occurrence in both alcoholism and chronic liver disease. It is important to remember that ethanol is a mucosal irritant and a potent stimulator of gastric secretion. Ethanol-induced mucosal irritation participates in the development of acute gastritis and peptic ulcer disease in patients with chronic liver disease. Portal hypertension and bleeding esophageal varices are common also in such individuals. Moreover, bleeding may be accelerated by the coexistent thrombocytopenia and coagulation abnormalities which are common in liver disease, and all these factors contribute to the anomalies seen in the hemopoietic system of the alcoholic.

Sullivan and Herbert (1964) demonstrated that the administration of ethanol to experimental subjects produced an increase in the serum iron level and saturation of the iron-binding proteins that did not decrease to normal or low values until after cessation of alcohol consumption. These abnormalities persisted in the presence of folic acid administration, with reticulocytosis suggesting an effect of alcohol on iron metabolism separate from changes in folate metabolism and hematopoiesis. Similarly, Lindenbaum and Lieber (1969a) studied volunteers who had been maintained on vitamin-supplemented diets for several months. During the administration of alcohol, they observed increases in the serum iron; this was followed by a statistically significant fall in iron levels during the withdrawal period. No diminution in the reticulocyte count, slowing of iron clearance rate, or diminution of red cell utilization of radioactive iron, such as would be anticipated with drug-induced erythrocyte depression, was observed. They postulated that the observed changes in serum iron might represent alcohol-induced abnormalities of hepatic iron storage or reticuloendothelial function rather than bone marrow abnormalities *per se* (Lindenbaum & Lieber, 1969a).

Increased hepatic storage of iron in patients consuming alcohol is not surprising, as many alcoholic beverages, particularly red wine, have a high iron content (MacDonald, 1966) and the absorption of ferric iron is enhanced by ethanol (Charlton *et al.*, 1964). The increased absorption of ferric but not ferrous or heme iron induced by ethanol may be due, at least in part, to enhanced gastric acid secretion. Acid is essential to maintain ferric iron in solution so that it can chelate with sugars, amino acids, and amides in the diet and the various intestinal secretions, all of which aid the solubility of iron so that it can be absorbed in the duodenum (Schade, Cohen, & Conrad, 1968). This acidification is not required for ferrous or heme iron, which are soluble at physiologic intestinal pHs. Diminished red cell production is clearly an important problem in alcoholics. Despite the prevalence of factors such as iron deficiency and hemolysis, which increase plasma iron turnover and red blood cell incorporation of iron, the majority of patients with alcohol-induced liver disease have a normal or diminished iron turnover and impaired incorporation of iron into red blood cells.

4.3. Vitamin Deficiency

Prolonged protein deprivation and deficiency of B vitamins—particularly riboflavin, pyridoxine and folic acid—play a role in the depression of hematopoiesis. In animal studies, it has been shown that protein deficiency or the removal of a single essential amino acid from the diet produces anemia with a hypoproliferative bone marrow, which disappears following administration of a normal diet (Ghitis, Piazuelo, & Vitale, 1963). Thus, protein deprivation probably plays an important role in the production of both anemia and the ferrokinetic abnormalities observed in alcoholics, particularly those with liver disease.

The relationship of folic acid deficiency to chronic alcoholism has been known for years. Consumption of a folate-poor diet for several months will deplete body stores, and the diet of most alcoholics contains significantly less than the daily minimum requirement. Folic acid deficiency is the primary cause of megaloblastic anemia in alcoholics. Since folic acid deficiency causes ineffective erythropoiesis, it is associated with an increased plasma iron turnover and a delayed red blood cell incorporation of iron. Folic acid deficiency produces increased iron absorption and may be reponsible for the increased iron stores observed in some chronic alcoholics.

Riboflavin deficiency is associated with a normocytic normochromic anemia with bone marrow hypoplasia and vacuolization identical to that observed in individuals ingesting alcohol (Alfrey & Lane, 1970). The importance of riboflavin deficiency in the pathogenesis of the hematopoeitic abnormalities seen in chronic alcoholics has not been studied.

Impaired conversion of pyridoxine to pyridoxine-5-phosphate and diminished plasma concentration of this biologically active coenzyme form of vitamin B_6 have been reported in chronic alcoholic individuals (Hines & Cowan, 1970). Deficiency of pyridoxal-5-phosphate has been causally implicated in several clinical problems seen in alcoholics, including sideroblastic changes in the bone marrow, peripheral neuropathy, convulsions, and worsening of liver disease (French & Castagna, 1967). The sideroblastic changes that ensue are associated with an increased serum iron concentration, increased iron absorption, and increased plasma iron turnover and subnormal or delayed red cell incorporation of iron. These manifestations can readily be mistaken for idiopathic hemochromatosis, and this diagnosis in alcoholics must be made with caution.

4.4. Macrocytosis

In the absence of coexistent iron deficiency resulting from hemorrhage, macrocytosis is seen in the majority of alcohol-abusing patients (Bingham, 1960).

In two recent studies of hospitalized malnourished alcoholics, macrocytosis was the most common type of anemia occurring alone or in combination with ringed sideroblasts in approximately 40% of patients. On the other hand, megaloblastic anemia was found in only 0% to 4% ambulatory nonhospitalized alcoholics or relatively well-nourished alcoholic patients admitted to hospitals for withdrawal (Eichner, Buchanan, & Smith, 1972). By the time folate deficiency has become severe enough to cause anemia, characteristic changes will already have appeared in the peripheral blood (i.e., hypersegmented neutrophils and macroovalocytic red cells will be prominent) (Lindenbaum & Nath, 1981). Therefore, neutrophil hypersegmentation is detectable in the blood smear of 98% of patients with megaloblastic anemia (Lindenbaum, 1980). Round macrocytosis in the absence of hypersegmentation in the alcoholic is usually not due to folate deficiency. The presence of a markedly elevated serum LDH activity, mild unconjugated hyperbilirubinenemia, and depression of serum haptoglobin levels in the absence of reticulocytosis are readily obtainable clues to the existence of the megaloblastic state in alcoholic individuals. Within three to seven days of initiation of therapy with folic acid, a reticulocytosis occurs and the megaloblastic marrow will be found to revert to normal (Lindenbaum, 1980). Hypersegmented polymorphonuclear leukocytes, however, persist unchanged or increase in number during the first 10 days of folic acid therapy; they begin to disappear only after two weeks or more. In an occasional alcoholic patient, serum folate levels will be normal, although the macrocytic anemia present will be found to respond to folate therapy. In Lindenbaum's (1980) experience, such patients have decreased red cell folate levels and normal or elevated serum B_{12} levels. He proposes, therefore, that erythrocyte folate levels are a better indicator of depletion of this vitamin's stores.

The factors that contribute to the pathogenesis of folate deficiency in alcoholics are many and impairment of hepatic function may contribute, at least in part, to negative folate balance in such individuals. In patients with alcoholic liver disease, increased release of folate from liver stores with loss of the vitamin in the urine (Tamura & Stokstad, 1979) and decreased retention of folate taken up from the plasma may play roles in the pathogenesis of folate deficiency. It should be noted, however, that megaloblastic anemia occurs almost exclusively in alcoholics who have been eating poorly. Thus, a very strong association has been noted between decreased dietary folate intake and the presence of megaloblastosis. Eichner and Hillman (1973) found that when alcohol was given along with a low folate diet, megaloblastic marrow conversion occurred much more rapidly than when the diet alone was taken. The failure of such morphologic changes to evolve when alcohol was given with folate supplements to well-nourished volunteers appears to indicate that ethanol accelerates the development of megaloblastic erythropoiesis only when folate stores are depleted (Cowan, 1973). The manner in which alcohol interferes with folate metabolism, however, has not been established fully (Lindenbaum, 1980).

Halstead, Romero, and Tamura (1979), studying monkeys fed ethanol for 12 to 24 hours, found, that following an intramuscular injection of ^{3}H-labeled polyglutamate (PGA), that there was a decreased hepatic retention and increased urinary excretion of the label. After 24 months of ethanol administration, total hepatic folate concentrations were reduced in alcohol-fed animals and ^{3}H-labeled PGA absorption after intergastric administration was impaired in animals fed ethanol. Another factor that may contribute to folate deficiency in the alcoholic is that ethanol interferes with folic acid absorption from the jejunum.

Clinically significant vitamin B_{12} deficiency rarely, if ever, occurs as a result of chronic alcoholism. Chronic pancreatitis, a well-known complication of chronic alcoholism, is associated with malabsorption of vitamin B_{12} as measured by the Schilling test (Matuchansky, Rombend, & Modigliani, 1974). The elegant studies of Allen and coworkers have shown that R binders present in saliva, gastric juice, bile, and intestinal fluids bind cobalamins with a greater affinity than intrinsic factor and that pancreatic proteases partially degrade R binders *in vitro,* allowing vitamin B_{12} to be transferred to intrinsic factor (Allen, 1975). Despite this fact, clinical B_{12} deficiency is rare in individuals with untreated pancreatic insufficiency, and most investigators believe that the low serum B_{12} levels encountered in a minority of alcoholics are due to folate deficiency rather than B_{12} deficiency. Low serum B_{12} levels have been reported in 30% or more of nonalcoholic patients with severe folate deficiency in the absence of B_{12} malabsorption or depletion. Serum B_{12} levels rapidly return to normal in such individuals after therapy with folic acid is begun. The mechanism by which folate deficiency depresses serum B_{12} levels is as yet unknown.

When the macrocytosis is associated with an increase in the mean corpuscular volume, "thick" macrocytes are present, suggesting that folic acid deficiency or reticulocytosis may be responsible for this finding. In most patients with alcoholic liver disease, however, the macrocytosis is associated with a normal mean corpuscular volume and the presence of a thin red blood cell with an increased cell diameter: the thin macrocyte. When such cells become exaggerated, the erythrocytes appear as target cells in peripheral smears. Thin macrocytes and target cells have an increased surface-to-volume ratio, an increased membrane cholesterol/phospholipid ratio, and enhanced resistance to osmotic lysis.

A few alcoholic patients with hypophosphatemia and a spherocytic anemia have been described. Markedly diminished erythrocyte adenosine triphosphate levels have been shown with diminished deformability of red blood cells in such individuals. It is postulated that the low serum phosphate level diminishes red blood cell ATP production, thereby shortening the red cell life span.

Diminished production of red blood cells due to a bone marrow hypofunction has been observed in alcohol-related anemias. This abnormality can be attributed partially to folic acid deficiency. The hematopoietic depression in such patients cannot be overcome without utilizing pharmacologic rather than the physiologic doses of folic acid, suggesting that factors other than folic acid deficiency play a role as well. In many studied cases, red cell utilization is subnormal even in the presence of iron deficiency and hemolysis. Ineffective erythropoiesis in the presence of a sideroblastic bone marrow is not uncommon in liver disease and may contribute, at least in part, to these abnormalities.

The syndrome of spur cell anemia represents an abnormality of red cell membrane cholesterol content that results from a primary disorder of plasma lipoprotein metabolism. It occurs in patients with severe liver disease, usually alcoholic cirrhosis. Hematocrits are generally less than 30% in these patients and can be as low as 16% to 18%. Reticulocytes range from 5% to 15% and jaundice is prominent. Splenomegaly is a constant feature and both ascites and hepatic encephalopathy are quite common.

The red blood cells in the individuals with spur cell anemia are bizarrely spiculated and undergo premature destruction *in vivo,* primarily in the spleen. Of the two major lipid classes of the red cell membrane, phospholipids are present in normal amounts, although with a disproportionate increase in the amount of lecithin; cholesterol, on the other hand, is increased by 25% to 65% (Cooper, Delong-Puray, & Lando, 1972), resulting in an increase in the membrane cholesterol-to-phospholipid ratio from normal values of 0.9 to 1.0 to values as high as 1.6. *In vivo* spur cells are retarded in their circulation through the spleen. The entrapment of such spur cells within the spleen leads to a progressive loss of their surface area and finally cell death. Splenectomy in individuals with spur cell anemia prevents both cell conditioning and premature cell death. Thus, the spur cell phenomenon seems to involve a two-phase process. The first phase is characterized by acquisition of cholesterol; the surface area develops a scalloped cell contour and a decrease in membrane fluidity which is, in part, dependent upon serum lipoproteins. The second or conditioning phase is characterized by a loss of cell surface area and transformation of the red cell to a spiculated cell contour, which leads to splenic entrapment and hemolysis. Although splenectomy corrects the hemolytic disorder in such individuals, the short-term benefit of such high-risk surgical intervention would rarely be indicated in patients with advanced alcoholic liver disease.

4.5. White Blood Cells

Leukopenia is relatively common in alcoholics (Cowan & Hines, 1971). Eichner and Hillman (1971) observed leukopenia (counts less than 5,000/mm³) in 8% of their cases. In another study of 112 ambulatory alcoholic subjects without serious illness, leukopenia (counts between 4,100 and 4,700 cells/mm³) was found in 1.6%. In yet another study of 82 ambulatory alcoholics without splenomegaly, infection, ascites, or other manifestations of gastrointestinal or hepatic disease, 8.5% were found to be leukopenic, with leukocyte counts ranging from 2,600 to

4,900. Only 2.4% had granulocytopenia defined as a granulocyte count less than $1,500/mm^3$.

Bone marrow smears obtained from such individuals consistently demonstrate hypocellularity, with markedly decreased numbers of mature granulocytes. The leukopenic episodes tend to be transient, lasting two to four days. Recovery is rapid and is often followed by a leukocytosis.

The morphological findings of decreased or normal cellularity with few mature granulocytes in the bone marrow and depleted functional marrow granulocyte reserve in alcoholics without splenomegaly, infection, or megaloblastic anemia suggest that decreased population of granulocytes could play a major role in the pathogenesis of the granulocytopenia in such individuals. This thesis is supported further by the observation that in vitro exposure of human bone marrow cells to ethanol in concentrations found in intoxicated individuals suppresses the growth of granulocyte colonies. The effect of alcohol on intravascular survival of granulocytes has not been evaluated.

It is unlikely that coexistent folic acid deficiency plays a role in the granulocytopenia, as a granulocytopenia has developed in patients receiving large doses of exogenous folic acid and, when measured, the erythrocyte folate levels have been found to be normal in leukopenic alcoholics. Furthermore, alcohol inhibits granulopoiesis in vitro despite the presence of a large amount of folic acid (Tisman & Herbert, 1973).

As long ago as 1938, Pickrell showed that the migration of leukocytes into sites of local pneumococcal infections in the skin and lung was impaired in rabbits during alcohol intoxication. Phagocytosis and intracellular killing of pneumococci by leukocytes obtained from alcohol-intoxicated rabbits, however, were normal. Subsequently, reduced mobilization of granulocytes into the peritoneal cavity after injection of coagulase-negative staphylococci was reported by Louria (1963) in acutely intoxicated mice having blood levels in the range of 125 to 250 mg/dL. In humans, Brayton, Stakes, and Schwartz (1970), using a modified Rebuck skin window technique, demonstrated that oral or intravenous administration of ethanol markedly inhibits the immigration of granulocytes into the area of traumatized skin. MacGregor, Spagnuolo, and Lentrek (1974) have shown that the exposure of human granulocytes to concentrations of ethanol ranging from 100 to 1,000 mg/dL in vitro is followed by a concentration-dependent reduction of the adherence of these cells to columns of packed nylon fiber. Subsequent study by the same investigators has indicated that the oral administration of ethanol over a period of 15 to 30 minutes to normal volunteers is also associated with inhibited granulocyte adherence (Gluckman & MacGregor, 1970). Finally, the exposure of granulocytes in vitro to high concentrations of ethanol has been shown to depress their chemotactic activity (Spagnuolo & MacGregor, 1975). The oral administration of ethanol for as little as six to eight days has been shown to be associated with inhibition of chemotactic function of granulocytes in normal volunteers

(Gluckman, Dvorak, & MacGregor, 1977). The mechanism by which alcohol impairs such granulocyte function remains unclear, although it has been suggested that increased intracellular concentrations of cyclic AMP occurring as a consequence of alcohol ingestion may be at least partly responsible for this phenomenon.

Evidence indicates that macrophages originate from the same stem cells that give rise to granulocytes. Thus, it would not be expected to find alterations in macrophage function as well as granulocyte function in response to ethanol. Following the administration of ethanol to experimental animals, the rate of clearance of bacteria within the peritoneal cavity and lung by macrophages can be shown to be reduced. In addition, alcohol administration to rats depresses the phagocytic capacity of the fixed macrophages lining the vascular sinusoids in the rat. As was the case with granulocytes, ethanol ingestion has been shown to reduce the motility of macrophages and to be associated with an increased intracellular cyclic AMP concentration. Lymphopenia (defined as a lymphocyte count less than 1,500/mm^3) is present in most alcoholic patients with leukopenia (Lindenbaum & Hargrove, 1968). In alcoholics admitted to a detoxification unit, the blood lymphocyte counts on admission are consistently reduced relative to counts observed one week after admission. Ethanol exposure *in vitro* suppresses the blastogenic transformation of lymphocytes induced by phytohemagglutinin, and studies involving alcoholic patients have indicated that there is a reduced percentage of thymus-derived lymphocytes in blood of such individuals and a reduced blastogenic transformation of such alcohol-exposed lymphocytes in response to phytohemagglutinin and concanavalin A. Moreover, studies involving experimental animals as well as humans during periods of alcohol ingestion reveal an inability to develop delayed dermal hypersensitivity to new antigens. *In vitro* exposure of human lymphocytes to alcohol at concentrations commonly seen in intoxicated individuals activates the membrane adenyl cyclase system and is associated with an increase in the intracellular concentration of cyclic AMP.

4.6. Coagulation and Platelet Disorder

Changes in the coagulation mechanism of patients with chronic alcoholism arise principally as a complication of advanced liver disease. These alterations are similar to those occurring in patients with other chronic liver diseases of any nature. The defects most commonly described are decreases in the circulating levels of clotting factors dependent on vitamin K and fibrinolysis with or without disseminated intravascular coagulation (Canoso, Hutton, & Deykin, 1979). Quantitatively abnormal fibrinogens may also be present (Weinstein & Deykin, 1978).

In contrast to the coagulopathies found in alcohol patients with cirrhosis, no significant coagulation abnormalities occur in noncirrhotic alcoholics or as a result of ethanol abuse *per se*. Platelet disorders accompany alcoholism and occur in association with active alcohol ingestion independently of liver disease. Thrombocytopenia in individuals with cirrhosis is usually attributed to the splenomegaly and hypersplenism or to dietary deficiency of folate. The suggestion that alcohol by itself might induce thrombocytopenia was initially made by Sullivan and Herbert (1964), who observed three patients with severe acute alcoholism and thrombocytopenia. Lindenbaum and Hargrove (1968) then described 10 episodes of thrombocytopenia in five alcoholics without evidence of cirrhosis or folate deficiency. Their observations were confirmed by those of Post and Desforges (1968), who proposed that ethanol directly impaired platelets. Thrombocytopenia, defined as a platelet count less than $100,000/\text{mm}^3$, exists in 3% of non-acutely ill patients with chronic alcoholism. The occurrence of thrombocytopenia in such individuals is unrelated to their socioeconomic or nutritional status. Platelet counts as low as 10,000 have been reported. Hepatomegaly and some degree of abnormality of liver function are present in the majority of these patients (50%). By contrast, splenomegaly is uncommon and when it occurs is usually related to the liver disease.

Folate deficiency exists in one-half of acutely ill alcoholic individuals; although folate deficiency may cause thrombocytopenia, the development of thrombocytopenia in an alcoholic patient is not dependent on low folate levels. Lindenbaum and Lieber (1969b) and Cowan (1973) have observed significant decreases in platelet counts in individuals fed alcohol and supplemental folic acid under metabolic ward conditions. The bone marrows of these folate-supplemented patients with thrombocytopenia all demonstrated normoblastic maturation. The thrombocytopenia in alcoholic individuals with congestive splenomegaly secondary to liver disease tends to persist. By contrast, the thrombocytopenia that is alcohol-related but not associated with liver disease tends to disappear with alcohol abstinence. Thus, the reappearance of platelets can be used to distinguish thrombocytopenia due to ethanol toxicity from that due to congestive splenomegaly. Two to three days usually are required after the last drink before the platelet count begins to rise. Thereafter, the number of circulating platelets increases at a rate of 20,000 to $60,000/\text{mm}^3/\text{day}$. Maximum counts occur 5 to 21 days after discontinuing alcohol; these peak counts are 2 to 19 times the initial count and are usually in the supernormal range. Such peak counts decline over the ensuing one to three weeks and stabilize thereafter within the range of normal individuals. The recovery from alcohol-related thrombocytopenia occurs spontaneously and is not dependent on provision of adequate nutrition or the administration of vitamins or corticosteroids.

The clinical significance of thrombocytopenia in alcoholism is difficult to determine. No hemorrhagic episodes were present in the 108 patients comprising the series reported by Cowan and Hines (1971) and Eichner and Hillman (1971). In contrast, bleeding other than petechiae or ecchymoses occurred in 60% of the patients as reported by Lindenbaum and Hargrove (1968) and in 65% of those reported by Post and Desforge (1968).

In addition to changes in platelet number, platelet dysfunction may also occur in individuals manifesting alcoholism. Such dysfunction may be related to cirrhosis, folate deficiency, or the direct effect of ethanol on platelets. Interpretations of bleeding time determinations in such patients are complicated by the multiplicity of factors that affect these results. Bleeding times in individuals with normal platelet counts who are ingesting ethanol are twice the times observed during control periods before ingestion of ethanol. Four- to fivefold increases in bleeding times over control values have been reported in patients ingesting alcohol who are also thrombocytopenic. The increases in their bleeding times exceed those predicted from studies in non-alcohol-ingesting individuals with similar platelet counts (Harker & Slichter, 1972).

Considerable evidence exists to suggest that effective platelet production— that is, delivery of newly formed platelets to the circulation from the bone marrow—is impaired by ethanol (Sullivan & Herbert, 1964; Cowan, 1973). Mean platelet size in patients admitted to hospital with acute alcoholism and thrombocytopenia is reduced and tends to increase to values greater than normal during recovery (Sahud, 1972). These data suggest that acute alcoholism suppresses platelet production and that withdrawal is associated with increased release. The total megakaryocyte mass in individuals ingesting alcohol can be shown, by quantitative methods, to be 1.9 times increased and that in patients with thrombocytopenia to be 3.6 times increased. Notwithstanding these increases in megakaryocyte mass, effective platelet production in these two groups of patients can be shown to be near normal (1.2 and 0.8 times normal respectively; Cowan, 1980). Such data in individuals ingesting ethanol document ineffective thrombocytopoiesis.

The survival of ^{51}Cr-labeled platelets is decreased in individuals ingesting alcohol (Cowan, 1973). Such reductions are modest in patients with normal platelet counts (75% of normal) but are substantially reduced in individuals who develop thrombocytopenia (50% of normal). Such reductions in platelet survival can be demonstrated in both folate-deficient and folate-supplemented patients, suggesting that folate deficiency is not responsible for this observation. Moreover, as compared with the pattern of linear disappearance of ^{51}Cr-labeled platelets observed in normal individuals, the pattern of disappearance in alcoholic thrombocytopenic patients is exponential. Thus, there is an accelerated rate of random destruction of platelets in patients ingesting large amounts of ethanol.

Two lines of evidence suggest that thrombocytopenia and the reduced platelet survival associated with alcohol ingestion are not due to a shift of platelets from the circulation to the splenic pool. First, in the platelet survival studies, the recovery of administered ^{51}Cr-labeled autologous platelets extrapolated to zero time after infusion is normal (Cowan, 1973). Second, the radioactivity over the spleen measured by external counting does not change. A number of ultrastructural alterations appear in platelets obtained from patients with alcohol-related thrombocytopenia (Cowan & Graham, 1975). As compared with normals, platelets in these individuals vary greatly in size. Many giant platelets can be seen. The circumferential band of microtubules is absent or fragmented, particularly in the giant platelets. Rod-shaped structures of undetermined origin are present in many of the larger platelets. After stimulation with adenosine-5'-diphosphate or collagen, migration of intracellular granules is delayed and incomplete relative to normal and degranulation is incomplete. The aggregates that form are smaller and less compact (Cowan & Graham, 1975). The aggregation of platelets exposed to adenosine-5'-disphosphate, epinephrine, thrombin, and collagen decreases 50% or more in patients whose blood ethanol level remains at or above 300 mg/dL. Impaired aggregation appears while the platelet count is normal and the impairment increases progressively as the platelet count decreases. Both the rate and the extent of the primary response to ADP and epinephrine are reduced. Secondary or release related aggregation is severely reduced or absent after stimulation with these agents. The aggregation of normal platelets exposed to moderately high levels of ethanol (240 to 400 mg/dL) *in vitro* is reduced significantly as well. Such *in vitro* abnormalities of platelet function induced by ethanol exposure primarily affect the secondary aggregation response. Intracellular concentrations of ADP and of ATP are reduced significantly with the development of thrombocytopenia during alcohol ingestion, and this finding accounts, at least in part, for the impaired secondary aggregation seen in the presence of ethanol.

Ingestion of ethanol is associated also with a number of changes in platelet metabolism. Thus, the oxidation of glucose by platelets obtained from alcoholic patients does not increase in response to epinephrine. In addition, after incubation with ^{14}C-labeled adenine, the percentage of total radioactivity recovered as cellular ATP in unstimulated platelets from patients ingesting alcohol is similar to that measured in collagen-stimulated platelets obtained from normals. The concentration of the adenosine-3', 5'-cyclic-monophosphate in platelets from alcoholic patients obtained during abstinence is normal. With alcohol ingestion, platelet cyclic AMP concentrations decrease by 50%. This decrease is associated with reduced adenylate cyclase activity and subnormal increases in activity after stimulation. The activity of cyclic nucleotide phosphodiesterase in platelets is unchanged by ethanol *in vivo* or *in vitro*. Thus, ethanol interferes with the production of cyclic AMP in platelets but not with its degradation.

Physiologic concentrations of ethanol do not affect the synthesis of thromboxane from exogenous arachidonic acid. In contrast, very high concentrations of ethanol produce a dose-dependent inhibition of thromboxane synthesis by human platelets. The activity of monoamine oxidase in platelets from alcoholic individuals is reduced significantly below normal and may remain subnormal for extended periods during abstinence. Moreover, ethanol competitively inhibits platelet monoamine oxidase activity *in vitro* (Cowan & Shook, 1977). Ethanol also decreases, by 50%, the initial rate of serotonin uptake into platelets. A three- to fivefold increase in the reflux of serotonin out of platelets also occurs in the presence of alcohol. The significance of these changes in serotonin fluxes remains uncertain, however, as the role of serotonin in terms of platelet function is unknown.

5. KIDNEY DISEASE AND ALCOHOLISM

Renal dysfunction is frequently seen in association with liver disease (Baldus & Summerskill, 1975). Oliguria, azotemia, reduced osmolar clearance and glomerular filtration, dilutional hyponatremia despite increased sodium retention, and abnormalities in renal tubular acidification in the presence of normal renal morphology characterize the renal abnormalities present in individuals with liver disease. Despite the general consensus on the apparently normal renal histology, individuals with ethanol-induced liver disease have been reported to have kidneys with an increased fat content (Lieber, Spritz, & DeCarli, 1966; Van Thiel, Gavaler, Little, & Lester, 1977), an increased protein and water content (Van Thiel, Gavaler, Little, & Lester, 1977), and gross nephromegaly (Van Thiel, Gavaler, Little, & Lester, 1977; Laube, Norris, & Robbins, 1967). Moreover, in a necroscopy study, renal papillary necrosis was found to occur in between 7% to 14% of chronic alcoholic patients examined. This increased prevalence of renal papillary necrosis is more apparent when compared with the prevalence of renal papillary necrosis found at autopsy in all patients, which is 0.15% to 0.66%. The great majority of these later cases had either diabetes mellitus (49.7%) or obstructive uropathy (25.6%). This increased prevalence of renal papillary necrosis among alcoholics has been confirmed in a second study (Longacre & Popky, 1968), in which radiologic as well as necropsy studies were used to identify cases. It is of some interest to note that in 90% of the cases in one series, renal papillary necrosis seemed to occur during the first attack of acute pyelonephritis and that the lower urinary tract was the source of the infection (Edmondson, Reynolds, & Jacobson, 1966). Moreover, 12 of the 20 cases occurred in individuals without cirrhosis, suggesting that chronic ethanol abuse and not liver disease was the predisposing factor. That such a conclusion is warranted is supported by the apparent failure to recognize renal papillary necrosis in other types of severe liver disease.

6. PULMONARY DISEASE AND ALCOHOLISM

Chronic obstructive pulmonary disease is common among males who abuse ethanol and especially among those who smoke. Until recently chronic alcohol abuse has been a disease limited to males, most of whom also smoke; thus the finding of an association between chronic obstructive lung disease and alcohol abuse would not be particularly surprising. Other pulmonary problems are also common in alcoholics. Alcoholics have an increased risk of developing pneumonia and pneumococcal sepsis than the general population. Moreover, probably as a consequence of poor dental health and recurrent episodes of aspiration, occurring during periods of intoxication, lung abscess due to anaerobic organisms is considerably more common in alcoholic individuals than in the general population. In addition, tuberculosis is a well-recognized health problem in the malnourished chronic alcohol-abusing population. With advanced liver disease, cyanosis, hyperventilation, and hypoxia due to pulmonary arteriovenous fistula are a common occurrence.

7. THE ENDOCRINE SYSTEM AND ALCOHOLISM

7.1. Gonadal and Adrenal Effects

Hypoandrogenization is commonly seen in chronic alcoholic men. Thus, 70% to 80% experience decreased libido and/or impotence (Lloyd & Williams, 1948; Van Thiel & Lester, 1979a,b). Reproductive failure as well as Leydig cell failure is common, with 70% to 80% of such men demonstrating both testicular atrophy and infertility (Lloyd & Williams, 1948; Van Thiel & Lester, 1979). Histologic studies of testicular tissue obtained from chronic alcoholic men demonstrate marked seminiferous tubular atrophy and loss of mature germ cells, many of which have an abnormal morphology (Van Thiel & Lester, 1976).

Evidence for hyperestrogenization is present also in such men, but to a lesser degree than the hypoandrogenization. Thus, a female escutcheon and palmar erythema develop in 50%, spider angioma in 40%, and gynecomastia in 20% of the alcoholics. These signs of chronic alcoholism, unlike the transient impotence commonly experienced with an acute alcoholic bout, persist in the absence of intoxication and are due to alcohol-induced tissue injury.

Until recently, liver disease was considered to be of primary importance in the pathogenesis of the sexual dysfunction present in chronic alcoholics (Van Thiel, 1980). However, during the past 10 years, this concept has been severely challenged and a diametrically opposite view of the pathogenesis of sexual dysfunction occurring in alcoholics has gained currency. This change in thinking has occurred as a result of the demonstration that sexual dysfunction can be present in alcoholic men with a spectrum of morphologic hepatic injury varying from essentially normal liver histology to that of severe alcoholic hepatitis and cirrhosis. Moreover, testosterone concentrations can be shown to fall in normal male volunteers within hours of their ingesting sufficient alcohol to produce hangover (Van Thiel, 1980; Gordon, Altman, Southren, Rubin, & Lieber, 1976). In addition, many of the features of the syndrome of alcohol-induced sexual dysfunction can be produced in experimental animals and appear at a time when hepatic biochemical function and morphologic appearance are altered only minimally (Van Thiel, Lester, & Vaitukaitis, 1978; Gavaler, Van Thiel, & Lester, 1980; Van Thiel, Gavaler, Lester, & Goodman, 1975; Van Thiel, Gavaler, Cobb, Sherins, & Lester, 1979). Thus, the concept that the sexual changes observed in chronic alcoholic men are the result of alcohol *per se,* rather than the indirect consequences of alcohol-induced liver disease, has gained considerable credence.

As noted earlier, confirmatory evidence has been developed in experimental animals; a dose-dependent decline in plasma testosterone is found in mice receiving graded amounts of alcohol over a five-day period, and alcohol-induced chronic testicular injury characterized by atrophy, loss of germ cells, and reduced testosterone levels has been found in alcohol-fed rats (Gavaler *et al.,* 1980; Van Thiel, Gavaler, Lester, & Goodman, 1975). When rats are fed a diet in which ethanol accounts for 36% of their caloric intake but which contains sufficient vitamins, trace metals, and protein for normal growth and development, they become hypogonadal. The hypogonadism is characterized by atrophy of androgen-dependent target organs and destruction of the germinal epithelium. The most direct evidence that alcohol and possibly acetaldehyde, the first metabolic product of ethanol metabolism, may disturb testicular function has been shown in studies utilizing the isolated perfused rat testes (Cobb, Ennis, Van Thiel, Gavaler, & Lester, 1980; Cobb, Ennis, Van Thiel, Gavaler, & Lester, 1978). Testes were perfused with a defined tissue culture medium that contained chorionic gonadotropin to stimulate testosterone production. When alcohol or acetaldehyde was added to the perfusion medium, in concentrations comparable to those found in the blood of chronically intoxicated individuals, testosterone production and secretion were reduced by 50%. The specific mechanisms by which alcohol adversely affects testicular function are being unraveled slowly (Cobb *et al.,* 1980; Cobb *et al.,* 1978). Vitamin A is essential for spermatogenesis, and alcohol may interfere with testicular vitamin A activation (Van Thiel, Gavaler, & Lester, 1974). In addition, alcohol metabolism may shift the balance between NAD and NADH in the testes, thereby secondarily limiting testosteronogenesis. Acetaldehyde produced in the testes or entering the testes from the plasma as a result of ethanol metabolism outside the testes may have deleterious effects upon testicular mitochondria, which are critical for steroidogenesis. Thus, it has been reported that the conversion of cholesterol to pregnenolone, a reaction that occurs in mitochondria, is inhibited as a result of preexposure of mitochondria to either alcohol or acetaldehyde. In addition, several groups have demonstrated reduced activity of microsomal 17-α-hydroxylase and 3-β-hydroxy steroid dehydrogenase/isomerase activity in microsomal preparations obtained from alcohol-fed rat testes (Chiao, Johnston, & Van Thiel, 1980; Johnston, Chiao, & Van Thiel, 1980; Cicero, Bell, Meyer, & Badger, 1980; Gordon, Vittek, & Southren, 1980). Not only is testicular testosterone production inhibited as a result of alcohol exposure but recent studies have demonstrated that ethanol interferes with gonadotropin (LH) binding to testicular tissue and that chronic alcohol exposure is associated with a hypothalamic–pituitary defect for gonadotropin secretion (Van Thiel, Lester, & Vaitukaitis, 1978; Van Thiel, Lester, & Sherins, 1974; Van Thiel & Lester, 1978). Thus, alcoholic individuals have inappropriately low plasma gonadotropin concentrations for the degree of gonadal failure present, and they demonstrate inadequate responses to stimuli that provoke gonadotropin release, such as clomiphene and luteinizing hormone releasing factor. Similar inadequate gonadotropin responses can be demonstrated in chronic alcohol-fed rats and following acute alcohol administration to normal rats (Van Thiel, Gavaler, Cobb, Sherins, & Lester, 1979). The foregoing suggests that chronic alcohol ingestion induces gonadal injury through its direct effects on the gonad as well as through indirect effects exerted through the hypothalamus and pituitary.

In addition to being hypogonadal, chronic alcoholic men are also often grossly hyperestrogenized. As noted above, palmar erythema, spider angiomata, a female escutcheon, and gynecomastia are common findings (Lloyd & Williams, 1948; Van Thiel & Lester, 1979). Biochemical evidence of hyperestrogenization can also be documented by increases in such estrogen-responsive proteins as sex-steroid-binding globulin and estrogen-responsive neurophysin (Van Thiel, Gavaler, Lester, Loriaux, & Braunstein, 1975). It is probable that the observed increases in prolactin seen in cirrhosis are estrogen-related also. Moreover, because testicular atrophy can be produced by estrogen administration, the testicular damage observed in alcoholic men with cirrhosis can, at least in part, be ascribed to a hyperestrogenic state. However, when plasma estradiol levels are determined in chronic alcoholic men, they are found to be either normal or only slightly increased. In contrast, plasma estrone levels are increased moderately (Van Thiel, Gavaler, Lester, Loriaux, & Braunstein, 1975). This finding of normal or near normal estrogen levels in the presence of androgen deficiency is paradoxical in that estrogens can only be produced by conversion from androgens. Thus, the presence of normal or moderately increased plasma estrogen levels in the presence of markedly reduced plasma androgen levels requires further explanation. Preliminary results would suggest that the hyperestrogenic state is the result of both the direct effects of alcohol and indirect effects of alcohol mediated through the development of liver disease. Unlike what was initially expected, the metabolic clearance rate for estradiol in men with Laennec's cirrhosis has been found to be normal, not reduced, and evidence is accumulating to suggest that adrenal overproduction of weak androgenic estrogen precursors regularly occurs in chronic alcoholic men (Olivo, Gordon, Rafii, & Southren, 1975). Moreover, signs and symptoms of adrenal glucocorticoid excess resembling Cushing's syndrome have been described in such men (Smals, Njo, Knoben, Ruland, & Kloppenborg, 1977; Frajria & Angeli, 1977). Thus, these patients not infrequently develop loss of peripheral muscle mass, truncal obesity, hypertension, facial erythema, increased plasma cortisol and androstenedione levels, loss of the normal diurnal variation of plasma cortisol, and release from dexamethasone suppression. The mechanism responsible for this overproduction of adrenocortical precursors of estrone is uncertain. Recent studies would suggest, however, that ethanol and acetaldehyde directly stimulate the adrenal cortex (Cobb, Van Thiel, Ennis, Gavaler, & Lester, 1979). Thus, in an isolated perfused rat adrenal system, concentrations of ethanol and acetaldehyde—observed in plasma of intoxicated males—have been shown to increase corticosterone excretion. Moreover, in clinical studies, weakly androgenic adrenocortical steroids such as androstenedione and dihydroepiandrosterone have been shown to undergo aromatization to estrogens in various tissues including skin, fat, muscle, bone, and brain. Such peripheral aromatization has been shown to be enhanced in men with Laennec's cirrhosis (Southren, Gordon, Olivo, Rafii, & Rosenthal, 1973; Gordon, Olivo, Rafik, Southren, 1976). In addition, aromatase activity in the liver and presumably other tissues is enhanced in experimental animals as a result of alcohol administration (Gordon, Southren, & Vittek, 1979). Thus, a normal metabolic clearance rate and an increased production rate of androstenedione and estrone account for the increases in the plasma concentrations of these two steroids seen in chronic alcoholic individuals (Southren et al., 1973; Gordon et al., 1976; Gordon et al., 1979).

Compounding this overproduction of adrenal androgens which can be converted to estrogens, portal systemic shunting occurring as a consequence of alcoholic liver disease has been shown to allow steroidal estrogen precursors secreted into the systemic circulation to escape the confines of the enterohepatic circulation such that they can be converted to an estrogen at peripheral sites where aromatase activity is increased (Van Thiel, Gavaler, Slone, Cobb, Smith, Bron, & Lester, 1980). The slight increase in plasma estrogen levels observed in alcoholics, therefore, predominantly reflects the levels that reflux back into the plasma from these peripheral sites after aromatization has occurred.

Compounding this increased peripheral aromatization is the observation that, at least in the liver, cytosolic estrogen receptor activity is disturbed in chronic alcohol-fed animals and presumably humans (Eagon, Porter, & Van Thiel, 1980). Normal male rat liver contains one-third the amount of cytoplasmic estrogen receptor present in normal female liver (Eagon, Fisher, Imhoff, Porter, Stewart, Van Thiel, & Lester, 1980). After castration of the male, cytoplasmic estrogen receptor activity increases towards female values (Eagon et al., 1980). Treatment of the castrated rat with dihydrotestosterone prevents this change toward the female pattern seen with castration. Chronic alcohol feeding of otherwise normal male rats is associated with a decline in male-specific estrogen-binding protein and an increase in the classic estrogen receptor, thus converting the male alcohol-fed rat liver to that of a female in terms of its estrogen-binding characteristics. Such increased estrogen-receptor activity allows the male liver to hyperrespond to the normal or only moderately increased plasma estrogen levels known to be present in alcohol-fed animals.

7.2. The Alcoholic Female

In contrast to the male, the alcoholic female is not superfeminized but instead shows severe gonadal failure commonly manifested by oligoamenorrhea, loss of secondary sexual characteristics such as breast and pelvic fat accumulation, and, in addition, infertility. Histologic studies of the ovaries obtained at autopsy from chronic alcoholic women who have died of cirrhosis while still in their reproductive years (20 to 40 years of age) have shown a paucity of developing follicles and few or no corpora lutea, thus documenting reproductive failure. Moreover, these findings have been reproduced in an animal model.

Endocrine failure of the ovaries of alcoholic women is manifested by reduced plasma levels of estradiol and progesterone, loss of secondary sex characteristics, and ovulatory failure. The biochemical mechanisms for such endocrine failure are probably the same as those occurring within the testes of the male, as the pathways for steroidogenesis are the same in the gonads of the two sexes, and an alcohol dehydrogenase has been reported to be present within the ovary.

In addition to demonstrating evidence of primary gonadal failure, chronic alcoholics, whether male or female, also showed evidence of a central hypothalamic–pituitary defect in gonadotropin secretion. Thus, despite severe gonadal injury, FSH levels in the female, although increased, are well below levels expected for the degree of reproductive failure present. Further, despite the marked reduction in sex steroid levels, LH concentrations range from normal to only moderately increased.

8. EFFECTS OF ETHANOL ON THE HYPOTHALAMIC-PITUITARY-ADRENAL AXIS

In normal subjects, ethanol at intoxicating doses produces an immediate increase in plasma cortisol (Fazekas, 1966; Jenkins & Connolly, 1968; Mendelson, Ogata, & Mello, 1971; Merry & Marks, 1972; Linkola, Fyhrquist, & Ylikahri, 1979). The cortisol response, moreover, appears to parallel the blood ethanol level (Jenkins & Connolly, 1968; Suzuki, Higashi, Hirose, Ikeda, & Tamura, 1972; Toro, Kolodny, Jacobs, Masters, & Daughaday, 1973). This acute response in normal individuals is probably due to hypothalamic "stress" reaction and pituitary release of ACTH. Such responses can be blocked in rats by pituitary stalk transsection.

In contrast to this acute stress reaction, ethanol intoxication and withdrawal have been shown to be associated with enhanced noradrenergic activity in the brain (known to inhibit hypothalamic release of corticotropin releasing factor, CRF) and impairment of the ACTH stress response (Tabakoff & Hoffman, 1980; Littleton, 1978; Bjorkquist, 1975).

A fascinating area of recent investigation is the study of the effect of endogenous opiate agonists (enkephalins and endorphins) on control of releasing factors. Activation of such opiate agonists appears to inhibit CRF and thereby ACTH release (Morley, Baranetsky, & Wingert, 1980) and could contribute to the reduced stress-induced ACTH release seen during alcohol intoxication and withdrawal. Moreover, the observation that the specific opiate antagonist naloxone improves the psychomotor impairment and depressed level of consciousness induced by ethanol strengthens such a hypothesis (Jeffcoate, Cullen, Herbert, Hastings, & Walder, 1979; Jefferys, Flanagan, & Volans, 1980).

Because acute exposure to ethanol causes an increase in plasma cortisol in normal persons, the effects of sustained ethanol levels on adrenal function are of interest. Plasma cortisol levels remain elevated in mice chronically fed alcohol (Cobb *et al.,* 1979a,b; Tabakoff, Jaffe, & Ritzmann, 1978; Kakihana, Butte, Hathaway, & Noble, 1971) and the presence of ethanol disturbs the normal diurnal variation of corticosterone levels (Kakihana & Moore, 1976). Studies using human subjects given ethanol for 4 to 29 days have similarly demonstrated persistent elevations of plasma cortisol. Moreover, a syndrome of "pseudo Cushing's" disease has been recognized recently in chronic alcoholics.

The state of the hypothalamic–pituitary–adrenal axis during alcohol withdrawal has been studied extensively. Cessation of chronic alcohol administration to mice is followed by an abstinence syndrome characterized by hyperactivity and seizures and increased plasma corticosterone levels (Kakihana *et al.,* 1971; Goldstein, 1972). Chronic alcoholics also experience hypercortisolism during ethanol withdrawal (Mendelson & Stein, 1966; Mendelson *et al.,* 1971; Stokes, 1973).

Interestingly, the pituitary reserve of ACTH in alcoholics experiencing withdrawal is frequently abnormal (Wright, Merry, Fry, & Marks, 1975). In contrast to the apparent lack of ACTH reserve seen with withdrawal, adrenal reserve of cortisol when stimulated by synthetic ACTH is normal (Wright *et al.,* 1975; Marks & Wright, 1977). Alcoholics who abstain from drinking often show persistent abnormalities of the hypothalamic–pituitary–adrenal axis (Oxenkrug, 1978).

9. EFFECTS OF ALCOHOL ON THE HYPOTHALAMIC-PITUITARY-THYROIDAL AXIS

The most consistent effect of alcohol on the function of the thyroid is to moderately decrease serum thyroxine (T_4) levels and to markedly decrease serum triiodothyronine (T_3) levels (Israel, Walfish, Orrego, Blake, & Kalant, 1979; Chopra, Solomon, Chopra, Young, & Chau Teco, 1974; Orrego *et al.,* 1979; Israel, Videla, MacDonald, & Bernstein, 1973; Nomura, Pittman, Chambers, Buck, & Shimivu, 1975). It appears that the low T_3 levels seen in alcoholics and normals after acute alcohol administration reflect hepatic injury and reduced hepatic deiodination of T_4 and T_3, since T_4 and TSH levels are only moderately reduced or are normal (Chopra et al., 1974; Green, Snitcher, Mowat, Elkins, Rees, & Dawson, 1977; Israel et al., 1973; Nomura et al., 1975; Orrego et al., 1979). Despite the considerable data suggesting that alcohol affects the hypothalamic–pituitary–thyroidal axis indirectly via hepatic injury, ethanol has been shown to increase the uptake of iodine by the thyroid. Moreover, Wright et al. (1975) and Van Thiel, Smith, Wight, and Abuid (1979) have reported a diminished TSH response to thyrotropin releasing factor (TRH) in chronic alcoholics.

Recent studies indicate that the administration of TRH to alcohol-naive male rats antagonizes the acute hypnotic and hypothalamic effects of ethanol. In another vein, Israel and colleagues have suggested that alterations in thyroid hormone metabolism may play a role in alcoholic hepatitis (Israel et al., 1979; Orrego et al., 1979; Israel et al., 1973; Israel et al., 1975a). In addition, they have reported that propylthiouracil reverses the adverse effects of alcohol on the liver (Israel et al., 1975; Bernstein, Videla, & Israel, 1975; Orrego et al., 1979; Israel et al., 1979).

10. THE EFFECTS OF ALCOHOL ON GROWTH HORMONE AND PROLACTIN

Considerable evidence has accrued to suggest that ethanol ingestion blocks stimulated growth hormone release in both normals and chronic alcoholics. Chronic alcoholics with cirrhosis, in contrast, have elevated basal levels of growth hormone and frequently show abnormal responses to stimuli of growth hormone release such as TRH (Van Thiel, Gavaler, Wight, Smith, & Abuid, 1978).

Several groups have reported increases in prolactin levels in normal volunteers after acute ethanol administration and in drinking alcoholics (Gordon & Southren, 1977; Wright, 1978; Van Thiel, Gaveler, Lester, Loriaux, & Braunstein, 1975; Van Thiel & Lester, 1976; Ylakahri, Huttunen, & Harkonen, 1976). Moreover, the responses of alcoholics to TRH stimulation have been reported to be excessive (Ylikahri et al., 1976; Ylikahri, Huttunen, Harkonen, Leino, Helenius, Liewerndahl, & Karonen, 1978; Van Thiel, McLain, Elson, & McMillin, 1978). Preliminary studies in the rat also suggest that ethanol administration increases plasma prolactin levels (Gordon & Southren, 1977).

11. EFFECTS OF ALCOHOL ON VASOPRESSIN AND OXYTOCIN

Acute alcohol administration to humans and animals produces an immediate diuresis, which seems to occur as a result of an inhibition of vasopressin secretion (Kleeman, 1973). Thus, several groups have reported finding reduced vasopressin levels in normal volunteers and animals after acute alcohol administration (Linkola, Fyhrquist, & Forsander, 1977; Linkola, Ylikahri, Fyhrquist, Wallenius, 1978; Helderman, Vestal, Rowe, Tobin, Andres, & Robertson, 1978). Little or no tolerance to the antidiuretic effects of ethyl alcohol or its inhibition of vasopressin release has been observed in chronic alcoholics (Marquis, Marchetti, Burlet, & Bowlange, 1975; Sereny, Rapaport, & Hudson, 1966). The site of alcohol's suppression of vasopressin release appears to be at the level of the hypothalamus. Thus, stimuli applied directly to the supraoptic nucleus can override the diuretic effects of alcohol. Moreover, alcohol inhibits the electrically evoked discharges of the supraoptic nucleus and prevents the degranulation produced by large doses of sodium chloride in animals (Raiba, 1960).

On the basis of bioassay data, ethanol would appear to inhibit the release of oxytocin (Wagner & Fuchs, 1968). No data, however, are available as yet on the actual blood levels of oxytocin during ethanol administration and withdrawal.

12. BIOLOGICAL MARKERS OF ALCOHOLISM

Until relatively recently, little emphasis has been placed on the development or identification of indicators that would permit detection of excessive drinking at a stage when intervention might be more effective and less costly. Although a worthwhile objective, the search for indicators of early alcohol abuse is complicated, since many of the medical sequelae of alcoholism are nonspecific and may be manifested only after a number of years of excessive drinking. Not unexpectedly, therefore, efforts to identify a single marker have been unsuccessful. In an effort to enhance reliability, the use of a composite profile of psychosocial and biochemical indicators of excess alcohol consumption has been promoted.

Most of the symptoms alcoholics complain of and the clinical signs as well as abnormal laboratory findings they express are nonspecific. Despite this, it is not unreasonable to assume that the more alcohol-related problems the patient has, the greater the probability is that excess alcohol consumption has been or is present. Moreover, because alcohol-related problems are known to be a common cause for medical consultation, the physician should be alert to the protean manifestations of hazardous alcohol consumption. Thus, the physician can compensate for the lack of specificity of most of the signs and symptoms of alcohol abuse by using combinations of psychosocial and biological markers. Psychosocial findings that suggest alcoholism are an increased incidence of sickness, absenteeism, and accidents, as all of these conditions are more prevalent in alcohol abusers than in control populations. Even more importantly, trauma and gastrointestinal disease tend to occur commonly in the course of alcohol abuse. Thus, morning retching, nausea, anorexia, and vomiting are common complaints of individuals who abuse alcohol. Similarly, it would appear that clinical manifestations of peptic ulceration and liver disease are common in alcoholics, with cirrhosis developing in 5% to 10%. It should be noted, however, that there is little or no correlation between clinical signs of liver disease and the severity of underlying alcohol-induced liver disease as assessed by liver biopsy. Thus there is no alternative to the percutaneous liver biopsy for a specific diagnosis.

Neurologic complaints are common in alcohol abusers and include acute intoxication withdrawal symptoms, hallucinations, epilepsy, delirium tremens, Wernicke-Korsakoff syndrome, cerebral degeneration, central pontine myelinolysis, Marchiafava-Bignami disease, cerebral atrophy, various neuropsychological impairments, and alcohol dementia. (See chapter by Freund.) It is especially important to be aware of mild withdrawal reactions such as tremor, anxiety, insomnia, hyperreflexia, and a lowered seizure threshold. All these symptoms may appear within a few hours of withdrawal, may last for approximately two days, and are frequently manifested in patients hospitalized for non-alcohol-related problems and should suggest the presence of an alcohol abuse problem in a patient who manifests them after admission to the hospital.

Past or present traumatic events are very common among chronic alcohol abusers and should suggest the diagnosis of alcoholism. It has been reported that 36% of regular drinkers reported at least two accidental injuries per year, compared with an accident rate of only 8% in nondrinkers. Rib or thoracic vertebral fractures or both are common in alcoholics, and their detection on routine roengenograms of the chest should suggest chronic alcohol abuse as a major health problem. Similarly, normal sleep patterns are not uncommonly disturbed by alcohol consumption, thus complaints of sleep disturbance, especially among young individuals, should prompt a clinician to inquire about the patient's drinking habits.

Finally, sexual dysfunction is quite common in alcohol-abusing individuals. Thus, complaints of impotence, loss of libido, or oligoamenorrhea should suggest that alcohol abuse may be a problem.

Physical signs of habitual alcohol use include persistent facial erythema with or without telangiectasias, capillary engorgement of the conjunctiva, edema of the forehead and periorbital regions, and an increased incidence of rosacea, neurodermatitis, dermatophytosis, seborrhea, acne, and psoriasis. Painless unilateral or bilateral enlargement of the parotid glands is common in alcohol-abusing individuals, and such enlargement has been shown to wax and wane in association with the amount of alcohol consumed.

Although the only true indicator of alcohol consumption is the detection of alcohol or one of its metabolites in the patient's body fluids, laboratory tests are occasionally useful in detecting early alcoholism. The National Council on Alcoholism's criteria regarding blood alcohol levels for the diagnosis of alcoholism are as follows: the finding of a blood alcohol level of 300 mg/dL or greater at any time; recording a blood alcohol of 100 mg/dL during a routine clinical examination; or a blood alcohol level greater than 150 mg/dL in an individual who is not obviously intoxicated.

The commonly ordered laboratory tests that have been found useful in identifying alcoholics include the mean corpuscular volume (MCV), serum level of alanine and asparate transaminases, uric acid, and triglyceride levels. The γ glutamyl transpeptidase activity also appears to be a good indicator of alcohol consumption but is very nonspecific. This is because any drug that is capable of microsomal induction will enhance the γ glutamyl transpeptidase activity.

Recent interest has focused on the use of the ratio of α amino isobutyric acid to leucine (AIB/L) in the plasma as a marker of alcohol abuse. Considerable evidence has accrued however, to suggest that this ratio is a nonspecific finding and relates either to malnutrition or liver disease rather than alcohol abuse *per se*.

Two possible markers of alcohol abuse that have been reported recently include the plasma transferrin and urinary salsolinol levels. Utilizing electrofocusing of plasma proteins, an abnormal transferrin with an isoelectric point at pH of 5.7 can frequently be found in alcohol-abusing patients and should suggest the diagnosis. Similarly, salsolinol, the product of condensation between acetaldehyde and dopamine, has been found to be 20 times more concentrated in the urine of alcohol-ingesting patients than in controls. However, the method for determining this unique transferrin and salsolinol requires sophisticated and expensive special equipment and is therefore not suitable for routine analysis and unlikely to become clinically valuable. As must be apparent from the preceding discussion, the ideal marker for alcohol abuse has yet to be identified.

13. REFERENCES

Ahmed, S. S., Levinson, G. E., & Regan, T. J. Depression of myocardial contractility with low doses of ethanol in normal men. *Circulation*, 1973, *48*, 378–385.

Alfrey, C. P., & Lane, M. The effect of riboflavin deficiency on erythropoiesis. *Seminars in Hematology*, 1970, *7*, 49–54.

Allen, R. H. Human vitamin B_{12} transport proteins. *Progress in Hematology*, 1975, *9*, 57–84.

Antonson, D. L., Barak, A. J., & Vanderhoof, J. A. Effect of acute and chronic alcohol ingestion on zinc absorption. *Clinical Research*, 1978, *26*, 660A.

Axon, A. T. R., & Clarke, A. Haematemesis: A new syndrome? *British Medical Journal*, 1975, *1*, 491–492.

Baldus, W. P., & Summerskill, W. H. J. Liver kidney interrelationships. In L. Schiff (Ed.), *Diseases of the liver*. Philadelphia: Lippincott, 1975.

Baraona, E., & Lieber, C. S. Effects of chronic ethanol feeding on serum lipoprotein metabolism in the rat. *Journal of Clinical Investigation*, 1970, *49*, 769–778.

Baraona, E., & Lieber, C. S. Intestinal lymph formation and fat absorption: stimulation by acute ethanol administration and inhibition by chronic ethanol feeding. *Gastroenterology*, 1975, *68*, 495–502.

Baraona, E., Pirola, R. C., & Lieber, C. S. Pathogenesis of postprandial hyperlipidemia in rats fed ethanol-containing diets. *Journal of Clinical Investigation*, 1973, *52*, 269–303.

Baraona, E., Pirola, R. C., & Lieber, C. S. Small intestine damage and changes in cell population produced by ethanol ingestion in the rat. *Gastroenterology*, 1974, *66*, 226–234.

Baraona, E., Pirola, R. C., & Lieber, C. S. Acute and chronic effects of ethanol on intestinal lipid metabolism. *Biochimica et Biophysica Acta*, 1975, *388*, 19–28.

Barboriak, J. J., & Meade, R. C. Impairment of gastrointestinal processing of fat and protein by ethanol in rats. *Journal of Nutrition*, 1969, *98*, 373–377.

Bernstein, J., Videla, L., & Israel, Y. Hormonal influences in the development of the hypermetabolic state of the liver produced by chronic administration of ethanol. *Journal of Pharmacology and Experimental Therapeutics*, 1975, *192*, 583–591.

Bingham, J. The macrocytosis of hepatic disease: Thick macrocytes. *Blood*, 1960, *15*, 244–254.

Bjorkquist, S. E. Clonidine in alcohol withdrawal. *Acta Psychiatrica Scandinavica*, 1975, *52*, 256–263.

Bode, J. C. H. Alcohol and the gastrointestinal tract. In J. C. H. Bode (Ed.), *Systemic illness and the gastrointestinal tract.* Stuttgart: Georg Thieme, 1981.

Brayton, R. G., Stakes, P. E., & Schwartz, M. S. Effect of alcohol and various diseases on leucocyte mobilization, phagocytosis and intracellular killing. *New England Journal of Medicine*, 1970, *282*, 123–128.

Brooks, F. P., & Thomas, J. E. The effect of alcohol on canine external pancreatic secretion. *Gastroenterology*, 1953, *23*, 36–42.

Burch, G. E., & Ansari, A. Chronic alcoholism and carcinoma of the pancreas. *Archives of Internal Medicine*, 1968, *122*, 273–275.

Canoso, R. T., Hutton, R. A., & Deykin, D. The hemostatic defect of chronic liver disease. Kinetic studies using ^{75}Se-selenomethionine. *Gastroenterology*, 1979, *76*, 540–547.

Carter, E. A., Drummery, G. D., & Isselbacher, K. J. Ethanol stimulates triglyceride synthesis by the intestine. *Science*, 1971, *174*, 1245–1247.

Cederbaum, A. I., Lieber, C. S., & Rubin, E. Effect of acetaldehyde on activity of shuttles for the transport of reducing equivalents into the mitochondria. *Federation of European Biochemical Societies Letters*, 1973, *37*, 89–92.

Chambers, J. W., & Piccrillo, V. J. Effects of alcohol on amino acid uptake and utilization by the liver and other organs of rats. *Quarterly Journal of Studies on Alcohol*, 1973, *34*, 707–717.

Charlton, R. W., Jacobs, P., & Seffel, H. Effect of alcohol on iron absorption. *British Medical Journal*, 1964, *2*, 1427–1429.

Cherrick, G. R., Baker, H., Frank, O., & Leevy, C. M. Observations on hepatic acidity for folate in Laennec's cirrhosis. *Journal of Laboratory and Clinical Medicine*, 1965, *66*, 446–451.

Chey, W. Y. Alcohol and gastric mucosa. *Digestion*, 1972, *7*, 239–245.

Chiao, Y-B., Johnston, D. E., & Van Thiel, D. H. Effect of chronic ethanol feeding on testicular content of enzymes required for testosteronogenesis. *Alcoholism: Clinical and Experimental Research*, 1980, *4*, 211A.

Chopra, I. J., Solomon, D. H., Chopra, U., Young, R. T., & Chua Teco, G. N. Alterations in circulating thyroid hormones and thyrotropin in hepatic cirrhosis. *Journal of Clinical Endocrinology and Metabolism*, 1974, *39*, 501–511.

Cicero, T. J., Bell, R. D., Meyer, E. R., & Badger, T. M. Ethanol and acetaldehyde directly inhibit testicular steroidogenesis. *Journal of Pharmacology and Experimental Therapeutics*, 1980, *213*, 228–233.

Cobb, C. F., Ennis, M. F., Van Thiel, D. H., Gavaler, J. S., & Lester, R. Acetaldehyde and ethanol are direct testicular toxins. *Surgical Forum*, 1978, *29*, 641–644.

Cobb, C. F., Van Thiel, D. H., Ennis, M. F., Gavaler, J. S., & Lester, R. Is acetaldehyde an adrenal stimulant? *Current Surgery*, 1979, *36*, 431–434. (a)

Cobb, C. F., Van Thiel, D. H., Ennis, M. F., Gavaler, J. S., & Lester, R. Pseudo Cushing's in alcoholics: A mechanism. *Clinical Research*, 1979, *27*, 448A. (b)

Cobb, C. F., Ennis, M. F., Van Thiel, D. H., Gavaler, J. S., & Lester, R. Isolated testes perfusion: A method using a cell-and protein-free perfusate useful for the evaluation of potential drug and/or metabolic injury. *Metabolism*, 1980, *29*, 71–79.

Cohen, B. I., & Raecht, R. F. Effect of ethanol on sterol metabolism in the rat. *Alcoholism: Clinical and Experimental Research*, 1980, *4*, 212–216.

Cooper, R. A., Delong-Puray, M., & Lando, P. An analysis of lipoproteins, bile acids, and red cell membranes associated with target cells and spur cells in patients with liver disease. *Journal of Clinical Investigation*, 1972, *51*, 3182–3192.

Coppage, W. S., Jr., Island, D. P., & Connor, A. E. The metabolism of aldosterone in normal subjects and in patients with hepatic cirrhosis. *Journal of Clinical Investigation*, 1962, *41*, 1672–1680.

Cowan, D. H. Thrombokinetic studies in alcohol-related thrombocytopenia. *Journal of Laboratory and Clinical Medicine*, 1973, *81*, 64–76.

Cowan, D. H. Effect of alcoholism on hemostasis. *Seminars in Hematology*, 1980, *17*, 137–147.

Cowan, D. H., & Graham, R. C., Jr. Studies on the platelet defect in alcoholism. *Thrombosis et Diathesis Haemorrhagica*, 1975, *33*, 310–327.

Cowan, D. H., & Hines, J. D. Thrombocytopenia of severe alcoholism. *Annals of Internal Medicine*, 1971, *74*, 37–43.

Cowan, D. H., & Shook, P. Effects of ethanol on platelet serotonin metabolism. *Thrombosis and Haemostasis.*, 1977, *38*, 33.

Darle, N., Ekholm, R., & Edlund, Y. Ultrastructure of the rat exocrine pancreas after long-term intake of ethanol. *Gastroenterology*, 1979, *58*, 62–72.

Davenport, H. W. Ethanol damage to canine glandular mucosa. *Proceedings of the Society for Experimental Biology*, 1967, *126*, 657–662.

Dhar, G. J., Selhub, J., & Gay, C. Characterization of the individual components of intestinal folate transport. *Gastroenterology*, 1977, *72*, 1049–1058.

Dinda, P. K., & Beck, I. T. On the mechanism of the inhibitory effect of ethanol on intestinal glucose and water absorption. *American Journal of Digestive Disorders*, 1977, *22*, 529–536.

Dinda, P. K., Beck, I. T., Beck, M., & McElligott, T. F. Effect of ethanol on sodium dependent glucose transplant in the small intestine of the hamster. *Gastroenterology*, 1975, *68*, 1517–1525.

Dowdle, E. B., Schachter, D., & Schenker, H. Requirement for vitamin D for the active transport of calcium by the intestine. *American Journal of Physiology*, 1960, *198*, 269–274.

Dreiling, D. A., & Bordalo, O. R. Secretory patterns in minimal pancreatic pathologies. *American Journal of Gastroenterology*, 1973, *60*, 60–69.

Eagon, P. K., Fisher, S. E., Imhoff, A. F., Porter, L. E., Stewart, R. R., Van Thiel, D. H., & Lester, R. Estrogen binding proteins of male rat liver: Influences of hormonal changes. *Archives of Biochemistry and Biophysics*, 1980, *201*, 486–499.

Eagon, P. K., Porter, L. E., & Van Thiel, D. H. Effect of hormonal alterations of level of a hepatic estrogen binding protein. *Alcoholism: Clinical and Experimental Research*, 1980, *4*, 213A.

Eastwood, G. L., & Erdmann, K. R. Effect of ethanol on canine epithelial ultrastructure and transmucosal potential difference. *American Journal of Digestive Diseases*, 1978, *23*, 429–435.

Eastwood, G. L., & Kirchner, J. P. Changes in the fine structure of mouse gastric epithelium produced by ethanol and urea. *Gastroenterology*, 1974, *67*, 71–84.

Eckardt, V. F., Grace, N. D., & Kantrowitz, P. A. Does lower esophageal sphincter incompetency contribute to esophageal variceal bleeding? *Gastroenterology*, 1976, *71*, 185–189.

Ederle, A., & Vantini, I. Fasting serum CCK immunoreactivity in chronic relapsing pancreatitis. *Richerca in Clinica e in Laboratorio*, 1978, *8*, 199–206.

Edmondson, H. A., Peters, R. L., & Telfer, B. R. Sclerosing hyaline necrosis of the liver in the chronic alcoholic. *Annals of Internal Medicine*, 1963, *59*, 646–673.

Edmondson, H. A., Reynolds, T. B., & Jacobson, H. G. Renal papillary necrosis with special reference to chronic alcoholism. *Archives of Internal Medicine,* 1966, *118,* 255–264.

Eichner, E. R., & Hillman, R. J. The evaluation of anemia in alcoholic patients. *American Journal of Medicine,* 1971, *50,* 218–232.

Eichner, E. R., & Hillman, R. J. Effect of alcohol on serum folate level. *Journal of Clinical Investigation,* 1973, *52,* 584–591.

Eichner, E. R., Buchanan, B., & Smith, J. W. Variation in the hematologic and medical status of alcoholics. *American Journal of Medical Science,* 1972, *263,* 35–42.

Ekbom, K., Hed, R., Kirsten, L., & Astrom, K. E. Muscular affections in chronic alcoholism. *Archives of Neurology,* 1964, *10,* 449–458.

Elwin, C. E. Some factors influencing the stimulatory effect of ethanol on gastric acid secretion during antrum application. *Acta Physiologica Scandinavica,* 1969, *75,* 12–25.

Engeset, A., Lygren, T., & Idsoe, R. The incidence of peptic ulcer among alcohol abusers and nonabusers. *Quarterly Journal of Studies on Alcohol,* 1963, *24,* 622–626.

Ettinger, P. O., Lyons, M., Oldewurtel, H. A., & Regan, T. J. Cardiac conduction abnormalities produced by chronic alcoholism. *American Heart Journal,* 1976, *91,* 66–78.

Ettinger, P. O., Wu, C. F., de la Cruz, C., Jr., Weisse, A. B., & Regan, T. J. Tachyarrhythmias associated with the preclinical cardiomyopathy of alcoholism. *American Journal of Cardiology,* 1976, *37,* 134.

Ettinger, P. O., Wu, C. F., de la Cruz, C., Jr., Weisse, A. B., Ahmed, S. S., & Regan, T. J. Arrhythmias and the holiday heart alcohol associated cardiac rhythm disorder. *American Heart Journal,* 1978, *95,* 555–562.

Faris, A. A., Reyes, M. G., & Abrams, B. M. Subclinical alcoholic myopathy: electromyographic and biopsy study. *Transactions of the American Neurological Association,* 1967, *92,* 102–106.

Fazekas, G. Hydrocortisone content of human blood and alcohol content of blood and urine, after wine consumption. *Quarterly Journal of Studies on Alcohol,* 1966, *27,* 439–446.

Ferrans, V. J., Rios, J. C., Gooch, A. S., Wintter, D., DeVita, V. T., & Datlow, D. W. Alcoholic cardiomyopathy. *American Journal of Medicine,* 1966, *252,* 123–136.

Findlay, J., Sellers, E., & Forstner, G. Lack of effect of alcohol on small intestinal binding of the vitamin B_{12}-intrinsic factor complex. *Canadian Journal of Physiology and Pharmacology,* 1976, *54,* 469–476.

Fischer, J. F., Yoshimura, N., & Aguirre, A. Plasma amino acids in patients with hepatic encephalopathy: Effects of amino acid infusions. *American Journal of Surgery,* 1974, *127,* 40–47.

Frajria, R., & Angeli, A. Alcohol-induced pseudo Cushing's syndrome. *Lancet,* 1977, *i,* 1050–1051.

French, S. W., & Castagna, J. Some effects of chronic ethanol feeding on vitamin B_6 deficiency in the rat. *Laboratory Investigations,* 1967, *16,* 526–531.

French, S. W., Sims, J. S., & Franks, K. E. Alcoholic hepatitis. In M. M. Fisher & J. G. Rankin (Eds.), *Alcohol and the liver.* New York: Plenum Press, 1977.

Friedman, G. D., Siegelaub, A. B., & Seltzer, C. C. Cigarettes, alcohol, coffee and peptic ulcer. *New England Journal of Medicine,* 1974, *290,* 469–473.

Galambos, J. T. The course of alcoholic hepatitis. In J. M., Khanna, Y. Israel, & H. Kalant (Eds.), *Alcoholic liver pathology.* Toronto: Addiction Research Foundation of Ontario, 1975.

Gangl, A., & Ockner, R. K. Intracellular compartmentation and mechanisms of control. *Journal of Clinical Investigation,* 1975, *55,* 803–813.

Gavaler, J. S., Van Thiel, D. H., & Lester, R. Ethanol, a gonadal toxin in the mature rat of both sexes: Similarities and differences. *Alcoholism: Clinical and Experimental Research,* 1980, *4,* 271–276.

Gerber, M. A., & Popper, H. Relation between central canals and portal tracts in alcoholic hepatitis. *Human Pathology,* 1972, *3,* 199–207.

Ghitis, J., Piazuelo, E., & Vitale, J. J. Cali-Harvard nutrition project IV. The erythroid atrophy of severe protein deficiency in monkeys. *American Journal of Clinical Nutrition*, 1963, *12*, 452–454.

Gluckman, S. J., & MacGregor, R. R. Effect of acute alcohol intoxication of granulocyte mobilization and kinetics. *Blood*, 1970, *52*, 551–559.

Gluckman, S. J., Dvorak, V. C., & MacGregor, R. R. Host defense during prolonged alcohol consumption in a controlled environment. *Archives of Internal Medicine*, 1977, *137*, 1539–1543.

Goldstein, D. B. An animal model for testing effects of drugs on alcohol withdrawal reactions. *Journal of Pharmacology and Experimental Therapeutics*, 1972, *183*, 14–22.

Gordon, G. G., & Southren, A. L. Metabolic effects of alcohol on the endocrine system. In C. S. Lieber (Ed.), *Metabolic aspects of alcoholism*. Baltimore: University Park Press, 1977.

Gordon, G. G., Altman, K., Southren, A. L., Rubin, E., & Lieber, C. S. Effect of alcohol on sex hormone metabolism in normal men. *New England Journal of Medicine*, 1976, *295*, 793–797.

Gordon, G. G., Olivo, J., Rafii, F., & Southren, A. L. Conversion of androgens to estrogens in cirrhosis of the liver. *Journal of Clinical Endocrinology and Metabolism*, 1976, *40*, 1018–1026.

Gordon, G. G., Southren, A. L., & Vittek, J. The effect of alcohol ingestion on hepatic aromatase activity and plasma steroid hormones in the rat. *Metabolism*, 1979, *28*, 20–24.

Gordon, G. G., Vittek, J., & Ho, R. Effect of chronic alcohol use on hepatic testosterone 5 α-A-ring reductase in the baboon and in the human being. *Gastroenterology*, 1979, *77*, 110–114.

Gordon, G. G., Vittek, J., & Southren, A. L. Effects of chronic alcohol ingestion on the biosynthesis of steroids in rat testicular homogenate in vitro. *Endocrinology*, 1980, *106*, 1880–1885.

Gottfried, E. B., Korsten, M. A., & Lieber, C. S. Gastritis and duodenitis induced by alcohol: An endoscopic and histologic assessment. *Gastroenterology*, 1976, *70*, 890–898.

Gottfried, E. B., Korsten, M. A., & Lieber, C. S. Alcohol-induced gastric and duodenal lesions in man. *American Journal of Gastroenterology*, 1978, *70*, 587–592.

Gould, L., Zahir, M., Mahmood, S., & Die Lieto, M. Cardiac hemodynamics in alcoholic heart disease. *Annals of Internal Medicine*, 1969, *71*, 543–553.

Green, J. R., Snitcher, E. J., Mowat, N. A., Ekins, R. P., Rees, L. H., & Dawson, A. M. Thyroid function and thyroid regulation in euthyroid men with chronic liver disease: Evidence of multiple abnormalities. *Clinical Endocrinology*, 1977, *7*, 453–461.

Halsted, C. H., Griggs, R. C., & Harris, J. W. The effect of alcoholism on the absorption of folic (H³PGA) evaluated by plasma levels and urine excretion. *Journal of Laboratory and Clinical Medicine*, 1967, *69*, 116–131.

Halsted, C. H., Robles, E. A., & Mezey, E. Intestinal malabsorption in folate deficient alcoholics. *Gastroenterology*, 1973, *64*, 526–532.

Halsted, C. H., Romero, J. J., & Tamura, T. Folate metabolism in the alcoholic monkey. *Gastroenterology*, 1979, *76*, 1149–1154.

Harker, L. A., & Slichter, S. J. The bleeding time as a screening test for evaluation of platelet function. *New England Journal of Medicine*, 1972, *287*, 155–159.

Hed, R., Lundmark, C., Fahlgren, H., & Orell, S. Acute muscular syndrome in chronic alcoholism. *Acta Medica Scandinavica*, 1962, *171*, 585–599.

Helderman, J., Vestal, R., Rowe, J., Tobin, J., Andres, R., & Robertson, G. The response of arginine vasopressin to intravenous ethanol and hypertoxic saline in man. *Journal of Gerontology*, 1978, *33*, 39–47.

Hines, J. D., & Cowan, D. H. Studies on the pathogenesis of alcohol-induced sideroblastic bone marrow abnormalities. *New England Journal of Medicine*, 1970, *283*, 441–446.

Hirschowitz, B. J., Pollard, H. M., Hartwell, S. W., & London, J. The action of ethyl alcohol on gastric acid secretion. *Gastroenterology*, 1956, *30*, 244–250.

Horwitz, L. D., & Atkins, J. M. Acute effects of ethanol on left ventricular performance. *Cardiology*, 1974, *49*, 124–128.

Howard, J. M., & Ehrlich, E. W. The etiology of pancreatitis. *Annals of Surgery*, 1960, *152*, 135–146.

Howard, L., Wagner, C., & Schenker, S. Malabsorption of thiamine in folate deficient rats. *Journal of Nutrition*, 1974, *104*, 1024–1032.

Hoyumpa, A. M., Breen, K. J., & Schenker, S. Thiamine transport across the rat intestine: II. Effect of ethanol. *Journal of Laboratory and Clinical Medicine*, 1975, *86*, 803–816.

Hoyumpa, A. M., Middleton, H. M., Wilson, F. A., & Schenker, S. Dual system of thiamine transport: Characteristics and effect of ethanol. *Gastroenterology*, 1974, *66*, 714–719.

Hoyumpa, A. M., Middleton, H. M., & Wilson, F. A. Thiamine transport across the rat intestine: I. Normal characteristics. *Gastroenterology*, 1975, *68*, 1218–1227.

Ishii, K. Epidemiological problems of pancreatic cancer. *Japanese Journal of Clinical Medicine*, 1968, *26*, 1839–1842.

Israel, Y., Kalant, H., Orrego, H., Khanna, J. M., Videla, L., & Phillips, J. M. Experimental alcohol induced hepatic necrosis suppression by propylthiouracil. *Proceedings of the National Academy of Sciences (USA)*, 1975, *72*, 1137–1141.

Israel, Y., Salazar, I., & Rosenmann, E. Inhibitory effects of alcohol on intestinal amino acid transport in vivo and in vitro. *Journal of Nutrition*, 1968, *96*, 499–504.

Israel, Y., Valenzuela, J. E., Salazar, I., & Ugarte, G. Alcohol and amino acid transport in human small intestine. *Journal of Nutrition*, 1969, *98*, 222–224.

Israel, Y., Videla, L., MacDonald, A., & Bernstein, J. Metabolic alterations produced in the liver by chronic ethanol administration: Comparison between the effects produced by ethanol and by thyroid hormones. *Biochemical Journal*, 1973, *134*, 523–529.

Israel, Y., Videla, L., & Bernstein, J. Liver hypermetabolic state after chronic ethanol consumption: Hormonal interrelationships and pathogenic implications. *Federation Proceedings*, 1975, *34*, 2052–2059.

Israel, Y., Walfish, P. G., Orrego, H., Blake, S., & Kalant, H. Thyroid hormones in alcoholic liver disease. *Gastroenterology*, 1979, *76*, 116–122.

Isselbacher, K. J. Metabolic and hepatic effects of alcohol. *New England Journal of Medicine*, 1977, *296*, 612–616.

Jeffcoate, W. J., Cullen, M. H., Herbert, M., Hastings, A. G., & Walder, C. P. Prevention of effects of alcohol intoxication by naloxone. *Lancet*, 1979, *2*, 1157–1159.

Jefferys, D. B., Flanagan, R. J., & Volans, G. N. Reversal of ethanol-induced coma with naloxone. *Lancet*, 1980, *1*, 308–309. (Letter)

Jenkins, J. S., & Connolly, J. Adrenocortical response to ethanol in man. *British Medical Journal*, 1968, *1*, 804–805.

Johnston, D. E., Chiao, Y-B, & Van Thiel, D. H. Ethanol and acetaldehyde inhibition of testosterone synthesis. *Alcoholism: Clinical and Experimental Research*, 1980, *4*, 219A.

Kakihana, R., & Moore, J. A. Circadian rhythm of corticosterone in mice: the effect of chronic consumption of alcohol. *Psychopharmacologia (Berl.)*, 1976, *46*, 301–305.

Kakihana, R., Butte, J. C., Hathaway, A., & Noble, E. P. Adrenocortical response to ethanol in mice: Modification by chronic ethanol consumption. *Acta Endocrinologica*, 1971, *67*, 753–764.

Kleeman, C. R. Water metabolism. In H. Maxwell & C. R. Kleeman (Eds.), *Clinical disorders of fluid and electrolyte metabolism*. New York: McGraw-Hill, 1973.

Korman, M. G., Soveny, C., & Hansky, J. Effect of food on serum gastrin evaluated by radioimmunoassay. *Gut*, 1971, *12*, 619–622.

Korsten, M. A., Matsuzaki, S., & Feinman, K. High blood acetaldehyde levels after ethanol administration: Difference between alcoholic and nonalcoholic subjects. *New England Journal of Medicine*, 1975, *292*, 386–389.

Kowarski, S., & Schachter, D. Vitamin D and adenosine triphosphate dependent divalent cations in rat intestinal mucosa. *Journal of Clinical Investigation*, 1973, *52*, 2765–2773.

Kowarski, S., Blair-Stanek, C. S., & Schachter, D. Active transport of zinc and identification of zinc-binding protein in rat jejunal mucosa. *American Journal of Physiology*, 1974, *226*, 401–407.

Krasner, N. Alcohol and the G.I. tract. *Journal of the Royal College of Surgeons of Edinburgh*, 1977, *12* (1), 15–20.

Krasner, N., Cochran, K. M., Russel, R. I., Carmichael, H. A., & Thompson, G. G. Alcohol and absorption from the small intestine. *Gut*, 1976, *17*, 245–251.

Krawitt, E. L. Ethanol inhibits intestinal calcium transport in rats. *Nature (Lond.)*, 1973, *243*, 88–89.

Krawitt, E. L. Effect of acute ethanol administration on duodenal calcium transport. *Proceedings of the Society for Experimental Biology and Medicine*, 1974, *146*, 406–408.

Krawitt, E. L. Effect of ethanol ingestion on duodenal calcium transport. *Journal of Laboratory and Clinical Medicine*, 1975, *85*, 665–671.

Krawitt, E. L., Sampson, H. W., & Katagiri, C. A. Effect of 1,25-dihydroxycholecalciferol on ethanol mediated suppression of calcium absorption. *Calcified Tissue Research*, 1975, *18*, 119–124.

Lane, F., Goff, P., McGuffin, R., Eichner, E. R., & Hillman, R. S. Folic acid metabolism in normal, folate deficient and alcoholic men. *British Journal of Haematology*, 1976, *34*, 489–500.

Laube, H., Norris, H. T., & Robbins, S. L. The nephromegaly of chronic alcoholics with liver disease. *Archives of Pathology*, 1967, *84*, 290–294.

Leevy, C. M., Baker, H., & Ten Hove, W. B-complex vitamin in liver disease of the alcoholic. *American Journal of Clinical Nutrition*, 1965, *16*, 339–346.

Li, T. K., Bosron, W. F., & Dafeldecker, W. P. Isolation of π-alcohol dehydrogenase of human liver: Is it a determinant of alcoholism? *Proceedings of the National Academy of Sciences (USA)*, 1977, *74*, 4378–4381.

Lieber, C. S., & Spritz, N. Effects of prolonged ethanol intake in man: Role of dietary, adipose and endogenously synthesized fatty acids in the pathogenesis of the alcoholic fatty liver. *Journal of Clinical Investigation*, 1966, *45*, 1400–1411.

Lieber, C. S., Spritz, N., & DeCarli, L. M. Accumulation of triglycerides in heart and kidney after alcohol ingestion. *Journal of Clinical Investigation*, 1966, *45*, 1041.

Lillibridge, C. B., Yoshimori, M., & Chey, W. Y. Observations on the ultrastructure of oxyntic cells in alcohol fed dogs. *American Journal of Digestive Disorders*, 1973, *18*, 443–448.

Lindenbaum, J. Folate and vitamin B_{12} deficiencies in alcoholism. *Seminars in Hematology*, 1980, *17*, 119–129.

Lindenbaum, J., & Hargrove, L. Thrombocytopenia in alcoholics. *Annals of Internal Medicine*, 1968, *68*, 526–532.

Lindenbaum, J., & Lieber, C. S. Alcohol induced malabsorption of vitamin B_{12} in man. *Nature (Lond.)*, 1969, *224*, 806–809. (a)

Lindenbaum, J., & Lieber, C. S. Hematologic effects of alcohol in man in the absence of nutritional deficiency. *New England Journal of Medicine*, 1969, *281*, 333–338. (b)

Lindenbaum, J., & Lieber, C. S. Effects of chronic ethanol administration: Intestinal absorption in man in the absence of nutritional deficiency. *Annals of the New York Academy of Science*, 1975, *252*, 228–234.

Lindenbaum, J., & Nath, B. J. Megaloblastic anemia and hypersegmentation. *British Journal of Haematology*, 1981, *47*, 628–634.

Lindenbaum, J., Saha, J. R., Shea, N., & Lieber, C. S. Mechanism of alcohol-induced malabsorption of vitamin B_{12}. *Gastroenterology*, 1973, *64*, 762–770.

Linkola, J., Fyhrquist, F., & Forsander, O. Effects of ethanol in urinary arginine vasopressin excretion in two rat strains selected for their different ethanol preferences. *Acta Physiologica Scandinavica*, 1977, *101*, 126–128.

Linkola, J., Ylikahri, R., Fyhrquist, F., & Wallenius, M. Plasma vasopressin in ethanol intoxication and hangover. *Acta Physiologica Scandinavica,* 1978, *104,* 180–187.

Linkola, J., Fyhrquist, F., & Ylikahri, R. Renin, aldosterone and cortisol during ethanol intoxication and hangover. *Acta Physiologica Scandinavica,* 1979, *106,* 75–82.

Littleton, J. Alcohol and neurotransmitters. *Clinical Endocrinology and Metabolism,* 1978, *7,* 369–384.

Lloyd, C. W., & Williams, R. H. Endocrine changes associated with Laennec's cirrhosis of the liver. *American Journal of Medicine,* 1948, *4,* 315–330.

Longacre, A. M., & Popky, G. L. Papillary necrosis in patients with cirrhosis: A study of 102 patients. *Journal of Urology,* 1968, *99,* 391–395.

Louria, D. B. Susceptibility to infection during experimental alcohol intoxication. *Transactions of the Association of American Physicians,* 1963, *76,* 102–110.

MacDonald, R. A. Primary hemochromatosis. In E. D. Brown & C. V. Moore (Eds.), *Progress in hematology.* New York: Grune & Stratton, 1966.

MacGregor, R. R., Spagnuolo, P. J., & Lentrek, A. L. Inhibition of granulocyte adherence by ethanol, prednisone and aspirin measured with an assay system. *New England Journal of Medicine,* 1974, *291,* 642–646.

Marks, V., & Wright, J. W. Endocrinologic and metabolic effects of alcohol. *Proceedings of the Royal Society of Medicine,* 1977, *70,* 337–344.

Marquis, C., Marchetti, J., Burlet, C., & Bowlange, M. Secretion urinaire et hormone antidiuretique chez des rats soumis à une administration repetée d' ethanol. *Comptes Rendus des Séances de la Société de Biologie et de ses Filiales,* 1975, *54,* 555–562.

Martin, J. L., Justus, P. G., & Mathias, J. R. Altered motility of the small intestine in response to ethanol (ETOH): An explanation for the diarrhea associated with the consumption of alcohol. *Gastroenterology,* 1980, *78,* 1218–1223.

Martini, G. A., & Weinback, M. Begunstigt Alkohol die Entstehung eines Barret-Syndromes: Endobrachyosaphagus? *Deutsche Medizinische Wochenschrift,* 1974, *99* (10), 434–439.

Matuchansky, C., Rombend, J. D., & Modigliani, R. Vitamin B_{12} malabsorption in chronic pancreatitis. *Gastroenterology,* 1974, *67,* 406–410.

Mayer, E. M., Grabowski, C. J., & Fisher, R. S. Effects of graded doses of alcohol upon esophageal motor function. *Gastroenterology,* 1978, *75,* 1133–1138.

McCurdy, P. R., Pierce, L. E., & Rath, C. E. Abnormal bone marrow morphology in acute alcoholism. *New England Journal of Medicine,* 1962, *266,* 505–506.

Mendelson, J. H., & Stein, S. Serum cortisol levels in alcoholic and non-alcoholic subjects during experimentally induced ethanol intoxication. *Psychosomatic Medicine,* 1966, *28,* 616–626.

Mendelson, J. H., Ogata, M., & Mello, N. K. Adrenal function and alcoholism: serum cortisol. *Psychosomatic Medicine,* 1971, *33,* 145–157.

Merry, J., & Marks, V. The effect of alcohol, barbiturate, and diazepam on hypothalamic/pituitary/adrenal function in chronic alcoholics. *Lancet,* 1972, *2,* 990–991.

Mezey, E. Ethanol: metabolism and adverse effects. *Viewpoints on Digestive Diseases,* 1979, *11* (2), 215–219.

Middleton, W. R. J., Carter, E. A., Drummery, G. D., & Isselbacher, K. J. Effect of oral ethanol administration on intestinal cholesterogenesis in the rat. *Gastroenterology,* 1971, *60,* 880–887.

Mistilis, S. P., and Ockner, R. K. Effects of ethanol on endogenous lipid and lipoprotein metabolism in small intestine. *Journal of Laboratory and Clinical Medicine,* 1972, *80,* 34–46.

Morgan, M. Y., & Sherlock, S. Sex-related differences among 100 patients with alcoholic liver disease. *British Medical Journal,* 1977, *1,* 939–941.

Morley, J. E., Baranetsky, N. G., & Wingert, T. D. Endocrine effects of naloxone-induced opiate receptor blockade. *Journal of Clinical Endocrinology and Metabolism,* 1980, *50,* 251–257.

Murray, M. J., & Stein, N. Effect of ethanol on absorption of iron in rats. *Proceedings of the Society for Experimental Biology and Medicine*, 1968, *120*, 816–819.

Nakamura, K., Sarles, H., & Payan, H. Three dimensional reconstruction of the pancreatic ducts in chronic pancreatitis. *Gastroenterology*, 1972, *62*, 942–949.

Ning, M., Lowenstein, L. M., & Davidson, C. S. Serum amino acid concentrations in alcoholic hepatitis. *Journal of Laboratory and Clinical Medicine*, 1967, *70*, 554–562.

Nishimo, K., & Itokawa, Y. Thiamine metabolism in B_6 and B_{12} deficient rats. *Journal of Nutrition*, 1977, *107*, 775–782.

Nomenclature, diagnostic criteria and diagnostic methodology for disease of the liver and biliary tract. Fogarty International Center, Proceeding 22. Washington, D.C.: U.S. Government Printing Office, 1976.

Nomura, S., Pittman, C. S., Chambers, J. B., Jr., Buck, M. W., & Shimivu, T. Reduced peripheral conversion of thyroxine to triiodothyronine. *Journal of Clinical Investigation*, 1975, *56*, 643–652.

Olivo, J., Gordon, G. G., Rafii, F., & Southren, A. L. Estrogen metabolism in hyperthyroidism and in cirrhosis of the liver. *Steroids*, 1975, *26*, 47–56.

Orrego, H., Kalant, H., Israel, Y., Blake, J., Medline, A., Rankin, J. G., Armstrong, A., & Kapur, B. Effect of short term therapy with propylthiouracil in patients with alcoholic liver disease. *Gastroenterology*, 1979, *76*, 105–115.

Oxenkrug, G. F. Dexamethasone test in alcoholics. *Lancet*, 1978, *2*, 795. (Letter)

Perin, A., & Sessa, A. In vitro effects of ethanol and acetaldehyde on tissue protein synthesis. In K. O. Lindroos & C. J. P. Eriksson (Eds.), *The role of acetaldehyde in the actions of ethanol*. Satellite Symposium—6th International Congress of Pharmacology, Helsinki. *The Finnish Foundation for Alcohol Studies*, 1975, *23*, 105–122.

Perlow, W., Baraona, E., & Lieber, C. S. Symptomatic intestinal disaccharidase deficiency in alcoholics. *Gastroenterology*, 1975, *68*, 935–942.

Peterson, R. E. Adrenocortical steroid metabolism and adrenal cortical function in liver disease. *Journal of Clinical Investigation*, 1960, *39*, 320–331.

Pfoffenbarger, R. S., Wing, A. L., & Hyde, R. T. Chronic disease in former college students: Early precursor of peptic ulcer. *American Journal of Epidemiology*, 1974, *100*, 307–312.

Pickrell, K. L. The effect of alcohol intoxication and other anaesthesia or resistance to pneumococcal infection. *Bulletin of the Johns Hopkins Hospital*, 1938, *63*, 238–260.

Pirola, R. C., & Davis, A. E. Effects of intravenous alcohol on motility of the duodenum and of the Sphincter of Oddi. *Australian Annals of Medicine*, 1970, *19*, 1–6.

Post, R. M., & Desforges, J. F. Thrombocytopenia and alcoholism. *Annals of Internal Medicine*, 1968, *68*, 1230–1236.

Puszkin, S., & Rubin, E. Adenosine diphosphate effect on contractility of human muscle actinomycin: Inhibition by ethanol and acetaldehyde. *Science*, 1975, *188*, 1319–1321.

Puszkin, S., & Rubin, E. Effect of ADP, ethanol and acetaldehyde on the relaxing complex of human muscle and its absorption by polystyrene particles. *Archives of Biochemistry and Biophysics*, 1976, *177*, 574–584.

Raiba, N. Effect of ethanol on cytological changes induced by salt load in nucleus supraoptcius of rat. *Proceedings of the Society for Experimental Biology and Medicine*, 1960, *103*, 387–391.

Reber, H. A. Chronic pancreatitis. In M. H. Slessenger & J. S. Fordtran (Eds.), *Gastrointestinal disease*. Philadelphia: Saunders, 1978.

Rich, A. R., & Duff, G. L. Experimental and pathological studies on the pathogenesis of acute hemorrhagic pancreatitis. *Bulletin of the Johns Hopkins Hospital*, 1936, *58*, 212–216.

Robert, A., Nezamis, J. E., Hanchar, A. J., & Lancaster, C. Aspirin combined with alcohol is ulcerogenic. *Gastroenterology*, 1980, *78*, 1245–1251.

Robles, E. A., Mezey, E., Halsted, C. H., & Schuster, M. M. Effects of ethanol on the motility of the small intestine. *Johns Hopkins Medical Journal*, 1974, *135*, 17–24.

Rodgers, J. B., & O'Brien, R. J. The effect of acute ethanol treatment on lipid-reesterifying enzymes of the rat small bowel. *American Journal of Digestive Diseases*, 1975, *20*, 354–358.

Rosen, H. M., Yoshimura, N., & Hodgman, J. M. Plasma amino acid patterns in hepatic encephalopathy of differing etiology. *Gastroenterology*, 1977, *72*, 483–488.

Rubin, E., Rybak, B. J., Lindenbaum, J., Gerson, C. D., Walker, G., & Lieber, C. S. Ultrastructural changes in the small intestine induced by ethanol. *Gastroenterology*, 1972, *63*, 801–810.

Sahud, M. A. Platelet size and number in alcoholic thrombocytopenia. *New England Journal of Medicine*, 1972, *286*, 355–356.

Saint-Blanquot, G. de, & Deroche, R. Action de l'ethanol sur la physiologie gastrique. *Biologie et Gastro-Enterologie (Paris)*, 1972, *57*, 247–256.

Sarles, H. *Pancreatitis*. Symposium of Marseille. Basel, Switzerland: Kager, 1963.

Sarles, H. Chronic calcifying pancreatitis—chronic alcoholic pancreatitis. *Gastroenterology*, 1974, *66*, 604–616.

Sarles, H. Alcohol and the pancreas. *Annals of the New York Academy of Science*, 1975, *252*, 171–182.

Sarles, H., & Sahel, J. Pathology of chronic calcifying pancreatitis. *American Journal of Gastroenterology*, 1976, *66*, 117–139.

Schachter, P. J. Distribution of serum zinc between albumin and alpha 2 macroglobulin in patients with decompensated hepatic cirrhosis. *European Journal of Clinical Investigation*, 1976, *6*, 147–150.

Schade, S. G., Cohen, R. J., & Conrad, M. E. Effect of HCI on iron absorption. *New England Journal of Medicine*, 1968, *279*, 672–674.

Schriber, S. S., Briden, K., & Oratz, M. Ethanol, acetaldehyde and myocardial protein synthesis. *Journal of Clinical Investigation*, 1972, *51*, 2820–2826.

Selhub, J., & Rosenberg, I. H. Isolation of folate binding protein from intestine with the aid of affinity chromatography. *Clinical Research*, 1976, *24*, 504–510.

Sereny, G., Rapaport, A., & Hudson, H. The effect of alcohol withdrawal on electrolyte and acid-base balance. *Metabolism*, 1966, *15*, 896–899.

Shaw, S., & Lieber, C. S. Plasma amino acid abnormalities in the alcoholic: Respective roles of alcohol, nutrition, and liver injury. *Gastroenterology*, 1978, *74*, 677–682.

Shirazi, S. S., & Platz, C. E. Effect of alcohol on canine esophageal mucosa. *Journal of Surgical Research*, 1978, *25*, 373–379.

Smals, A. G. H., Njo, K. T., Knoben, J. M., Ruland, C. M., & Kloppenborg, P. W. E. Alcohol-induced Cushingoid syndrome. *Journal of the Royal College Physicians*, 1977, *12*, 36–41.

Smith, B. M., Skillman, J. J., & Edwards, B. G. Permeability of the human gastric mucosa: Alteration by acetylsalicylic acid and ethanol. *New England Journal of Medicine*, 1971, *285*, 716–721.

Smith, M. E., Matty, A. J., & Blair, J. A. The transport of pteroglutamic acid across the small intestine of the rat. *Biochimica et Biophysica Acta*, 1970, *219*, 37–46.

Sorrell, M. F., Tuma, D. J., & Barak, A. J. Evidence that acetaldehyde irreversibly impairs glycoprotein metabolism in liver slices. *Gastroenterology*, 1977, *73*, 1138–1141.

Sorrell, M. F., Tuma, D. J., & Schafer, E. C. Role of acetaldehyde in the ethanol-induced impairment of glycoprotein metabolism in rat liver slices. *Gastroenterology*, 1977, *73*, 137–144.

Southren, A. L., Gordon, G. G., Olivo, J., Rafii, F., & Rosenthal, W. S. Androgen metabolism in cirrhosis of the liver. *Metabolism*, 1973, *22*, 695–702.

Spagnuolo, P. J., & MacGregor, R. R. Acute ethanol effect of chemotaxis and other components of host defense. *Journal of Laboratory and Clinical Medicine*, 1975, *86*, 24–31.

Sporn, M. B., Dunlop, N. M., Newton, D. L., & Smith, J. M. Prevention of chemical carcinogenesis by vitamin A and its synthetic analogs (retinoids). *Federation Proceedings,* 1976, *35,* 1332–1338.

Stein, W. S., Lieber, C. S., & Leevy, C. M. The effect of ethanol upon systemic and hepatic blood flow in man. *American Journal of Clinical Nutrition,* 1963, *13,* 68–74.

Steinbert, S., Campbell, C., & Hillman, R. Disruption of folate metabolism by alcohol. *Alcoholism: Clinical and Experimental Research,* 1980, *4,* 229–234.

Stokes, P. E. Adrenocortical activation in alcoholics during chronic drinking. *Annals of the New York Academy of Science,* 1973, *215,* 77–83.

Straus, E., Urbach, H. J., & Yalow, R. S. Alcohol-stimulated secretion of immunoreactive secretin. *New England Journal of Medicine,* 1975, *293,* 1031–1032.

Strum, W. B., & Spiro, H. M. Chronic pancreatitis. *Annals of Internal Medicine,* 1971, *74,* 264–277.

Sullivan, J. F. Effect of alcohol on urinary zinc excretion. *Quarterly Journal of Studies on Alcohol,* 1962, *23,* 216–220.

Sullivan, L. W., & Herbert, V. Suppression of hematopoeisis by ethanol. *Journal of Clinical Investigation,* 1964, *43,* 2048–2062.

Sullivan, L. W., Adams, W. H., & Liu, Y. K. Induction of thrombocytopenia by thrombopheresis in man: Patterns of recovery in normal subjects during ethanol ingestion and abstinence. *Blood,* 1977, *49,* 197–207.

Suzuki, T., Higashi, R., Hirose, T., Ikeda, H., & Tamura, K. Adrenal 17-hydroxycorticosteroid secretion in the dog in response to ethanol. *Acta Endocrinologica,* 1972, *70,* 736–740.

Tabakoff, B., & Hoffman, P. L. Alcohol and neurotransmitters. In H. Rigter & J. Crabbe (Eds.), *Alcohol tolerance and dependence.* Amsterdam: Biomedical Press, 1980.

Tabakoff, B., Jaffe, R. C., & Ritzmann, R. F. Corticosterone concentrations in mice during ethanol drinking and withdrawal. *Journal of Pharmacy and Pharmacology,* 1978, *30,* 371–374.

Tamura, T., & Stokstad, E. L. R. Increased folate excretion in acute hepatitis. *American Journal of Clinical Nutrition,* 1979, *30,* 1378–1379.

Tapper, E. J., Bushi, S., & Ruppert, R. D. Effect of acute and chronic ethanol treatment on the absorption of iron in rats. *American Journal of Medical Science,* 1968, *255,* 46–52.

Thompson, A. D. Alcohol and nutrition. *Clinics in Endocrinology and Metabolism,* 1978, *7,* 405–428.

Thomson, A. D., Baker, H., & Leevy, C. M. Patterns of ^{35}S-thiamine hydrochloride absorption in the malnourished alcoholic patient. *Journal of Laboratory and Clinical Medicine,* 1970, *76,* 34–45.

Thompson, A. D., Frank, D., & De Angelis, B. Thiamine depletion induced by folate deficiency in rats. *Nutrition Reports International,* 1972, *6,* 107–110.

Tisman, G., & Herbert, V. In vitro myelosuppression and immunosuppression in ethanol. *Journal of Clinical Investigation,* 1973, *52,* 1410–1414.

Tomasulo, P. A., Kater, R. M., & Iber, F. L. Impairment of thiamine absorption in alcoholism. *American Journal of Clinical Nutrition,* 1968, *21,* 1341–1344.

Toro, G., Kolodny, R. C., Jacobs, L. S., Masters, W. H., & Daughaday, W. H. Failure of alcohol to alter pituitary and target organ hormone levels. *Clinical Research,* 1973, *21,* 505. (Abstract)

U.S. Department of Health, Education, and Welfare, National Center for Health Statistics. *Monthly Vital Statistics Report, Advance Report.* Final mortality statistics. *25* (11) Supplement, February 1975.

U.S. Department of Health, Education, and Welfare. *Third special report of the U.S. Congress of alcohol and health from the Secretary of Health, Education, and Welfare,* Washington, D.C.: June 1978.

Van Thiel, D. H. Alcohol and its effect upon endocrine function. *Alcoholism: Clinical and Experimental Research*, 1980, *4*, 44–49.

Van Thiel, D. H., & Lester, R. Alcoholism: Its effect on hypothalamic–pituitary–gonadal function. *Gastroenterology*, 1976, *71*, 318–327.

Van Thiel, D. H., & Lester, R. Further evidence for hypothalamic–pituitary dysfunction in alcoholic men. *Alcoholism: Clinical and Experimental Research*, 1978, *2*, 265–269.

Van Thiel, D. H., & Lester, R. The effect of chronic alcohol abuse on sexual function. *Clinical Endocrinology and Metabolism*, 1979, *8*, 499–510.

Van Thiel, D. H., & Stremple, J. R. Lower esophageal sphincter pressure in cirrhotic men with ascites before and after diuresis. *Gastroenterology*, 1977, *72*, 842–844.

Van Thiel, D. H., Gavaler, J. S., & Lester, R. Ethanol inhibition of vitamin A metabolism in the testes: Possible mechanism for sterility in alcoholics. *Science*, 1974, *186*, 941–942.

Van Thiel, D. H., Lester, R., & Sherins, R. J. Hypogonadism in alcoholic liver disease: Evidence for a double defect. *Gastroenterology*, 1974, *67*, 1188–1199.

Van Thiel, D. H., Gavaler, J. S., Lester, R., & Goodman, M. D. Alcohol-induced testicular atrophy: An experimental model for hypogonadism occurring in chronic alcoholic men. *Gastroenterology*, 1975, *69*, 326–332.

Van Thiel, D. H., Gavaler, J. S., Lester, R., Loriaux, D. L., & Braunstein, G. D. Plasma estrone, prolactin, neurophysin and sex steroid binding globulin in chronic alcoholic men. *Metabolism*, 1975, *24*, 1015–1019.

Van Thiel, D. H., Gavaler, J. S., Little, J. M., & Lester, R. Alcohol: Its effect on the kidney. *Metabolism*, 1977, *26*, 857–886.

Van Thiel, D. H., Gavaler, J. S., Wight, C., Smith, W. I., Jr., & Abuid, J. Thyrotropin releasing hormone (TRH) induced growth hormone (hGH) responses in cirrhotic men. *Gastroenterology*, 1978, *75*, 66–70.

Van Thiel, D. H., Lester, R., & Vaitukaitis, J. Evidence for a defect in pituitary secretion of luteinizing hormone in chronic alcoholic men. *Journal of Clinical Endocrinology and Metabolism*, 1978, *47*, 499–507.

Van Thiel, D. H., McClain, C. J., Elson, M. K., & McMillin, M. J. Hyperprolactinemia and thyrotropin releasing factor responses in men with alcoholic liver disease. *Alcoholism: Clinical and Experimental Research*, 1978, *2*, 344–348.

Van Thiel, D. H., Gavaler, J. S., Cobb, C. F., Sherins, R. J., & Lester, R. Alcohol induced testicular atrophy in the adult male rat. *Endocrinology*, 1979, *105*, 888–895.

Van Thiel, D. H., Smith, W. I., Jr., Wight, C., & Abuid, J. Elevated basal and abnormal thyrotropin releasing hormone induced thyroid stimulating hormone secretion in chronic alcoholic men with liver disease. *Alcoholism: Clinical and Experimental Research*, 1979, *3*, 302–308.

Van Thiel, D. H., Gavaler, J. S., Slone, F. L., Cobb, C. F., Smith, W. I., Jr., Bron, K. M., & Lester, R. Is feminization in alcoholic men due in part to portal hypertension? A rat model. *Gastroenterology*, 1980, *78*, 81–91.

Verdy, M., & Caron, D. Effect et absorption du calcium chez l'humain. *Biologie Gastro-Enterologie (Paris)*, 1973, *6*, 157–160.

Videla, L., Bernstein, J., & Israel, Y. Metabolic alterations produced in the liver by chronic ethanol administration: Increased oxidative capacity. *Biochemical Journal*, 1973, *134*, 507–514.

Wagner, G., & Fuchs, A. R. Effects of ethanol on uterine activity during suckling in post partum women. *Acta Endocrinologica*, 1968, *58*, 133–141.

Wasserman, R. H., & Taylor, A. N. Vitamin D-dependent calcium binding protein. *Journal of Biological Chemistry*, 1968, *243*, 3987–3993.

Watts, H. D. Lesions brought on by vomiting. The effect of hiatal hernia on site of injury. *Gastroenterology*, 1976, *71*, 683–688.

Weinstein, M. J., & Deykin, D. Quantitative abnormality of an Aα-chain molecular weight form on the fibrinogen of cirrhotic patients. *British Journal of Haematology*, 1978, *40*, 617–630.

Weise, R. R., Schapiro, H., & Woodward, E. R. Effect of parenteral alcohol on gastric secretion. *Surgical Forum*, 1961, *12*, 281–284.

Whang, G., & Pierson, R. M. Distribution of zinc in skeletal muscle and liver tissue in normal and dietary control alcoholic rats. *Journal of Laboratory and Clinical Medicine*, 1975, *85*, 50–58.

Wright, J. Endocrine effects of alcohol. *Clinical Endocrinology and Metabolism*, 1978, *7*, 351–367.

Wright, J., Merry, J., Fry, D., & Marks, V. Pituitary function in chronic alcoholism. *Advances in Experimental Medicine and Biology*, 1975, *59*, 253–255.

Wynder, E. L. Toward the prevention of laryngeal cancer. *Laryngoscope*, 1975, *85* (7), 1190–1196.

Wynder, E. L., & Chan, P. C. The possible role of riboflavin deficiency in epithelial neoplasia II: Effect on skin tumor development. *Cancer*, 1970, *26*, 1221–1224.

Ylikahri, R. H., Huttunen, M. O., & Harkonen, M. Effect of alcohol on anterior pituitary secretion of trophic hormones. *Lancet*, 1976, *I*, 1353.

Ylikahri, R. H., Huttunen, M. O., Harkonen, M., Leino, T., Kelenius, T., Liewerndahl, K., & Karonen, S. L. Acute effects of alcohol on anterior pituitary secretion of the trophic hormones. *Journal of Clinical Endocrinology and Metabolism*, 1978, *46*, 715–720.

5

Ethanol and the Central Nervous System

WALTER A. HUNT

The effect of ethanol on the central nervous system is most certainly the first to be recognized. Since it was discovered that putting fruit and grain in water in the warm sun produced a drink whose consumption resulted in pleasant feelings, alcoholic beverages have been an integral part of many cultures. It is the pharmacological effects of ethanol on the brain that make necessary this book and the expanding research in the area of alcoholism.

This chapter will survey the various ways in which ethanol alters neural function. It will begin by exploring ethanol's behavioral effects and then approach the possible mechanisms that might mediate its effects. The discussion begins with the effects of ethanol at the molecular level and then proceeds to higher levels of organization, including the effects on electrical properties of cells, sleep, synaptic transmission, and brain metabolism. A section concerning the long-term effects of ethanol consumption is also included, but only as it pertains to the development of neurological diseases and brain damage. Discussions of tolerance and dependence and of fetal alcohol syndrome can be found in other chapters in this book. This chapter is not meant to be an exhaustive review of the literature but rather an overview of the various ways in which ethanol affects the brain. Specific reviews of a given area are cited; the reader can refer to these for more detailed information.

WALTER A. HUNT • Behavioral Sciences Department, Armed Forces Radiobiology Research Institute, Bethesda, Maryland 20014.

1. ETHANOL AND BEHAVIOR

1.1. General Aspects

Ethanol has a variety of effects on behavior that are dependent on the blood ethanol concentration (see reviews of Barry, 1979; Alkana & Malcolm, 1980). These effects fall into several categories and relate to motor function, mental processes, emotion, and consciousness.

Although ethanol is a depressant, biphasic effects in response to ethanol can be observed (see review of Pohorecky, 1977). This occurs, apparently, because inhibitory processes are more sensitive to ethanol than excitatory ones, although direct neuronal stimulation by ethanol has not been ruled out. Thus, at low doses of ethanol, excitation can be found, while at high doses the nervous system is progressively depressed. At low doses of ethanol, excitation in humans is expressed in a number of ways. In general, one's inhibitions are reduced. There is a greater degree of social interaction, feelings of euphoria, and reduced tension (Ekman, Frankenhauser, Goldberg, Bjerver, Jarpe, & Myrsten, 1963). Certain behaviors, such as gambling, are increased because of the release of inhibitions (Sjoberg, 1969). At higher doses of ethanol there is a progressive motor and behavioral decrement that is dependent on the blood ethanol concentration. Although there can be considerable variability in the blood ethanol concentration that results in a particular decrement, certain general relationships between decrement and blood ethanol concentrations can be derived (Barry, 1979). At blood levels of 50 mg/dL, there is an impairment of attention to a task and an increased failure to perceive an infrequent stimulus, accompanied by some disruption in balance. As blood levels increase to the range of 100 to 150 mg/dL, motor and cognitive function declines, with the development of disturbances in gait and coordination (ataxia), impaired mental skills and short-term memory, and slurred speech. The ability to respond to stimuli is abolished at 200 mg/dL. Consciousness is lost at 250 mg/dL and death can occur above 500 mg/dL.

1.2. Motor Function

The effect of ethanol on motor function can be measured in several ways. One sensitive method is the Rombert test, which measures the ability of a subject to stand steadily. The subject stands with his feet side by side on a platform balance and attempts to remain as steady as possible. With increasing intoxication, it becomes progressively more difficult to remain steady. This test is sensitive enough to detect a decrement in balance at blood ethanol concentrations of 69 mg/dL (Franks, Hensley, Hensley, Starmer, & Teo, 1976). Another important test of motor coordination is the walking test that requires a subject to walk in a straight line heel-to-toe. This test is frequently used by law enforcement officers to detect drunk drivers. Impairment of this task is difficult to detect at blood ethanol concentrations below 100 mg/dL (Burns & Moskowitz, 1977).

Reaction time is also sensitive to ethanol. This test requires the subject to perform some simple motor task, such as pressing a button as soon as a visual or auditory stimulus is perceived. Reaction times increase when blood ethanol concentrations reach 50 to 100 mg/dL (Sutton & Burns, 1971; Franks et al., 1976).

A more complex motor task is driving an automobile. It is well known that ethanol impairs driving capabilities and is a major cause of traffic fatalities. Actual measurements of driving impairment do not really show much of an effect of ethanol below a blood ethanol concentration of 100 mg/dL (Perrine, 1976). However, accidents have been reported which involved drivers with blood ethanol concentration below 50 mg/dL. Such accidents could be accounted for by an increased willingness to make risky decisions while driving, thereby enhancing the likelihood of an accident (Barry, 1979).

1.3. Mental Processes

Learning and memory are generally disrupted at relatively low doses of ethanol. Various tests that examine the ability to learn have uniformly shown that the number of tasks required to reach a predetermined criterion of performance is increased at low doses of ethanol. Retention of learned information is also affected. Immediate recall involving lists of words or nonsense syllables is disrupted, the decrement being greater as the difficulty of the task is increased. Short- and long-term memory using tests of free and cued (paired associations or picture recognition) recall are impaired at blood ethanol concentrations of 50 to 80 mg/dL (Alkana & Malcolm, 1980).

Intellectual tasks that require the processing of information and executing prelearned procedures, such as arithmetic calculations, are difficult to perform under the influence of ethanol. With increasing amounts of ethanol, the number of errors rises (Barry, 1979). On the other hand, under certain conditions memory can be enhanced after ethanol treatment. Memory of information acquired before ingestion of ethanol is enhanced after low doses of ethanol (Parker, Birnbaum, Weingartner, Hartley, Stillman, & Wyatt, 1980).

1.4. Psychological Reactions

The feeling that one attains after the consumption of alcoholic beverages is one factor which promotes drinking. Drinking presumably has some reinforcing quality (i.e., some pleasant feeling results and stimulates continued drinking). It is generally believed that people drink to relieve anxiety and to facilitate social interactions. With blood ethanol concentrations of 50 to 150 mg/dL, drinkers report feelings of exhilaration and euphoria. In terms of social behavior, people become cheerful and talkative. More direct studies of the effect of ethanol on anxiety have not been conclusive; results seem to depend on the experimental design used. For example, using the psychiatric outpatient mood scale, tension and anxiety were reported to be decreased (Warren & Raynes, 1972). On the other hand, the Spielberger state anxiety inventory indicated an increase in anxiety with drinking (Logue, Gentry, Linnoilla, & Erwin, 1978). An increase in social interactions is likely to be the result of disinhibition which involves the suppression of normal inhibitory influences, leaving excitatory ones predominant.

The degree to which ethanol alters mood depends on several factors. One is the person's expectations. The power of the mind to create a psychological reaction in the absence of a drug is quite strong. If one expects to become intoxicated, intoxication is much more likely to occur (e.g., the person who sobers up very quickly when stopped by the police while driving). Other factors, such as drinking history, the amount of food consumed, race (flushing in Orientals; see Li, Chapter 3 of this volume), and personality contribute to the level of intoxication after drinking.

Ethanol has been reported to elicit aggressive behavior and alter sexual arousal (see review of Carpenter & Armenti, 1972). Drinking can enhance the likelihood of aggression between individuals, again presumably a result of disinhibition. However, the extent to which this is observed depends on the social situation. Aggression is much more likely when there is perceived competition or threat than in a more benign encounter, such as a casual interaction between a man and a woman. Sexual arousal generally decreases with drinking. This is expressed in the physiological responses needed to engage in sexual activity. However, evidence from mostly anecdotal origin suggests that sexual desire increases.

1.5. Hangover

Anyone who has consumed ethanol in excess has probably experienced a hangover. The most common complaints associated with hangover are headache, nausea, sweating, and tremor. The cause of this malady is unknown, but two general hypotheses have been advanced to explain it.

Alcoholic beverages contain not only ethanol, but congeners as well. Congeners generally other alcohols and aldehydes are substances similar to ethanol and have some of the same physical and pharmacological properties. They also have toxic properties of their own. A few studies have been reported comparing the degree of hangover experienced after consumption of different types of alcoholic beverages. When bourbon was compared with vodka, more hangover symptoms were reported after drinking bourbon and the symptoms were more severe (Damrau & Liddy, 1960; Chapman, 1970).

Another mechanism that can explain hangover is the possibility that it reflects a mild withdrawal syndrome (see Tabakoff, this volume). Some experimental evidence in rodents has suggested that a small increase in the susceptibility to seizures is obtained even after a single large dose of ethanol. In mice treated orally with a 4 g/kg dose, pentylenetetrazol-induced seizures were reduced during the first few hours; eight hours after treatment, however, a significant increase in seizures was observed (McQuarrie & Fingl, 1958).

2. ETHANOL AND MEMBRANE STRUCTURE AND FUNCTION

2.1. Ethanol–Membrane Interactions

The primary site of action of ethanol in the central nervous system is believed to be on membranes surrounding cells. This interaction would, in turn, disrupt the normal processes of electrical conduction and chemical transmission (see reviews of Kalant, 1971; Seeman, 1972; Grenell, 1972; Hunt, 1975). In order to understand how ethanol can interact with membranes, it is important to have a basic knowledge of how membranes are structured.

The cellular membrane is generally described as a fluid mosaic structure (Singer & Nicolson, 1972) consisting of a lipid bilayer with functional proteins embedded in or through it (Figure 1). The lipid bilayer is composed of phospho-

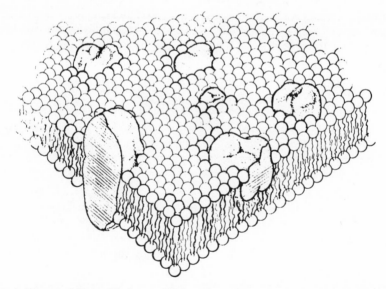

Figure 1. Diagram of Singer–Nicolson model of membrane organization. The membrane consists of a lipid bilayer with globular proteins embedded through it. (Reproduced from Singer & Nicolson, 1972.)

lipids, which have hydrocarbon chains oriented toward the interior of the membrane and polar head groups in contact with the aqueous phase. The proteins are globular in nature and penetrate the membrane to different depths depending on their physicochemical properties. There are other important constituents to membranes, including cholesterol. Membranes are asymmetric and are not entirely rigid (Rothman & Lenard, 1977). Components of the membrane are able to diffuse to some extent in a lateral direction, which may relate to some aspects of cellular function.

Ethanol has such a simple molecular structure that it probably does not interact with a specific receptor. Its pharmacological properties are determined by its physicochemical characteristics and in this context ethanol is similar to anesthetics. The various theories of the mechanism of action of anesthetics have been reviewed elsewhere (e.g., Seeman, 1972; Roth, 1979). The best known of these is the Meyer–Overton theory. It states that the potency of an anesthetic is proportional to its lipid solubility.

Alcohols have been shown by both *in vitro* and *in vivo* experiments to conform to the Meyer–Overton theory (Rang, 1960; Lindbohm & Wallgren, 1962; Israel, Kalant, & LeBlanc, 1966; McCreery & Hunt, 1978). With increasing lipid solubility, the potency of the alcohols increases no matter what experimental endpoint is being measured. However, if lipid solubility exceeds a certain level, as would be obtained with aliphatic alcohols of six to eight carbons, the potency progressively declines. This latter phenomenon is known as "cutoff." The mechanism of action of cutoff is not understood but could reflect an inability of the alcohol to fit in a bilayer or a relocation of the alcohol to a region of the membrane that is less functional. Because of the amphiphilic nature of alcohols (i.e., presence of both hydrophilic and hydrophobic properties), only a certain area in the membrane—which could be near the aqueous-membrane interface—might be the relevant site of action.

The nature of the interaction of ethanol with membranes is beginning to be better understood. Ethanol appears to dissolve physically in the membrane. This results in the expansion of membranes, thereby altering their normal internal structure (Seeman, 1974), and may lead to or involve conformational changes of various membrane constituents, such as proteins.

More recently, the ability of ethanol to affect membrane structure has been investigated with the use of "molecular" probes. Molecular probes are compounds containing a structural moiety that can report on the environment in which it resides. These probes have a known molecular orientation and can be inserted into membranes. Their properties can then be studied by a number of physical techniques.

One technique that has been particularly useful is electron spin resonance spectroscopy (ESR) (Chignell, 1973). ESR employs a compound with an attached free radical which has an unpaired electron. Measuring the mobility of this free radical in its environment can determine whether ethanol interacts with membranes through alterations in membrane fluidity. Fluidity is an index of how freely constituents of membranes can diffuse and rotate.

Chin and Goldstein (1977) utilized the probe 5-doxylsteric acid to examine ethanol–membrane interactions. This probe contains a nitroxide free radical attached to a fatty acid backbone and was inserted into erythrocyte or synaptosomal membranes *in vitro*. When ethanol was added in concentrations of 10 to 320 mmol, there was a dose-dependent reduction in the order parameter, an index of fluidity. This indicated that the environment in which the spin label resided became more fluid in the presence of ethanol; thus the probe could move more freely in the membrane. When other aliphatic alcohols were tested, their potency in increasing membrane fluidity was directly related to their lipid solubility, similar to the relationship observed with their biological activity (Lyon, Schreurs, & Goldstein, 1980).

2.2. Effect of Ethanol on Electrical Properties and Ion Translocation

Electrophysiological approaches have also suggested that ethanol interacts with membranes. Experiments have been carried out in which the ability of ethanol to influence the rate of recovery from posttetanic potentiation (PTP) was studied. PTP is the increased neuronal response to a stimulus that occurs after repetitive stimulation of a synapse. When ethanol in concentrations of 800 mmol was added to the bathing medium of an abdominal ganglion of *Aplysia* and recordings were made in cell R15, the decay of PTP was accelerated (Woodson, Traynor, Schlapfer, & Barondes, 1976). The response was also observed with several short-chain aliphatic alcohols and correlated significantly with their lipid solubility.

What consequences the above-mentioned membrane effects might have on normal cell function is not clear, but a number of studies have appeared suggesting that ethanol might alter ion translocation. Neurons transmit impulses by the progressive and sequential influx of sodium ions along the axon, resulting in depolarization. Repolarization occurs with the subsequent efflux of potassium ions. Studies with invertebrate neurons have indicated that ethanol blocks the transient inward sodium conductance that results from nerve stimulation without a significant effect on the resting membrane potential (Armstrong & Binstock, 1964; Moore, Ulbricht, & Takata, 1964; Bergmann, Klee, & Faber, 1974). In addition, [22]sodium influx into electrically stimulated brain slices is inhibited by ethanol (Wallgren, Nikander, von Boguslawsky, & Linkola, 1974). No change in potassium influx has been detected.

In order to maintain a proper sodium gradient, intracellular sodium is pumped out of the neuron, using energy derived from sodium and potassium-stimulated adenosine triphosphatase (Na-K ATPase) (Schwartz, Lindenmayer, &

Allen, 1975). There are reports that Na-K ATPase activity is also affected by ethanol. Early studies have shown that ethanol *in vitro* has an inhibitory effect on this enzyme system (Israel, Kalant, & Laufer, 1965; Israel *et al.*, 1966; Sun & Samorajski, 1970). This inhibition could be blocked by increasing the potassium concentration in the medium. In addition, other short-chain aliphatic alcohols were inhibitors of Na-K ATPase activity and their potency was correlated with their thermodynamic activity, that is, the effective concentrations in the membrane (Israel *et al.*, 1966). Taken together, these data have been interpreted as suggesting that ethanol might exert its depressant effects through inhibition of Na-K ATPase activity. This view has recently been questioned, however, because inhibition of Na-K ATPase activity by a variety of different means consistently leads to a hyperexcitable state (Hunt, 1975). After chronic treatment with ethanol, an elevation in Na-K ATPase activity has been reported (Israel, Kalant, LeBlanc, Bernstein, & Salazar, 1970; Roach, Khan, Coffman, Pennington, & Davis, 1973). However, these data have not been confirmed (Goldstein & Israel, 1972; Akera, Rech, Marquis, Tobin, & Brody, 1973). It appears, therefore, that ethanol-induced alterations in Na-K ATPase reflect the level of excitability in the brain. A depressed nervous system would have less need for ion transport than usual; conversely, a hyperactive nervous system would need a greater ability to transport ions to function normally. Na-K ATPase activity may, therefore, decrease as a *result* rather than being a *cause* of reduced neuronal activity. Conversely, enzymatic activity may increase after chronic ethanol treatment to accommodate elevated neuronal activity that might be seen after withdrawal (See Tabakoff, this volume).

It is generally accepted that calcium is important in neurotransmitter release (Rubin, 1970) and in stabilizing excitable membranes (Rothstein, 1968). Calcium in ionic form has a large hydrated radius and, as such, will not readily diffuse through membranes. However, calcium can be taken up into depolarized brain tissue (Cooke & Robinson, 1971; Stahl & Swanson, 1971). This influx provides the source of calcium necessary for neurotransmitter release. Under resting conditions, calcium bound to membranes reduces the permeability to sodium in order to stabilize electrical activity (i.e., reduce the effectiveness of stimuli to modify electrical activity).

A number of studies have explored the effect of ethanol on the interaction of calcium and membranes from the central nervous system. Some reports have indicated that calcium levels in different areas of the brain are reduced by ethanol in a dose-dependent manner (Ross, Medina, & Cardenas, 1974; Ross, 1976). However, these findings have not been reproduced in other laboratories (Boggan, Meyer, Middaugh, & Sparks, 1979; Ferko & Bobyock, 1980). More consistent results have been found when the ability of calcium to bind to membranes *in vitro* was examined. Studies have consistently shown that ethanol in concentrations as low as 10 mM enhances calcium binding to erythrocyte ghosts and synaptosomal membranes (Seeman, Chan, Goldberg, Sanko, & Sax, 1971; Michaelis & Myers, 1979). In addition, the potency of other aliphatic alcohols to increase calcium binding is dependent on their lipid solubility, suggesting that this effect may relate to alcohol-induced changes in membrane fluidity. With greater binding of calcium to excitable membranes, an increase in electrical stability would result, making it more difficult for neurons to fire. This would then be followed by a reduced neurotransmitter release.

3. ETHANOL AND ELECTRICAL CELLULAR ACTIVITY

3.1. Electrophysiological Studies

In order to begin to understand how ethanol affects behavior, it is necessary to take a progressively broader, integrated approach to neural function—including an examination of how cells interact with one another—and to determine how ethanol disrupts these interactions. It also becomes important to view the actions of ethanol in light of what specific areas of the central nervous system might mediate certain behavioral and physiological alterations produced by ethanol. One approach has been to examine the electrical properties of neurons in various parts of the brain in an attempt to ascertain if specific areas are more sensitive than others to the effects of ethanol and whether an effect of ethanol in one area disrupts the activity of neurons in another area.

There are a number of electrophysiological techniques that have been used to assess the actions of ethanol on cellular function (see reviews of Himwich & Callison, 1972; Begleiter & Platz, 1972; Klemm, 1979). The most commonly employed are single-unit and multiple-unit recordings, evoked potentials, and electroencephalographic (EEG) recordings. Single-unit recordings usually involve the impalement of single cells and the subsequent recording of electrical activity in these cells. Extracellular recordings can also be performed. Large cells such as cortical or hippocampal pyramidal cells or cerebellar Purkinje cells are most easily used for this purpose. The approach also has the particular benefit of allowing the injection of various substances, such as neurotransmitters and drugs, into or onto a cell to determine how a response might be modified by ethanol treatment. Multiple-unit recordings are extracellular and monitor the activity of a number of cells. The information derived from such measurements reflects the average response of all the cells in a given recording area. Evoked potentials can be induced in appropriate areas of the brain when an appropriate stimulus is presented—for example, photic or auditory stimulation. The EEG is a tracing of the changes in voltage generated by the brain over time and represents the activity of millions of cells. EEG measurements can be taken from the surface of the skull or from electrodes implanted in specific areas of the brain.

In many cases a biphasic response in electrical activity is observed after ethanol treatment, with some neuronal types being depressed while others are excited. At low doses of ethanol, spontaneous electrical activity is elevated, whereas at high doses activity is reduced (Horsey & Akert, 1953; Hadji-Dimo, Edberg, & Ingvar, 1968). More specifically, spontaneous activity of spinal interneurons and motor neurons, cerebellar cortical and Purkinje cells, and cells of the lateral vestibular nucleus of the brainstem is depressed, while the activity of cerebellar interneurons and climbing fibers is increased (Eidelberg, 1971, Eidelberg, Bond, & Kelter, 1971; Rogers, Siggins, Schulman, & Bloom, 1980).

By using several physiological approaches, some areas of the brain have been found to be more sensitive to ethanol than others. In anesthetized cats, evoked potentials resulting from radial nerve stimulation and recorded in the reticular formation are more easily blocked by ethanol than those recorded in the primary somatosensory cortex (DiPerri, Dravid, Scherigerat, & Himwich, 1968). Evoked potentials recorded from the lateral funiculus of the spinal cord are more resistant to ethanol inhibition. With photic stimulation, evoked potentials recorded from the visual cortex are more easily inhibited than those recorded in the geniculate body of the thalamus.

Measurements of multiple-unit activity from different areas of the brain have also suggested a differential sensitivity to ethanol. With electrodes inserted in many areas of the brain, it has been determined that multiple-unit activity is most sensitive to ethanol in cortical areas of cerebral, cerebellar, and limbic origin (Klemm & Stevens, 1974; Klemm, Mallari, Dreyfus, Fisk, Forney, & Mikeska, 1976b; Hyvarinen, Laakso, Roine, Leinonen, & Sippel, 1978). At high doses, the effects of ethanol are inhibitory; but at low doses an increase in multiple-unit activity can be seen, especially in the limbic areas (Klemm, Dreyfus, Forney, & Mayfield, 1976a). Single-unit recordings have also demonstrated that the hippocampus is particularly sensitive to ethanol (Grupp & Perlanski, 1979). Also, a biphasic response after ethanol treatment similar to that obtained with multiple-unit recordings has been reported (Grupp, 1980).

On the whole, the experimental evidence does not conclusively support the notion that ethanol works first in the higher centers of the cerebral cortex; then, as blood and brain ethanol concentrations rise, subcortical and cerebellar areas become affected and finally the brainstem. This supposition had been based on the clinical observation that low doses of ethanol interfere with speech and cognitive functions, which are presumably mediated by the cerebral cortex. At higher doses, motor coordination is impaired, suggesting a site of action which is cerebellar in origin. Finally, at the highest doses, respiration and consciousness, controlled at the brainstem level, are depressed involving the brainstem. As previously stated, cells in the cerebellum and reticular formation, which is an area involved in arousal, are particularly sensitive to ethanol.

The difficulty in finding parallel observations at the cellular and behavioral levels may involve several factors. First of all, it is often difficult to distinguish between primary and secondary effects. Although a certain behavioral change would suggest that a particular area of the brain might be responsible for that effect, that area may be at the end of a neural network that originates somewhere else. The cells in this distant region could be especially sensitive to ethanol. Another factor relates to the fact that the activity of neurons depends on the algebraic summation of all excitatory and inhibitory input exerted on them. Depending on whether single- or multiple-unit recordings are employed, the response measured may represent one of these influences in a few cells or the average response of a larger number of cells. Since excitatory and inhibitory influences tend to cancel each other, different sensitivities of different neuronal populations may result in an average response that does not accurately reflect the sensitivity of single neuronal types. On the other hand, single-unit recordings usually represent the activity of a small percentage of the total number of cells and may not accurately reflect the mean activity of all the cells in the population.

3.2. Sleep Studies

One area of electrophysiological research on the effects of ethanol that has had considerable attention is the EEG and sleep (see reviews of Williams & Salamy, 1972; Mendelson, 1979). It has also been an area where it has been possible to obtain information from human subjects as well as experimental animals.

It is well accepted that sleep can be divided into several discrete stages related to EEG patterns, eye movements, and muscular tension. In an awake but resting stage, the EEG records voltage activity at 8 to 12 cps (alpha waves) and is asynchronous. At Stage 1 of sleep, lower-voltage synchronous recordings are obtained with frequencies of 4 to 6 cps (theta waves). After a few minutes and a gradual slowing in frequency, an increase in the amplitude of the EEG pattern, Stage 2, appears. At this point there are intermittent spindles of activity with frequencies of 12 to 15 cps and high-voltage patterns called K-complexes. These may represent momentary periods of arousal. As Stages 3 and 4 develop, a progressively greater incidence of high-voltage, low-frequency patterns (1 to 4 cps, delta waves) are observed. Movement through the first three stages is relatively rapid, with a progressive reduction in muscular tension, as shown by the electromyogram. Stage 4 lasts about one-half hour. At this point the EEG shifts back to low-voltage, higher-frequency patterns until it resembles a conscious state. However, the muscles are relaxed, and there is rapid movement of the eyes. This stage of sleep is called paradoxical or rapid eye movement (REM) sleep. Throughout a normal sleeping period, an oscillation between REM and non-REM sleep develops, with each cycle lasting about 90 to 100 min. As the cycle is repeated, the amount of time spent in non-REM sleep is reduced and that in REM sleep increases. REM sleep is a time during which dreaming occurs.

One of the earlier studies in which the effect of ethanol on sleep was performed utilized human subjects (Gresham, Webb, & Williams, 1963). Ethanol was administered to healthy volunteers for five nights. A consistent reduction in REM sleep was observed. Other investigations demonstrated similar results but provided more details. The inhibitory effect of ethanol on REM sleep appeared to occur only during the first half of the sleeping session (Yules, Freedman, & Chandler, 1966). In fact, a rebound in REM sleep was observed during the last half. Upon closer examination, it appeared that the reduction in REM sleep was related to the blood ethanol concentration, while the rebound in REM sleep was not (Yules, Lippman, & Freedman, 1967). With higher doses of ethanol, the rebound in REM sleep was not observed, and REM sleep was reduced throughout the sleeping period (Knowles, Laverty, & Knechler, 1968).

Studies with experimental animals have generally yielded results similar to those found in humans. Sleep latency is decreased, total sleep is increased, and REM sleep is reduced with no rebound (Yules, Ogden, Gault, & Freedman, 1966; Branchey, Begleiter, & Kissin, 1970; Mendelson & Hill, 1976). This reduced REM sleep is dose-dependent. To date no evidence as to the mechanism by which acute doses of ethanol disrupt REM sleep has been forwarded.

4. ETHANOL AND SYNAPTIC TRANSMISSION

4.1. Neurotransmitters

Communication between neurons in the nervous system is accomplished by the release of a chemical mediator called a neurotransmitter. A number of substances have been identified as neurotransmitters, although it appears likely that there are many more that have not yet been discovered. Over the last decade, increasing attention has been given to the role of neurotransmitters in mediating the behavioral effects of ethanol. However, unequivocal results have been difficult to obtain. When dose and time factors are taken into account, a clearer picture emerges.

The study of the effect of ethanol on neurotransmission has been approached by a number of means (see reviews of Feldstein, 1971; Lahti, 1975; Hunt & Majchrowicz, 1979). Before discussing the reports addressing ethanol–transmitter interactions, a brief summary of the rationale of these approaches will be given.

Initial studies involving transmitters usually begin with measurements of the endogenous concentrations in the whole brain or in regional structures. It should be emphasized that these concentrations represent the net concentration that results from the continuous process of synthesis and degradation through enzymatic reactions. This approach has the limitation that it would reflect alterations in the metabolic process but would not necessarily provide information on the degree of neural activity mediated by a given transmitter.

A procedure that is better designed to assess the degree of utilization of a transmitter involves the concept of turnover. "Turnover" is defined as the rate at which a given store of transmitter is replaced by newly synthesized transmitter. The assumption is that turnover provides an index of the activity of certain neurons. An increased turnover would suggest greater activity in a neural pathway, while a reduction in turnover would suggest less activity. Measurements of turnover have provided valuable information on neural function. However, some erroneous conclusions can be drawn from turnover experiments if some prerequisite conditions are not met—for example, if steady-state conditions are not established.

The ability of a transmitter to interact with its receptor, which leads to the initiation of electrical activity in the postsynaptic neuron, is one of the important factors in neurotransmission. Uptake and release of transmitter determine the availability of transmitter for interaction with receptors. Uptake into the presynaptic neuron is the process by which many transmitters are inactivated—that is, removed from receptor sites—thus terminating their action. Release is the actual event of ejecting the transmitter from its presynaptic storage compartments into the synaptic cleft.

The neurotransmitters that have received the most attention in ethanol research have been the catecholamines norepinephrine and dopamine. Although there does not appear to be any substantial effect of ethanol on the concentrations of these substances in the brain, profound alterations have been observed in their measured turnover rates following ethanol treatments. The most interesting aspect of ethanol's actions on catecholamine turnover is that the effect is biphasic. When a single dose of ethanol is administered, there is an initial acceleration of norepinephrine turnover followed by a subsequent reduction in turnover (Hunt & Majchrowicz, 1974a; Pohorecky & Jaffe, 1975). Similar results are obtained with dopamine turnover. After low doses of ethanol, dopamine turnover is elevated (Karoum, Wyatt, and Majchrowicz, 1976; Lai, Makous, Horita, & Leung, 1979), whereas, after high doses of ethanol, dopamine turnover is reduced (Hunt & Majchrowicz, 1974a; Bacopoulos, Bhatnager, & Van Orden, 1978). Dopamine release appears to be affected in the same manner. Release is increased at low doses and reduced at high doses (Darden & Hunt, 1977). All the above effects are closely related to the blood ethanol concentration.

The biphasic effects of ethanol on transmitter turnover are of particular interest because a similar biphasic effect in behavior occurs after ethanol administration, as discussed earlier. It would be tempting to suggest that the responses of catecholamine systems are somehow related to these behavioral changes. However, little information is available on this point. One study of interest does demonstrate that neurons in the locus coeruleus, an area of the brain involved in arousal, are inhibited by a 2-g/kg intraperitoneal dose of ethanol (Pohorecky & Brick, 1977). The locus coeruleus contains a large number of noradrenergic cell bodies.

Cholinergic function has also been shown to be affected by ethanol treatment. A number of studies in this area involved measurements of acetylcholine release, both *in vitro* (Kalant & Grose, 1967; Carmichael & Israel, 1975) and *in vivo* (Erickson & Graham, 1973; Morgan & Phillis, 1975). In all cases ethanol was able to depress acetylcholine release. In addition, EEG synchrony accompanied this reduction in release (Erickson & Graham, 1973). The data suggest that acetylcholine may be involved in ethanol-induced alterations in the EEG. Further support of this hypothesis comes from the observation that the cholinesterase inhibitor physostigmine, which would increase the amount of acetylcholine at its receptor, can block the development of EEG synchrony by ethanol treatment (Klemm, 1974; Erickson & Chai, 1976). The role of acetylcholine in ethanol-induced behavioral depression is not clear, since physostigmine could not antagonize this depression (Klemm, 1974; Graham & Erickson, 1974).

The effect of ethanol on cholinergic activity does not appear to be exclusively inhibitory. Using measurements of high-affinity choline uptake, which provides an index of acetylcholine release, cholinergic neurons in the caudate nucleus may be excited by ethanol (Hunt, Majchrowicz, & Dalton, 1979). This is seen only at high blood ethanol concentrations. Since dopamine release in the caudate nucleus is inhibited under these conditions (Darden & Hunt, 1977), the effect on choline uptake may reflect a lack of inhibitory input that nigrostriatal dopaminergic fibers normally provide on striatal cholinergic neurons.

Other neurotransmitters have been studied after ethanol treatment, but the results have not been as consistent as those obtained for catecholamines and acetylcholine. Reports addressing serotonin turnover have been inconclusive, showing an increase (Palaic, Desaty, Albert, & Panisset, 1971), decrease (Tyce, Flock, Taylor, & Owens, 1970; Hunt & Majchrowicz, 1974b), or no change (Kuriyama, Rauscher, & Sze, 1971; Frankel, Khanna, Kalant, & LeBlanc, 1974) following ethanol treatment. Differences in experimental designs have made it difficult to evaluate the discrepancies. However, a more recent study has shed light on the problem. When serotonin levels were examined at various times after ethanol treatment, it was found that a biphasic effect of ethanol was obtained (Badawy & Evans, 1976). At early time points, serotonin levels were elevated, while at later periods levels were reduced. More detailed studies of functional parameters related to serotonin activity might resolve these differences.

γ-Aminobutyric acid (GABA) is an inhibitory neurotransmitter that has also received some attention. After some conflicting reports on the effects of ethanol on GABA concentrations in the brain had appeared, it was found that there was also a biphasic effect of ethanol on GABA concentrations (Syntinsky, Guzikov, Gomanko, Eremin, & Konovalova, 1975). Thus, at low doses of ethanol, GABA concentrations were elevated, and at high doses they were reduced.

With a better understanding of how ethanol influences synaptic transmission, it may be possible to develop specific pharmacological approaches to the treatment of various behavioral and physiological maladies induced by ethanol.

4.2. Cyclic Nucleotides

Another area of neurotransmission that has been a focus of ethanol research is the cyclic nucleotides (see reviews of Volicer & Gold, 1975; Hunt, 1979). Cyclic nucleotides are substances that have been implicated as "second messengers" in the actions of neurotransmitters on their receptors (see reviews of Dismukes & Daly, 1976; Nathanson, 1977; Williams & Rodnight, 1977). It is now believed that in some cases, when a neurotransmitter interacts with its receptor, an accumulation of cyclic nucleotides occurs in postsynaptic cells. The cyclic nucleotide stimulates a cyclic nucleotide-dependent protein kinase, which, in turn, catalyzes the phosphorylation of proteins located in synaptosomal membranes. This phosphorylation is believed to change the conformation of the membrane in a manner that alters the ability of ions to pass through it and thus regulates its excitability. There are two known cyclic nucleotides in the brain, adenosine-3', 5'-cyclic monophosphate (cAMP) and guanosine-3', 5'-cyclic monophosphate (cGMP). These are derived from adenosine triphosphate (ATP) or guanosine triphosphate (GTP), respectively.

Considerable controversy surrounds the effect of ethanol on cAMP concentrations in the brain. Some laboratories have reported a reduction (Volicer & Gold, 1973; Volicer & Hurter, 1977; Shen, Pathman, Jacobyansky, & Thurman, 1977), while others could find no effect (Redos, Hunt, & Catravas, 1976; Breese, Lundberg, Mailman, Frye, & Mueller, 1979). The reasons for the discrepancies are not clear, but they appear to be related to methodology. Because cAMP is quite sensitive to postmortem changes, fairly sophisticated technology is required to minimize these changes. The conditions for these studies are possibly not yet optimal. A detailed discussion of the problems associated with these types of experiments can be found elsewhere (Hunt, 1979).

The effects of ethanol on cGMP are more consistent. Single doses deplete cGMP in most areas of the brain studied in a dose-dependent manner (Redos, Catravas, & Hunt, 1976; Hunt, Redos, Dalton, & Catravas, 1977; Volicer & Hurter, 1977). The effect can be quite dramatic, with cGMP concentrations reduced by as much as 95% under some experimental conditions. The effect is directly related to the blood ethanol concentrations. Full recovery is obtained once the ethanol has been eliminated.

The mechanisms that mediate the changes in cyclic nucleotide content are unknown. The activity of enzymes that are responsible for their synthesis and degradation are not directly affected by ethanol (Kuriyama & Israel, 1973; Hunt et al., 1977). Two other indirect possibilities could explain these observations. Alterations in neurotransmitter functions can lead to changes in cyclic nucleotide levels. If transmitter activity were to increase or decrease, a corresponding change in cyclic nucleotide levels would occur as well, responding to whatever need existed at the time. Since ethanol affects transmitter activity, changes in cyclic nucleotide concentrations could just reflect that. Another possibility may relate to the action of ethanol on membranes. Guanylate cyclase, the enzyme that catalyzes the synthesis of cGMP, is calcium-dependent. As pointed out earlier, ethanol disrupts calcium metabolism and in so doing could reduce calcium availability to modulate the reaction that converts GTP into cGMP.

Some recent experiments have suggested that cGMP levels in the brain can be a function of locomotor activity (Lundberg, Breese, Mailman, Frye, & Mueller, 1979). When animals were paralyzed with curare, cGMP concentrations decreased. In addition, the effect of ethanol on cGMP depletion was considerably reduced. It is possible, therefore, that the depletion of cGMP might be a consequence of depressed motor function by the action of ethanol on the brain. On the other hand, it cannot be ruled out that the depletion of cGMP mediates some aspect of behavioral depression.

5. ETHANOL AND METABOLISM

5.1. Intermediary Metabolism

Ethanol is a natural by-product of glucose metabolism by microorganisms and it is generally present in low concentrations in humans due to its production by the bacterial flora of the gut. When high concentrations of ethanol are imbibed, a number of alterations in intermediary metabolism of the brain have been observed (see reviews of Rawat, 1975; Reitz, 1979). The major effect of ethanol on intermediary metabolism is the suppression of glucose utilization. A single dose of ethanol increases glucose concentrations, reduces lactate and pyruvate concentrations, and decreases the conversion of ^{14}C-glucose into lactate and amino acids derived from the citric acid cycle (Flock, Tyce, & Owen, 1970; Roach & Reese, 1971; Veloso, Passanneau, & Veech, 1972). Also, there is a reduction in $^{14}CO_2$ formation, total CO_2, and oxygen uptake (Majchrowicz, 1965).

Two hypotheses have been advanced to explain these findings: (1) that the effect of ethanol is indirect and related to its metabolism and (2) that the effect of ethanol is related to its action on membranes.

When ethanol is metabolized by the liver, it is converted to acetaldehyde and then to acetate, with the reduction of NAD to NADH (see Li, this volume). Since much of the glycolytic pathway and citric acid cycle requires NAD to function normally, the depletion of NAD could inhibit glucose metabolism. This can occur in liver because there is an active alcohol dehydrogenase (ADH) there. However, there is little ADH in brain (Raskin & Sokoloff, 1968), it is difficult to conceive how such a shift in the overall redox state could occur. The possibility of a redox imbalance in brain has been tested directly in a number of laboratories, but the results have depended on methodology. When an animal is immersed in liquid nitrogen after ethanol treatment, the ratios of reduced oxidized redox pairs are increased and coenzyme A (CoA) and acetyl-CoA are reduced (Ammon, Estler, & Heim, 1969; Rawat & Kuriyama, 1972; Rawat, 1974). Furthermore, these changes could be blocked by the prior administration of pyrazole, an inhibitor of ADH. On the other hand, when brain tissue was obtained using the freeze-blowing technique, which inactivates the brain much faster than immersion in liquid nitrogen (Veech, Harris, Veloso, & Veech, 1973), these effects were not observed (Veloso et al., 1972; Guynn, 1976). The reasons for these discrepancies have not been determined.

Another approach to explaining the inhibition of glucose metabolism in the brain relates to the functioning of excitable membranes. An effect of ethanol on excitable membranes is suggested by the finding that, in vitro, the inhibition of intermediary metabolism occurs only if the tissue is stimulated (Majchrowicz, 1965). Thus, the metabolism in the neuron is not affected in the resting state but only when the neuron is excited. As discussed in Section 2.1, ethanol directly disrupts membrane function through changes in membrane fluidity. One consequence of this action appears to be a reduction in the transient inward sodium current accompanying excitation. With the subsequent reduction in ion transport, a relationship could be envisioned between ethanol–membrane interactions and ethanol-induced alterations in intermediary metabolism involving the degree of neuronal activity in the brain after ethanol treatment. Indeed, rates of glucose metabolism in the brain can vary widely and have been reported to range from 0.15 mmol/kg/min during anesthesia to 10 mmol/kg/min in the initial phase of convulsions (Balazs, 1970). A major function of intermediary metabolism in the brain is to provide, via glucose metabolism, the ATP needed for ion transport, which maintains the proper ion balance across excitable membranes. This ion transport is mediated by the Na-K ATPase. It has been estimated that 10% to 50% of the energy produced by cellular metabolism is used for ion transport (Whittam, 1961; Whittam, 1962). Consequently, the rate of glucose metabolism may change depending on the needs of the brain to maintain normal neuronal function.

5.2. Aberrant Neurotransmitters

One area that has been the object of a great deal of attention and controversy is the possible ethanol-induced formation of condensation products between dopa-

mine and its aldehyde metabolite or dopamine and acetaldehyde (see reviews of
Deitrich & Erwin, 1980; Hamilton & Hirst, 1980). A diagram of the relevant
metabolic pathways can be found in Figure 2. It has been known for some time
that ethanol treatment can lead to a shift in the peripheral metabolism of biogenic
amines from normally oxidative to reductive (Davis, Brown, Huff, & Cashaw,
1967a,b). It has been hypothesized that the aldehyde metabolite accumulates and
condenses with the amine to form complex alkaloids called tetrahydroisoquinolines (TIQs) (Davis & Walsh, 1970). A similar suggestion has been advanced
suggesting a reaction between biogenic amines and acetaldehyde (Cohen & Collins, 1970). Because some of the TIQs are intermediates in the formation of morphine in plants (Battersby, 1961), the possibility that alcohol and morphine
dependence are related in some way was postulated (Davis & Walsh, 1970).

A particularly interesting report has indicated that TIQs will induce ethanol
drinking in rats that normally do not drink ethanol. When TIQs were infused
chronically into the lateral ventricle for 14 days, the animals significantly
increased their preference for ethanol (Myers & Melchior, 1977; Melchior &
Myers, 1977). The most potent TIQ tested was tetrahydropapaveroline (THP).

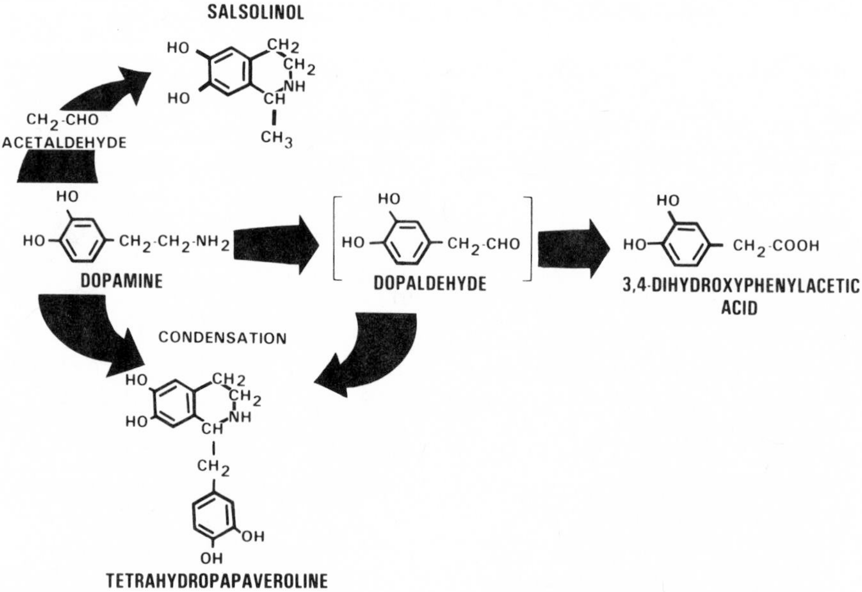

Figure 2. Pathways of the metabolism of dopamine to tetrahydroisoquinolines. The diagram shows
how acetaldehyde and dopaldehyde can condense with dopamine to form salsolinol and tetrahydropapaveroline, respectively. All possible reactions are not included.

In fact, one daily dose of THP for 14 days was sufficient to produce increased drinking (Myers & Oblinger, 1977). A single dose was ineffective. Reports from other laboratories have both supported and refuted these results (Duncan & Deitrich, 1980; Smith, Brown, & Amit, 1980). However, technical differences seem to account for the discrepancies (Myers, Melchior, & Swartzwelder, 1980). Although these findings are, on the surface, intriguing, their significance is not very clear. In any event, it would still be important to know why laboratory animals drink something they normally do not voluntarily consume.

The ultimate test of the relevance of these findings is the detection of TIQs in the brain after treatment with ethanol. There are, however, theoretical considerations to keep in mind (i.e., the availability of aldehyde intermediates of biogenic amines and acetaldehyde). Without these substances, TIQs cannot be formed. Not only must these precursors be present in the brain but their concentration must increase after ethanol treatment.

An increase in the aldehyde intermediates could come from a shift in central biogenic amine metabolism analogous to that obtained in the periphery after ethanol treatment. Several lines of evidence do not support this possibility. For the aldehydes to accumulate, the enzymes responsible for their metabolism, aldehyde dehydrogenase and/or aldehyde reductase, would have to be inhibited. Ethanol has not been reported to have any direct effect on these enzymes.

The presence of acetaldehyde, which has been shown to inhibit aldehyde dehydrogenase in the liver (Lahti & Majchrowicz, 1967), could lead to an accumulation of aldehyde intermediates or to a direct reaction with the parent amines to form TIQs. The question of whether acetaldehyde exists in any appreciable quantities in brain has been debated for some time (see review of Lindros, 1978). As pointed out earlier (Section 5.1), the brain has little ADH activity, making it difficult to picture how the brain could synthesize enough acetaldehyde to have any physiological consequences. A recent report, however, of the presence of a catalase in brain which will, in conjunction with hydrogen peroxide, metabolize ethanol to acetaldehyde, may revive this possibility (Cohen, Sinet, & Heikkila, 1980).

Acetaldehyde in the brain could, of course, be derived from peripheral sources. Most studies, however, find very little acetaldehyde in the brain (Sippel, 1974; Tabakoff, Anderson, & Ritzman, 1976; Eriksson & Sippel, 1977). In fact, very high concentrations must exist in the blood before acetaldehyde will accumulate in the brain (Sippel, 1974). Also, acetaldehyde is barely detectable in the cerebrospinal fluid of intoxicated alcoholics (Lindros & Hillbom, 1979). Thus, there would not seem to be enough precursor available to allow significant amounts of TIQs to form following ethanol ingestion.

There have been several attempts to detect the presence of TIQs in brain directly after chronic alcohol treatment. Because of expected low values, sophisticated technology has been employed, involving gas and liquid chromatography with electron capture and electrochemical detection, respectively, and mass spectrometry. The present limits of detection by these methods are 2 to 8 ng/g of brain. The administration of a single dose of ethanol did not lead to the formation of salsolinol (Collins & Bigdeli, 1975). However, if the animals were pretreated with pyrogallol, a catechol-O-methyltransferase inhibitor, salsolinol could be detected following ethanol administration (O'Neill & Rahwan, 1977; Riggin & Kissinger, 1977). In animals treated chronically with ethanol, salsolinol could not be detected under similar conditions. On the other hand, there has been one report indicating the presence of a compound that appears to be O-methylsalsolinol (Hamilton, Blum, & Hirst, 1978). However, this metabolite of salsolinol was not positively identified. It is possible, though, that TIQs are metabolized to other biologically active compounds.

At this point, there is promise that some of the actions of ethanol, such as the compulsion to drink ethanol, may be mediated by an aberrant metabolite. Much more research will be needed to demonstrate its importance.

6. CONSEQUENCES OF LONG-TERM ETHANOL CONSUMPTION

6.1. Clinical Effects

Long-term use of alcoholic beverages can lead to a number of problems in central nervous system function. The most prevalent is the development of tolerance and dependence on ethanol. This topic will be covered in another chapter (see Chapter 7). Another major area of chronic toxicity concerns the development of various neurological diseases (see reviews of Freund, 1973; Dreyfus, 1974; Freund, Chapter 6 of this volume). The study of the contribution of ethanol to the etiology of these diseases is confounded by the presence of other factors, such as malnutrition and the normal aging process.

Neurological disturbances resulting from chronic ethanol consumption fall into two general categories, consequences of (1) nutritional deficiencies and (2) organic brain damage. Wernicke's syndrome, the most commonly observed malady, appears to develop after a long-term deficiency of thiamine (vitamin B_1). This conclusion is based on successful treatment of the disease with B_1 vitamins (Phillips, Victor, Adams, & Davidson, 1952) and on its similarity to disorders related to malnutrition but unrelated to alcoholism (Victor, Adams, & Collins, 1971). Other disorders related to brain damage include Korsakoff's syndrome and cerebellar cortical degeneration. Further details on these diseases can be found elsewhere in this volume (see Chapter 6).

6.2. Animal Models for Brain Damage

Attempts have been made over the past few years to reproduce in experimental animals some of the abnormalities that are observed in long-term alcoholics. The most direct studies have examined the effect of chronic ethanol consumption on the morphology of neurons in the hippocampus and cerebellum. These areas were chosen because of their involvement with learning, memory, and motor coordination. If rats were permitted to consume a nutritionally balanced diet containing ethanol for four months, the number of dendritic spines on hippocampal pyramidal cells and granule cells in the dentate gyrus were reduced (Riley & Walker, 1978). After five months of ethanol consumption, there was a significant loss of both hippocampal pyramidal and cerebellar Purkinje cells (Walker, Barnes, Zornetzer, Hunter, & Kubanis, 1980; Walker, Barnes, Riley, Hunter, & Zornetzer, 1980). Under similar experimental conditions, the ability to learn a shock-avoidance task, timing behavior, and problem-solving abilities are considerably reduced (Freund, 1970; Walker & Freund, 1973; Bond & DiGiusto, 1976). These results demonstrate that, in experimental animals, ethanol can have a direct neurotoxic effect in spite of adequate nutrition.

The mechanism by which ethanol can damage cells is unknown. One thought is that the site of action is at the level of the membrane (French, 1971). One way membrane defects have been studied is through the assessment of the ability of neurotransmitters to interact with their receptors. This can be done with the use of radiolabeled ligands which specifically bind to the desired receptor. In one study, rats consumed ethanol in a nutritionally balanced diet for 18 weeks and displayed an increased density of muscarinic cholinergic receptors with a concomitant reduction in choline acetylase activity, the enzyme responsible for acetylcholine synthesis (Pelham, Marquis, Kuglemann, & Munsat, 1980). The effects remained for at least four weeks after ethanol withdrawal and were found in the caudate nucleus and mammillary bodies but not in the cerebral cortex or hippocampus. After 13 months of ethanol consumption, the density of dopaminergic receptors in the caudate nucleus was also reduced. Since dopaminergic fibers in the basal ganglia synapse onto cholinergic fibers, the data were interpreted to reflect cellular damage. After short-term ethanol treatment that has not been demonstrated to induce brain damage, the changes in receptor binding have not been observed (Hunt & Dalton, 1981).

Another interesting study addressed the possibility that brain damage could contribute to increased drinking due to a higher level of anxiety resulting from a reduced density of anxiolytic receptors (Freund, 1980). It is now known that benzodiazepines, which are common tranquilizers, interact with a specific receptor which, presumably, is normally acted upon by some naturally occurring endogenous ligand. It was reasoned that if brain damage following chronic ethanol consumption reduced these receptors, a higher level of anxiety might result, thereby increasing the level of drinking in order to relieve this anxiety. To test this possibility, mice were allowed to consume ethanol in a nutritionally balanced diet for seven months, followed by one month of abstinence. It was found that both the density and affinity of benzodiazepine receptors were reduced (Freund, 1980). Although the drinking patterns of these animals were not reported, this study provides some very interesting clues for further research in this area. Again, short-term ethanol treatment did not lead to changes in ^{3}H-diazepam binding (Karobath, Rogers, & Bloom, 1980).

Other studies that indicate a number of biochemical or metabolic changes after chronic ethanol treatment have appeared. However, for the most part, the role of these changes in brain damage has not been apparent. An area that may have relevance is the study of ethanol's effects on protein and RNA metabolism in brain (Tewari & Noble, 1979). Prolonged ethanol treatment inhibits incorporation of amino acids into protein; the site of inhibition was found to be at the level of the ribosome, the place where amino acids are attached to a lengthening protein chain. Amino acids are first bound to a tRNA before protein synthesis can take place. It is this reaction that is reduced by chronic ethanol administration. Also suppressed is the synthesis of mRNA, which contains the genetic code for the synthesis of a specific protein. It is possible, then, that ethanol administration interrupts the normal synthesis of important cell constituents and that the loss of these constituents ultimately contributes to cell death.

7. SUMMARY

Ethanol has a most profound effect on the central nervous system. It acts as a depressant of neural function in a number of ways, an effect that is made obvious by ethanol's disruption of behavior. Apparent stimulatory effects—which include feelings of euphoria, talkativeness, and relief of tension—are observed after low doses of ethanol. Aggressiveness can also be seen after ethanol consumption. The stimulatory responses reflect the suppression of inhibitory influences in the brain (disinhibition) or possibly direct neuronal stimulation and are blocked when greater amounts of ethanol are consumed. With increasing doses of ethanol, there is a progressive reduction in motor coordination, including disturbances in gait, equilibrium, and reaction time. Learning, memory, and speech are impaired as well. Hangover can be experienced after a drinking session and is characterized by headache and nausea. It may result from congeners in alcoholic beverages or may be the expression of a mild withdrawal syndrome.

The mechanism by which ethanol exerts its action on the brain is not well understood. Its primary site of action appears to be on excitable membranes in the brain. The available evidence suggests that the fluidity of membranes is increased by ethanol, resulting in a reduction in the transient inward sodium conductance that accompanies nerve stimulation. Also, calcium metabolism is altered by ethanol, and this phenomenon may have an effect on the electrical stability of the membrane.

The action of ethanol on the brain has been studied by several disciplines in order to gain insight into what causes the depression in neural activity. Electrophysiological techniques have shown that cellular activity is reduced in the brain, with some areas being more sensitive to ethanol than others. Sleep is disrupted and a reduction in REM sleep is observed after ethanol consumption.

Synaptic transmission is altered by the actions of ethanol. At high doses of ethanol, neurotransmitter activity tends to be depressed; but because of complexities of neuronal interactions, this effect is not always evident.

Biphasic behavioral effects seen after consumption of ethanol do have their parallels in cellular activity and transmitter turnover. Turnover of some of the transmitters, particularly the catecholamines, is increased at low doses of ethanol but reduced at high doses.

Furthermore, a result of lower neural activity may be coupled to a decrease in the rate of intermediary metabolism. This is seen as a decreased utilization of glucose and may reflect a changing need for glucose, whose metabolism provides the supply of energy for ion translocation. Other alterations in metabolism may lead to the formation of complex alkaloids, called tetrahydroisoquinolines, which may in some way initiate and perpetuate excessive ethanol consumption. Still quite controversial, their ultimate importance is far from proven.

Long-term consumption of alcoholic beverages can lead to a number of pathologic conditions of the brain. Among them are a number of neurological diseases, such as Wernicke-Korsakoff syndrome, and organic brain damage. Some of these diseases result from nutritional deficiencies, while others result from a direct neurotoxic effect of ethanol. Studies in both humans and experimental animals have demonstrated the presence of cerebral atrophy after long-term ethanol consumption and the loss of cells in certain parts of the brain, especially the hippocampus and cerebellum. Other investigations suggest that the loss of certain receptors specific for a given neurotransmitter or other biologically active substances might contribute to some of the medical complications associated with chronic ethanol usage.

8. REFERENCES

Akera, T., Reech, R. H., Marquis, W. J., Tobin, T., & Brody, T. M. Lack of relationship between brain ($Na^+ + K^+$) activated adenosine triphosphatase and the development of tolerance to ethanol in rats. *Journal of Pharmacology and Experimental Therapeutics,* 1973, *185,* 594–601.

Alkana, R. L., & Malcolm, R. D. Comparison of the effects of acute alcohol intoxication on behavior in humans and other animals. In K. Eriksson, J. D. Sinclair, & K. Kiianmaa (Eds.), *Animal models in alcohol research.* London: Academic Press, 1980.

Ammon, H. P. T., Estler, C. J., & Heim, F. Inactivation of coenzyme-A by ethanol: 1. Acetaldehyde as mediator of the inactivation of coenzyme-A following the administration of ethanol *in vivo*. *Biochemical Pharmacology*, 1969, *18*, 29–33.

Armstrong, C. M., & Binstock, L. The effects of several alcohols on the properties of the squid giant axon. *Journal of General Physiology*, 1964, *48*, 265–277.

Bacopoulos, N. G., Bhatnagar, R. K., & Van Orden, L. S. III. The effects of subhypnotic doses of ethanol on regional catecholamine turnover. *Journal of Pharmacology and Experimental Therapeutics*, 1978, *204*, 1–10.

Badawy, A. A., & Evans, M. The role of free serum tryptophan in the biphasic effect of acute ethanol administration on the concentrations of rat brain tryptophan, 5-hydroxytryptamine and 5-hydroxyindol-3-ylacetic acid. *Biochemical Journal*, 1976, *160*, 315–324.

Balazs, R. Carbohydrate metabolism. In A. Lajtha, (Ed.), *Handbook of Neurochemistry* (Vol. 3). New York: Plenum Press, 1970.

Barry, H. III. Behavioral manifestations of ethanol intoxication and physical dependence. In E. Majchrowicz & E. P. Noble (Eds.), *Biochemistry and pharmacology of ethanol* (Vol. 2). New York: Plenum Press, 1979.

Battersby, A. R. Alkaloid biosynthesis. *Quarterly Reviews*, 1961, *25*, 259–286.

Begleiter, H., & Platz, A. The effects of alcohol on the central nervous system in humans. In B. Kissin & A. Begleiter (Eds.), *The biology of alcoholism*. New York: Plenum Press, 1972.

Bergmann, M. C., Klee, M. R., & Faber, D. S. Different sensitivities to ethanol of three early transient voltage clamp currents of Aplysia neurons. *Pflugers Archives and European Journal of Physiology*, 1974, *248*, 139–153.

Boggan, W. O., Meyer, J. S., Middaugh, L. D., & Sparks, D. L. Ethanol, calcium and naloxone in mice. *Alcoholism: Clinical and Experimental Research*, 1979, *3*, 158–161.

Bond, N. W., & DiGiusto. Impairment of Hebb–Williams maze performance following prolonged alcohol consumption in rats. *Pharmacology, Biochemistry and Behavior*, 1970, *5*, 85–86.

Branchey, M. H., Begleiter, H., & Kissin, B. The effects of various doses of alcohol on sleep in the rat. *Communications in Behavioral Biology*, 1970, *5*, 75–79.

Breese, G. R., Lundberg, D. B. A., Mailman, R. B., Frye, G. D., & Mueller, R. A. Effect of ethanol on cyclic nucleotides *in vivo*: Consequences of controlling motor and respiratory changes. *Drug and Alcohol Dependence*, 1979, *4*, 321–326.

Burns, M., & Moskowitz, H. Psychophysical tests for DWI arrests, *DOT Publication HS-802424*, National Technical Information Service, Virginia, 1977.

Carmichael, F. J., & Israel, Y. Effects of ethanol on neurotransmitter release by rat brain cortical slices. *Journal of Pharmacology and Experimental Therapeutics*, 1975, *193* 824–843.

Carpenter, J. A., & Armenti, N. P. Some effects of ethanol on human sexual and aggressive behavior. In B. Kissin & H. Begleiter (Eds.), *The biology of alcoholism* (Vol. 2). New York: Plenum Press, 1972.

Chapman, L. F. Experimental induction of hangover. *Quarterly Journal of Studies on Alcohol, Supplement*, 1970, *5*, 67–86.

Chignell, C. F. New applications of electron spin resonance to problems in biochemistry and pharmacology. *Life Sciences*, 1973, *13*, 1299–1314.

Chin, J. H., & Goldstein, D. B. Effects of low concentrations of ethanol on the fluidity of spin-labeled erythrocyte and brain membranes. *Molecular Pharmacology*, 1977, *13*, 435–441.

Cohen, G., & Collins, M. Alkaloids from catecholamines in adrenal tissue: Possible role in alcoholism. *Science*, 1970, *167*, 1749–1751.

Cohen, G., Sinet, P. M., & Heikkila, R. Ethanol oxidation by rat brain *in vivo*. *Alcoholism: Clinical and Experimental Research*, 1980, *4*, 366–370.

Collins, M. A., & Bigdeli, M. G. Tetrahydroisoquinolines *in vivo*. I. Rat brain formation of salsolinol, a condensation product of dopamine and acetaldehyde under certain conditions during ethanol intoxication. *Life Sciences*, 1975, *16*, 585–602.

Cooke, W. J., & Robinson, J. D. Factors influencing calcium movements in rat brain slices. *American Journal of Physiology*, 1971, *221*, 218–225.

Damrau, F., & Liddy, E. Hangovers and whiskey congeners: Comparison of whiskey and vodka. *Journal of National Medical Association*, 1960, *52*, 262–265.

Darden, J. H., & Hunt, W. A. Reduction of striatal dopamine release during an ethanol withdrawal syndrome. *Journal of Neurochemistry*, 1977, *29*, 1143–1145.

Davis, V. E., Brown, H., Huff, J. A., & Cashaw, J. L. Ethanol-induced alterations of norepinephrine in man. *Journal of Laboratory and Clinical Medicine*, 1967, *69*, 787–797. (a)

Davis, V. E., Brown, H., Huff, J. A., & Cashaw, J. L. The alteration of serotonin metabolism to 5-hydroxytryptophol by ethanol ingestion in man. *Journal of Laboratory and Clinical Medicine*, 1967, *69*, 132–140. (b)

Davis, V. E., & Walsh, M. J. Alcohol, amines, and alkaloids: A possible biochemical basis for alcohol addiction. *Science*, 1970, *167*, 1005–1007.

Deitrich, R., & Erwin, V. Biogenic amine-aldehyde condensation products: Tetrahydroisoquinolines and tryptolines (β-carbolines). *Annual Reviews of Pharmacology and Toxicology*, 1980, *20*, 55–80.

DiPerri, R. Dravid, A. Scherigerat, A., & Himwich, H. F. Effects of alcohol on evoked potentials of various parts of the central nervous system of the cat. *Quarterly Journal of Studies on Alcoholism*, 1968, *29*, 20–37.

Dismukes, R. K., & Daly, J. W. Adaptive responses of brain cyclic AMP-generating systems to alterations in synaptic input. *Journal of Cyclic Nucleotide Research*, 1976, *2*, 321–336.

Dreyfus, P. M. Diseases of the nervous system in chronic alcoholics. In B. Kissin & H. Begleiter (Eds.), *The biology of alcoholism* (Vol. 3). New York: Plenum Press, 1974.

Duncan, C., & Deitrich, R. A. A critical evaluation of tetrahydroisoquinoline induced ethanol preference in rats. *Pharmacology, Biochemistry and Behavior*, 1980, *13*, 265–282.

Eidelberg, E. Effects of ethanol upon central nervous system neurons. In N. K. Mello & J. H. Mendelson (Eds.), *Recent advances in studies of alcoholism*. Washington, D.C.: U.S. Government Printing Office, 1971.

Eidelberg, E., Bond, M. L., & Kelter, A. Effects of alcohol on cerebellar and vestibular neurons. *Archives Internationales de Pharmacodynamie et de Therapie*, 1971, *152*, 213–214.

Ekman, G., Frankenhauser, M., Goldberg, H., Bjerver, K., Jarpe, G., & Myrsten, A. H. Effects of alcohol intake on subjective and objective variables over a five-hour period. *Psychopharmacologia (Berl.)*, 1963, *4*, 23–28.

Erickson, C. K., & Chai, K. J. Cholinergic modification of ethanol-induced electroencephalographic synchrony in the rat. *Neuropharmacology*, 1976, *15*, 39–43.

Erickson, C. K., & Graham, D. J. The alteration of cortical and reticular acetylcholine release by ethanol *in vivo*. *Journal of Pharmacology and Experimental Therapeutics*, 1973, *185*, 583–593.

Eriksson, C. J. P., & Sippel, H. W. The distribution and metabolism of acetaldehyde in rats during ethanol oxidation-I. The distribution of acetaldehyde in liver, brain, blood and breath. *Biochemical Pharmacology*, 1977, *26*, 241–247.

Feldstein, A. Effect of ethanol on neurohumoral amine metabolism. In B. Kissin & H. Begleiter (Eds.), *The biology of alcoholism* (Vol. 1). New York: Plenum Press, 1971.

Ferko, A. P., & Bobyock, E. A. study on regional brain calcium concentrations following acute and prolonged administration of ethanol in rats. *Toxicology and Applied Pharmacology*, 1980, *55*, 179–187.

Flock, E. V., Tyce, G. M., & Owen, C. A., Jr. Effects of ethanol on glucose utilization in rat brain. *Proceedings of the Society for Experimental Biology and Medicine*, 1970, *135*, 325–333.

Frankel, D., Khanna, J. M., Kalant, H., & LeBlanc, A. E. Effect of acute and chronic ethanol administration on serotonin turnover in rat brain. *Psychopharmacologia (Berl.)*, 1974, *37*, 91–100.

Franks, H. M., Hensley, V. R., Hensley, W. J., Starmer, G. A., & Teo, R. K. The relationship between alcohol dosage and performance decrement in humans. *Journal of Studies on Alcoholism*, 1976, *37*, 284–297.

French, S. W. Acute and chronic toxicity of alcohol. In B. Kissin & H. Begleiter (Eds.), *The biology of alcoholism* (Vol. 1). New York: Plenum Press, 1971.

Freund, G. Impairment of shock avoidance learning after long-term alcohol ingestion in mice. *Science*, 1970, *168*, 1599–1601.

Freund, G. Chronic central nervous system toxicity of alcohol. *Annual Reviews of Pharmacology*, 1973, *13*, 217–227.

Freund, G. Benzodiazepine receptor loss in brains of mice after chronic alcohol consumption. *Life Sciences*, 1980, *27*, 987–992.

Goldstein, D. B., & Israel, Y. Effects of ethanol on mouse brain (Na + K)- activated adenosine triphosphatase. *Life Sciences*, 1972, *11*, 957–963.

Graham, D. T., & Erickson, C. K. Alteration of ethanol-induced CNS depression: Ineffectiveness of drugs that modify cholinergic transmission. *Psychopharmacologia (Berl.)*, 1974, *34*, 173–180.

Grenell, R. G. Effects of alcohol on the neuron. In B. Kissin & H. Begleiter (Eds.), *The biology of alcoholism* (Vol. 2). New York: Plenum Press, 1972.

Gresham, S. C., Webb, W. B., & Williams, R. L. Alcohol and caffeine: Effect on inferred visual dreaming. *Science*, 1963, *140*, 1266–1267.

Grupp, L. A. Biphasic action of ethanol on single units of the dorsal hippocampus and the relationship to the cortical EEG. *Psychopharmacology*, 1980, *70*, 95–103.

Grupp, L. A., & Perlanski, E. Ethanol-induced changes in the spontaneous activity of single units in the hippocampus of the awake rat: A dose–response study. *Neuropharmacology*, 1979, *18*, 63–70.

Guynn, R. W. Effect of ethanol on brain CoA and acetyl-CoA. *Journal of Neurochemistry*, 1976, *27*, 303–304.

Hadji-Dimo, A. A., Edberg, R., & Ingvar, D. H. Effects of ethanol on EEG and cortical blood flow in the cat. *Quarterly Journal of Studies on Alcoholism*, 1968, *29*, 828–838.

Hamilton, M. G., Blum, K., & Hirst, M. Identification of an isoquinoline alkaloid after chronic exposure to ethanol. *Alcoholism: Clinical and Experimental Research*, 1978, *2*, 133–137.

Hamilton, M. G., & Hirst, M. Alcohol-related tetrahdroisoquinolines: Pharmacology and identification. *Substance and Alcohol Actions/Misuse*, 1980, *1*, 121–144.

Himwich, H. E., & Callison, D. A. The effects of alcohol on evoked potentials of various parts of the central nervous system of the cat. In B. Kissin & H. Begleiter (Eds.), *The biology of alcoholism* (Vol. 2). New York: Plenum Press, 1972.

Horsey, W. J. & Akert, K. The influence of ethyl alcohol on the spontaneous electrical activity of the cerebral cortex and subcortical structures of the cat. *Quarterly Journal of Studies on Alcohol*, 1953, *14*, 363–377.

Hunt, W. A. The effects of aliphatic alcohols on the biophysical and biochemical correlates of membrane function. In E. Majchrowicz (Ed.), *Biochemical pharmacology of ethanol*. New York: Plenum Press, 1975.

Hunt, W. A. Effects of acute and chronic administration of ethanol on cyclic nucleotides and related systems. In E. Majchrowicz & E. P. Noble (Eds.), *Biochemistry and pharmacology of ethanol* (Vol. 2). New York: Plenum Press, 1979.

Hunt, W. A., & Dalton, T. K. Neurotransmitter–receptor binding in various brain regions in ethanol-dependent rats. *Pharmacology, Biochemistry and Behavior*, 1981, *14*, 733–739.

Hunt, W. A., & Majchrowicz, E. Alterations in the turnover of brain norepinephrine and dopamine in alcohol-dependent rats. *Journal of Neurochemistry*, 1974, *23*, 549–552. (a)

Hunt, W. A., & Majchrowicz, E. Turnover rates and steady-state levels of brain serotonin in alcohol-dependent rats. *Brain Research*, 1974, *72*, 181–184. (b)

Hunt, W. A. & Majchrowicz, E. Alterations in neurotransmitter function after acute and chronic treatment with ethanol. In E. Majchrowicz & E. P. Noble (Eds.), *Biochemistry and pharmacology of ethanol* (Vol. 2). New York: Plenum Press, 1979.

Hunt, W. A., Majchrowicz, E., & Dalton, T. K. Alterations in high-affinity choline uptake in brain after acute and chronic ethanol treatment. *Journal of Pharmacology and Experimental Therapeutics*, 1979, *210*, 259–263.

Hunt, W. A., Redos, J. D., Dalton, T. K., & Catravas, G. N. Alterations in brain guanosine-3′,5′-cyclic monophosphate levels after acute and chronic treatment with ethanol. *Journal of Pharmacology and Experimental Therapeutics*, 1977, *201*, 103–109.

Hyvarinen, J., Laakso, M., Roine, R., Leinonen, L., & Sippel, H. Effect of ethanol on neuronal activity in the parietal association cortex of alert monkeys. *Brain*, 1978, *101*, 701–715.

Israel, Y., Kalant, H., & Laufer, I. Effect of ethanol on microsomal Na-K ATPase activity. *Biochemical Pharmacology*, 1965, *14*, 1803–1814.

Israel, Y., Kalant, H., & LeBlanc, A. E. Effects of lower alcohols on potassium transport and microsomal adenosine triphosphatase activity of rat cerebral cortex. *Biochemical Journal*, 1966, *100*, 27–33.

Israel, Y., Kalant, H., LeBlanc, E., Bernstein, J. C., & Salazar, I. Changes in cation transport and (Na + K)-activated adenosine triphosphatase produced by chronic administration of ethanol. *Journal of Pharmacology and Experimental Therapeutics*, 1970, *174*, 330–336.

Kalant, H. Absorption, diffusion, distribution and elimination of ethanol: Effects on biological membranes. In B. Kissin & H. Begleiter (Eds.), *The biology of alcoholism* (Vol. 1). New York: Plenum Press, 1971.

Kalant, H., & Grose, W. Effects of ethanol and pentobarbital on release of acetylcholine from cerebral cortex slices. *Journal of Pharmacology and Experimental Therapeutics*, 1967, *158*, 386–393.

Karobath, M., Rogers, J., & Bloom, F. Benzodiazepine receptors remain unchanged after chronic ethanol administration. *Neuropharmocology*, 1980, *19*, 125–128.

Karoum, F., Wyatt, R. J., & Majchrowicz, E. Brain concentrations of biogenic amine metabolites in acutely treated and ethanol-dependent rats. *British Journal of Pharmacology*, 1976, *56*, 403–411.

Klemm, W. R. Dissociation of EEG and behavioral effects of ethanol provide evidence for a non-cholinergic basis of intoxication. *Nature*, 1974, *251*, 234–236.

Klemm, W. R. Effects of ethanol on nerve impulse activity. In E. Majchrowicz & E. P. Noble (Eds.), *Biochemistry and pharmacology of ethanol* (Vol. 2). New York: Plenum Press, 1979, 243–267.

Klemm, W. R., & Stevens, R. E. III. Alcohol effects on EEG and multiple-unit activity in various brain regions of rats. *Brain Research*, 1974, *70*, 361–368.

Klemm, W. R., Dreyfus, L. R., Forney, E., & Mayfield, M. A. Differential effects of low doses of ethanol on the impulse activity in various regions of the limbic system. *Psychopharmacology*, 1976, *50*, 131–138.

Klemm, W. R., Mallari, C. G., Dreyfus, L. R., Fiske, J. C., Forney, E., & Mikeska, J. A. Ethanol-induced regional and dose-dependent differences in multiple-unit activity in rabbits. *Psychopharmacology*, 1976, *49*, 235–244.

Knowles, J. B., Laverty, S. G., & Knechler, H. A. Effects of alcohol on REM sleep. *Quarterly Journal of Studies on Alcohol*, 1968, *29*, 342–349.

Kuriyama, K., & Israel, M. A. Effect of ethanol administration on cyclic 3′, 5′-adenosine monophosphate metabolism in brain. *Biochemical Pharmacology*, 1973, *22*, 2919–2922.

Kuriyama, K., Rauscher, G. E., & Sze, P. Y. Effect of acute and chronic administration of ethanol on the 5-hydroxytryptamine turnover and tryptophan hydroxylase activity of the mouse brain. *Brain Research*, 1971, *26*, 450–454.

Lahti, R. A. Alcohol, aldehydes and biogenic amines. In E. Majchrowicz (Ed.), *Biochemical Pharmacology of ethanol*. New York: Plenum Press, 1975, 239–253.

Lahti, R. A., & Majchrowicz, E. The effects of acetaldehyde on serotonin metabolism. *Life Sciences*, 1967, *6*, 1399–1406.

Lai, H., Makous, W. L., Horita, A., & Leung, H. Effects of ethanol on turnover and function of striatal dopamine. *Psychopharmacology*, 1979, *61*, 1–9.

Lindbohm, R., & Wallgren, H. Changes in respiration of rat brain cortex slices induced by some aliphatic alcohols. *Acta Pharmacologica et Toxicologica*, 1962, *19*, 53–58.

Lindros, K. O. Acetaldehyde—Its metabolism and role in the actions of alcohol. In Y. Israel, F. B. Glaser, H. Kalant, R. E. Popham, W. Schmidt, & R. G. Smart, (Eds.), *Research advances in alcohol and drug problems* (Vol. 4). New York: Plenum Press, 1978.

Lindros, K. O., & Hillbom, M. E. Acetaldehyde in cerebrospinal fluid: Its near-absence in ethanol-intoxicated alcoholics. *Medical Biology*, 1979, *57*, 246–247.

Logue, P. E., Gentry, W. D., Linnoila, M., & Erwin, C. W. Effect of alcohol consumption on state anxiety change in male and female nonalcoholics. *American Journal of Psychiatry*, 1978, *135*, 1079–1081.

Lundberg, D. B. A., Breese, G. R., Mailman, R. B., Frye, G. D., & Mueller, R. A. Depression of some drug-induced *in vivo* changes of cerebellar guanosine-3′,5′-monophosphate by control of motor respiratory responses. *Molecular Pharmacology*, 1979, *15*, 246–256.

Lyon, R. C., Schreurs, J., & Goldstein, O. B. Disordering of spin-labeled synaptosomal plasma membranes by several short-chain alcohols. *Drug and Alcohol Dependence*, 1980, *6*, 69–70.

Majchrowicz, E. Effects of aliphatic alcohols and aldehydes on the metabolism of potassium-stimulated rat brain cortex slices. *Canadian Journal of Biochemistry*, 1965, *43*, 1041–1051.

McCreery, M. J., & Hunt, W. A. Physicochemical correlates of alcohol intoxication. *Neuropharmacology*, 1978, *17*, 451–462.

McQuarrie, D. G., & Fingl, E. Effects of single dose and chronic administration of ethanol on experimental seizures in mice. *Journal of Pharmacology and Experimental Therapeutics*, 1958, *124*, 264–271.

Melchior, C. L., & Myers, R. D. Preference for alcohol evoked by tetrahydropapaveroline (THP) chronically infused in the cerebral ventricle of the rat. *Pharmacology, Biochemistry, and Behavior*, 1977, *7*, 19–35.

Mendelson, W. B. Pharmacologic and electrophysiologic effects of ethanol in relation to sleep. In E. Majchrowicz & E. P. Noble (Eds.), *Biochemistry and pharmacology of ethanol* (Vol. 2). New York: Plenum Press, 1979, 467–484.

Mendelson, W., & Hill, S. Y. A dose-response study of the acute effects of ethanol on the sleep of rats. *Sleep Research*, 1976, *5*, 75.

Michaelis, E. K., & Myers, S. L. Calcium binding to brain synaptosomes: Effects of chronic ethanol intake. *Biochemical Pharmacology*, 1979, *28*, 2081–2087.

Moore, J. W., Ulbricht, W., & Takata, M. Effect of ethanol on the sodium and potassium conductance of the squid axon membrane. *Journal of General Physiology*, 1964, *48*, 279–295.

Morgan, E. P., & Phillis, J. W. The effects of ethanol on acetylcholine release from the brain of unanesthetized cats. *General Pharmacology*, 1975, *6*, 281–284.

Myers, R. D., & Melchior, C. L. Alcohol drinking: Abnormal intake caused by tetrahydropapaveroline in brain. *Science*, 1977, *196*, 554–556.

Myers, R. D., & Oblinger, M. M. Alcohol drinking in the rat induced by acute intracerebral infusion of two tetrahydroisoquinolines and a β-carboline. *Drug and Alcohol Dependence*, 1977, *2*, 469–483.

Myers, R. D., Melchior, C., & Swartzwelder, H. S. Amine-aldehyde metabolites and alcoholism: Fact, myth or uncertainty? *Substance and Alcohol Actions/Misuse*, 1980, *1*, 223–238.

Nathanson, J. A. Cyclic nucleotides and nervous system function. *Physiological Reviews*, 1977, *57*, 157–256.

O'Neill, P. J., & Rahwan, R. G. Absence of formation of brain salsolinol in ethanol-dependent mice. *Journal of Pharmacology and Experimental Therapeutics*, 1977, *200*, 306–313.

Palaic, D. J., Desaty, J., Albert, J. M., & Panisset, J. C. Effect of ethanol on metabolism and subcellular distribution of serotonin in rat brain. *Brain Research*, 1971, *25*, 381–386.

Parker, E. S., Birnbaum, I. M., Weingartner, H., Hartley, J. T., Stillman, R. C., & Wyatt, R. J. Retrograde enhancement of human memory with alcohol. *Psychopharmacology*, 1980, *69*, 219–222.

Pelham, R. W., Marquis, J. K., Kugelmann, K., & Munsat, T. L. Prolonged ethanol consumption produces persistent alterations of cholinergic function in rat brain. *Alcoholism: Clinical and Experimental Research*, 1980, *4*, 282–287.

Perrine, M. W. Alcohol and highway crashes: Closing the gap between epidemiology and experimentation. *Modern Problems of Pharmacopsychiatry*, 1976, *11*, 23–41.

Phillips, G. B., Victor, M., Adams, R. D., & Davidson, C. S. A study of the nutritional defect in Wernicke's syndrome. *Journal of Clinical Investigation*, 1952, *31*, 859–871.

Pohorecky, L. A. Biphasic action of ethanol. *Biobehavioral Reviews*, 1977, *1*, 231–240.

Pohorecky, L. A., & Brick, J. Activity of neurons in the locus coeruleus of the rat: Inhibition by ethanol. *Brain Research*, 1977, *131*, 174–179.

Pohorecky, L. A., & Jaffe, L. S. Noradrenergic involvement in the acute effects of ethanol. *Research Communications in Chemical Pathology and Pharmacology*, 1975, *12*, 433–448.

Rang, H. P. Unspecific drug action: The effects of a homologous series of primary alcohols. *British Journal of Pharmacology*, 1960, *15*, 185–200.

Raskin, N. H., & Sokoloff, L. Brain alcohol dehydrogenase. *Science*, 1968, *162*, 131–132.

Rawat, A. K. Brain levels and turnover rates of presumptive neurotransmitters as influenced by administration and withdrawal of ethanol in mice. *Journal of Neurochemistry*, 1974, *22*, 915–922.

Rawat, A. K. Effects of ethanol on brain metabolism. In E. Majchrowicz (Ed.), *Biochemical Pharmacology of ethanol*. New York: Plenum Press, 1975.

Rawat, A. K., & Kuriyama, K. Ethanol oxidation: Effect on the redox state of brain in mouse. *Science*, 1972, *176*, 1133–1135.

Redos, J. O., Catravas, G. N., & Hunt, W. A. Ethanol-induced depletion of cerebellar guanosine-3',5'-cyclic monophosphate levels. *Science*, 1976, *193*, 58–59.

Redos, J. D., Hunt, W. A., & Catravas, G. N. Lack of alteration in regional brain adenosine-3',5'-cyclic monophosphate levels after acute and chronic treatment with ethanol. *Life Sciences*, 1976, *18*, 989–992.

Reitz, R. C. Effects of ethanol on the intermediary metabolism of liver and brain. In E. Majchrowicz & E. P. Noble (Eds.), *Biochemistry and pharmacology of ethanol* (Vol. 2). New York: Plenum Press, 1979.

Riggin, R. M. & Kissinger, P. T. Determination of tetrahydroisoquinoline alkaloids in biological materials with high performance liquid chromatography. *Analytical Chemistry*, 1977, *49*, 530–533.

Riley, J. N., & Walker, D. W. Morphological alterations in hippocampus after long-term alcohol consumption in mice. *Science*, 1978, *201*, 646–648.

Roach, M. K., & Reese, W. N., Jr. Effect of ethanol on glucose and amino acid metabolism in brain. *Biochemical Pharmacology*, 1971, *20*, 2805–2812.

Roach, M. K., Khan, M. M., Coffman, R., Pennington, W., & Davis, D. L. Brain Na-K ATPase activity and neurotransmitter uptake in alcohol-dependent rats. *Brain Research,* 1973, *63,* 323–329.

Rogers, J., Siggins, G. R., Schulman, J. A., & Bloom, F. E. Physiological correlates of ethanol intoxication, tolerance, and dependence in rat cerebellar Purkinje cells. *Brain Research,* 1980, *196,* 183–198.

Ross, D. H. Selective action of alcohols on cerebral calcium levels. *Annals of the New York Academy of Sciences,* 1976, *273,* 280–294.

Ross, D. H., Medina, M. A., & Cardenas, H. L. Morphine and ethanol: Selective depletion of regional brain calcium. *Science,* 1974, *186,* 63–65.

Roth, S. H. Physical mechanisms of anesthesia. *Annual Reviews of Pharmacology and Toxicology,* 1979, *19,* 159–178.

Rothman, J. E., & Lenard, J. Membrane asymmetry. *Science,* 1977, *195,* 743–753.

Rothstein, A. Membrane phenomena. *Annual Reviews of Physiology,* 1968, *30,* 15–72.

Rubin, R. P. The role of calcium in the release of neurotransmitter substances and hormones. *Pharmacological Reviews,* 1970, *22,* 389–428.

Schwartz, A., Lindenmayer, G. E., & Allen, J. C. The sodium-potassium adenosine triphosphatase: Pharmacological, physiological and biochemical aspects. *Pharmacological Reviews,* 1975, *27,* 3–134.

Seeman, P. The membrane actions of anesthetics and tranquilizers. *Pharmacological Reviews,* 1972, *24,* 583–655.

Seeman, P. The membrane expansion theory of anesthesia: Direct evidence using ethanol and a high-precision density meter. *Experientia,* 1974, *30,* 759–760.

Seeman, P., Chan, M., Goldberg, M., Sanko, T., & Sax, L. The binding of calcium to the cell membrane increased by volatile anesthetics (alcohol, acetone, ether), which induce sensitization of nerve and muscle. *Biochimica Biophysica Acta,* 1971, *225,* 185–193.

Shen, A., Pathman, D., Jacobyansky, A., & Thurman, R. G. Kinetics of alterations in brain cyclic AMP levels during ethanol treatment and withdrawal. In R. G. Thurman, J. R. Williamson, H. R. Orott, & B. Chance (Eds.), *Alcohol and aldehyde metabolizing systems* (Vol. 3). New York: Academic Press, 1977.

Singer, S. J., & Nicolson, G. L. The fluid mosaic model of the structure of cell membranes. *Science,* 1972, *175,* 720–731.

Sippel, H. W. The acetaldehyde content in rat brain during ethanol metabolism. *Journal of Neurochemistry,* 1974, *23,* 451–452.

Sjoberg, L. Alcohol and gambling. *Psychopharmacologia (Berl.),* 1969, *14,* 284–298.

Smith, B. R., Brown, Z. W., & Amit, Z. Chronic intraventricular administration of tetrahydroisoquinoline alkaloids: Lack of effect on voluntary ethanol consumption in the rat. *Substance and Alcohol Actions/Misuse,* 1980, *1,* 209–221.

Stahl, W. L., & Swanson, P. D. Movements of calcium and other cations in isolated cerebral cortex. *Journal of Neurochemistry,* 1971, *18,* 415–427.

Sun, A. Y., & Samorajski, T. Effects of ethanol on the activity of ATPase and AChE in synaptosomes isolated from guinea-pig brain. *Journal of Neurochemistry,* 1970, *17,* 1365–1372.

Sutton, D., & Burns, J. Alcohol dose effects on feedback-maintained simple reaction time. *Journal of Psychology,* 1971, *78,* 151–159.

Syntinsky, I. A., Guzikov, B. M., Gomanko, M. V., Eremin, V. R., & Konovalova, N. N. The gamma-aminobutyric acid (GABA) system in brain during acute and chronic ethanol intoxication. *Journal of Neurochemistry,* 1975, *25,* 43–48.

Tabakoff, B., Anderson, R. A., & Ritzman, R. E. Brain acetaldehyde after ethanol administration. *Biochemical Pharmacology,* 1976, *25,* 1305–1309.

Tewari, S., & Noble, E. P. Effects of ethanol on cerebral protein and ribonucleic acid synthesis. In

E. Majchrowicz & E. P. Noble (Eds.), *Biochemistry and pharmacology of ethanol* (Vol. 1). New York: Plenum Press, 1979.

Tyce, G. M., Flock, E. V., Taylor, W. F., & Owens, C. A., Jr. Effects of ethanol on 5-hydroxy-tryptamine turnover in rat brain. *Proceedings of the Society for Experimental Biology and Medicine*, 1970, *134*, 40–44.

Veech, R. L., Harris, R. L., Veloso, D., & Veech, E. H. Freeze-blowing: A new technique for the study of brain *in vivo*. *Journal of Neurochemistry*, 1973, *20*, 183–188.

Veloso, D., Passaneau, J. V., & Veech, R. L. The effects of intoxicating doses of ethanol upon intermediary metabolism. *Journal of Neurochemistry*, 1972, *19*, 2679–2686.

Victor, M., Adams, R. D., & Collins, H. G. *The Wernicke–Korsakoff syndrome*. Philadelphia: Davis, 1971.

Volicer, L., & Gold, B. I. Effect of ethanol on cyclic AMP levels in the rat brain. *Life Sciences*, 1973, *13*, 269–280.

Volicer, L., & Gold, B. I. Interactions of ethanol with cyclic AMP. In E. Majchrowicz, (Ed.), *Biochemical pharmacology of ethanol*. New York: Plenum Press, 1975.

Volicer, L., & Hurter, B. P. Effects of acute and chronic ethanol administration and withdrawal on adenosine-3′,5′-monophosphate and guanosine-3′,5′-monophosphate levels in the rat brain. *Journal of Pharmacology and Experimental Therapeutics*, 1977, *200*, 298–305.

Walker, D. W., & Freund, G. Impairment of timing behavior after prolonged alcohol consumption in rats. *Science*, 1973, *182*, 597–599.

Walker, D. W., Barnes, D. E., Zornetzer, S. F., Hunter, B. E., & Kubanis, P. Neuronal loss in hippocampus induced by prolonged ethanol consumption in rats. *Science*, 1980, *209*, 711–713.

Walker, D. W., Barnes, D. E., Riley, J. N., Hunter, B. F., & Zornetzer, S. F. The neurotoxicity of chronic ethanol consumption. In M. Sandler (Ed.), *Psychopharmacology of alcohol*. New York: Raven Press, 1980.

Wallgren, H., Nikander, P., von Boguslowsky, P., & Linkola, J. Effects of ethanol, tert-butanol and clomethiazole on net movement of sodium and potassium in electrically stimulated cerebral tissue. *Acta Physiologica Scandinavica*, 1972, *33*, 979–989.

Warren, G. H., & Raynes, A. E. Mood changes during three conditions of alcohol intake. *Quarterly Journal of Studies on Alcohol*, 1972, *33*, 979–989.

Whittam, R. Active cation transport as a pace-maker of respiration. *Nature*, 1961, *191*, 603–604.

Whittam, R. The dependence of the respiration of brain cortex on active cation transport. *Biochemical Journal*, 1962, *82*, 205–212.

Williams, M., & Rodnight, R. Protein phosphorylation in nervous tissue: Possible involvement in nervous tissue function and relationship to cyclic nucleotide metabolism. *Progress in Neurobiology*, 1977, *8*, 183–250.

Williams, H. L., & Salamy, A. Alcohol and sleep. In B. Kissin & H. Begleiter (Eds.), *The biology of alcoholism* (Vol. 2). New York: Plenum Press, 1972.

Woodson, P. B. J., Traynor, M. E., Schlapfer, W. T., & Barondes, S. H. Increased membrane fluidity implicated in acceleration of decay of post-tetanic potentiation by alcohols. *Nature*, 1976, *260*, 797–799.

Yules, R. B., Freedman, D. X., & Chandler, K. A. The effect of ethyl alcohol on man's electroencephalographic sleep cycle. *Electroencephalography and Clinical Neurophysiology*, 1966, *20*, 109–111.

Yules, R. B., Lippman, M. E., & Freedman, D. X. Alcohol administration prior to sleep: The effect on EEG sleep stages. *Archives of General Psychiatry*, 1967, *16*, 94–97.

Yules, R. B., Ogden, J. A., Gault, F. P., & Freedman, D. X. The effect of ethyl alcohol on electroencephalographic sleep cycles in cats. *Psychonomic Science*, 1966, *5*, 97.

6

Neurologic Diseases Associated with Chronic Alcohol Abuse

GERHARD FREUND

1. INTRODUCTION

1.1. Scope

Many physical illnesses are in some way related to alcohol abuse and occur more often in alcohol abusers than in the general population. The different interactions between alcohol consumption and disease will be reviewed in this chapter and, I hope, will stimulate the reader to think about the gaps in our knowledge of alcohol-related diseases. These physical illnesses interact in many ways with psychological and social aspects of alcohol abuse, which is why professionals involved with problem drinkers need to be aware of these physical illnesses. Because of space limitations, the description of the various diseases is brief; the reader is referred to appropriate sources for in-depth study. These sources include the current editions of textbooks of internal medicine and its subspecialties as well as current literature reviews cited in the text (Kissin & Begleiter, 1974; Seixas, Williams, & Eggleston, 1975; Tarter & Sugerman, 1976).

1.2. Types of Interactions between Alcohol and Disease

After absorption, ethanol is rapidly distributed throughout the total body water space in every cell. Because ethanol is also lipid-soluble, it is present in every

GERHARD FREUND • Veterans Administration Medical Center and Departments of Medicine and Neuroscience, College of Medicine, University of Florida, Gainesville, Florida 32602.

biological membrane of the body. It is therefore not surprising that the drug ethanol can impair the function and structure of every tissue. Fortunately, living organisms have many mechanisms to cope with chemicals foreign to their normal metabolism. Therefore, pathological abnormalities are rare unless these adaptive mechanisms are overwhelmed or otherwise impaired. It is nevertheless totally unexplained why chronic alcohol abuse causes disease of a particular tissue (e.g., pancreas) in only a small proportion of heavy drinkers. What are the conditions that make a particular individual vulnerable or protect the majority of unaffected ones? Why does alcohol abuse affect exclusively the liver in one person, the heart in another, the brain in still another? Clearly, conditions other than the presence of ethanol are necessary to induce tissue damage. Such predisposing conditions could be genetic—for example, inherited enzyme defects that predispose to the effects of thiamin deficiency (Blass & Gibson, 1977). They could also be environmental (toxic chemicals including congeners and drugs, viral infections, nutritional deficiencies, etc.) or might stem from an interaction between genetic and environmental conditions (Figure 1). A well-known example of the latter is the development of overt diabetes mellitus caused in the genetically predisposed person by excessive food consumption and obesity. In general, there is a minimum amount

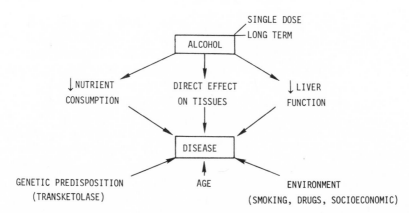

Figure 1. Simplified diagram of possible causal relations between alcohol consumption and diseases. "Alcohol" represents alcohol itself as well as its metabolites (acetaldehyde). "Impaired or altered liver function" includes changes in NADH/NAD ratio as well as protein, lipid, carbohydrate, and steroid metabolism in the liver, with a host of resulting secondary effects. A "single dose" of alcohol may cause an arrhythmia in a patient with coronary artery disease, but long-term alcohol consumption is necessary to induce alcoholic cardiomyopathy. "Direct effects" of alcohol include changes in fluidity of cell membranes (bulk or at specific protein–lipid interphases), ion channels, and others. Not indicated is the possibility that several alcohol-induced diseases may interact with each other (i.e., pancreatitis caused by a direct effect of alcohol may result in malabsorption, which further enhances the effects of decreased nutrient consumption).

of alcohol that must be consumed before toxic effects can occur (Turner, Mezey, & Kimball, 1977). But after that condition has been fulfilled, predisposing factors, rather than only the amount of alcohol consumed, become important.

The situation is more complicated because many alcohol-associated diseases may occur in the complete absence of alcohol consumption. Prominent examples of this are pancreatitis, acute hepatitis (viral, toxic), and cirrhosis of the liver. If even small amounts of alcohol are consumed, these disorders may be aggravated, even if alcohol did not originally cause them. For instance, when rats are exposed to harmless doses of halogenated hydrocarbons, an acute cell necrosis may be induced after alcohol is administered subsequently (Cornish & Adefuin, 1966). This suggests that without alcohol abuse, a mild case of any one of these diseases might have healed spontaneously and gone unnoticed. Therefore, it is sometimes impossible to determine whether or not a disease has been caused by alcohol consumption. Finally, a disease and alcohol consumption can coexist fortuitously where the alcohol is not the cause but only a coincidental finding. Thus it is appropriate to refer to alcohol-*related* (associated) rather than alcohol-caused diseases.

The liver has a central role in the toxicity of ethanol. Although ethanol is present in all tissues, it is metabolized almost exclusively in the liver. Therefore, the toxic effects of ethanol in tissues other than the liver must be the result of (1) a direct physical effect of ethanol molecules; (2) the presence in the cells of minute, currently undetectable amounts of ethanol which is metabolized to acetaldehyde elsewhere than in the liver, as in neurons; or (3) metabolism of ethanol in the liver, which causes indirect effects—for instance, release of acetaldehyde into the systemic circulation or changes of the redox status of body metabolism (Table 1). Many of the complex metabolic events resulting from the metabolism of ethanol in the liver could potentially cause alcohol-related liver diseases (Lieber, 1978).

The central nervous system (CNS) also occupies a unique role in alcohol toxicity because ethanol is an anesthetic; that is, it suppresses and alters the electrical activity in the brain that is necessary for normal function. Acute toxicity that includes coma and death is not considered here. It is currently unclear what relationships exist between recurrent acute episodes of reversible intoxication and the permanent, mostly irreversible structural and functional changes of the brain that result from prolonged alcohol consumption. Chronic brain damage is possibly the cumulative effect of multiple small, irreversible insults. Or the damage could be the result of a mechanism unrelated to the intoxicating properties of ethanol, for instance, acetaldehyde formation.

1.3. Pathogenetic Mechanisms

The term "mechanism" is defined here as an orderly, predictable sequence of events beginning at the molecular level of biological organization and proceeding to structural and behavioral changes at the end of the chain (Freund, 1982b).

Table 1. Potential Mechanisms of Ethanol Toxicity

  I. Direct toxicity of ethanol molecules
     A. Physical membrane fluidity—expansion
        1. Bulk fluidity
        2. At protein–lipid interphases
     B. Membrane transport (ions, amino acids)
     C. Local tissue irritation
     D. Free radical formation
 II. Metabolism of ethanol
     A. Acetaldehyde formation
        1. Hepatic–systemic circulation
        2. Intracellular
        3. Condensation products (salsolinol)
     B. NADH:NAD ratio
        1. Lipogenesis
        2. Gluconeogenesis
        3. Other
     C. Drug-metabolizing enzyme induction
        1. Metabolites
        2. Drugs, chemicals
III. Physiological effects
     A. Blood flow
     B. CNS depression
     C. Stress
 IV. Nutritional effects of ethanol consumption
     A. Total calories (devoid of other nutrients)
     B. Effects on protein, vitamins, mineral metabolism
        1. Consumption
        2. Absorption
        3. Utilization
        4. Requirements

Table 1 gives an overview of physical and chemical events that may cause alcohol-induced diseases. Several of these mechanisms are not mutually exclusive and may also interact with one another. These molecular events are reviewed in several recent publications (Majchrowicz, 1975; Majchrowicz & Noble, 1979; Begleiter, 1980).

1.4. Prevalence of Alcohol-Associated Diseases

Autopsy studies give some insight into the prevalence of alcohol-related diseases (Schmidt & deLint, 1972; Corrigan, 1976). For instance, Jolliffe and Jellinek (1941) estimated that approximately 8% of chronic alcoholics develop cirrhosis of the liver. In turn, the prevalence of alcoholism has been estimated from the prevalence of alcohol-related diseases in certain populations (Single, 1979).

An analysis of hospital admissions is another source of information. One of the difficulties, however, is that alcohol abuse is either not recognized or is purposely omitted from the official hospital record. For instance, Nolan (1965) found that in 14% of medical admissions to a university hospital, alcoholism was judged to be a significant problem. But this high prevalence emerged only as a result of a prospective study that included family and close friends verifying alcohol use by the patient. In university-affiliated Veterans Administration Medical Centers, this figure is over 30% (McAllister & Dzur, 1974) and up to 50% (Gomberg, 1975). One study compared diseases in populations of alcoholics with those in nonalcoholic controls matched by age, sex, occupation, and geographical location; the alcoholic/control case ratios were 29 for cirrhosis of the liver, 1.9 for ulcer of the stomach, 1.4 for ulcer of the duodenum, 1.6 for diabetes mellitus, 1.7 for gout, and 1.6 for neuritis (Pell & D'Alonzo, 1968). The usual acute complications of alcohol withdrawal were not considered but occur in approximately 23% to 29% of alcoholics in other studies (German, 1973). Obviously, these various selected hospital populations do not indicate the true prevalence in the population as a whole or the degree to which alcohol abuse contributes to pathogenesis.

One should keep in mind that the prevalence of any one of the diseases to be discussed here will vary greatly, depending on variables in the patient population—that is, socioeconomic and educational background, age, sex, race, drinking history, duration of sobriety, concomitant use of other drugs (e.g., ulcerogenic salicylates), climate (hypothermia), availability of medical care, and many others. It is well known that an institution or agency will selectively attract certain types of patients. Data from one institution cannot necessarily be extrapolated to those from another, which may be quite different. For example, data on the prevalence of anemia in alcoholic patients admitted to an inner-city hospital will be quite different from those reported from a private hospital in a wealthy surburb where patients are likely to eat more meat and take vitamin and iron supplements.

2. PHYSICAL DEPENDENCE

The biological aspects of physical dependence are discussed elsewhere in this volume. Alcohol withdrawal syndromes are clinically important because they are often precipitated by a medical or surgical illness that prevents the patient from obtaining or consuming alcohol. Once physical signs and symptoms of withdrawal develop, they become superimposed over the manifestations of the precipitating disease and may thereby interfere with diagnosis and management (Salum, 1972). For instance, fever, diaphoresis, and tachycardia may develop with uncomplicated alcohol withdrawal (Isbell, Frazer, Wikler, Belleville, & Eisenman, 1955), but these signs may also be caused by pneumonia, which often precipitates alcohol withdrawal syndromes. It must be remembered that even moderate and infrequent alcohol consumption, which does not lead to physical dependence, may precipitate seizures in epileptic patients (Victor, 1970).

3. CHRONIC DISEASES OF THE CENTRAL NERVOUS SYSTEM

There is a tendency to attribute a disorder of the CNS to alcohol when it occurs in an alcohol abuser. However, alcoholics are subject to the same spectrum of CNS diseases as is the general population. The statistical prevalence of a disease may be somewhat different in alcoholics compared with nonalcoholics. Except, perhaps, for trauma to the head and subdural hematoma, such statistical differences are too slight to be of help in diagnosing an individual case. The clinical features (Freund, 1976) and pathogenesis (Freund, 1973) of alcohol-related brain diseases have been reviewed.

Some alcohol-related diseases of the CNS are correctly diagnosed on clinical grounds alone; others may be diagnosed with certainty only after autopsy. Although a large overlap exists, clinical disorders may have primarily psychiatric or neurologic aspects. The subsequent classifications are therefore divided into a psychiatric–behavioral or clinical classification used by psychiatrists and a neurologic–neuropathologic section used primarily by pathologists to classify autopsy findings.

3.1. Psychiatric-Behavioral Diagnoses (DSM-III)

The current clinical classification is based on the ninth edition of *The International Classification of Diseases, Clinical Modification* (ICD-9-CM) (1979), which corresponds with the third edition of the *Diagnostic and Statistical Manual of Mental Disorders* (DSM-III) of the American Psychiatric Association (1980). Alcohol-related diseases are classified and coded as follows:

> Alcohol Intoxication: 303.0X
> Alcohol Abuse: 305.0X
> Alcohol Dependence: 303.9X

The last digit, here shown as X, is entered as follows: 0 = unspecified, 1 = continuous, 2 = episodic, 3 = in remission.

> Alcohol Withdrawal Delirium: 291.0
> Alcohol Amnestic Disorder (Korsakoff's Psychosis): 291.1X
> Alcohol Dementia (Organic Brain Syndrome): 291.2X
> Alcohol Withdrawal Hallucinosis: 291.3X
> Alcohol Withdrawal Syndrome: 291.8X

The last digit (X) indicates severity: 0 = unspecified, 1 = mild, 2 = moderate, 3 = severe.

> Thiamine Deficiency (Wernicke's Encephalopathy): 265.1

The exact definitions for each diagnosis are explained in detail in DSM-III; various organic brain syndromes are described as follows: *Hallucinations* are visual, auditory, or sensory (skin sensations) perceptions of things that are not really there. Illusions are misinterpretations of things that are there; for example, a fold of a bedsheet is perceived to be a mouse. This must occur in the absence of a clouded sensorium (delirium) or cognitive impairment (dementia). The individual may be aware that the hallucinations are not real or may have the firm conviction, which cannot be corrected by reason, that they are real (delusion).

Delirium is defined as a clouded state of consciousness, a reduction in the clarity of awareness of the environment. This is manifested by difficulty in sustaining attention to both external and internal stimuli, sensory misperceptions, and a disordered stream of thought. This was formerly called "acute brain syndrome."

The amnestic syndrome is an isolated impairment of memory in the absence of clouded sensorium (delirium) or dementia. Short-term memory deficit (anterograde amnesia) is the inability to retain any new information for more than a few minutes—that is, to learn new material. Inability to recall material that was known in the past is called *long-term memory deficit* or *retrograde amnesia*.

Alcohol amnestic disorder due to thiamine deficiency is also known as *Korsakoff's disease*. . . . The alcohol amnestic disorder often follows an acute episode of Wernicke's encephalopathy, a neurological disease manifested by confusion, ataxia, eye movement abnormalities (gaze palsies, nystagmus), and other neurological signs. Gradually, these manifestations subside, but the major impairment of memory, alcohol amnestic disorder, remains. If Wernicke's disease is treated early with large doses of thiamine, alcohol amnestic disorder may not develop. (DSM-III, p. 137)

Dementia associated with alcoholism, in contrast, is not limited to memory impairment but involves higher cortical intellectual functions. This diagnosis should not be made until at least three weeks after the patient has stopped drinking. This condition was formerly called *chronic brain syndrome* or *alcoholic deterioration* (DSM-II). Dementia is characterized by (1) impairment of abstract thinking (difficulties with interpreting proverbs); (2) impaired judgment and impulse control (reckless behavior); (3) impoverished language and capacities for verbal expression; and (4) personality changes, including apathy, irritability, and combativeness—often an accentuation of premorbid traits. In severe cases, there may be aphasia (language disorder), apraxia (inability to carry out motor activities despite intact comprehension and motor function), agnosia (failure to recognize or identify objects despite intact sensory function), and constructional difficulty (inability to copy three-dimensional figures, assemble blocks, or arrange sticks in specific designs). All of this results in impairment of vocational and social function to the extent that institutionalization is required.

The degree of dementia may range from mild, demonstrable only with sensitive tests of cognitive behavior, to a severe, disabling ablation of all higher cortical functions. Mild and moderate degrees of dementia are defined by the severity of impairment of social and occupational functions. Severe dementia includes marked deterioration of personality and inability to function independently. Specific lists have been designed to quantify the severity of dementia on a "dementia scale" (Blessed, Tomlinson, & Roth, 1968). The degree of impairment of cognitive function may be partially related to the amount and duration of alcohol consumed; it ranges from mild impairment in social drinkers (Parker & Noble, 1980) to a continuum of severe impairment in the alcohol abuser (Parsons, 1980; Ryan & Butters, 1980).

3.1.1. Differential Diagnosis

Many systemic and brain diseases can cause dementia. They range from metabolic hypothyroidism to mechanical normal-pressure hydrocephalus (Wells, 1977). The largest number of cases are associated with aging. Patients with cerebrovascular disease may be classified as having vascular or multi-infarct dementia. In the absence of vascular disease, and if the patient is under age 65, the classification is presenile dementia (Alzheimer's disease). If the dementia begins after age 65, it is diagnosed as senile dementia of the Alzheimer's type (SDAT) (Katzman, Terry, & Bick, 1978). Alcohol-induced dementia has no specific characteristics and requires a history of heavy alcohol consumption and the exclusion of all the other causes of dementia. It is the cause of approximately 9% of all male admissions to state and county mental hospitals (Bachrach, 1976a). An additional estimated 10% of all male admissions, "while not assigned primary alcoholic diagnosis, were reported as having drinking problems. These latter admissions may be regarded as 'missed' alcoholic admissions" (Bachrach, 1976b). The possible interactions between alcohol consumption and normal or pathological aging of the CNS are only beginning to be explored at the molecular level of biological organization. It is conceivable that the alcohol-induced changes are a model for biological aging and vice versa (Freund, 1982b; Freund & Butters, 1982).

3.1.2. Pathogenesis

There is much controversy about what role alcohol itself has in the causation of alcohol-related dementia. No doubt thiamin deficiency causes the acute, reversible Wernicke's encephalopathy (Jolliffe, Wortis, & Fein, 1941; Phillips, Victor, Adams, & Davidson, 1952) whether accompanied by alcohol use or not (Freund, 1982a). However, there is no convincing evidence that the permanent amnestic syndrome (Korsakoff's dementia) is also caused by thiamine deficiency rather than by concomitant alcohol abuse (Freund, 1973). Wernicke's syndrome is characterized by lesions in the central gray structures in the absence of significant changes in the cerebral cortex (Victor, Adams, & Collins, 1971).

The noninvasive, radiologic technique known as computerized axial tomography (CAT) has made it possible to visualize neural structures on X-ray film and to quantify cerebral cortical and ventricular atrophy *in vivo*. CAT indicates that the cerebral cortex atrophies in patients who abuse alcohol (Carlen, Wortzman, Holgate, Wilkinson, & Rankin, 1978; Lee, Hardt, Moller, Haubek, & Jensen, 1979). Since the introduction of this technique, a large data base is rapidly accumulating (Idestrom, 1981) and has led to the recognition that the cortex as well as the central gray structures is affected by alcohol abuse (Editorial, 1981). There is a rough correlation between the degree of cognitive impairment, the amount of alcohol consumed, and the degree of cortical atrophy. However, atrophy explains the variance of cognitive tests only on the order of 30%. Predictably, the correlation is not perfect in such cross-sectional studies for a variety of reasons. To mention only a few: the prealcohol baseline of behavioral performance and therefore the real extent of the cognitive loss is not known. Often the behavioral tests are too insensitive to measure real differences between alcohol abusers and controls. Control populations may differ by many factors other than alcohol consumption. Gross morphological measurements cannot take into consideration micromorphological or molecular changes in the synapses, which can also alter cognitive function profoundly. In spite of these limitations, however, CAT will make important contributions to our understanding of the effects of alcohol abuse on the brain. Cortical atrophy and diminished performance in some psychometric tests also occur with normal aging. This raises the intriguing possibility that the underlying biochemical changes in aging and alcoholism also may be similar or identical and that the two processes may interact (Freund, 1982a).

3.2. Neurologic-Neuropathologic Diagnoses (SNOMED)

Autopsy findings are classified according to Systematized Nomenclature of Medicine (SNOMED), College of American Pathologists (1978). The findings are coded in four categories: topography (T), morphology (M), etiology (E), and diagnosis (D). For instance, central pontine myelinolysis caused by alcohol may be classified as T-X5400 (central pons), M-50510 (histological type of degeneration), E-5512 (ethanol). Alternatively a disease (D) with a characteristic combination of pathological findings, such as Wernicke's disease, may be classified as D-8777; or alcoholic cerebellar degeneration syndrome as D-8785; or Marchiafava–Bignami disease, callosum degeneration syndrome, as D-8787.

3.3. Nutritional Deficiencies

3.3.1. Wernicke's Syndrome

That acute hemmorhagic superior polioencephalitis (clinically designated as Wernicke's syndrome) is clearly secondary to thiamine deficiency is based on three observations: (1) This acute syndrome may occur in patients who have not consumed alcohol but whose diets are vitamin-deficient (Drenick, Joven, & Swend-seid, 1960; Mancall & McEntee, 1965) or after depletion by hemodialysis (Lopez & Collins, 1968). (2) Thiamine administration can reverse this syndrome within hours unless it is not recognized and therapy is delayed until irreversible brain changes have occurred (Joliffe et al., 1941; Phillips et al., 1952; Victor et al., 1971) or when liver disease slows the conversion of thiamine to its active metabolite (Cole, Turner, Frank, Baker, & Leevy, 1969). Therefore, to prevent this serious complication, 100 mg of thiamine should be administered parenterally immediately to every ill alcoholic patient when admitted to the hospital. This should be followed by multivitamin therapy, because vitamin deficiency almost invariably involves a combination of several vitamins that occur together in natural foods. (3) The syndrome has been induced in animals by thiamine deficiency (McCandless & Schenker, 1968; Robertson, Wasan, & Skinner, 1968).

The clinical picture has been described and extensively correlated with histopathological data by Victor et al. (1971). The presenting complaints develop over several days or weeks (or, rarely, within a day) and consist of confusion (90% of patients), loss of memory, staggering gait, and inability to focus eyes. Objective signs include (1) ataxia; (2) ophthalmoplegia, resulting in bilateral ptosis of eyelids and impaired lateral and upward gaze; and (3) horizontal and vertical nystagmus. Hypothermia with temperatures ranging from 97°F to 85°F (36°C to 29.5°C) is uncommon (Philip & Smith, 1973). These findings may be associated with those of withdrawal syndromes, alcohol-associated dementias (organic brain syndromes), malnutrition other than thiamine deficiency, liver diseases, and other medical diseases often encountered in an alcoholic patient population. The prevalence of fever in a predominantly skid-row type of population was approximately 12% (Victor et al., 1971). Other vitamin deficiencies may occur in alcoholics with severe undernutrition. Pellagra (niacin deficiency) is characterized by dermatitis, stomatitis, and diarrhea. In the late stages, confusion, hallucinations, delirium, and tremors may develop. Vitamin B_{12} and folic acid deficiencies may also be present.

Because of the frequent association of the acute Wernicke's syndrome, malnutrition, and the chronic Korsakoff amnestic syndrome in their patient population, Victor and colleagues (1971) consider both syndromes to have the same nutritional cause; they designate the combination as Wernicke–Korsakoff syndrome. Modern use of the term "Korsakoff's psychosis" ("Alcohol Amnestic Disorder," 291.10, ICD-9-CM or DSM-III) is quite different from Korsakoff's original description (Victor & Yakovlev, 1955) of "psychosis polyneuritica" which "usually develops in the course of other disease—post partum, during acute infections and some chronic diseases." According to Korsakoff, the psychosis occurs in three types:

> increased irritability and agitation, with relatively good preservation of consciousness; in other cases, on the contrary, confusion predominates, either apathetic or associated with excitement; and finally, a third group, a characteristic disturbance of memory—a peculiar form of amnesia—stands in the foreground.

In contrast, the DSM-III (p. 112) more narrowly specifies that

> Amnestic Syndrome is not diagnosed if memory impairment exists in the context of clouded consciousness (Delirium) or in association with a more general loss of intellectual abilities (Dementia). . . . Apathy, lack of initiative and emotional blandness are common. Although the individual is superficially friendly and agreeable, his or her affect is shallow.

The diagnosis of Dementia Associated with Alcoholism (291.2x) "should not be made until at least three weeks have elapsed since the cessation of alcohol use" (p. 137).

A recent paper (Blass & Gibson, 1979) cites three reports as demonstrating that "patients with Wernicke's syndrome typically went on to develop Korsakoff psychosis if they lived long enough." However, to prove this point, it is necessary to show: (1) that the patients did not have a poor memory from chronic alcohol abuse *before* they developed acute Wernicke's syndrome—that is, that the Korsakoff amnesia did not precede Wernicke's syndrome; and (2) that the patients truly had Korsakoff's syndrome, which in the DSM III is defined as amnesia with a *clear* sensorium that persists long *after* the deliriums from ethanol withdrawal and Wernicke's syndrome have subsided. By these criteria, none of the three cited reports show that Korsakoff's syndrome usually follows Wernicke's encephalopathy. The first paper (Kant, 1932–1933) reports 17 cases (one nonalcoholic) of autopsy-proven Wernicke's encephalopathy. All patients were admitted to the hospital in various stages of delirium (both withdrawal and Wernicke-related), stupor, or coma. By definition, all died in the acute phase of their illness, making prolonged follow-up impossible. Intellectual abilities were assessed before the acute phase of the disease only in patient 11, whose poor memory *predated* his admission by more than half a year. In contrast with current definitions stating that amnestic syndromes are associated with clear sensorium (DSM III), the author of this paper uses the term "Korsakoff's syndrome" loosely to include amnesia associated with delirium, disorintation, and confusion.

DeWardener and Lennox (1947) reported 52 cases of beriberi in prisoners of war receiving deficient diets. Again the "memory loss for recent events"— together with the neurological signs of nystagmus, ophthalmoplegia, and ataxia— were associated with confusion, hallucinations, and "occasionally preceded the onset of coma." In the typical patient treated with thiamine, "loss of memory for recent events returned within 2 days to a week." In patients with advanced confusional states, it

> was likely to take up to 3 months to return to normal mentality, losing successively confabulation, disorientation and lastly, loss of memory for recent events. In these patients there was apt to be a permanent amnesia *for the time during which they were most confused.* (Emphasis added).

Again, this is not permanent amnesia associated with a clear sensorium characteristic of Korsakoff's amnestic syndrome (DSM III). The same is true of the retrospective clinical study of 27 cases of Wernicke's syndrome (3 nonalcoholic), by Jolliffe *et al.* (1941), in which 14 patients died in the acute phase and only 1 of the surviving patients was observed for more than a few days after the delirium (patient 15). The one survivor was a 38-year-old alcoholic who was left with a "Korsakoff picture" (no data) 28 days after the onset of Wernicke's syndrome. It is not reported what this patient's mental status was before the admission, whether the amnesia was restricted to the delirious phase, or whether it persisted after a three-month follow-up. The lack of reliable data regarding poor memory in time periods before and after Wernicke's encephalopathy as well as the inclusion of delirium-related memory deficits does not permit the conclusion that chronic Korsakoff's amnesia usually follows the acute Wernicke's syndrome (Freund, 1973).

3.4. Degenerative Syndromes

Cerebellar degeneration is clinically manifested by the gradual development of ataxic gait, incoordination, spasticity, tremors of arms and legs, nystagmus, and dysarthria (speech described as "thick," gait as broad-based and halting; Victor, Adams, & Mancall, 1959). In the absence of alcohol consumption, cerebellar degeneration may occur—either isolated or in association with degeneration of a variety of other related structures in the CNS—in the form of various characteristic syndromes described in the neurology literature. When cerebellar degeneration is associated with chronic alcoholism, it may also be associated with Wernicke's encephalopathy (in 6 of 7 cases) or pontine myelinolysis (in 1 of 7 cases; Allsop & Turner, 1966). Victor and associates (1959) speculated that malnutrition, rather than ethanol *per se,* is the cause of this syndrome. However, no history or evidence of malnutrition was found in 11 of 50 patients in one series (Victor *et al.,* 1959) and in none out of 3 patients in another series (Martin, 1965). Perhaps these discrepancies simply reflect the variable prevalence of malnutrition within a particular population of alcoholics.

With the advent of CAT scans, it is now possible to make the diagnosis of cerebellar degeneration with assurance *in vivo* and at an earlier stage of development. For instance, in 41 male alcoholics under the age of 35, atrophy of the cerebellar vermis was present in 12 patients, and 8 of them also had atrophy of the cerebellar hemisphere (Haubek & Lee, 1979). Only one of those patients had a clinically gross ataxic gait.

Degeneration of the corpus callosum (Marchiafava–Bignami disease) is clinically suggested by an insidious onset of psychosis (manic, depressive, or paranoid) and by dementia and focal neurological signs, such as grand mal seizures, paresis, aphasia, and apraxia. Death usually ensues within three to six years after onset. Marchiafava–Bignami disease was originally described in Italy in 1903 and blamed on the drinking of wine. It is a very rare disease (Ironside, Bosanquet, & McMenemey, 1961), only one case having been described among the millions of wine drinkers in Germany (Walter, 1978). The rarity of this syndrome, together with the fact that it can occur in (malnourished) subjects who never consumed any alcohol (Leong, 1979), suggests that the originally described association of this syndrome with wine drinking was probably fortuitous, since almost everyone in Italy drinks wine. However, because this syndrome has been carried in the textbooks for nearly a century as being caused by alcohol, it will probably continue this way indefinitely.

Central pontine myelinolysis was first described by Adams, Victor, and Mancall (1959). Clinically, there is an acute onset of quadriplegia and pseudobulbar palsy, manifested by nystagmus, slurring of speech, impaired ocular convergence, dysphagia, nasal regurgitation, and diminished cough and gag reflexes. Since this diagnosis is based on the histological changes at autopsy, the *in vivo* diagnosis can only be suspected on clinical grounds.

3.5. Hepatic Encephalopathy

Severe liver disease, acute or chronic and irrespective of the cause, may induce a syndrome characterized by disturbed consciousness ranging from mild lethargy to profound coma. Personality changes are nonspecific, range from depression to euphoria, and may be associated with anxiety and paranoid features. Intellectual function may be impaired, as evidenced by an inability to concentrate, remember, and think abstractly. Neurological impairment may consist of dysphasia; slow, slurred speech; apraxia; a characteristic (but not pathognomonic) flapping tremor of the outstretched hands ("asterixis"); ataxia; and hyperreflexia. Characteristically, the severity of all these manifestations may fluctuate rapidly within minutes or hours, apparently as a result of concurrent metabolic fluctuations such as rate of ammonia absorption from the bowel and its disposition, pH of the blood as determined by respiration, and others.

The clinical course varies with the degree of acuteness of the underlying liver disease. Fulminant hepatitis may cause death in deep coma preceded by convulsions and decerebrate rigidity. Chronic cirrhosis of the liver may have a variable course, with either improvement of encephalopathy or progression to paraplegia or dementia over a period of years.

The cause of the neurological and psychiatric manifestations of hepatic encephalopathy appears to be toxic substances (including ammonia) from the gastrointestinal tract and the intermediary metabolism that are normally detoxified in the liver (Plum, 1974).

3.6. Subdural Hematoma

Subdural hematoma following head trauma is not an uncommon cause of death (due to slow venous bleeding) in alcoholics. Death is preventable if surgical drainage is done promptly. Symptoms of the chronic subdural hematoma may begin several weeks after the often trivial head injury, which by then may have been forgotten. Headaches (in 90% of cases), confusion, and irritability are insidiously followed by drowsiness, urinary incontinence, and stupor, all of which may be erroneously attributed to deterioration as a result of alcoholism or to senescence. The course may fluctuate for weeks or months, finally terminating in sudden coma and death. The presence of a subdural hematoma can now be diagnosed with such noninvasive techniques as the CAT scan and echoencephalography. This disorder is mentioned here because a high index of suspicion is a necessary prerequisite for early referral and successful surgical treatment.

3.7. Other CNS Disorders

Alcohol consumption may also affect the course of disorders not usually thought to be associated with alcohol. For instance, it has been suggested that acute ethanol intoxication may promote brain infarction in young adults (Hillbom & Kaste, 1978).

4. PERIPHERAL POLYNEUROPATHY

Manifestations of disorders of the peripheral nervous system may be classified according to its functional divisions—motor, sensory, and autonomic. In severity, these disorders may range from impairment detectable only by nerve conduction velocity studies in clinically asymptomatic patients to clinically overt neuropathy of various degrees of severity and disability. Most patients with chronic alcoholism have no detectable impairment of the peripheral nervous system.

The development of clinical manifestations is usually slow, extending over a period of weeks or months and, rarely, days. Typically the involvement is symmetrical; it begins and is most severe in the lower rather than upper extremities and in the distal rather than proximal extremities. Sensory manifestations—paresthesias, pain, numbness, hyperesthesia upon pressure—are usually followed but sometimes preceded by motor involvement, including weakness, muscle atrophy, foot drop, and ataxic gait. Vibration and position sense and reflexes become impaired. In extreme cases, cranial nerves may become involved, resulting in scotomas, pupil abnormalities, visual impairment, and paresis of ocular, facial, and pharyngeal muscles. Autonomic nervous system involvement (Novak & Victor, 1974) may manifest itself by paralysis of urethral and rectal sphincters, vocal cord palsy (hoarseness, weak voice), and persistent hypotension. As usual, peripheral neuropathy may be associated with other nutritional, neurological, and nonneurological diseases common in alcoholic patients. One again should be reminded that a neuropathy in an alcoholic patient is not necessarily "alcoholic neuropathy"; it may be caused by a spinal cord tumor, a degenerated intervertebral disk or many other disorders.

The incidence of clinically significant peripheral neuropathy as usual depends on the population from which the sample is drawn. In one study, the incidence was approximately 5% of patients requiring admission for chronic alcoholism to a neuropsychiatric hospital (Niedermeyer & Prokop, 1959). In another study it was 80 of 25,000 (0.3%) patients referred to a university neurology outpatient clinic in Hamburg over a 12-year period (Janzen & Balzereit, 1968). A third survey of 451 skid-row alcoholics consecutively admitted to a correctional institution found only 7 cases of "possible nutritional polyneuropathy," though 23% of the subjects were judged to be underweight (Figueroa, Sargent, Imperiale, Morey, Paynter, Vorhaus, & Kark, 1953). The unexpectedly low incidence was attributed to the enrichment of bread with vitamins, which was started in 1940 in the United States.

Neurophysiological studies demonstrated impairment in asymptomatic alcoholic patients of motor (Wanamaker & Skillman, 1966) and sensory (Casey & LeQuesne, 1972) nerve conduction velocities, generally associated with degeneration of the myelin sheaths of peripheral nerves. But the nerve axons themselves (and by implication the associated nerve cells) may also be damaged, as evidenced by reduced amplitudes of nerve action potentials and by nerve biopsy (Casey & LeQuesne, 1972; Bischoff, 1971; Walsh & McLeod, 1970).

The usual controversy exists regarding the pathogenetic roles of vitamin deficiencies and of direct toxic effects of alcohol. Those who favor the nutritional etiology cite three facts: (1) vitamin deficiencies alone may cause peripheral neuropathies in humans and animals (Spillane & Riddoch, 1947; Denny-Brown, 1947); (2) vitamin deficiencies are commonly associated with neuropathy in chronic alcoholic patients; (3) peripheral nutritional neuropathy may improve if vitamin therapy is instituted before irreversible damage has occurred (Spillane & Riddoch, 1947; Denny-Brown, 1947). Authors who postulate that alcohol *per se* has a direct toxic effect base their opinions on the following: (1) the clinical picture of the vitamin deficiency polyneuropathies is somewhat different from that encountered in alcoholic patients (for discussion, see Novak & Victor, 1974); (2) not all patients with alcoholic polyneuropathy show evidence or have a history of malnutrition (Walsh & McLeod, 1970; Bischoff, 1971); and (3) experimental vitamin deficiency causes a demyelination of nerve fibers with axonal involvement in only the final stages (Zimmerman, 1956; Robertson et al., 1968). In contrast, patients with alcoholic polyneuropathy frequently have a primary axonal degeneration (Bischoff, 1971). The lack of uniformity of the clinical and histopathologic picture suggested to Bischoff a variety of pathogenetic factors in alcoholic polyneuropathy. As is self-evident, inferences about pathogenetic mechanisms cannot be made with certainty from associations alone. The relative contributions of malnutrition and direct toxic alcohol effects must be elucidated by further experiments.

5. NUTRITIONAL DEFICIENCIES

Chronic alcohol abuse can lead to altered consumption of calories, protein, vitamins, or minerals in food. In addition, absorption, transport, storage, and utilization of each nutrient can be altered. A prolonged and marked deficit of a nutrient can cause abnormalities in tissue structure, function, or both (malnutrition). However, as Hillman (1974) commented: "The patient is an alcoholic: therefore, he is malnourished. This aphorism, while credible and convenient, no longer deserves the deference reserved for traditional stereotypes." Many alcoholics today are well nourished (Figueroa *et al.*, 1953; Neville, Eagles, Samson, & Olson, 1968), but alcohol may, under certain conditions, interfere with absorption of ingested nutrients.

5.1. Gastrointestinal Tract

The effect of either a single dose or chronic consumption of ethanol on the small intestine is essentially a slowing of the transport rate of some vitamins (Wilson & Hoyumpa, 1979). Currently available evidence indicates that prolonged, deficient consumption of proteins and vitamins (thiamine, folic acid, and vitamin B_{12}) leads to deficiency states that, in turn, impair the function of the small intestine, specifically its absorptive capacity (Figure 2). For instance, in the patient who is not drinking alcohol, vitamin B_{12} deficiency may impair vitamin B_{12} absorption by the vitamin-deficient bowel (Lindenbaum, Pezzimenti, & Shea, 1974). In such a self-perpetuating circle, vitamin deficiency begets further vitamin deficiency. These absorption deficits are reversible with parenteral administration of vitamins. In addition, there is evidence that alcohol itself may have an independent, direct toxic effect on absorptive processes in the small bowel (Figure 2). Two

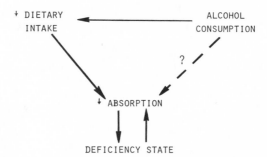

Figure 2. Alcohol and malnutrition. Alcohol calories replace regular food calories that have associated proteins and vitamins. Alcohol in very large doses may also, under some conditions, directly interfere with the absorption of some nutrients. More importantly, once vitamin deficiencies from any cause are established, the vitamin-depleted intestine is then unable to absorb vitamins normally, and a self-perpetuating cycle is established.

types of effects are possible—an acute effect while alcohol is present in the blood perfusing the small bowel and a chronic structural effect that persists for various periods of time after prolonged ethanol consumption has ceased.

In malnourished alcoholics, direct alcohol toxicity and nutritional deficiencies may independently contribute to the development of clinical malnutrition (Figure 2). To determine the relative contributions of each, it is necessary first to correct the deficiencies and continue alcohol consumption. Under these conditions, only vitamin B_{12} absorption is inhibited in some subjects, not thiamine, folic acid, xylose, or fat (Mezey, 1975; Lindenbaum & Lieber, 1975).

In the study by Lindenbaum and Lieber (1975), the duration of heavy ethanol consumption ranged from 13 to 37 days. There was no suppression of vitamin absorption in 2 of 8 subjects and, in the remaining subjects, vitamin absorption was decreased to a mean of 55% of baseline when compared with values before or 8 to 22 days after ethanol consumption. Although neither a diet low in folate content nor alcohol consumption alone may reduce the absorption of folate, the two combined may result in decreased folate absorption, with recovery after folic acid administration despite continuation of alcohol consumption (Mezey, 1975). On the basis of these studies, it is unlikely that healthy people with an adequate vitamin and protein intake would suffer deficiencies from malabsorption induced by alcohol consumption.

5.2. Calories

Ethanol contains 7 kcal/g (5.5 kcal/mL) compared with fat, which has approximately 9 kcal/g, and protein and carbohydrates, which have 4 kcal/g. In energy balance, when calorie intake equals expenditure and body weight does not change, an increase in calories derived from ethanol must be balanced against a decrease of non-ethanol-derived calories like protein. Alternatively, if ethanol calories are consumed in addition to a constant diet, body weight will increase because of a positive energy balance. A person drinking a pint of 80 proof spirits consumes 150 g of absolute ethanol, which equals 1,050 kcal or 50% of a 2,000-kcal diet. Because alcoholic beverages contain no significant amounts of protein or vitamins, deficiencies may ensue unless the diet is appropriately supplemented.

5.3. Vitamins

The possibility that alcohol consumption may alter the absorption of vitamins has been described above and in the chapter by Van Thiel. Thiamine deficiency causes Wernicke's encephalopathy, particularly in the genetically predisposed individual (Blass & Gibson, 1977). There is no evidence that thiamine absorption is significantly impaired by moderate alcohol consumption in the otherwise healthy person (Wilson & Hoyumpa, 1979). While large, single doses of ethanol in various *in vivo* and *in vitro* preparations do have several effects on thiamine transport and metabolism (Hoyumpa, 1980), the clinical significance of these observations is less clear. In one acute clinical study widely quoted as demonstrating impaired thiamine absorption in alcoholics (Tomasulo, Kater, & Iber, 1968), the decrease in thiamine excretion in urine in alcoholics as compared with controls is of small magnitude and overlaps widely between the two groups. This difference may also be attributable to factors other than diminished absorption, such as renal impairment, increased uptake by tissues, liver diseases, and others. In another study (Thomson, Baker, & Leevy, 1970), thiamine excretion in urine was diminished after the concomitant administration of a single concentrated dose of oral thiamine and oral or intravenous ethanol. However, the blood thiamine concentrations in the first 1.5 hours were almost identical in both groups. The subsequent, more rapid decline of thiamine concentrations in blood and urine in the alcoholic group are more compatible with an increased uptake in tissues rather than impaired absorption. There is currently no evidence—in the absence of liver disease, pancreatitis, or gross, severe malnutrition—that clinically relevant thiamine deficiency is common among alcoholic patients. Thiamine requirements are actually reduced if alcohol replaces carbohydrates in the diet (Westerfield & Lawrow, 1953).

6. CONCLUSIONS

In this review of alcohol-related neurological diseases, I have attempted to bring to the readers' attention the great extent and complexity of the potential consequences of alcohol consumption. These diseases have a great psychological and socioeconomic impact on the individual, family, and society. The misery inflicted by some of these diseases may induce some people to seek relief by drinking alcohol and may, thereby, contribute to the perpetuation of alcohol consumption. A consequence becomes a cause, and a self-perpetuating circle is established. Therefore, it is perhaps not advisable, although fashionable, to draw the line too sharply between causes and effects of alcohol abuse.

Very little is known about why and how a small and simple molecule like ethanol can induce so large a spectrum of biological responses. Therefore, little can be done to prevent and treat some of these disorders. It has been stated simplistically that to prevent these diseases people should stop drinking alcohol. In analogy, one might suggest that marital problems be solved by abolishing marriage or traffic accidents be prevented by abolishing cars. Drug-seeking behavior is a powerful psychological force. It is not eliminated by prohibition or the distant threat of a physical disease. Instead, research must be directed toward understanding and intercepting the alcohol-tissue interactions that cause diseases. Society must learn that the price of research is small compared with the price of treatment and of the disabling consequences of alcohol-related diseases.

7. REFERENCES

Adams, R. D., Victor, M., & Mancall, E. L. Central pontine myelinolysis. *AMA Archives of Neurology and Psychiatry*, 1959, *81*, 154–172.

Allsop, J., & Turner, B. Cerebellar degeneration associated with chronic alcoholism. *Journal of Neurological Sciences*, 1966, *3*, 238–258.

American Psychiatric Association. *Diagnostic Statistical Manual of Mental Disorders (DSM-III)*, (3rd ed.). Washington, D.C.: American Psychiatric Association, 1980.

Bachrach, L. L. Educational level of male admissions with alcohol disorders: state and county mental hospitals—1972. *NIMH Mental Health Statistical Note*, January 1976, No. 123. Washington, D.C.: National Institute of Mental Health. (a)

Bachrach, L. L. Characteristics of diagnosed and missed alcoholic male admissions to state and county mental hospitals—1972. *NIMH Mental Health Statistical Note*, February 1976, No. 124. (b)

Begleiter, H. (Ed.). Biological effects of alcohol. *Advances in Experimental Medicine and Biology*, 1980, *126*, 1–832.

Bischoff, A. Die alkoholische Polyneuropathie [Alcoholic polyneuropathy]. *Deutsche Medizinische Wochenshrift*, 1971, *96*, 317–322.

Blass, J. P., & Gibson, G. E. Abnormality of a thiamine-requiring enzyme in patients with Wernicke–Korsakoff syndrome. *New England Journal of Medicine*, 1977, *297*, 1367–1370.

Blass, J. P., & Gibson, G. E. Genetic factors in Wernicke-Korsakoff syndrome. *Alcoholism*, 1979, *3*, 126–134.

Blessed, G., Tomlinson, B. E. & Roth, M. The association between quantitative measures of dementia and senile change in the cerebral grey matter of elderly subjects. *Journal of Psychiatry*, 1968, *114*, 797–811.

Carlen, P. L., Wortzman, G., Holgate, R. C., Wilkinson, D. A., & Rankin, J. G. Reversible cerebral atrophy in recently abstinent chronic alcoholics measured by computed tomography scans. *Science*, 1978, *200*, 1076–1078.

Casey, E. B., & LeQuesne, P. M. Electrophysiological evidence for a distal lesion in an alcoholic neuropathy. *Journal of Neurology, Neurosurgery and Psychiatry*, 1972, *35*, 624–630.

Cole, M., Turner, A., Frank, O., Baker, H., & Leevy, C. M. Extraocular palsy and thiamine therapy in Wernicke's encephalopathy. *American Journal of Clinical Nutrition*, 1969, *22*, 44–51.

College of American Pathologists. *Systematized Nomenclature of Medicine* (4 vols.). Skokie, Ill.: College of American Pathologists, 1978.

Cornish, H. H., & Adefuin, J. Ethanol potentiation of halogenated aliphatic solvent toxicity. *American Industrial Hygiene Association Journal*, 1966, *27*, 57–61.

Corrigan, G. E. Autopsy pathology of alcoholism. *Annals of the New York Academy of Sciences*, 1976, *273*, 385–387.

DeWardener, H. E., & Lennox, B. Cerebral beriberi (Wernicke's encephalopathy). *Lancet*, 1947, *1*, 11–17.

Drenick, J. E., Joven, C. B., & Swendseid, M. E. Occurrence of acute Wernicke's encephalopathy during prolonged starvation for the treatment of obesity. *New England Journal of Medicine*, 1960, *247*, 937–939.

Editorial. Alcoholic brain damage. *Lancet*, 1981, *1*, 477–478.

Figueroa, W. G., Sargent, F., Imperiale, L., Morey, G. R., Paynter, C. R., Vorhaus, L. J., & Kark, R. M. Lack of avitaminosis among alcoholics: Its relation to fortification of cereal products and general nutrition status of the population. *Journal of Clinical Nutrition*, 1953, *1*, 179–199.

Freund, G. The interaction of chronic alcohol consumption and aging on brain structure and function. *Alcoholism: Clinical and Experimental Research*, 1982, *6*, 13–21. (a)

Freund, G. & Butters, N. Alcohol and aging: Challenges for the future. *Alcoholism: Clinical and Experimental Research*, 1982, *6*, 1–2. (Editorial)

German, E. Medical problems in chronic alcoholic men. *Journal of Chronic Diseases*, 1973, *26*, 661–668.

Gomberg, E. S. Prevalence of alcoholism among ward patients in a Veterans Administration hospital. *Journal of Studies on Alcohol*, 1975, *36*, 1458–1467.

Haubek, A., & Lee, K. Computed tomography in alcoholic cerebellar atrophy. *Neuroradiology*, 1979, *18*, 77–79.

Hillbom, M., & Kaste, M. Does ethanol intoxication promote brain infarction in young adults? *Lancet*, 1978, *2*, 1181–1183.

Hoyumpa, A. M., Jr. Mechanisms of thiamine deficiency in chronic alcoholism. *American Journal of Clinical Nutrition*, 1980, *33*, 2750–2761.

Idestrom, C. M. Alcohol and brain research. *Acta Psychiatrica Scandinavica Suppl*, 1980, *62*, 286.

Ironside, R., Bosanquet, F. D., & McMenemey, W. H. Central demyelination of the corpus callosum (Marchiafava–Bignami disease): With report of a second case in Great Britain. *Brain*, 1961, *84*, 212–217.

Isbell, H., Fraser, H. F., Wikler, A., Belleville, R. E., & Eisenman, A. J. An experimental study of the etiology of "rum fits" and delirium tremens. *Quarterly Journal of Studies on Alcohol*, 1955, *16*, 1–33.

Janzen, R., & Balzereit, F. Polyneuropathie bei Alkoholabusus [Polyneuropathy in alcohol abuse]. *Internist (Berl.)*, 1968, *9*, 260–263.

Jolliffe, N., & Jellinek, E. M. Vitamin deficiencies and liver cirrhosis in alcoholism: Cirrhosis of liver. *Quarterly Journal of Studies on Alcohol*, 1941, *2*, 544–583.

Jolliffe, N., Wortis, H., & Fein, H. D. The Wernicke syndrome. *Archives of Neurology and Psychiatry*, 1941, *46*, 569–597.

Kant, F. Wernicke's pseudoencephalitis of alcoholics (polioencephalitis haemorrhagica superior acuta). *Archiv fuer Psychiatrie und Nervenkrankheiten*, 1932–1933, *98*, 702–768.

Lee, K., Hardt, F., Moller, L., Haubek, A., & Jensen, E. Alcohol-induced brain damage and liver damage in young males. *Lancet*, 1979, *2*, 759–761.

Leong, A. S. Machiafava–Bignami disease in a non-alcoholic Indian male. *Pathology*, 1979, *11*, 241–249.

Lindenbaum, J., & Lieber, C. S. Effects of chronic ethanol administration on intestinal absorption in man in the absence of nutrition deficiency. *Annals of the New York Academy of Sciences*, 1975, *252*, 228–234.

Lindenbaum, J., Pezzimenti, J. F., & Shea, N. Small intestinal function in vitamin B_{12} deficiency. *Annals of Internal Medicine*, 1974, *80*, 236–331.

Lopez, R. I., & Collins, G. H. Wernicke's encephalopathy: A complication of chronic hemodialysis. *Archives of Neurology*, 1968, *18*, 248–259.

Majchrowicz, E. (Ed.). Biochemical pharmacology of ethanol. *Advances in Experimental Medicine and Biology*, 1975, *56*, 1–367.

Majchrowicz, E., & Noble, E. P. (Eds.). *Biochemistry and pharmacology of ethanol* (Vols. 1 & 2). New York: Plenum Press, 1979.

Mancall, E. L., & McEntee, W. J. Alterations of the cerebellar cortex in nutritional encephalopathy. *Neurology*, 1965, *15*, 303–313.

Martin, E. A. Alcoholic cerebellar degeneration: A report of three cases. *Journal of the Irish Medical Association*, 1965, *56*, 172–175.

McAllister, R. G., Jr., & Dzur, J. Medical admissions to a teaching service: A six months' review in a veterans hospital. *Southern Medical Journal*, 1974, *67*, 388–392.

McCandless, D. W., & Schenker, S. Encephalopathy of thiamine deficiency: Studies of intracerebral mechanisms. *Journal of Clinical Investigation*, 1968, *47*, 2268–2280.

Mezey, E. Intestinal function in chronic alcoholism. *Annals of the New York Academy of Sciences*, 1975, *252*, 215–227.

Neville, J. N., Eagles, J. A., Samson, G., & Olson, R. E. Nutritional status of alcoholics. *American Journal of Clinical Nutrition*, 1968, *21*, 1329–1340.

Niedermeyer, E., & Prokop, H. Über die Alkoholpolyneuritis und deren Stellung im Rahmen chronischer Alkoholschaden des gesamten Nervensystems [On alcohol polyneuritis and its place among chronic alcohol injuries of the entire nervous system]. *Wiener Klinische Wochenschrift*, 1959, *71*, 267–268.

Nolan, J. P. Alcohol as a factor in the illness of university service patients. *American Journal of Medical Science*, 1965, *249*, 135–142.

Novak, D. J., & Victor, M. The vagus and sympathetic nerves in alcoholic polyneuropathy. *Archives of Neurology*, 1974, *30*, 273–284.

Parker, E. S., & Noble, E. P. Alcohol and the aging process in social drinkers. *Journal of Studies on Alcohol*, 1980, *41*, 170–178.

Parsons, O. A. Cognitive dysfunction in alcoholics and social drinkers: Introduction. *Journal of Studies on Alcohol*, 1980, *41*, 107–118.

Pell, S., & D'Alonzo, C. A. The prevalence of chronic disease among problem drinkers. *Archives of Environmental Health*, 1968, *16*, 679–684.

Phillip, G., & Smith, J. F. Hypothermia and Wernicke's encephalopathy. *Lancet*, 1973, *2*, 122–124.

Phillips, G. B., Victor, M., Adams, R. D., & Davidson, C. S. A study of the nutritional defect in Wernicke's syndrome: The effect of a purified diet, thiamine, and other vitamins on the clinical manifestations. *Journal of Clinical Investigation*, 1952, *31*, 859–871.

Robertson, D. M., Wasan, S. M., & Skinner, D. B. Ultrastructural features of early brain stem lesions of thiamine-deficient rats. *American Journal of Pathology*, 1968, *52*, 1081–1097.

Ryan, C. & Butters, N. Further evidence for a continuum-of-impairment encompassing male alcoholic Korsakoff patients and chronic alcoholic men. *Alcoholism (New York)*, 1980, *4*, 190–198.

Salum, I. Delirium tremens and certain other acute sequels of alcohol abuse. *Acta Psychiatrica Scandinavica (Supplementum)*, 1972, *235*, 1–145.

Schmidt, W., & de Lint, J. Causes of death of alcoholics. *Quarterly Journal of Studies on Alcohol*, 1972, *33*, 171–185.

Single, E. W. Estimating the number of alcoholics in Ontario: A replication and extension of an earlier study. *Journal of Studies on Alcohol*, 1979, *40*, 1046–1052.

Thomson, A. D., Baker, H., & Leevy, C. M. Patterns of ^{35}S-thiamine hydrochloride absorption in the malnourished alcoholic patient. *Journal of Laboratory and Clinical Medicine*, 1970, *76*, 34–45.

Tomasulo, P. A., Kater, R. M. H., & Iber, F. L. Impairment of thiamine absorption in alcoholism. *American Journal of Clinical Nutrition*, 1968, *11*, 1340–1344.

Victor, M. The role of alcohol in the production of seizures. *Modern Problems in Pharmacopsychiatry*, 1970, *4*, 185–199.

Victor, M., & Yakovlev, P. I. S. S. Korsakoff's psychiatric disorder in conjunction with peripheral neuritis: A translation of Korsakoff's original article with brief comments on the author and his contribution to clinical medicine. *Neurology*, 1955, *5*, 394–406.

Victor, M., Adams, R. D., & Mancall, E. L. A restricted form of cerebellar cortical degeneration occurring in alcoholic patients. *Archives of Neurology*, 1959, *1*, 579–688.

Walsh, J. C., & McLeod, J. G. Alcoholic neuropathy: An electrophysiological and histological study. *Journal of Neurological Sciences*, 1970, *10*, 457–469.

Walter, G. I. Marchiafava–Bignami disease: First case in Germany. *Archiv für Psychiatrie und Nervenkrankheiten*, 1978, *226*, 75–78.

Wanamaker, W. M., & Skillman, T. G. Motor nerve conduction in alcoholics. *Quarterly Journal of Studies on Alcohol*, 1966, *27*, 16–22.

Westerfield, W. W., & Lawrow, J. The effect of caloric restriction and thiamine deficiency on the voluntary consumption of alcohol by rats. *Quarterly Journal of Studies on Alcohol,* 1953, *14,* 378–384.

Zimmerman, H. M. Neuropathies due to vitamin deficiency. *Journal of Neuropathology and Experimental Neurology,* 1956, *15,* 335–339.

7.1. Monographs and Reviews

Denny-Brown, D. Neurological conditions resulting from prolonged and severe dietary restriction. *Medicine,* 1947, 26, 41–113.

Freund, G. Chronic central nervous system toxicity of alcohol. *Annual Review of Pharmacology,* 1973, *13,* 217–227.

Freund, G. Diseases of the nervous system associated with alcoholism. In R. E. Tarter and A. A. Sugerman (Eds.), *Alcoholism: Interdisciplinary approaches to an enduring problem.* Reading, Mass.: Addison-Wesley, 1976.

Freund, G. Interactions of aging and chronic alcohol consumption on the central nervous system. In W. G. Wood & M. F. Elias (Eds.), *Alcoholism and aging: Advances in research.* Boca Raton, Fla.: CRC Press, 1982. (b)

Hillman, R. W. Alcoholism and malnutrition. In B. Kissin & H. Begleiter (Eds.), *The biology of alcoholism* (Vol. 3). *Clinical pathology.* New York: Plenum Press, 1974.

Katzman, R., Terry, R. D., & Bick, K. L. *Alzheimer's disease: Senile dementia and related disorders.* New York: Raven Press, 1978.

Kissin, B., & Begleiter, H. (Eds.). *The biology of alcoholism* (Vol. 3). *Clinical pathology.* New York: Plenum Press, 1974.

Plum, F. (Ed.) *Brain dysfunction in metabolic disorders (Proceedings of the Association for Research in Nervous and Mental Disease,* Vol. 53). New York: Raven Press, 1974.

Seixas, F. K., Williams, K., & Eggleston, S. (Eds.). Medical consequences of alcoholism. *Annals of the New York Academy of Sciences,* 1975, *252,* 1–399.

Spillane, J. D., & Riddoch, G. *Nutritional disorders of the nervous system.* Baltimore: Williams and Wilkins, 1974.

Tarter, R. E., & Sugerman, A. A. (Eds.) *Alcoholism: Interdisciplinary approaches to an enduring problem.* Reading, Mass.: Addison-Wesley, 1976.

Turner, T. B., Mezey, E., & Kimball, A. W. Measurement of alcohol-related effects in man: Chronic effects in relation to levels of alcohol consumption (Part A). *Johns Hopkins Medical Journal,* 1977, *141,* 235–248.

United States Public Health Service. *The international classification of diseases* (9th ed.). *Clinical modification* (ICD-9-CM). Washington, D.C.: United States Public Health Service, 1980.

Victor, M., Adams, R. D., & Collins, G. H. *The Wernicke-Korsakoff syndrome.* Philadelphia: Davis, 1971.

Wells, C. E. (Ed.). *Dementia* (2nd ed.). Philadelphia: Davis, 1977.

Wilson, F. A., & Hoyumpa, A. M., Jr. Ethanol and small intestinal transport. *Gastroenterology,* 1979, *76,* 388–403.

7

Biology of Tolerance and Dependence

BORIS TABAKOFF AND JEFFREY D. ROTHSTEIN

Alcoholism is a heterogeneous phenomenon that involves maladaptive behavior, medical complications, and cultural attitudes, but all realistic definitions of alcoholism include reference to an individual's tolerance to and dependence on ethanol (see Chapter 1). Alcohol tolerance and dependence, however, are not unidimensional entities; therefore it will be the purpose of this chapter to introduce the reader to the various facets of tolerance and dependence on ethanol, to discuss the implications of tolerance and dependence in promoting aberrant drinking behavior and alcohol-induced pathologies, and to describe the current treatment approaches used to manage the acute alcohol withdrawal syndrome.

1. INTRODUCTION TO TOLERANCE AND DEPENDENCE

Tolerance to ethanol or to other pharmacological agents is present if one witnesses a *diminished response* to a particular dose of a drug (e.g., ethanol) *after* one or more prior administrations of this drug (see further discussion below). Tolerance can also be said to be present if a *larger dose* of ethanol is necessary to produce a particular intensity of physiologic or behavioral response in an individual who has previously consumed ethanol as compared to the dose that was necessary to produce such response in this individual prior to the consumption of

BORIS TABAKOFF • Westside Veterans Administration Medical Center, Chicago, Illinois 60612, and Alcohol and Drug Abuse Research and Training Program, Department of Physiology and Biophysics, University of Illinois at the Medical Center, Chicago, Illinois 60680. JEFFREY D. ROTHSTEIN • Department of Physiology and Biophysics, University of Illinois at the Medical Center, Chicago, Illinois 60680.

ethanol. The definitions of tolerance have also included a distinction between metabolic and functional tolerance. Functional tolerance describes a resistance to ethanol's effects at the cellular level, while metabolic tolerance is concerned with changes in the absorption, distribution, degradation, and excretion of ethanol that would contribute to an increased rate of elimination of ethanol in an individual with a history of prior ethanol ingestion. A demonstration of a *decreased* effect of ethanol in the tolerant individual at cellular levels of ethanol that produce a greater effect in the ethanol "naive" individual is necessary before concluding that *functional* tolerance is present. If tolerance is monitored by changes in the *duration* of the effects of ethanol, rather than by the extent of an effect at particular tissue levels of ethanol, one has to consider that metabolic tolerance (i.e., increased elimination rate) could be responsible for a diminished duration of ethanol's effects.

Dependence on ethanol has been, on many occasions, subclassified into psychological dependence and physical dependence. Psychological dependence is an imprecise term encompassing the difficult-to-define concepts of "need" or "craving" for ethanol in an individual with a prior history of heavy ethanol consumption. It is now well established that ethanol possesses reinforcing properties—that is, particular behaviors will be maintained or accelerated if ethanol administration is used as a "reward" for performance of that behavior; thus, behaviors leading to self-administration of ethanol can be established and maintained in a human or animal, with ethanol acting as the "reinforcer." The voluntary self-administration of ethanol by an animal or human, even in lieu of performing other behaviors, does not, however, characterize the more complex meanings that have been attached to the terms "need" or "craving." These terms indicate that there exists some underlying biologic necessity for ethanol in the psychologically dependent individuals and that these individuals would be adversely affected were ethanol to be withheld from them. Little evidence exists—within the context of either human or animal studies on ethanol self-administration—to support such contentions. Humans or animals will voluntarily terminate ethanol ingestion in paradigms designed to show the reinforcing properties of ethanol, and no adverse symptoms accompany such cessation of ethanol intake (see reviews by Mello, 1972; Spealman & Goldberg, 1978). Thus, although "psychological dependence" is a term that is often used within the discussion of factors responsible for ingestion of ethanol, it has, at present, little or no scientific basis for definition.

The term "physical dependence" has been used, in distinction to "psychological dependence," to describe the fact that either humans or animals, given sufficiently large amounts of ethanol for varying periods of time, will exhibit characteristic physiologic disturbances if the intake or administration of ethanol suddenly ceases. The presence of the "withdrawal reaction" (see description below) has been used as *a priori* evidence that an individual was physically dependent on ethanol. In other words, the presence of high amounts of ethanol in the body for prolonged periods results in tissue *adaptation,* which could then be responsible for the signs and symptoms of the ethanol withdrawal syndrome upon termination of ethanol ingestion.

2. FACTORS CONTRIBUTING TO TOLERANCE AND DEPENDENCE

In trying to conceptualize the biochemical factors responsible for functional tolerance and physical dependence, experimenters have, in the past, considered that development of functional tolerance was inexorably linked to the development of physical dependence (i.e., tolerance and physical dependence were thought to be processes that had identical biologic determinants; Himmelsbach, 1942). Thus, the intake of ethanol would produce intoxication by interfering with the function of the CNS. The CNS would adapt in an as yet undefined way to the presence of ethanol, such that functional, CNS *tolerance* developed. The ethanol-adapted (tolerant) CNS, however, could not function properly in the absence of ethanol and, upon ethanol withdrawal, a syndrome indicative of the altered CNS function would become evident. A number of possible cellular sites have been proposed for the adaptive response(s) leading to the development of functional tolerance and physical dependence. Neurotransmitter receptor changes that occur during the time that ethanol is present in the CNS have formed the basis of theories of tolerance and physical dependence, such as those proposed by Jaffe and Sharpless ("denervation supersensitivity hypothesis"; 1968), and by Collier ("receptor proliferation hypothesis"; 1968). Adaptive changes in enzymes functioning in neurotransmitter metabolism have been hypothesized by Goldstein and Goldstein (1968) to be the factors responsible for the development of tolerance and physical dependence (the "enzyme expansion theory"), and the "redundant neuronal pathway theory" proposed by Martin (1970) suggested that tolerance and physical dependence were related to the recruitment of additional neuronal networks to maintain normal function in the presence of ethanol. Although the proposed theories were parsimonious and are still adhered to by a significant number of researchers, there exists substantial recent evidence that functional tolerance and physical dependence may be distinct and separable phenomena.

Studies that have monitored the time course for development of tolerance and signs of physical dependence after ethanol withdrawal in animals have found that the time courses for development and dissipation of these phenomena do not follow each other as closely as would be predicted from the above "homeostatic adaptation" hypotheses. One must, however, be careful in coming to conclusions from the studies which show differences in the time course of development or dissipation of tolerance and dependence, since the investigators usually monitored tolerance by using only one or two measures, and withdrawal symptoms were also crudely measured. As will be discussed below, the rate of tolerance development can vary, depending on the measure used to monitor tolerance. Similarly, the time course of the development or duration of physical dependence varies with the measure used to characterize the withdrawal syndrome. Thus, by using behavioral or physiological tests that are not equally sensitive for demonstrating tolerance and physical dependence, one may draw erroneous conclusions. This argument has, however, been overcome by studies of tolerance and dependence on the molecular and cellular level, where adaptive, compensatory changes (tolerance) leading to resistance to ethanol's disruptive effects on cellular membranes (Goldstein, 1973) or synaptic transmission events (Curran & Seeman, 1977; Traynor, Schlapfer, & Barondes, 1980) have been shown not to be accompanied by "rebound" phenomena that could be described as signs of withdrawal or physical dependence.

Further evidence indicating that functional tolerance and physical dependence are separable phenomena comes from studies demonstrating that tolerance development in an ethanol-consuming mouse can be blocked by partial destruction of the noradrenergic systems of brain but that physical dependence will develop as usual in such animals (Tabakoff & Ritzmann, 1977). Tolerance to ethanol can also be maintained for long periods in animals given small daily doses of the peptide hormone arginine vasopressin (Hoffman, Ritzmann, & Tabakoff, 1979), but there is no evidence that the same treatment will prolong the presence of physical dependence to any comparable degree if physical dependence is measured by the presence of withdrawal symptoms.

One can, at present, conclude that the "homeostatic adaptation" hypothesis, which forms the foundation for the conceptualization of functional tolerance and physical dependence as expressions of a singular biologic process, is not supported by a substantial number of current studies. We will, therefore, address the phenomena of tolerance and physical dependence as separate issues. In our discussion of tolerance, we will also attempt to define several subclasses of CNS (functional) tolerance; it is hoped that this discussion will not only indicate the salient features of the development of alcohol tolerance in humans and animals but also point to the gaps in knowledge regarding alcohol tolerance.

3. CLASSIFICATIONS AND DEFINITIONS OF TOLERANCE

Tolerance can be demonstrated within the time that a single dose of ethanol is cleared from an individual. This "within session" tolerance has been referred to as acute tolerance, and the initial description of the phenomenon can be attributed to Mellanby (1919). Acute tolerance is usually exemplified by a diminished effect of ethanol during the descending portion of the blood alcohol curve (BAC) as compared with the effect witnessed at the same tissue concentrations of ethanol on the ascending portion of the BAC. Within the context of acute tolerance, one should also consider that tolerance may well be evidenced, even during the rising portion of the BAC if the rate of increase in the BAC is sufficiently slow.

Chronic tolerance (i.e., between-session tolerance) can be defined as tolerance which develops *after* a single dose or repeated dosing with ethanol. Chronic tolerance is exemplified by the fact that a particular dose of ethanol, given after the initial dose or after repeated dosing with this drug, produces less of an effect than it would in a drug-naive animal. Studies now available do not clearly answer the questions of whether *acute* tolerance is a precursor to *chronic* tolerance or in any other way related to it. The studies of Kalant, LeBlanc, and Gibbins (1971) demonstrated that the asymptotic value for tolerance achieved with chronic ethanol administration to rats was greater than tolerance achieved with a single dose; the authors therefore postulated that acute tolerance may be an additive component of chronic tolerance. The elucidation of the relationship between acute and chronic tolerance will, however, be achieved only by clarifying the biochemical mechanisms that underlie the various forms of tolerance.

3.1. Environment-Dependent and -Independent Tolerance

Recent studies have also demonstrated the necessity of subdividing chronic tolerance into at least two components: *environment-dependent* and *environment-independent*. The classification of environment-dependent tolerance was initially necessitated by studies showing that the *rate of development* of chronic tolerance to the behavior-modifying effects of ethanol in both animals and humans could be increased by repeated testing under particular environmental conditions. LeBlanc, Gibbins, and Kalant (1975) concluded from their studies of tolerance development in rats that "adaptive changes responsible for tolerance to ethanol are influenced by the functional demand imposed upon the central nervous system during the period of drug effect, but are *not* totally dependent on such demands." That is, they found that although the rate of tolerance development is influenced by the conditions under which the animal receives ethanol, tolerance will eventually develop regardless of these conditions.

On the other hand, the studies of Siegel (1975) suggested that tolerance to morphine can be *totally* controlled by environmental cues and that the pharmacologic effect of morphine alone may not be sufficient to initiate tolerance development. Recent studies presented by Wenger, Tiffany, Bombardier, Nicholls, and Woods (1981) further question the conclusions of LeBlanc and his coworkers (1975), indicating that tolerance to the behavioral effects of ethanol *cannot* be demonstrated without exposing an animal to the effects of ethanol within the test situation (i.e., tolerance is a learned phenomenon).

On basis of the studies of Siegel and others a Pavlovian conditioning model of alcohol tolerance has been proposed by a number of investigators. According to this model, each drug administration represents a conditioning trial: the drug administration constitutes the unconditioned stimulus which, in turn, elicits an unconditioned physiological response(s) from the organism. The total *environmental context* in which the drug is given—such as the experimental apparatus, preparatory procedures, and so on—serves as conditioned stimuli.

In the course of repeated drug administration or even possibly during the prolonged presence of a single drug dose, a conditioned response develops in association with those environmental stimuli that have been paired with the unconditioned, pharmacological stimulus. This conditioned response represents an attempt to compensate for the physiological perturbation produced by the drug. As a result, the conditioned response effectively counteracts the direct drug effect. The conditioning model proposes that the development of such a compensatory response eventually attenuates the direct pharmacological drug action and that the observed result of such attenuation is tolerance. Therefore, as a consequence of repeated drug administration within a consistent, predictable environment, tolerance can be demonstrated *only in the environment with which the drug has been paired.* If the drug is administered outside the environment with which it has previously been associated, the organism will not be tolerant (Melchior & Tabakoff, 1981). It is clear that such environment-dependent ethanol tolerance does occur under proper conditions (Melchior & Tabakoff, 1981). However, environment-independent forms of ethanol tolerance have also been demonstrated.

Tolerance to ethanol has been shown to develop under conditions where ethanol is administered as part of a liquid diet or by inhalation techniques; the animals are tested for tolerance after injection of ethanol. Within such paradigms, learning would be expected to play an insignificant role in tolerance development and, consonant with this fact, tolerance in such studies has been demonstrated to be independent of the testing environment. Examination of experimental protocols of studies of environment-dependent and -independent forms of ethanol tolerance indicates that continuous exposure to *significantly higher amounts of ethanol* is necessary to produce environment-independent tolerance as compared to environment-dependent tolerance, but further distinction of these subclasses of tolerance and assessment of the determinants of these tolerances will require additional studies.

Environment-dependent and environment-independent forms of tolerance can be further subdivided into the functional and metabolic (dispositional) components, defined above. Although prior studies indicated that chronic administration of ethanol was necessary to induce dispositional tolerance (see Chapter 3), the recent studies of Yuki, Bradford, and Thurman (1980) indicate that the rate of ethanol metabolism can be increased during the time that a single, initial dose of ethanol is being removed from the animal. It is of interest that *environment-dependent* or "learned" tolerance to barbiturates has been shown in certain cases to be mediated by altered *metabolism* of the administered hexobarbital (Roffman & Lal, 1974); recent studies on environment-dependent ethanol tolerance indicate that altered distribution of ethanol may be the underlying determinant of this tolerance. Dispositional tolerance can, therefore, contribute to both environment-dependent and environment-independent forms of tolerance.

Figure 1, a flowchart, shows the contribution of various components to acute and chronic tolerance development.

Although it is quite important to distinguish between the various forms of tolerance when the determinants of tolerance are being analyzed, the construction of most published studies, either of humans or animals, does not allow for making such distinctions. Therefore, in the following discussion, "tolerance" will often be used as a generic term to denote differences between the initial sensitivity to ethanol in an ethanol-naive individual and measures of sensitivity subsequent to the initial exposure to a particular level of ethanol.

3.2. Acute Tolerance

The ability to demonstrate the development of acute tolerance in either humans or animals seems to be related to the task being used as a measure of

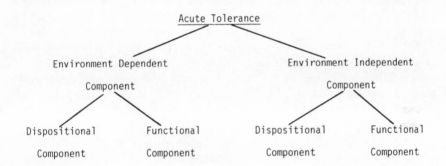

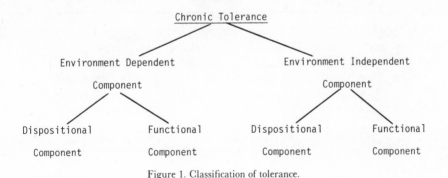

Figure 1. Classification of tolerance.

ethanol's actions and to the individual's genetic constitution (see below). Acute tolerance has been demonstrated to occur in humans when ethanol's actions have been measured by tests of motor performance, cognitive function, standing steadiness, and self-reports of intoxication. On the other hand, no acute tolerance was noted if a pursuit rotor task was used as a measure of ethanol's effect (see review by Tabakoff, 1980). A difficult problem, ignored in earlier studies of acute tolerance, concerns the relationship between venous blood levels of ethanol, which are usually measured, and ethanol levels at the site of action (e.g., the brain). During the absorption phase after ingestion or administration of ethanol, ethanol rapidly partitions into the brain, therefore brain ethanol levels are not well reflected by ethanol levels in venous or mixed venous/arterial blood samples. This problem may be somewhat ameliorated by determining ethanol levels in capillary blood samples or using Breathalyzer samples for ethanol determinations. These sampling methods give better correlation to brain levels of ethanol at any particular time and are necessary to derive appropriate conclusions on the development of acute tolerance.

An individual's genetic constitution may control his or her ability to develop acute tolerance. Studies utilizing inbred strains of mice demonstrated that mice of the C57B1 strain easily developed acute tolerance, while DBA mice did not. Measures of the duration of acute tolerance are few and are confounded by lack of attention to environment-dependent variables. Human studies by Vogel-Sprott (1979) have indicated that tolerance developed during a single exposure to ethanol, as measured by a coding task, was carried over to a subsequent alcoholization occurring one week later. Animal studies demonstrate that the administration of a single inebriating dose of ethanol does not alter an animal's response to a second dose of ethanol (measured by performance on a moving-belt test or by loss of righting reflex) if the administrations are separated by three or more days. However, if the injections of ethanol are spaced 24 hours apart, a significant diminution of the effects of the second dose of ethanol has been noted. Thus, at least for certain measures, acute tolerance can be maintained for periods significantly longer than the period during which a single dose of ethanol is present in the human or animal. These studies may also provide the initial evidence that acute tolerance may be an additive component of chronic tolerance.

An initial cycle of tolerance development may also "prime" the adaptive machinery of an individual so that, during subsequent consumption of ethanol, tolerance can develop at a greater rate or to a greater extent (Kalant, LeBlanc, & Gibbins, 1978a). Acute tolerance may, in this manner, act to promote the development of chronic tolerance.

3.3. Chronic Tolerance

At one time, it was commonly believed that chronic tolerance in humans develops only after long exposure to ethanol, and most of the early studies on tolerance in human volunteers used relatively long periods (several weeks) of ethanol administration prior to testing for tolerance. Tolerance, in these studies, was demonstrated to be present by hospital staff's subjective impressions of intoxication and by measures of the EEG effects of ethanol. However, little information was gathered on either the rate of tolerance development in humans or the rate of dissipation of tolerance once established. On the other hand, studies with animals have determined that chronic tolerance can develop to its maximal levels even during several days of ethanol administration. As discussed above, it is important to recognize that the actual rate of tolerance development is a function of the measure being used to ascertain the presence of chronic tolerance. This statement pertains to both environment-dependent and environment-independent forms of functional tolerance. For instance, tolerance to the hypothermic effects of ethanol was evidenced much sooner than tolerance to ethanol's hypnotic effects in paradigms which used either discrete injections of ethanol (environment-dependent method) or administration of ethanol within a liquid diet to mice (environment-independent method) to establish tolerance. Additional data have also been presented indicating that although mice become tolerant to the hypnotic effects of ethanol, they do not, under the same conditions of ethanol administration, become tolerant to ethanol's activating effects on their locomotor behavior. Direct extrapolation from these animal studies to the human situation is not, at present, possible, but one can conclude that both humans and animals consuming ethanol exhibit a *slowly developing component of tolerance* that reaches a plateau within a few days to three weeks of daily intoxication. A very crude generalization can also be made regarding the extent to which ethanol tolerance develops. Once tolerance reaches an asymptote, both humans and animals improve their performance about 50% to 100% under the influence of ethanol (Kalant *et al.*, 1971; also other references cited above). These figures are dependent on both the task and the extent of initial performance impairment.

Once maximal tolerance had been established within a particular paradigm, studies using mice and rats as experimental animals demonstrated that tolerance disappeared within a seven-day period after discontinuation of the chronic ethanol treatment. LeBlanc, Kalant, Gibbins, and Berman (1969) also noted a phase of increased sensitivity to ethanol among rats that occurred approximately 12 days after a 28-day treatment with ethanol. Although the increased sensitivity did not reach statistical significance, it should be considered within the context of anecdotal reports on increased sensitivity to ethanol of some alcoholics after a period of withdrawal. The response of the ethanol-withdrawn rats to ethanol in the studies of LeBlanc *et al.* (1969) became indistinguishable from that of the controls after a 17- to 21-day ethanol-free period. Tolerance was, however, shown to develop more rapidly during a second cycle of ethanol administration, even when a 17-day drug-free period intervened between cycles, and tolerance developed even more rapidly in subsequent cycles (Kalant, LeBlanc, Gibbins, & Wilson, 1978b). This finding has been substantiated by others (Masur & Boerngen, 1980); one can thus postulate that long-lasting, subliminal changes occur in the CNS during chronic ethanol administration to animals, and that these changes contribute to tolerance formation in subsequent exposures to ethanol. Although quantitation of such effects in humans is lacking, Mendelson and LaDou (1964) noted that alcoholics attain a higher level of alcohol consumption in a lesser time compared to nonalcoholic subjects.

3.4. Neuronal Systems Responsible for Development of Tolerance

The development of functional tolerance, and particularly environment-dependent functional tolerance, can be viewed as a process similar to other CNS adaptive phenomena, including memory consolidation. To determine the contribution of particular neuronal systems to ethanol tolerance, one can, therefore, consider studies that have examined the effects on tolerance development of agents known to disrupt memory consolidation.

In animals, ablations of the frontal cortex and treatment with cycloheximide, an inhibitor of protein synthesis, have been shown to inhibit the development of alcohol tolerance (LeBlanc & Cappel, 1977). Both these procedures have previously been shown to interfere with consolidation of learned responses. The generalized destruction of neuronal systems or interference with neuronal function does not, however, give insight into whether or not particular neuronal systems are responsible for the development of tolerance. Several of the neurotransmitter systems of the brain—for example, serotonin (5-HT), norepinephrine (NE) and acetylcholine (ACh)—have been demonstrated to play an integral role in memory consolidation processes; the effects of selective destruction of these systems have also been examined with respect to ethanol tolerance development.

The *development of tolerance* to ethanol in rats was slowed by chronic administration of *p*-chlorophenylalanine (*p*CPA) in a dosage regimen that produced and maintained approximately 95% depletion of brain serotonin (Frankel, Khanna, LeBlanc, & Kalant, 1975). Similarly, selective destruction of serotonergic neurons with the neurotoxin 5,7-dihydroxytryptamine significantly slowed tolerance development (Frankel, Khanna, Kalant, & LeBlanc, 1979). Tolerance to both the hypothermic and motor-impairing effects of ethanol was evaluated in these studies. Once tolerance was established, pCPA did not affect its expression, but it did increase the rate of loss of tolerance. Thus, part of the inhibitory effect on tolerance development could have been due to the accelerated loss of tolerance during the induction phase. The depletion of brain 5-HT did not affect the metabolism of ethanol after the test dose.

Partial destruction of mouse brain catecholamine systems with the selective neurotoxin 6-hydroxydopamine (6-OHDA) also blocked the development of tolerance to the hypothermic and sedative effects of ethanol in studies where mice were fed an ethanol-containing liquid diet (Ritzmann & Tabakoff, 1976; Tabakoff & Ritzmann, 1977). In these studies, the rate of acquisition of tolerance was not determined, so that a decrease in the rate of tolerance development cannot be ruled out. On the other hand, in a paradigm that produced environment-dependent tolerance, 6-OHDA treatment was shown to slow tolerance development (Melchior & Tabakoff, 1981). In all studies with 6-OHDA, noradrenergic systems, rather than dopaminergic systems, were postulated to be of importance for development of ethanol tolerance, but the destruction of noradrenergic systems after tolerance had developed did not affect expression of this tolerance (Tabakoff & Ritzmann, 1977).

The involvement of cholinergic systems in the *development* of ethanol tolerance has not been as extensively investigated, but Wahlstrom and Ekwall (1976) did demonstrate that injections of hemicholinium, which depleted brain acetylcholine, postponed the appearance of tolerance during chronic treatment of rats with barbiturates.

The above results may seem to indicate that specific neuronal systems are necessary for normal development of ethanol and barbiturate tolerance, but it must be remembered that both pharmacological and histochemical experiments have described interactions between noradrenergic and serotonergic systems in the CNS (Renaud, Buda, Lewis, & Pujol, 1975; Antelman & Caggiola, 1977). Interactions also exist between NE and DA systems—and ACh, NE, and DA systems—in which each system modulates the activity of the other. Thus, it is quite likely that the development and/or expression of ethanol tolerance is ultimately controlled by interactions between NE and 5-HT networks and between these and other systems.

These studies on the effect of neurotoxins on the *development* of tolerance also bring out the important fact that the presence of ethanol in the milieu of neuronal systems is a necessary but not, in itself, sufficient factor for the development of tolerance. The appropriate activity of certain neuronal systems (e.g., noradrenergic neurons), as well as the interaction of the various neuronal systems in the presence of ethanol, seems to be a controlling factor for tolerance development, at least in animals.

Additional evidence of similarities between neurobiological processes that modulate memory and ethanol tolerance has recently been obtained with the use of vasopressin and related peptides. Administration of vasopressin, which has previously been shown to prevent extinction of learned behaviors (Walter, Hoffman, Flexner, & Flexner, 1975; De Wied, Bohus, van Wimersma Griedanus, & Gispen, 1975), to mice chronically treated with ethanol, postponed the disappearance of ethanol tolerance after termination of the ethanol administration (Hoffman *et al.*, 1979; Hoffman, Ritzmann, Walter, & Tabakoff, 1978).

4. BIOCHEMICAL DETERMINANTS OF ETHANOL TOLERANCE

To elucidate the biochemical systems that actually become tolerant to ethanol (i.e., to identify systems in which tolerance actually resides), investigators have utilized the concept that tolerance (resistance to ethanol) should be demonstrable in systems that are initially inhibited or disrupted by the presence of ethanol. The neuronal membrane contains entities that modulate ion permeabilities and recognize transmitter molecules, and these entities are important for conduction and transmission of information in the CNS. Ethanol has been shown to affect ion permeabilities in excitable tissues (Seeman, 1972), and ethanol added to neuronal membranes has been shown to produce a disordering effect (increased "fluidity") in such membranes (see Chapter 5). On the other hand, neuronal membranes derived from ethanol-fed mice were found to be resistant to such disordering effects of ethanol, and this resistance (tolerance) has been postulated to be the result of increased cholesterol levels or changes in phospholipid composition in the membranes of the ethanol-tolerant animals (Goldstein & Chin, 1981). Cholesterol interacts with the hydrocarbon chains of the phospholipid in the neuronal membranes, and changes in either the hydrocarbon chain saturation *per se* or membrane cholesterol content would markedly affect fluidity of neuronal plasma membranes. Such changes can impart to the membrane a resistance to ethanol's effects.

The lipids of the neuronal membrane are its major structural components, but the major functional components (i.e., ionophores, receptors, and transport enzymes) are proteinacious in nature. Changes in membrane lipid composition can, however, alter the activity of these membrane-bound, functional proteins Tabakoff & Hoffman, 1983). For instance, the function of neurotransmitter-sensitive adenylate cyclase and the sodium-potassium–activated ATPase have both been shown to be sensitive to changes in membrane lipids, and the activity of both of these enzymes has been shown to be altered by chronic ethanol administration. Thus, it may be postulated that chronic ethanol administration produces adaptive changes in the lipids of neuronal membranes and that these changes in lipids may, in turn, alter the function of certain enzymes and receptors residing in the neuronal membranes. Changes in the activity of the functional components of the neuronal membranes and their resistance to ethanol's actions would contribute to the expression of the ethanol-tolerant state. The postulated changes in the lipids of neuronal membranes offer a testable hypothesis regarding the determinants of ethanol tolerance, but it must be recognized that this is not the only possible explanation of tolerance development. A wide array of other neurochemical parameters have been examined in relation to tolerance development. However, no definitive data now exist to indicate a predominant responsibility to any neurochemical system for being the repository of the various forms of functional ethanol tolerance. For further discussion on the acute and chronic effects of ethanol on the CNS, the reader is referred to several recent reviews (Tabakoff & Hoffman, 1980; Tabakoff & Hoffman, 1983), including Chapter 5 in this volume. Similarly, no consensus has been reached on the mechanisms by which metabolic tolerance is manifested, but Chapter 3 in this volume provides some viable possibilities.

5. CHARACTERISTICS OF PHYSICAL DEPENDENCE ON ETHANOL

As already stated, the presence of physical dependence on ethanol is, in large part, defined by the fact that a characteristic syndrome, consisting of symptoms which are, in most cases, opposite to the signs of acute intoxication, becomes evident in a dependent human or animal upon cessation of ethanol intake. It is, at present, generally accepted in the United States that the symptoms that have been referred to as delirium tremens (see below) are a result of *withdrawal* from consumption of large amounts of ethanol. On the other hand, a number of clinicians and researchers in Europe adhere to the position that several of the symptoms that comprise the "withdrawal syndrome" are actually pathological signs of intoxication. One should, from the outset, be aware that such disagreements center on only certain symptoms noted after cessation of ethanol intake, and that the data on this subject can be reconciled into an integrated picture of intoxication and withdrawal (see Gross, Rosenblatt, Chartoff, Hermann, Schachter, Sheinkin, & Broman, 1971).

The initial detailed description of the "acute" (i.e., three to eight days' duration) alcohol withdrawal syndrome has been attributed to the British physician Joseph Sutton, who, in 1813, noted the three cardinal signs of the alcohol withdrawal syndrome to be tremors, clouding of the sensorium, and visual hallucinations. He also stated that these symptoms were a result of cessation of heavy consumption of alcoholic beverages. Although the studies of Sutton and other early investigators were for a time forgotten, the fact that alcohol withdrawal produces a characteristic syndrome of physiologic and behavioral pathology in humans was clearly established in the early 1950s by the studies of Victor and Adams (1953) and Isbell, Fraser, Wikler, Belleville, and Eisenman (1955). Prior to the early 1950s, the acute withdrawal syndrome had been categorized into three major entities: (1) "impending delirium tremens," a state characterized by mild to severe clouding of the sensorium, tremor, sweating and insomnia; (2) "delirium tremens," consisting of visual hallucinations, moderate to marked clouding of the sensorium, moderate to marked alterations in temperature regulation, and marked sweating; and (3) "acute alcoholic hallucinosis," a rare phenomenon consisting primarily of auditory hallucinations with few if any other derangements in physiologic function. Acute alcoholic hallucinosis has been considered by some clinicians to represent a primary schizoid problem which is uncovered during alcohol withdrawal. The categorization of the alcohol withdrawal syndrome into impending delirium tremens and delirium tremens implies a progression from mild to severe symptomatology. However, a significant number of patients show severe tremors and diaphoresis during the early stages of alcohol withdrawal and may even demonstrate convulsions but not hallucinations. Thus, the above categorization does not clearly classify the symptomatology of a large number (25% to 50%)

of patients undergoing withdrawal from ethanol. To improve diagnostic classification, Victor and Adams (1953) devised a scale for ethanol withdrawal symptoms based on the time of their appearance after withdrawal. This classification also grouped the symptoms along a continuum from lesser to greater severity. The symptoms ranged from tremulousness to epileptiform seizures and hallucinatory behavior to delirious states. Each patient could manifest any combination of symptoms, but symptoms were expected to occur in a particular sequence after withdrawal. For instance, tremulousness and seizures were characteristic of the early (up to 72 hours) period after withdrawal of ethanol, while delirium would not be expected until after this initial withdrawal period. The sequence of appearance of symptoms of ethanol withdrawal led Wolfe and Victor (1971) to modify Victor and Adams's (1953) earlier classification and to designate a dichotomous classification of symptoms of ethanol withdrawal. Currently, this is the most common classification of the symptoms of ethanol withdrawal. The ethanol withdrawal symptoms are divided into an early (minor) and a later (major, delirium tremens) withdrawal syndrome (Figure 2). The nomenclature of "minor" and "major" syndrome is unfortunate, since life-threatening situations can occur both early and late in withdrawal. Thus, epileptiform seizures are characteristic of the early stages of ethanol withdrawal, while severe autonomic malfunctions (tachycardia, profuse perspiration, fever, etc.) occur in conjunction with delirium in the later stages of withdrawal. The utility of the Wolfe and Victor (1971) designation is, however, in predicting the course of the symptomatology and improving the capability of the clinician to develop a prognosis for the individual undergoing withdrawal from ethanol. More recently, even more precise and extensive systems for classifying clinical variables of the ethanol withdrawal syndrome have been devel-

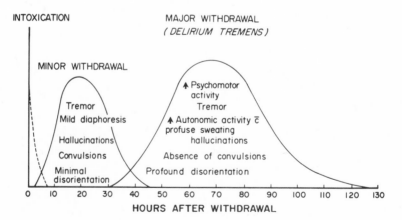

Figure 2. Clinical manifestations of the minor (early) alcohol withdrawal syndrome and the major withdrawal syndrome (delirium tremens). (From Wolfe and Victor, 1971.)

oped. The utility of these newer approaches, particularly the classifications and severity scales developed by Gross, Lewis, and Hastey (1974), is that an understanding of the relationship between various symptoms can be obtained by statistical methods such as factor analysis. Such analysis can indicate which symptoms occur in clusters or which are prognostic for others. The analysis can also be utilized to generate hypotheses regarding the underlying biochemical or physiological mechanisms that may generate particular clusters of symptoms.

Gross and coworkers defined 30 signs and symptoms of the ethanol withdrawal syndrome. By using a statistical analysis of these symptoms in patients undergoing withdrawal, they were able to identify three factors. Each factor contained related symptoms which were independent of symptoms contained within other factors. These factors and some of the symptoms contained therein are as follows (Gross *et al.,* 1974):

1. *Factor I:* Nausea and vomiting; tinnitus, visual disturbances; pruritus, paresthesias, muscle pain, sleep disturbances, *hallucinations,* and agitation
2. *Factor II:* *Tremor,* sweats, depression, and anxiety
3. *Factor III:* Level of consciousness, attention, and awareness; nystagmus, gait disturbance, and *clouding of sensorium*

A more thorough description of this approach and its utility is contained in a chapter authored by Gross *et al.* (1974). It is, however, interesting that each of the factors contains one of the cardinal signs that were used in the earlier classifications of the ethanol withdrawal syndrome. Thus, Factor I contains symptoms related to hallucinatory behavior, Factor II contains tremor as one of the component symptoms, while Factor III contains clouding of the sensorium as one of its components. Such factor analysis allows one to hypothesize that the related symptoms within each factor may be determined by common mechanisms. This is particularly important for conducting animal studies that examine the biochemical determinants of particular symptoms of ethanol withdrawal. Analysis of hallucinatory behavior or clouding of the sensorium is an inherently difficult task in animals. Yet, *if* it can be determined that another, easily measured symptom can be used as a marker for an array of phenomena which are more difficult to quantitate, then correlative studies between physiology, behavior, and biochemistry would certainly be made easier.

The cardinal signs of the ethanol withdrawal syndrome bear some further description. Tremor occurs in a majority of patients undergoing withdrawal from ethanol; this is characteristically a postural tremor with a frequency of 8 to 10 Hz. The tremor may fluctuate in intensity, and is worsened by emotional stress or physical anxiety. Tremor may be assessed by having the patient maintain arms in an outstretched position; when the tremor is severe, it may also manifest itself as an intention tremor during voluntary motor activity, as in the finger-to-nose test. It has been suggested that the tremor of alcohol withdrawal is an exaggerated form of normal physiologic tremor with a contribution from anxiety, fatigue, and thyrotoxic factors (Mellor & Ganguli, 1979). However, other medical conditions may be responsible for tremor in an individual who has ceased imbibing large quantities of ethanol and should also be considered when one is presented with a tremulous patient. These include normal physiologic tremor, tremors of anxiety, thyrotoxicosis, hypomagnesemia, Wilson's disease, and benign essential tremor. Diagnostic tests—such as measurements of thyroxine and triiodothyronine levels, serum magnesium levels, serum ceruloplasmin levels—as well as liver function studies may be helpful. Alcohol withdrawal has also been shown to provoke transient Parkinsonism, characterized by slow speech, resting tremor, cogwheel rigidity, and bradykinesia (Carlen, Lee, Jacob, & Livshits, 1981).

The seizures which occur in some individuals (12% of 266 patients in the study of Victor & Adams, 1953) during ethanol withdrawal are characteristically grand mal in nature, with a loss of consciousness and without a preceding prodromal aura. EEG recordings during sober periods reveal a normal EEG, as opposed to the abnormal EEG found in epileptics. Additionally, 50% of patients with seizures during withdrawal exhibit generalized myoclonus or convulsive seizures following photic stimulation. Conversely, idiopathic epileptics rarely respond to this activating procedure.

Seizures are most likely to occur if there has been a history of withdrawal seizures or epilepsy. Withdrawal seizures do not, however, produce epilepsy, and many patients having withdrawal seizures do not have seizures at other times. Since withdrawal from alcohol *lowers seizure threshold*, patients with idiopathic or posttraumatic epilepsy are especially susceptible to withdrawal seizures. Although there may be only a single seizure during withdrawal, they usually occur in bursts of two to six. Status epilepticus (continuous seizures without a recovery of consciousness) may occur occasionally. More than 90% of seizures occur within 48 hours of the onset of withdrawal, with a peak incidence at 24 hours. It has been suggested that seizures may be due to a hyperexcitable state of the CNS, produced by the combined effect of low serum magnesium levels and respiratory alkalosis that are often observed during early withdrawal (Victor & Wolfe, 1973).

It is extremely important to determine whether seizures during withdrawal are the result of conditions other than ethanol withdrawal. A major problem is that the alcoholic population has a high incidence of seizure disorders due to head trauma from falls, producing brain trauma and subdural hematomas. In addition, epilepsy, systemic infections, brain abscesses, low serum potassium, or low serum magnesium may be responsible for seizures. The appearance of focal seizures, due to localized damage or disturbance within the brain, should signal the possibility of these conditions; in general, all patients exhibiting seizures during ethanol withdrawal should receive careful neurological and systemic examinations.

About 25% of patients undergoing ethanol withdrawal manifest symptoms of sensory disorganization. These patients may suffer from nightmares and from illusions or hallucinations that may be visual, auditory, or tactile or a combination of the three. In addition, these patients may be mildly disoriented in time and have difficulty recalling events over the few days prior to withdrawal. Hallucinations may occur even while the patient is clear-thinking and oriented. Typically the hallucinations begin one to two days after withdrawal and last for no longer than three days.

Visual hallucinations are evident in approximately 5% of hospitalized alcoholics undergoing withdrawal from ethanol. The patient often misinterprets the surrounding environment—objects appear distorted, sounds and shadows may become confusing. Visual hallucinations often appear in either human, animal, or insect forms; they may appear normal or ugly and distorted. Patients with delirium tremens hallucinations may be difficult to distinguish from those with schizophreniform disorders. Aside from a history of alcohol abuse, an EEG is useful, since functional disorders would not be expected to show the diffuse, abnormal background activity often found in patients suffering from delirium.

Auditory hallucinations are more rare than visual hallucinations but are notable in that they occur in the presence of a clear sensorium. The hallucinations may be vocal, musical, or of random sounds. Vocal hallucinations often address the patient in the third person. Occasionally, they may address the patient in a maligning or threatening way. Patients often report that the voices come from the external environment rather than from within, and they may be quite fearful of their presence. These hallucinations are most common at night; they may last from a few minutes to hours or recur for days throughout the withdrawal. Rarely, auditory hallucinations may persist after an individual has recovered from symptoms of alcohol withdrawal and is no longer drinking. This syndrome is known as alcoholic hallucinosis, and these patients may go on to develop schizophrenia.

Clouding of the sensorium is especially prominent during late-withdrawal episodes of delirium tremens. Patients may have disturbances of attention, memory, coherent thinking, perception, and psychomotor behavior. Orientation, in general, is impaired and patients may have difficulty in correctly stating the date, day of the week or time of day, in describing their surrounding location, or in identifying familiar people.

Visual hallucinations that arise during withdrawal have, in some cases, been attributed to the "intrusion of dreams into the waking state." Alcohol intoxication has a profound effect on sleep, and sleep disturbances are certainly another important feature of the ethanol withdrawal syndrome. Ingestion of ethanol by nonalcoholic humans in doses of 0.8 to 1.0 g/kg or more prior to bedtime results in a decreased sleep latency and a decrease in the percentage of REM sleep, either in the first half of the sleep period or throughout the sleep period. The ethanol-induced changes in sleep in nonalcoholic subjects are diminished with time (tolerance), so that the percentage of REM sleep returns to normal values during three days of drinking. If drinking is continued for a period of up to five days and then abruptly terminated, a REM rebound effect (increased percentage of REM sleep) becomes evident on the night subsequent to the termination of drinking.

Alcohol ingestion to the point of the development of physical dependence results in significantly more severe disturbances in sleep patterns upon termination of ethanol ingestion. Alcohol withdrawal results initially in a decrease in total sleep. As the duration of withdrawal progresses, REM sleep begins to comprise the major portion of the nonwaking EEG record. REM sleep usually begins to increase on the second or third night after withdrawal and may, on the fourth through sixth nights of withdrawal, constitute more than 90% of sleep time (Gross, Goodenough, Hastey, & Lewis, 1973; Johnson, Burdick, & Smith, 1970). This increase in REM sleep is characterized by an increased number of REM episodes and a decrease in time between episodes. Even after three weeks of abstinence, alcoholics have been demonstrated to have more REM sleep and less Stage 3 sleep than normal age-matched volunteers (Lester, Rundell, Cowden, & Williams, 1973). Sleep disturbances in alcoholics may persist, with less slow-wave sleep, more arousals, and increased number of stage changes for up to one or two years after termination of chronic drinking.

The sleep disturbances during the early phases of alcohol withdrawal have been proposed to be (1) related to the hallucinations evident in withdrawing individuals (the REM intrusion hypothesis) (Vogel, 1968); (2) correlated with the development of delirium tremens (Greenberg & Pearlman, 1967); and (3) causally related to the irritability and emotional hyperreactivity during abstinence (Zarcone, Schreier, Mitchell, Orenberg, & Barchas, 1980). Although these disturbances in sleep patterns are among the most characteristic CNS signs of prolonged, excessive intake of ethanol and subsequent withdrawal, sleep patterns have seldom been monitored during withdrawal and few therapies are specifically directed at correcting these symptoms (see section below on treatment of acute withdrawal).

6. ETIOLOGICAL FACTORS CONTRIBUTING TO THE DEVELOPMENT OF PHYSICAL DEPENDENCE

Factors such as the availability of distilled spirits, in contrast to beer or wine, and the socioeconomic status of an individual play an important role in contributing to the development of the alcohol withdrawal syndrome at times of abstinence in the drinking population. It can be generalized that the first time a patient is admitted to the hospital for symptoms of ethanol withdrawal he or she is usually 35 to 50 years old with a history of more than 5 to 10 years of alcohol use. At this point, however, it is useful to reiterate the results of the studies by Isbell and coworkers (1955), Mendelson and LaDou (1964), and Gross et al. (1974), which demonstrate that even a week or several weeks of continuous, heavy consumption of ethanol (about 200 to 300 g/day) will produce, in most individuals, the full gamut of withdrawal symptoms once ethanol consumption is terminated. These observations of a rapid development of physical dependence, given sufficient and continuous consumption of ethanol, are well supported by studies with animals; here, it has been found that continuous intoxication of rats or mice for periods of four to seven days is quite sufficient to produce an ethanol withdrawal syndrome characterized by symptoms similar to those witnessed in withdrawing alcoholics (see Table 1).

Observations of both the withdrawing human and animal clearly demonstrate that given equal amounts of ethanol, some individuals exhibit a significantly more severe withdrawal syndrome than others. A number of factors contribute to this phemonenon. Gross, Rosenblatt, Lewis, Chartoff, and Malenowski (1972) have noted that a prior episode of delirium tremens predisposes an individual to develop more severe symptomatology after terminating a subsequent period of heavy ethanol consumption. Studies with rats have clearly supported these observations. Using both behavioral and electrophysiologic techniques, the animal studies have shown that a prior period of heavy ethanol consumption and withdrawal will increase the rate at which physical dependence develops and will increase the severity of the witnessed withdrawal symptoms when the second period of ethanol administration is terminated.

Animal studies also support the anecdotal information gathered in work with humans which points to a genetically determined predisposition for some individuals to develop severe symptoms of ethanol withdrawal. Inbred strains of mice given equivalent quantities of ethanol exhibit withdrawal symptoms of significantly different severity, depending on their genotype. More recent work has, in addition, demonstrated that animals can be selectively bred for developing more severe withdrawal symptoms after a standard period of ethanol consumption. It is important to realize, however, that the current studies are unable to distinguish

Table 1. Symptomatology Associated with Acute (Early) Withdrawal Syndrome

Humans	Animals
Tremors	Tremors
Anorexia	Anorexia
Insomnia	Insomina
REM rebound	REM rebound
Convulsions	Convulsions
Temperature aberrations	Temperature aberrations
Agitation	Agitation
Diaphoresis	Piloerection
Hallucinations	Mydriasis

whether the genetic constitution of an animal predisposes to a more rapid or more extensive development of physical dependence or simply allows for a greater expression of the withdrawal symptoms.

In addition to the genetic constitution of an individual, a number of other factors have been noted to modulate the severity of the ethanol withdrawal syndrome in humans given equivalent quantities of ethanol (Mello, 1972). Individual drinking patterns, and factors such as food intake, are reflected in blood ethanol levels and severity of the symptoms upon withdrawal from ethanol. The pattern or method of withdrawal is another critical variable, and it has been a universal observation that involuntary, abrupt withdrawal, such as would be produced by trauma and subsequent hospitalization, greatly increases the gravity of the withdrawal symptoms. A gradual diminution of blood ethanol levels by a controlled decrease in intake results in a substantially reduced threat of severe withdrawal symptoms.

7. NEUROCHEMICAL SYSTEMS DETERMINING PHYSICAL DEPENDENCE

The biological mechanisms responsible for producing the symptoms of withdrawal are therefore, by definition, the factors responsible for physical dependence; at present, they are being avidly investigated. However, only a speculative appraisal of these factors is currently possible. The reader interested in the neurochemical alterations witnessed upon withdrawal of an animal or human from ethanol is referred to the review by Tabakoff and Hoffman (1983). In this section, we will discuss only the few systems that have demonstrated adaptation and subsequent "rebound" phenomena which would be expected to characterize the activity of a system exhibiting physical dependence on ethanol.

The activity of brain noradrenergic neurons, as measured by the turnover of norepinephrine (NE), is depressed by a high dose of ethanol. This depression of CNS norepinephrine turnover has been noted in various areas of brain in animals and through measures of 3-methoxy-4-hydroxyphenylglycol (MOPEG) levels in CSF after ethanol administration to humans (Borg, Kvande, & Sedvall, 1981). On the other hand, chronic treatment of animals with high doses of ethanol was found to produce an increase in the turnover of NE in brain. The changes in NE turnover were evident at the time of withdrawal and persisted for 48 to 72 hours after the termination of ethanol administration to the experimental animals. The increased NE turnover in humans and animals after *chronic* consumption of high doses of ethanol may be viewed as an adaptation to the initial depression in NE turnover caused by an acute dose of ethanol. After clearance of an acute ethanol dose, the NE turnover rates return rapidly to normal, but the adaptive response to chronic ethanol exposure may involve changes in neuronal properties and/or feedback control systems which require substantial time for readjustment. The decreased turnover of NE evident during the initial period of intoxication and the higher-than-normal turnover of NE witnessed during withdrawal constitute good examples of "rebound" phenomena. One has to, however, be careful in drawing conclusions regarding the overall functional significance of the increased NE turnover during ethanol withdrawal, since the effectiveness of a transmitter at a synapse is determined not only by the quantity of that transmitter being released but also by the "sensitivity" of the synaptic receptors for that transmitter.

The kinetic characteristics of the binding of radioactive ligands to the NE receptor or the analysis of effectiveness of certain NE receptor agonists in stimulating adenylate cyclase activity in brain tissue can be used as a measure of NE receptor status. The NE-sensitive adenylate cyclase in the cortex of ethanol-withdrawn rats has been found to be subsensitive to stimulation by NE. This "subsensitivity" was witnessed during the first 24 hours after withdrawal, but within 72 hours after withdrawal the cortical adenylate cyclase activity was shown to become more sensitive than normal to stimulation by NE. Specific binding of the β-adrenergic antagonist ^{3}H-dihydroalprenolol was decreased in the brains of ethanol-treated rats immediately after ethanol withdrawal, but it was significantly increased as compared to control rats at 48 and 72 hours after ethanol withdrawal. The changes in binding of this radioactive ligand were reflective of changes in the number of β-adrenergic receptors in brains of the ethanol-withdrawn animals at different times after withdrawal. The reported changes in receptor number seem to fit well the biphasic changes in the functional state of NE-sensitive adenylate cyclase in the cortex of ethanol-withdrawn rats. When changes in NE receptors are considered together with the reported changes in NE turnover, it becomes clear that changes in NE receptors seem, at the early stages of withdrawal, to compensate for the increased NE turnover but may be overshooting their normal limits after NE turnover returns to the normal range. Thus, the altered balance of several related factors, rather than the singular alteration in NE metabolism, may be the determinant of the NE involvement in physical dependence and the development of certain symptoms (e.g., sleep disturbances) of withdrawal. In this respect, it is of interest that the β-receptor blocker propranolol has, under certain conditions, proved to be efficacious in ameliorating certain aspects of the ethanol withdrawal symptomatology (Sellers, Zilm, & Degani, 1977).

The cholinergic neurons have also been shown to be sensitive to ethanol and to show changes indicative of adaptation and rebound phenomena following chronic treatment with ethanol. Acute ethanol administration decreases acetylcholine release from brain cortical tissue in animals, and the findings that a single dose of ethanol increases brain acetylcholine levels can, in a great part, be attributed to the decreased release of acetylcholine from cholinergic neurons in the presence of intoxicating levels of ethanol. When brain acetylcholine levels are measured during and after chronic treatment of animals with ethanol, decreases in levels of acetylcholine are noted in a number of brain areas. These changes in acetylcholine levels, which can be interpreted to result from *increased* release of acetylcholine, returned to normal within one or two days after withdrawal. As with the noradrenergic system, changes in characteristics of cholinergic receptors were found to accompany the changes noted in the metabolism of the neurotransmitter acetylcholine. Muscarinic cholinergic receptors in the hippocampus and cortex of mice withdrawn from chronic treatment with ethanol are increased in number (20% to 25%) at the time of withdrawal, and this increase in receptor number remains evident for the initial day after ethanol withdrawal in these animals. Since most of the overt symptoms of the ethanol withdrawal syndrome in mice (e.g., seizures) occur within 24 hours after withdrawal of animals from the chronic treatment with ethanol, the increased "sensitivity" of cholinergic receptors has been postulated to be related to susceptibility to seizures in the withdrawing animals. Again, however, it is important to exercise caution in considering this information, since not only the cholinergic receptor characteristics but also the release of transmitter are altered in brain during the withdrawal period. A great number of other neurotransmitter receptors and the metabolism of most known neurotransmitters have come under scrutiny in searching for the causative factors of the ethanol withdrawal syndrome. Most of the work, however, is still in its formative period, and a number of untested and uncontrolled variables preclude definitive conclusions at this time.

Another factor that has been hypothesized to contribute to the symptomatology (particularly the seizures) witnessed during the ethanol withdrawal syndrome is magnesium. The symptoms of magnesium deficiency are quite similar to certain symptoms witnessed during ethanol withdrawal. Plasma levels of magnesium have been reported to be decreased after chronic ingestion of ethanol by humans, and the withdrawal of individuals from chronic ethanol consumption results in a further decrease in serum magnesium concentrations (Wolfe & Victor, 1971). Controversy, however, surrounds the relationship between the lowered plasma magnesium levels and the appearance and severity of the various symptoms of the ethanol withdrawal syndrome. The controversy cannot, at present, be resolved, since little information is available on *brain* magnesium levels during withdrawal, and it is known that the circulating levels of magnesium, and even CSF levels of magnesium, may not accurately reflect brain tissue levels of this cation. For instance, the feeding of rats with a magnesium-deficient diet produced a hyperexcitable state (Chutkow, 1974a) and concomitantly lowered brain concentrations of magnesium. The administration of magnesium to the animals rapidly returned *serum* and *cerebrospinal fluid* magnesium levels to normal, while the increase in brain tissue magnesium concentrations was relatively slow and the hyperexcitable state persisted beyond the time that cerebrospinal fluid magnesium levels became normal (Chutkow, 1974a,b). At the present time, only one study has measured *brain* magnesium levels in animals during a period in which animals were exhibiting maximum alcohol withdrawal symptoms (Belknap, Berg, & Coleman, 1978). The results of this study showed a small but statistically significant decrease in brain magnesium levels during the withdrawal period (Belknap *et al.*, 1978). More studies of this nature will have to be performed before conclusions are drawn regarding the role of magnesium in the etiology of the symptoms of ethanol withdrawal.

8. PHARMACOLOGIC MANAGEMENT OF THE ACUTE ALCOHOL WITHDRAWAL SYNDROME

The search for the biochemical determinants of the symptoms of the ethanol withdrawal syndrome is directed not only toward the elucidation of the factors responsible for physical dependence on ethanol but also toward the development of more specific and efficacious treatments of the withdrawal syndrome. One might not expect that a single substance would ameliorate the whole gamut of the withdrawal symptoms unless that substance had the pharmacological properties (and dependence-producing liabilities) of ethanol itself. However, the development of drugs that lack dependence-producing properties and are specific for the more threatening groups of symptoms of withdrawal may provide a significant improvement over the current management of the ethanol withdrawal syndrome.

In clinical practice, one is many times confronted with the need to treat the symptoms of alcohol withdrawal under two distinct sets of circumstances. The first circumstance involves patients who present themselves in an inebriated state, wherein the first goal of therapy is to alleviate the toxic effects of ingested ethanol. The second circumstance involves patients who have been admitted for treatment of conditions ostensibly unrelated to their use of alcohol and who, during the course of therapy, begin to exhibit the signs and symptoms of the acute alcohol withdrawal syndrome.

Although the ultimate treatment of the alcohol withdrawal symptoms under the two sets of circumstances may be similar, the diagnostic skills of the physician are certainly going to be tested more severely under the second circumstance. It should, therefore, be recommended that a history of a patient's prior alcohol consumption or laboratory data indicative of heavy use of alcohol (see chapter by Van Thiel) not be overlooked by physicians.

The severely intoxicated patient should also be treated with diagnostic caution. A number of concomitant disturbances—including head injury, hepatic insufficiency, concurrent intoxication with other drugs, and diabetic coma—may be obscured by the apparent alcohol intoxication. Complications should be suspected particularly when the determined blood-alcohol levels do not correspond to the clinical state of the patient (i.e., if the patient is incoherent at blood ethanol levels well below 200 mg/100 mL, or is comatose at blood ethanol levels below 400 mg/ 100 mL). Under such conditions, extreme care should be taken to determine the cause of the witnessed symptoms as quickly as possible.

If alcohol is determined to be the sole agent responsible for a state of severe intoxication or coma, the situation should be treated with measures that generally pertain to the treatment of coma or shock (see Adams, 1980) and specific therapies should be undertaken to correct acid-base, electrolyte, temperature, and glucose abnormalities that are a particular hallmark of alcohol intoxication. Hypoglycemia is many times present in malnourished individuals intoxicated with ethanol (Searle, Shames, Cavalier, Bagdade, & Porte, 1974), and this condition can usually be corrected by intravenous administration of 5% glucose solutions. The administration of glucose should, however, be accompanied by administration of thiamine (100 mg IM), since thiamine deficiencies may also be present in the alcoholic patient. The administration of glucose to thiamine-deficient individuals can further divert thiamine from its function in the sodium-gating mechanisms on neuronal membranes to being utilized as a cofactor for the metabolism of the administered glucose. Such a removal of the limited supplies of thiamine from the neuronal membranes in brain may certainly exacerbate the coma present in severely intoxicated patients. It is, therefore, advisable to administer thiamine in conjunction with the glucose being administered to correct any evident hypoglycemia.

Alcohol elimination by humans proceeds approximately at a rate of 10 g/hr for a 70-kg individual (although this rate may be increased in the chronic drinker). At this rate, one would expect that it would take more than ten hours to return an individual with blood ethanol levels of over 200 mg/100 mL to levels that are below those considered to be intoxicating in most areas of the United States (i.e., <100 mg/100 mL). Although it may, at times, be efficacious to attempt to quickly lower blood ethanol levels (e.g., by dialysis in cases where blood ethanol levels exceed 600 mg/100 mL), the rapid removal of ethanol from an intoxicated alcoholic will encourage the appearance of a more severe alcohol withdrawal syndrome. Other factors that contribute to the severity of the acute alcohol withdrawal syndrome include the magnitude (in quantity and duration) of the preceding period of intoxication (see above), but it is, in general, difficult to ascertain from an intoxicated individual the extent of the various predisposing factors. Therefore a physician should be prepared to manage a syndrome that varies in intensity from symptoms which are primarily discomforting to the patient (such as agitation, diaphoresis, insomnia, nausea, and anorexia) to those which are potentially fatal (such as severe abnormalities in the control of body temperature and seizures of the grand mal type). The milder symptoms of the acute alcohol withdrawal syndrome respond well to bed rest, normalization of electrolytes and water balance, and judicial use of anxiolytic drugs (see below) to promote sleep. The objectives for the use of any drugs in the management of alcohol withdrawal are to relieve subjective symptoms and to *prevent* or treat the more serious complications of withdrawal. Since most drugs used in the treatment of withdrawal have sedative properties, their potential interactions with ethanol should be recognized and great care should be taken to avoid administering the drugs while significant amounts of ethanol are still present in an individual. One should also be aware that many alcoholics have liver disorders that will alter the normal metabolism of administered drugs and that the administered drugs may, on the other hand, further compromise the function of an already damaged liver in the alcoholic. Additional criteria for judging a drug as being useful in treating alcohol withdrawal have been listed by Kissin and Gross (1968); these criteria state that the drug should not mask preexisting medical problems and should not increase the possibility of convulsions (see discussion of the use of phenothiazines below).

8.1. Treatment Strategy

The major, currently utilized pharmacologic treatment strategy for management of the more severe manifestations of alcohol withdrawal is based on the work of Isbell (1967). This work suggested that "cross-dependent" drugs would be efficacious in treatment of alcohol withdrawal; these drugs were so grouped because their chronic use and later abrupt withdrawal result in a syndrome similar to the withdrawal syndrome witnessed after abrupt cessation of ethanol ingestion by the alcoholic. Therapy with such drugs constitutes a substitution of one CNS depressant drug (alcohol) by another, and the choice of the "other" drug is governed by considerations of its efficacy, therapeutic index, and duration of action. The patient is reintoxicated (titrated) with the "cross-dependent" drug to the point of clinical suppression of symptoms of the withdrawal syndrome. The dose of the drug is then gradually reduced, over a period of days, ostensibly to allow time for the maladapted (dependent) CNS to readjust to normal function. The titration of patients with cross-dependent "drugs" has, in general, proved to be an effective means for treating the early signs of the acute alcohol withdrawal syndrome and has reduced the incidence of the later development of delirium tremens symptomatology. Most drug therapies are, however, ineffective in the treatment of delirium tremens if the drug therapy is instituted after these later symptoms of alcohol withdrawal are already in progress. Victor (1966) has provided a fine summary of the important aspects of the treatment of delirium tremens once they occur and has stressed the importance of closely monitoring blood pressure and body temperature and the major role that dehydration plays in mortality associated with this condition.

8.2. Benzodiazepines

With regard to the treatment of the early phase of alcohol withdrawal, the specific drugs that fall into the category of substances that are "cross-dependent" with ethanol can be subdivided into the sedative–hypnotics and the anxiolytic drugs. The benzodiazepines, which were introduced into medical practice in the late 1950s for the treatment of anxiety, have become the mainstay of treatment of the acute alcohol withdrawal syndrome in the United States. The use of these agents was based primarily on empirical observations of their efficacy, but current research into the mechanism of action of the benzodiazepines and other drugs which have marked utility in treatment of the early signs of the withdrawal syndrome has demonstrated that many of these drugs potentiate the effectiveness of transmission at the γ-aminobutyric acid (GABA) synapses. The potentiation of GABA transmission may be the common mechanism by which many agents ameliorate the early signs of the acute alcohol withdrawal syndrome. The benzodiazepines interact with two classes of specific CNS receptors that are coupled to GABA receptors. The binding of benzodiazepines to their receptors potentiates the binding of GABA to its receptor, and the enhanced GABA binding may produce the anxiolytic and anticonvulsant effects which characterize the actions of the benzodiazepines.

The efficacy of benzodiazepines in treating the acute alcohol withdrawal syndrome has been demonstrated in a number of studies where these agents have been compared with other drugs (phenothiazines, butyrophenones, sedative–hypnotics) or placebo treatment (see Gessner, 1979, for review). The benzodiazepines provide several advantages over sedative–hypnotics (i.e., barbiturates, paraldehyde–chloral hydrate mixtures). Used in doses that effectively decrease anxiety and agitation, they do not suppress REM sleep and, thus, do not further postpone the reinstatement of normal sleep patterns in the withdrawing patient. Given orally or parenterally, these drugs do not produce excessive sedation or stupor in patients being treated for anxiety; thus, psychotherapy can be instituted at a significantly earlier time than with patients receiving the sedative–hypnotics. The benzodiazepines, even in large doses (30 to 60 mg) also produce little respiratory or cardiovascular depression. Respiratory depression can be a significant complicating feature of treatment of alcohol withdrawal with the barbiturates, since many alcoholics present with obstructive pulmonary disease and would be prone to develop respiratory failure if given large doses of barbiturates. The benzodiazepines are effective anticonvulsants that increase the seizure threshold for both electrically induced and chemically (pentylenetetrazol, or Metrazol) induced seizures in experimental animals.

Studies with animals have demonstrated that alcohol withdrawal produces a lowering of the seizure threshold for convulsants such as Metrazol, and it is of interest that agents such as benzodiazepines and barbiturates, which are particularly effective in controlling such *chemically* induced seizures, are also most effective in controlling the seizures that are evident in the withdrawing human. On the other hand, hydantoins (e.g., diphenylhydantoin) are primarily effective in modifying the pattern of electrically induced seizures and are not effective against Metrazol-induced seizures. The hydantoin derivatives are not efficacious in preventing seizures that occur strictly as a result of ethanol withdrawal (Gessner, 1979; see further discussion below). The major consideration for the choice of a particular benzodiazepine for treatment of the alcohol withdrawal syndrome is the speed of onset and the duration of action. For these reasons, diazepam has become the drug of choice. Diazepam is rapidly absorbed after oral administration, and peak plasma concentrations can be achieved through this route of administration within one hour. Chlordiazepoxide, on the other hand, is slowly absorbed after oral administration, and several hours may elapse before peak blood concentrations are reached. Chlordiazepoxide is eliminated relatively quickly, its half-life (the time for half the dose to be eliminated) being one to two days. Diazepam, on the other hand, is metabolized in a biphasic pattern, the slow phase of which has a half-life of two to eight days. Furthermore, diazepam is metabolized to an active metabolite, oxazepam, which is then further metabolized or excreted. Thus, diazepam well fulfills the necessary criteria for drugs useful in control of the early phase of the acute alcohol withdrawal syndrome. The "titration" of the patient can be rapidly achieved by parenteral or oral administration; then the diazepam or its active metabolites are slowly eliminated from the patient during the recovery period. Several cautions should, however, be kept in mind when using diazepam. Sellers and Kalant (1976) have well described the dangers of a cumulative pharmacologic effect caused by slowly metabolized drugs such as the benzodiazepines; therefore diazepam doses should be reduced over time to prevent toxic accumulation of this drug. It must also be remembered that the benzodiazepines are themselves compounds that are liable to produce physical dependence, and care must be taken not to create another, substitute, dependence in the patient. This caution applies fully to all drugs that fall within the category of "cross-dependent" compounds used for the treatment of alcohol withdrawal.

8.3. Paraldehyde

The use of paraldehyde or the combination of paraldehyde and chloral hydrate to treat the symptoms of the acute alcohol withdrawal syndrome constitutes one of the older but more efficient therapies of this syndrome. More recently, the use of paraldehyde has fallen into disrepute due to this compound's unpleasant taste and odor and to reports of deaths associated with the clinical use of paraldehyde. When used properly, paraldehyde is a relatively safe medication. Paraldehyde is a cyclic polymer of acetaldehyde which, however, decomposes to acetaldehyde when improperly stored. The acetaldehyde then oxidizes in solution to acetic acid, and this acetic acid further catalyzes the depolymerization of paraldehyde. It is the use of such decomposed solutions of paraldehyde that constitutes the greatest danger associated with paraldehyde treatment. Care should, therefore, be exercised to use only fresh or properly stored paraldehyde; if the drug is to be administered parenterally, no more than a 7% concentration should be used. The solubility of paraldehyde in water at 37°C is 7.8%; if this solubility is exceeded, droplets of irritating pure paraldehyde are likely to occur at the site of injection or in the blood.

When properly administered, paraldehyde is an excellent anticonvulsant and rapidly acting hypnotic agent. Several studies, including one by Golbert, Sanz, Rose, and Leitschuh (1967), have demonstrated that paraldehyde given in combination with chloral hydrate is as effective as or more efficacious than the commonly used benzodiazepines or the phenothiazines in managing the early phases of the acute alcohol withdrawal syndrome and in preventing the development of delirium tremens. An extensive discussion of the merits of the use of paraldehyde in treating alcohol withdrawal is contained in the review of Gessner (1979).

8.4. Barbiturates

Barbiturates constitute the third major class of drugs of "cross-dependence" that are commonly used to treat symptoms of alcohol withdrawal. The long-acting barbiturates, phenobarbital and mephobarbital, are the more efficacious agents due to their excellent anticonvulsant properties. The longer-acting barbiturates are also less likely to initiate a substitute dependence, since they do not produce the initial euphoria sometimes experienced by patients treated with the shorter-acting barbiturates. Although phenobarbital and mephobarbital will prevent or suppress the convulsions that may accompany ethanol withdrawal, these agents have little effect on alleviating anxiety or agitation unless used in hypnotic doses. As already mentioned, the use of higher doses of barbiturates is accompanied by risk of respiratory depression, and the sedation ("sleep") induced by the barbiturates lacks the REM component. After the administered barbiturate is eliminated by the patient, the REM suppression by barbiturates can further accentuate the REM rebound usually evident in the withdrawing individual. The need to use sedating doses of barbiturates to overcome anxiety or agitation in the withdrawing patient also prevents the initiation of supportive psychotherapy until treatment with the barbiturates is terminated.

Barbiturates are metabolized primarily in the liver; prior, chronic ingestion of alcohol can certainly alter this metabolism. Alcohol can induce the enzymes responsible for the degradation of barbiturates in a "healthy" liver or can significantly slow the metabolism of barbiturates by damaging the liver (see chapter by Deitrich). One should, therefore, have an indication of the state of a patient's liver function prior to initiating a regimen of treatment with the barbiturates.

8.5. Antipsychotics

The phenothiazines and butyrophenones were introduced as antipsychotic agents in the 1950s and soon thereafter began to be utilized for the treatment of the acute alcohol withdrawal syndrome. These drugs do not fall into the category of agents that exhibit "cross-dependence" with ethanol; this has led to their further acceptance by clinicians. Controlled clinical trials of the phenothiazines, however, have uncovered several disturbing features which accompany the use of these compounds in withdrawing patients. It is well known that chlorpromazine, which is prototypic of the phenothiazines, lowers convulsive thresholds, particularly in patients who have had a history of seizure disorders. Two studies (Thomas & Freedman, 1964; Golbert et al., 1967) have clearly documented excessive mortality among patients being treated for alcohol withdrawal with phenothiazines as compared to those being treated with paraldehyde or benzodiazepines; other studies have confirmed these results. This added threat to the well-being of the withdrawing patient should be seriously considered prior to use of the phenothiazines.

The phenothiazines have proved to be of some utility in controlling agitation associated with alcohol withdrawal, but sedative doses of the phenothiazines have to be used for this purpose, and the potency of the various phenothiazines, in this respect, is more correlated with their ability to sedate than with their antipsychotic actions. The phenothiazines have also been found to be useful in the control of "alcoholic hallucinosis," but, as stated above, the rarely occurring auditory hallucinations characteristic of this state are most probably an indication of a primary psychotic disorder which is obscured by the patient's alcoholism. The butyrophenones (e.g., haloperidol) have not received the careful evaluation in clinical situations that was given the phenothiazines, but preliminary animal screening has indicated that haloperidol significantly enhances convulsions in mice withdrawn from chronic dosing with ethanol (Blum, Eubanks, Wallace, & Hamilton, 1976).

8.6. Chlormethiazole

The chemical structure of chlormethiazole is somewhat similar to the thiazole part of thiamine (vitamin B_1); this agent possesses anticonvulsant and sedative properties. Although quite popular for treatment of alcohol withdrawal in Europe, it is not available in the United States. Several studies have demonstrated the superiority of chlormethiazole as opposed to phenothiazine treatment, and chlormethiazole has been suggested to be as efficacious as benzodiazepines in preventing the development of delirium tremens. However, success with chlormethiazole is predicated on keeping patients heavily sedated during the first days of therapy.

8.7. Anticonvulsants

Since the convulsions that occur during the course of the acute alcohol withdrawal syndrome resemble grand mal seizures, the hydantoin anticonvulsant agents (e.g., diphenylhydantoin) have been recommended for use during alcohol withdrawal. The efficacy of the hydantoins in specifically controlling the seizures which are a direct result of ethanol withdrawal has been put in doubt by studies of these drugs in animals being withdrawn from chronic treatment with ethanol. The work with animals has indicated that the hydantoins are ineffective in suppressing alcohol withdrawal seizures. Clinical assessment of hydantoins in treating seizures occurring during ethanol withdrawal has demonstrated the effectiveness of these compounds, but this effectiveness seems to be primarily evident in patients with a prior history of convulsion caused by preexisting epilepsy or the prior incidence of alcohol withdrawal.

Dipropylacetate (sodium valproate), on the other hand, has been shown to be an effective anticonvulsant in both animals and humans being withdrawn from ethanol. This anticonvulsant agent has minimal sedative properties, and its mode of action seems to be related to its ability to increase the levels of GABA in the CNS. As pointed out above, a drug's ability to potentiate the effects of GABA in the brain seems to be positively correlated with efficacy in controlling the early symptoms of the acute alcohol withdrawal syndrome.

8.8. Miscellaneous

A number of other agents—such as antihistamines (hydroxyzine), beta adrenergic-receptor blocking agents (propranolol), antidepressants (lithium carbonate), as well as ethanol itself—have been utilized for the treatment of the acute alcohol withdrawal syndrome. These agents may, under certain conditions, have utility, but due to objections to either their pharmacology or moral issues regarding their use (e.g., ethanol) these compounds have not gained popularity. The characteristics of these drugs are, therefore, not described here; however, the interested reader is referred to a review by Gessner (1979) for further information. We also advise the perusal of several other reference texts (Goodman & Gilman, 1980; AMA Drug Evaluations, 1980) for explicit information on the dosage schedules and further cautions regarding the use of the drugs described above. Our intent in the later sections of this chapter was primarily to provide an overview of the positive and negative characteristics of the drugs commonly employed for the treatment of ethanol withdrawal. Based on this overview, one can conclude that the most effective, currently available (in the United States) drugs for treatment of the more severe cases of acute alcohol withdrawal are (1) the benzodiazepines and (2) paraldehyde given in combination with chloral hydrate. This conclusion certainly does not offer a great armamentarium of medications for the treatment of alcohol withdrawal; it may be noted that the most efficacious drugs are also those that are "cross-dependent" with ethanol. Further research and clinical trials are, therefore, certainly warranted to discover more effective agents with less dependence-producing properties.

9. REFERENCES

Adams, R. D. Coma and related disturbances of consciousness. In K. J. Isselbacher, R. J. Adams, E. Braunwald, R. G. Petersdorf, & J. D. Wilson (Eds.), *Harrison's principles of internal medicine* (9th ed.). New York: McGraw-Hill, 1980.

American Medical Association. *American Medical Association drug evaluations* (4th ed.). Chicago: American Medical Association, 1980.

Antelman, S. M. & Caggiola, A. R. Norepinephrine–dopamine interactions and behavior. *Science*, 1977, *195*, 646–653.

Belknap, J. R., Berg, J. H., & Coleman, R. R. Alcohol withdrawal and magnesium deficiency in mice. *Pharmacology, Biochemistry and Behavior*, 1978, *9*(1), 1–6.

Blum, R., Eubanks, J. D., Wallace, J. E., & Hamilton, H. Enhancement of alcohol withdrawal convulsions in mice by haloperidol. *Clinical Toxicology*, 1976, *9*, 427–434.

Borg, S., Kvande, H., & Sedvall, G. Central norepinephrine metabolism during alcohol intoxication in addicts and healthy volunteers. *Science*, 1981, *213*, 1135–1137.

Carlen, P. L., Lee, M. A., Jacob, M., & Livshits, O. Parkinsonism provoked by alcoholism. *Annals of Neurology*, 1981, *9*, 84–86.

Chutkow, J. G. Clinical–chemical correlations in encephalopathy of magnesium deficiency: Effect of reversal of magnesium deficits. *Mayo Clinic Proceedings*, 1974, *49*, 244–247. (a)

Chutkow, J. G. Metabolism of magnesium in central nervous system: Relationship between concentrations of magnesium in cerebrospinal fluid and brain in magnesium deficiency. *Neurology (Minn.)*, 1974, *24*, 780–787. (b)

Collier, H. O. J. Supersensitivity and dependence. *Nature*, 1968, *220*, 228–231.

Curran, M., & Seeman, P. Alcohol tolerance in a cholinergic nerve terminal: Relation to the membrane expansion–fluidization theory of ethanol action. *Science*, 1977, *197*, 910.

DeWied, D., Bohus, B., van Wimersma Griedanus, Tj. B., & Gispen, W. H. Pituitary peptides and memory. In R. Walter & J. Meienhofer (Eds.), *Peptides, chemistry, structure, biology.* Ann Arbor, Mich.: Ann Arbor Scientific Publications, 1975.

Frankel, D., Khanna, J. M., LeBlanc, A. E., & Kalant, H. Effect of *p*-chlorophenylalanine on the acquisition of tolerance to ethanol and pentobarbital. *Psychopharmacology*, 1975, *44*, 247–252.

Frankel, D., Khanna, J. M., Kalant, H., & LeBlanc, A. E. Effect of *p*-chlorophenylalanine on the acquisition of tolerance to the hypothermic effects of ethanol. *Psychopharmacology*, 1979, *57*, 239–242.

Gessner, P. R. Drug therapy of the alcohol withdrawal syndrome. In E. Majchrowicz & E. P. Noble (Eds.), *Biochemistry and pharmacology of ethanol* (Vol. 2). New York: Plenum Press, 1979.

Golbert, T. M., Sanz, C. J., Rose, H. D., & Leitschuh, T. H. Comparative evaluation of treatments of alcohol withdrawal syndromes. *Journal of the American Medical Association*, 1967, *201*, 99–102.

Goldstein, D. B. Alcohol withdrawal reactions in mice: Effects of drugs that modify neurotransmission. *Journal of Pharmacology and Experimental Therapeutics*, 1973, *186*, 1–9.

Goldstein, D. B., & Chin, J. H. Interaction of ethanol with biological membranes. *Federation Proceedings*, 1981, *40*, 2073–2076.

Goldstein, A., & Goldstein, D. B. Enzyme expansion theory of drug tolerance and physical dependence. In A. Wikler (Ed.), *The addictive states.* Baltimore: Williams & Wilkins, 1968.

Goodman, L. S., & Gilman, A. (Eds.). *The pharmacological basis of therapeutics* (6th ed.). New York: Macmillan, 1980.

Greenberg, R., & Pearlman, C. Delirium tremens and dreaming. *American Journal of Psychiatry*, 1967, *124*, 133–142.

Gross, M. M., Rosenblatt, S. M., Chartoff, S., Hermann, A., Schachter, M., Sheinkin, D., & Broman, M. Evaluation of acute alcohol psychoses and related states. The daily clinical course rating scale. *Quarterly Journal of Studies of Alcohol, 32,* 1971, 611–619.

Gross, M. M., Rosenblatt, S. M., Lewis, E., Chartoff, S., & Malenowski, B. Acute alcoholic psychoses and related syndromes—Psychosocial and clinical characteristics and their implications. *British Journal of Addiction,* 1972, *67,* 15–31.

Gross, M. M., Goodenough, D. R., Hastey, J., & Lewis, E. Experimental study of sleep in chronic alcoholics before, during and after four days of heavy drinking, with a nondrinking comparison. *Annual New York Academy of Science,* 1973, *215,* 254–265.

Gross, M. M., Lewis, E., & Hastey, J. Acute alcohol withdrawal syndrome. In B. Kissin & H. Begleiter (Eds.), *The biology of alcoholism* (Vol. 3), *Clinical pathology.* New York: Plenum Press, 1974.

Himmelsbach, C. R. Clinical studies of drug addiction. *Archives of Internal Medicine, 69,* 1942, 766–772.

Hoffman, P. L., Ritzmann, R. F., & Tabakoff, B. The influence of arginine vasopressin and oxytocin on ethanol dependence and tolerance. In M. Galanter (Ed.), *Currents in alcoholism* (Vol. 5). New York: Grune & Stratton, 1979.

Hoffman, P. L., Ritzmann, R. F., Walter, R., & Tabakoff, B. Arginine vasopressin maintains ethanol tolerance. *Nature (London),* 1978, *276,* 614–616.

Isbell, H. Alcohol proteins and alcoholism. In R. B. Beeson & W. McDermott (Eds.), *Loeb's textbook of medicine* (12th ed.). Philadelphia: Saunders, 1967.

Isbell, H., Fraser, H. F., Wikler, A., Belleville, R. E., & Eisenman, A. J. An experimental study of the etiology of "rum fits" and delirium tremens. *Quarterly Journal of Studies of Alcohol,* 1955, *16,* 1–33.

Jaffe, J. H., & Sharpless, S. K. Pharmacological denervation supersensitivity in the central nervous system: A theory of physical dependence. In A. Wikler (Ed.), *The addictive states.* Baltimore: Williams & Wilkins, 1968.

Johnson, L. C., Burdick, A., & Smith, J. Sleep during alcohol intake and withdrawal in the chronic alcoholic. *Archives of General Psychology,* 1970, *22,* 406–418.

Kalant, H., LeBlanc, A. E., & Gibbins, R. J. Tolerance to, and dependence on, some non-opiate psychotropic drugs. *Pharmacology Review,* 1971, *23,* 135–191.

Kalant, H., LeBlanc, A. E., & Gibbins, R. J. Repetitive development of ethanol tolerance. *Psychopharmacology,* 1978, *60,* 59–65. (a)

Kalant, H., LeBlanc, A. E., Gibbins, R. J., & Wilson, A. Accelerated development of tolerance during repeated cycles of ethanol exposure. *Psychopharmacology,* 1978, *60,* 59–65. (b)

Kissin, B., & Gross, M. M. Drug therapy in alcoholism. *American Journal of Psychiatry,* 1968, *125,* 31–41.

LeBlanc, A. E., & Cappell, H. Tolerance as adaptation: Interactions with behavior and parallels to other adaptive processes. In K. Blum (Ed.), *Alcohol and opiates: Neurochemical and behavior mechanisms.* New York: Academic Press, 1977.

LeBlanc, A. E., Kalant, H., Gibbins, R. J., & Berman, N. D. Acquisition and loss of tolerance to ethanol by the rat. *Journal of Pharmacology and Experimental Therapeutics,* 1969, *168,* 244–250.

LeBlanc, A. E., Gibbins, R. J., & Kalant, H. Generalization of behaviorally augmented tolerance to ethanol and its relation to physical dependence. *Psychopharmacology,* 1975, *44,* 241–246.

Lester, B. K., Rundell, O. H., Cowden, L. C., & Williams, H. L. Chronic alcoholism, alcohol and sleep. In M. M. Gross (Ed.), *Alcohol intoxication and withdrawal: Experimental studies* (Vol. 1). New York: Plenum Press, 1973.

Martin, W. R. Pharmacological redundancy as an adaptive mechanism in the CNS. *Federation Proceedings,* 1970, *29,* 13–18.

Masur, J., & Boerngen, R. The excitatory component of ethanol in mice: A chronic study. *Pharmacology, Biochemistry and Behavior*, 1980, *13*, 777–780.

Melchior, C. L., & Tabakoff, B. Modification of environmentally cued tolerance to ethanol in mice. *Journal of Pharmacology and Experimental Therapeutics*, 1981, *219*, 175–180.

Mellanby, E. Alcohol: Its absorption into and disappearance from the blood under different conditions. *Medical Research Council, Special Report Series (London)*, 1919, *15*, 1–48.

Mello, N. K. Behavioral studies of alcoholism. In B. Kissin & H. Begleiter (Eds.), *The biology of alcoholism* (Vol. 2). New York: Plenum Press, 1972.

Mellor, C. S., & Ganguli, R. Semiography of tremor in alcohol withdrawal. In M. Galanter (Ed.), *Currents in alcoholism* (Vol. 5). New York: Grune & Stratton, 1979.

Mendelson, J. H., & LaDou, J. Experimentally induced chronic intoxication and withdrawal in alcoholics. Part 2—Psychophysiological findings. *Quarterly Journal on Studies of Alcohol*, 1964, Suppl. 2, 14–39.

Renaud, B., Buda, M., Lewis, B. P., & Pujol, J. K. Effects of 5,6-dihydroxytryptamine on tyrosine-hydroxylase activity in central catecholaminergic neurons of the rat. *Biochemical Pharmacology*, 1975, *24*, 1739–1742.

Ritzmann, R. F., & Tabakoff, B. Body temperature in mice: A quantitative measure of alcohol tolerance and physical dependence. *Journal of Pharmacology and Experimental Therapeutics*, 1976, *199*, 158–170.

Roffman, M., & Lal, H. Stimulus control of hexobarbital narcosis and metabolism in mice. *Journal of Pharmacology and Experimental Therapeutics*, 1974, *191*, 358–369.

Searle, G. L., Shames, D., Cavalier, R. R., Bagdade, J. D., & Porte, D., Jr. Evaluation of ethanol hypoglycemia in man: Turnover studies with C-6-^{14}C glucose. *Metabolism*, 1974, *23*, 1023–1035.

Seeman, P. The membrane actions of anesthetics and tranquilizers. *Pharmacology Review*, 1972, *24*, 583–655.

Sellers, E. M., & Kalant, H. Drug therapy: Alcohol intoxication and withdrawal. *New England Journal of Medicine*, 1976, *294*, 757–762.

Sellers, E. M., Zilm, D. H., & Degani, N. C. Comparative efficacy of propranolol and chlordiazepoxide in alcohol withdrawal. *Journal of Studies in Alcohol*, 1977, *38*, 2096–2108.

Siegel, S. Evidence from rats that morphine tolerance is a learned response. *Journal of Comparative and Physiological Psychology*, 1975, *89*, 498–506.

Spealman, R. D., & Goldberg, S. R. Drug self-administration by laboratory animals: Control by schedules of reinforcement. *Annual Review of Pharmacological Toxicology*, 1978, *18*, 313–339.

Tabakoff, B. Alcohol tolerance in humans and animals. In K. Eriksson, J. D. Sinclair, & K. Kiianmaa (Eds.), *Animal models in alcohol research*. New York: Academic Press, 1980.

Tabakoff, B., & Hoffman, P. L. Alcohol and neurotransmitters. In H. Rigter & J. C. Crabbe (Eds.), *Alcohol tolerance and dependence*. Amsterdam: Elsevier/North Holland, 1980.

Tabakoff, B., & Hoffman, P. L. Neurochemical aspects of tolerance and physical dependence on alcohol. In B. Kissin & H. Begleiter (Eds.), *The biology of alcoholism* (Vol. 7). New York: Plenum Press, 1983.

Tabakoff, B., & Ritzmann, R. F. The effects of 6-hydroxydopamine on tolerance to and dependence on ethanol. *Journal of Pharmacology and Experimental Therapeutics*, 1977, *203*, 319–331.

Thomas, D. W., & Freedman, D. X. Treatment of alcohol withdrawal syndrome: Comparison of promazine and paraldehyde. *Journal of the American Medical Association*, 1964, *188*, 316–318.

Traynor, A. E., Schlapfer, W. T., & Barondes, S. H. Stimulation is necessary for the development of tolerance to a neuronal effect of ethanol. *Journal of Neurobiology*, 1980, *11*, 633–637.

Victor, M. Treatment of alcoholic intoxication and the withdrawal syndrome. *Psychosomatic Medicine*, 1966, *28*, 636–650.

Victor, M., & Adams, R. D. The effect of alcohol in the nervous system. *Research Publication, Association Research on Nervous and Mental Disorders,* 1953, *32,* 526–573.

Victor, M., & Wolfe, S. M. Causation and treatment of the alcohol withdrawal syndrome. In P. B. Bourne & R. Fox (Eds.), *Alcoholism progress in research and treatment.* New York: Academic Press, 1973.

Vogel, G. W. REM deprivation. III. Dreaming and psychosis. *Archives of General Psychiatry,* 1968, *18,* 312–329.

Vogel-Sprott, M. Acute and chronic tolerance to low doses of alcohol: Differences in cognitive and motor skill performance. *Pscychopharmacology,* 1979, *61,* 287–291.

Wahlstrom, G., & Ekwall, T. Tolerance to hexobarbital and supersensitivity to pilocarpine after chronic barbital treatments in the rat. *European Journal of Pharmacology,* 1976, *38,* 123–129.

Walter, R., Hoffman, P. L., Flexner, J. B., & Flexner, L. B. Neurohypophyseal hormones, analogs and fragments: Their effects on puromycin-induced amnesia. *Proceedings of the National Academy of Science, USA,* 1975, *72,* 4180–4184.

Wenger, J. R., Tiffany, T. M., Bombardier, C., Nicholls, K., & Woods, S. C. Ethanol tolerance in the rat is learned. *Science,* 1981, *213,* 575–577.

Wolfe, V. M., & Victor, M. The physiological basis of the alcohol withdrawal syndrome. In N. K. Mello & J. H. Mendelson (Eds.), *Recent advances in studies of alcoholism: An interdisciplinary symposium.* Washington, D.C.: U.S. Government Printing Office, Pub. No. (HSM) 71-9045, 1971.

Yuki, T., Bradford, B. V., & Thurman, R. G. Role of hormones in the mechanism of the swift increase in alcohol metabolism in the rat. *Pharmacology, Biochemistry and Behavior, 13*(Suppl. 1), 1980, 67–71.

Zarcone, V. P., Schreier, L., Mitchell, G., Orenberg, E., & Barchas, J. Sleep variables, cyclic AMP and biogenic amine metabolites after one day of ethanol ingestion. *Journal of Studies on Alcoholism,* 1980, *41,* 318–324.

8

Alcohol Consumption and Prenatal Development

ERNEST L. ABEL, CARRIE L. RANDALL, AND EDWARD P. RILEY

References to the association between alcohol and inferior offspring development and/or birth defects date back several hundred years in the scientific literature. For instance, during England's gin epidemic of 1720–1750, considerable concern was expressed over alcohol's adverse effects on unborn children; by the turn of the 20th century, epidemiological studies had actually documented alcohol's risk to the developing fetus. During the early 1900s, a number of laboratory studies were also conducted to test alcohol's effects on embryonic development in animals. However, these studies do not seem to have been prompted by a concern about alcohol's role as a teratogen in humans but rather by practical considerations. Alcohol was considered representative of general anesthetic agents with the advantage of being readily available, soluble in water, and volatile.

Stockard (1932), using guinea pigs as subjects, performed the most systematic studies of alcohol's prenatal effects on mammals. Administration of alcohol by vapor to pregnant animals resulted in smaller litters due to an increase in prenatal deaths. Birth weights, however, were comparable to controls, and only occasional reference was made to defective embryos. On the basis of several years of experimentation, it was concluded that the action of alcohol (as well as other anesthetics) on the embryo was to retard development. The result was abnormal development

ERNEST L. ABEL • Research Institute on Alcoholism, 1021 Main Street, Buffalo, New York 14203.   CARRIE L. RANDALL • Research Services, Veterans Administration Medical Center, 109 Bee Street, Charleston, South Carolina 29403.   EDWARD P. RILEY • Department of Psychology, State University of New York at Albany, Albany, New York 12222.

of various parts of the body. The type of abnormality was thought to be related to time of alcohol exposure and not to alcohol itself, since several agents produced the same type of defect when given at identical developmental stages: "There can be no specific action for alcohol on the embryo. If effective, alcohol acts as other effective agents do to slow the rate of development" (Stockard, 1932).

Despite the epidemiological and laboratory evidence supporting the recurrence of warnings and clinical observations of alcohol's potential as a teratogen, alcohol's potential for causing birth defects never seems to have generated much attention among physicians, scientists, or the public. The reasons for this apathy are moot. Skepticism, inconsistencies in the data, unawareness of the evidence, the Prohibition era, and so on, may all have contributed to the lack of concern or interest regarding alcohol's teratogenicity until rediscovery of the "fetal alcohol syndrome" by Jones and Smith (1973).

The remainder of this chapter will be devoted to an overview of both the clinical and animal literature regarding the effects of alcohol on fetal growth and development. A literature review on the topic will not be presented, however, since many reviews already exist (e.g., Warner & Rosett, 1975; Randall, 1977, 1981; Randall & Noble, 1980). Where possible, clinical and animal results will be discussed together, but the chapter is divided for simplicity into separate clinical and animal sections. The critical discussion at the end will tie the results together and discuss future directions and concerns.

1. FETAL ALCOHOL SYNDROME/FETAL ALCOHOL EFFECTS

In 1973 Jones and Smith described a pattern of defects in children born to alcoholic women which has come to be known as the fetal alcohol syndrome (FAS). For a diagnosis of FAS to be made, the patient must exhibit three main characteristics. These are (1) growth deficiencies (>2 standard deviations for length and weight), (2) facial anomalies, and (3) evidence of central nervous system (CNS) dysfunction (Clarren & Smith, 1978).

Patients who exhibit all three main characteristics are sometimes described as having the "full blown" FAS. (However, the criteria for determining presence or absence of one or more of these general characteristics have not yet been rigidly defined, e.g., which facial anomalies, extent of CNS dysfunction.) Those who exhibit only one or two of these characteristics, however, are sometimes described as exhibiting "fetal alcohol effects" (FAE) or the "partial FAS." Some of the more common FAE are summarized in Table 1.

The degree of mental retardation tends to be related to the severity of physical anomalies associated with *in utero* alcohol exposure (Streissguth, Herman, & Smith, 1978a; Majewski, Bierich, Loser, Michaelis, Leiber, & Bettecken, 1976). However, CNS anomalies may also be present in the absence of observable phys-

Table 1. Main Characteristics of FAS and FAE

Growth deficiency
  Intrauterine growth retardation
  Postnatal growth retardation

Facial characteristics
  Short palpebral fissures
  Indistinct philtrum
  Epicanthic folds
  Ptosis
  Shortened nasal bridge/upturned nose
  Thin upper lip
  Underdeveloped jaw
  High arched palate
  Cleft palate/lip

Microcephaly

Limb/joint anomalies
  Abnormal palmar creases
  Clinodactyly
  Camptodactyly
  Hypoplasia of nails
  Hip dislocation

Cardiovascular defects

Urogenital defects

Central nervous system dysfunction
  Mental retardation
  Hyperactivity
  Fine motor dysfunction

ical signs (Landesman-Dwyer, Keller, & Streissguth, 1978; Majewski *et al.,* 1976). This observation poses a serious problem in diagnosing FAE at birth, since mental retardation is difficult to diagnose at this time.

On the basis of numerous clinical and epidemiological studies, it appears that *in utero* alcohol exposure can result in a wide range of effects, with the full-blown FAS at one extreme and the only barely perceptible FAE as the other end of the continuum is approached. Such variability may be due to differences in *in utero* blood alcohol exposure, daily exposure versus binge drinking, genetic sensitivity, gestational time of exposure, interactions with other drugs, nutritional status, and so on.

Estimates of the incidence of the full-blown FAS may vary with the population studied. In the United States, for example, the incidence is placed at 0.4 per 1,000 (Sokol, Miller, & Reed, 1980), 1 per 1,000 (Hanson, Streissguth, & Smith, 1978), and 3.5 per 1,000 (Ouellette, Rosett, Rosman, & Weiner, 1977). Among some American Indian tribes the incidence is estimated at 20 per 1,000 (Aase,

1980). In Europe, estimates vary from 3.3 per 1,000 in France (Dehaene, Samaille-Villette, Samaille, Crepin, Walbaum, Deroubaix, & Blanc-Garin, 1977) to 1.7 per 1,000 in Sweden (Olegard, Sabel, Aronsson, Sandin, Johansson, Carlsson, Kyllerman, Iversen, & Hrbek, 1979). However, if focus is shifted from the full-blown to the partial FAS, the incidence would no doubt be considerably higher. In summary, it is clear that any epidemiologic study of FAS is limited by the population studied and estimates vary accordingly.

1.1. Major Characteristics Associated with FAS and FAE

1.1.1. Growth Deficiency

Pre- and postnatal growth deficiencies are the most common characteristics associated with FAS. FAS children are lighter in weight and shorter in length than other children of the same gestational age. Clinical (Ouellette et al., 1977) and animal studies (Abel, 1979a; Lochry, Randall, Goldsmith, & Sutker, 1982) suggest that this alcohol-induced intrauterine growth retardation occurs during the last third of gestation.

Following birth, most FAS children remain below weight and height for their age. Animal studies suggest that growth retardation is not due to metabolic deficiencies in assimilation or utilization of food (Abel, 1981) but might be the result of decreased cell numbers (Henderson, Hoyumpa, McClain, & Schenker, 1979). Growth hormone levels and other endocrine functions are within the normal range (Root, Reiter, Andriola, & Duckett, 1975; Tze, Friesen, & MacLeod, 1976). More information concerning growth retardation associated with the FAS is contained in the review by Abel and Greizerstein (1981).

1.1.2. Facial Features

Some of the more commonly encountered facial features associated with the FAS are listed in Table 1. Although there is considerable variation in these facial features from patient to patient, in the experience of Clarren and Smith (1978), most FAS patients are characterized by three "key features": (1) short palpebral fissures, (2) thin upper lip and thinned vermilion, and (3) diminished to absent philtrum. Majewski and Bierich (1979), however, consider short palpebral fissures a very infrequent (<10%) characteristic of the FAS. A more extended discussion of the facial anomalies associated with the FAS is contained in a review by Clarren and Smith (1978).

1.1.3. Cardiopathy

The incidence of cardiopathy associated with FAE appears to range between 41% and 74% (Sandor, Smith, & MacLeod, 1980; Steeg & Woolf, 1979; Depuis, Dehaene, Deroubaix-Tella, Blanc-Garin, Rey, & Carpenter-Couralt, 1978). The most common anomalies are septal defects, especially ventricular septal defect. Ventricular septal defect is also the most common anomaly in mice exposed to alcohol *in utero* (Chernoff, 1977; Randall, Taylor, & Walker, 1977). In most cases, the septal defects in FAS children are small and not life-threatening; they frequently close spontaneously.

1.1.4. Liver Anomalies

There are very few clinical reports of liver damage resulting from *in utero* alcohol exposure (Habbick, Zaleski, Casey, & Murphy, 1979; Moller, Brandt, & Tygstrup, 1979; Newman, Flannery, & Caplan, 1979; Peiffer, Majewski, Fischbach, Bierich, & Volk, 1979). No consistency was evident in the kind of abnormalities noted in these reports.

1.1.5. Kidney and Urogenital Tract Anomalies

Anomalies of the kidney and/or genitourinary tract have not been noted often in connection with the FAS, but they do seem to occur more frequently in children of alcoholic mothers than in the general population (Havers, Majewski, Olbing, & Eickenberg, 1980). The most commonly occurring abnormalities are hydronephrosis, hypoplasia or renal agenesis, and obstruction of the uteropelvic junction. The frequency of occurrence of kidney and urogenital tract anomalies in patients with FAS is unknown but is probably greater than that which has been reported, since renal evaluations are not routine. In animal studies as many as 86% of litters of mice exposed to alcohol *in utero* had at least one pup with a hydronephrotic kidney, and 33% had urogenital tract defects (Boggan, Randall, & DeBeukelaer, 1978; cf. also Boggan, Randall, DeBeukelaer, & Smith, 1979).

1.1.6. Neuropathological Anomalies

The most dramatic indication of alcohol's teratogenic effects on the brain of the developing fetus comes from autopsy studies of children prenatally exposed to alcohol who were either aborted or died shortly after birth. The anomalies identified thus far are incomplete cortical development, enlarged lateral ventricles, fusion of ventricles, aberrant neuronal and glial migration, absence or underdevelopment of corpus callosum, absence of anterior commissure, rudimentary cerebellum, absence of olfactory bulbs, and underdevelopment of the caudate nucleus. It is clear from this diversity of observed defects that the brain is a primary target of ethanol's teratogenic action.

With regard to neural tube disorders, Clarren (1979) noted that the frequency of such births in conjunction with the fetal alcohol syndrome in the Pacific northwest was 31 per 1,000, or 63 times greater than normal. In reference to this incidence of occurrence, however, Arulanantham and Goldstein (1979) caution that this may be a biased estimate, since children with neural tube defects are more likely to be referred to a particular center, thereby increasing the apparent association.

1.1.7. Behavioral Teratology

Although most FAS patients do not experience the profound neurological damage described in the previous section, many suffer from behavioral anomalies suggestive of functional CNS disorders.

Mental retardation is among the most serious CNS consequence of prenatal alcohol exposure. Studies reported from France, Sweden, Germany, and the United States have noted a high frequency of low IQ scores for FAS children. Scores average about 70 and tend to remain stable over time (Streissguth, Herman, & Smith, 1978b). The effect of enriched environments and special education on IQ scores in these children remains to be evaluated, as does the contribution of genetic factors.

In addition to, or quite apart from, the mental retardation occurring in children born to alcoholic women, there are also numerous reports of "hyperactivity," also called "minimal brain dysfunction" or "attentional deficit disorder" in FAS children. This behavioral problem is associated with attentional deficits, distractibility, impulsiveness, and disciplinary problems. It is not necessary that the FAS child be mentally retarded to display hyperactivity. In a recent study, Shaywitz, Cohen, & Shaywitz (1980) reported that 15 patients diagnosed as FAS children were "hyperactive" despite normal intelligence. Thus, hyperactivity is not necessarily a result of mental insufficiency but, rather, is a separate problem also indicative of CNS dysfunction. Whether pharmacotherapy is successful in treating FAS children with hyperactivity or whether the condition is permanent remains to be determined.

Sleep disorders are also commonly encountered in conjunction with prenatal alcohol exposure (Rosett, Snyder, Sander, Lee, Cook, Weiner, & Gould, 1979). During all stages of sleep, EEG activity tends to be hypersynchronous, almost to the point that infants can be diagnosed as being offspring of alcoholic women on the basis of EEG activity alone (Havlicek, Childiaeva, & Chernick, 1977). EEGs during periods when children are awake are also abnormal, being characterized by excessive slowing, poor organization of background rhythm, and rhythmical delta; in some cases, "sleep" EEG activity was suggestive of possible epilepsy (Root et al., 1975; Puschel & Seifert, 1979).

Other behavioral anomalies observed in children prenatally exposed to alcohol include slow habituation to stimuli (Streissguth, Martin, & Barr, 1977), weak sucking ability (Martin, Martin, Streissguth, & Lund, 1979), poor operant learning (Martin, Martin, Lund, & Streissguth, 1977), and decreased alertness (Landesman-Dwyer et al., 1978). It is likely that these behavioral problems, in turn, affect maternal behavior and the mother–infant bond, so it may be necessary to offer special counseling to parents with FAS children. Results from animal studies recently reviewed by Riley (1981) strongly suggest that many behavioral deficits will be mitigated with age.

1.2. Risk Factors

1.2.1. Undernutrition

Alcohol-induced undernutrition probably is not responsible for the pattern of defects associated with FAS. Children born during the Dutch famine of 1944 (Smith, 1947) do not resemble FAS children except for lowered birth weights (but detailed neurological examinations were not conducted). Conceivably, however, chronic alcohol consumption may cause deficiencies in essential nutrients such as thiamine, folic acid, and so on, that are greater than those that occurred in conjunction with the Dutch famine. Thus, undernutrition could conceivably exacerbate the effects of alcohol.

1.2.2. Maternal Disease

There is no indication that mothers of FAS children share any diseases in common which could result in the birth of a child with FAS. Although liver damage is not uncommon among this population of women (Abel & Greizerstein, 1981), there are many instances in which maternal liver function is normal.

1.2.3. Amount of Consumption

Although Majewski et al. (1976) were unable to correlate consumption levels with severity of symptoms among their clinical case populations, such correlations have been noted in more controlled studies in terms of spontaneous abortions (Harlap & Shiono, 1980), birth weight (Little, 1977; Russell, 1977), and frequency of abnormalities in animal studies (cf. Randall, 1981).

In a prospective study, for example, Little (1977) reported that daily consumption of 1 oz of absolute alcohol (approximately two drinks) during late pregnancy resulted in a decrease in birth weight of 160 g. In a retrospective study, Russell (1977) reported a decrease of 53 g in birth weight after a daily consumption of 1 to 2 oz of absolute alcohol per day during pregnancy and a progressively greater decrease in birth weight with maternal daily intakes of 5 to 6 oz of absolute alcohol (approximately 11 drinks per day).

1.2.4. Genetic Factors

One reason for the variability in severity of FAS symptoms despite equivalent levels of alcohol consumption during gestation may be a genetic factor, which predisposes some women to differences in the actual blood alcohol levels attained, differences in the levels of acetaldehyde, and/or differences in maternal or fetal sensitivity to alcohol and/or its metabolites. For example, despite equivalent levels of alcohol consumption, maternal blood alcohol levels may vary considerably due to differences in maternal stature, diet, metabolic efficiency, and so on.

Veghelyi, Osztovics, and Szaszovsky (1978) have argued that the critical factor in determining whether or not a child will develop FAS is not the blood alcohol level but rather the blood acetaldehyde levels achieved by the mother. They point out that whereas blood acetaldehyde levels are normally between 21 and 30 μmol, levels may be considerably higher in alcoholics. For example, Veghelyi et al. (1978) cite a case in which a female patient achieved a blood acetaldehyde level of 140 μmol after consuming only 0.5 mL/kg alcohol. On the basis of their studies, they propose that blood acetaldehyde levels above 40 μmol constitute a serious factor for development of FAS.

The human placenta does not provide as adequate a metabolic barrier to acetaldehyde as the rat placenta (Kouri, Koivula, & Koivusalo, 1977). Thus, studies such as those of Kesaniemi and Sippel (1975), which demonstrate little or no acetaldehyde in rat fetuses after the mother received alcohol, may not reflect the situation encountered in humans. Mouse fetuses, in addition, have been found to contain acetaldehyde after the mother received ethanol (Randall, Taylor, Tabakoff, & Walker, 1977). If hepatic metabolic function is genetically deficient in terms of aldehyde dehydrogenase activity, blood acetaldehyde levels could rise to a point at which the fetus could be exposed to acetaldehyde.

Related to the issue of genetic factors in terms of aldehyde dehydrogenase activity is that of genetically determined sensitivity to alcohol and/or acetaldehyde. Three reports of twins born to alcoholic mothers are illustrative. Two cases involved dizygotic twins and the third concerned monozygotic twins. In the first report of FAS in dizygotic twins, one of the infants had many features of the FAS whereas the other was only minimally affected (Christoffel & Salafsky, 1975). The authors state that the latter child's condition would have escaped detection had his twin not been so severely affected. The second case of FAS in dizygotic twins occurred in Spain (Santolaya, Martinez, Gorostiza, Aizpiri, & Hernandez, 1978). As in the previous case, the twins differed in terms of severity of FAS-related stigmata. Interestingly, one twin had less pronounced FAS facial features and his height and weight were less depressed at 11 months of age, but his psychomotor disturbances were greater than the other's. The third case involved monozygotic rather than fraternal twins. While these twins shared the same placenta and exhibited many of the same characteristics of FAS, they did differ in the severity of some features (Palmer, Ouellette, Warner, & Leichtman, 1974).

These twin studies thus suggest that there are genetic differences in susceptibility to alcohol's teratogenicity. These could be due to differences in tissue susceptibility, fetoplacental circulation, placental ability to metabolize alcohol, or preventing transmission of acetaldehyde to the fetus.

Some other genetic considerations which also warrant attention are the contributions of paternal factors and abnormal maternal characteristics apart from chronic alcoholism. With respect to paternal alcoholism, there is a general tendency for alcoholic women to have spouses who are also alcoholic (Gomberg, 1975). Lester and Van Thiel (1977) have reported that sperm samples from alcoholic men are often grossly abnormal. This observation raises the possibility that some of the characteristics of the FAS may be due to paternal factors. This possibility is also suggested by a number of animal studies that observed poor growth and behavioral anomalies in offspring sired by males who consumed alcohol prior to breeding (Anderson, Beyler, & Zaneveld, 1978; Badr & Badr, 1975; Pfeifer, MacKinnon, & Seiser, 1977). However, results from teratologic studies in animals have, for the most part, failed to find an increase in birth defects in offspring sired by alcohol-treated males (Anderson, Furby, Oswald, & Zaneveld, 1981; Randall, Burling, & Lochry, 1982).

Apart from their use of alcohol, alcoholic women may be more at risk for giving birth to children with lower IQ. For example, Streissguth, Little, Herman, and Woodell (1979) found that children born to alcoholic women after they stopped drinking had significantly lower IQ scores than those born to nondrinkers. Lower birth weights of children born to recovered alcoholics relative to nondrinkers have also been reported (Little, Streissguth, Woodell, & Norden, 1979). However, these reports are open to criticism, since parental IQ or body size was not considered.

In general, these studies suggest the possibility that maternal "constitutional" factors may in some way contribute to the birth of a child with features of FAS. Conceivably, many FAS children have lower IQs because of lower parental IQs.

2. ALCOHOL AS A TERATOGEN IN ANIMALS, 1973–1979

Difficulties in separating cause and effect with regard to alcohol and reproductive dysfunction, and especially the problem of assessing mechanisms of action, are among the many reasons effort has been devoted to the development of "animal models." By studying the effects of *in utero* alcohol exposure under controlled laboratory conditions, researchers are able to isolate critical variables that may contribute to the teratogenicity of alcohol *per se*.

Since 1973, animal studies investigating the effects of prenatal alcohol exposure on the development of offspring have proliferated. Some of the studies were designed with the specific intention of developing an animal model of the FAS. Others were more concerned with determining whether alcohol was, in fact, a teratogen as evidenced by its ability to alter morphologic development when administered during the period of organogenesis. Despite the differences in objectives of these studies, the basic issue under investigation has been and continues to

·be the teratogenicity of alcohol in animals. Traditional teratological investigations of congenital malformations have been conducted, as well as studies of the structural, functional, and biochemical anomalies that may manifest themselves either at birth or some time afterwards.

Before discussing the results of animal studies, it is necessary to describe briefly some of the background methodologies, especially those related to route of administration, and to mention the different species that have been employed. For a more detailed evaluation of the advantages and disadvantages of these methods, see Abel (1980a), Boggan (1981), and Randall and Riley (1981).

Currently, the most common method of alcohol administration to laboratory rodents is with a liquid diet. Alcohol, in known concentrations, is added to a commercially available liquid diet (e.g., Sustacal) and is fortified with additional vitamins. This diet replaces the animal's solid chow and usually water as well. Daily consumption is monitored to determine caloric and alcohol intake per day. Control animals are fed an identical liquid diet except for the isocaloric replacement of the ethanol with sucrose or other carbohydrates in the experimental diets. Each control animal receives the same volume of diet that an experimental animal, with which it has been paired, has consumed on a particular day of pregnancy. In this way, caloric intake is equated between groups. An ad lib pair-fed group is often included as well to assess the role of maternal undernutrition itself. This method of alcohol administration is convenient to the experimenter and not stressful to the animal, the latter point being of primary concern in experiments employing pregnant animals.

Another frequently used method of administration is intubation. With this procedure, a known dose of alcohol is intubated directly into the stomach. Control animals are intubated with an equal volume of an isocaloric sucrose solution. In some studies, the amount of solid food and water consumed by the experimental animal is measured and the same amount is presented to the control animal in order to equate daily caloric and fluid intake in the two groups. Ideally, an ad lib group is included for comparison. Once again, as with the liquid-diet technique, there is emphasis on controlling for nutritional variables. This procedure is more stressful to pregnant animals than the liquid diet technique but allows the experimenter to control the amount of alcohol each animal receives.

Two lesser used methods of alcohol administration are to replace the animal's water with a dilute alcohol solution or to inject alcohol intraperitoneally. The former method is of dubious value because it results in relatively low blood alcohol levels (e.g., <100 mg/100 mL). The latter method is not recommended for pregnant animals because of possible puncture of the fetus or amniotic sac and the risk of peritonitis.

Mice and rats have been the most commonly studied animals for developing models of FAS and in animal teratology in general; other animals that have also been studied include the dog (Ellis & Pick, 1980), monkey (Jacobson, Rich, &

Tovsky, 1978), rabbit (Schwetz, Smith, & Staples, 1978), miniature swine (Dexter, Tumbleson, Decker, & Middleton, 1979), and cat (Himwich, Hall, & MacArthur, 1977).

2.1. Effects on Growth and Development and Postnatal Mortality

Litter size is frequently overlooked as a measure of teratogenesis, yet it is an extremely powerful index, since fetuses most affected by a teratogen die *in utero* or are stillborn. Although decreases in the number of pups born to alcohol-treated mothers might be expected, such decreases have not been consistently observed. As Abel (1980b) points out in his review article, this is surprising, since *in utero* alcohol exposure has been reported to increase the number of prenatal deaths observed in mice and rats when animals are sacrificed immediately prior to delivery. While it appears incongruous to find increased prenatal mortalities on the one hand and no differences in litter size at birth on the other, there is a possible explanation: determination of litter size at birth includes only dams that deliver pups. Thus, data concerning litter size are based only on actual births. Females who do not give birth are excluded but may actually comprise a relatively large proportion of the treated subjects. If, instead, uterine contents were examined for all animals, it is conceivable that the prenatal death rate (as reflected by the number of resorptions) would be increased by alcohol use, whereas litter size would not be affected.

Maternal alcohol consumption reliably produces dose-dependent decreases in progeny weight. It should be noted that alcohol exposure during the third week of gestation seems to have a more severe effect on birth weight than exposure earlier in gestation (Abel, 1979a; Lochry *et al.*, 1982). Not surprisingly, the degree of effect on birth weight is related to genotype (Yanai & Ginsburg, 1977). These findings corroborate clinical observations of FAS progeny and indicate that critical periods of susceptibility to the action of alcohol depend on the variable being assessed. That is, while morphological defects are more pronounced after first-trimester alcohol exposure in humans and second-trimester exposure in rodents, growth impairment is evident following third-trimester exposure. It is clear that a "safe" period for consuming alcohol during pregnancy probably does not exist.

Although the factor(s) responsible for alcohol-induced growth impairment have not yet been identified conclusively, recent studies suggest that *in utero* alcohol exposure results in decreased cell number (hypoplasia) and size (hypotrophy). This conclusion stems from reports of decreased organ DNA and protein content as well as decreased incorporation of leucine into protein in rat fetuses exposed to alcohol *in utero* (Henderson & Schenker, 1977; Henderson *et al.*, 1979; Henderson, Hoyumpa, Rothschild, & Schenker, 1980; Rawat, 1975, 1976). Further studies have also demonstrated decreased body DNA and protein content in rat embryos exposed to alcohol *in vitro* (Brown, Goulding, & Fabro, 1979).

Since DNA content per diploid cell is constant, a decrease in total DNA reflects a decrease in cell number. Decreases in protein content per cell (protein/ DNA) reflect decreased cell size. Whereas decreases in cell size do not result in permanent growth deficits, decreased cell number does result in permanent post-natal growth retardation. Since permanent postnatal growth retardation occurs in both children and animals exposed to alcohol *in utero*, the pre- and postnatal growth retardation characteristic of FAS is likely the result of inhibition of cellular proliferation (hypoplasia).

Postnatal mortality is a second index of teratologic insult. Functional anom-alies not observable at birth may become manifest with maturation. If the defect is serious enough, death will occur. Increased postnatal mortality in progeny of alcohol-treated pregnant rats has been reported in several studies that have been reviewed by Abel (1980b). The effect appears to be dose-related and is not due to residual effects of alcohol on maternal behavior or lactational performance (Abel & Dintcheff, 1978).

In summary, the most reliable effect of prenatal alcohol exposure in animals, as in humans, is a decrease in birth weight that is probably the result of a reduced number of body cells. This cellular hypoplasia is reflected by a postnatal growth retardation in animals which is thought to be comparable to the "failure to thrive" observed in FAS children. Depending on amount of *in utero* alcohol exposure, there is also an increase in postnatal mortality in animals, which is also compa-rable to the increased postnatal mortality occurring in FAS children (Jones & Smith, 1973).

2.2. Morphologic Anomalies

By definition, a teratogen is an agent that produces anomalous development, not only in growth patterns but in structural and functional development as well. Skeptics of FAS have claimed that the congenital defects observed in the offspring of alcoholic mothers could have been caused by maternal undernutrition, vitamin deficiency, nicotine, infection, or a number of other adverse conditions frequently associated with alcohol abuse (Mendelson, 1978). The results from animal studies, however, strongly support the notion that alcohol is, in fact, a teratogen. These studies have been reviewed recently by Randall (1981).

Briefly, defects observed in mice and dogs exposed to alcohol *in utero* include hydrocephaly, cardiac anomalies, hydronephrosis, digit peculiarities, cleft palate, and so on. The defects are dose-related. That is, low doses of alcohol are not asso-ciated with an increase in birth defects in the offspring, while moderate-to-high doses produce a deleterious effect. Excessively high doses, however, result in fail-ure to maintain pregnancy rather than inducing birth defects in 100% of the litter, as might be expected. Taken together, these animal studies are significant because they demonstrate alcohol's teratogenicity under controlled conditions and in the absence of confounding factors.

2.3. Behavioral Teratogenic Effects

The scope of teratology has been broadened to include functional as well as structural abnormalities. Although it is presumed that functional anomalies are the result of structural or biochemical anomalies, such structural anomalies may not be visible because they involve subtle neuroanatomical or neurochemical changes in the brain. These neuroanatomical/neurochemical changes are inferred from functional deficits. On the basis of functional deficits, it may be possible to determine where in the brain such structural deficits may be located. Thus far, activity and learning/memory performance have commanded the most attention as far as studies of functional deficits are concerned. Studies in this area have been reviewed recently by Riley (1981), and the reader is referred to his work for greater detail.

2.3.1. Activity

Most studies have reported that prenatal alcohol exposure increases activity and/or exploratory behavior in animals. Although many of these studies are methodologically flawed, similar studies employing control procedures not included in the less-controlled studies have essentially arrived at similar conclusions.

While these activity data appear to corroborate the clinical accounts of hyperactivity in children prenatally exposed to alcohol, the underlying processes responsible for these behaviors in children and animals have yet to be identified and may not necessarily be similar. Despite this caveat, the concurrence of animal and human data is intriguing and provides a firm experimental foundation for the behavioral teratogenicity of alcohol with respect to "hyperactivity" in humans.

One of the major characteristics of the FAS is cognitive deficits. In most instances, studies in animals are consistent with reports of intellectual impairment in children associated with *in utero* alcohol exposure. For example, Shaywitz, Klopper, and Gordon (1976), Bond and DiGiusto (1977), and Abel (1979b) have reported impaired learning in an active shock avoidance task in animals prenatally exposed to alcohol. In the Abel (1979b) study, deficits in two-way shock avoidance were observed in animals six months after *in utero* alcohol exposure, indicating that prenatal alcohol exposure can have long-lasting effects on behavior.

Riley, Lochry, and Shapiro (1979) and Lochry and Riley (1980) have also observed, in animals prenatally exposed to alcohol, learning deficits in a passive avoidance task wherein the animal must withhold responding to avoid an aversive event. These results suggest that *in utero* alcohol exposure adversely affects response-inhibition mechanisms (Riley, Lochry, & Shapiro, 1979; Riley, Lochry, Shapiro, & Baldwin, 1979). Deficits in reversal learning reported by Lochry and Riley (1980) and Anandam and Stern (1980) are also compatible with the response-inhibition deficit hypothesis (Riley, Lochry, & Shapiro, 1979; Riley, Lochry, Shapiro, & Baldwin, 1979).

Studies of operant behavior can also be examined with respect to learning/ memory function, although this may not have been the original intention of these studies. For example, after an animal has been trained to operate a manipulandum for reinforcement (e.g., food, water), it will cease ("extinguish") to operate the manipulandum when it no longer receives any rewards for its efforts. "Extinction" represents a general form of learning, namely, that the contingencies between output and reinforcement no longer exist. In this context, Riley, Shapiro, Lochry, and Broida (1980) reported that food-deprived male rat offspring prenatally exposed to alcohol continued to bar press for food reward during extinction more often than control offspring. This increased level of responding was not due to a higher level of responding prior to extinction, since alcohol-exposed animals were actually bar pressing at a slower rate at this time compared to pair-fed controls.

In summary, many of the effects of *in utero* alcohol exposure in animals corroborate the behavioral effects observed in conjunction with FAS. The most consistent findings involve hyperactivity and deficits in learning/memory performance. Moreover, the wide variety of appetitive and aversive reinforcements used to motivate behavior in these studies suggests that these impairments are not due to differences in motivational factors. Differences in activity also do not appear to be a confounding factor in learning tasks, since in many of the tests the criterion is errors, not speed of responding. Not all the studies in this area have reported deficits in learning (e.g., Osborne, Caul, & Fernandez, 1980), however, and the reasons for these discrepancies are not apparent. Differences in test procedures, methods and levels of alcohol exposure, age of testing, and so on, are factors that may account for these conflicting observations.

2.3.2. Miscellaneous Behavioral Effects

The effects of prenatal exposure to alcohol on aggression in animals are inconsistent. In a recent study that included a nutritional control group, Abel (1980a) reported decreased aggressiveness toward prey on the part of female animals prenatally exposed to alcohol as compared with control animals born to dams given *ad lib* access to food and water. Compared with pair-fed controls, however, alcohol-exposed animals were not less aggressive. The results of this study illustrate the need to control for alcohol-related undernutrition in animal models.

Data with regard to the effects of *in utero* alcohol exposure on subsequent preference for alcohol are also inconsistent (Bond & DiGiusto, 1976; Abel & York, 1979). At present the reasons for this inconsistency cannot be accounted for unequivocally, since these studies differed in many dimensions.

Several studies have examined the sensitivity of animals to alcohol as a result of prenatal alcohol exposure. When sensitivity is evaluated by means of "sleep time" (alcohol-induced narcosis), animals prenatally exposed to alcohol do not exhibit altered sensitivity to alcohol as compared with control animals (Abel, 1979c; Anandam, Strait, & Stern, 1980; Boggan & Randall, 1980; Harris & Chase, 1979; Da Silva, Ribeiro, & Masur, 1980). However, when hypothermic response to a challenge dose of alcohol is evaluated, prenatally exposed animals have been reported to exhibit less (Abel, Bush, & Dintcheff, 1981; Anandam *et al.*, 1980) or more (Taylor, Branch, Liu, Weichmann, Hill, & Kokka, 1981) of a drop in body temperature as compared with pair-fed controls. The reason for those discrepant results remains to be elucidated in future experiments.

2.4. Neuroanatomical Changes

Observable alterations in structural or biochemical mechanisms could conceivably indicate the locus or mechanism(s) underlying the physical or behavioral anomalies noted in animals and humans prenatally exposed to alcohol. As noted above, a number of autopsy studies have been performed on FAS children. These studies have demonstrated that *in utero* alcohol exposure can produce marked structural changes in the brain. Brain anomalies similar to those noted in these clinical reports have also been observed in animals prenatally exposed to alcohol. These defects include hydrocephalus, absence of the corpus callosum, and dilated ventricles.

In addition to these gross anatomical defects, histopathological effects in CNS tissue have also been observed in conjunction with *in utero* alcohol exposure. West, Hodges, and Black (1981), Barnes and Walker (1981), and Abel, Jacobson, and Sherwin (1981) have each observed aberrations in the organization of neuronal fibers in the hippocampus of rats exposed to alcohol *in utero*. Nutritional control groups were included in each of these studies and offspring were raised by non-drug-treated surrogate dams after birth. Since the hippocampus is involved in learning/memory performance and inhibitory control of behavior (Douglas, 1967), these observations suggest that damage to the hippocampus is a possible explanation for the behavioral aberrations noted in conjunction with *in utero* alcohol exposure.

Myelination has also been reported to be affected by prenatal alcohol exposure. Despite absence of either adequate nutritional controls or controls for postnatal maternal factors, reports of delayed neuronal and myelin development in animals prenatally exposed to alcohol are consistent with the behavioral observations of delayed functional development discussed above.

In summary, neuroanatomical studies of the effects of *in utero* alcohol exposure in animals corroborate many of the gross changes observed in the brains of FAS children. Neurohistopathological studies have also consistently demonstrated that such exposure produces alterations in the neuronal circuitry of the hippocampus. There is also considerable evidence that *in utero* alcohol exposure causes delays in neuronal maturation. These studies provide solid support for the likelihood that the behavioral deficits observed in FAS children (e.g., mental retardation, delayed psychomotor development, impaired fine motor coordination, attentional deficit syndrome) may be directly due to alcohol-induced structural changes in the brain.

2.5. Neurochemical Alterations

Although a number of studies have been reported concerning the effects of *in utero* alcohol exposure on neurochemicals in animals, these studies are contradictory. The literature on this topic has been reviewed by Boggan (1981). The reader is referred to this source for specific details and methodological issues.

To summarize, changes in brain serotonin (5-hydroxytryptophan) levels following prenatal alcohol exposure have been reported to decrease, increase, and remain unchanged relative to pair-fed controls.

Changes in catecholamine levels are similarly inconsistent, with increases, decreases, and no changes in brain levels of norepinephrine being reported in conjunction with *in utero* alcohol exposure. In the case of dopamine, most studies have reported no significant changes in brain levels resulting from *in utero* alcohol exposure, but there is also a report of decreased brain dopamine levels. With respect to tyrosine hydroxylase, the rate-limiting enzyme in the synthesis of dopamine and norepinephrine, both increases and no changes in brain tissue have been reported.

At present no conclusions can be reached concerning the *in utero* effects of alcohol on neurochemical levels or turnover. Different treatment periods, routes of alcohol administration, amount of alcohol ingested or administered, age of testing, and other methodological procedures preclude resolution of the numerous contradictions apparent in the literature.

2.6. Effects on Biochemistry

Alcohol is metabolized primarily by the hepatic enzyme alcohol dehydrogenase (ADH). The metabolite acetaldehyde is further metabolized by the hepatic enzyme aldehyde dehydrogenase. ADH can be increased in adult animals as a result of chronic alcohol exposure (Hawkins, Kalant, & Khanna, 1966); several studies have been directed at the possibility that a comparable induction of ADH activity may also occur in offspring exposed to alcohol *in utero*. The data from these studies, however, are inconsistent, since both increases in ADH activity (Sze, Yanai, & Ginsburg, 1976; cf. also Niimi, 1973) and decreases have been reported (Duncan & Woodhouse, 1978) in animals prenatally exposed to alcohol, using the same period and regimen of exposure, the same strain of animals, and the same methods of analyses. No significant differences in ADH activity in rat fetuses or neonates exposed to alcohol *in utero* have also been reported by Raiha, Koskinen,

and Pikkarainen (1967) and by Sjoblom, Oisund, and Morlund (1979). In contrast to the previous studies, the study by Sjoblom *et al.* (1979) is noteworthy for
the fact that nutritional controls were employed.

An increase in aldehyde dehydrogenase has been reported in rats prenatally
exposed to alcohol (Burke & Fenton, 1978). Activity of this enzyme was detected
on day 1 postpartum in alcohol-exposed offspring but not until day 8 in control
(not pair-fed) offspring. By day 8, differences in activity of this enzyme were no
longer significant between alcohol- and non-alcohol-treated animals. This result
was not corroborated by Sjoblom *et al.* (1979). In summary, prenatal alcohol
exposure does not appear to affect metabolism of alcohol postnatally. Whether this
is true in children with FAS remains to be determined.

2.7. Protein and Nucleic Acid Synthesis

Thadani, Lau, Slotkin, and Schanberg (1977) and Thadani, Slotkin, and
Schanberg (1977) reported that ornithine decarboxylase (ODC) levels in neonatal
rat brain following *in utero* alcohol exposure were initially increased, followed by
a decrease. This enzyme is involved in polyamine synthesis, beginning with the
metabolism of the amino acid ornithine. Changes in its activity may thus be
reflected in nucleic acid and protein synthesis.

Impairment of amino acid transport across the placenta may also result in
altered protein synthesis. Such impairment with respect to transfer of α-amino-
isobutyric acid following alcohol administration in rats has been reported (Lin &
Maddatu, 1980). Transport of other amino acids may similarly be impaired. Henderson, Hoyumpa, Patwardhan, and Schenker (1981) have also reported
decreased uptake of α-aminobutyric acid into placental tissue in rat dams ingesting
alcohol throughout pregnancy. Decreases in uptake of l-alanine, cycloleucine, and
l-lysine were also noted. Measurements of amino acid levels in fetal tissues, however, are not consistent with these observations. Thus, while alterations in amino
acid uptake and transport across the placenta appear to occur in conjunction with
maternal alcohol consumption, no conclusions concerning the significance of these
changes are yet apparent.

Rawat (1975, 1976) has reported that perinatal alcohol exposure decreases
^{14}C-leucine incorporation into fetal and neonatal liver, heart, and brain tissues.
These observations suggest that alcohol reduces protein synthesis in developing
fetal tissue. Decreased fetal organ DNA and protein content in conjunction with
in utero alcohol exposure have been reported (Henderson & Schenker, 1977; Henderson *et al.*, 1979, 1980; Woodson & Ritchey, 1979) and are consistent with
Rawat's data of decreased incorporation of amino acids into fetal tissue.

There is thus considerable evidence that alcohol inhibits net protein synthesis
in fetal tissues. Since accumulation of protein is essential for increased cellular
growth and number, such inhibition is probably related to the intrauterine and

postnatal growth retardation observed in FAS children and offspring born to animals prenatally exposed to alcohol.

3. CRITICAL DISCUSSION AND GENERAL CONCLUSIONS

Interest in alcohol's potential as a teratogen has a long history, but this interest has been cyclic rather than sustained. While many early reports suggested that alcohol could produce teratogenic effects, these reports were subject to numerous interpretations and not much significance was attached to them.

In the last 10 years, considerable clinical attention has been directed specifically to alcohol's teratogenicity. There is now little doubt that alcohol is capable of producing birth defects in humans, but there are many issues that still remain unresolved, such as mechanism of action for these effects, the question of genetic susceptibility, critical periods for exposure, and so on.

Because many of these issues are difficult to answer in human studies, considerable effort has been devoted to developing animal models for FAE. These current studies represent an improvement over earlier studies in that many have controlled for alcohol-related effects on nutritional variables; they have included more than one dose of alcohol or strain of animal; and they have determined blood alcohol levels associated with alcohol dosages. On the negative side, postnatal fostering procedures have been included in only a few studies, so that it is difficult to partition pre- and postnatal factors. However, to date, there is very little evidence suggesting that the residual effects of alcohol exposure during pregnancy significantly influence maternal behavior or lactational performance. Overall, despite the discrepancies between some studies, there is enough consistency in some of the data to draw a number of conclusions.

First, alcohol is a teratogen in the classic sense of producing morphological anomalies in animals exposed to alcohol *in utero*. These anomalies are similar to those reported in conjunction with FAS/FAE and support the continued use of animals to a further exploration of alcohol's teratogenic effects and the variables that may contribute to these effects (e.g., genotype, acetaldehyde levels).

Second, alcohol is also a behavioral teratogen in that it can produce behavioral anomalies in offspring even in the absence of morphological anomalies. Current evidence suggests that some of these behavioral anomalies may be related to structural change in neurons in the area of the hippocampus.

Third, there is obviously a continuum of fetal alcohol effects ranging from perinatal death and morphological anomalies at one extreme (i.e., FAS) to more subtle behavioral anomalies in the absence of physical anomalies at the other (FAE). The extent of both the morphologically and behaviorally teratogenic effects has been shown to be dose-related. Other variables that determine the severity of expression of these effects—for example, genotype—still await clarification.

Fourth, these studies demonstrate that maternal nutritional factors are not primarily responsible for the effects occurring in conjunction with maternal alcohol consumption during pregnancy. While nutritional factors may particularly contribute to these observed effects—such as lower birth weight—alcohol's teratogenicity has been clearly established.

3.1. Future Trends

Continued clinical and epidemiological interest in alcohol as a teratogen will, no doubt, be sustained for many years. Several prospective studies evaluating alcohol's teratogenic effects have already been reported and provide valuable information regarding the incidence of FAS and FAE in the general population, characteristics of mothers of FAS and FAE children, risk factors, and so on. Before conclusive statements can be made regarding the effects of parental alcohol consumption on fetal development, additional studies need to be conducted on parents to determine, for instance, if the lower IQ scores of FAS children are due to "nature" and/or "nurture." More attention also needs to be paid to the possible paternal contributions to FAS/FAE.

There is also little doubt that more studies of alcohol's teratogenic effects will be conducted in animals. The validity of animal models already in use as accurate models of the human situation with respect to FAE has been clearly demonstrated. Furthermore, the results of such studies have stimulated testable hypotheses concerning the mechanisms of alcohol's teratogenicity while also involving scientists from many disciplines. For example, there are some suggestions that acetaldehyde may be responsible for the adverse effects in humans and animals associated with maternal alcohol consumption. This hypothesis is intriguing but needs to be tested under properly controlled conditions. Other possible mechanisms that warrant attention include possible mediation of effects via hypoxia, altered transport of nutrients across the placenta, inhibited utilization of nutrients, and so forth. If the mechanisms of action for alcohol's teratogenicity could be identified, it is conceivable that some of the alcohol-related effects on fetal development could be prevented or minimized through therapeutic intervention.

Currently, most animal-model studies in this area have involved the mouse and rat. While these two species will undoubtedly continue to be widely used, future studies will undoubtedly see the development of other animal models as well. In fact, animal models using dogs, miniature swine, and nonhuman primates are already being used in this area and will certainly contribute further understanding to the mechanisms of alcohol's teratogenic actions.

4. REFERENCES

Aase, J. *FAS in American Indians: A high risk group.* Paper presented at the Fetal Alcohol Syndrome Workshop, Seattle, Wash., May 2–4, 1980.

Abel, E. L. Effects of ethanol exposure during different gestation weeks of pregnancy on maternal weight gain and intrauterine growth retardation in the rat. *Neurobehavioral Toxicology*, 1979, *1*, 145–151. (a)

Abel, E. L. Prenatal effects of alcohol on adult learning in rats. *Pharmacology, Biochemistry and Behavior*, 1979, *10*, 239–243. (b)

Abel, E. L. Prenatal effects of alcohol on open-field behavior, step-down latencies and "sleep time." *Behavioral and Neural Biology*, 1979, *25*, 406–410. (c)

Abel, E. L. Procedural considerations in evaluating prenatal effects of alcohol in animals. *Neurobehavioral Toxicology*, 1980, *2*, 167–174. (a)

Abel, E. L. The fetal alcohol syndrome: Behavioral teratology. *Psychological Bulletin*, 1980, *87*, 29–50. (b)

Abel, E. L. Prenatal exposure to beer, wine, whiskey, and ethanol: Effects on postnatal growth and food and water consumption. *Neurobehavioral Toxicology*, 1981, *3*, 49–51.

Abel, E. L., & Dintcheff, B. A. Effects of prenatal exposure to ethanol on growth and development in rats. *Journal of Pharmacology and Experimental Therapeutics*, 1978, *207*, 916–921.

Abel, E. L., & Greizerstein, H. B. Growth and development in animals prenatally exposed to alcohol. In E. L. Abel (Ed.), *Fetal alcohol syndrome* (Vol. 2). Boca Raton, Fla.: CRC Press, 1982.

Abel, E. L., & York, J. L. Absence of effect of prenatal ethanol on adult emotionality and ethanol consumption in rats. *Journal of Studies on Alcohol*, 1979, *40*, 547–553.

Abel, E. L., Bush, R., & Dintcheff, B. A. Exposure of rats to alcohol *in utero* alters drug sensitivity in adulthood. *Science*, 1981, *212*, 1531–1533.

Abel, E. L., Jacobson, S., & Sherwin, B. *In utero* alcohol exposure produces functional and structural damage. Manuscript in preparation, 1981.

Anandam, N., & Stern, J. M. Alcohol *in utero:* Effects on preweanling appetitive learning. *Neurobehavioral Toxicology*, 1980, *2*, 199–205.

Anandam, N., Strait, T., & Stern, J. M. *In utero* ethanol retards early discrimination learning and decreases adult responsiveness to ethanol. *Teratology*, 1980, *21*, 25A.

Anderson, R. A., Jr., Beyler, S. A., & Zaneveld, L. J. D. Alterations of male reproduction induced by chronic ingestion of ethanol: Development of an animal model. *Fertility and Sterility*, 1978, *30*, 103–105.

Anderson, R. A., Jr., Furby, J. E., Oswald, C., & Zaneveld, L. J. D. Teratological evaluation of mouse fetuses after paternal alcohol ingestion. *Neurobehavioral Toxicology and Teratology*, 1981, *3*, 117–120.

Arulanantham, K., & Goldstein, G. Neural tube defects with fetal alcohol syndrome—Reply. *Journal of Pediatrics*, 1979, *95*, 329.

Badr, F. M., & Badr, R. S. Induction of dominant lethal mutation in male mice by ethyl alcohol. *Nature*, 1975, *253*, 134–136.

Barnes, D. E., & Walker, D. W. Prenatal ethanol exposure permanently reduces the number of pyramidal neurons in rat hippocampus. *Developmental Brain Research*, 1981, *1*, 3–24.

Boggan, W. O. Animal models of the fetal alcohol syndrome. In E. L. Abel (Ed.), *Fetal alcohol syndrome* (Vol. 3). Boca Raton, Fla.: CRC Press, 1982.

Boggan, W. O., & Randall, C. L. Effect of low-dose prenatal alcohol exposure on behavior and the response to alcohol. *Alcohol: Clinical and Experimental Research*, 1980, *4*, 226.

Boggan, W. O., Randall, C. L., & DeBeukelaer, M. *Renal abnormalities in mice prenatally exposed to ethanol.* Paper presented at the National Alcoholism Forum, St. Louis, Mo., 1978.

Boggan, W. O., Randall, C. L., DeBeukelaer, M., & Smith, R. Renal anomalies in mice prenatally exposed to ethanol. *Research Communications in Chemical Pathology and Pharmacology*, 1979, *23*, 127–142.

Bond, N. W., & DiGiusto, E. L. Effects of prenatal alcohol consumption on open-field behavior and alcohol preference in rats. *Psychopharmacology*, 1976, *46*, 163–168.

Bond, N. W., & DiGiusto, E. L. Prenatal alcohol consumption and open-field behavior in rats: Effects of age at time of testing. *Psychopharmacology*, 1977, *52*, 511–512.

Brown, N. A., Goulding, E. H., & Fabro, S. Ethanol embryotoxicity: Direct effects on mammalian embryos *in vitro*. *Science*, 1979, *206*, 573–575.

Burke, J. P., & Fenton, M. R. The effect of maternal ethanol consumption on aldehyde dehydrogenase activity in neonates. *Research Communications in Psychiatry and Behavior*, 1978, *3*, 169–172.

Chernoff, G. F. The fetal alcohol syndrome in mice: An animal model. *Teratology*, 1977, *15*, 223–229.

Christoffel, K. K., & Salafsky, I. Fetal alcohol syndrome in dizygotic twins. *Journal of Pediatrics*, 1975, *87*, 963–967.

Clarren, S. K. Neural tube defects and fetal alcohol syndrome. *Journal of Pediatrics*, 1979, *98*, 328.

Clarren, S. K., & Smith, D. W. The fetal alcohol syndrome. *New England Journal of Medicine*, 1978, *298*, 1063–1067.

Da Silva, V. A., Ribeiro, M. J., & Masur, J. Developmental, behavioral, and pharmacological characteristics of rat offspring from mothers receiving ethanol during gestation and lactation. *Developmental Psychobiology*, 1980, *13*, 653–660.

Dehaene, P. H., Samaille-Villette, C. H., Samaille, P.-P., Crepin, G., Walbaum, R., Deroubaix, P., & Blanc-Garin, A. P. Le syndrome d'alcoolisme foetal dans le nord de la France. [The fetal alcohol syndrome in the north of France.] *Revue de l'Alcoolisme*, 1977, *23*, 145–158.

Depuis, C., Dehaene, P., Deroubaix-Tella, O., Blanc-Garin, A. P., Rey, C., & Carpenter-Couralt, C. Les cardiopathies des enfants nés de mère alcoolique. [The heart diseases of children born to alcoholic mothers.] *Archives des Maladies du Coeur et des Vaisseaux*, 1978, *71*, 656–672.

Dexter, J. D., Tumbleson, M. E., Decker, J. D., & Middleton, C. C. Morphologic comparisons of piglets from first and second litters in chronic ethanol consuming Sinclair (S-1) miniature dams. *Alcoholism: Clinical and Experimental Research*, 1979, *3*, 171.

Douglas, R. J. The hippocampus and behavior. *Psychological Bulletin*, 1967, *67*, 416–442.

Duncan, R. J. S., & Woodhouse, B. The lack of effect on liver alcohol dehydrogenase in mice of early exposure to alcohol. *Biochemical Pharmacology*, 1978, *27*, 2755–2756.

Ellis, F. W., & Pick, J. R. An animal model of the fetal alcohol syndrome in beagles. *Alcoholism: Clinical and Experimental Research*, 1980, *4*, 123–134.

Gomberg, E. S. *Alcoholism and women: State of knowledge today*. Paper presented at the National Alcoholism Forum, Milwaukee, Wisc., 1975.

Habbick, B. F., Zaleski, W. A., Casey, R., & Murphy, F. Liver abnormalities in three patients with fetal alcohol syndrome. *Lancet*, 1979, *1*, 580–581.

Hanson, J. W., Streissguth, A. P., & Smith, D. W. The effects of moderate alcohol consumption during pregnancy on fetal growth and morphogenesis. *Journal of Pediatrics*, 1978, *92*, 457–460.

Harlap, S., & Shiono, P. H. Alcohol, smoking, and incidence of spontaneous abortions in the first and second trimester. *Lancet*, 1980, *2*, 173–176.

Harris, R. A., & Chase, J. Maternal consumption of ethanol, barbital, chlordiazepoxide: Effects on behavior of the offspring. *Behavioral and Neural Biology*, 1979, *26*, 234–247.

Havers, W., Majewski, F., Olbing, H., & Eickenberg, H.-U. Anomalies of the kidneys and genitourinary tract in alcohol embryopathy. *Journal of Urology*, 1980, *124*, 108–110.

Havlicek, V., Childiaeva, R., & Chernick, V. E.E.G. frequency spectrum characteristics of sleep rates in infants of alcoholic mothers. *Neuropadiatrie*, 1977, *8*, 360–373.

Hawkins, D., Kalant, H., & Khanna, I. M. Effects of chronic intake of ethanol on rate of ethanol metabolism. *Canadian Journal of Physiology and Pharmacology*, 1966, *44*, 241.

Henderson, G. I., & Schenker, S. The effects of maternal alcohol consumption on the viability and visceral development of the newborn rat. *Research Communications in Chemical Pathology and Pharmacology*, 1977, *16*, 15–32.

Henderson, G. I., Hoyumpa, A. M., Jr., McClain, C., & Schenker, S. The effects of chronic and acute alcohol administration on fetal development in the rat. *Alcoholism: Clinical and Experimental Research*, 1979, *3*, 99–106.

Henderson, G. I., Hoyumpa, A. M., Jr., Rothschild, M. A., & Schenker, S. Effect of ethanol and ethanol-induced hypothermia on protein synthesis in pregnant and fetal rats. *Alcoholism: Clinical and Experimental Research*, 1980, *4*, 165–177.

Henderson, G. I., Hoyumpa, A., Patwardhan, R., & Schenker, S. Effect of acute and chronic ethanol exposure on placental uptake of amino acids. *Alcoholism: Clinical and Experimental Research*, 1981, *5*, 153.

Himwich, W. A., Hall, J. S., & MacArthur, W. F. Maternal alcohol and neonatal health. *Biological Psychiatry*, 1977, *12*, 495–505.

Jacobson, S., Rich, J. A., & Tovsky, N. J. Retardation of cerebral cortical development as a consequence of the fetal alcohol syndrome. *Alcoholism: Clinical and Experimental Research*, 1978, *2*, 193.

Jones, K. L., & Smith, D. W. Recognition of the fetal alcohol syndrome in early infancy. *Lancet*, 1973, *2*, 999–1001.

Kesaniemi, Y. A., & Sippel, H. W. Placental and fetal metabolism of acetaldehyde in rat. 1. Contents of ethanol and acetaldehyde in placenta and foetuses of the pregnant rat during ethanol oxidation. *Acta Pharmacologica et Toxicologica*, 1975, *37*, 43–48.

Kouri, M., Koivula, T., & Koivusalo, M. Aldehyde dehydrogenase activity in human placenta. *Acta Pharmacologica et Toxicologica*, 1977, *40*, 460–463.

Landesman-Dwyer, S., Keller, L. S., & Streissguth, A. P. Naturalistic observations of newborns: Effects of maternal alcohol intake. *Alcoholism: Clinical and Experimental Research*, 1978, *2*, 171–177.

Lester, R., & Van Thiel, D. H. Gonadal function in chronic alcoholic men. *Advances in Experimental Medicine and Biology*, 1977, *85a*, 399–414.

Lin, G. W.-J., & Maddatu, A. P., Jr. Effect of ethanol feeding during pregnancy on maternal-fetal transfer of alpha-aminoisobutyric acid in the rat. *Alcoholism: Clinical and Experimental Research*, 1980, *4*, 222.

Little, R. E. Moderate alcohol use during pregnancy and decreased infant birth weight. *American Journal of Public Health*, 1977, *67*, 1154–1156.

Little, R. E., Streissguth, A. P., Woodell, S., & Norden, R. Birth weights of infants born to recovered alcoholic women. *Alcoholism: Clinical and Experimental Research*, 1979, *3*, 184.

Lochry, E. A., & Riley, E. P. Retention of passive avoidance and T-maze escape in rats exposed to alcohol prenatally. *Neurobehavioral Toxicology*, 1980, *2*, 107–115.

Lochry, E. A., Randall, C. L., Goldsmith, A. A., & Sutker, P. B. The effects of acute alcohol exposure during selected days of gestation in C3H mice. *Neurobehavioral Toxicology and Teratology*, 1982, *4*, 15–19.

Majewski, F., & Bierich, J. R. Auxological and clinical findings in alcohol embryopathy: Experience with 76 patients. *Acta Medica Scandinavica*, 1979, *206*, 413–423.

Majewski, F., Bierich, J. R., Loser, H., Michaelis, R., Leiber, B., & Bettecken, F. Zur Klinik und Pathogenase der Alkohol-Embryopathie. Bericht uber 68 Falle. [Clinical aspects and pathogenesis of alcohol embryopathy: A report of 68 cases.] *Münchener Medizinische Wochenschrift*, 1976, *118*, 1635–1642.

Martin, D. C., Martin, J. C., Streissguth, A. P., & Lund, C. A. Sucking frequency and amplitude in newborns as a function of maternal drinking and smoking. In M. Galanter (Ed.), *Currents in alcoholism* (Vol. 5): *Biomedical issues and clinical effects of alcoholism.* New York: Grune & Stratton, 1979.

Martin, J. C., Martin, D. C., Lund, C. A., & Streissguth, A. P. Maternal alcohol ingestion and cigarette smoking and their effects on newborn conditioning. *Alcoholism: Clinical and Experimental Research,* 1977, *1,* 243–247.

Mendelson, J. H. The fetal alcohol syndrome. *New England Journal of Medicine,* 1978, *299,* 556.

Moller, J., Brandt, N. J., & Tygstrup, I. Hepatic dysfunction in patient with fetal alcohol syndrome. *Lancet,* 1979, *1,* 605–606.

Niimi, Y. Studies on effects of alcohol on fetus. *Sanfujinka No Shimpo,* 1973, *25,* 55–78.

Newman, S. L., Flannery, D. B., & Caplan, D. B. Simultaneous occurrence of extrahepatic biliary atresia and fetal alcohol syndrome. *American Journal of Diseases of Children,* 1979, *133,* 101.

Olegard, R., Sabel, K. G., Aronsson, M., Sandin, B., Johansson, P. R., Carlsson, C., Kyllerman, M., Iversen, K., & Hrbek, A. Effects on the child of alcohol abuse during pregnancy. *Acta Paediatrica Scandinavica,* 1979, *275,* 112–121.

Osborne, G. L., Caul, W. F., & Fernandez, K. Behavioral effects of prenatal ethanol exposure and differential early experience in rats. *Neurobehavioral Toxicology,* 1980, *12,* 393–401.

Ouellette, E. M., Rosett, H. L., Rosman, N. P., & Weiner, L. Adverse effects on offspring of maternal alcohol abuse during pregnancy. *New England Journal of Medicine,* 1977, *297,* 528–530.

Palmer, R. H., Ouellette, E. M., Warner, L., & Leichtman, S. R. Congenital malformations in offspring of a chronic alcoholic mother. *Pediatrics,* 1974, *53,* 490–494.

Peiffer, J., Majewski, F., Fischbach, H., Bierich, J. R., & Volk, B. Alcohol embryo- and fetopathy: Neuropathology of three children and three fetuses. *Journal of Neurological Sciences,* 1979, *41,* 125–137.

Pfeifer, W. D., MacKinnon, J. R., & Seiser, R. L. Adverse effects of paternal alcohol consumption on offspring in the rat. *Bulletin of the Psychonomic Society,* 1977, *10,* 246.

Puschel, K., & Seifert, H. Bedeutung des Alkohols in der Embryofetalperiode und beim Neugeborenen. [Effects of alcohol on the embryo, fetus, and newborn.] *Zeitschrift fuer Rechtsmedizin,* 1979, *83,* 69–76.

Raiha, N. C. R., Koskinen, M., & Pikkarainen, P. Developmental changes in alcohol-dehydrogenase activity in rat and guinea-pig liver. *Biochemical Journal,* 1967, *103,* 623–626.

Randall, C. L. Teratogenic effects on *in utero* ethanol exposure. In K. Blum, D. L. Bard, & M. G. Hamilton (Eds.), *Alcohol and opiates: Neurochemical and behavioral mechanisms.* New York: Academic Press, 1977.

Randall, C. L. Alcohol as a teratogen in animals. In National Institute on Alcohol Abuse and Alcoholism, *Biomedical processes and consequences of alcohol use.* Alcohol and Health Monograph No. 2. Rockville, Md.: The Institute, 1981.

Randall, C. L., & Noble, E. P. Alcohol abuse and fetal growth and development. In N. Mello & J. Mendelson (Eds.), *Advances in substance abuse* (Vol. 1). Greenwich, Conn.: JAI Press, 1980.

Randall, C. L., & Riley, E. P. Prenatal alcohol exposure: Current issues and the status of animal research. *Neurobehavioral Toxicology and Teratology,* 1981, *3,* 111–115.

Randall, C. L., Taylor, W. J., Tabakoff, B., and Walker, D. W. Ethanol as a teratogen. In R. G. Thurman, J. R. Williamson, H. R. Drott, & B. Chance (Eds.), *Alcohol and aldehyde metabolizing systems* (Vol. 3): *Intermediary metabolism and neurochemistry.* New York: Academic Press, 1977.

Randall, C. L., Taylor, W. J., & Walker, D. W. Ethanol-induced malformations in mice. *Alcoholism: Clinical and Experimental Research,* 1977, *1,* 219–223.

Randall, C. L., Burling, T. A., & Lochry, E. A. The effect of paternal alcohol consumption on fetal development: A mouse model. *Drug and Alcohol Dependence,* 1982, *9,* 89–95.

Rawat, A. K. Ribosomal protein synthesis in the fetal and neonatal rat brain as influenced by maternal ethanol consumption. *Research Communications in Chemical Pathology and Pharmacology,*
1975, *12,* 723-732.

Rawat, A. K. Effect of maternal ethanol consumption of foetal and neonatal rat hepatic protein
synthesis. *Biochemical Journal,* 1976, *160,* 653-661.

Riley, E. P. Alcohol induced behavioral teratogenesis in the rat. In National Institute on Alcohol
Abuse and Alcoholism, *Biomedical processes and consequences of alcohol use.* Alcohol and
Health Monograph No. 2. Rockville, Md.: The Institute, 1982.

Riley, E. P., Lochry, E. A., & Shapiro, N. R. Lack of response inhibition in rats prenatally exposed
to alcohol. *Psychopharmacology,* 1979, *62,* 47-52.

Riley, E. P., Lochry, E. A., Shapiro, N. R., & Baldwin, J. Response perseveration in rats exposed
to alcohol prenatally. *Pharmacology, Biochemistry and Behavior,* 1979, *10,* 255-259.

Riley, E. P., Shapiro, N. R., Lochry, E. A., & Broida, J. P. Fixed-ratio performance and subsequent
extinction in rats prenatally exposed to ethanol. *Physiological Psychology,* 1980, *8,* 47-50.

Root, A. W., Reiter, E. O., Andriola, M., & Duckett, G. Hypothalamic-pituitary function in the
fetal alcohol syndrome. *Journal of Pediatrics,* 1975, *87,* 585-588.

Rosett, H. L., Snyder, P., Sander, L. W., Lee, A., Cook, P., Weiner, L., & Gould, J. Effects of
maternal drinking on neonate state regulation. *Developmental Medicine and Child Neurology,*
1979, *21,* 464-473.

Russell, M. Intrauterine growth on infants born to women with alcohol-related psychiatric diagnoses. *Alcoholism: Clinical and Experimental Research,* 1977, *1,* 225-231.

Sandor, S., Smith, D. F., & MacLeod, P. M. Cardiac malformations in the fetal alcohol syndrome.
Clinical Research, 1980, *28,* 118a.

Santolaya, J. M., Martinez, G., Gorostiza, E., Aizpiri, J., & Hernandez, M. Alcoholismo fetal.
[Fetal alcohol syndrome.] *Drogalcohol,* 1978, *3,* 183-192.

Schwetz, B. A., Smith, F. A., & Staples, R. E. Teratogenic potential of ethanol in mice, rats, and
rabbits. *Teratology,* 1978, *18,* 385-392.

Shaywitz, B. A., Klopper, J. H., & Gordon, J. W. A syndrome resembling minimal brain dysfunction (MBD) in rat pups born to alcoholic mothers. *Pediatric Research,* 1976, *10,* 451.

Shaywitz, S. E., Cohen, D. J., & Shaywitz, B. A. Behavior and learning deficits in children of normal
intelligence born to alcoholic mothers. *Journal of Pediatrics,* 1980, *96,* 978-982.

Sjoblom, M., Oisund, J. F., & Morlund, J. Development of alcohol dehydrogenase and aldehyde
dehydrogenase in the offspring of female rats chronically treated with ethanol. *Acta Pharmacologica et Toxicologica,* 1979, *44,* 128-131.

Smith, C. A. Effects of maternal undernutrition upon the newborn infant in Holland. *Journal of
Pediatrics,* 1947, *30,* 229-243.

Sokol, R. J., Miller, S. I., & Reed, G. Alcohol abuse during pregnancy: An epidemiologic study.
Alcoholism: Clinical and Experimental Research, 1980, *4,* 135-145.

Steeg, C. N., & Woolf, P. Cardiovascular malformations in the fetal alcohol syndrome. *American
Heart Journal,* 1979, *98,* 635-637.

Stockard, C. R. The effects of alcohol in development and heredity. In H. Emerson (Ed.), *Alcohol
and man.* New York: Macmillan, 1932.

Streissguth, A. P., Martin, D. C., & Barr, H. M. Neonatal Brazleton assessment and relationship
to maternal alcohol intake. Fifth International Congress on Birth Defects, *International Congress Series,* 1977, *426,* 62.

Streissguth, A. P., Herman, C. S., & Smith, D. W. Intelligence and dysmorphogenesis in the fetal
alcohol syndrome: A report on 20 clinical cases. *Journal of Pediatrics,* 1978, *92,* 363-367. (a)

Streissguth, A. P., Herman, C. S., & Smith, D. W. Stability of intelligence in the fetal alcohol
syndrome: A report on 20 clinical cases. *Journal of Pediatrics,* 1978, *92,* 363-367. (b)

Streissguth, A. P., Little, R. E., Herman, C. S., & Woodell, B. S. IQ in children of recovered alcoholic mothers compared with maternal controls. *Alcoholism: Clinical and Experimental Research*, 1979, *3*, 197.

Sze, P. Y., Yanai, J., & Ginsburg, P. W. Effects of early ethanol input on the activities of ethanol-metabolizing enzymes in mice. *Biochemical Pharmacology*, 1976, *25*, 215–217.

Taylor, A. N., Branch, B. J., Liu, S. H., Weichmann, A. F., Hill, M. A., & Kokka, N. Fetal exposure to ethanol enhances pituitary-adrenal and temperature responses to ethanol in adult rats. *Alcoholism: Clinical and Experimental Research*, 1981, *5*, 237–246.

Thadani, P. V., Lau, C., Slotkin, T. A., & Schanberg, S. M. Effects of maternal ethanol ingestion on neonatal rat brain and heart ornithine decarboxylase. *Biochemical Pharmacology*, 1977, *26*, 523–527.

Thadani, P. V., Slotkin, T. A., & Schanberg, S. M. Effects of late prenatal or early postnatal ethanol exposure on ornithine decarboxylase activity in brain and heart of developing rats. *Neuropharmacology*, 1977, *16*, 289–293.

Tze, W. J., Friesen, H. G., & MacLeod, P. M. Growth and hormone response in fetal alcohol syndrome. *Archives of Disease in Childhood*, 1976, *51*, 703–706.

Veghelyi, P. V., Osztovics, M., & Szaszovsky, E. Maternal alcohol consumption and birth weight. *British Medical Journal*, 1978, *2*, 1365–1366.

Warner, R. H., & Rosett, H. L. The effects of drinking on offspring: An historical survey of the American and British literature. *Journal of Studies on Alcohol*, 1975, *36*, 1395–1420.

West, J. R., Hodges, C. A., & Black, A. C., Jr. Prenatal exposure to ethanol alters the organization of hippocampal mossy fibers in rats. *Science*, 1981, *211*, 957–959.

Woodson, P. M., & Ritchey, S. J. Effect of maternal alcohol consumption on fetal brain cell number and cell size. *Nutrition Reports International*, 1979, *20*, 225–228.

Yanai, J., & Ginsburg, B. E. A developmental study of ethanol effect on behavior and physical development in mice. *Alcoholism: Clinical and Experimental Research*, 1977, *1*, 325–333.

9

Interaction of Ethanol with Other Drugs

RICHARD A. DEITRICH AND DENNIS R. PETERSEN

1. INTRODUCTION

1.1. Definitions

The interactions between alcohol and other drugs can be categorized into (1) pharmacological interactions, where ethanol and the second drug act on the same biochemical system; (2) physiological interactions, where ethanol and a second drug act on different systems; and (3) metabolic interactions, where the interaction takes place at the level of *metabolism* of ethanol or the second drug. Of course, more than one mechanism may be operative for any given drug–ethanol combination.

There are a few other terms that need definition; although these have been variously defined by others, we do need to specify how we will use them.

Agonist: A compound that brings about a biologic response
Partial agonist: A compound incapable of producing a full biologic response
Antagonist: A compound that blocks the action of an agonist
Additive effect: The case whereby the response to two compounds, present simultaneously, is a summation of the separate responses
Synergism: The case whereby the response of the body to two compounds is greater than that expected by a simple summation of the effects of both (e.g., compounds that inhibit alcohol metabolism and are also depressants)

RICHARD A. DEITRICH • Alcohol Research Center, Department of Pharmacology, University of Colorado Medical Center, Denver, Colorado 80262. DENNIS R. PETERSEN • Alcohol Research Center, School of Pharmacy, University of Colorado, Boulder, Colorado 80309.

Potentiation: Applies to a compound with no intrinsic activity of its own as an agonist but which, when combined with ethanol, increases the effect of ethanol (e.g., an inhibitor of alcohol metabolism that has no intrinsic ethanollike activity).

1.2. Dose–Response Curves

There are important dose–response considerations to all the above-mentioned situations, and the response obtained is directly dependent upon where on the dose–response curve the measurements are taken. If drugs interact with specific receptors by classical reversible kinetics, the following equation describes this interaction:

$$\frac{e}{E_{\max}} = \frac{\{D\}}{\{D\} + Kd}$$

The variable e is the effect observed at any concentration of drug D which has a dissociation constant for a receptor whose value is the Kd. $E_{\max}$ is the maximal response of which the system is capable. A linear as well as a log–dose plot of this equation is found in Figure 1.

The log-dose-response curve is usually used for reasons of convenience. As can be seen, there is a nearly linear portion of the curve in the middle of the dose range, and the points for higher and doses are compressed so that the graph is not unnecessarily wide.

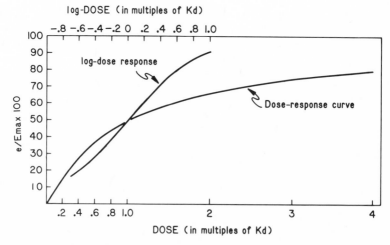

Figure 1. Dose–response curves plotted as both linear and log functions.

If this equation is strictly adhered to, the entire response is produced within a hundred fold change of drug concentrations. If two drugs are acting on the same system and the same endpoint is used to measure the effect of both drugs, then the response at any given drug concentration is a function of the dose of both drugs. The important point is that the response is not a linear function of dose nor is the response to two drugs a linear function of the additive doses of the two drugs.

Perhaps the simplest way of looking at this is to visualize the situation where the dose of drug B, which is such as to produce 90% of E_{max}, is combined with a dose of drug A, also calculated to yield 90% of E_{max}. Obviously the combination cannot yield over 100% of E_{max}. If we assume, as do the simplest theories, that the response is proportional to the fraction of receptors occupied, then we can use the values in Table 1.

A linear function is most closely approximated at low doses of both compounds. When each drug is present at concentration 0.1 times its Kd value, the effects come close to being strictly linear ($9 + 9 = 16.6$ instead of 18), while at higher doses there is a progressively greater deviation from the linearity. This is true, of course, only if we do not redefine the response we are measuring.

Synergism will exist whenever the observed e/E_{max} values (i.e., assumed to be proportional to the fraction of receptors occupied) are significantly above those calculated for the doses of the two drugs.

Unfortunately dose–response curves for ethanol do not conform to this ideal situation. Ethanol behaves as a compound that does not bind to specific receptors. The dose–response curve is very steep. Doses that bring about a just-noticeable effect, need to be increased as little as tenfold to reach lethal levels. Many of the drugs that interact with ethanol, such as gaseous anesthetics, have similarly steep dose–response curves. The margin for error in such a situation can be very small. Other drugs—such as opiates, benzodiazepines, antihistamines, and so on—follow

Table 1. Drug–Receptor Interactions

Dose of drug A	Percentage of receptors occupied if A were alone	Dose of drug B	Percentage of receptors occupied if B were alone	Theoretical percentage of receptors occupied if A and B were together	Actual percentage of receptors occupied
$0.1 \times Kd$	9	$0.1 \times Kd$	9	18	17
$0.5 \times Kd$	33	$0.5 \times Kd$	33	66	50
$1 \times Kd$	50	$1 \times Kd$	50	100	66
$5 \times Kd$	83	$5 \times Kd$	83	166	90
$10 \times Kd$	90	$10 \times Kd$	90	180	95

more conventional dose–response curves by virtue of the presence of specific receptors for these agents.

In practical terms, the nature of drug interactions with ethanol can be roughly estimated by administering together doses of both ethanol and the second drug which separately bring about a 50% response (ED_{50}, or roughly the Kd value). One would expect a response of 60% to 70% of the E_{max} in such a situation if the combination were additive. If the response is greater or less than that, then either synergism or antagonism is indicated.

1.2.1. Isobolograms

More detailed investigations can be carried out by the use of isobolograms (Curry, 1977). These plots are constructed by choosing a particular endpoint (e.g., death, a certain duration of loss of righting response, drop in temperature etc.). The dose of ethanol that will achieve the defined endpoint in the presene of varying doses of the second drug is then determined. The resulting situation is shown in Figure 2. Additive, partial agonist, antagonist, and synergist combinations produce characteristic curves. The situation with potentiating agents that have no intrinsic activity may require more explanation. In combination with a potentiating agent, there will be some dose of ethanol which will fail to produce an effect; at this point, the curve will become vertical, since the potentiating drug has no intrinsic activity of its own in this system.

Unfortunately, in practice such experiments are rarely carried out because of the large numbers of animals required to produce full curves. There are, however, several examples of the use of these techniques, which are illustrated later in this chapter. Analysis of several of these experiments indicates that pure additive effects with ethanol are rare; the more usual response is that of a partial agonist interaction.

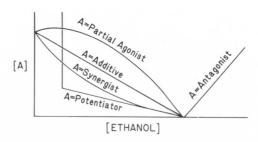

Figure 2. Isobolograms for interactions between drug A and ethanol. Figure drawn in idealized curves.

1.3. Metabolic Principles

There are a great many possible metabolic interactions between ethanol and its metabolites and the metabolism of the drugs. No study of ethanol–drug interactions should be considered complete until it is either demonstrated that there is no metabolic interaction or the effects that are found are defined. In general, ethanol, acetaldehyde, acetate, or the increased NADH levels in the liver (see Chapter 3) may directly inhibit some metabolic step necessary for metabolism of a second compound. In a few cases there may be increased metabolism of a given drug as a result of the presence of ethanol or any one of ethanol's metabolites; for instance, chronic administration of ethanol may induce the cytochrome P_{450} drug metabolizing system.

Another and potentially important interaction between ethanol and other drugs is that of altered compartmentalization of drugs. Ethanol can alter protein binding, active transport processes, or diffusional barriers and thus alter the distribution of a compound even if overall metabolism is not markedly affected. Thus, brain levels (corrected for blood content) of drugs should be measured in the presence and absence of ethanol whenever possible.

More detailed information concerning specific drug–ethanol interaction may be found by way of a comprehensive bibliography published by the Addiction Research Foundation in Toronto, Canada, entitled *Interaction of Alcohol and Other Drugs*. This volume contains 15,000 references. A recent study of sleeping pills by the Institute of Medicine has resulted in a report entitled *Sleeping Pills, Insomnia and Medical Practice*, available from the Office of Publications of the National Academy of Sciences, Washington D.C. It contains much detailed data about ethanol–hypnotic interactions with other hynotics. All good textbooks of pharmacology and all compendiums of drug interactions at least list the various therapeutically important interactions with ethanol. In this chapter we will discuss interactions of ethanol with other centrally active compounds that act primarily on the central nervous system.

2. CENTRALLY ACTING COMPOUNDS

2.1. Depressants

2.1.1. Barbiturates and Methaqualone

Clinically, the interaction of ethanol with barbiturates represents the classic example of occasional synergism between these two pharmacological agents. At the same time, this well-documented interaction is a complex function of both functional and dispositional tolerance to either one or both drugs.

There is a reduction in therapeutic margin of both alcohol and barbiturates when ingested in combination by an individual who is not tolerant to either. For instance, barbiturate overdose usually results in death when phenobarbital concentrations in the blood approach 100 μg/mL. When the barbiturate is ingested in combination with alcohol, barbiturate blood levels of 50 μg/mL will prove fatal. Likewise, lethal blood levels of alcohol in humans are reduced from 650 mg/100 mL to 150 mg/100 mL when alcoholic beverages are consumed in combination with barbiturates. Of course this effect would depend on the sedative–hypnotic potency and pharmacokinetics of the barbiturates. The relationships of the sedative–hypnotic properties of a barbiturate in combination with alcohol to specific central nervous system (CNS) parameters is difficult to interpret, since both agents affect a multitude of neurochemical and neurophysiological pathways. However, given the fact that alcoholics display an increased tolerance to sedative–hypnotics, there seems little doubt that there is some degree of pharmacodynamic cross-tolerance between alcohol, barbiturates, and general anesthetics (Caldwell & Sever, 1974). It is generally believed that this cross tolerance may be a function of barbiturate half-life. The tolerance to the shorter-acting barbiturates (e.g., hexobarbital) could be explainable on the basis of enhanced barbiturate metabolism, while tolerance to longer-acting barbiturates such as phenobarbital is most likely due to functional or CNS tolerance. Unfortunately, few conclusive studies have been performed to characterize the functional cross-tolerance between alcohol and barbiturates in humans.

It is widely accepted that acute or chronic alcohol ingestion can have a pronounced effect on barbiturate metabolism. First, the ability of acute ethanol administration to inhibit hepatic drug-metabolizing enzymes *in vivo* and *in vitro* has been demonstrated in laboratory animals and humans (Rubin, Bacchin, Ganrg, & Lieber, 1970; Rubin, Gang, Misra, & Lieber, 1970). In these studies, acute ethanol administration of 1 g/kg to humans significantly prolonged the half-life of pentobarbital and meprobamate. The inhibitory effect of acute ethanol treatment on hepatic drug metabolism—in particular those drugs metabolized by hydroxylation—has been used to explain the increased sensitivity of inebriated persons to the effect of barbiturates and tranquilizers. However, it should be stressed that this effect is observed only when both alcohol and a barbiturate are present simultaneously.

On the other hand, it has been clearly demonstrated that chronic ethanol ingestion in humans and rats results in a proliferation of hepatic smooth endoplasmic reticulum, which is associated with enhanced activities of microsomal drug-metabolizing enzymes (Lieber, 1977; Pirola, 1978). It is not surprising, then, that a person who uses alcohol extensively but is *not* under the direct influence of alcohol at a particular time requires very large doses of barbiturates and other anesthetics to produce surgical anesthesia.

Given the above potential interactions of ethanol and barbiturates, it is evident that acute ingestion of alcohol impairs barbiturate metabolism and reduces the therapeutic margin of both drugs. The situation becomes even more complicated for the alcoholic who is not alcohol-free and may receive barbiturates for therapeutic purposes. Given the possibility of CNS cross-tolerance, it could be very difficult to administer effective doses of barbiturates and at the same time maintain an adequate margin between therapeutic and lethal doses. Thus, in the treatment of delirium tremens in alcoholics, barbiturates have largely been replaced by benzodiazepines, which have smaller additive effects with alcohol and are themselves less addictive than the barbiturates (Isbell & Chrusciel, 1970; see also discussion in chapter by Tabakoff).

Ho and Ho (1978) have carried out a careful analysis of the interaction of ethanol and methaqualone. They found that methaqualone inhibited disappearance of ethanol and increased ethanol toxicity. One would expect a synergistic effect, since both drugs are CNS depressants; in fact, however, isobolograms constructed from these investigators' data show an only partial agonistic relationship, indicating some degree of antagonism between the two compounds.

2.1.2. Gaseous Anesthetics

Gaseous anesthetics are thought to be additive in their effects with ethanol. A recent review by Cullen and Miller (1979) is interesting in that it contains an isobologram for the interaction between isoflurane and ethanol. The presented data resemble a curve for only a partial agonistic relationship between alcohol and the gaseous anesthetic agents in mice and do not resemble a strictly additive interaction. It has been presumed for many years that the mechanism of action of ethanol and these agents depended on their interactions with the cell membrane and that it was the same for all gaseous anesthetics (Ritchie, 1980). Differences in potency were explained n the basis of physical–chemical properties of these anesthetics. Recent evidence, however, indicates that some differences in the mechanism of action of ethanol and gaseous anesthetics exist. Using mice selectively bred for either sensitivity or resistance to ethanol narcosis, Baker, Melchior, and Deitrich (1980) demonstrated that, while the ED_{50} for loss of righting response differed by twofold for ethanol, the ED_{50} of halothane in these animals was the same. Koblin and Deady (1981) found a smaller difference in the ED_{50} for nitrous oxide (1.34 fold) and enflurane (1.12 fold) but no difference for isoflurane (1.01 fold) between these same lines of mice. Apparently there is some fundamental difference between the CNS-depressant actions of ethanol and these agents.

On the other hand animals can demonstrate cross-tolerance between ethanol and these agents (Adriani & Morton, 1968). Koblin and associates have demonstrated that animals made tolerant to nitrous oxide were also tolerant to ethanol and that animals genetically resistant to ethanol were also resistant to nitrous oxide (Koblin & Deady, 1981; Koblin, Deady, Dong, & Eger, 1980).

2.1.3. Opiates

As with other depressants, opiate compounds are generally regarded as being additive with ethanol in CNS-depressant effects. Based on statistical information, there have been warnings to physicians that the combination of propoxyphene (Darvon) and alcohol may be lethal (Rosser, 1980). Individuals on methadone maintenance who also consume ethanol are reported to have an increased death rate (Jackson & Richman, 1973). Study of the interactions of alpha-1-acetylmethadol (LAAM) and ethanol by Ho, Chen, and Ho (1978) yield interesting effects in that, at low doses of ethanol (0.5 and 1 gm/kg), there is clearly antagonism of the lethal effect of LAAM. An isobologram constructed from the data presented in this paper is given in Figure 3. While there an effect of morphine, methadone, LAAM, and levorphanol on brain ethanol levels to increase them slightly, there was no effect of ethanol on brain morphine levels except at 150 minutes after a dose of 4 g/kg of ethanol, when a small increase was found. A word of caution should be noted concerning the reported blood and brain levels of ethanol in this paper. The levels of alcohol in the brain are nearly twice as high as in the blood at all time points. Such a condition is not consistent with data from many other investigators, where blood and brain levels come into equilibrium at nearly the same levels within 30 to 60 minutes after injection and never differ by more than twofold.

The possibility of some common mechanism between the actions of ethanol and opiates is of considerable interest. Mendelson (1980) has recently reviewed the evidence that opiate antagonists such as naloxone may reverse some of the

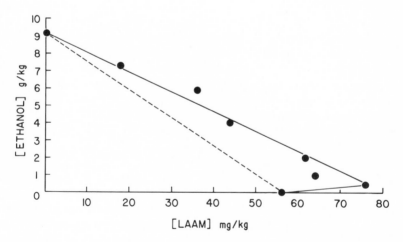

Figure 3. Isobologram for the interaction between ethanol and LAAM. (Plotted from data presented in Ho *et al.*, 1978.)

effects of ethanol on human intoxication (Moss, 1973; Sorenson & Mattison, 1978; Mackenzie, 1979; Jeffcoate, Cullen, Herbert, Hasting, & Walder, 1979; Barros & Rodriguez, 1981) as well as having effects on preference for ethanol by rats (Myers & Melchior, 1977; Altshuler, Phillips, & Feinhandler, 1981). Ho et al. (1978) showed that naloxone decreased brain ethanol levels slightly. Also, ethanol sleep time is reduced and the ED_{50} increased by naloxone (Ho & Ho, 1979). Middaugh, Read, and Boggan (1978), on the other hand, found that naloxone blocked only ethanol-induced excitatory effects.

Another interaction of potential therapeutic importance is that reported between the synthetic opiate diphenoxylate (a component of Lomotil, used for control of diarrhia) and ethanol (McGuire, Awourters, & Miemeegers, 1978). An isobologram plotted from their data reveals that diphenoxylate appears to be a potentiator of ethanol's effect rather than possessing the ability to act in an additive fashion.

At the level of metabolism, acute administration of ethanol inhibits methadone metabolism, but chronic treatment speeds methadone degradation (Borowsky & Lieber, 1978). Apparently the opposite is not true; that is, methadone or LAAM treatment does not alter ethanol metabolsim (Downs, 1979), although Kreek (1981) presents preliminary data to the contrary.

Thus there may be more to the interaction between opiates and alcohol than nonspecific physiological interactions. The molecular basis for ethanol–opiate interactions may include the specific action of these drugs on calcium metabolism (Ross, Medina, & Cardenas, 1974), or there interactions may be mediated by endogenous alkaloids (see review by Deitrich & Erwin, 1980) or endogenous peptides.

2.1.4. Meprobamate

Meprobamate is the prototype of the drugs classified as propanediol carbamates. These drugs are used primarily as antianxiety agents and have a pharmacological effect nearly identical to that of the barbiturates. The relative efficacy of meprobamate as an antianxiety agent is questionable; the chronic use of this drug is associated with a high potential for dependence. In spite of these disadvantages, meprobamate is still widely used (Harvey, 1980).

The results of most studies concerned with the interactions of alcohol and meprobamate indicate at least additive depressant effects when these agents are coadministered (Goldberg, 1970; Zirkle, McAtee, & King, 1960). It is generally assumed that this interaction is mediated in part by the influence of ethanol on meprobamate disposition. Meprobamate pharmacokinetics have been studied in human volunteers in the absence and presence of an acute ethanol dose (Rubin, Bacchin, Gang, & Lieber, 1970). When coadministered with meprobamate, ethanol increased the half-life of meprobamate two- to fivefold. The results of this study are apparently explained by the finding that acute ethanol ingestion appears to impair meprobamate metabolism significantly, a situation similar to that observed when alcohol and barbiturates are coadministered.

Chronic alcohol ingestion also significantly alters *in vivo* meprobamate metabolism. This effect is attributed to the induction of hepatic drug-metabolizing enzymes by habitual alcohol consumption. This mechanism is further supported by the study of Misra, Lefèvre, Ishil, Rubin, & Lieber (1974), which demonstrated that the blood clearance of meprobamate is nearly twice as rapid in chronic alcoholics as in nonalcoholic individuals. It is important to note that blood clearance of meprobamate was determined in alcoholics and nonalcoholics under conditions where alcohol was not present in the body, so as to avoid the inhibitory interactions of ethanol on meprobamate metabolsim noted above. This point must be kept in mind, since many observations indicate that even alcoholics who have developed metabolic tolerance to such agents as meprobamate and barbiturates still present a reduced margin of safety to these therapeutic agents during intoxication.

Undoubtedly, the interactions of ethanol and meprobamate are complex and may involve alterations in pharmacokinetic properties of both agents; these interactions may also affect the duration and time course of ethanol ingestion with respect to the schedule and dose of meprobamate therapy.

2.1.5. Benzodiazepines

Like the phenothiazines, the benzodiazepines are among the most commonly prescribed medications in the United States. In fact, it has been estimated that benzodiazepines account for nearly 75% of all the hypnotics currently prescribed in the United States (Baldessarini, 1980). Factors partially responsible for the widespread use of benzodiazepines in clinical medicine include the following: (1) these agents display a wide range of pharmacological responses, rendering them useful as sedative hypnotics (flurazepam and nitrazepam) or antianxiety agents (chlordiazepoxides, diazepam, and oxazepam); (2) there is a remarkable margin of safety associated with the use of these agents, which results in a very low occurrence of clinical toxicities; (3) by comparison with other drugs, they are generally considered to have a low potential for the development of dependence; and (4) interactions of other drugs with benzodiazepines are infrequent. Of the above factors, the low frequency of side effects and near absence of interactions with other drugs make the benzodiazepines the drugs of choice in the treatment of anxiety.

Generally, when taken in combination with CNS depressants, benzodiazepines exhibit interactions classified as additive. However, older data concerning the interactions between benzodiazepines and alcohol are conflicting, with reports of additivity, no additivity, and mild antagonism (Linnoila & Hakkinen, 1974; Bowes, 1960; Vaapatalo & Karppunen, 1969). A number of more recent studies have established that therapeutic doses of diazepam or chlordiazepoxide taken in combination with alcohol result in significant impairment of many psychomotor, driving, and mental skills (Linnoila & Mattila, 1973; Mørland, Setekleiv, Haffner, Strømsaether, Danielsen, and HolstWethe, 1974; Palva, Linnoila, & Mattila, 1976). The duration of the benzodiazepine–alcohol interactions may be much greater than originally anticipated. The results of one study (Mendelson, Goodwin, Hill, & Reichman, 1976) indicate that 16 hours following the administration of flurazepam and alcohol to human volunteers, EEG abnormalities were still detectable. Since the effect was not observed in individuals exposed only to either ethanol or to flurazepam, these data suggest that the manifestations of benzodiazepine–alcohol interaction may have a relatively long half-life in the CNS. A newer benzodiazepine, tofisopam, may not have as great an interaction with ethanol (Seppälä, Palva, Mattila, Korttila, & Shrotriya, 1980).

It appears that ethanol and benzodiazepines may also interact at a level that influences benzodiazepine pharmacokinetics. Results from one study indicate that human subjects ingesting diazepam and ethanol maintained significantly higher plasma diazepam levels up to four hours following administration than did individuals ingesting diazepam and water. A recent study by Hoyumpa, Desmond, Roberts, Nichols, Johnson, and Shenker (1980) in dogs clearly shows that ethanol decreases the clearance of orally administered diazepam and chlordiazepoxide. These data suggest that in addition to interactions of diazepam and ethanol in the CNS, ethanol may also enhance absorption or inhibit metabolism of diazepam (Hayes, Pablo, Radomski, & Palmer, 1977). Macleod, Giles, Patzalek, Thiessen, and Sellers (1977) obtained evidence of an effect of ethanol on diazepam absorption or distribution kinetics; Sellers, Naranjo, Giles, Frecker, and Beeching (1980) found that ethanol slowed elimimation of chlordiazepoxide in humans.

The majority of studies examining ethanol–benzodiazepine interactions have been conducted in humans receiving the drug only on an acute basis. However, since benzodiazepines have become the drug of choice to treat the symptoms of alcohol withdrawal including delirium tremens (Favazza & Martin, 1974) it may be important to consider the interactions of benzodiazepines and alcohol in the chronic alcoholic as a special case. A recent report has noted that alcoholics who were classified as having a mixed alcohol–benzodiazepine addiction experienced a withdrawal syndrome atypical of alcoholics who consumed only alcohol 2 to 10 days after discontinuation of both drugs. The timing and nature of the specific symptoms more closely resembled benzodiazepine withdrawal (Benzer & Cushman, 1980). The factors responsible for these delayed withdrawal reactions have yet to be determined; however, they indicate that, during withdrawal, the therapeutic management of alcoholics suffering from benzodiazepine addiction should be carefully considered.

2.1.6. Phenothiazines

The phenothiazines are antipsychotic agents and as a class represent one of the more commonly prescribed medications in the United States. Chlorpromazine is considered the prototype drug of the phenothiazines; therefore, this discussion will be limited to the interaction of alcohol and chlorpromazine. Taken alone, chlorpromazine produces a variety of pharmacological effects which are complex and involve both the central and peripheral nervous systems. With respect to interactions with alcohol, the sedative effects are of greatest importance.

Numerous studies in laboratory animals and humans demonstrate that interactions related to the depressant effects of chlorpromazine and alcohol are synergistic (Berger, 1969; Milner & Landauer, 1971; Seppälä, 1976). However, investigators do not all agree about the synergistic interactions of alcohol and chlorpromazine in humans. This is most likely related to the fact that the observed interactions originate in the CNS as well as the ability of chlorpromazine to affect alcohol pharmacodynamics. For instance, humans receiving chlorpromazine for seven days prior to ethanol were found to maintain higher arterial ethanol concentrations than individuals who received only ethanol. Individuals pretreated with chlorpromazine also exhibited higher blood acetaldehyde levels during this same period of time (Sutherland, Burbridge, Adams, & Simon, 1960). These *in vivo* results are consistent with *in vitro* experiments indicating that chlorpromazine is an inhibitor of alcohol dehydrogenase; this observation could partially account for the above results (Khouw, Burbridge & Sutherland, 1963). However, since blood acetaldehyde levels were also elevated in the humans pretreated with chlorpromazine, some of the observed interactions may also be mediated through the inhibition of aldehyde dehydrogenase.

Given the diverse pharmacological actions of chlorpromazine, it is also possible that this drug may alter the pharmacodynamics of ethanol by altering the ethanol absorption rate or perturbing peripheral blood flow rather than through a direct effect on ethanol metabolism itself.

Although a number of studies have been performed to determine the influence of chlorpromazine on ethanol metabolism, few investigators have considered the potential effects of ethanol on chlorpromazine pharmacokinetics. Like the barbiturates, chlorpromazine is metabolized by the hepatic microsomal drug-metabolizing system. Thus it is possible that, as in the case of barbiturates, ethanol could significantly inhibit the metabolism of chlorpromazine at the microsomal level. Such a metabolic interaction would have an effect similar to that observed with the barbiturates, where the margin of safety for ethanol and the drug with which it is interacting is reduced. Further complications could also arise if chronic ethanol ingestion enhanced the hepatic microsomal metabolism of chlorpromazine, an effect that would make it difficult to maintain therapeutic concentrations of chlorpromazine in the sober alcoholic. The picture could be further complicated by impaired microsomal drug metabolism as a result of extensive alcohol-induced liver damage in the alcoholic (see Chapter 4).

In summary, the synergistic depressant interactions of chlorpromazine and alcohol have been well documented. It remains to be established whether these interactions are principally mediated directly through the CNS or indirectly through alterations in ethanol or chlorpromazine metabolism.

2.1.7. Ethanol–Antihistamine Interactions

Since most antihistamines possess some sedative properties, it is not surprising that there may be an interaction between ethanol and antihistamines. Perhaps the most serious problem is the combined effect of ethanol and antihistamines on driving skills and skills necessary for the operation of dangerous equipment. A recent study by Burns and Moskowitz (1980) demonstrated the additive effect of the interaction between diphenydramine (Benadryl), a common over-the-counter antihistamine, and ethanol on such skills. The number of subjects (12) was small, but a repeated-measures double-blind procedure was followed and blood levels of both ethanol and diphenhydramine were taken. The antihistamines had no effect on blood alcohol levels. However, ethanol ingestion produced higher blood diphenhydramine levels in subjects who were given alcohol than in alcohol-free control subjects.

2.2. Stimulants

2.2.1. Tricyclic Antidepressants

The tricyclic antidepressants are currently the most widely used for the treatment of depression; their effectiveness in this respect is well recognized. Despite their efficacy in treating affective disorders, their exact mechanism of action remains to be determined. Their pharmacological actions are manifested principally in the CNS, the autonomic nervous system, and the cardiovascular system.

An interesting feature of the tricyclic antidepressants is that within this class of drugs, therapeutic responses depend upon the sedative potency of the specific tricyclic antidepressant (Hollister, 1980). Thus it is not surprising that in a review of the pertinent literature, Kissin (1974) noted that, overall, the tricyclic antidepressants varied in their degrees of synergistic interactions with alcohol. A survey of the literature on humans supports this hypothesis in that ingestion of amitriptyline, the most sedative of the tricyclic antidepressants, results in the greatest potentiation of ethanol effects as measured by impaired motor-skill performance. However, nortriptyline, a tricyclic antidepressant about one order of magnitude less effective in terms of sedative potency than amitriptyline, has been reported to antagonize slightly the depressant actions of alcohol. It is difficult to attribute the synergistic actions of tricyclic antidepressants and ethanol to depression or stimulation of specific neurochemical pathways since individual tricyclic antidepressants differ in their respective sedative properties, anticholinergic effects, and effects on presynaptic neurotransmitter transport.

It also remains to be determined whether ethanol–tricyclic antidepressant interaction can be attributed to a disturbance in metabolism of either or both agents. The *in vivo* metabolism of tricyclic antidepressants is mediated by the hepatic microsomal drug-metabolizing enzymes. As a general rule, tricyclic antidepressants are metabolized by demethylation and hydroxylation. Since these metabolic conversions are also typical of barbiturate and meprobamate metabolism, which seems to be sensitive to inhibition by ethanol, it is tempting to speculate that ethanol might have a similar effect on the metabolism of tricyclic antidepressant metabolism also. However, additional studies are necessary to determine whether acute doses of ethanol significantly alter tricyclic antidepressant metabolism in humans. Likewise, it is of importance to determine whether chronic ethanol ingestion alters tricyclic antidepressant metabolism in a manner similar to that observed for barbiturates and meprobamate.

One recognized feature of tricyclic antidepressant therapy is the large interpatient variation in steady-state concentrations of these drugs within the individual. This variation is genetically determined, since identical but not fraternal twins show nearly identical plasma concentrations and half-lives after oral administration. Therefore it is likely that therapeutic responses to tricyclic antidepressants, and possibly interactions with ethanol, may be attributed to genetically determined parameters. Given the complexity of pharmacological actions of tricyclic antidepressants and the apparent lack of knowledge concerning CNS, and metabolic interactions with ethanol, the coadministration of ethanol and tricyclic antidepressants should be avoided. As pointed out by Pirola (1978), a number of fatalities have been reported which were associated with ingestion of therapeutic doses of tricyclic antidepressants and blood concentrations of ethanol that, in themselves, could not be considered lethal.

2.2.2. CNS Stimulants

Given the popularity of both ethanol and stimulants such as amphetamine, methylphenidate, cocaine, and caffeine, it is not surprising that they are used together in the hope of either "sobering up" or altering the CNS effects of the stimulant. In an extensive study of some of these compounds in combination with ethanol, Rech, Vomachka, and Rickert (1978) demonstrated that roto-rod performance of both rats and mice after ethanol were impaired significantly longer when ethanol was combined with either cocaine, amphetamine, or methylphenidate. These compounds had no influence on ethanol disappearance but ethanol did have an effect on amphetamine levels.

A similar study by Todzy, Coper, and Ferandes (1978) showed, however, that amphetamine decreased sleep time after a dose of 3.2 g/kg ethanol. Apparently the more subtle measure achieved by use of the roto-rod performance demonstrates additive behavioral effects, whereas the time to regain the righting reflex demonstrates antagonism. The term "wide-awake drunk" might be applied to an individual receiving both amphetamine and ethanol.

The study by Todzy *et al.* (1978) demonstrated that ethanol prolonged amphetamine half-life, apparently by inhibiting parahydroxylation. It is impossible to tell from the data presented whether amphetamines had an effect on ethanol absorption or metabolism.

Femetozole is an interesting and potentially useful antidepressant. Frye, Breese, Mailman, Vogel, Ondrusek, and Mueller (1980) found that it would antagonize locomotor stimulation produced by low doses of ethanol and also antagonize depression produced at high doses of ethanol. They demonstrated that femetozole had no effect on the pharmacokinetics of ethanol.

A potentially serious metabolic interaction between ethanol and cocaine has been studied by Smith, Freeman, and Harbison (1981). It was found that following chronic ethanol treatment, acute toxicity due to cocaine was reduced; however, there was a delayed hepatic necrosis which produced a 30% mortality seven days later. The authors attributed both these effects to an induction of cytochrome P_{450} systems by ethanol. While cocaine itself is thought to be responsible for the initial toxicity of this compound, its metabolite N-desmethyl-cocaine may be responsible for the liver damage.

The traditional use of a cup of black coffee to sober someone up is without experimental support. Numerous studies have failed to detect any beneficial effect of caffeine in this regard (see review by Deitrich & Petersen, 1979).

2.3. Neurotransmitters

There is a substantial literature describing the interactions between neurotransmitter agonists or antagonists and ethanol (see review by Deitrich & Petersen, 1979). In general, these studies are undertaken to elucidate the mechanism of action of ethanol. Thus most of them are of potential but not immediate therapeutic importance.

One aim of studies of this kind is to discover compounds that will function as ethanol antagonist or amethystic agents. There are a number of technical pitfalls in such investigations. The first is that the duration of ethanol-induced anesthesia on "sleep" is used as a measure of the effect of ethanol. This is usually measured as the time from loss of righting response to its recovery following a dose of ethanol. Often the sleep times recorded are so short as to preclude distribution and equilibration of ethanol between blood and brain. Sleep time of less than 30 minutes should be regarded with a good deal of skepticism.

Sleep time alone should not be used; instead, blood and preferably brain alcohol levels at the time of "waking" should be the criteria for an interactive and especially antagonistic effect of any drug toward ethanol. For example, a recent paper (Munoz & Guivernau, 1980) reported that d-l but not d-propranolol reduced the sleep time following ethanol doses of 3.75, 4.4, and 5 gm/kg in mice. Propanolol reduced sleep time from 27.5 to 14.9 minutes but there was no difference in blood levels at the times that the animals regained their righting reflex (436 *versus* 437 mg/100mL). Thus the difference in sleep times must be accounted for by inadequate diffusion of ethanol into the brain, more rapid metabolism, or some other factor.

Liljequist, Berggren, and Engel (1981) have studied the antagonistic effect of the central-adrenergic and dopamine-receptor blocking agents on the stimulation produced by low doses of ethanol. These studies, coupled with their finding that the dopamine-hydroxylase inhibitor FLA-63 also blocked ethanol-induced locomotor stimulation, led to the conclusion that adrenergic and dopamine receptors are involved in the stimulatory actions of ethanol. Interpretation of this study is difficult because brain ethanol levels were not measured. Another mechanism of FLA-63 action is also possible, since Sharkawi (1980) showed that FLA-63 inhibits mouse liver alcohol dehydrogenase and alters the disposition of ethanol.

2.4. Metabolic Interactions

2.4.1. Ethanol–Chloral Hydrate and Paraldehyde

The combination of ethanol and chloral hydrate known as a "Mickey Finn" has a widespread reputation as a particularly potent hypnotic combination. It is often depicted as bringing about unconsiousness within a few seconds. The possibilities for interactions between ethanol and chloral hydrate, both metabolic and pharmacological, are indeed numerous, as shown in Figure 4. Compounds with known pharmacological actions are shown in boldface. The older work in this area has been reviewed previously (see Deitrich & Petersen, 1979); hence we will concentrate only on more recent developments.

The possible metabolic interactions are clearly evident in Figure 4. Chloral hydrate (CLH) is reduced by ADH–NADH complex, giving rise to trichloroethanol (TCE). Since this metabolic step results in an ADH–NAD complex, it bypasses the rate-limiting step of ethanol oxidation, which is the dissociation of NADH from ADH (see Chapter 3). The rapid generation of the ADH–NAD complex in the presence of chloral hydrate cannot, however, speed the metabolism of ethanol greatly *in vivo,* because the dose of chloral hydrate is only about 0.1 that of of ethanol. Reduction of chloral hydrate is, of course, favored by increased NADH/NAD ratios, which exist during ethanol metabolism (Owen & Taberner, 1980). Whatever increase there is in alcohol metabolism, it must also increase the

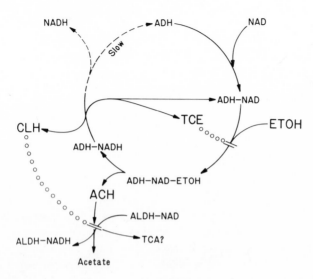

Figure 4. Metabolic interaction between ethanol (ETOH), chloral hydrate (CLH), trichloroethanol (TCE), and trichloroacetic acid (TCA). (o o o = inhibitory action.)

rate of formation of acetaldehyde. Coupled with inhibition of aldehyde dehydrogenase by chloral hydrate, there should be an increase in blood acetaldehyde. This effect has been reported (Creaven & Roach, 1969), but others find lower blood acetaldehyde levels. It is known that trichloracetic acid is a metabolite of chloral hydrate, but the pathway to this product is not certain (Deitrich & Petersen, 1979). Trichloroethanol should be oxidized by alcohol dehydrogenase, but this is not observed; in fact, trichloroethanol functions as an inhibitor of ethanol oxidation (Owen & Taberner, 1980). Presumably the failure to find oxidation of trichloroethanol is a problem of thermodynamics, since there is little doubt that chloral hydrate is a substrate for reduction since Wong and Biemann (1978) demonstrated that a deuterium atom in d_6 labeled ethanol is transferred to chloral hydrate, presumably via NADH(D), to form trichloroethanol. Pyrazole, an inhibitor of ADH, prolonged the action of trichloroethanol, indicating but not proving that ADH plays a role in the metabolism of trichloroethanol. Other enzymes capable of reducing aldehydes are the aldehyde reductase enzymes. These enzymes can catalyze the reduction of chloral hydrate to trichloroethanol using NADPH rather than NADH (Tabakoff, Vugrincic, Anderson, & Alvisatos, 1974; Ikeda, Ezaki, Kokeguchi, & Ohmori, 1981).

Since trichloroethanol has a longer half-life in the brain than chloral hydrate and is about equipotent with chloral hydrate in terms of its hypnotic effects, any procedure which causes reduction of the chloral hydrate mechanism—such as administration of ethanol—should prolong the action of administered chloral hydrate. In addition, the CNS-depressant actions of trichloroethanol, chloral hydrate, and ethanol will be additive.

Paraldehyde, a compound with CNS-depressant properties, has been widely used for treatment of alcohol withdrawal. It is a polymer of acetaldehyde and is widely assumed to give rise to acetaldehyde *in vivo*. The evidence for this is not substantial, however (Deitrich & Petersen, 1979), and any interaction with ethanol probably occurs because of additive CNS-depressant effects.

2.4.2. Hypoglycemic Agents

Ingestion of ethanol in combination with the more commonly used hypoglycemic agents can result in a number of different pharmacological and physiological responses. These responses depend, to some extent, on the carbohydrate regulatory capabilities of the individual and the specific hypoglycemic agent involved.

First, it should be pointed out that ethanol alone can cause hypoglycemia. Ethanol is thought to interfere with gluconeogenesis primarily through the ability to increase the ratio of reduced to oxidized nicotinamide adenine dinucleotide (NADH/NAD) within the hepatocyte during ethanol oxidation. Thus, most metabolic transformations in pathways of gluconeogenesis that require NAD would be significantly inhibited. Cytosolic gluconeogenic reactions—such as the oxidation of glycerol phosphate and lactate—are inhibited significantly, the end result being a deficiency of acetyl CoA.

Although the hypoglycemic actions of ethanol may be subtle in an individual who is able to regulate his or her glucose metabolism the same actions of ethanol may result in irreversible damage or death in a diabetic or acutely malnourished individual. The severe hypoglycemia in a diabetic who is taking hypoglycemic drugs and ingesting alcohol can result in irreversible neurological damage or death (Arkey, Veverbrants, & Abrason, 1968).

Of the hypoglycemic agents, sulfonylurea–alcohol interactions have been most frequently reported. The effect most commonly reported from coingesting alcohol and sulfonylureas resembles a disulfiram reaction, which is characterized by malaise and flushing.

A controversy has developed in the literature as to the value of the chloropropamide–ethanol flushing reaction as a tool for predicting the severity of retinopathy in diabetics (Leslie, Barnett, & Pyle, 1979; Barnett & Pyke, 1980, 1981; DeSilva, Tunbridge, & Alberti, 1981; Barnett, Leslie, & Pike, 1981; Barnett, Mace, & Pyke, 1981; Kobberbling, Bengsh, & Bruggeboes, 1980). There was also a report that the flushing reaction was an inherited response (Leslie & Pyke, 1978) but this idea was discounted (Dreyer, Kuhnau, & Rudiger, 1980). In fact, one report indicates that the symptoms of flushing have been observed in 16% to 33% of diabetics maintained on sulfonylureas (Logie, Galloway, & Petrie, 1976). Since these symptoms appear to be similar to disulfiram–alcohol reactions, which are elicited by hepatic aldehyde dehydrogenase inhibition, it is possible that sulfonlureas may also be inhibitors of these same enzyme systems (Deitrich & Hellerman, 1963).

Chronic alcohol ingestion has been reported to influence the pharmacokinetics of tolbutamide. It appears that when alcohol is consumed chronically, the hepatic microsomal drug-metabolizing enzymes become induced. Tolbutamide half-life is only half as long in alcoholics as in appropriate healthy control individuals (Kater, Zieve, Tobon, Roggin, & Iber, 1969; Carulli, Manenti, Gallo, & Salvioli, 1971).

In summary, it is evident that the interactions observed in individuals consuming alcohol concurrently with hypoglycemic drugs depend on several parameters, such as the severity of diabetic symptoms, the dose and nature of the hypoglycemic agent prescribed, and the drinking habits of the patient. Given the severity of either the hypoglycemic symptoms, the potential disulfiramlike reactions, or simply the caloric contributions of ethanol itself, the diabetic should be cautioned about drinking alcohol alone or in combination with hypoglycemic drugs.

2.4.3. Analgesics–Antipyretics

The problem of blood loss following ingestion of aspirin is well known. Several reports have appeared indicating that ethanol may aggravate this situation (Bouchier & Williams, 1969; Goulston & Cooke, 1968; Needham, Kyle, Jones, Johnston, & Kerridge, 1971; DeSchepper, Tjandramaga, Verhaest, Dauro, & Steelman, 1978). The problem would be particularly acute for individuals with blood clotting defects.

Another potential but as yet unresolved problem is the interaction between acetaminophen and ethanol in humans. It is well established that acetaminophen can cause liver damage when taken in an acute or chronic overdose, but there is no agreement that a combination of alcohol and acetaminophen is more toxic than acetaminophen alone (Barker, deCarle, & Anuras, 1977; Medical News, 1980).

Experimental evidence in animals of an increased toxicity of the combination seems well established (Teschke, Stutz, & Strohmeyer, 1979; Sato, Matsuda, & Lieber, 1981). Presumably the basis for the increased toxicity is the induction of microsomal drug-metabolizing systems by chronic administration of ethanol. The role of decreased conjugation by glutathione, sulfate, and glucuronic acid has not been studied in detail.

2.4.4. Antialcohol Compounds

There are other important metabolic interactions with compounds that are used therapeutically for their antialcohol effect, specifically disulfiram (Antabuse) and cyanamide (Temposil). Metranidozole (Flagyl) is a widely used amebicide and cure for trichomoniasis which was widely regarded as having disulfiramlike action (Goldman, 1980) and thus was recommended as being effective in treating alcoholism. Evidence for such an effect was originally based on case reports and uncontrolled clinical studies. Double-blind studies in humans have been carried out (Linton & Hain, 1967) or outlined, (Lehman, Ban, & Naltchayan, 1966), and studies in animals (Kalant, LeBlanc, Guttman, & Khanna, 1972) fail to provide any evidence for a disulfiramlike action. Indeed, we have not found any double-blind placebo-controlled study in humans unequivocally demonstrating that metronidazole has an adverse interaction with ethanol.

Both cyanamide and disulfiram act to inhibit acetaldehyde metabolism (Kitson, 1977). As a result blood acetaldehyde levels rise to very high levels and contribute to symptoms of flushing, nausea, vomiting, fall in blood pressure, and even death following intake of ethanol (Antabuse–alcohol reaction). The mechanism of this action is primarily by inhibition of the action of aldehyde dehydrogenase, but other actions—such as inhibition of dopamine β hydroxylase by disulfiram—may contribute to the reaction. Under normal circumstances, the level of acetaldehyde in human blood following ethanol intake is extremely low, of the order of a few micromoles per liter. In fact, considerable debate has evolved around the accuracy of the measurement of acetaldehyde in human blood. Since there is artifactual formation of acetaldehyde from ethanol following collection and treatment of blood, there may, in fact, be no detectable (< 1 μmol) acetaldehyde in blood following ethanol intake in humans. If this is true, then the levels of acetaldehyde found following disulfiram or cyanamide treatment represent even greater increases than previously thought.

The mechanism of the inhibition of acetaldehyde metabolism is presumed to be mediated by inhibition of aldehyde dehydrogenase. In the case of disulfiram, the inhibition of the enzyme is essentially irreversible and probably accounts for the long-term effect of disulfiram (Deitrich & Erwin, 1971). One finds in the literature various statements that the inhibition of the enzyme is due to diethyldithiocarbamate, a reduced metabolite of disulfiram. There is no evidence that this is the case; the metabolite fails to inhibit the enzyme *in vitro* (Deitrich & Erwin, 1971). The misconception probably arose because disulfiram is quickly metabolized and little appears in blood (Kitson, 1977) and also because diethyldithiocarbamate given *in vivo* does produce inhibition of liver aldehyde dehydrogenase. It is possible that some mixed disulfide between disulfiram and an endogenous sulfhydryl-containing compound such as glutathione or cysteine is the active inhibitor.

There are different degrees of susceptibility of aldehyde dehydrogenase enzymes to inhibition by disulfiram. In order to be effective in raising blood acetaldehyde levels, the inhibition of the enzymes with high affinity for acetaldehyde must be accomplished. Given the effectiveness of relatively low doses of disulfiram in humans (250 to 500 mg), the affected human enzyme must be very sensitive to the inhibition or be present only in slight excess over what is required to oxidize acetaldehyde as it is formed. In this situation as with many others, it is important to realize that there are a multitude of aldehyde dehydrogenase enzymes capable of oxidizing acetaldehyde, but with lower affinities. Thus, as the level of acetaldehyde rises, a greater fraction of the enzyme activity is called into play; then there is no further increase in acetaldehyde levels. Ultimately, if acetaldehyde concentrations reach high enough levels, alcohol oxidation is shut off by reversal of the alcohol dehydrogenase reaction.

The mechanism of the action of cyanamide is even less well understood. Initially it was presumed that a metabolite of cyanamide was responsible for inhibition of aldehyde dehydrogenase, since the compound was effective *in vivo* but not *in vitro* with purified enzyme (Deitrich, Troxell, & Worth, 1976). Since that time, others have shown that incubation of crude enzyme mixtures of aldehyde dehydrogenase, NAD, and cyanamide does result in inhibition of the enzyme (Tottmar, Marchner, & Lindberg, 1977). The active species of the inhibitor has not been identified, however.

In contrast, much more is known about the mechanism of action of coprine, the active component of inky cap mushrooms, which have long been reported to cause a reaction when taken with alcohol. The mechanism of the inhibition of aldehyde dehydrogenase is thought to involve the cyclopropanone ring structure in coprine and lead to essentially irreversible inhibition of the enzyme. This mechanism has thus far been studied using only yeast aldehyde dehydrogenase (Wiseman, Tayrien, & Abeles, 1980).

Likewise, the inhibition of mitochondrial aldehyde dehydrogenase by pargyline has been traced to a metabolite, propargyl aldehyde (Shirota, DeMaster, Elberling, & Nagasawa, 1980).

3. REFERENCES

Altshuler, H. L., Phillips, P. E., & Feinhandler, D. A. Alteration of ethanol self-administration by naltrexone. *Life Science*, 1980, *26*, 679–688.

Adriani, J., & Morton, R. C. Drug dependence: Important considerations from the anesthesiologist's viewpoint. *Anesthesia and Analgesia*, 1968, *47*, 472–481.

Arkey, R. A., Veverbrants, E., & Abrason, A. Irreversible hypoglycemia: A complication of alcohol and insulin. *Journal of the American Medical Association*, 1968, *206*, 575–578.

Baker, R., Melchior, C., & Deitrich, R. The effect of halothane on mice selectively bred for differential sensitivity to alcohol. *Pharmacology, Biochemistry and Behavior*, 1980, *12*, 691–695.

Baldessarini, R. J. Drugs used in the treatment of psychiatric disorders. In A. G. Gilman, L. S.

Goodman, & A. Gilman (Eds.), *The pharmacological basis of therapeutics* (6th ed.). New York: Macmillan, 1980.

Barker, J. D., Jr., deCarle, D. J., & Anuras, S. Chronic excessive acetaminophen use and liver damage. *Annals of Internal Medicine,* 1977, *87,* 299–301.

Barnett, A. H., Leslie, R. D. G., & Pyke, D. A. Chlorpropamide–alcohol flushing and proteinuria in non-insulin-dependent diabetics. *British Medical Journal,* 1981, *282,* 522–523.

Barnett, A. H., Mace, P. J. E., & Pyke, D. A. Chlorpropamide–alcohol flushing and microangiopathy in insulin-dependent diabetes. *British Medical Journal,* 1981, *282,* 523.

Barnett, A. H., & Pyke, D. A. Chlorpropamide alcohol flushing and large vessel disease in noninsulin dependent diabetes. *British Medical Journal,* 1980, *281,* 261–262.

Barnett, A. H., & Pyke, D. A. Chloropropamide alcohol flushing. *Lancet,* 1981, *I,* 222.

Barros, S., & Rodriguez, G. Naloxone as an antagonist in alcohol intoxication. *Anesthesiology,* 1981, *54,* 174.

Benzer, D., & Cushman, P. Alcohol and benzodiazepine: Withdrawal syndromes. *Alcoholism: Clinical and Experimental Research,* 1980, *4,* 243–247.

Berger, H. J. Chlorpromazine and ethanol combination: Effects on respiration, random motor activity and conditioned avoidance-escape in mice. *Quarterly Journal of Studies on Alcohol,* 1969, *30,* 862–869.

Borowsky, S. A., & Lieber, C. S. Interaction of methadone and ethanol metabolism. *The Journal of Pharmacology and Experimental Therapeutics,* 1978, *207,* 123–129.

Bouchier, I. A. D., & Williams, H. S. Determination of faecal blood loss after combined alcohol and sodium salicylate intake. *Lancet,* 1969, *1,* 178–180.

Bowes, H. A. The role of librium in an outpatient psychiatric setting. *Diseases Nervous System,* 1960, *21*(Suppl.), 20–22.

Burns, M., & Moskowitz, H. Effects of diphenhydramine and alcohol on skills performance. *European Journal of Clinical Pharmacology,* 1980, *17,* 259–266.

Caldwell, J., & Sever, P. S. The biochemical pharmacology of abused drugs. II. Alcohol and barbiturates. *Clinical Pharmacology and Therapeutics,* 1974, *16,* 737–749.

Carulli, N., Manenti, F., Gallo, M., & Salvioli, G. F. Alcohol–drugs interaction in man: Alcohol and tolbutamide. *European Journal of Clinical Investigation,* 1971, *1,* 421–424.

Creaven, P. J., & Roach, M. K. Effect of chloral hydrate on the metabolism of ethanol. *Journal of Pharmacy and Pharmacology,* 1969, *21,* 332–333.

Cullen, B. F., & Miller, M. G. Drug interactions and anesthesia: A review. *Anesthesia and Analgesia,* 1979, *58,* 413–423.

Curry, S. H. Homergic interactions, isobols and drug concentrations in blood. In D. G. Grahame-Smith (Ed.), *Drug interactions.* London: University Park Press, 1977.

Deitrich, R. A., & Erwin, V. G. Mechanism of the inhibition of aldehyde dehydrogenase *in vivo* by disulfiram and deithyldithiocarbamate. *Molecular Pharmacology,* 1971, *7,* 301–307.

Deitrich, R. A., & Erwin, V. G. Biogenic amine-aldehyde condensation products tetrahydroisoquinolines and tryptolines (β carbolines). *Annual Review of Pharmacology and Toxicology,* 1980, *20,* 55–80.

Deitrich, R. A., & Hellerman, L. Diphosphopyridine nucleotide-linked liver aldehyde dehydrogenase: II. Inhibitors. *Journal of Biological Chemistry,* 1963, *238,* 1683–1689.

Deitrich, R. A., & Petersen, D. R. Interaction of ethanol with other drugs. In E. Majchrowicz & E. P. Noble (Eds.), *Biochemistry and pharmacology of ethanol* (Vol. 2). New York: Plenum Press, 1979.

Deitrich, R. A., Troxell, P. A., & Worth, W. S. Inhibition of aldehyde dehydrogenase in brain and liver by cyanamide. *Biochemical Pharmacology,* 1976, *25,* 2733–2737.

DeSchepper, P. J., Tjandramaga, T. B., Verhaest, L., Dauro, C., & Steelman, S. L. Diflunisal versus aspirin: A comparative study of their effect on faecal blood loss, in the presence and absence of alcohol. *Current Medical Research and Opinion*, 1978, *5*, 520–524.

DeSilva, N. E., Tunbridge, W. M. G., & Alberti, K. G. M. M. Low incidence of chlorpropamide-alcohol flushing in diet-treated non-insulin-dependent diabetes. *Lancet*, 1981, *1*, 128–131.

Desmond, P. V., Patwardhan, R. V., Schenker, S., & Hoyumpa, A. M. Short-term ethanol administration impairs the elimination of chlordiazepoxide (Librium[R]) in man. *European Journal of Clinical Pharmacology*, 1980, *18*, 275–278.

Downs, D. A. Interactions of acetylmethadol or methadone with oher drugs in Rhesus monkeys. *Pharmacology, Biochemistry and Behavior*, 1979, *10*, 407–414.

Dreyer, M., Kuhnau, J., & Rudiger, H. W. Chlorpropamide–alcohol flushing is not useful for individual genetic conseling of diabetic patients. *Clinical Genetics*, 1980, *18*, 189–190.

Favazza, A. R., & Martin, P. Chemotheapy of delirium tremens: A survey of physicians preferences. *American Journal of Psychiatry*, 1974, *131*, 1031–1033.

Frye, G. D., Breese, G. R., Mailman, R. B., Vogel, R. A., Ondrusek, M. G., & Mueller, R. A. An evaluation of the selectivity of fenmetozole (DH-524) reversal of ethanol induced changes in central nervous system function. *Psychopharmacology*, 1980, *69*, 149–155.

Goldberg, L. Effects of ethanol in the central nervous system. In R. E. Popham (Ed.), *Alcohol and Alcoholism*. University of Toronto Press, 1970.

Goldman, P. Metronidazole. *New England Journal of Medicine*, 1980, *303*, 1212–1217.

Goulston, K., & Cooke, A. R. Alcohol, aspirin and gastrointestinal bleeding. *British Medical Journal*, 1968, *4*, 664–665.

Harvey, S. Hypnotics and sedatives. In A. G. Gilman, L. S. Goodman & A. Gilman (Eds.), *The pharmacological basis of therapeutics* (6th ed.). New York: Macmillan, 1980.

Hayes, S. L., Pablo, G., Radomski, T., & Palmer, R. Ethanol and diazepam absorption. *New England Journal of Medicine*, 1977, *296*, 186–189.

Ho, A. K. S., & Ho, C. C. Toxic interactions of ethanol with other central depressants: Antagonism by naloxone to narcosis and lethality. *Pharmacology, Biochemistry and Behavior*, 1979, *11*, 111–114.

Ho, A. K. S., Chen, R. C. A., & Ho, C. C. Interaction toxicity between ethanol and narcotics in mice with reference to alpha-1-acetyl-methadol (LAAM). *Pharmacology, Biochemistry and Behavior*, 1978, *9*, 195–200.

Ho, C. C., & Ho, A. K. S. Interaction between methaqualone and ethanol in rats and mice during acute and chronic states. *Clinical and Experimental Pharmacology and Physiology*, 1978, *5*, 665–671.

Hollister, L. E. Psychiatric Disorders. In G. S. Avery (Ed.), *Drug Treatment* (2nd ed.). New York: Avery Press, 1980.

Hoyumpa, A. M., Jr., Desmond, P. V., Roberts, R. K., Nichols, S., Johnson, R. F., & Schenker, S. Effect of ethanol on benzodiazepine disposition in dogs. *Journal of Laboratory and Clinical Medicine*, 1980, *95*, 310–322.

Ikeda, M., Ezaki, M., Kokeguchi, S., & Ohmori, S. Studies on NADPH-dependent chloral hydrate reducing enzymes in rat liver cytosol. *Biochemical Pharmacology*, 1981, *30*, 1931–1939.

Isbell, H., & Chrusciel, T. L. Dependence liability of nonnarcotic drugs. *World Health Organization*, 1970, 5–31.

Jackson, G. W., & Richman, A. Alcohol use among narcotic addicts. *Alcohol World*, 1973, *1*, 25–28.

Jeffcoate, W. J., Cullen, M. H., Herbert, M., Hasting, A. G., & Walder, C. P. Prevention of effects of alcohol intoxication by naloxone. *Lancet*, 1979, *2*, 1157–1159.

Kalant, H., LeBlanc, A. E., Guttman, M., & Khanna, J. M. Metabolic and pharmacologic inter-action of ethanol and metronidazole in the rat. *Canadian Journal of Physiology and Pharma-cology*, 1972, *50*, 476–484.

Kater, R. M. H., Zieve, P., Tobon, F., Roggin, G., & Iber, F. L. Accelerated metabolism of drugs in alcoholics. *Gastroenterology*, 1969, *56*, 412.

Khouw, L. B., Burbridge, T. N., & Sutherland, V. C. The inhibition of alcohol dehydrogenase. I Kinetic Studies. *Biochimica Biophysica Acta*, 1963, *73*, 173–185.

Kissin, B. Interactions of ethyl alcohol and other drugs. In B. Kissin & H. Begleiter (Eds.) *The biology of alcoholism* (Vol. 3). New York: Plenum Press, 1974.

Kitson, T. M. The disulfiram–ethanol reaction. A review. *Journal Studies on Alcohol*, 1977, *38*, 96–113.

Kobberling, J., Bengsh, N., & Bruggeboes, B. The chlorpropamide alcohol flush. Lack of specificity for familial non-insulin-dependent diabetes. *Diabetologia*, 1980, *19*, 359–363.

Koblin, D. D., & Deady, J. E. Anaesthetic requirement in mice selectively bred for differential ethanol sensitivity. *British Journal Anaesthesia*, 1981, *53*, 5–10.

Koblin, D. D., Deady, J. E., Dong, D. E., & Eger, E. I. II. Mice tolerant to nitrous oxide are also tolerant to alcohol. *Journal of Pharmacology and Experimental Therapeutics*, 1980, *213*, 309–312.

Kreek, M. J. Metabolic interactions between opiates and alcohol. *Annals of the New York Academy of Sciences*, 1981, *362*, 36–49.

Lehman, H. E., Ban, T. A., & Naltchayan, E. Metronidazole in the treatment of the alcoholic. *Psychiatric Neurology*, 1966, *152*, 395–401.

Leslie, R. D. G., & Pyke, D. A. Chlorpropamide–alcohol flushing: A dominantly inherited trait associated with diabetes. *British Medical Journal*, 1978, *2*, 1519–1521.

Leslie, R. D. G., Barnett, A. H., & Pyke, D. A. Chlorpropamide alcohol flushing and diabetic retinopathy. *Lancet* 1979, *1*, 997–999.

Lieber, C. S. Metabolism of ethanol. In C. S. Lieber (Ed.), *Metabolic aspects of alcoholism*. Balti-more: University Park Press, 1977.

Linton, P. H., & Hain, J. D. Metronidazole in the treatment of alcoholism. *Quarterly Journal of Studies on Alcohol*, 1967, *28*, 544–546.

Liljequist, S., Berggren, U., & Engel, J. The effect of catecholamine receptor antagonists on ethanol-induce locomotor stimulation. *Journal of Neural Transmission*, 1981, *50*, 57–67.

Linnoila, M., & Hakkinen, S. Effects of diazepam and codeine alone and in combination with alco-hol on simulated driving. *Clinical Pharmacology and Therapeutics*, 1974, *15*, 368–373.

Linnoila, M., & Mattila, M. J. Drug interaction on psychomotor skills related to driving: diazepam and alcohol. *European Journal of Clinical Pharmacology*, 1973, *5*, 186–194.

Logie, A. W., Galloway, D. B., & Petrie, J. C. Drug interactions and long-term antidiabetic therapy. *British Journal of Clinical Pharmacology*, 1976, *3*, 1027–1032.

MacKenzie, A. I. Naloxone in alcohol intoxication. *Lancet* 1979, *1*, 733–734.

MacLeod, S. M., Giles, H. G., Patzalek, G., Thiessen, J. J., & Sellers, E. M. Diazepam actions and plasma concentrations following ethanol ingestion. *European Journal of Clinical Pharma-cology*, 1977, *11*, 345–349.

McGuire, J. L., Awourters, F. & Niemegeers, C. J. E. Interaction of loperamide and diphenoxylate with ethanol and methohexital. *Archives International Pharmacodynamics*, 1978, *236*, 51–59.

Medical News. Alcohol-acetaminophen issue explored. *Journal American Medical Association*, 1980, *244*, 636–642.

Mendelson, J. H. The search for alcohol antagonists: New research possibilities. *Advances in Alco-holism*, 1980, *1*(23).

Mendelson, W. B., Goodwin, D. W., Hill, S. Y., & Reichman, J. D. The morning after: Residual

EEG effects of triazolam and flurazepam alone and in combination with alcohol. *Current Therapeutic Research,* 1976, *19,* 155–163.

Middaugh, L. D., Read, E., & Boggan, W. O. Effects of naloxone on ethanol induced alterations of locomotor activity in C57BL/6 mice. *Pharmacology, Biochemistry and Behavior,* 1978, *9,* 157–160.

Milner, G., & Landauer, A. A. Alcohol, thioridazine and chlorpromazine effects on skills related to driving behavior. *British Journal of Psychiatry,* 1971, *118,* 351–352.

Misra, P. S., Lèfevre, A., Ishil, H., Rubin, E., & Lieber, C. S. Increase of ethanol, meprobamate and pentobarbital metabolism after chronic ethanol administration in man and rats. *American Journal of Medicine,* 1971, *51,* 346–351.

Mørland, J., Setekleiv, J., Haffner, J. F. W., Strømsaether, C. F., Danielsen, A., & HolstWethe, G. Combined effects of diazepam and ethanol on mental and psychomotor functions. *Acta Pharmacologica et Toxicoogica,* 1974, *34,* 5– 15.

Moss, L. M. Naloxone reversal of non-narcotic induced apnea. *Journal of the American College of Emergency Physicians,* 1973, *1,* 46–48.

Munoz, C., & Guivernau, M. Antagonistic effects of propranolol upon ethanol-induced narcosis in mice. *Research Communications in Chemical Pathology and Pharmacology,* 1980, *29,* 57–65.

Myers, R. D., & Melchior, C. L. Alcohol drinking: Abnormal intake caused by tetrahydropapaveroline. *Science,* 1977, *196,* 554–556.

Needham, C. D., Kyle, J., Jones, P. F., Johnston, S. J., & Kerridge, D. F. Aspirin and alcohol in gastrointestinal haemorrhage. *Gut,* 1971, *12,* 819–821.

Owen, B. E., & Taberner, P. V. Studies on the hypnotic effects of chloral hydrate and ethanol and their metabolism in vivo and in vitro. *Biochemical Pharmacology,* 1980, *29,* 3011–3016.

Palva, E. S., Linnoila, M. & Mattila, M. J. Effect of active metabolites of chlordiazepoxide and diazepam alone or in combination with alcohol. *Modern Problems in Pharmacopsychiatry,* 1976, *11,* 79–90.

Pirola, R. C. *Drug metabolism and alcohol.* Baltimore: University Park Press, 1978.

Rech, R. H., Vomachka, M. K., & Rickert, D. E. Interactions between depressants (alcohol-type) and stimulants (amphetamine-type). *Pharmacology, Biochemistry and Behavior,* 1978, *8,* 143–151.

Ritchie, J. M. The aliphatic alcohols. In A. G. Gilman, L. S. Goodman, & A. Gilman (Eds.), *The pharmacological basis of therapeutics* (6th ed.) New York: Macmillan, 1980.

Ross, D. H., Medina, M., & Cardenas, H. L. Morphine and ethanol: Selective depletion of regional brain calcium. *Science,* 1974, *186,* 63–65.

Rosser, W. W. The interaction of propoxyphene with other drugs. *Canadian Medical Association Journal,* 1980, *122,* 149–150.

Rubin, E., Bacchin, P., Gang, H., & Lieber, C. S. Induction and inhibition of hepatic microsomal and mitochondrial enzymes by ethanol. *Laboratory Investigations,* 1970, *22,* 569–580.

Rubin, E., Gang, H., Misra, P. S., & Lieber, C. S. Inhibition of drug metabolism by acute ethanol intoxication: A hepatic microsomal mechanism. *American Journal of Medicine,* 1970, *49,* 801–806.

Sato, C., Matsuda, Y., & Lieber, C. S. Increased hepatotoxicity of acetaminophen after chronic ethanol consumption in the rat. *Gastroenterology,* 1981, *80,* 140–148.

Sellers, E. M., Naranjo, C. A., Giles, H. G., Frecker, R. C., & Beeching, M. Intravenous diazepam and oral ethanol interaction. *Clinical Pharmacology and Therapeutics* 1980, *28,* 638–645.

Seppälä, T. Effect of chlorpromazine or sulpiride and alcohol on psychomotor skills related to driving. *Archives Internationales de Pharmacodynamie et de Theapie,* 1976, *223,* 311–323.

Seppälä, T., Palva, E., Mattila, M. J., Korttila, K., & Shrotriya, R. C. Tofisopam, a novel 3,4,-

benzodiazepine: Multiple-dose effects on psychomotor skills and memory. Comparison with diazepam and interactions with ethanol. *Psychopharmacology,* 1980, *69,* 209–218.

Sharkawi, M. Pharmacological and metabolic interactions between ethanol and the dopamine-β-hydroxylase inhibitor FLA 63 in mice. *Neuropharmacology,* 1980, *19,* 277–280.

Shirota, F. N., DeMaster, E. G., Elberling, J. A., & Nagasawa, H. T. Metabolic depropargylation and its relationship to aldehyde dehydrogenase inhibition *in vivo. Journal of Medicinal Chemistry,* 1980, *23,* 669–673.

Smith, A. C., Freeman, R. W., & Harbison, R. D. Ethanol enhancement of cocaine-induced hepatotoxicity. *Biochemical Pharmacology,* 1981, *30,* 453–458.

Sorensen, S. C., & Mattisson, K. Naloxone as an antagonist in severe alcohol intoxication. *Lancet,* 1978, *2,* 688–689.

Sutherland, V. C., Burbridge, T. N., Adams, J. E., & Simon, A. Cerebral metabolism in problem drinkers under the influence of alcohol and chlorpromazine hydrochloride. *Journal of Applied Physiology,* 1960, *15,* 189–196.

Tabakoff, B., Vugrincic, C., Anderson, R., & Alvisatos, S. G. A. Reduction of chloral hydrate to trichloroethanol in brain extracts. *Biochemical Pharmacology,* 1974, *23,* 455–460.

Teschke, R., Stutz, G., & Strohmeyer, G. Increased paracetamol-induced hepatotoxicity after chronic alcohol consumption. *Biochemical and Biophysical Research Communication,* 1979, *91,* 368–374.

Todzy, I., Coper, H., & Fernandes, M. Interaction between d-amphetamine and ethanol with respect to locomotion, stereotypes, ethanol sleeping time, and the kinetics of drug elimination. *Psychopharmacology,* 1978, *59,* 143–149.

Tottmar, O., Marchner, H., & Lindberg, P. Inhibition of rat-liver aldehyde dehydrogenases *in vivo* by disulfiram, cyanamide and the alcohol-sensitizing compound coprine. In R. G. Thurman, J. R. Williamson, H. R. Dratt, & B. Chance (Eds.), *Alcohol and aldehyde metabolizing systems* (Vol 2). New York: Plenum Press, 1977.

Vapaatalo, H,, & Karppunen, H. Combined toxicity of ethanol with chlorpromazine, diazepam, chlormethiozole or pentobarbital in mice. *Agents and Actions,* 1969, *1,* 43–45.

Wiseman, J. S., & Abeles, R. H. Mechanism of inhibition of aldehyde dehydrogenase by cyclopropanone hydrate and the mushroom toxin coprine. *Biochemistry,* 1979, *18,* 427–435.

Wiseman, J. S., Tayrien, G., & Abeles, R. H. Kinetics of the reaction of cyclopropanone hydrate with yeast aldehyde dehydrogenase: A model for enzyme–substrate interaction. *Biochemistry,* 1980, *19,* 4222–4231.

Wong, L. K., & Biemann, K. A study of drug interaction by gas chromatography–mass spectrometry–synergism of chloral hydrate and ethanol. *Biochemical Phamacology,* 1978, *27,* 1019–1022.

Zirkle, G. A., McAtee, O. B., & King, P. D. Meprobamate and small amounts of alcohol. Effects on human ability. Coordination and judgment. *Journal of the American Medical Association,* 1960, *173,* 1823–1825.

10

Psychological Correlates and Explanations of Alcohol Use and Abuse

R. LORRAINE COLLINS AND G. ALAN MARLATT

There are a number of psychological correlates and explanations for the excessive consumption of alcohol. The selection of topics covered in this chapter represents the major psychological approaches used to explain excessive alcohol use, namely, the psychodynamic, disease, and behavioral/social learning models. Research on the psychological aspects of alcohol consumption is relatively new. An attempt has been made to present the basic ideas of each of the models along with research evidence and methodological issues pertaining to their evaluation. Each of the models presented has contributed to our continuing attempts to understand the complex mechanisms and issues involved in excessive alcohol use. As our theoretical and methodological sophistication increases, further refinement of each of these approaches seems likely. For the present, they represent laudable initial efforts to develop psychological frameworks within which one can study and treat problem drinking.

1. PSYCHODYNAMIC MODELS

This section includes a discussion of psychoanalytic theory as well as motivational and personality explanations of the etiology of excessive alcohol use. The term "psychodynamic" encompasses the common focus of the above mentioned

R. LORRAINE COLLINS • Department of Psychology, State University of New York at Stony Brook, Stony Brook, New York 11794. **G. ALAN MARLATT** • Department of Psychology, University of Washington, Seattle, Washington 98195.

explanations on the uncovering of inner forces related to alcohol use. However, each explanation differs in its total scope. Psychoanalytic theory focuses on the role of early experiences and unconscious dynamics, while motivational theory assumes that the need for power is an important influence on drinking. Personality theorists seek to describe a set pattern of characteristics which predisposes the individual to drink heavily or distinguishes the alcoholic from the nonalcoholic individual. These approaches, however, share common investigative methods, many of which involve the gathering and interpretation of self-report data.

1.1. Psychoanalytic Theory

Psychoanalytic approaches to alcohol use have offered a number of ways of conceptualizing the etiology of alcoholism. A common theme is the notion that addiction to alcohol or other substances results from dependency needs caused by deficiences in psychosexual development (Fenichel, 1945). These may involve fixation at a particular stage of growth or regression to a previously outgrown stage. The severity of drinking problems and developmental fixation are seen as inversely related, such that more severe problems occur at earlier stages and vice versa. Among the causes of alcoholism outlined in a comprehensive review of the psychoanalytic approach (Blum, 1966) are the following:

1. Excessive dependency due to frustration, spoiling, or a combination of the two that prevents the successful management of the move to independence.
2. Overly punitive parents who serve as models for the development of attitudes of self-punishment, which are expressed via excessive drinking.
3. Fixation or regression to one of three developmental stages. Fixation at the oral stage may be expressed via narcissism and the need for immediate pleasure characteristic of some alcoholics. Regression to or fixation at the anal stage may result in traits such as aggressiveness and rebelliousness, also characteristic of some alcoholics. Individuals fixated at this stage may also attempt to disguise or repress their homosexual tendencies. Last, fixation at the phallic stage leads to the development of alcoholics whose superficial friendliness may mask feelings of low self-esteem, rebelliousness, and anger.

Other psychodynamic models that have discounted the causative role of failures in psychosexual development have also focused on the fulfillment of dependency needs. McCord and McCord (1960) based their model of the etiology of alcoholism on a longitudinal study of lower-class boys. Using a variety of data collected over a five-year period, they were able to distinguish the personality, familial, and physiological traits that differentiated boys who became adult alcoholics from the rest of the sample.

The resulting model of alcoholism postulated that three types of external pressure—family background, cultural pressure, and adult situation—interacted to cause alcoholism. The family situation of the prealcoholic was likely to be stressful; furthermore, it was not likely to meet dependency needs consistently or to offer a clear model of the male role. Cultural pressures are derived from the contradiction between the male role depicted by society (responsible, courageous) and the behavior exhibited by the father (cowardly and deviant). The child resolved this conflict by attempting to enact the stereotypic male role while covertly satisfying dependency needs. This resolution being incomplete, the conflict continued into adulthood, where alcoholism developed as a result of the collapse of the stereotypic self-image and the emergence of dependency needs. The consumption of alcohol served to satisfy dependency needs by evoking feelings of warmth, comfort, and power while decreasing feelings of inadequacy through the presentation of the manly image of a "hard drinker."

These and related psychoanalytic theories concerning the development of alcoholism have been criticized for possessing a number of limitations. Psychoanalytic models have been described as tautological, as subscribing to the logical fallacy of deducing etiology from outcome (Blum, 1966). Due to reliance on retrospective self-reports and individual case studies, psychoanalytic models tend to lack empirical support. Not only are psychoanalytic models purely theoretical but they have led to no consistent diagnostic, treatment, or outcome criteria for alcoholism. Last, similar personality syndromes and family constellations have been proposed as the antecedents for alcoholism and a number of other forms of psychopathology. Given the outlined limitations, the contributions of psychoanalytic theory have been limited and range afield from current views of the etiology and treatment of alcoholism.

1.2. The Alcoholic Personality

A recent review on the alcoholic personality (Cox, 1979) outlined a number of reasons for interest in this line of research. They include investigation of the etiology of alcoholism, detection and prediction of alcoholic tendencies to facilitate prevention and early treatment, differential assignment of alcoholic types to optimally effective treatment, and assessment of personality antecedents and consequents of alcohol use. It is not surprising, then, that a number of personality scales have been applied to the investigation of alcoholics' characteristics and of distinctions between alcoholics and various nonalcoholic control groups. Among the assessment instruments employed are self-report measures, projective tests (e.g., the Rorschach and Thematic Apperception Test, or TAT), picture drawing, locus-of-control measures, alcoholism scales, and personality inventories, (e.g., the Minnesota Multiphasic Personality Inventory, or MMPI). Due to limitations in study design and contradictions in resulting findings, many behavioral psychologists view the yield of such studies over the past fifty years as relatively limited in terms of explaining the etiology of excessive alcohol use.

A good example of inconsistency in findings is provided by review of work employing the Rorschach. These studies have produced results supporting oral dependency needs in alcoholics (Bertrand & Masling, 1969; Tahka, 1966; Weiss & Masling, 1970), and results finding no support for distinctions between alcoholics and nonalcoholic psychiatric patients (Ackerman, 1971; Freed, 1976). The research on locus of control has also produced inconsistent results (Barnes, 1979). Some studies have suggested that alcoholics have greater internal locus of control than nonalcoholics (Costello & Manders, 1974; Distefano, Pryer, & Garrison, 1972; O'Leary, Donovan, & Hague, 1974), while others indicate that alcoholics show tendencies toward greater external locus of control (Butts & Chotlos, 1973) or report no differences in the control orientation of alcoholics and nonalcoholics (Donovan & O'Leary, 1975).

Limited support for the notion of an alcoholic personality as well as failure to isolate a personality pattern specific to alcoholics have emerged from personality investigations employing the MMPI. As Butcher and Owen (1978) noted, as many as 96 publications addressing alcohol and drug abuse issues using the MMPI were published in the period 1972–1977, reflecting the great interest in this type of research. Most of these, however, are cross-sectional, biased by extreme samples, limited by problems inherent in retrospective self-reporting, and void of multivariate, multimethod assessment. Nevertheless, the literature does suggest that there are clearly defined subtypes of alcoholics which have been replicated across samples (Brown, 1950; Goldstein & Linden, 1969). Further, other researchers have shown that differences in self-reported alcohol consumption among groups other than alcoholics can be predicted by MMPI profile types.

For example, Whitelock, Overall, and Patrick (1971) examined self-reported alcohol use and MMPI responding among psychiatric patients and found that three of four identified profile types resembled those described by Goldstein and Linden (1969). In this study more severe alcohol use was associated with report of greater subjective distress such as anxiety and depression, while lower use scores were more common among patients whose profiles were indicative of antisocial or sociopathic features. Complementary results were reported by Sutker, Brantly, and Allain (1980), who found that self-reported alcohol use among 500 "driving under the influence" male offenders was significantly related to MMPI prototypic profile types. These investigators identified two profile patterns associated with comparatively high levels of alcohol consumption. Most pronounced was the relationship between higher drinking levels and profile patterns characterized by prominent elevations on Scale 2, indicating depressed affect and pessimistic mentation. Second, individuals defined by a peak elevation on Scale 2 and a less exaggerated score on Scale 4 also estimated significantly more average alcohol consumption.

The MMPI features that have been found to distinguish alcoholics from other groups include high psychopathic deviance or sociopathy, depression, anxiety, and psychasthenia (Clopton, 1978; Cox, 1979). However, personality comparisons of alcoholics and heroin addicts show that depressive symptomatology is probably more characteristic of alcoholics, whereas sociopathy may be more fundamental to illicit drug use (Overall, 1973; Sutker, Archer, Brantly, & Kilpatrick, 1979). In any event, it is likely that tests of depression or other negative affect are significantly influenced by chronic alcohol or drug use, among other factors; therefore the extent to which negative affect states/traits or proclivities toward social deviance are predictive of maladaptive alcohol use is yet to be determined. Attempts to distinguish alcoholics from nonalcoholics using a variety of alcoholism scales (e.g., MacAndrew, 1965) have met with some success. However, use of the scales often yields large percentages of false positives and false negatives (Cox, 1979) and may not distinguish typically antisocial groups such as addicts and prisoners from alcoholics (Butcher & Owen, 1978).

At present, the consensus of opinion concerning evidence for a single, unique configuration of personality characteristics in alcoholics is negative (Cox, 1979; Keller, 1972a; Sutherland, Schroeder, & Tordella, 1950; Syme, 1957). However, studies have identified several personality profile types that are common across alcoholic and alcohol use groups. Hence, researchers have largely abandoned the search for a specific alcoholic personality in favor of a more sophisticated multitrait, multivariate explanatory framework which takes into account personal as well as situational factors and their interaction. Certainly, inconsistent findings have been a major problem for research on the alcoholic personality, reflecting methodological limitations of personality research in general. Common errors include the lack of controlled comparisons, failure to match on demographic characteristics of alcoholic and nonalcoholic samples, and use of restricted samples from which generalizations are derived. Additionally, responses to personality measures are susceptible to variations in test-taking situations and conditions as well as to such personal factors as intelligence, race, and gender.

The question of cause versus effect has been a ticklish one for personality research. Since few longitudinal studies (e.g., McCord & McCord, 1960) have been conducted, it is difficult to make decisions about whether a specific personality characteristic plays a role in predisposing an individual to alcohol misuse or results from the behavior in question. Assumptions concerning the nature of personality also suggest some possible conceptual limitations in personality research, particularly as it has been developed historically. Much of the research on the alcoholic personality is conceived within a framework that views personality as a set of consistent characteristics generalized across situations. This trait approach has been criticized for not taking into account personal and situational variables, which may have profound effects on individual responses within and across situations (Mischel, 1968; 1973). Mischel (1973) has suggested that use of a cognitive social-learning approach that incorporates environmental conditions, personal variables, and phenomenological events maximizes the likelihood that personality will be predictive of behavior. The use of this more comprehensive approach offers promise for future research on personality and alcohol use. Hence, researchers are turning to more sophisticated conceptual frameworks, multivariate in scope, to investigate both initial and sustained alcohol use (Kandel, 1978; Nathan & Lansky, 1978; Sadava & Forsyth, 1977; Sutker, 1982).

1.3. Power Motivation

McClelland and his colleagues began their work on the relationship of fantasies to alcohol use with no plan to question the widely held psychoanalytic view that dependency needs were the motivation for alcohol use (Kalin, McClelland, & Kahn, 1965). However, by the end of their 10-year program to investigate the psychological motivation for excessive alcohol use, they had reached the conclusion that the need for power, not dependency, was the primary motivation for excessive alcohol use in males (McClelland, Davis, Kalin, & Wanner, 1972). This power motivation theory was based on data gathered through a variety of methods, including content analysis of folktales, cross-cultural comparisons, and experimental investigations in which male subjects were administered the TAT before and after drinking alcohol in a variety of situations. Summarized, these sources suggested "that drinking serves to increase power fantasies and that heavy liquor drinking characterizes those whose personal power needs are strong and whose level of inhibition is low" (McClelland *et al.*, 1972, p. 276). It was hypothesized that generally the

> ingestion of alcohol cues off thoughts of strength and power in men everywhere, apparently for physiological reasons. Taken in distilled form, it creates burning sensations in the throat, stimulates the secretions of adrenalin which has broad mobilizing effects throughout the body. . . . These diffuse sensations of increased strength, particularly those induced by distilled liquor, are readily elaborated into fantasies of increased power—by some men more readily than others and in some situations more than in others. (p. 334)

A distinction was also made between the effects of light and heavy drinking. Though both forms of drinking increase thoughts of power, light drinking is said to increase thoughts of "socialized power" while heavy drinking produces thoughts of "personalized power." Socialized power thoughts involve having influence with others for their own or a social good. Thoughts of personal power involve seeing the world as being highly competitive and as requiring the ability to win out over one's adversaries. Such thoughts are sometimes expressed in an aggressive or sexual manner.

The male alcoholic, who by definition is addicted to alcohol, is said to be one whose concerns about personal power are much greater than his concerns about socialized power. Such an individual may also lack inhibition and/or behave impulsively because large amounts of alcohol tend to decrease inhibitory thoughts. Excessive drinking serves as one of a number of outlets for the need for power. For example, a study of working-class men found that gambling, aggressive behavior, and the collection of prestige objects were alternative outlets for the need for personal power (McClelland et al., 1972).

Power motivation theory suggests that the exaggerated desire for personalized power develops as a result of a power conflict. This conflict may result from a number of factors including (1) a demand for the male to be strong and assertive; (2) little social support for the male role, which undercuts the demand for assertiveness; (3) lack of outlets for socialized power. A concern with personal power may also develop as a result of the male sex role, a demanding occupation, or increasing age. Men may then attempt to compensate for situations created by these and related factors by presenting a facade of strength while suppressing feelings of weakness and powerlessness. Alcohol may represent a way of fulfilling this purpose. Thus, events that continue to heighten the need for personal power would also serve to increase the tendency to consume alcohol. Alcohol can then be seen as reinforcing the feeling of power while decreasing the sense of personal responsibility for behavior.

Power motivation theory has certain implications for the treatment of excessive alcohol use. If it were possible to decrease the need for personalized power, it is likely that excessive drinking would also decrease. McClelland et al. (1972) proposed a number of solutions for an increased preoccupation with personal power. These include satisfying the power drive vicariously by collecting prestige items, socializing the personal power drive by joining an organization and working with others to gain collective power, or borrowing strength from powerful movements such as organized religion.

Many of these solutions were developed into a treatment program that has been applied to alcoholics (McClelland et al., 1972). In an initial attempt to facilitate the socialization of power needs, 20 problem drinkers were involved in a three-day didactic program consisting of small group meetings in which they were taught to recognize increased thoughts of power as a result of drinking and to develop alternative ways of satisfying the need for power. Data on the first six drinkers in the program include a four-month follow-up and eight-month telephone contact. It was reported that treatment had some short-term effects, such as improved interpersonal relationships and a return to the job market. For the most part, drinking continued but was more controlled.

Other studies in which power motivation training (PMT) has been applied to alcoholics have produced inconsistent results. Cutter, Boyatzis, and Clarey (1977) compared PMT to a treatment package consisting of individual and group therapy, meetings of Alcoholics Anonymous (AA), and disulfarim (Antabuse). The PMT program was described as an intensive educational–therapeutic experience designed to teach patients alternative ways of feeling powerful. Treatment interventions included behavioral exercises, group discussion, role playing, and lectures. One hundred inpatient alcoholics were randomly assigned to one of the two treatments. Days intoxicated and weeks worked 6 and 12 months following treatment served a outcome measures. Results indicated no significant effects for the type of treatment received or for the follow-up periods, and there were no significant interactions. Further analyses suggested that personality characteristics indicating authoritarianism were the most important factor in accounting for response to the two treatments. Patients with a need for authority responded well to the standard treatment, while more rebellious patients responded to the PMT, which was presented in a more didactic format. McClelland's (1977) reanalysis of these outcome data used both ability to work and sobriety as outcome measures. He reported a significantly higher rate of improvement at the 12-month period for PMT patients than for those in standard treatment. Even given this promising long-term outcome, the efficacy of PMT seems limited.

McClelland et al.'s (1972) conceptualization of the power motive as a mediator for excessive alcohol consumption has been challenged by the findings of Cutter, Key, Rothstein, and Jones (1973). Using TATs administered to 54 male hospitalized alcoholics, these investigators assessed expressions of power needs as well as inhibition before and after drinking. The results suggested that alcohol had no effect on power needs. However, the inhibition measure indicated that alcohol consumption led to a decrease in inhibition. It was concluded that inhibition rather than a need for power was more relevant to both the prediction of alcohol consumption and the treatment of alcoholism.

Overall, alternative explanations of the behaviors attributed to the need for power and the limited efficacy of PMT suggest a lack of empirical validation of power motivation theory. Though the need for power may be expressed by some social drinkers and alcoholics, the data presently available suggest that power motivation theory does not account fully for excessive alcohol use.

2. THE DISEASE MODEL

The disease concept of alcoholism has often been attributed to E. M. Jellinek (1952, 1960), one of its more articulate proponents. In his early writings on the subject, Jellinek, 1952) described both the disease of alcoholism and its phases. He defined the disease of alcoholism as involving addiction to alcohol that included loss-of-control drinking. Drinkers who did not experience loss of control but evidenced the psychological problems which led to excessive drinking were said to be nonaddictive alcoholics. Jellinek then proceeded to outline an elaborate model of the four major phases of alcoholism and to specify the behaviors and symptoms characteristic of each phase. Jellinek's conceptualization of the phases of alcohol addiction was based on questionnaires administered to 2,000 male members of AA. Though he sought to limit his presentation by indicating that not all symptoms occurred in all alcoholics or occurred in the same sequence, Jellinek did indicate that the following phases and sequence of symptoms were "characteristic of the great majority of alcohol addicts" (p. 676).

The four phases of alcoholism were said to be progressive, beginning with the prealcoholic, symptomatic phase and moving through the prodromal, crucial, and chronic phases. The *prealcoholic phase* involves the experience of relief from tension via alcohol on an almost daily basis. Tolerance for alcohol may also begin to occur. During the *prodromal phase*, the alcoholic may experience "blackouts" and become so preoccupied with alcohol that he begins to engage in behaviors such as surreptitious drinking and to experience guilt because of his drinking. In the *crucial phase*, the drinker experiences loss of control, which marks the beginning of the disease process. Jellinek defines loss of control as meaning "that any drinking of alcohol starts a chain reaction which is felt by the drinker as a physical demand for alcohol" (p. 679). Loss of control is established after a number of intoxicating experiences; although it is said to occur after the individual has begun to drink, it does not in itself lead to the initiation of drinking. Though loss-of-control drinking is balanced by periods of abstinence, the alcoholic's behavior is now so centered around alcohol that he engages in grandiose behavior and rationalization while exhibiting social isolation and neglect of health care behaviors (e.g., nutrition) as well as family relationships. The final, *chronic phase* involves engaging in obsessive drinking that results in prolonged periods of intoxication marked by cognitive impairment, physical symptoms such as tremors, psychomotor inhibition, and a loss of alcohol tolerance.

In his later work, Jellinek (1960) elaborated on the disease model of alcoholism. He revised his earlier definition of alcoholism to "any use of alcoholic beverages that causes any damage to the individual, or society or both" (p. 35). Building on this broad conceptualization, he further specified five species of alcoholism. The first is *alpha alcoholism,* defined as psychological dependence on the effects of alcohol to relieve physical or emotional distress. Though drinking in alpha alcoholism is said to be "undisciplined," it is not seen as progressive or as an illness. *Beta alcoholism* is described in terms of development of medical complications related to alcohol use (e.g., gastritis, cirrhosis of the liver) without physical or psychological dependence on alcohol. *Gamma alcoholism* is said to involve (1) increased tissue tolerance to alcohol; (2) physical dependence manifested by withdrawal symptoms and craving; (3) loss-of-control drinking within a drinking bout; and (4) adaptation of cell metabolism. Gamma alcoholism produces the most serious physical and social damage and is the preeminent form of alcoholism found in the United States. *Delta alcoholism* shares many of the characteristics of gamma alcoholism, but rather than exhibiting a loss of control, delta alcoholics are unable to abstain from drinking for any extended period of time. Last, the *epsilon alcoholic* is one who engages in periodic excessive drinking. In Jellinek's view, this list, although not exhaustive, described the most prevalent types of excessive alcohol use.

After presenting his broad definition and further describing the most common species of alcoholism, Jellinek became more restrictive in his designation of what species of alcoholism constituted a disease. He designated gamma and delta alcoholism as disease processes because they involved physical symptoms such as increased tissue tolerance, craving, loss-of-control drinking, adaptive cell metabolism, and withdrawal symptoms. Alpha, beta, and epsilon alcoholism were designated nonaddictive forms of excessive drinking. Jellinek was relatively cautious in his presentation of the disease model. For example, he limited his definition of alcoholism as a disease to the two species in which physical symptoms occurred. The other species of alcoholism (alpha, beta, and epsilon) were not seen as disease processes even though they are marked by excessive drinking. He was also careful to mention other determinants of excessive drinking, ranging from cultural and socioeconomic factors to learning. The role of psychological factors such as learning was seen as relevant predominantly to the initiation of the addictive process. In discussing the role of learning, Jellinek wrote,

> There remains the fact that a learning theory of drinking in the well-defined terms of psychological discipline is essential to all species of alcoholism, including addiction. The learning process ... is a prerequisite to bring about the conditions which are necessary for the development of addiction in the pharmacological sense.... Neither would it (learning theory) conflict with a disease conception of one or the other species of alcoholism. (p. 77)

The disease model has become accepted as the basis of excessive alcohol use (Criteria Committee, National Council on Alcoholism, 1972). One reason for the popularity of Jellinek's model is the fact that it facilitated the trend away from moral models of alcohol use to less judgmental medical models. The presentation of Jellinek's model also coincided with the growth of movements such as AA and offered "medical legitimization" (Hershon, 1974, p. 125) of popular lay notions about the nature of alcoholism. This legitimization led to the establishment of medical treatment as the proper treatment for excessive alcohol use. Viewing alcoholism as an illness requiring medical treatment reduced the stigma attached to alcoholics (Glatt, 1976). The alcoholic was offered a sick role which removed the responsibility for many actions, thereby reducing the burdens of guilt and remorse. It also provided a socially accepted excuse for abstinence from social drinking. Last, those aspects of alcoholism that conformed to the characteristics of a disease requiring medical treatment (e.g., cirrhosis) and mechanisms (tolerance and withdrawal) that suggested a physiological basis for alcoholism served to substantiate disease notions.

The acceptance of Jellinek's model led to the simplification and reification of what had originally been presented as a series of working hypotheses. Alcoholism became popularly viewed as a disease characterized by craving for alcohol and loss-of-control drinking for which the only acceptable treatment was total abstinence. The existence of a disease process was interpreted to mean that alcoholics were somehow constitutionally different from social drinkers (e.g., AA's notion of an allergy to alcohol) and thus could never touch alcohol.

After much reinterpretation and reification, the current disease model of alcoholism may be said to incorporate the following propositions:

1. There is a unitary phenomenon which can be identified as alcoholism.
2. Alcoholics and prealcoholics are essentially different from nonalcoholics.
3. Alcoholics may sometimes experience an irresistible physical craving for alcohol or a strong psychological compulsion to drink.
4. Alcoholics gradually develop a process called "loss of control" over drinking and possibly even an inability to stop drinking.
5. Alcoholism is a permanent and irreversible condition.
6. Alcoholism is a progressive disease which follows an inexorable development through a distinct series of phases. (Pattison, Sobell, & Sobell, 1977, p. 2)

Many researchers have questioned the nature of the disease process outlined by Jellinek and his followers. Their concerns have encompassed a number of critical issues. Some critics pointed out that whether or not alcoholism is seen as a disease is dependent on the definition used for both alcoholism and disease (Glatt, 1976; Robinson, 1972). It is also reasoned that if the disease model focuses on purely organic pathology and physical symptoms, it should not be applied to alcoholism (Glatt, 1976). Such a limited focus is seen as being too simplistic because it does not include complex nonphysiological factors and does not consider the multiple etiologies of alcoholism. It also shifts emphasis away from social, cultural, and psychological factors which could lead to improved techniques for prevention and treatment (Davis, 1974). There are also objections to inadequacies in the methodology of Jellinek's work, much of which was based on clinical experience and retrospective self-reports of individuals already converted to a disease-oriented view of alcoholism, for example, AA members. Those who believe that drinking behavior is subject to personal control also object to the fact that the disease model provides the alcoholic with a convenient excuse for drinking and denies the opportunity of accepting responsibility for the drinking behavior (Hershon, 1974).

Although debates concerning the disease model have been heated, they are often based on differences in theoretical orientation and opinion. However, Jellinek has provided researchers with two potentially verifiable manifestations of the disease process, the notion of craving for alcohol and loss-of-control drinking. Both proponents and opponents of the model have sought to prove or disprove the existence of these phenomena.

2.1. Craving/Loss of Control

Research on craving and loss-of-control drinking has often been confused by definitional problems that have limited attempts to validate these constructs empirically (Maisto & Schefft, 1977). For example, Jellinek's (1952) early definition of these constructs involved a unidimensional model in which minimal amounts of alcohol triggered craving and loss-of-control drinking. Later Jellinek (1960) described a multidimensional model in which alcohol consumption figured as only one of a number of factors (e.g., situational, psychological, cultural) which triggered craving and loss-of-control drinking. Similarly, other traditional models of alcoholism (e.g., that of AA) have defined craving, loss of control, and alcoholism as interdependent constructs without first defining each construct independently. The resulting circularity impedes both the identification and prediction of either of these phenomena. Even given these methodological problems, attempts to examine the mechanism and processes involved in craving and loss-of-control drinking have provided some insight into excessive alcohol use.

Merry (1966) was the first investigator to assess empirically the relationship between consuming a single dose of alcohol and loss-of-control drinking in alcoholics. Over a three-week period, he provided nine inpatient alcoholics with a drink containing an orange flavor and either vodka or water. After consuming this "vitamin mixture," subjects were asked to rate their degree of craving. Merry found no significant differences in craving for alcohol between days when the alcoholics received a mixture containing vodka versus when they received a water mixture. There were also no signs of physical dependence on alcohol. It was concluded that loss of control in the alcoholic was not brought about by a single drink. The author suggested that "psychological and environmental factors may be more important influences in initiating loss of control drinking" (p. 1258).

Subsequently, Engle and Williams (1972) reached a similar conclusion using a more elaborate research design. Forty alcoholics were randomly assigned to four groups in which the alcohol content of a vitamin mixture and information about the content of the mixture were systematically varied. The only significant difference found in ratings of cravings following consumption of this beverage was between the two groups who had received the mixture containing alcohol. The group given alcohol but given no information about the alcohol content of the mixture reported less craving than the group that had been informed that they were receiving alcohol. It was again concluded that psychological factors have an important effect on the alcoholic's desire for a drink. A reanalysis of these data substantiated the role of cognitive factors (Maisto, Lauerman, & Adesso, 1977).

Marlatt, Demming, and Reid (1973) assessed the role of cognitive factors in loss-of-control drinking by providing alcoholics and social drinkers with ad lib access to a beverage that contained tonic or vodka and tonic. In a taste-rating task, the subject's expectancy concerning the alcoholic content of the beverage was varied via instructions to create four groups: told alcohol/given alcohol; told alcohol/ given tonic; told tonic/given tonic; told tonic/given alcohol. This four-group design, which permits assessment of the independent effects of both psychological (expectancy) and pharmacological (beverage content) factors, is called the "balanced placebo design" (Marlatt & Rohsenow, 1980). In the Marlatt *et al.* (1973) study, a primer dose of the beverage to which the subject had been assigned was administered 20 minutes before the beginning of the taste-rating task. It was found that for both social drinkers and alcoholics, the subject's *expectancy* of the content of the beverage determined the amount of beverage consumed, regardless of the actual beverage content. The results highlighted the role of cognitive factors, such as expectancy, in loss-of-control drinking. Taken along with previous research in this area, pharmacologically mediated explanations of loss of control were cast in doubt. Berg, Laberg, Skutle, and Ohman (1981) elaborated on this design and also reported that the behavioral and physiological responses of alcoholics were controlled by instruction-induced expectancies rather than the pharmacological properties of alcohol. Further research employing the balanced placebo design will be discussed later in this chapter.

Other researchers (Glatt, 1967, 1976; Ludwig & Wikler, 1974; Rankin, Hodgson, & Stockwell, 1979) have attempted to maintain the validity of the constructs of craving and loss of control by reinterpreting them. Glatt (1967, 1976) chose to expand the definition of loss-of-control drinking beyond the physiologically mediated construct hypothesized by Jellinek (1960). His multifactorial model (Glatt, 1976) involves psychosocial and pharmacological factors as well as physiology. Loss of control is defined as meaning that an alcoholic "can never be certain that he will be able to stop on a given occasion once he has started to drink" (p. 140). Loss-of-control drinking may be said to be physiologically mediated only after an unspecified critical blood alcohol level has been reached. At blood alcohol levels below this critical threshold, alcohol consumption is mainly influenced by psychological, sociocultural, or environmental factors. This modification of his earlier model (Glatt, 1967) does not include the critical blood alcohol threshold; instead, physiological factors are seen as but one of a number of variables that determine loss of control.

A classical conditioning model of craving has been proposed by Ludwig and Wikler (1974). They describe craving for alcohol as representing the cognitive correlate of a "subclinical withdrawal syndrome" similar to that found with opiates. Craving, which occurs during withdrawal from alcohol, is classically conditioned to a wide variety of environmental stimuli and emotional states associated with drinking and/or the process of withdrawal. Exposure to the conditioned stimuli associated with withdrawal elicits the symptoms of craving. This mechanism is said to protect the alcoholic against a potential source of threat (e.g., anxiety, withdrawal symptoms) by alerting him or her to a potential source of relief (alcohol).

In Ludwig and Wikler's model, the relationship between craving and alcohol consumption is not always a direct one because craving can be modified by a number of factors including setting, the availability of alcohol, and the alcoholic's ability to correctly label his or her internal state of arousal as craving for alcohol. Thus craving does not invariably lead to alcohol consumption. Usually, however, the first drink sets off a sequence of responses and behaviors developed in previous drinking episodes. Under the proper set of circumstances, craving will lead to drinking and associated loss of control. Loss of control is described as the alcoholic's "relative inability to regulate ethanol consumption" (p. 122). Thus consumption of the first drink may act as an "appetizer," stimulating craving and thus increasing the probability that loss of control will occur.

In an empirical test of this theory of craving, Ludwig, Wikler, and Stark (1974) conducted a study in which 24 detoxified male alcoholics were administered one of three doses of alcohol (no-alcohol placebo, low dose, high dose) under a label (favorite alcoholic beverage) or a nonlabel (ethyl alcohol in sweetened mixture) condition designed to heighten the external cues associated with prior drinking. In order to determine the effects of the independent variables on craving and alcohol-seeking behavior, a variety of subjective behavioral and physiological measures were assessed. It was hypothesized that the low-dose alcohol would produce greater craving for alcohol than the high dose, since the high dose would be more likely to satisy craving while the low dose would act as an appetizer stimulating a craving for more alcohol. It was also hypothesized that craving and alcohol-seeking behavior would be highest in the labeled condition, in which external cues relating to alcohol consumption were maximized.

Findings were not always consistent with these hypotheses. It was found that in the label condition both the high and low doses of alcohol induced similar alcohol acquisition behavior. The label condition also led to significantly higher levels of craving than the nonlabel condition. This finding provides support for the role of cognitive factors such as expectancy in the experience of craving and loss of control (Maisto et al., 1977; Marlatt, 1978; Marlatt et al., 1973). Physiological measures (EEG, heart and respiratory rate) also did not support the hypothesis that "an adequate amount of alcohol . . . should elicit conditioned withdrawal responses (or comparable states of CNS–ANS 'arousal') that, in turn, serve as interoceptive cues for increased craving and alcohol seeking behavior" (p. 544). Keller (1972b) has similarly modified Jellinek's model to include the role of learning, with loss of control being triggered by an unspecified complex of internal and external stimuli.

Another multifactorial model of craving, based on learning theory, has recently been proposed (Hodgson, Rankin, & Stockwell, 1979; Rankin, Hodgson, & Stockwell, 1979). In a formulation somewhat similar to Ludwig and Wikler's (1974), this model suggests that craving may be a learned compulsion resulting from repeated consumption of alcohol in order to escape and avoid withdrawal symptoms. Exposure to the cognitive or physiological cues associated with the termination of drinking leads to the experience of craving. Craving is said to be governed by a set of complex variables such as consequences of the behavior, the setting, and psychological and social factors. The overt behavior related to craving (e.g., loss-of-control drinking) is just one of a number of responses available to the alcoholic. Thus, loss of control is relative and is dependent on how the alcoholic interprets a particular situation. Physiological, biochemical, and cognitive correlates of craving also exist.

Rankin *et al.* (1979), employed speed of consuming the first drink as a behavioral measure of craving. They reported the existence of a priming effect in "severely dependent" alcoholics who were informed of the type of alcoholic beverage being consumed. Even given these results, which could be interpreted to support the disease model, the authors stressed that craving is only one of a number of factors contributing to excessive drinking.

The development of a behavioral measure of craving may provide a means of empirically assessing the existence of craving. However, the continued use of research designs that fail to assess the role of cognitive factors such as expectancy present methodological barriers to the interpretation of the research on craving. For the most part models of the mechanism underlying craving and loss-of-control drinking have provided descriptive rather than empirically verifiable constructs and may be best described as "unproductive" (Maisto & Schefft, 1977). Whatever the outcome of the debate concerning the existence of craving and loss of control, the finding that one drink of alcohol does not automatically trigger excessive drinking has been replicated (Engle & Williams, 1972; Marlatt *et al.,* 1973; Merry, 1966). When interpreted within a social-learning-theory framework, this finding has reinforced the development of controlled drinking as a promising alternative treatment strategy for some problem drinkers (Lloyd & Salzberg, 1975; Miller & Caddy, 1977; Pattison, 1976; Sobell, 1978).

3. BEHAVIORAL AND SOCIAL-LEARNING APPROACH

Behavioral models of the determinants of alcohol consumption share common assumptions concerning the central role of learning in the development of patterns of excessive drinking. Though developed within a similar empirically derived mode of inquiry, they vary in the significance assigned to a variety of social, environmental, and cognitive factors. The four topics to be presented here represent the variety of behavioral viewpoints. The traditional behavioral approach is presented in our discussion of the tension reduction hypothesis which was derived from research on the Hullian model of learning and reinforcement. Social learning theory is represented by our discussion of the role of modeling, while the section on the role of expectancy reflects the continuing expansion of behavioral researchers into the realm of cognition. Last, our discussion of relapse prevention presents an intervention strategy which incorporates a variety of cognitive and behavioral factors into a comprehensive model that may also have implications for etiology.

3.1. Social Learning: The Role of Modeling

The consumption of alcohol has often been described as a socially mediated activity (Bandura, 1969; MacAndrew & Edgerton, 1969). Social-learning approaches to alcohol use endorse this view and describe excessive drinking as a habit developed via the mechanisms of learning. In essence, adaptive and maladaptive styles and levels of alcohol use are said to develop via mechanisms such as vicarious learning, modeling, and the positively reinforcing pharmacological properties of alcohol. For example, Bandura (1969) defines the alcoholic as someone who has acquired "through differential reinforcement and modeling experience, alcohol consumption as a widely generalized dominant response to aversive stimulation" (p. 536). The individual variation in such learning experiences results in a variety of drinking styles that can be placed on a continuum ranging from abstinence on the one hand to the problem drinker or alcoholic on the other. On such a continuum the "social drinker" represents a moderate level of alcohol consumption.

The role of modeling in the development of drinking habits is complex. According to social-learning theory (Bandura, 1969; 1977a), models can serve to teach new behaviors, strengthen or weaken the performance of previously learned responses, or enhance the value of a particular stimulus or behavior. The observed consequences (positive or negative reinforcement) of a particular behavior also have an impact on its subsequent performance. Thus, a behavior that is followed by a reward or a lack of negative consequences is likely to be modeled by the observer. A behavior that is followed by punishment or other negative consequences is likely to be inhibited by the observer. Drinking styles as well as cultural norms and subgroup mores about alcohol use are said to be transmitted via the modeling of socializing agents such as the family, the media, and peers. Since drinking behavior as well as the circumstances in which drinking occurs has an impact on future drinking, the role of such models is very important. For example, it has often been reported that parental drinking habits are predictive of the drinking patterns of adolescents, such that adolescent problem drinkers frequently have heavy-drinking parents (Briddle, Bank, & Marlin, 1980; O'Leary, O'Leary, & Donovan, 1976; Wechsler & McFadden, 1979). On the other hand, adolescents who abstain from alcohol or drink lightly tend to have parents who are nondrinkers (Wechsler & McFadden, 1979). Genetic explanations have not fully accounted for such similarities in drinking habits.

Social-learning theory provides a viable framework for explaining similarity, which suggests the following. In a family where alcohol is used only on specific occasions, as during special meals or religious rituals, offspring learn to moderate alcohol use and are likely to develop patterns of light social drinking. In a family where alcohol is used as a means of coping with a variety of emotional states and environmental stresses, offspring are likely to develop similar patterns of alcohol usage. If alcohol proves even intermittently reinforcing on these occasions, its use is likely to be maintained. Once habituated to heavy social drinking, physical or psychological dependence can develop and lead to problem drinking.

The role of the media, particularly television, in modeling patterns of alcohol use is also now being assessed (Garlington, 1977; Lowery, 1980). This research suggests that media portrayals of alcohol use may also be a powerful form of social influence, both providing information about drinking behavior and reinforcing notions that alcohol use is a socially approved means of solving problems. Lowery analyzed alcohol use on daytime soap operas in terms of portrayals of alcohol as a means of social facilitation (enhanced enjoyment of social interaction, reduction of social tension), crisis management, and escape from chronic stress. It was found that a majority of the portrayals involved social facilitation, with escape from reality and crisis management second and third in frequency. In a majority of cases alcohol use was either reinforced or had no consequences. The only type of drinking that received negative consequences was escape-from-reality drinking, and these consequences were usually only temporary. Social-learning theory suggests that televised presentations of alcohol as a means of (1) facilitating social interaction, (2) coping with stress and negative emotional states, or (3) reinforcing masculine identity are likely to increase alcohol use and abuse, since such presentations portray alcohol as being pleasurable and rewarding.

Since alcohol consumption often takes place in the presence of friends or peers who can serve as models for excessive alcohol use, researchers have also studied the mechanisms of this social influence process. Much of the research has focused on the impact of light- or heavy-drinking models on the alcohol consumption of heavy-drinking males who are most likely at risk to become problem drinkers. The research in this area has recently been reviewed (Collins & Marlatt, 1981). A brief overview of these findings indicates the following.

Initial research on the effects of modeling on social drinking involved male college students classified as heavy social drinkers. In the first study of modeling influences on alcohol consumption (Caudill & Marlatt, 1975), the subjects were asked to participate in a taste-rating task in which they made discriminations between the taste characteristics of three wines. The taste-rating task had previously served as an unobtrusive measure of alcohol consumption (Marlatt, 1978). Ratings were made in the presence of a confederate of the experimenter who modeled a predetermined rate of consumption. During the 15-minute taste-rating task, subjects were exposed to either a heavy-consumption model (700 ml of wine), a light-consumption model (100 ml of wine), or no model. The results showed that subjects exposed to a heavy-drinking model consumed significantly more than subjects exposed to a light-drinking model or no model. There was no significant difference between the light-drinking and the no-model control condition. Caudill and Marlatt hypothesized that the modeling effect may have occurred as a result of social pressure, including competition and/or the fact that the model provided cues concerning appropriate performance in an ambiguous situation.

Subsequently, the taste-rating task has been used in a number of studies designed to assess the role of modeling and other social influence processes in alcohol consumption (Cooper, Waterhouse, & Sobell, 1979; Hendricks, Sobell, & Cooper, 1978; Lied & Marlatt, 1979). The results of these studies have replicated and extended those reported by Caudill and Marlatt (1975). For example, Hendricks, Sobell, and Cooper (1978) sought to determine the nature of the social influence process that produced the modeling effect by varying the presence or absence of the confederate model. They created three social conditions consisting of (1) coaction, in which the subject and confederate simultaneously performed an art-rating task followed by the taste-rating task (wine); (2) audience facilitation, in which the subject and confederate performed the two tasks in reverse order from one another; and (3) imitation, in which the confederate first performed the taste-rating task and then left the room while it was performed by the subject. Subjects were also exposed to heavy- (700 ml) or light- (100 ml) consumption models. The results indicated that subjects exposed to a heavy-consumption confederate drank significantly more than subjects in the light-consumption condition. This was due mainly to the fact that subjects exposed to a heavy-consumption confederate in the coaction social condition drank significantly more than subjects in other heavy-consumption social conditions. It was concluded that the modeling effect was a result of coaction rather than imitation.

Other researchers have studied the modeling effect in natural (Reid, 1978) or seminaturalistic settings (Caudill & Lipscomb, 1980; Collins & Marlatt, 1982; DeRicco & Garlington, 1977; DeRicco & Nieman, 1980; Garlington & DeRicco, 1977; Parks, Collins, & Marlatt, 1982) and have produced results similar to that found in laboratory analogue studies. For example, Marlatt and his colleagues (Collins & Marlatt, 1982; Parks et al., 1982) have made use of a cocktail bar setting (The BARLAB) in which dim lights, music, waitresses, and ad lib access to alcoholic beverages provide the subject with a relatively natural drinking experience. In a typical study done in the BARLAB, subjects may spend 30 to 40 minutes sitting at one of a number of tables engaged in friendly conversation with a confederate, just as they might in a bar. Reid (1978) went so far as to plant experimental confederates in a real bar. Differences between a laboratory and a bar setting have been shown to influence both the quantity of alcohol consumed and the drinking style of individuals. For example, Strickler, Dobbs, and Maxwell (1979) reported that subjects drink significantly more alcohol at a significantly faster rate in a bar than in a laboratory setting. The fact that studies conducted in both of these settings have produced similar results suggests the existence of a powerful effect wherein an individual's consumption of alcohol will vary to match that of a drinking partner. This effect is so potent that even providing subjects with the information that an attempt to influence their behavior is being made does not seem to have any impact (DeRicco & Garlington, 1977).

Researchers have also found a number of characteristics that modify the modeling effect, including gender (Cooper et al., 1979; Lied & Marlatt, 1979), drinking history (Lied & Marlatt, 1979) and the nature of the interaction between the drinking partners (Parks et al., 1982; Reid, 1978). The research on gender effects suggests that both males and females drink more when exposed to a heavy-drinking model of either sex than when exposed to a nondrinking partner. However, male subjects drink more than female subjects when exposed to a heavy-drinking male model (Cooper et al., 1979; Lied & Marlatt, 1979). The modeling of light consumption occurs when subjects are exposed to models of the same sex or of the opposite sex.

Most importantly, drinking history has been found to have an effect on the modeling of heavy drinking. When exposed to a heavy-drinking model, light drinkers have shown a nonsignificant increase in alcohol consumption while heavy drinkers (particularly males) have shown a significant increase (Lied & Marlatt, 1979). This finding and the other pieces of evidence concerning the modeling effect suggest a powerful mechanism for the development of problem drinking. The individual who develops heavy-drinking habits (via learning) and who consumes alcohol with other heavy- or problem-drinking friends is likely to increase his or her consumption (via modeling) to match or outdo such friends and thus move into the realm of problem drinking. The fact that modeling influences have also been found with alcoholics, particularly when the confederate was seen as a peer who could also drink heavily (Caudill & Lipscomb, 1980), substantiates this hypothesis.

3.2. Tension-Reduction Hypothesis

The tension-reduction hypothesis (TRH) is one of the first learning-based theories of alcohol use. The TRH states that alcohol serves to reduce tension and that this relief of tension reinforces further alcohol use. Once this learned relationship is established, experiences of tension (anxiety, stress, etc.) increase the probability of drinking, which in turn may lead to the development of excessive alcohol use.

Much of the initial research on the tension-reducing properties of alcohol is based on laboratory studies with animals. One of the early proponents of the TRH (Conger, 1956) described a series of experiments in which alcohol was shown to reduce avoidance behavior in rats subjected to an approach–avoidance conflict. These results were generalized to humans, and it was concluded that alcoholism in humans resulted from the reinforcement provided by reductions in either primary (physiological) or learned drives.

With the emphasis on Hullian drive-reduction theories current in the 1950s, this learning-theory approach to alcoholism was readily accepted. Further support for the TRH was also provided by commonsense notions of the effects of alcohol as a tension reducer and by the pharmacologically depressant properties of alcohol. Since its origin, the TRH has been subjected to rigorous research attempts to test and substantiate its basic assumptions. Interpretation of the results of this research has been contradictory.

Cappell and Herman (1972) reviewed the animal research literature, assessing such behavioral indexes of the TRH as avoidance and escape learning, conditioned suppression, and risk-taking behavior. It was concluded that in each of these areas empirical support for the TRH was either "negative, equivocal or contradictory" (p. 59). The only area where results with animals were said to be consistent with the TRH was research on conflict and experimental neurosis. Brown and Crowell (1974) have questioned this assessment of the relationship between tension reduction and conflict resolution. In their reanalysis of the conflict literature, it was suggested that alcohol's reduction of avoidance due to fear in an approach–avoidance conflict could actually increase conflict as approach to the goal increased. Thus, in humans, increased approach to a tension-producing situation could produce excessive drinking via increases in tension. In such a situation, alcohol consumption increases as a result of increased tension rather than from the reinforcement provided by the release of tension. Hodgson, Stockwell, and Rankin (1979) have also questioned the conclusions reached by Cappell and Herman. Their review of the animal research states that "the literature on experimental conflict, avoidance behavior, conditioned suppression, extinction and partial reinforcement has forced us to conclude that alcohol *can* inhibit fear and frustration" (p. 463). These contradictory conclusions seem based on methodological differences in interpretation of the research paradigms used in the animal literature. Hodgson *et al.* suggested that the lack of distinction between active and passive avoidance and one-way and two-way avoidance had created the inconsistencies found in the animal literature. By making distinctions between these avoidance paradigms, they were able to conclude that active avoidance was not reduced by alcohol but that passive avoidance was.

Similar methodological problems exist in the research on alcohol and tension reduction in humans. Beyond the problems of definition of terms and comparable research designs, Marlatt (1976) outlined problems associated with a lack of multiple outcome measures, variations in alcohol dosage, subject characteristics and situational factors, and a failure to control for expectancy effects. Thus, reviewers of the human research (Cappell, 1975; Higgins, 1976; Marlatt, 1976) have reported a paucity of clear empirical support for the TRH. Higgins (1976) concludes his review by stating that "despite an extensive and complex body of research, it must be concluded that the specific role of tension-reduction in the etiology of either normal or abusive drinking remains obscure. The research aimed at delineating the tension-reducing effects of alcohol is currently so entangled in a host of methodological and interpretational problems that very few generalizations are warranted" (p. 69). Resolution of these methodological problems often leads to the further undermining of the support for the claim that the pharmacological effects of alcohol reduce tension. The example of expectancy effects is a case in point.

Even in questioning the validity of the TRH, Cappell (1975) referred to its plausibility due to its consistency with our commonplace experiences. These commonplace experiences and other notions about the effects of alcohol often become reified into a system of beliefs about the positive effects of alcohol (Brown, Goodman, Inn, & Anderson, 1980; Isaacs, 1979; Southwick, Steele, Marlatt, & Lindell, 1981; Tamerin, Weiner, & Mendelson, 1970). Researchers have controlled for expectancy effects by independently varying these cognitive beliefs and the pharmacological effects of alcohol (Marlatt & Rohsenow, 1980). The results of studies of social anxiety, designed to test the TRH, have consistently indicated that beliefs about having consumed alcohol predominate over the pharmacological effects of alcohol (e.g., Abrams & Wilson, 1979; Wilson & Abrams, 1977). The inconsistency between beliefs and the pharmacological properties of alcohol may be due to the biphasic effects of alcohol. Light to moderate doses of alcohol act as a CNS stimulant while large amounts of alcohol act as a depressant (Russell & Mehrabian, 1975). Positive expectancies may develop from the initial stimulating effects of alcohol. Whatever the source, it seems that the anticipated effects of alcohol do not always correspond to its actual effects. These expectancies may not only motivate alcohol use but also mediate the effects of alcohol on a wide range of behaviors.

3.3. Cognitive Factors: The Role of Expectancy

Much of the confusion concerning the effects of alcohol has occurred because researchers tended to ignore the role of psychological factors in alcohol use. Initially, the effects of alcohol were attributed to its pharmacological properties. However, findings inconsistent with pharmacological explanations often occurred. Coincidental with a movement in behavioral psychology to incorporate cognitive phenomena into research design and treatment, researchers began to investigate the role of cognitive factors, particularly expectancy, in alcohol use.

In alcohol research, "expectancy" refers to the beliefs about the effects of alcohol that are held by an individual or sociocultural group. Our expectations about alcohol effects result from learning about factors such as the social situations in which alcohol can be consumed, the behavioral effects of alcohol, and societal reactions to the behavioral effects associated with alcohol use. For example, a belief held in a variety of cultures is that intoxication leads to a "time out" from accountability for transgressing social norms of appropriate behavior (MacAndrew & Edgerton, 1969). Generally, research on expectancy suggests that both social drinkers and alcoholics expect alcohol to have positive effects on affect and socially mediated behaviors (Brown, Goldman, Inn, & Anderson, 1980; Isaacs, 1979; Southwick *et al.,* 1981; Tamerin *et al.,* 1970).

The balanced placebo design was developed as a means of assessing expectancy effects by separating the pharmacological and psychological effects of a substance. It combined the traditional placebo design with an "antiplacebo" design. In the traditional placebo control design, all subjects are led to expect that they will receive an active substance. However, only half the subjects receive the active substance and half receive an inert substance. The antiplacebo procedure involves the expectation of receiving an inert substance while actually receiving either the inert substance or an active substance. The result is a 2 × 2 design in which the actual substance consumed and instructions concerning the substance are indepen-

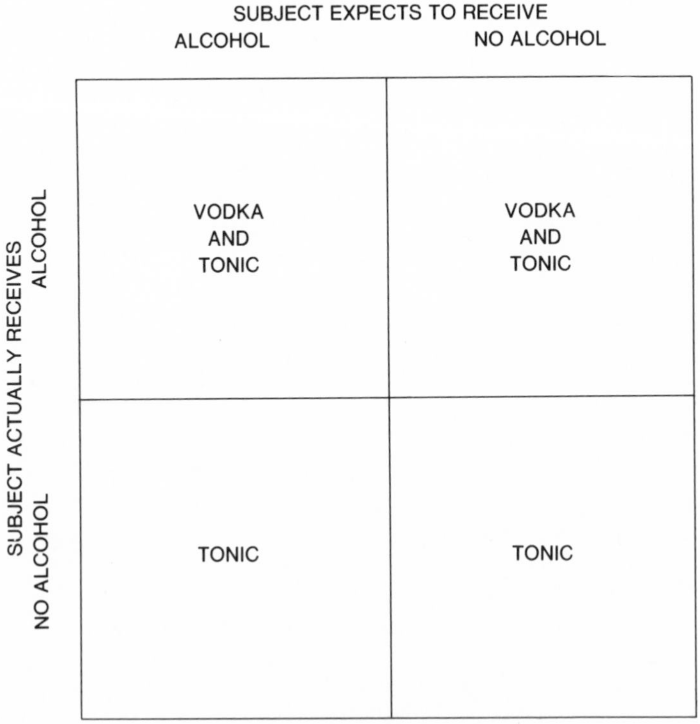
SUBJECT EXPECTS TO RECEIVE
ALCOHOL
NO ALCOHOL
SUBJECT ACTUALLY RECEIVES
ALCOHOL
NO ALCOHOL
VODKA AND TONIC
VODKA AND TONIC
TONIC
TONIC

Figure 1. The balanced placebo design.

dently varied. In alcohol research, the four groups of the balanced placebo design are expect alcohol/receive alcohol; expect alcohol/receive placebo; expect placebo/ receive alcohol; and expect placebo/receive placebo.

In many of the studies to date, the beverage used is that originally developed by Marlatt *et al.* (1973). A mixture of one part 80 proof vodka to five parts tonic water with a squirt of lime was found to be indistinguishable from tonic water and thus provided an effective means of disguising the presence of alcohol. The expectancy manipulation was also heightened by a beverage administration procedure in which subjects saw their drinks being prepared from bottles appropriately labeled as containing vodka or tonic. In truth, when the subject was in the expect alcohol/receive tonic condition, the vodka bottle contained decarbonated tonic. In the expect tonic/receive alcohol condition, the tonic bottle contained a premixed vodka and tonic mixture. For a more comprehensive discussion of the methodology of the balanced placebo design, the reader is referred to Rohsenow and Marlatt (1981).

The balanced placebo design has been used to investigate the role of cognitive versus pharmacological factors in a number of areas, including loss-of-control drinking, craving for alcohol, mood states, sexual behavior, and motor responses. Based on a recent review of this literature (Marlatt & Rohsenow, 1980), a description of the highlights of this line of research is presented below.

3.3.1. Craving/Loss of Control

As previously described in our discussion of the disease model, Engle and Williams (1972) employed the balanced placebo design to study craving of alcoholic subjects. It was found that instructions concerning the presence of alcohol affected self-reports of craving, such that subjects expecting to receive alcohol reported significantly greater craving than those not expecting alcohol. The study by Marlatt *et al.* (1973) used the balanced placebo design to study loss-of-control drinking in alcoholics and social drinkers. The amount of alcohol consumed by both alcoholics and social drinkers was found to be determined by the subject's expectations concerning the content of the beverage. A recent extension of these two studies (Berg *et al.*, 1981) provides further support for the role of cognitive factors in the alcoholics' response to alcohol. In this study, 12 hospitalized alcoholics and 12 social drinking males were observed over an eight-day period. Each subject took part in four sessions, one session in each of the conditions of the balanced placebo design. During each session a triplet of the same three subjects were observed while watching a soccer game. Subjects were given ad lib access to an alcoholic or tonic beverage similar to that used by Marlatt *et al.* (1973). The use of subject triplets having ad lib access to alcohol was said to provide a more naturalistic drinking situation than that provided in previous studies. A number of dependent measures were assessed. They included behavioral observation, measures of alcohol consumption (duration, frequency), ratings of craving and emotional states (e.g., anxiety, mood), and physiological measures (heart rate, blood pressure). Data analyses indicated that in almost all cases, "instructions were much more potent than alcohol in affecting the dependent variables, and this effect was more obvious among alcoholics than among social drinkers" (p. 60). Alcoholics were found to consume significantly more alcohol, drink faster, and take fewer sips when they expected alcohol than when they expected tonic. Experimenter ratings of craving reactions were also higher after alcohol instructions than after tonic instructions. It was concluded that expectancy rather than the pharmacological properties of alcohol determined the alcoholics' response to alcohol. The results for social drinkers were not consistent with the expectancy hypothesis but may have been due to these subject's knowledge of the experimental design.

3.3.2. Sexual Arousal

Findings of research concerning the role of expectancy in sexual responsivity have varied as a function of the gender of the subjects. In the studies conducted to date, expectancy has been found to potentiate sexual arousal in male subjects and to decrease sexual arousal in female subjects. Wilson and Lawson (1976) randomly assigned male social drinkers to the four conditions of the balanced placebo design and then exposed them to either of two erotic films. One film depicted a heterosexual interaction and the other depicted a male homosexual interaction. Penile tumescence served as the behavioral/physiological measure of sexual arousal. The results indicated that expectancy significantly affected penile tumescence during both types of erotic films. Alcohol effects were not significant. It was concluded that the subjects' "cognitive set" about the nature of the beverage consumed accounted for significant differences in sexual arousal.

A similar conclusion was reported by Bridell, Rimm, Caddy, Kravitz, Sholis, and Wunderlin (1978), who exposed male social drinkers to audiotaped descriptions of normal (mutually enjoyable heterosexual intercourse) and deviant (forcible rape and sadistic aggression) sexual behavior. Their results indicated that an increase in penile tumescence in response to the erotic recordings occurred for subjects who were instructed that they were consuming alcohol. Expectancy effects also facilitated increased sexual responding to deviant stimuli. Alcohol did not produce significant increases in sexual arousal. Lang, Searles, Lauerman, and Adesso (1980) and Lansky and Wilson (1981) have also reported that beliefs about having consumed alcohol facilitated sexual arousal in males viewing erotic stimuli.

The single study employing the balanced placebo design to assess expectancy effects in the sexual arousal of females (Wilson & Lawson, 1978) was a replication of the Wilson and Lawson (1976) study. Female social drinkers were exposed to films of erotic heterosexual or homosexual stimuli: vaginal pressure pulse, obtained using a vaginal photoplethysmograph, served as a physiological measure of sexual arousal. The results indicated that the actual consumption of alcohol significantly decreased sexual arousal regardless of instructions.

A number of reasons for gender differences in sexual response to the expectancy manipulation have been proposed. It may be that women are more physiologically vulnerable to the effects of alcohol, that their beliefs about alcohol effects are weaker due to social programming and/or drinking history, or that men have stronger cognitive control over their sexual arousal (Wilson & Lawson, 1978). Limitations of the vaginal photophethysmograph as a measure of sexual arousal may also have contributed to these findings.

3.3.3. Emotional Expression and Mood States

The balanced placebo design has been employed in studying alcohol's effects on the expression of emotions, including aggression (Lang, Goeckner, Adesso, & Marlatt, 1975), mood states (Connors & Maisto, 1979; McCollam, Burish, Maisto, & Sobell, 1980; Vuchinich, Tucker, & Sobell, 1979) and social anxiety (Abrams & Wilson, 1979; Polivy, Schueneman, & Carlson, 1976; Wilson & Abrams, 1977). In much of this research, expectancy effects have been shown to have greater influence on emotional expression than have the pharmacological properties of alcohol. For example, in the Lang *et al.* (1975) study on aggression, male social drinkers who believed they had consumed alcohol exhibited greater aggression (duration and intensity of electric shocks) than did subjects who believed that they had consumed a nonalcoholic beverage. The research on mood states has produced less consistent findings. Methodological changes in the implementation of the balanced placebo design used in these studies may account for these inconsistencies (Marlatt & Rohsenow, 1980).

The research on anxiety provides illustrative examples of two major problems in research on expectancy effects: gender differences and inconsistent findings due to limitations in research design. In the initial study employing the balanced placebo design (Polivy *et al.*, 1976), light-social-drinking males were exposed to a high-anxiety (threatened with a painful electric shock) or low-anxiety (painless electrical stimulation) condition. A self-report anxiety scale served as the dependent measure. The results indicated that subjects who believed they had consumed alcohol reported significantly greater anxiety than those expecting a nonalcoholic substance (vitamin C). Subjects who actually received alcohol reported less anxiety than subjects receiving the placebo.

As an example of a study that produced findings inconsistent with the expectancy effect, this study contains certain crucial methodological limitations which hamper the interpretation of the results. Since most subjects are unlikely to have specific beliefs about the effects of alcohol on electric shock, the choice of anxiety manipulation is unlikely to have provided the opportunity for the expression of expectancy effects. The choice of subject (light drinkers) also decreases the likelihood of a strong expectancy effect. Since light drinkers are likely to have limited experience with alcohol, expectations concerning its effects may also be limited. Last, the use of a single self-report measure of anxiety adds another confounding factor to the interpretation of these results. Subsequent studies have improved on these methodological limitations by employing subjects with more drinking experience, using multiple measures (self-report, physiological arousal, and behavioral measures), and by providing exposure to a source of anxiety about which individuals are likely to have developed expectations—social anxiety. Results have shown a strong effect for expectancy; however, differences due to subject gender have been reported.

Wilson and Abrams (1977) asked moderate-drinking male subjects to try to make a favorable impression while speaking to a female confederate. Their results indicated changes in both physiological (heart rate) and self-reported indicators of anxiety that were attributable to expectancy effects. Subjects who believed they had consumed alcohol showed decreases in heart rate relative to those who believed they had consumed a nonalcoholic beverage. The expectancy effects for self-rated anxiety were marginally significant, with subjects expecting alcohol rating themselves as less anxious than those expecting tonic.

A replication of this study employing female subjects and a male confederate (Abrams & Wilson, 1979) reported that subjects expecting alcohol exhibited more anxiety in both physiological and behavioral measures. There were no significant differences in self-reported anxiety. As with the findings for sexual arousal, the results for social anxiety in males and females were reversed. However, in both cases expectancy was shown to be a significant determinant of a socially mediated response.

3.3.4. Motor and Cognitive Skills

The use of the balanced placebo design to study motor and cognitive skills has produced findings suggesting the primacy of the pharmacological effects of alcohol. For example, in the Lang et al. (1975) study of aggression, response latency after a confederate's signal was significantly influenced by the actual beverage consumed and not by expectancy. Similarly, Vuchinich and Sobell (1978) reported impairment due to alcohol effects on a pursuit-motor-tracking task and a divided attention task. However, both the consumption of alcohol and the expectation of consuming alcohol interacted to produce increased errors on a reaction-time task. It seems that expectancy can play some role in alcohol effects on motor task. On purely cognitive skills, Miller, Adesso, Fleming, Gino, and Lauerman (1978) have reported that expectancy had no effect on immediate recall or relearning of word lists, while alcohol produced performance deficits.

It seems that the pharmacological effects of alcohol have more effect on physiologically mediated skills, while expectancy effects are more pronounced with socially mediated behaviors. An oft-proposed reason for this difference is the individual's limited experience with alcohol and the performance of cognitive and motor skills. This lack of experience inhibits the development of a belief system concerning alcohol effects. The opposite is true for socially mediated behaviors, where a variety of experiences with alcohol lead to the development of strong individual and/or sociocultural beliefs concerning the effects of alcohol.

A theoretical explanation of the expectancy effect has been provided by Valins's (1966) extension of Schacter's (1964) attributional theory of emotion (Marlatt & Rohsenow, 1980). Schacter's theory proposed that emotional arousal is relatively diffuse and that differentiation of emotional states was a function of the individual's choice of label to explain the arousal. Valins modified Schacter's formulation to suggest that the belief that one is psysiologically aroused can influence emotional responding, even in the absence of a pharmacologically induced state of physiological arousal. Marlatt and Rohsenow (1980) have interpreted the results of studies employing the balanced placebo design within Valins's framework. They suggest that "the physiological arousal levels obtained in the balanced placebo studies are insufficient in intensity to override the compelling labelling effects of expectancy" (p. 189). This interpretation of expectancy effects has recently been critiqued by Vuchinich and Tucker (1980).

Another alternative explanation of expectancy effects may be provided by conditioning theories of drug dependence (Siegel, 1975; Siegel, Hinson, & Krank, 1978). In such a formulation, instructions concerning beverage consumption elicit a conditoned state of intoxication regardless of the actual content of the beverage. Drinking history would mediate the strength of the conditioned response such that heavy drinking would produce a more pronounced conditioned response. Thus, in the Berg et al. (1981) study, alcoholic subjects in the told alcohol/given placebo condition may have drunk more in order to alleviate withdrawal symptoms elicited by the instructions. Alcoholics in the told placebo/given alcohol condition would have exhibited a clear drug response unmediated by the conditioned antagonistic response.

Whatever the theoretical explanations for the expectancy effects, the research suggests that fixed beliefs about the effects of alcohol can influence behavioral reactions to consuming alcohol. This effect is particularly pronounced in socially mediated behaviors (e.g., aggression, social anxiety, sexual arousal). Given the pervasiveness of expectancy effects, it seems crucial that cognitive factors be included in our theories of alcohol use and abuse (Marlatt, 1978; Wilson, 1978).

3.4. Relapse Prevention

Cognitive–behavioral approaches to alcohol abuse view problem drinking as being multiply determined. They expand on the strict learning model, which focuses on the observable determinants and consequences of drinking, by also examining the role of internal factors such as cognitions and expectancy.

Marlatt (1979) is one of the proponents of a cognitive–behavioral approach.

In his model the probability of the occurrence of excessive drinking in a particular situation was said to vary as a function of the following factors:

1. The degree to which the drinker feels controlled by or helpless relative to the influence of others. The role of social influence has previously been discussed, but it should be reiterated that subtle (e.g., modeling cues) or overt (e.g., peer pressure) social variables can have a profound effect on alcohol consumption.
2. The individual's view of self in relation to environmental events that are perceived as being beyond his or her control. (For example, feelings of powerlessness, fatalism, learned helplessness.)
3. The availability of alcohol and constraints on drinking in a particular situation.
4. The availabliity of adequate coping responses as alternatives to drinking.
5. The drinker's expectancies about the effects of alcohol as one means of attempting to cope with the situation. Individuals who have positive beliefs that alcohol will facilitate coping are more likely to use alcohol.

Marlatt and Gordon (1980) expanded on this model of the determinants of excessive alcohol use. Their relapse-prevention model was based on an examination of the limited maintenance of treatment outcome for substance abuse. In examining the actual process of relapse, a model describing precipitants of excessive alcohol use was developed.

The examination of relapse began with an assessment of the situational and environmental determinants of relapse. The individual's cognitive interpretation of the relationship between the initial relapse episode and subsequent alcohol use was also assessed. Detailed accounts of relapse episodes were obtained from individual individuals who were in treatment for alcohol, smoking, or heroin addiction. The alcoholic sample consisted of 70 male chronic alcoholics from treatment programs in which abstinence was the primary goal of treatment. Information concerning the circumstances associated with the initial use of alcohol following treatment was analyzed and categorized. It was found that the majority of relapses (61%) fell into the category of intrapersonal/environmental determinants. Important subcategories included negative emotional states (e.g., frustration, anger, anxiety, fear), which accounted for 38% of the relapses, and urges and temptations (e.g., craving, exposure to cues associated with the use of alcohol), which accounted for 11% of the relapses. In the interpersonal determinants category, the subcategories of interpersonal conflict and social pressure (direct influence and/or modeling) each accounted for 18% of relapses. The enhancement of positive emotional states (intrapersonal and interpersonal) accounted for relatively few relapses (3%), suggesting that few problem drinkers used alcohol as a means of feeling good in the absence of stress.

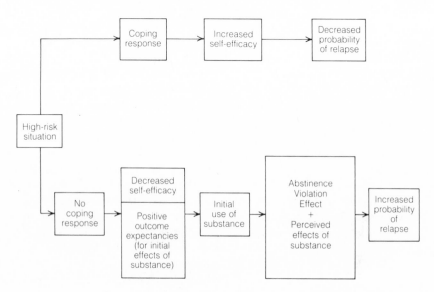

Figure 2. Cognitive–behavioral model of the relapse process.

The theoretical model based on these data assumes that the individual has voluntarily made a choice to abstain or to control alcohol consumption. The maintenance of that choice leads to a sense of personal control over drinking.

Relapses are said to occur if this perception of control diminishes, particularly when the individual encounters a high-risk situation. A high-risk situation is broadly defined as one posing a threat or challenge to the individual's sense of control. The likelihood that a relapse will occur in such situations depends on the individual's capacity to engage in adequate coping responses. If the individual is able to cope with a high-risk situation, his or her sense of personal control and self-efficacy (Bandura, 1977b) tends to increase. A strong sense of personal control will tend to decrease the probability of relapse when the individual is faced with future high-risk situations.

The lack of a coping response initiates a negative cycle in which a loss of confidence and a sense of helplessness leads to initial alcohol use. Drinking is even more likely to occur if the individual also has positive expectancies about the effects of alcohol as a means of coping. After consuming alcohol following a period of abstinence, the individual may experience a reaction to transgressing self-imposed limits on alcohol use, called the abstinence-violation effect (AVE). The AVE is made up of two components: cognitive dissonance and a personal attribution effect. The cognitive dissonance component involves a conflict between the individual's self-image as an abstainer or moderate alcohol user and the behavior of drinking beyond self-imposed limits. The cause of this infraction is attributed to a personal weakness (e.g., lack of will power, a disease process) or failure. Having failed once, there is the expectation for continued failure. The initial stimulating effects of alcohol are experienced as pleasant and add to the likelihood of its continued use.

Though the relapse-prevention model was developed as an intervention strategy geared towards the initial use of alcohol following treatment, its application to the description of the etiology of excessive alcohol use seems very appropriate. For example, research on expectancy suggests that both alcoholics and social drinkers have positive beliefs about the effects of alcohol (Brown *et al.*, 1980; Isaacs, 1979; Tamerin *et al.*, 1970). Tamerin *et al.* found that alcoholics expected alcohol to make them feel more pleasant and to behave more sociably. Similarly, Brown *et al.* found that social drinkers expected alcohol to "transform experiences in a positive way, enhance social and physical pleasure, enhance sexual performance and experience, increase power and aggression, increase social assertiveness and reduce tension" (p. 419). Social drinkers who possess such beliefs are likely to increase alcohol consumption when faced with stressful situations similar to the high-risk situations found to precipitate relapses in alcoholics. If alcohol becomes the habitual response to coping with stress, patterns of excessive alcohol use may develop. For the heavy social drinker, initial episodes of excessive drinking may elicit an experience similar to the abstinence violation effect. The conflict between self-definition as a social drinker and the behavioral consequences of excessive alcohol use plus the attribution of such alcohol consumption to internal mechanisms can serve as potent facilitators for continued excessive alcohol use. The initial positive effects of alcohol may further aid in the establishment of patterns of excessive drinking.

The validity of applying Marlatt and Gordon's (1980) relapse-prevention model to the development of problem drinking can be tested empirically, (cf. Chaney, O'Leary, & Marlatt, 1978). Longitudinal assessment of the situational determinants of heavy social drinking can yield a description of high-risk situations similar to that found with alcoholics. Such information may provide a useful predictor of the likelihood of the development of a drinking problem in particular individuals.

4. FUTURE DIRECTIONS

We have described the theoretical approaches presented in this chapter as initial efforts in the search for the etiology and psychological correlates of excessive alcohol use. Researchers must now focus on the means of capitalizing on our present knowledge in order to develop more cogent theories of etiology. The building of reasonable theories is profoundly important for increasing our understanding of drinking disorders and the development of more successful methods of preventing and treating excessive alcohol use.

Each of the models covered offers implications for future research and theory construction. Our review of psychodynamic approaches suggests that continued assessment of the characteristics related to excessive alcohol use may be more fruitful if studied within a framework that considers state and situational factors. There is also a need for longitudinal studies in which prospective data can be collected. These may involve individuals considered to be at high risk (e.g., children of alcoholics) and low risk (e.g., children of light drinkers) who could be studied over time using personality, social, and behavioral measures.

We have also seen that social factors can play a significant role in the etiology of problem drinking. Even so, the majority of individuals who consume alcohol are social drinkers who never develop drinking problems. Continued study of the social drinker will contribute to our ongoing assessment of the role of social factors in the maintenance of moderate drinking and the development of problem drinking.

Findings concerning the role of cognitions, particularly beliefs about the effects of alcohol, also suggest another rewarding path for future investigation. Researchers must continue to examine the development of such beliefs and the mediating role of cognitive factors in the development of moderate and/or problem drinking styles. It is likely that only by incorporating research from these and other approaches will we finally develop a model that addresses the complex factors related to excessive alcohol consumption.

5. REFERENCES

Abrams, D. B., & Wilson, G. T. Effects of alcohol on social anxiety in women: Cognitive versus physiological processes. *Journal of Abnormal Psychology,* 1979, *88,* 161–173.

Ackerman, M. J. Alcoholism and the Rorschach. *Journal of Personality Assessment,* 1971, *35,* 224–228.

Bandura, A. *Principles of behavior modification.* New York: Holt, 1969.

Bandura, A. *Social learning theory.* Englewood Cliffs, N.J.: Prentice-Hall, 1977. (a)

Bandura, A. Self-efficacy: Toward a unifying theory of behavioral change. *Psychological Review,* 1977, *84,* 191–215. (b)

Barnes, G. E. The alcoholic personality: A reanalysis of the literature. *Journal of Studies on Alcohol,* 1979, *40,* 571–634.

Berg, G., Laberg, J. C., Skutle, A., & Ohman, A. Instructed versus pharmacological effects of alcohol in alcoholics and social drinkers. *Behaviour Research and Therapy,* 1981, *19,* 55–66.

Bertrand, S., & Masling, J. Oral imagery and alcoholism. *Journal of Abnormal Psychology,* 1969, *74,* 50–53.

Blum, E. M. Psychoanalytic views of alcoholism. *Quarterly Journal of Studies on Alcohol,* 1966, *27,* 259–299.

Briddle, B. J., Bank, B. J., & Marlin, M. M. Social determinants of adolescent drinking. *Journal of Studies on Alcohol*, 1980, *41*, 215–241.

Bridell, D. W., Rimm, D. C., Caddy, G. R., Krawitz, G., Sholis, D., & Wunderlin, R. J. Effects of alcohol and cognitive set on sexual arousal to deviant stimuli. *Journal of Abnormal Psychology*, 1978, *87*, 418–430.

Brown, J. S., & Crowell, C. R. Alcohol and conflict resolution: A theoretical analysis. *Quarterly Journal of Studies on Alcohol*, 1974, *35*, 66–85.

Brown, M. A. Alcoholic profiles on the Minnesota Multiphasic. *Journal of Clinical Psychology*, 1950, *6*, 266–269.

Brown, S. A., Goldman, M. S., Inn, A., & Anderson, L. R. Expectations of reinforcement from alcohol: Their domain and relation to drinking patterns. *Journal of Consulting and Clinical Psychology*, 1980, *48*, 419–426.

Butcher, J. N., & Owen, P. L. Objective personality inventories: Recent research and some contemporary issues. In B. B. Wolman (Ed.), *Clinical diagnosis of mental disorders: A handbook*. New York: Plenum Press, 1978.

Butts, S. V., & Chotlos, J. A comparison of alcoholics and nonalcoholics on perceived locus of control. *Quarterly Journal of Studies on Alcohol*, 1973, *34*, 1327–1332.

Cappell, H. An evaluation of tension models of alcohol consumption. In R. J. Gibbins, Y. Israel, H. Kalant, R. E. Popham, W. Schmidt, & R. G. Smart (Eds.), *Research advances in alcohol and drug problems* (Vol. 2). New York: Wiley, 1975.

Cappell, H., & Herman, C. P. Alcohol and tension reduction: A review. *Quarterly Journal of Studies on Alcohol*, 1972, *33*, 33–64.

Caudill, B. D., & Lipscomb, T. R. Modeling influences on alcoholics' rates of alcohol consumption. *Journal of Applied Behavior Analysis*, 1980, *13*, 355–365.

Caudill, B. D., & Marlatt, G. A. Modeling influences in social drinking: An experimental analogue. *Journal of Consulting and Clinical Psychology*, 1975, *43*, 405–415.

Chaney, E. F., O'Leary, M. R., & Marlatt, G. A. Skill training with alcoholics. *Journal of Consulting and Clinical Psychology*, 1978, *46*, 1092–1104.

Clopton, J. R. Alcoholism and the MMPI. *Journal of Studies on Alcohol*, 1978, *39*, 1540–1558.

Collins, R. L., & Marlatt, G. A. Social modeling as a determinant of drinking behavior: Implications for prevention and treatment. *Addictive Behaviors*, 1981, *6*, 233–240.

Collins, R. L., & Marlatt, G. A. *Social determinants of alcohol consumption: The effects of model status on the self-administration of alcohol*. In preparation, University of Washington, 1982.

Conger, J. J. Reinforcement theory and the dynamics of alcoholism. *Quarterly Journal of Studies on Alcohol*, 1956, *17*, 296–305.

Connors, G. J., & Maisto, S. A. Effects of alcohol, instructions, and consumption rate on affect and physiological sensations. *Pharmacology*, 1979, *62*, 261–266.

Cooper, A. M., Waterhouse, G. J., & Sobell, M. B. Influence of gender on drinking in a modeling situation. *Journal of Studies on Alcohol*, 1979, *40*, 562–570.

Costello, R. M., & Manders, K. R. Locus of control and alcoholism. *British Journal of Addiction*, 1974, *69*, 11–17.

Cox, W. M. The alcoholic personality: A review of the evidence. In B. Maher (Ed.), *Progress in experimental personality research* (Vol. 9). New York: Academic Press, 1979.

Criteria Committee, National Council on Alcoholism. Criteria for the diagnosis of alcoholism. *American Journal of Psychiatry*, 1972, *129*, 127–135.

Cutter, H. S., Boyatzis, R. E., & Clancy, D. D. Effectiveness of power motivation training in rehabilitating alcoholics. *Journal of Studies on Alcohol*, 1977, *38*, 131–141.

Cutter, H. S. G., Key, J. C., Rothstein, E., & Jones, W. C. Alcohol, power and inhibition. *Quarterly Journal of Studies on Alcohol*, 1973, *34*, 381–389.

Davis, D. L. Alcoholism as a disease. *Psychological Medicine*, 1974, *4*, 130–132.

DeRicco, D. A., & Garlington, W. K. The effects of modeling and disclosure of experimenter's intent on drinking rate in college students. *Addictive Behaviors*, 1977, *2*, 135–139.

DeRicco, D. A., & Niemann, J. E. In vivo effects of peer modeling on drinking rate. *Journal of Applied Behavior Analysis*, 1980, *13*, 149–152.

Distefano, M. K., Pryer, M. W., & Garrison, J. L. Internal-external control among alcoholics. *Journal of Clinical Psychology*, 1972, *28*, 36–37.

Donovan, D. M., & O'Leary, M. R. Comparison of perceived and experienced control among alcoholics and nonalcoholics. *Journal of Abnormal Psychology*, 1975, *84*, 726–728.

Engle, K. B., & Williams, T. K. Effects of an ounce of vodka on alcoholics' desire for alcohol. *Quarterly Journal of Studies on Alcohol*, 1972, *33*, 1099–1105.

Fenichel, O. *The psychoanalytic theory of neurosis*. New York: Norton, 1945.

Freed, E. X. Alcoholism and the Rorschach Test: A review. *Journal of Studies on Alcohol*, 1976, *37*, 1633–1654.

Garlington, W. K. Drinking on television: A preliminary study with emphasis on method. *Journal of Studies on Alcohol*, 1977, *38*, 2199–2205.

Garlington, W. K., & DeRicco, D. A. The effect of modeling on drinking rate. *Journal of Applied Behavior Analysis*, 1977, *10*, 207–211.

Glatt, M. M. The question of moderate drinking despite "loss of control." *British Journal of Addiction*, 1967, *62*, 267–274.

Glatt, M. M. Alcoholism disease concept and loss of control revisited. *British Journal of Addiction*, 1976, *71*, 135–144.

Goldstein, S. G., & Linden, J. D. Multivariate classification of alcoholics by means of the MMPI. *Journal of Abnormal Psychology*, 1969, *74*, 661–669.

Hendricks, R. D., Sobell, M. B., & Cooper, A. M. Social influences on human ethanol consumption in an analogue situation. *Addictive Behaviors*, 1978, *3*, 253–259.

Hershon, H. Alcoholism and the concept of disease. *British Journal of Addiction*, 1974, *69*, 123–131.

Higgins, R. L. Experimental investigations of tension reduction models of alcoholism. In G. Golstein & C. Neuringer (Eds.), *Empirical studies of alcoholism*. Cambridge, Mass.: Ballinger, 1976.

Hodgson, R., Rankin, H., & Stockwell, T. Alcohol dependence and the priming effect. *Behaviour Research and Therapy*, 1979, *17*, 379–387.

Hodgson, R. J., Stockwell, T. R., & Rankin, H. J. Can alcohol reduce tension? *Behaviour Research and Therapy*, 1979, *17*, 459–479.

Isaacs, M. College students' expectations of the results of drinking. *Journal of Studies on Alcohol*, 1979, *40*, 476–479.

Jellinek, E. M. Phases of alcohol addiction. *Quarterly Journal of Studies on Alcohol*, 1952, *18*, 673–684.

Jellinek, E. M. *The disease concept of alcoholism*. New Brunswick, N.J.: Hillhouse Press, 1960.

Kalin, R., McClelland, D. C., & Kahn, M. The effects of male social drinking on fantasy. *Journal of Personality and Social Psychology*, 1965, *1*, 441–452.

Kandel, D. B. Convergences in prospective longitudinal surveys of drug use in normal populations. In D. B. Kandel (Ed.), *Longitudinal research on drug use*. Washington, D.C.: Hemisphere, 1978.

Keller, M. The oddities of alcoholics. *Quarterly Journal of Studies on Alcohol*, 1972, *33*, 1147–1148. (a)

Keller, M. On the loss-of-control phenomenon in alcoholism. *British Journal of Addiction*, 1972, *67*, 153–166. (b)

Lang, A. R., Goeckner, D. J., Adesso, V. J., & Marlatt, G. A. Effects of alcohol on aggression in male social drinkers. *Journal of Abnormal Psychology*, 1975, *84*, 508–518.

Lang, A. R., Searles, J., Lauerman, R., & Adesso, V. Expectancy, alcohol and sex guilt as determinants of interest in and reaction to sexual stimuli. *Journal of Abnormal Psychology*, 1980, *89*, 644–653.

Lansky, D., & Wilson, G. T. Alcohol, expectations and sexual arousal in males: An information processing analysis. *Journal of Abnormal Psychology*, 1981, *90*, 35–45.

Lied, E. R., & Marlatt, G. A. Modeling as a determinant of alcohol consumption: Effect of subject sex and prior drinking history. *Addictive Behaviors*, 1979, *4*, 47–54.

Lloyd, R. W., & Salzberg, H. C. Controlled social drinking: An alternative to abstinence as a treatment goal for some alcohol abusers. *Psychological Bulletin*, 1975, *82*, 815–842.

Lowery, S. A. Soap and booze in the afternoon. *Journal of Studies on Alcohol*, 1980, *41*, 829–838.

Ludwig, A. M., & Wikler, A. "Craving" and relapse to drink. *Quarterly Journal of Studies on Alcohol*, 1974, *35*, 108–130.

Ludwig, A. M., Wikler, A., & Stark, L. H. The first drink: Psychobiological aspects of craving. *Archives of General Psychiatry*, 1974, *30*, 539–547.

MacAndrew, C. The differentiation of male alcoholic outpatients from nonalcoholic psychiatric outpatients by means of the MMPI. *Quarterly Journal of Studies on Alcohol*, 1965, *26*, 238–246.

MacAndrew, C., & Edgerton, R. B. *Drunken comportment*. Chicago: Aldine, 1969.

Maisto, S. A., Lauerman, R., & Adesso, V. J. A comparison of two experimental studies of the role of cognitive factors in alcoholics' drinking. *Journal of Studies on Alcohol*, 1977, *38*, 145–149.

Maisto, S. A., & Schefft, B. K. The construct of craving for alcohol and loss-of-control drinking: Help or hindrance to research. *Addictive Behaviors*, 1977, *2*, 207–217.

Marlatt, G. A. Alcohol, stress and cognitive control. In I. G. Sarason, & C. D. Spielberger (Eds.), *Stress and anxiety* (Vol. 3). Washington, D.C.: Hemisphere, 1976.

Marlatt, G. A. Craving for alcohol, loss of control and relapse: A cognitive–behavioral analysis. In P. E. Nathan, G. A. Marlatt, & T. Løberg (Eds.), *Alcoholism: New directions in behavioral research and treatment*. New York: Plenum Press, 1978.

Marlatt, G. A. Alcohol use and problem drinking: A cognitive–behavioral analysis. In P. C. Kendall & S. P. Hollon (Eds.), *Cognitive–behavioral interventions: Theory, research and procedures*. New York: Academic Press, 1979.

Marlatt, G. A., Demming, B., & Reid, J. B. Loss of control drinking in alcoholics: An experimental analogue. *Journal of Abnormal Psychology*, 1973, *81*, 233–241.

Marlatt, G. A., & Gordon, J. R. Determinants of relapse: Implications for the maintenance of behavior change. In P. Davidson & S. Davidson (Eds.), *Behavioral medicine: Changing health lifestyles*. New York: Brunner/Mazel, 1980.

Marlatt, G. A., & Rohsenow, D. J. Cognitive processes in alcohol use: Expectancy and the balanced placebo design. In N. K. Mello (Ed.), *Advances in substance abuse: Behavioral and biological research* (Vol. 1). Greenwich, Conn.: JAI Press, 1980.

McClelland, D. C. The impact of power motivation training on alcoholics. *Journal of Studies on Alcohol*, 1977, *38*, 142–144.

McClelland, D. C., Davis, W. N., Kalin, R., & Wanner, E. *The drinking man*. New York: Free Press, 1972.

McCollam, J. B., Burish, T. G., Maisto, S. A., & Sobell, M. B. Alcohol's effects on physiological arousal and self-reported affects and sensations. *Journal of Abnormal Psychology*, 1980, *89*, 224–233.

McCord, W., & McCord, J. *Origins of alcoholism*. Stanford, Calif.: Stanford University Press, 1960.

Merry, J. The "loss of control" myth. *Lancet*, 1966, *1*, 1257–1258.

Miller, M. E., Adesso, V. J., Fleming, J. P., Gino, A., & Lauerman, R. The effects of alcohol on the storage and retrieval processes of heavy social drinkers. *Journal of Experimental Psychology: Human Learning and Memory*, 1978, *4*, 246–255.

Miller, W. R., & Caddy, G. R. Abstinence and controlled drinking in the treatment of problem drinkers. *Journal of Studies on Alcohol*, 1977, *38*, 986–1003.

Mischel, W. *Personality and assessment.* New York: Wiley, 1968.

Mischel, W. Toward a cognitive social learning reconceptualization of personality. *Psychological Review,* 1973, *80,* 252–283.

Nathan, P. E., & Lansky, D. Common methodological problems in research on the addictions. *Journal of Consulting and Clinical Psychology,* 1978, *46,* 713–726.

O'Leary, D. E., O'Leary, M. R., & Donovan, D. M. Social skill acquisition and psychosocial development of alcoholics: A review. *Addictive Behaviors,* 1976, *1,* 111–120.

O'Leary, M. R., Donovan, D. M., & Hague, W. M. Interpersonal differentiation, locus of control and cognitive style among alcoholics. *Perceptual and Motor Skills,* 1974, *39,* 978–998.

Overall, J. E. MMPI personality patterns of alcoholics and narcotic addicts. *Quarterly Journal of Studies on Alcohol,* 1973, *34,* 104–111.

Parks, G., Collins, R. L., & Marlatt, G. A. The effect of social atmosphere on the modeling of alcohol consumption. Manuscript in preparation, University of Washington, 1982.

Pattison, E. M. Nonabstinent drinking goals in the treatment of alcoholics. In R. J. Gibbins, Y. Israel, H. Kalant, R. E. Popham, W. Schmidt, & R. G. Smart (Eds.), *Research advances in alcohol and drug problems* (Vol. 3). New York: Wiley, 1976.

Pattison, E. M., Sobell, M. B., & Sobell, L. C. *Emerging concepts of alcohol dependence.* New York: Springer, 1977.

Polivy, J., Schueneman, A. L., & Carlson, K. Alcohol and tension reduction: Cognitive and physiological effects. *Journal of Abnormal Psychology,* 1976, *85,* 595–600.

Rankin, H., Hodgson, R., & Stockwell, T. The concept of craving and its measurement. *Behaviour Research and Therapy,* 1979, *17,* 389–396.

Reid, J. B. Study of drinking in natural settings. In G. A. Marlatt & P. E. Nathan (Eds.), *Behavioral approaches to alcoholism.* New Brunswick, N.J.: Rutgers Center of Alcohol Studies, 1978.

Robinson, D. The alcoholologist's addiction: Some implications of having lost control over the disease concept of alcoholism. *Quarterly Journal of Studies on Alcohol,* 1972, *33,* 1028–1042.

Rohsenow, D. M., & Marlatt, G. A. The balanced placebo design: Methodological considerations. *Addictive Behaviors,* 1981, *6,* 107–122.

Russell, J. A., & Mehrabian, A. The mediating role of emotions in alcohol use. *Journal of Studies on Alcohol,* 1975, *36,* 1508–1531.

Sadava, S. W., & Forsyth, R. Person–environment interaction and college student drug use: A multivariate longitudinal study. *Genetic Psychology Monographs,* 1977, *96,* 211–245.

Schacter, S. The interaction of cognitive and physiological determinants of emotional state. In L. Berkowitz (Ed.), *Advances in experimental social psychology* (Vol. 1). New York: Academic Press, 1964.

Siegel, S. Evidence from rats that morphine tolerance is a learned response. *Journal of Comparative and Physiological Psychology,* 1975, *89,* 498–506.

Siegel, S., Hinson, R. E., & Krank, M. D. The role of predrug signals in morphine analgesic tolerance: Support for Pavlovian conditioning model of tolerance. *Journal of Experimental Psychology: Animal Behavior Processes,* 1978, *4,* 188–196.

Sobell, M. B. Alternatives to abstinence: Evidence, issues, and some proposals. In P. E. Nathan, G. A. Marlatt, & T. Løberg (Eds.), *Alcoholism: New directions in behavioral research and treatment.* New York: Plenum Press, 1978.

Southwick, L., Steele, C. M., Marlatt, G. A. & Lindell, M. Alcohol-related expectancies: Defined by phase of intoxication and drinking experience. *Journal of Consulting and Clinical Psychology,* 1981, *49,* 713–721.

Strickler, D. P., Dobbs, S. D., & Maxwell, W. A. The influence of setting on drinking behaviors: The laboratory vs. the barroom. *Addictive Behaviors,* 1979, *4,* 339–344.

Sutherland, E. H., Schroeder, H. G., & Tordella, C. L. Personality traits and the alcoholic: A critique of existing studies. *Quarterly Journal of Studies on Alcohol,* 1950, *11,* 547–561.

Sutker, P. B. Adolescent drug and alcohol behaviors. In T. Field, A. Huston, H. Quary, L. Troll, & H. Finley (Eds.), *Review of human development.* New York: Wiley, 1982.

Sutker, P. B., Archer, R. P., Brantley, P. J., & Kilpatrick, D. G. Alcoholics and opiate addicts: Comparison of personality characteristics. *Journal of Studies on Alcohol,* 1979, *40,* 635–644.

Sutker, P. B., Brantley, P. J., & Allain, A. N. MMPI response patterns and alcohol consumption in DUI offenders. *Journal of Consulting and Clinical Psychology,* 1980, *48,* 350–355.

Syme, L. Personality characteristics and the alcoholic: A critique of current studies. *Quarterly Journal of Studies on Alcohol,* 1957, *18,* 288–302.

Tahka, V. *The alcoholic personality: A clinical study.* Helsinki: Finnish Foundation for Alcohol Studies, 1966.

Tamerin, J. S., Weiner, S., & Mendelson, J. H. Alcoholics' expectancies and recall of experiences during intoxication. *The American Journal of Psychiatry,* 1970, *126,* 1697–1704.

Valins, S. Cognitive effects of false heart-rate feedback. *Journal of Personality and Social Psychology,* 1966, *4,* 400–408.

Vuchinich, R. E., & Sobell, M. B. Empirical separation of physiologic and expected effects of alcohol on complex perceptual motor performance. *Psychopharmacology,* 1978, *60,* 81–85.

Vuchinich, R. E., & Tucker, J. A. A critique of cognitive labeling explanations of the emotional and behavioral effects of alcohol. *Addictive Behaviors,* 1980, *5,* 179–188.

Vuchinich, R. E., Tucker, J. A., & Sobell, M. B. Alcohol, expectancy, cognitive labeling, and mirth. *Journal of Abnormal Psychology,* 1979, *88,* 641–651.

Wechsler, H., & McFadden, M. Drinking among college students in New England. *Journal of Studies on Alcohol,* 1979, *40,* 969–996.

Weiss, L., & Masling, J. Further validation of a Rorschach measure of oral imagery: A study of six clinical groups. *Journal of Abnormal Psychology,* 1970, *76,* 83–87.

Whitelock, P. R., Overall, J. E., & Patrick, J. H. Personality patterns and alcohol abuse in a state hospital population. *Journal of Abnormal Psychology,* 1971, *78,* 9–16.

Wilson, G. T. Booze, beliefs, and behavior: Cognitive processes in alcohol use and abuse. In P. E. Nathan, G. A. Marlatt, & T. Løberg (Eds.), *Alcoholism: New directions in behavioral research and treatment.* New York: Plenum Press, 1978.

Wilson, G. T., & Abrams, D. B. Effects of alcohol on social anxiety and physiological arousal: Cognitive versus pharmacological processes. *Cognitive Therapy and Research,* 1977, *1,* 195–210.

Wilson, G. T. & Lawson, D. M. Expectancies, alcohol, and sexual arousal in male social drinkers. *Journal of Abnormal Psychology,* 1976, *85,* 587–594.

Wilson, G. T., & Lawson, D. M. Expectancies, alcohol and sexual arousal in women. *Journal of Abnormal Psychology,* 1978, *87,* 358–367.

11

Alcoholism Treatment Approaches
Patient Variables, Treatment Variables

BARBARA S. McCRADY AND KENNETH J. SHER

This chapter is organized into four major sections. In the first section, a brief critical review of the alcoholism treatment outcome literature is provided, in which particular attention is paid to the limitations of evaluating heterogeneous patients and treatment. In Section 2, the focus is on three major alcoholism treatment models: Alcoholics Anonymous, behavior therapy, and psychoanalytically oriented psychotherapy. The ways in which these three models treat biological, individual, and interpersonal problems of patients are presented. In Section 3, the discussion turns to a consideration of patient variables in treatment, using three illustrative special patient populations—the elderly, women, and the psychiatrically impaired alcohol abuser. For each population, biological, individual, and interpersonal treatment implications are presented. Section 4 examines the research and treatment implications of studying specific patient-variable–treatment-interventions interactions.

1. CRITICAL VIEW OF TREATMENT OUTCOME EVALUATION

The alcoholism treatment literature is vast and mostly descriptive, introducing new approaches and providing details about various treatment methods. It

BARBARA S. McCRADY • Brown University and Butler Hospital, Providence, Rhode Island 02906. KENNETH J. SHER • Department of Psychology, University of Missouri, Columbia, Missouri 65211. Preparation of this chapter was supported in part by NIAAA grant RO1 AA 03984, "Marital, Spouse and Self-Control Treatment of Alcoholism," awarded to Dr. McCrady.

appears that every treatment available to the health and mental health fields, ranging from LSD treatment to self-help groups, has been applied to alcoholics and alcohol abusers at one time or another. Within this morass of treatment literature, there are many studies that evaluate the efficacy of single treatments that compare two or more different treatments. The majority of these studies have used a "horserace" approach in which two or more heterogeneous treatments are applied to a heterogeneous population of alcohol abusers and the results are evaluated on a number of global measures of "success" or "failure."

1.1. Evaluation of Heterogeneous Treatments: The "Horserace" Approach

Using this horserace approach to treatment outcome evaluation, Emrick (1974, 1975) reviewed 374 studies in which a minimum of three subjects were followed for at least six months after the completion of treatment. He concluded that there were no appreciable differences in the efficacy of different treatment approaches. Only a handful of studies (five) found one treatment to be clearly more effective than another, but he concluded that these findings were due to decreased effectiveness of the control treatment because the control subjects were disappointed when they found that they were not in the experimental group. Emrick (1975) further concluded in his review that treatment is more effective than minimal or no treatment (minimal treatment was defined as less than five outpatient visits or less than two weeks of inpatient treatment) in helping subjects to reduce their drinking but that treatment has no appreciable effect on abstinence rates six months after therapy is terminated. Similarly pessimistic conclusions can be drawn from a recent study by Edwards *et al.* (1977). This research group compared giving a single session of "advice" to the alcoholic and family (about the need to abstain from the use of alcohol) with providing access to a range of therapeutic services over a one-year period. There were no differences in outcomes between these two experimental groups.

One conclusion that can be drawn from these studies is that it makes no difference what one does with an alcoholic in treatment as long as *something* is done. However, there is a danger of oversimplification in interpreting these results. First, the treatments studied are complex and heterogeneous and usually have attempted to intervene in many areas of the patient's life functioning. Also, interventions have been applied to heterogeneous patient populations. It is likely that some element of the treatment might be effective in helping some members of the patient population with one set of problems, that another element of the treatment might be effective with another group of patients with another set of problems, and so on. One would expect that the various interactions between effective combinations of treatment–patient variables would be balanced by another group of ineffective treatment–patient interventions, obscuring any true differences in treatment effectiveness for specific interventions with specific patient problems. Thus, no differences are found between treatments because we are looking in the wrong place for differences.

A third problem with the conventional horserace approach involves the measures used to evaluate outcomes. Many of the measures are alcohol-specific, and some studies have classified subjects as "abstinent" or "not abstinent," not allowing for gradations in improvement. Since most studies find that more than half of the subjects consume at least some alcohol during a year of posttreatment follow-up (e.g., Emrick, 1975), important improvements in patterns of drinking behavior may be masked. In addition to the problem with the method for measuring drinking behavior, many other measures of outcome have been global and applied equally to all subjects being studied. Thus, occupational functioning, physical health, interpersonal relationships, and subjective life satisfaction may be measured for all subjects. However, no specific attention is paid to the areas in which subjects initially presented problems or to changes in these problem areas. In effect, measuring the same dimensions of outcome for all subjects may not truly reflect the differential success of different treatments for subjects with different presenting problems.

The basis for these global evaluations seems to originate from an erroneous assumption that "alcoholism" is a unitary syndrome. This assumption may be grounded in the disease concept of alcoholism (e.g., Jellinek, 1951), which regards alcoholism as a disease with recognizable symptoms and an inevitable course. Thus, the alcoholism of the board-room executive is the same as that of the housewife, with the same course and cure. This is similar to the assumption made about many physical diseases, in that, for example, the course of pneumococcal pneumonia is not much different from one socioeconomic class to another, and the treatment, in the form of medications and other appropriate interventions, will be effective, if followed, no matter who is the host of the pneumococcus.

Unfortunately, alcohol abuse and alcoholism are not as simple as the disease concept would superficially suggest. First, a great deal of evidence has now accumulated (e.g., Cahalan & Cisin, 1976) indicating that the course of alcoholism does not run as smoothly and inevitably as was once believed. Many adult Americans develop alcohol problems or alcoholism, but their problems lessen or disappear over time. Others may periodically have severe exacerbations of their problems, followed by relatively problem-free periods. A distinction, therefore, must be made between alcoholism, which is characterized by physical dependence on alcohol, and alcohol abuse, characterized by adverse emotional, vocational, interpersonal, or health consequences of drinking but with no symptoms of physical dependence. Second, many of the subjects in treatment outcome studies do not even meet Jellinek's criteria for being alcoholics, and therefore would not necessarily be expected to follow the progression of symptoms he outlined. By inference, they would not necessarily need the same types of interventions to deal with their drinking problems successfully. The reasons or original causes for drinking also appear to be quite varied (cf. Noble, 1978). It seems that a complex interaction of genetic factors, early learning experiences, family pattern, personality factors, social support systems, ethnic background, cultural norms, availability, and so on all interact differently in different individuals. It is therefore not at all surprising that this complicated pool of people with problems would have different treatment needs and would respond differently to the same treatment approach.

It can be seen that the approach to outcome evaluation that compares heterogeneous treatments has many limitations. Patient–treatment interactions are obscured, treatments and patients are heterogeneous, and measures of outcome have been global rather than problem-specific.

1.2. Patient–Treatment Matching

An alternate approach to placing heterogeneous groups of patients into the same treatment would be to match particular types of patients more carefully to particular treatment programs on the basis of patient problems or patient characteristics.

Glaser and his colleagues (1978, 1980; Ogborne & Glaser, 1981), in discussing the rationale for patient–treatment matching in the treatment of alcohol problems, describe three variations: (1) matches between attributes of clients and attributes of therapists, (2) matches between attributes of clients and treatment goals, and (3) matches between problems of clients and specific capabilities of treatments. While much of the data and discussion to follow are related to the third variation of the matching approach, there are some applications of both the first (e.g., McLachan, 1972) and the second approach (e.g., Miller & Caddy, 1977) to alcohol treatment efforts.

Several strategies for matching patients to treatment have been suggested. For example, Ewing (1977) has discussed the "cafeteria plan" of patient–treatment matching. The rationale of this approach is that patients, if provided with sufficient alternatives, will select those treatment alternatives that best fit their needs. Treatment programs following this model would provide a wide range of services and therapeutic modalities, and the staff and patients would select that combination which seemed optimal for each patient. While this plan appears attractive, Ewing provides no data to support the effectiveness or the cost-effectiveness of such an approach. One potential danger not mentioned by Ewing is that patients may select the easiest or least noxious treatment rather than the one most effective for them.

A somewhat different approach can be derived from a study by Price and Curlee-Salisbury (1975). Subjects in this study rated various components of treatment on a variety of subjective dimensions such as pleasantness, participation, and perceived worth. Using the ratings made by patients of the therapeutic benefits of the various treatment activities, the investigators identified three clusters of patients who differed systematically on their views of what treatment components were most valuable. Each of these clusters was identified by a different MMPI profile. It is conceivable that using a similar methodology, other investigators could replicate or extend these findings (also using more objective outcome criteria) to isolate predictors of success with specific types of patients in specific treatment modalities.

Two studies have used *post hoc* analyses to find differential outcomes for specific patient–treatment matches. For example, Wallerstein and his colleagues (1957) compared four treatment modalities (Antabuse, chemical aversion, group hypnotherapy, and "milieu" therapy) and their differential effectiveness with different diagnostic groupings. They found, for example, that compulsive character traits predicted good outcomes with Antabuse (disulfiram) treatment and passivity tended to predict a good outcome with group hypnotherapy.

A similar *post hoc* analysis of the subjects involved in the "advice" versus treatment study described above (Edwards *et al.,* 1977 Orford, Oppenheimer, & Edwards, 1976) found that patients who showed evidence of physical dependency on alcohol did better with treatment than they did with advice; the reverse was true for non-physically dependents subjects, who did better with advice than with treatment.

A third study of matching patient to treatments is found in the work of Reynolds, Merry, and Coppen (1979). These investigators examined the effectiveness of lithium carbonate in the treatment of alcoholism. As with the above two studies, they found no overall evidence of differential treatment effectiveness when comparing lithium with placebo. However, when the 16 patients who had scores greater than 15 on the Beck Depression Inventory were considered, patients on lithium were found to have drunk less and been intoxicated less than patients on placebo. Both in this study and in another (Kline & Cooper, 1979), lithium did not have a measurable effect on symptoms of depression. Thus, although lithium may be differentially effective in the treatment of depressed alcoholics, its mode of action is not at all clear.

As noted above, one study has examined the possibility of matching patients and therapists. McLachan (1972) posited that patients whose therapists provided conditions that matched the patient's "conceptual level" (which ranges from undifferentiated personality, through concerns with "right" versus "wrong," to integrated personality) would have better therapeutic outcomes than patients who were mismatched. His results indicated that patients who matched their therapists on conceptual level did show greater improvement than mismatched patients.

1.3. An Alternative Model for Treatment Evaluation

While these studies that match patients on some identified characteristics are an improvement over the global horserace approach, they still have many limitations. One important limitation is that the treatments themselves were heterogeneous. For example, group hypnotherapy has many active elements, as did the treatment program utilized by Edwards *et al.* (1977). The ideal approach might be to identify active elements in treatment and match these active elements to certain patient characteristics or presenting problems. Clinicians would identify specific areas to target for interventions and would then select the interventions with the best proven effectiveness for these particular problems. Outcome measurement would then become specific to the intervention in the targeted problem areas in addition to more global measures of drinking behavior and overall life functioning.

The approach proposed above sounds like a utopian dream. At this point, knowledge about the effectiveness of specific interventions is limited, and the majority of alcoholism treatment practitioners are most interested in testing their own theories or defending their own camps. Apart from these "political" considerations, the kind of evaluation model described here is time-consuming and tedious and does not allow rapid treatment of large numbers of clients in distress, who are seeking treatment regardless of whether any practitioners can currently deliver highly effective treatments. This chapter is an attempt to diverge from the conventional approaches to thinking about alocholism treatment. Three commonly used treatment approaches will be discussed in terms of their similar or different approaches to a range of specific patient problems. How these problems differ in different populations will then be considered. The final section of the chapter examines how the detailed consideration of treatment elements and partient elements can be integrated into a new framework that may be helpful to the study of alcoholism treatment and eventually to the clinical treatment of people with drinking problems.

2. TREATMENT VARIABLES

In this section, various levels of systems organization, from the biological to the interpersonal system level, will be used to organize an analysis of treatment approaches. The ways in which three major therapeutic approaches address each level of organization will be considered. This approach is undertaken to highlight the similarities and differences among theoretical models of treatment. In considering the crucial issue of matching patients and treatments, a systems analysis will highlight the differing emphases of these models which, in turn, will highlight some of the potentially productive patient–therapy matches that could be explored. The systems to be considered here will be the biological, individual, and interpersonal systems. The larger social system, while important, will not be emphasized in this chapter.

This section will describe how three major treatment models—Alcoholics Anonymous (AA), behavior therapy, and psychoanalytically oriented psychotherapy—intevene at each of the three systems levels described above. These particular treatment models were selected because they represent the most widely employed, widely discussed, and widely studied therapeutic modalities (cf. Noble, 1978). It will be assumed here that the reader is familiar with the basic tenets of these three treatments. For descriptions of these systems, the reader is referred to the excellent reviews of AA by Leach and Norris (1977), of behavioral models by Nathan and Briddell (1977), and of psychoanalytic psychotherapy approaches by Blum (1966). Table 1 summarizes the similarities and differences among these treatment models.

2.1. Biological Variables

The first system level is the biological system. The concern here is with the treatment implications of certain biological findings about alcoholics and alcohol abusers and with types of biological interventions that may be used in the treatment of alcoholism. Theories about biological or genetic bases for alcohol abuse or alcoholism will not be considered. The three psychological theories of treatment approach these issues quite differently.

2.1.1. Role of Medications

AA takes a fairly clear position about the use of psychoactive drugs. While drug therapies are recognized as part of the treatment of alcohol withdrawal syndrome, the use of other psychoactive drugs (such as antianxiety agents) is viewed negatively. In general, AA suggests that alcoholics use other drugs the same way they use alcohol—abusively and as a way to avoid learning to cope with life without chemicals. Thus, the ability to place faith in a higher power, the ability to make a personal inventory, and the ability to be willing to have God remove "defects" of character would be interfered with by using other psychoactive drugs to deal with personal "shortcomings." The use of disulfiram (Antabuse) is seen as undesirable as well, although many AA members seem to be quite pragmatic about its use. Generally however, internal change is strongly emphasized in the AA approach (see section on individual variables), and the establishment of artificial, external controls is viewed as less desirable.

Behavior therapists, by contrast, have said little about the use of psychoactive drugs in the treatment of alcoholism, although disulfiram has frequently been used in behavioral programs. Most of these treatments have used an operant approach, in which specific contracts have been developed to maintain a person on disulfiram. Reinforcers have been both positive and negative, including taking Antabuse as an alternative to jail for chronic DWI (driving while intoxicated) offenders (e.g., Haynes, 1973), contracting with spouses (e.g., O'Farrell & Cutter, 1979), or contracting with an Antabuse "buddy" (e.g., Azrin, 1976). Most of these programs thus assume that long-term compliance in taking disulfiram is desirable.

Table 1. Comparison of Three Alcoholism Treatment Models

	AA	Behavioral Therapy	Psychoanalytic Psychotherapy
BIOLOGICAL SYSTEM			
Psychoactive drugs	Does not use—believes that it continues dependence	No comment	May use intially, then does not use—continues dependence
Disulfiram	Discourages its use	May use with contingencies and then teach self-control usage	No comment
Neuropsychological deficits: Abstraction and new learning	Contains abstract concepts and concrete suggestions	Contains concepts shaped from concrete to abstract; suggestions are concrete	Contains abstract concepts; some insights may be concrete
Visual-spatial	Clients may have trouble finding meetings	No comment	No comment
INDIVIDUAL SYSTEM			
Personality change	Emphasizes self-reflection, confession, and restitution	Sees change in person variables as a process of situation-specific change goals	Stresses the reexperiencing and resolving of conflicts through the therapeutic relationship
Cognitive change Beliefs about self	Teaches clients to: accept self attribute blame to powerlessness Believe in no *self*-control Decrease self-esteem—"pride" a liability	Believe in self-control Learn problem solving Learn to think positive thoughts Learn new coping skills Increase activities	Teaches clients to: Support ego, build better (adult) defenses Increase activities to increase self-esteem
Beliefs about own drinking	Stresses belief that client is an alcoholic with no control over drinking	Labels alcohol use as a problem	No comment
Affective change	Teaches that: Negative feelings are a normal part of recovery One can decrease negative feelings by removing blame and by sharing with others Restituion of past wrongs is helpful	Change negative cognitions that precede negative affects Learn coping skills to deal with negative feelings Negative feelings as cues Relaxation training	Teaches clients to: Pace the experience of negative affects See negative feelings as a sign of progress in therapy Accept negative feelings as normal

Table 1. (Continued)

	AA	Behavioral Therapy	Psychoanalytic Psychotherapy
Skills acquisition:			
Environmental management	Urges clients to: Attend daily meetings Get a sponsor Avoid drinking environments	Urges clients to: Avoid drinking environments or repeated exposure to drinking environments Rearrange drinking environment Access environments incompatible with drinking	Leaves decision up to patient after insight is achieved
Communication	Encourages: "Twelfth step work" Talking in meetings Self-revelation Making restitution to others	Teaches: Social skills training Drink refusal training	Aims to increase self-revelation by talking in therapy
Treatment goals:			
Drinking	Seeks life long abstinence	Seeks controlled drinking under special circumstances Abstinence	Seeks controlled drinking or abstinence (individual decision)
Other life changes	Sees change as an essential part of treatment	Sees change as an essential part of treatment	Sees change as a consequence of successful therapy
THERAPEUTIC RELATIONSHIP			
The relationship	Achieves through sponsor: Self-revelation Directive Acceptance Sponsor self-awareness	Achieves through therapist: Limit-setting on noncompliance Directive Accepting, supportive	Achieves through therapist and therapist self-awareness May use self-revelation Patient works through reactions to the therapist
Response to drinking	Minimizes blame Moves on Increases AA involvement Client may come to meetings drunk	Minimizes blame Analyzes drinking and identify alternatives Reschedules if client is drunk	Interprets as testing of limits or of trust May meet if client is drunk
INTERPERSONAL SYSTEM			
Family	Urges family to: Build relationships within family Not blame Give feedback about actions Be understanding during recovery	Attempts to: Establish contingencies for drinking and sobriety Improve communication skills Improve parenting skills	Seeks to help spouse resolve conflicts by self or through therapy

(continued)

Table 1. (*Continued*)

	AA	Behavioral Therapy	Psychoanalytic Psychotherapy
Employer	Understands that alcoholism is a disease Encourages limit setting when drinking, support when sober	Establishes contingencies for drinking Teaches "healthy" behavior	No comment
Other Social Networks	Helps clients to develop through AA and to find new friends	Teaches clients to learn new social skills and to find new friends Contingency management in the criminal justice system	No comment

None have described techniques to assist clients in effectively discontinuing the use of disulfiram. A novel behavioral approach to the use of Antabuse has been suggested informally by Sobell (1979). Here Antabuse is used as a behavior alternative to drinking. Clients are taught to identify those cues for drinking that are most difficult to resist. They are then instructed that they may take Antabuse just prior to anticipated exposure to high-risk situations, making it easier to avoid drinking at those times.

Psychoanalytically oriented psychotherapists have somewhat complicated views of the use of medications in treatment. Since many believe that alcohol abusers have dependency conflicts, they may see the use of psychoactive medications early in treatment as a way to gratify dependency needs (by having the therapist give to the client) and to satisfy the problem drinker's hypothesized need for immediate gratification. However, long-term use of such drugs would inhibit the anxiety believed to be necessary for effective work in psychotherapy and would also interfere with the client's ability to "work through" dependency needs and associated needs for immediate gratification of impulses.

It should be noted, however, that many practitioners are much more pragmatic, rather than theoretical, in their approach to psychotropic medications. Thus, many therapists will refer their clients for antidepressant medications, lithium carbonate or antipsychotic medications if they show severe psychotic, manic, or depressive symptoms no matter what their primary theoretical allegiance is.

In summary, psychoanalytically oriented psychotherapists may be most amenable to the use of psychoactive drugs in treatment; AA is least amenable to their use. Behavioral treatments have most enthusiastically embraced the use of disulfiram in treatment.

2.1.2. Neuropsychological Deficits

Although there are at least five major organic states associated with alcoholism (including acute intoxication, alcohol withdrawal syndrome, alcoholic blackouts, the effects of chronic alcohol ingestion on neuropsychological functioning, and Wernicke–Korsakoff syndrome), the one most pertinent to psychosocial interventions is that associated with chronic alcohol ingestion. Studies suggest that chronic, non-Wernicke–Korsakoff patients show no overall impairment of intellectual functioning (Parsons & Farr, 1981). However, when neuropsychological functioning as measured by the Halsted–Reitan Neuropsychological Test Battery is examined, certain areas of impairment appear. Alcoholics consistently score lower than normals on measures of ability to learn, to form concepts, and to benefit from informational feedback (the Categories test) as well as on measures of spatial reasoning (the Tactual Performance Test), of ability to make fine auditory discrimination (the Speech Sounds Perception Test), and of ability to use simple concepts efficiently and flexibly in a visual–spatial task (Trails A and B) (Birnbaum & Parker, 1977). Thus, visual–spatial deficits and impaired ability to shift from one concept to another or to plan and implement cognitive strategies appear to be characteristic of alcoholics. These results are most salient for older alcoholics and for those with a history of drinking for more than ten years. Some data seem to suggest that most of these functions recover after one year of abstinence from the use of alcohol (Goldman, Whitman, Rosenbaum, & Vandevusse, 1978).

While the three treatment systems being considered here have not specifically developed interventions for these deficits, the models might differ in their ability to be effective with clients exhibiting these deficits. AA, for example, may be both helpful and confusing for a person with an impaired ability to abstract and learn new concepts. The core AA readings, *Alcoholics Anonymous* (1976) and *Twelve Steps and Twelve Traditions* (1972), are quite abstract and contain some difficult concepts. For example, the concepts of powerlessness (Step 1) and turning one's life over to God (Step 3) might be difficult to understand. However, AA also provides concrete, simple advice and catchwords or phrases that are easier to grasp. Newcomers (who probably have the most neuropsychological deficits) are told to attend meetings daily, join a group, and get a sponsor. They are told to just try to stay sober for 24 hours, to pray for guidance in the morning, and to thank God in the evening for the day. These prescriptions are all clear, fairly unambiguous, easy to implement, and probably well suited for the person who cannot abstract well. New members are told to get involved in the Twelve Steps, the most abstract part of AA, later in their recovery.

Behavioral interventions differ in how helpful or confusing they are for mildly impaired alcoholics or alcohol abusers. Most operantly based programs focus on fairly concrete discrete behaviors (such as drinking no alcohol), which are specified for the client to engage in so as to gain access to certain discrete reinforcers (such as job, friends, or a social club; e.g., Azrin, 1976; Hunt & Azrin, 1973). In contrast, programs that are more social-learning based (e.g., Sobell, Sobell, & Sheahan, 1976) may be more confusing to clients. Learning to identify subtle environmental cues for drinking, learning that cognitions and affects are related to drinking behavior and learning and practicing new thoughts are all fairly abstract concepts. Learning behavioral alternatives to drinking and learning how to apply these differentially in a complex environment may also be a Herculean task for the mildly organic client. However, behavior therapists frequently produce treatment manuals that explain these concepts and provide many concrete examples (e.g., Miller & Muñoz, 1976). These manuals may make it easier for clients to learn these complex concepts. Learning can also be assisted by breaking down behavior change into small steps (shaping) and making the abstract concepts somewhat easier to understand. Also, repeated practice in the form of role playing and homework may help.

Psychoanalytically oriented psychotherapy places a variety of cognitive demands on the patient. To observe one's inner life and one's reactions to a therapist and other significant figures in the environment as well as to be able to understand the relationship between these reactions and one's problems are all tasks requiring the patient to abstract far beyond his or her present reality. Indeed, the process of "making the unconscious conscious" is such a long-term and global goal that the actual ability to transfer therapeutic insights to the patient depends in large part on the skill and patience of the therapist and client.

In sum, psychoanalytically oriented psychotherapy appears least adaptable to alcoholics who suffer neuropsychological deficits and need immediate and concrete assistance. AA and behavior therapy may be suitable, but they both have the potential to be abstract and confusing to such patients. In the next section, we will move from a consideration of individual biological variables to individual psychological variables in treatment.

2.2. Individual Psychological Variables

The focus of this level of analysis will be on the defense mechanisms as well as emotional and cognitive experiences of the alcoholic and how the three treatments intervene with defenses and emotional or cognitive problems. Additionally, the degree of emphasis of each treatment model on the behavioral skills that alcohol abusers and alcoholics have or lack will be considered. Discussion will then turn to treatment goals and the therapeutic relationship.

Alcoholics have been described as using a range of defense mechanisms (e.g., Blum, 1966), including: (1) denial of unpleasant realities, (2) projection of responsibility for problems, (3) sublimation, and (4) repression. Alcoholics' personalities have been described as including primary features of narcissism, low frustration tolerance, hostility, and rebelliousness.

Several affective variables have frequently been described as significant for alcohol abusers. The variables considered here include guilt, remorse, depression, anxiety, and restlessness.

Cognitive variables of particular interest in this section fall into two major categories:

1. General beliefs about self and abilities, including (a) self-esteem (e.g., Beckman, 1978), (b) beliefs about the ability to control one's environment or life course, and (c) expectancies about the outcomes of attempts to cope with stressful situations.

2. Thoughts related to alcohol and one's own drinking problems, including (a) the client's belief about his or her status as an alcohol abuser or alcoholic, (b) the client's beliefs about his or her ability to control drinking, and (c) the way in which the client handles thoughts about wanting to drink, or "cravings."

In addition to different emphases on personality—cognitive and affective variables—the three treatments differ in the degree of focus on teaching alcoholics skills to change their external environments or to cope with stressful situations. The skills considered here include (1) rearranging or seeking out new environments, (2) expressing positive and negative feelings to others, (3) relaxation, (4) vocational skills, and (5) drink refusal.

The three treatment approaches differ dramatically in the ways and degrees to which they address these personality, cognitive, affective, and behavioral skills issues.

2.2.1. Personality Variables and Defense Mechanisms

Psychoanalytically oriented psychotherapy and AA both have a major focus on defense mechanisms and personality variables. Step 4 in AA requires alcoholics to examine their personalities and to identify "character defects." These are said to include, among others, pride, grandiosity, guilt, and self-pity. AA also stresses recognizing how one blames others for problems or rationalizes ("self-justification") one's own behavior. AA emphasizes that it is difficult to recognize one's own "character defects" and that many of these interfere with the alcoholic's abilities to complete this inventory. After one recognizes these defects, AA prescribes a specific course of change. The AA member is to admit his or her "wrongs" to another person (Step 5) and then to make amends directly to any person who was harmed if making amends will not cause any further pain to the other person involved (Step 9). Thus, AA stresses the necessity of personality change to help the alcoholic recover, the mechanism of change being self-awareness, confession, and restitution. The steps that involve these actions (Steps 4, 5, and 9) are surrounded by steps that emphasize the continuing need for the alcoholics to be honest with themselves, to rely on a "higher power," and to be willing to change. Thus, a strong spiritual component and a giving up of a sense of personal control are important elements in the personality change component of AA.

Psychoanalytically oriented psychotherapies, in contrast to AA, place a strong emphasis on the patient–therapist relationship as a vehicle for change. This component will be discussed fully in a later section.

Psychoanalytically oriented psychotherapy of alcoholism varies a great deal. One major source of variation is in the degree of uncovering of unconscious conflicts and early experiences as opposed to the strengthening of ego functions. All psychoanalytically oriented therapies have in common a fundamental assumption that alcoholics experience strong conflicts in dependency needs and in their relationships to authority figures. Thus, treatment initially focuses on meeting immediate dependency needs. This may be accomplished through hospitalization (e.g., Moore, 1972), through responding to whatever immediate and reality-based needs the patient has (e.g. Chafetz *et al.*, 1962), through an initially firm but overtly caring response from the therapist, or through the judicious use of medications. Intrapsychic conflicts are aroused through the transference, but treatment often focuses more on the patient's current actions. Confrontation of denial is seen as extremely important.

Group therapy and residential treatment are strongly advocated by psychoanalytically oriented therapists. The residential setting allows the patient to reexperience being in a family, to regress in a safe environment, and to experience and resolve feelings of rivalry, excessive dependence on powerful figures, anger, and other intense and overdetermined feelings. Delivering treatments in groups (e.g., Martensen-Larsen, 1956) often dilutes the intensity of negative transference feelings that might otherwise result in the patient's premature termination of treatment.

Thus, in contrast to AA, which emphasizes self-reflection and then changing current or past relationships through specific actions, psychoanalytically oriented psychotherapies see the process of personality change as occurring within the therapeutic relationship, whether this involves a single therapist, a therapy group, or a residential program. Both approaches, however, assume that alcoholics have enduring personality problems that must be dealt with if the alcoholic is to be able to change his or her drinking habits.

Behavioral approaches, by contrast, do not assume enduring personality problems and do not explicitly attempt to modify personality "traits." However, some behavioral approaches place a significant emphasis on modifying cognitions; these will be discussed next.

2.2.2. Cognitive Variables

As noted above, many studies and descriptive reports about alcoholics have focused on the important role of self-esteem, beliefs about self, and thoughts about alcohol. Again, the three treatment models differ in the emphasis they place on treating these beliefs and in the types of interventions used.

AA places a major emphasis on changing the alcoholics' beliefs about themselves. Step 1 in involvement in AA is reflected in the statement "We admitted we were powerless over alcohol—that our lives had become unmanageable." This step requires a major shift in the alcoholic's belief about self. AA suggests that until alcoholics are able to admit that they are powerless, they will be "the victim(s) of a mental obsession" (p. 22). This obsession involves the desire to drink and an inability to recognize that one's daily life is controlled by the use of alcohol. Therefore, the crucial first step in treatment involves a major change in beliefs about one's drinking and self-control. In this first step, AA has a fairly unique approach to dealing with alcoholics' problems with self-esteem. Self-confidence is labeled as "a liability," and the alcoholic is told that almost no one recovers alone.

Steps 2 and 3 continue the process of changing beliefs about one's ability to control one's actions. These steps emphasize developing a belief that a higher power can lead the person back to "sanity" and that individuals can decide to turn their lives over to this power to make decisions. These steps specifically state that the alcoholic has no internal resources to stay sober, that rational decision making is not possible, and that his or her previous approach to God (and other aspects of life) has been self-centered and narcissistic. The sum effect of these three steps is to leave the alcoholic with many negative views of self. This cognitive set probably facilitates a change in belief structure to one in which the alcoholic looks to a "higher power" for control.

Thus, AA explicitly teaches alcoholics to believe that they do not have control over their own lives and that having a sense of self-control is probably dangerous. Pride is labeled as a character defect and self-confidence, a liability. Instead of attempting to enhance self-esteem, AA paradoxically attempts to decrease it. This decreased self-esteem may enhance the alcoholic's involvement with AA and strengthen spiritual beliefs as well. AA also stresses the importance of recognizing and admitting one's alcoholism and labels any hope of being able to continue to drink in a controlled fashion as an indication that the person has not fully accepted Step 1.

AA and behavioral approaches are virtually at polar opposites in relation to these cognitive variables. First, the behavior therapist does not require that clients accept themselves as alocholics nor do they necessarily label alcohol use as a problem. If the client is willing to make a contract for treatment and can label any problem areas on which she or he is willing to work, that may be sufficient to begin treatment. If the client *is* labeling alcohol use as a problem needing treatment, this level of self-belief about one's alcohol use is sufficient to proceed.

There are a variety of behavioral approaches to modifying cognitions. For example, classical conditioning approaches focus primarily on internal change. Originally it was believed that aversion therapies actually resulted in new conditioned responses to alcohol and the cues associated with it. However, it is less clear today whether a new automatic response is being conditioned (e.g., Elkins, 1976), or whether clients are learning to anticipate negative consequences of drinking more effectively by learning new cognitive strategies. Thus, for example, in covert conditioning treatments (Cautela, 1967), the therapist will have the client imagine various behavioral sequences that previously had led to alcohol use. These will include various environmental as well as internal cues. The therapist then has the client imagine extreme aversive consequences and, through this process, hopes to condition a new response to these cues. Other forms of aversion therapy use a similar model but involve the client in actually experiencing an aversive event rather than imagining it. Thus, in chemical aversion programs (Madill, Campbell, Laverty, Sanderson, & Vanderwater, 1966), the client ingests an emetic drug and then alcohol just as the emetic properties take effect, so that the client begins to vomit just after taking a drink. It is believed that this sequence will condition a response of nausea to the sight and smell of alcohol. A similar model has been used in electrical aversion programs (Rachman & Teasdale, 1969), where electric shock is the aversive stimulus rather than nausea and vomiting from a drug.

A different conditioning approach has been taken in cue exposure programs (Blakey & Baker, 1980). This approach postulates that, instead of teaching alcoholics to avoid cues for alcohol, they should be exposed to these cues repeatedly, until the desire for alcohol in response to these cues extinguishes. As with the aversion therapy programs, it is not clear whether the potential effectiveness of this approach results from the extinction paradigm or from clients' learning new cognitions about drinking environments—such as thinking "I can handle this without alcohol"—or both.

In contrast to classical conditioning based treatments in which new cognitions may be an effect of the intervention, social-learning therapists deliberately teach clients to modify their cognitions. These interventions emphasize learning strategies to increase positive self-statements and decrease negative thoughts. For example, for a client who experiences strong feelings of depression, a behavior therapist might identify the kinds of negative self-statements that generate these feelings, such as thoughts that the client cannot cope with the problems or beliefs that he or she is bad or unworthy; then the therapist might help the client to generate more rational and positive alternative thoughts. A system to practice these positive thoughts and to practice countering the negative thoughts with more positive ones would then be established, and the client's progress in rehearsing these thoughts would be monitored. Additionally, the therapist would focus on modifying environmental conditions that cued these thoughts (the reinforcement schedules that maintained the depressive cognitions) and might also help the client increase his or her involvement in enjoyable activities. Similarly, if a client has frequent thoughts about wanting to drink or thoughts that a few drinks would not hurt (in a client where the treatment goal is abstinence—see below), the therapist might develop a cognitive restructuring program to counter these thoughts. For example, the client might list all the negative consequences of drinking and all the positive consequences of sobriety and then cognitively rehearse these consequences.

It can be seen that the behavioral approach does not address the global notion of self-esteem. Rather, behavioral approaches identify specific components of what might be called self-esteem, such as beliefs about competency, and directly intervene in changing the discrete problematic thoughts or behaviors. Social-learning models may also teach clients new skills (see below) which help clients to be more successful and would also indirectly change their beliefs about their competencies. In contrast to AA, believing that one is an alcoholic is deemphasized and replaced by a requirement that the client identify some problem behaviors that he or she wishes to change.

Just as behavioral interventions do not focus directly on global personality change, psychoanalytically oriented therapies do not directly deal with modifying beliefs. An emphasis on the client's recognition of his or her alcoholism does not exist. In general, therapy focuses on affective responses and helping a patient to understand the source of these responses. However, more ego-psychoanalytic interventions may focus on enhancing a patient's self-esteem and increasing the patient's involvement in reality-oriented activities rather than emphasizing negative and "baser" aspects of the self.

2.2.3. Affective Variables

The clinical picture of an alcoholic in the beginning of treatment is often that of a remorseful, guilty, and depressed person. Restlessness and anxiety are also often evident, especially during alcohol withdrawal. Many alcoholics present histories of depression and anxiety while drinking: for some, the history of these problems may actually predate the drinking problems. Again, the three models approach these affective phenomena differently.

AA does not directly intervene in the affective sphere, but much of the program has a strong indirect effect on negative emotions. For example, Step 1, which emphasizes that a person is powerless over alcohol, also implies that the person did not choose to be an alcoholic and had no control over drinking. One result of accepting this belief may be a decrease in the alcoholic's sense of guilt and remorse. Similarly, sharing one's "inventory" (Step 5) with another who is able to hear about past wrongs and not judge or punish the person for his or her actions or feelings may further serve to decrease guilt and depression. Making restitutions to others for past wrongs would also serve to decrease the negative affects.

AA also teaches its members to expect many painful feelings during recovery. Episodes of acute anxiety may be labeled as "dry drunks." If a newly recovering member talks about depression or anxiety, older members may share stories about their own experience of these feelings, reassuring the newcomer that these are a normal part of recovery and will pass as long as the person does not drink and keeps "working the program."

Behavioral models also intervene indirectly with negative affective states. As described above in the discussion of cognitive variables, the kinds of thoughts that lead to negative emotional states may be identified and strategies to change these beliefs introduced. Or, as described below, clients may be taught active coping skills, such as relaxation or assertiveness, to deal more effectively with these feelings when they do occur. Clients may also be taught to utilize negative affective states as cues that the situation they are in, or their response to it, is problematic. Thus, instead of labeling negative affects as undesirable, these emotions are seen as providing useful information to the client.

Psychoanalytically oriented psychotherapists see many of the negative feelings—such as depression, guilt, and anxiety—as initially overwhelming to the patient, and the therapist may attempt to control the pace at which the patient experiences these painful feelings (e.g., Blum, 1966). However, later in treatment the patient is allowed to experience these feelings more fully. The experience of negative feelings would be viewed positively, as an indication that the patient is becoming aware of painful impulses and conflicts, thus facilitating their eventual working through.

These first sections have focussed on the ways in which three treatments effect change in internal events—personality traits, cognitions, and affect. The next section will examine the differing ways in which the three models teach alcoholics how to deal wih the external world.

2.2.4. Skills Acquisition

An individual needs many skills in order to function most effectively in the world: vocational skills, leisure skills, communication skills, self-care skills, relaxation, and so on. Alcoholics who are trying not to drink also need to be able to say no to offers of alcohol and to find activities, occupations, and friends that are conducive to nonalcoholic drinking or abstinence. Both AA and behavior therapy specifically recognize and attempt to intervene directly in this area; psychoanalytically oriented psychotherapies intervene much more indirectly.

The final step in AA (Step 12) focuses on bringing the AA message to other alcoholics. Thus, members are encouraged to talk to other nonrecovering alcoholics and to "sponsor" new members. Thus, the persons engaging in "twelfth step work" are given specific guidance in how to talk to other people about their own alcoholism and engage in behaviors designed to help another person not drink (through sponsorship). In addition to providing some specific skills, "twelfth step work" probably has an impact on many of the internal variables discussed above. Giving to others is a way of constantly reinforcing one's own beliefs about AA and alcoholism and also of countering the narcissism that according to AA is a part of alcoholism. Bringing help to others is also a way to enhance one's own sense of self-worth. Step 5, in which the alcoholic shares his or her personal inventory with another, is also a way to indirectly improve communication skills by specifically emphasizing self-revelation.

AA's formal program almost exclusively focuses on internal change. However, the program is also structurd in a way that emphasizes making changes in how one deals with the environment. For example, a newcomer is given a number of prescriptions for behavior change. These include such advice as going to "90 meetings in 90 days" at the beginning of AA involvement. The result is that the newcomer spends a great deal of time in an activity that is incompatible with drinking and is with nondrinkers rather than drinkers. If a person has "cravings" for alcohol or experienes any dysphoric states, action is recommended: go to an AA meeting, read the "Big Book," call a fellow AA member, or do something incompatible with drinking (e.g., scrubbing a floor, hanging out laundry). AA writings and folklore are somewhat contradictory about what environments an alcoholic should enter. For example, the book *Alcoholics Anonymous* (1976) states that a recovering alcoholic should be able to go anywhere, whether or not alcohol is being served, including a bar, *if* she or he has a legitimate reason for being there. At the same time, many older members will confront a new member who wants to go to bars and suggest that going to old drinking haunts is inadvisable when one is first gaining sobriety.

Behavioral models also have many "prescriptions" for behavior change and provide skills training to help clients implement these changes. The interventions are usually tailored to the specific skills which the client appears to be lacking. For example, therapy might focus on what environmental situations cue drinking behavior, and therapy would help the client to develop alternate strategies to cope with these environments. The client may be taught to avoid strong discriminative stimuli for drinking, such as bars, parties, or weddings. Alternate skills training might also be emphasized to enable the client to generate new responses in these situations, as through practicing drink refusal, learning to obtain a nonalcoholic beverage as soon as the situation is entered, or mixing his or her own drinks. Another strategy is to teach the client to rearrange the contingencies of the situation. For example, the client might be taught to arrange to be picked up after being in a high-risk-for-drinking situation for a short period of time or to schedule a highly desirable activity that is incompatible with drinking to come immediately after spending time in that situation. The client will also most likely be taught strategies to rearrange the consequences of drinking: learning to get involved in enjoyable activities that are incompatible with drinking, learning to seek out a job or develop job skills that would lead to a job that is highly incompatible with drinking, and learning ways to provide self-reinforcement contingent on specific behavior changes such as not drinking for a specified period of time.

In addition to the focus on rearranging environments, and rearranging contingencies for drinking and not drinking, another form of externally focused intervention is the behavior therapists' emphasis on teaching clients skills that may serve as alternatives to drinking. For example, for a client who frequently drinks in response to situations involving hurt feelings or anger, assertiveness training or rational restructuring might be a focus of treatment. Or, for a client who drinks in response to feelings of anxiety, relaxation or meditation methods might be taught. Similarly, treatments might be structured to help the client to meet new people, learn how to carry on conversations, compliment people, or develop other such skills that the client lacks in order to remain sober.

In contrast to behavioral approaches, psychoanalytic approaches regard the patient's environmental changes as a logical outgrowth of internal changes. Thus, the psychotherapist would not explicitly address changing the patient's patterns of daily living. Many behavior patterns provide grist for the therapeutic mill, allowing the therapist to recognize and interpret the denial that might be symbolized by a patient's plan to go to bars each day but just not drink. Or an interaction sequence with a boss might be seen as evidence for continued conflicts in relationships with authority figures. The therapist, however, would be extremely unlikely to forbid the client to go to bars or to attempt to "teach" the paient a new way to request a raise.

2.2.5. Summary

In summary, the three approaches clearly differ in their emphasis. Both psychoanalytic and AA approaches see internal reconstruction as the essential vehicle for change. AA, however, also offers explicit and concrete instructions to alcoholics on how to change their environments and their daily actions. Behavior therapists may also focus on internal change, but they see this more as changing cognitive strategies than changing personality traits. To the degree that similar cognitive strategies are used in different situations, they are more similar to personality variables than are situation-specific acts, but they are not seen to be as pervasive or enduring as traditionally conceived personality variables. Much greater emphasis is placed on the client's learning how to change environments, actions, and internal cognitions, and explicit ways of doing so are structured into the therapy.

This section reviewed the focus and process of the individual aspects of alcoholism treatment. In the next section, the goals of the treatment will be discussed.

2.2.6. Treatment Goals

Nowhere in the alcoholism treatment field has more controversy been generated than in discussion of treatment goals. Pragmatic, ideological, and scientific issues have all been involved. There are two main dimensions to consider in relation to treatment goals: drinking goals and the relevance of establishing goals for change in other areas.

2.2.6a. Drinking Goals. The issue of whether or not an alcoholic can drink in a moderate fashion has generated a great deal of empirical research (e.g., Sobell & Sobell, 1973; Polich, Armor, & Braiker, 1980). Much discussion, however, has focused more on the philosophical views of the discussants than on research findings. AA is very clear in its views of drinking goals. AA subscribes to the disease concept of alcoholism, stating that alcoholics have an "allergy" to alcohol, that they crave alcohol when not drinking—experiencing loss of control when they start drinking—and that there is a biological basis for these observed phenomena. Their conclusion is that lifelong abstinence is the only hope for an alcoholic. However, since lifelong abstention is a formidable goal, AA advocates the "24-hour plan," which suggests that a person attempt to remain abstinent for that day and not set long-term goals.

In contrast, clinicians and researchers operating from a social-learning perspective have been most vocal in challenging and questioning the disease concept. Early behavioral researchers strongly advocated the notion that drinking was a learned behavior and that, therefore, even an addicted alcoholic should be able to learn how to drink in a controlled manner. Several clinical research programs have had moderate degrees of success in teaching "controlled drinking" (e.g., Sobells, W. R. Miller), although others have reported unsuccessful results (e.g., Ewing & Rouse, 1976). Guidelines for selection of candidates for controlled drinking training have been suggested (e.g., Miller & Caddy, 1977) but remain untested. Similarly, a number of strategies for teaching controlled drinking, such as training in the discrimination of blood alcohol levels, training in self-control procedures, training in changing drinking topography (such as changing the rate, frequency, and amount consumed per drink), contingency management procedures, and aversive conditioning procedures have all been utilized but not systematically compared.

Recently, however, behavioral researchers have begun to develop a more sophisticated, biological–behavioral view of drinking behavior. Genetic studies of tolerance to alcohol are contributing to a view that drinking and alcoholic drinking are much more complex phenomena than originally suggested. The implications for treatment offered by these lines of research are still not definitive, but may result in an increased interest in abstinence as a treatment goal while also pointing to more empirically based means of determining appropriate treatment goals.

Traditional psychoanalytic models of the treatment of alcoholism are very specific in *not* advocating abstinence from alcohol as a treatment goal. The rationale is twofold. First, drinking is seen as a defense mechanism that protects the patient against more severe forms of disorganization, such as psychosis, overwhelming anxiety, depression, or suicidal or homicidal behavior. Therefore, *traditional* psychoanalytic views would specifically forbid requiring the patient to be abstinent from the beginning of treatment. The second implication in regard to treatment goals is that abstinence is seen as less than a completely healthy adaptation and therefore an indication that the patient has not fully resolved the unconscious conflicts that led to the drinking problems in the first place. Thus, the ability to drink moderately was traditionally seen as the most desirable outcome in terms of drinking behavior.

Many modern alcoholism therapists who subscribe to psychoanalytic theory have modified their views about drinking and now support the notion that abstinence may be a necessary prerequisite for successful treatment. These modified notions are based partly on recognition of the disruptive effects that drinking has on the patients' ability to recognize and work through conflictual material, the disruptive effects of alcohol on new learning, as well as on an increasing emphasis on strengthening ego functions through activity and supportive treatment, rather than focusing on uncovering and reconstructive work in treatment. Psychoanalytic psychotherapists have also recognized that severe psychological disorganization does not necessarily occur when an alcoholic stops drinking.

Thus AA is the only one of the three models which has consistently viewed abstinence as the only appropriate drinking goal. Both behaviorally and psychoanalytically oriented clinicians have considered moderate drinking as an appropriate or desirable alternative goal for some patients, although respect for abstinence as a goal appears to be increasing among clinicians of both these perspectives.

2.2.6b. Other Life Change Goals. All three treatment models emphasize the importance of life changes other than changing drinking behavior. AA sees other life changes as equally essential as abstinence to true recovery, or what AA calls "sobriety," as opposed to being "dry." Thus, the self-examination described in the previous section—as well as constant attempts to change, continue to develop one's spirituality, and to help others—are really seen as the core of the recovery process.

Behavior therapists, like AA, have paid a great deal of attention to other life changes as necessary to support changes in drinking. Thus, learning new skills to handle social–interpersonal situations, new ways to cope with negative affects, changing cognitions, and developing alternative reinforcement systems are all integral parts of behavioral treatment.

Whatever the psychoanalytically oriented therapists' view of drinking goals, this treatment also clearly encompasses much more than modifying drinking behavior. The need to confront unacceptable impulses as well as to work through conflicts aroused by the relationship with the therapist, with other group members, or with others outside of treatment are the main issues of treatment. Change in these areas is seen as a prerequisite to recovery.

Thus, the three models differ greatly on their views of drinking goals, ranging from a belief that complete abstinence is an essential and lifelong goal, to a consideration of alternative outcomes in terms of drinking behavior, to a view that moderation is the most desirable outcome of treatment. At the same time, all three models view extensive changes in a number of life areas as an integral part of total "recovery." However, the content of these life changes and the changes that are most valued vary from model to model.

In order to effect change, there clearly must be an agent of change. The identiy of that change agent and how that person relates to the alcoholic on a number of dimensions are the focus of the next section.

2.2.7. Role of the Therapeutic Relationship

Most forms of psychological intervention require a therapist. (Although computers and self-help manuals are now being used to deliver some structured forms of treatment, people still seem to predominate.) However, controversy arises in considering who should provide treatment, what is appropriate and inappropriate behavior for the therapist, or whether the person should indeed even be viewed as a therapist. Some of the dimensions of interest include the questions of the nature of the relationship between alcoholic and therapist, especially in terms of how directive the therapist is; the role of self-revelation by the therapist; and how the setting of limits is handled, especially in how the therapist responds to drinking episodes.

2.2.7a. The Therapeutic Relationship. In AA, a new member is not assigned a specific "helper." An alcoholic can attend meetings, talk to people, select meetings, and come as often or as rarely as he or she wishes. It is up to the individual to decide that he or she wants to have a "sponsor." The sponsor is chosen by the individual alcoholic on the basis of whether the alcoholic feels comfortable with the person and if that person seems to be helpful. The relationship of the sponsor to the new AA member is fairly unique. First, the sponsor may be extremely directive with his or her "pigeon" (new member). The number of meetings that the person should attend is prescribed; also, the person is told to read the book *Alcoholics Anonymous* (1976) or other AA literature and instructed to call day or night if he or she feels like having a drink. The sponsor interacts frequently with the new member by relating his or her own experiences with alcohol. Whenever the new member is experiencing, for example, urges to drink, doubts, depression, "resentments," and so on, the sponsor may respond by talking about similar experiences and sometimes may refer to things in AA that were helpful, such as reading certain passages in the AA literature or contemplating a certain step of the "Twelve Steps." The sponsor rarely challenges, preaches, or requires acceptance of particular beliefs. For example, if the member is uncertain about the notion of a "higher power," the sponsor might suggest that such a power can be anything that is outside of the alcoholic, even if it is only the power of AA. Rather than confronting and driving the person away or making him or her feel ashamed of feeling doubt, all these feelings are presented as normal, acceptable, and part of the process or recovery. Clearly, only another AA recovering alcoholic can be a sponsor.

While AA provides a great deal of advice to sponsors on how to relate to the member whom they are sponsoring, the relationship of the behavior therapist to the alcoholic is not carefully defined (however, see Hay & Nathan, 1982). Establishing a warm, empathic relationship is stressed. Obtaining compliance so that the client will engage in homework, try out new behaviors, and attend treatment regularly are important elements of treatment. The therapist may attempt to use differential reinforcement of desired therapeutic behaviors of the client and will often set limits on noncompliance. For example, the therapist may reschedule a session if the client has not completed homework that was assigned in the previous session. Similarly to AA, the behavior therapist is usually quite directive in treatment. Specific actions may be identified as important, and the therapist will often then expect the client to engage in these new behaviors. The sessions themselves are quite structured and may involve teaching the client a new skill in the session by describing the skill and then having the client rehearse it in the session.

While AA and behavior therapy may have some guidelines or usual practices to define the therapeutic relationship, one of the *keys* to psychoanalytic psychotherapy of alcoholism lies in the therapeutic relationship (e.g., Gottesfeld & Yager, 1950). Traditional models of treatment require the therapist to present a neutral image to the client onto which the client can then project his or her own distorted images. More contemporary psychotherapists however, may present a more open, emotional image (e.g., Moore, 1972) and may be described as "an active intervenor, participant, reality interpreter—very open of his own feelings, willing to say no, available, nondoctrinaire. He is a problem-solver, not an objective and diffident observer . . ." (Moore, 1972, p. 229). Within this relationship, the therapist can confront the patient's reality distortions, how he or she relates to the therapist, and how this relationship relates to deeper conflicts and to repetitive patterns of interaction in the patient's life outside therapy.

An alternative approach advocated by some psychoanalytically oriented treatment programs is to hospitalize the patient and allow him or her to regress and experience conflicts with both "maternal" and "paternal" figures among the staff. By constantly being helped to discriminate between present reality and his or her distortions, and by learning how these reactions and distortions relate to repetitive experiences, the patient is supposed to learn more adult defenses, which will, in turn, permit a wider range of adaptive behavior.

Since the patient–therapist relationship is so crucial to psychoanalytically oriented psychotherapy, some emphasis is also placed on helping psychotherapists be aware of their own reactions and needs and how these may interfere with treatment. For example, some authors have suggested that the therapist may be controlled, successful, and ambitious but may also shelter an "unsatisfied oral child" (Moore, 1972, p. 228). The alcoholic's gratification of "infantile" needs through drinking may elicit envy on some level from the therapist, which could lead to overmotivated attacks on the patient or, conversely, overindulgence and lack of limit setting even when very appropriate and necessary in treatment. Thus. the therapist must be well trained to be able to recognize countertransference reactions and know how to deal with these effectively without harming the treatment. Many psychoanalytically oriented psychotherapists might suggest that the recovered alcoholic should be the last person to treat the alcoholic, because these particular needs and conflicts may be so close to the surface that the therapist might not be able to establish and maintain the necessary distance to engage in this intensive form of therapy.

Thus, the general nature of the relationship between therapist or sponsor and the alcoholic is quite different in the three therapeutic modalities. However, how the therapist responds to drinking episodes is somewhat more similar across these three treatments.

2.2.7b. Therapeutic Response to Drinking. Many alcoholics and alcohol abusers consume alcohol during treatment or return to addictive drinking patterns. AA recognizes this phenomenon in several ways. First, they predict that a person will inevitably return to an alcoholic drinking pattern once he or she consumes any alcohol. If an AA member does drink, guilt and self-blame are minimized by emphasizing that the alcoholic should be living "one day at a time." However, length of sobriety is counted in AA, and the "counter" goes back to zero after a drinking day. Sponsors often will not talk to the persons whom they are sponsoring when these people are drunk; instead, they will talk about the episode the next day and will reemphasize commitment to AA and following the AA program. However, people may attend AA meeting while they are intoxicated if they are not disruptive.

Behavior therapists set fairly firm limits in treatment and may reschedule a meeting if the client comes into a treatment session intoxicated. This, of course, is in marked contrast to the AA approach, which will allow a person to stay at the meeting even if drunk. At the same time that the therapist sets limits and directs the sessions, he or she also attempts to communicate an acceptance of the client. For example, if a client has a drinking episode during treatment (if the goal is abstinence) or if a client drinks beyond the level set (if the goal is controlled drinking), the therapist will, after the client is sober, help him or her analyze what conditions led to the drink, what the person was thinking and feeling, and what the consequences were. The therapist and client will then work together to identify alternative strategies that would have led to more positive consequences than did drinking or overdrinking. Similar to AA, the client is not punished for drinking.

If a client drinks during psychoanalytically oriented treatment, this may be viewed in a number of ways (e.g., Blane, 1977). It may be seen as acting out in the therapy, in which case limit setting is required, as well as interpretation of the meaning of the behavior for the patient and within the present context of the therapeutic relationship. The behavior may also be seen as a way of testing the relationship to see if the therapist will really be accepting of the more undesirable aspects of the patient's being. If this testing of trust is seen as the primary feature of the drinking, it may be accepted and interpreted at a much later date in the treatment.

This section of the chapter has focused on the role of the individual change system in treatment. In the next section we will consider the role of external, environmental changes in treatment.

2.3. The Interpersonal System

Although the focus of each of the three systems may be on individual change, treatment may also focus on creating new environments for alcoholics as they recover or on ways of rearranging or recreating old environments in order to support nondrinking or reduced drinking. The previous section discussed how the individual could reconstruct his or her own environment. The focus in this section is on how the therapist or agent of change might rearrange the patient's environment. Three different interpersonal systems will be considered in this section: the family of procreation, the employer, and other social networks.

2.3.1. The Family

AA is very explicit in defining who has responsibility for changing relationships; it lies with the individual alcoholic. However, there are two full chapters in the major AA book (*Alcoholics Anonymous*, 1976) devoted to the family. The counsel to the families on how to change is clear. Wives (the chapter is written "To Wives" instead of "To Spouses") are advised to focus on changing their own behavior: they are told to not become angry and to avoid giving advice to their spouses on how to change their drinking. Focusing on building and maintaining their own relationships with their children is also seen as an important part of the wives' actions. Giving the husband feedback about the effects of his drinking is suggested. Giving him information about AA is also advised if the husband expresses an interest in doing something about this drinking. Also, letting friends and family know about the alcoholic's "sickness" is suggested as a way to increase their understanding and therefore their support. Thus, the initial focus of AA for the spouse is on changing his or her own behavior vis à vis the drinking. Advice is offered on how to begin to create a different social network around the alcoholic by engaging friends and family in understanding what is happening.

AA also provides a great deal of advice to the family on how to respond to a recovering alcoholic. Tolerance, understanding, and patience are emphasized. Joining the alcoholic in meditation or other spiritual experiences is also seen as important. While AA acknowledges that it is difficult for the family to readjust to the alcoholic as he or she recovers, the message to the family is on adjustment and acceptance, just as the message to the alcoholic is on his or her own responsibility in restoring relationships with the family. Thus, AA firmly emphasizes the responsibility of each side in rebuilding relationships in the family. Most of the focus of this rebuilding is on learning how to deal with sobriety rather than on building a new relationship system.

The discussion here has presented what AA suggests to spouses of alcoholics. It should be noted that since AA began and since their original literature was produced, separate organizations have developed to help the families of alcoholics. Alanon, Alateen, and Alatot are, respectively, for the adult family members, teenage children, and preteenage children of alcoholics. While these organizations have no formal affiliation with AA, the philosophies are extremely similar—as is the advice to families, although much more detailed than what is presented here.

Treatment interventions based on social-learning principles which are aimed at the social networks of the alcoholic have used one of two approaches: (1) to change the interactions between the alcoholic and the significant other or (2) to rearrange the contingencies of reinforcement to reinforce sobriety or reduced drinking and to punish or withdraw reinforcement as a consequence of inappropriate drinking.

Virtually all behavioral interventions with families have focused exclusively on the marital relationship. In early case reports (e.g., Miller, 1972), the focus was on contingency management, in which the alcoholic and spouse drew up a contract whereby the alcoholic would have to pay a monetary fine to the spouse for engaging in inappropriate drinking. Relationship issues were considered somewhat in that the wife was to stop "nagging" about the drinking. When she broke the contract, she was to pay a fine to her alcoholic mate. Other early programs focused on interventions for spouses only (e.g., Burtle, Whitlock, & Franks, 1974) and tried to teach them how to apply positive and negative consequences to the drinking behavior as well as other desired or undesired behaviors of their alcoholic mates. More contemporary approaches to behavioral interventions in alcoholic marriages focus on relationship change as well as contingency management. For example, O'Farrell and Cutter (1979) teach couples to establish and maintain contracts around the use of Antabuse, but they also teach communciation skills to improve their ability to solve problems and increase the rate of positive rather than negative exchanges in the relationship. This latter change is seen as important because it is postulated that the negative, coercive interactions that characterize alcoholic marriages actually may cue further drinking. Other investigators, (e.g., McCrady, 1978), are focusing on ways to teach spouses more effective ways to cope with drinking and nondrinking. Thus, behavioral therapists have seen the involvement of the spouse system as important, in order to teach new skills to the spouse or the couple. These skills have included both communication and contingency management skills.

In contrast to AA and behavioral approaches, which teach spouses coping skills to deal with an alcoholic mate, psychoanalytically oriented therapists have taken a different view of the spouse. Psychoanalytic writers became interested in alcoholic marriages, and especially the wives of alcoholic men, as early as the 1930s (Paolino & McCrady, 1977). These women were seen as neurotic, experiencing significant psychosexual conflicts as expressed through being overcontrolling, needing to dominate a weakened male, ravaged by sexual fears and inadequacies, or defending against deep dependency needs. Marriage to an alcoholic mate was conceptualized as a defense against these unconscious conflicts or needs; some writers believed that such women would decompensate to psychosis or severe depression were their husbands to stop drinking permanently. While many clinical and research studies (reviewed, for example, in Paolino & McCrady, 1977) have found little support for this view of wives of alcoholics, a more contemporary psychoanalytic view of alcoholism and marriage has not emerged.

Based on these early notions, treatment interventions directed at the marital system were focused on the individual conflicts of the wife. She was provided with individual or group therapy to help her resolve her own conflicts as related to her marriage, but no specific prescriptions were offered on how she might change her own actions vis à vis the alcoholic or his drinking episodes. Some studies have reported that involving the wives of alcoholics in such a treatment program improves the probability of a good treatment outcome for the alcoholic (e.g., Smith, 1967), but these studies have not had appropriate control groups for comparison.

We now turn our attention to a second type of system intervention: the employer system.

2.3.2. The Employer

AA has a specific message to employers about alcoholic employees. First, an understanding of alcoholism as a disease, not controlled by will and self-control, is emphasized. Then, limit setting and support are both counseled. If an employer believes that the employee does not want to stop drinking, firing is advised. It is suggested that the firing might be an important "jolt" in helping the alcoholic to realize the seriousness of his or her drinking. However, if the employer believes that the employee wants help, different advice is provided. Honest discussion with the employee about the alcoholism, its effects on his or her work, and the employee's value when sober are all part of the initial conversation. Supporting the employee in getting to a doctor for necessary medical treatment is the next step. Then, talking freely with him or her about problems, indiscretions, or "shocking" actions are all seen as part of the employer's role in supporting recovery. As the alcoholic's sobriety increases, the employer is encouraged to use the alcoholic to talk with other employees troubled by alcohol. Also, it is advised that the employer give AA literature to junior executives so that they can be more knowledgeable and helpful with alcoholic employees.

Despite the supportive attitude advised, AA still suggests that the employer should consider firing the employee who returns to the use of alcohol if the employer does not feel that the employee "sincerely" wants to stop drinking.

Behavioral approaches to modifying the employer system have usually followed strict contingency management procedures. In such programs, employers are taught to apply clearly discriminable consequences for drinking and not drinking. For example, Hunt and Azrin (1973) taught employers to withhold pay from alcoholic employees for days missed due to drinking. Other clinical programs may establish contracts between employer and alcoholic that require the employee to take Antabuse at work and to be forbidden to work or be paid on days on which the Antabuse is not taken.

More recently, behavioral psychologists have begun to approach many health problems from a new perspective, often called "behavioral medicine" or "behavioral health psychology" (e.g., Matarazzo, 1980). Programs are developed to teach positive life-style habits, which are believed to be a way to prevent the development of serious health problems. Many such health behavior programs have been begun in industries. One component of many programs teaches non-alcohol-abusing employees skills to moderate and control their alcohol intake. Companies offer employees the opportunity to participate in such programs but do not establish any monitoring of subsequent behavior change. Thus, in contrast to the behavioral contingency management approach, which focuses on reinforcement and punishment, behavioral health programs focus on providing employees with opportunities to learn positive, health-producing behavior patterns in a noncontingent setting.

AA and behavioral programs have paid a great deal of attention to the social systems surrounding the alcoholic or alcohol abuser. Psychoanalytic theory is fundamentally a model of internal processes, and the treatment focuses on internal changes. To our knowledge, no programs have been developed on the basis of psychoanalytic notions to intervene in industry.

2.3.3. Other Social Networks

AA gives no specific advice to the friends of alcoholics. However, the whole organization of AA results in a reorganization of an alcoholic's friend and social network. For example, since daily attendance at AA is advised, the alcoholic is regularly exposed to a different social network than the old network of drinking buddies or social-drinking friends. Obtaining a sponsor provides a close relationship associated with abstinence, honesty, and spending a great deal of time together. Thus, if an alcoholic becomes fully involved in AA, he or she will find friends who do not drink, who share common beliefs, and who accept the alcoholic almost *because of* common weaknesses and faults. Thus, it is clear that AA gives a great deal of attention to ways of reordering the alcoholic's interpersonal world. Understanding and acceptance are key concepts in rearranging this world, and individual responsibility for change is also central. Because of this latter emphasis, the key to sobriety is still seen to lie with the alcoholic and the process of internal change described earlier. However, AA does attempt to make this process easier and more effective by counseling those around the alcoholic as well.

In intervening in other social networks, behavioral therapists and researchers have shown a gradual shift in emphasis over the past ten years which, in some ways, parallels the shift in employer interventions. Early interventions taught friends of an alcoholic to leave a bar if their friend ordered an alcoholic beverage. As noted above, contemporary approaches teach the alcoholic client skills to increase the quality and range of his or her social interacting, thus placing the responsibility for changed social interactions more with the alcoholic than the friends. Similarly, early interventions through the legal system rearranged contingencies. For example, in one typical program (Haynes, 1973), chronic public drunkenness offenders were given the option of taking the required one-year jail sentence or becoming involved in an outpatient Antabuse clinic to which they reported daily for their medication. If they failed to report, the consequence was jail. In contrast, Miller and his colleagues (e.g., 1978, 1980) provide services to DUI offenders, offering a program to teach them skills to decrease their alcohol consumption and learn adaptive skills to handle various problem areas (as through relaxation training or assertiveness training).

In summary, ten years ago behavioral and AA approaches to the alcoholic's environment were very different, with a behavioral focus on rearranging consequences and making punishment contingent on drinking, and with AA recommending support and feedback while still emphasizing that responsibility lay with the individual alcoholic. Behavioral approaches have moved closer to this view, now teaching the alcoholic self-control skills to rearrange his or her own environment and to maximize access to reinforcers when not drinking rather than having the therapist initiate this rearrangement.

In this early part of the chapter, we have identified major components of alcoholism and alcohol abuse treatment, highlighting the similarities and differences among our three models on these components. In the next section, we will consider some of the major issues of concern in different populations.

3. PATIENT VARIABLES

In the preceding sections we have discussed how alcoholism treatment approaches differ in the nature and extent to which they address biological, individual, and interpersonal factors relevant to the treatment and rehabilitation of problem drinkers. In a complementary way, problem drinkers can be thought to differ from each other along similar dimensions. For example, in the *biological* domain, problem drinkers can differ in genetic predisposition, neuropsychological impairment, tolerance to and dependence on ethanol, and abuse of other psychoactive substances. In the *individual* domain, differences in affect, drinking pattern, personality, and beliefs and attitudes about alcohol's effects have been noted among problem drinkers. Problem drinkers also differ on *interpersonal* variables such as socioeconomic status, social support, and role functioning. Many more areas of indivdual differences could be added to these brief lists.

Each of these three domains of individual differences in problem drinkers have been shown to have prognostic significance. For example, neuropsychological impairment (e.g., Abbott & Gregson, 1981), personality (e.g., O'Leary, Donovan, Chaney, & O'Leary, 1980), attitudes about alcohol (e.g., Cahalan, 1970), and sociodemographic variables such as marital and socioeconomic status (e.g., Mindlin, 1959; Bromet, Moos, Bliss, & Wuthmann, 1977) are important predictors of outcome and suggest that treatment efforts should address these factors. In the discussion to follow, important characteristics of subtypes of alcoholics will be examined, using the biological–individual–interpersonal framework as a guide for focusing on potential patient–treatment matching opportunities. Specifically, we will consider the characteristics and explore the treatment implications of these characteristics for the older problem drinker, the female problem drinker, and the problem drinker with other significant psychopathology. These three subtypes were chosen because they differ from the more prototypical younger, male primary alcoholic in a number of respects and thus illustrate much of the heterogeneity of persons with alcohol problems. Limited space precludes us from considering other important subtypes such as problem drinkers who are members of ethnic minorities, child and adolescent problem drinkers, and homosexual problem drinkers. However, it is hoped that our discussion of the older problem drinker, the female problem drinker, and the problem drinker with other significant psychopathology will illustrate many significant issues in patient–treatment matching that have wide applicability. The general research implications that patient–treatment matching raises will be addressed in the final section of this chapter.

3.1. Problem Drinking in Old Age

Determining the prevalence of problem drinking in the elderly is complicated by several factors. The terms "old age" and "elderly" do not have universally shared meanings, and investigators vary widely in how they use them. Furthermore, since older people are less likely to be employed, married, or involved in as many informal social networks as younger people, definitions of problem drinking that rely heavily upon traditional criteria of social or vocational impairment may not be well suited for studying drinking in the elderly. In addition to these definitional problems, rates of problem drinking in the elderly vary across the geographical regions and settings that have been surveyed. We would therefore not be too surprised to see that estimates of rates for problem drinking in older people vary from 2% in community surveys to almost 50% in hospitalized patients (Gomberg, 1980; Mishara & Kastenbaum, 1980).

Despite these widely varying estimates, one consistent finding to emerge in the literature is that older people drink less and have lower rates of problem drinking than younger people. Most existing evidence suggests that this reflects a tendency for individuals to drink less or give up drinking as they get older (Cahalan, Cisin, & Crossley, 1969) and/or a tendency for heavier drinkers to have a higher mortality and therefore be less likely to live until old age (Schmidt & deLint, 1969). If alcohol problems are relatively less frequent in older people, why should this group be singled out for special consideration? Certain reasons are apparent: (1) as the proportion of older people in the U.S. continues to increase, the proportion of problem drinkers who are elderly should also be expected to rise, and (2) because older people are frequently confronted with other complicating problems such as reduced social supports, physical illness, and reduced income or poverty, the impact of alcohol problems is apt to be severe.

3.1.1. Special Characteristics of Older Problem Drinkers

The population of older problem drinkers is by no means homogeneous. Experts in the area find it useful to mention possible differences among older problem drinkers who differ in gender, ethnicity, and duration of problem drinking (Gomberg, 1980). However, some general statements can probably be safely made about older problem drinkers as a group, with the recognition that certain statements may be more applicable to specific subgroups.

Comparisons of the kinds of drinking problems most often experienced by younger versus older individuals reveal both similarities and differences (Gomberg, 1980; Mishara & Kastenbaum, 1980). In a national study of American drinking practices, Cahalan et al., (1969) showed that older men less often reported related alcohol problems than their young counterparts. The most frequently reported problems were frequent intoxication (9%), problems with spouse and relatives (5%), psychological dependence (4%), and health problems (4%).

3.1.1a. Biological. Physical illness, when present, can magnify the toxic effects of alcohol through impaired alcohol metabolism, lower vulnerability of diseased organs to alcohol effects, and toxic interactions between alcohol and medications (both prescribed and nonprescribed). Even in the absence of physical illness, certain effects of alcohol appear to be more pronounced in older people. Obviously, the older alcoholic who has been drinking for much of his or her adult life will often have physical problems, including neurological deficits, resulting from a long history of alcohol abuse.

3.1.1b. Individual. Although—as opposed to younger alcohol abusers— relatively little is known about the personality characteristics and desciptive psychopathology of older problem drinkers, it is generally felt that psychiatric symptomatology plays less of a role in their drinking than in the problem drinking of younger people (Rosin & Glatt, 1971). In general, early-onset alcoholism is associated with greater psychopathology than later-onset alcoholism (Abelsohn & Van der Spuy, 1978). The older problem drinker who begins drinking or develops drinking problems late in life often appears to be drinking in response to life crises characteristic of old age, such as bereavement, retirement, social isolation, physical illness, and marital discord (Rosin & Glatt, 1971). While the older problem drinker whose alcohol problems began years earlier has been found to have more psychological maladjustment and more dependence on alcohol (Rosin & Glatt, 1971), the developmental crises and circumstances of old age may actively contribute to these older people's current drinking problems.

3.1.1c. Interpersonal. Older people are more likely to have diminished social networks and ranges of activities due to retirement, loss of spouse, reduced income, restricted opportunities for transportation, and physical illnes. Additionally, family problems are a frequently cited difficulty among older problem drinkers (Gomberg, 1980; Cahalan, *et al.,* 1969). Thus, older problem drinkers may be more likely to have diminished and chaotic social support systems than younger problem drinkers. Given the importance of social support in predicting outcome in drinking problems in general (Mindlin, 1959; Bromet, *et al.,* 1977), this would appear to be an important factor to consider in developing treatment interventions for this population.

Because many older problem drinkers are retired or unemployed, alcohol-related work difficulties are not common problems among these individuals (Cahalan *et al.,* 1969). The social system that is most likely to encounter the older problem drinker is probably the health care system. Gomberg (1980) reviews evidence showing that older patients in both general medical and psychiatric hospitals frequently have alcohol-related problems, with estimates of problem drinking ranging from 15% to 49%. The legal system is also likely to become involved with the older problem drinker. "Difficulties with the police" were found by Cahalan *et al.* (1969) to be among the most prevalent problems for older problem drinkers. In fact, there is some evidence to indicate that when older people do run into problems with the police, it is likely to be because of drinking (Epstein, Mills, & Simon, 1970).

3.1.2. Treatment Implications for Older Problem Drinkers

3.1.2a. Biological.   A number of treatment issues are raised by the use of a wide variety of drugs in the treatment of elderly alcoholics. These involve both practical difficulties in using drugs with these patients as well as the appropriateness of instituting drug treatment with them. In regard to the practical aspect, both because of physical disease and normal aging, the metabolic rates of certain drugs can be relatively slow, possibly resulting in overly prolonged effects and/or an accumulation of the drug to toxic levels. Also, many commonly used sedative/hypnotic drugs can interfere with cognitive and motor functioning and result in unintended subjective distress to the patient. To make matters even more complex, the elderly alcoholic may be on a variety of drugs for other ailments, and the addition of another medication may cause toxic drug interactions or unwanted blocking of the therapeutic effect of a drug.

As alluded to above, the use of psychoactive drugs may not be most appropriate in the treatment of older problem drinkers if, as some data indicate, problem drinking in this population may be part of a stress response to the biological, psychological, and social consequences of aging. From this perspective, drug treatment may be construed as a palliative, which is ultimately antitherapeutic because it reduces motivation for (1) taking direct action to remedy a difficult developmental and environmental situation, (2) "working through" the meanings and implications of the stress event, or (3) learning coping skills for dealing with stressful situations in nondestructive ways. Studies comparing the effectiveness of these different treatment options for elderly problem drinkers could be quite informative.

The use of Antabuse with older problem drinkers raises several important questions. Perhaps most importantly, for which population of older drinkers is Antabuse treatment safe and/or effective? Memory impairment could conceivably render Antabuse ineffective because the patient might forget to take his or her daily doses. Alternatively, the patient with memory impairment might inadvertently take more than the prescribed dosage. Memory problems might lead a patient to drink while on Antabuse if he or she forgets about having taken it or about the consequences of an Antabuse–alcohol reaction. Research examining the effect of memory impairment on the ability to use Antabuse appropriately would be quite helpful.

The physical state of the older problem drinker has implications for psychosocial as well as pharmacological treatment. The older problem drinker, especially one who has been drinking for many years, is more likely than the younger prob-

lem drinker to have a range of neuropsychological deficits that may impede traditional therapeutic approaches. While the cognitive and perceptual abilities of
many problem drinkers may be relatively undiminished in later life, many older
problem drinkers will have significantly impaired perceptual, information processing, and memory capabilities. Treatment approaches with these patients
should be adapted accordingly. Research examining the kinds of modifications that
help to minimize these possible impediments to treatment would be especially useful. Research questions of possible importance include the following: Do older
problem drinkers with memory difficulties require more extensive treatment (e.g.,
more sessions, more conditioning trials) because of possible learning problems? Is
the repetitiousness of AA particularly well suited for the older alcoholic with
learning and memory problems? Are insight-oriented treatments to be avoided
because of the extent of cognitive demands? To what extent is it useful for treatment to focus on cognitive impairment, if present, as a disability to be coped with?

3.1.2b. Individual. As discussed above, problem drinking in the elderly
often appears to be related to stressful life events and life-style changes. This
would suggest that a variety of coping-oriented techniques such as stress management training, stress inoculation training, relaxation, "grief work," and other techniques designed to help an individual "process" past stressors and prepare for new
ones could be adapted and evaluated for effectiveness with the elderly. Research
evaluating the extent to which treatment should focus on environmental influences
rather than on drinking behavior itself (Droller, 1964; Rosin & Glatt, 1971; and
Zimberg, 1978) would be valuable.

As previously mentioned, the older problem drinker with neuropsychological
deficits may present problems for the therapist interested in bringing about internal changes by means of cognitive interventions. The processes of perceiving,
understanding, and remembering might be limited, precluding successful treatment. Research evaluating the effect of different neuropsychological deficits on the
ability to learn and apply different treatment approaches would be extremely valuable. Freud's (1905) early claim that "near or above the age of 50 the elasticity
of the mental processes on which the treatment depends is, as a rule, lacking—old
people are no longer educable" (p. 264) is not accepted by many contemporary
psychoanalytically oriented psychotherapists (e.g., Cohen, 1981). However, the
need to adapt cognitive types of interventions to the perceptual–cognitive abilities
of the patient remains an important issue.

3.1.2c. Interpersonal. Some writers (Zimberg, 1978; Gomberg, 1980) have
stressed the utility of "social therapies" (e.g., family and group therapy) in the
treatment of the older problem drinker. This position is based on the observations
that family problems are frequent in this population and that the older problem
drinker often has impoverished social networks. Research comparing the effectiveness of individual therapy versus "social therapies" with older problem drinkers is needed to determine which approach is most effective. It would be important

to determine if social network variables (i.e., high versus low social support) predicted treatment outcome differentially for individual versus group or family treatment. The extent of treatment gains related to changes in patients' social networks would also be useful to determine.

Given the important role that lack of social support is thought to play in problem drinking among the elderly, it would be perhaps useful to evaluate whether intensive alcohol treatment programs could be matched in effectiveness by more informal social groups with less professional support. Because the prevalence of drinking problems in the elderly is low, it would be helpful to determine whether effective treatment with these patients can take place in groups or programs not composed exclusively of problem drinkers. That is, can effective group or milieu treatment of the elderly alcoholic take place in treatment settings primarily composed of non-problem-drinking elderly (psychiatric) patients. Comparisons of the effectiveness of treatment geared primarily for the alcoholic (e.g., traditional alcoholism treatment centers) versus treatment focused primarily on problems of the elderly (cf. Zimberg, 1978) would prove useful for planning treatment services and referrals. An important related issue is the match between therapist and patient. If elderly patients were found to have better outcomes with older therapists, it would be extremely useful to determine whether older nonprofessional persons could be trained to provide effective service in paraprofessional roles.

Because many elderly problem drinkers are often socially isolated, it seems likely that alcohol problems in these persons often go undetected. Thus, in addition to being relatively rare, older individuals with drinking problems are also hard to identify. An evaluation of various ways to increase case finding among services frequently used by older people, such as health and social services, would be extremely helpful. For older people dependent upon human service agencies and institutions, effective treatment strategies could possibly be based upon utilizing these services as community reinforcers (e.g., along the line of Hunt & Azrin, 1973). Because older people typically underutilize mental health services (Gatz, Snyder, & Lawton, 1980), it will be important to develop treatment services that older alcoholics will view as relevant and potentially helpful.

3.1.3. Summary

Although drinking problems are not as prevalent among the elderly as among younger people, there is strong reason to believe that when problems do occur, their impact is apt to be severe. Several differences between younger and older problem drinkers have been noted. Perhaps most salient is the probable role played by biological, individual, and social stresses of growing old in our culture. Cognitive and physical problems resulting from alcohol abuse can be magnified in the elderly. The social support network of the elderly alcoholic is often fragmented or depleted. The design of effective treatment programs for this population will need to take into account their specific problems and needs.

3.2. Problem Drinking in Women

Community survey data reported by Cahalan and Cisin (1976) estimate that severe drinking problems occur in about 4% of women, while rates for women in treatment for alcoholism are usually estimated to range from 0.1% to 1%. Across a variety of settings, female problem drinkers are less prevalent than male problem drinkers. Keller and Efron (1955) reported the ratio of male to female alcoholics ranged from 3:1 for private physicians to 11:1 for police custody. Although alcoholism is less prevalent among women than among men, there is some evidence to suggest that alcoholism among women is increasing. Cahn (1970) reported that between 1963 and 1968 the ratio of male to female alcoholics admitted to mental hospitals decreased from 5.5:1 to 4.2:1. Corrigan (1980) conservatively estimates the number of women problem drinkers in the United States at a million or more.

3.2.1. Special Characteristics of Female Alcoholics

The age of onset and the course of problem drinking have frequently been noted to differ between men and women. Reviews of the empirical literature (e.g., Beckman, 1975; Gomberg, 1976) report that women are likely to become problem drinkers at a later age than men. These same reviewers also report data suggesting that women's problem drinking progresses more rapidly than men's, a phenomenon referred to as "telescoping." "Telescoping" has been used to describe the frequently observed accelerated course of women's problem drinking both from abstinence or social drinking to problem drinking and from the onset of problem drinking to obtaining treatment services. The clinical importance of this phenomenon is difficult to determine. It has been proposed that the rapid progression of drinking problems in women reflects greater "psychopathology" in female as compared to male alcohol abusers (Beckman, 1975). However, rather than focusing upon possible differences in the amount of psychopathology, it is probably more useful to specify differences in the kinds of behavioral problems that women problem drinkers are especially likely to have at the time of treatment. As is true in our discussion of other types of problem drinkers, the category of women problem drinkers is quite heterogeneous and the following generalizations are probably more true for certain subgroupings than others.

To begin with, the kinds of problems that women face as a consequence of their drinking differ from those of men to the extent that their traditional social roles differ. It is not surprising that women are less likely to have financial, vocational, and legal problems resulting from their problem drinking (e.g., Mulford,

1977) given that they are less likely to work outside the home, be the principal breadwinner, or have contact with the police. Even when women are confronted by police or employers because of their drinking problem, they are less likely than men to encounter the same degree of negative consequences (McCrady, in press). To further complicate matters, women problem drinkers have been noted frequently to hide their excessive drinking from others, presumably because of the social stigma attached to heavy drinking among females (Curlee, 1970). Because of these factors, many women problem drinkers may not *appear* to have incurred as many kinds of problems as their male counterparts. Thus, traditional problem-drinking assessment instruments may not be especially sensitive to the problem drinking of women. Even quantity–frequency measures of alcohol consumption will tend to underestimate effective differences between male and female levels of alcohol intake if appropriate adjustments for sex and body weight are not made. In short, assessment of problem drinking in women needs to take into account the specific social roles of the individual women and the consequences of their drinking in relationship to these roles.

3.2.1a. Biological. Women alcoholics appear to be especially sensitive to the negative medical consequences of alcohol abuse. Bourne and Light (1979) review a number of studies documenting the fact that various alcohol-related diseases, including pancreatitis, cirrhosis, ulcers, and cardiovascular disorders are more prevalent among women than among men alcoholics. This higher level of physical problems does not seem to be related to a longer history of alcohol abuse among women, since they were noted to have a more accelerated development of physical problems resulting from heavy drinking than men drinkers in one study (Ashley, Olin, leRiche, Kornaczewski, Schmidt, & Rankin, 1977). In addition, women alcoholics have been reported to suffer a much higher proportion of gynecological problems than other women. However it is not known if these problems are an antecedent or a consequence (or both) of the patients' excessive drinking (Gomberg, 1976). It has been suggested that some women increase their drinking in response to premenstrual and menstrual discomfort, with alcohol possibly serving as an analgesic or diuretic, but this has not been well demonstrated.

Women problem drinkers have been noted often to abuse drugs other than alcohol. For example, Corrigan (1980) reports that 71% of her sample abused minor tranquilizers. As calculated from Corrigan's (1980) data, significant proportions of these women alcohol abusers were found to abuse a variety of other drugs including sleeping pills (43%) and stimulants (21%).

3.2.1b. Individual. Although reviewers (e.g., Beckman, 1975; Gomberg, 1976; Bourne & Light, 1979) are quick to point out the possibly more salient similarities, male and female problem drinkers have often been noted to differ on the kinds of psychological symptoms they exhibit. Most notably, women drinkers have been observed to have more depressive symptoms than their male counterparts, possibly reflecting a greater incidence of affective disorder. Receiving almost as much attention are the findings that alcoholic women report higher levels of guilt and anxiety and lower levels of self-esteem than men (Beckman, 1975; Gomberg, 1976; Bourne & Light, 1979). Because of the apparent predominance of dysphoric affect in female alcohol abusers, it has been said that they drink to cope with their symptoms, in contrast to their male counterparts who drink to express their (characterological) psychopathology (Tamerin, 1978).

The notion that many female alcoholics are drinking to cope with a sex-role conflict has received a good deal of attention (Wilsnack, 1973, 1976). Although it is felt that such a conflict can take many forms (Scida & Vanicelli, 1979; Beckman, 1978) and may also be characteristic of male alcoholics (Gomberg, 1976), a basic difficulty in the integration of masculine and feminine traits and strivings is posited. While the conflict is considered psychological, it is though to be strongly affected by changing sex roles and cultural values. Although writers on female problem drinking have emphasized the importance of the sex-role conflict, little about the specific therapeutic implications of this posited factor has been written.

There is a body of evidence suggesting that environmental factors are of greater importance in female than in male problem drinking. First, while a genetic component has been demonstrated for male alcoholism, this has not been shown for female alcoholism (Goodwin, Schulsinger, Knop, Mednick, & Guze, 1977). More importantly, women alcoholics tend to report more specific life stresses, particularly stresses that can be thought of as object losses or blows to self-esteem, than male alcoholics (Beckman, 1975). Whether or not such stresses are truly related to drinking problems is difficult to say, since women tend to report more life stress events and to assign more impact to these events than do men in general (Horowtiz, Schaefer, Hiroto, Wilner, & Levin, 1977). Given the prevailing negative social attitudes about female drinking, it would also seem likely that women have more reason to attribute their problem drinking to external causes (Corrigan, 1980).

3.2.1c. Interpersonal. One area of frequently reported problems among female problem drinkers is marital relations. For example, in a recent study, female problem drinkers were more than twice as likely as their male counterparts to report a poor relationship with their spouse (Mulford, 1977). In this same study, female problem drinkers were also found to be married more than once more frequently than male problem drinkers. It is not clear what this tendency toward marital disruption reflects. Is the impact of female problem drinking on the family particularly severe? Are males less supportive of their problem-drinking spouses than females are? Are female alcoholics more "sensitive" or accurate reporters of their domestic life than their male counterparts? Although at present there are no clear answers to these questions, empirical research aimed at explicating these issues would be valuable clinically.

For a number of reasons discussed above, female alcoholics are less likely than males to have vocational or legal problems resulting from their drinking. Because female alcoholics are often found to have high rates of physical symptomatology (Bourne & Light, 1979) as well as psychological symptomatology (Beckman, 1975), it is likely many of them have contact with the health care and mental health systems.

3.2.2. Treatment Implications

3.2.2a. Biological.   Female problem drinkers coming in for treatment will frequently report the use of other drugs, particularly minor tranquilizers and sleeping pills and, to a lesser extent, stimulants or marijuana. Whether or not it is useful to prescribe psychoactive medications for these women is an important research and clinical question. It is possible to view the continued use of drugs such as minor tranquilizers as a major impediment to treatment. However, some writers (e.g., Tamerin, 1978) claim it is important to reach a compromise on the female alcoholic's request for tranquilizers with the feeling that an outright refusal is countertherapeutic. At present, we know of no empirical studies relating use of tranquilizers to therapeutic outcome. Such studies seem important, given the salience of this issue in the treatment of female alcoholics. Research elucidating when minor tranquilizers may be helpful (e.g., during alcohol withdrawal, at the beginning of therapy, during situational crises) and how it should be administered (as needed or at regular intervals) would be valuable additions to the literature.

Furthermore, since the nonprescribed use of drugs may be denied or minimized, it would be useful to determine whether blood or urine screens for measuring the extent of other drug abuse would increase the "hit rate" of diagnoses of other drug problems.

It would also be helpful to determine whether patients with diagnosable affective disorders benefit from a trial of antidepressant or lithium (see below, under "Implications for Treatment"). When such treatment should be initiated, how, and for how long it should be maintained are also important unanswered questions.

As noted above, female problem drinkers have frequently been noted to conceal their drinking from family and friends. Is Antabuse an important treatment adjunct for these women? Is it useful for the female alcoholic to make an explicit Antabuse contract between herself and other family members? In assessing the effectiveness of Antabuse with the female alcoholic, particularly the one who has a history of concealed drinking, it would be important to evaluate the effect on those family members who in the past may have feared that the patient would drink if left alone. These other family members might have responded to such concerns by either seeking to overprotect or by distancing themselves from the patient. Antabuse treatment could conceivably allay these concerns somewhat and lead to positive changes in family environment.

There is some evidence that certain women drink excessively in response to premenstrual tension and that some women increase their drinking during and after menopause (Belfer, Shader, Carroll, & Harmatz, 1971) Where such an association is suspected, it would be important to discover whether some form of biological intervention (e.g., hormonal, analgesic, or diuretic) would be helpful.

3.2.2b. Individual. It is usually thought that the "female alcoholic is drinking to medicate a symptom of psychic distress" (e.g., Tamerin, 1978). As discussed above, the female problem drinker has often been described as exhibiting high levels of guilt, depression, and anxiety. How these problems should be approached in therapy are important issues.

While most therapeutic approaches conceptualize some relationship between psychological distress and problem drinking, they often differ on the extent to which they focus on these painful affects versus overt drinking behavior. Does the problem drinker who has high levels of psychic distress require special treatment? Should treatment attempt to reduce negative affects directly by focusing therapy efforts on these problems? What techniques are most useful for reducing guilt, depression, and anxiety and for increasing self-esteem? Is it most productive for the therapist to strive for internal changes in the form of new self-statements, restructured object relations, or submission to a higher power or to strive for external changes such as increases in pleasurable activities, adoption of drinking-incompatible recreation, avoidance of drinking cues, improved social communication skills, and development of new interpersonal relationships?

Considering the amount of attention sex-role conflict has received in the literature on female problem drinking, it is surprising that the therapeutic implications of these findings have not been well explored. What types of techniques are useful for "resolving" such conflict? Should such conflicts be resolved through attempting internal or external changes? To what extent is the sex of the therapist an important variable in the identification and treatment of these issues? Given the amount of interest that sex-role conflict has elicited in those who study alcohol problems in women, it would seem extremely important to measure this construct when treating alcoholic women, attempting to relate treatment components to changes in sex-role conflict, and to ultimately relate changes in sex-role conflict to changes in drinking status and treatment outcome broadly defined.

The finding that women tend to report environmental events as antecedents to problem drinking also deserves mention. This finding suggests that there is a set of women problem drinkers who may be experiencing an acute adjustment reaction or stress-response syndrome. For these women, is some form of brief psychotherapy or crisis intervention an effective treatment option? Would training in stress management techniques such as relaxation or stress inoculation training (Meichenbaum, 1977) reduce the probability of relapse in these patients?

3.2.2c. Interpersonal. For those problem drinkers who are married or involved in similar kinds of intimate relationships, it might be very important to involve the spouse in treatment. This is particularly true for female problem drinkers, since they are likely to report marital difficulties as a specific problem and are less likely than men to have an occupation or significant activities to draw support from outside of the home. There are a number of important questions concerning how best to do couples therapy with female problem drinkers. For example, under what conditions is it best to proceed with couples treatment as opposed to individual treatment? Factors such as the willingness of the spouse to participate in treatment, the extent to which the spouse is supportive of sobriety, whether or not the spouse also has drinking problems, and presumably many others would appear to be variables worthy of future study. Given that couples treatment is desirable for many female problem drinkers, what is the best way to involve the spouse in treatment? Research examining the optimal role for spouse involvement in treatment would provide useful information for the practicing clinician.

A substantial proportion of women problem drinkers will become progressively socially isolated as their drinking problem develops; this pattern would seem to be particularly true for unmarried, younger women (Corrigan, 1980). Furthermore, existing relationships are often based around drinking. Thus, for many problem-drinking women, there is a lack of adequate nondrinking social support, particularly support for attempts at sobriety. For these women, providing or helping to develop new social networks might be of high therapeutic priority. This could conceivably be brought about in several ways: participation in AA, group therapy, development of social skills, employment for those unemployed drinkers, and so on. The relative effectiveness of different strategies for developing social support networks is clearly an important research question. Important dimensions for comparing social support networks might include material support (e.g., money, shelter, employment), emotional support, the extent to which the network is supportive of the patient's drinking goal, the extensiveness of the social-support network, and the degree to which the network is achieved through individual effort and skill or provided by family or social agencies.

The findings that women alcoholics tend to hide their drinking from friends, relatives, and employers and are less likely to experience employment or legal difficulties as a result of their drinking suggest that the identification and referral of problem-drinking women is a very difficult undertaking. Although there are probably no easy solutions, greater public recognition of drinking problems in women and a greater encouragement of police and employer to take a more active role in dealing constructively with these problems would probably be of help. Thus, it would be useful to determine whether efforts to develop explicit contingencies surrounding alcoholic behavior with police and business could result in reduced rates of women's problem drinking or increased referral to and follow-through with treatment.

3.2.3. Summary

The female alcoholic has been found to differ from her male counterparts in a number of ways that may have important implications for effective treatment.

Many women alcoholics have been reported to have high levels of painful affects, significant sex-role conflicts, other drug abuse, a tendency to conceal drinking, discrete life events precipitating drinking episodes, and marital problems. They have also been noted to be less likely than male alcoholics to have legal or vocational problems resulting from their drinking. Several important questions that are discussed include the following: Are traditional problem-drinking assessment techniques adequate for use with female populations? How is it best to deal with other drug abuse in the female alcoholic? How can Antabuse be used to curtail concealed drinking? How can issues of "sex-role conflict" be identified and successfully resolved? How and when should a spouse become involved in treatment? How can new social networks be developed for the female alocholic?

3.3. Problem Drinking in Persons with Other Psychiatric Disorders

Problem drinking is frequently noted to coexist with a variety of psychiatric disorders. In most of these cases it is assumed that alcohol abuse is a consequence or "complication" of the other disorder. Less frequently considered is the possibility that alcoholism might precipitate psychiatric disorder. In fact, Bowman and Jellinek (1941) have claimed that excessive drinking could not bring about psychosis by itself. Such a claim may be premature in light of evidence showing that certain types of life events likely to be a consequence of problem drinking (loss of job, separation, and divorce) have been found to precipitate depressive episodes (Paykel, Myers, Dienelt, Klerman, Lindenthal, & Pepper, 1969) and other psychiatric disorders.

Those psychiatric disorders that have been shown to be correlated with the diagnosis of alcoholism include affective disorders and sociopathy (e.g., Winokur, Rimmer, & Reich, 1971) as well as anxiety disorders (e.g., Quitkin, Rifkin, Kaplan, & Klein, 1972; Mullaney & Trippett, 1979). The following discussion will focus on these. Schizophrenia and other diagnoses also have been shown to be associated with alcoholism, but less frequently; therefore they will not be discussed here.

3.3.1. Special Characteristics of Problem Drinkers with Other Psychiatric Disorders

3.3.1a. Affective Disorder.   Affective disorder can be frequently diagnosed in samples of female alcoholics. Studies by Winokur *et al.* (1971) and Schuckit and Morrissey (1979a) found from 14 to 25% of female alcoholic patients meeting diagnostic criteria for affective disorder. In contrast, Winokur *et al.* (1971), found that only 3% of male alcoholics could be diagnosed as suffering from an affective disorder. Winokur points out that the kind of affective disorder manifested by these patients is primarily depression and that mania occurs in alcoholics and their relatives no more frequently than chance. There is some evidence (e.g., Freed,

1970; Reich, Davies, & Himmelhoch, 1974) that a significant proportion of bipolar patients (about one-third) drink excessively during manic episodes. Because of this it has been suggested that these manic episodes may present as episodic drinking binges or what is often referred to as dipsomania.

Determining the presence of an affective disorder in an individual does not merely rely on establishing the presence of depressive symptomatology. The problem drinker appearing for treatment can be depressed for a number of reasons other than the presence of an affective disorder. Woodruff, Guze, and Clayton (1973) have reported that even when alcoholic patients with diagnosable affective disorders were excluded from their study sample, 11 of 14 (79%) of their alcoholics showed depressed mood. Depressed mood can be a direct consequence of recent heavy drinking. It can also result from situational difficulties or a realistic assessment of the severity of a drinking problem. In order to establish a diagnosis of affective disorder with alcoholism, these other sources of depressed affect must be ruled out and a history of signs and symptoms of a depressive disorder either antedating or existing independently of problem drinking must be established. While it may be clinically useful to determine the sequencing of the development of problem drinking and affective disorder, determining which problem is "primary" can often prove to be a difficult task. Both may have existed for many years prior to the patient's entry into treatment, and both may have sporadic courses, with periods of remission alternating with symptomatic periods. Thus primary–secondary distinctions will often be difficult to make with certainty.

3.3.1b. Anxiety Disorders. Alcohol abuse is often listed as a complication of the anxiety disorders (e.g., *Diagnostic and Statistical Manual of Mental Disorders,* 1980; Marks, 1978a). Woodruff, Guze, & Clayton (1972) found that 25% of their sample of 62 anxiety neurotics were heavy drinkers and about 15% were alcoholics. Marks, Birley, and Gelder (1966) found that 2 of 38 (5%) of the agoraphobics they studied were alcoholics. In a recent study in England, Mullaney and Trippett (1979) reported that 32% of the alcoholics they studied were rated as having agoraphobia or a social phobia and an additional 36% were rated as having borderline phobic disorders of these types. These figures reported by Mullaney and Trippett (1979) would seem too high, especially in light of the fact that other investigators have not reported a substantial proportion of alcoholic patients as suffering from anxiety disorders.

Mullaney and Trippett (1979) reported that in their sample, phobic symptoms tended to precede the development of problem drinking. Quitkin *et al.* (1972) stress the importance of undertaking a thorough psychiatric history with a good deal of attention focused on the preproblem drinking period, since the "true clinical picture will be obscured by the more obvious drug abuse." An incomplete psychiatric history might be one reason that some investigators do not report a substantial prevalence of anxiety disorders among problem drinkers.

3.3.1c. Sociopathy. Problem drinking and sociopathy (antisocial personality disorder) often coexist, particularly in men. In a study of patients in treatment at an alcoholism treatment center, Winokur, Reich, Rimmer, and Pitts (1970) found that 20% of the male alcoholics had primary diagnoses of sociopathy. The strong relationship between alcoholism and sociopathy can be illustrated by data from a recent study in Finland. Virkkunen (1979) found that 79% of adult male prisoners and 87% of juvenile delinquents who met the criteria for sociopathy also met the criteria for alcoholism.

Sociopathic alcoholism as defined by Schuckit (1973) "involves the onset of alcohol abuse . . . in a person with ongoing antisocial personality or sociopathy" (p. 159). In this definition, the primacy of the sociopathy and the secondary aspect of the alcoholism, at least chronologically, is explicit. Many alcoholics without sociopathy may exhibit antisocial or criminal behavior, especially when intoxicated, and it is imperative that the diagnosis of sociopathy be made only if an individual meets the diagnostic criteria for sociopathy. Although technically a detailed history is needed to assess whether a pattern of antisocial behavior antedates abusive drinking, since sociopathy is defined as having an early onset (prior to age 15 according to DSM-III; 1980), sociopathy would rarely be diagnosed as occurring secondary to alcoholism.

3.3.1d. Biological. Schuckit and Morrissey (1979b) have recently shown that female alcoholics with primary affective disorder or sociopathy are more likely than primary alcoholics to report using both depressants and stimulants. This was especially true for sociopathic alcoholics in his sample. Of these patients, 75% reported using depressants and 85% reported using stimulants. People with anxiety disorders are also likely to abuse other depressant drugs, perhaps to a greater extent than alcohol (Quitkin *et al.,* 1972). Thus it would appear that alcoholics with other psychiatric problems are at high risk for drug abuse in addition to their alcoholism.

The combined use of drugs and alcohol may have more debilitating physical effects than those of alcohol by itself. For example, Schuckit and Morrissey (1979b) found that drug-abusing women alcoholics were more likely to have liver damage than nonabusing alcoholics. Polydrug abuse, particularly of CNS depressants, has been found to result in high rates of neuropsychological impairment that persists over at least three months of abstinence and possibly longer (Grant, Adams, Carlin, Rennick, Judd, Schooff, & Reed, 1978). Therefore, many alcoholics who abuse other drugs may have significant organic impairment.

To varying extents, each of the psychiatric disorders under consideration has been related to underlying biological factors, and alcohol intake can be conceptualized as having an ameliorative effect on the biological substrate of each subtype. For example, alcohol has been thought to act as a euphoriant through its effect on central catecholaminergic mechanisms (e.g., Kissin, 1974). Alcohol has also been shown to have anxiolytic properties, and these may be related to its GABA-ergic activity (Gray, 1977, 1979; Nestoros, 1980). Finally, alcohol has been posited to increase cortical arousal in the chronically underaroused sociopath (Tarter, 1978). Thus, alcohol may have some beneficial effects for depressed, anxious, and antisocial people. Furthermore, the pharmacological mode of each of these effects might be mediated by different actions of alcohol.

3.3.1e. Individual. By definition, painful affects play a prominent role in the problem drinking of persons with affective or anxiety disorders. Surprisingly, in Schuckit and Morrissey's (1979a) sample of female alcoholics, "depressive symptoms—relatively persistent sadness that did not qualify for a diagnosis of affective disorder—were seen most frequently in the subjects with antisocial personality" (p. 614). Clearly, high levels of subjective distress, especially depression, are relatively frequent in alcoholics with affective disorder, anxiety, and sociopathy. Depression may be a motivating factor in bringing alcoholics into treatment. Woodruff *et al.* (1973) found that the major difference between alcoholics who did and did not seek treatment was the presence of depression.

The sociopath has been described as having deficits in learning to associate events and behaviors with aversive consequences (e.g., Hare, 1970). Therefore, the sociopathic alcoholic may lack awareness of the problematic nature of his or her drinking. Such learning deficits could hamper efforts to attempt covert (cognitive) and overt (e.g., chemical aversion) conditioning of negative consequences. The sociopath has also been viewed as having deficits in impulse control (e.g., Gorenstein & Newman, 1980), as demonstrated by a tendency to behave in ways that maximize short-term (immediate) gains irrespective of long-term (delayed) gains or losses. It is not clear whether these impulse-control and learning deficits represent two different phenomena or are merely different views of the same one. In either case, helping the sociopathic alcoholic to acquire greater self-control would appear to be an important goal. In addition to these deficits, the sociopathic individual may be chronically underaroused (e.g., Hare, 1970) and engage in antisocial acts and other sensation-seeking behaviors as a means of providing a more optimal level of stimulation. As mentioned in the preceding section, Tarter (1978) has suggested that alcohol consumption might serve an arousal-increasing function for the sociopath.

3.3.1f. Interpersonal. By definition, the sociopathic alcoholic is less likely to appear for treatment with current social assets such as marital or vocational stability or a well-established social network, characteristics that bode well for outcome. In addition, the behavioral tendencies likely to be exhibited by the sociopath, including tendencies to lie or be aggressive, may make the establishment of a strong working therapeutic relationship difficult. Sociopathic alcoholics also often come to treatment by way of coercion from schools, courts, and employers. Thus the sociopath often has few of the resources that are good predictors of treatment outcome.

Depressed patients, in general, both withdraw from relationships with others and seem to alienate others by their behavior (Coyne, 1976; Price, 1978). Presumably, depressed patients with secondary alcoholism share these characteristics. Although this pattern of interpersonal behavior could conceivably lead to marital and vocational difficulties, whether or not depressed alcoholics show more impairment in marital, social, and vocational adjustment than other alcoholics has yet to be reported. Similarly, it is difficult to comment on the interpersonal system of the problem drinker with anxiety disorder.

3.3.2. Implications for Treatment

3.3.2a. Biological. One might suspect that some alcoholics with other psychiatric disorders could be successfully treated psychopharmacologically. Although this may be true, especially when the other psychiatric disorder is depression, there is little empirical evidence to justify psychopharmacological intervention at present. In a double-blind treatment study of alcoholics (Kline & Cooper, 1979), lithium was found to be more effective than placebo at reducing problem drinking over a 48-week period. Reynolds *et al.* (1979) report that lithium was effective in preventing relapse in depressed alcoholics. Because of the small number of depressed alcoholics in this study, it is probably premature to start recommending this treatment, although the initial results appear promising. In both studies, it is noteworthy that lithium was not found to reduce rated levels of depression more than placebo.

Although there has been some suggestion that tricyclic antidepressants may be of benefit to the patient with primary affective disorder and secondary alcoholism (Schuckit, 1979), there are no data yet in support of this position. The use of antidepressants for alcoholics *in general* has not been found useful in controlled trials (Viamontes, 1972). There is a clear need to delineate when lithium and antidepressant drugs may be of benefit. Equally needed are studies examining the interactive effects of psychotherapy, behavior therapy, and drug treatment. Even when a severe psychiatric disorder is primary to problem drinking, alleviation of the "underlying" psychiatric disorder may not necessarily reduce problem drinking, since abusive drinking may be maintained by a number of factors other than the psychiatric problem by the time an individual presents for treatment.

The use of psychoactive medications in problem drinkers with anxiety disorders has not been well studied. There is some evidence suggesting that antidepressant medications including MAO inhibitors and tricylcic antidepressants are helpful in a number of anxiety and phobic conditions, particularly those characterized by panic attacks (e.g., Klein, 1964; Zitrin, Klein, & Woerner, 1980). Quitkin *et al.* (1972) report some preliminary data suggesting the usefulness of antidepressants in the treatment of "phobic anxiety syndrome complicated by alcohol abuse." It should be pointed out that even when anxiety patients respond favorably to antidepressants, maintenance of treatment gains appears dependent on continued use of the drug (Marks, 1978b). Thus, whether alcoholics with anxiety and panic symptoms would be helped by these drugs is still an unanswered empirical question. Although minor tranquilizers are often prescribed and routinely used for detoxification, their use is very controversial. These drugs appear to have high abuse potential and might be expected to be abused by problem drinkers who had previously abused alcohol in attempts to cope with anxiety. There might be a group of problem drinkers with anxiety problems that could receive substantial benefit from minor tranquilizers without going on to abuse them. Identifying these individuals and establishing optimal length of pharmacological treatment for them could be useful. Assuming that such people exist, it might be recommended that the drugs be taken on a regular schedule and not on an "as needed" basis, so that patients do not take their medications in a way that is functionally equivalent to drinking. Whether such a strategy could reduce the abuse potential of these drugs is another question deserving of study.

As discussed in a previous section, sociopathic alcoholics and, to a somewhat lesser extent, depressed alcoholics are more likely than primary alcoholics to abuse both stimulant and depressant drugs. Polydrug abuse appears to have deleterious consequences on neuropsychological functioning (Grant et al., 1978); therefore alcoholics with primary psychopathology and secondary alcoholism may often have a number of cognitive deficits due to neuropsychological impairment. Some of the treatment questions that the issue of neuropsychological impairment raise are discussed above, in the section on problem drinking in the elderly.

Because the psychopathic alcoholic is often brought to treatment under coercion, the use of Antabuse may seem desirable, because this treatment adjunct might satisfy the forces bringing the patient into treatment as well as supply external controls for the individual who feels unable to exercise optimal internal control. Thus the use of Antabuse in psychopaths could conceivably be a very useful intervention with this population. However, because of the high degree of impulsivity often characterizing the psychopath, it is also possible that these individuals are at high risk for drinking on Antabuse, possibly precipitating a medical crisis as well as a psychotherapeutic one. Although the prediction of which patients would be likely to drink on Antabuse might be useful for alcoholics in general, it would probably be particularly useful in deciding on the role of Antabuse in psychopathic individuals.

3.3.2b. Individual.   Are patients with significant psychopathology more difficult to engage in alcohol treatment than primary alcoholics? Patients with high levels of depression, anxiety, and impulsivity may tend to see these difficulties as their major problems and downplay the significance of their problem drinking (also, many alcohol counselors are not trained to deal with these other issues). While this would not, perhaps, be problematic for patients in psychoanalytic or behavioral treatment, this kind of perception *could* be problematic for patients in group or milieu settings in alcohol treatment programs. If group discussion or contact with treatment staff focuses primarily upon drinking problems, the secondary alcoholic with primary psychopathology could conceivably become disenfranchised and at high risk for dropping out of treatment. Similarly, is referral to AA for these patients to be avoided? The necessary first step of admitting helplessness over alcohol and labeling the self an alcoholic may be difficult for the patient who sees his or her other psychiatric problems as primary. In short, the strategies for engaging the alcoholic with other serious psychopathology in treatment may be somewhat different from those found most effective with primary alcoholics and should be investigated.

There are a number of cognitive and behavioral techniques that have been demonstrated to be useful for anxiety and, to a somewhat lesser extent, depressive disorders (Marks, 1978b). Many behavioral alcoholism treatment programs offer a "broad spectrum" approach (Nathan, 1976), where a variety of techniques such as skill training, relaxation, cognitive restructuring, contingency management, and other strategies are employed. While these treatment programs may be effective for alcoholics in general (e.g., Hamburg, 1975), their effectiveness with problem drinkers with depressive and anxiety disorders remains to be demonstrated. Studies examining the effect of cognitive and behavioral interventions with depressed and anxious subtypes of alcoholics will need to pay particular attention to outcome in both the domains of drinking behavior and psychiatric symptomatology. If the often-found phenomenon of weak relations between different domains of outcome criteria holds true, there is little reason to suspect that improvement in affective functioning will necessarily lead to improvement in drinking behavior. In fact, one might speculate that rapid mood improvement without alcoholism-focused treatment might predict a poor prognosis for changing drinking behavior, since research indicates that depressive affect is a motivation for treatment for many alcoholics. That is, subjects who quickly experience affective improvement may lose their motivation for examining or attempting to change the way in which they drink. Again, the timing and relative degree of emphasis on specific drinking behavior versus other psychopathology is an area that may be useful to study.

There is a body of research evidence suggesting that alcohol consumption serves a specific need to the sociopath, namely to increase arousal to optimal levels. Although this is at present a theoretical formulation, some data exist to warrant examining possible therapeutic implications of this formulation. Perhaps cognitive strategies where these patients are taught ways to monitor their arousal level or sensation-seeking tendencies and to engage in alternate, nonantisocial behavior could be of value. Clearly, a better knowledge of the function of alcohol for these individuals will assist in the search for effective treatments.

The sociopathic problem drinker who presents for treatment may lack internal motivation and the social skills and assets that facilitate the development of a good therapeutic relationship. Are treatment approaches that rely heavily upon such relationships (e.g., psychoanalytic) useful with this population? Outcome studies comparing the effectiveness of relationship-oriented treatment approaches with more explicit, concrete, and directive approaches with this population would help clarify this point. Because the sociopathic alcoholic is often in treatment because of external pressure, it would be useful to study the optimal ways of using this pressure to therapeutic advantage. Does contracting with the schools, courts, families, or employers for specific behavioral requirements improve compliance with treatment? Are behavioral changes motivated by coercion generalized to new settings or durable over time?

3.3.2c. Interpersonal. Because sociopathic individuals lack the interpersonal attachments and good work history predictive of good outcome, devising strategies for improving the sociopath's track record in interpersonal and vocational achievements appears to be a sound approach. However, the intervention to attain this goal is not at all clear. It does not seem likely that the sociopath's interpersonal difficulties stem from social-skills deficits since, at least on a superficial level, they are able to "simulate" situation-specific appropriate behaviors. Although able superficially to behave appropriately in many situations, the sociopath is typically undependable; programs that provide a high degree of structure and explicit contingencies for goal-directed behavior might be particularly useful. Research examining the importance of structure and limit setting on treatment outcome with sociopaths is clearly needed. Determining how to optimally involve available significant others and institutions in the treatment plan might be especially important in ensuring consistency in treatment approach and generalization across settings.

There may be a variety of interpersonal forces contributing to the maintenance of abusive drinking in anxious and depressed alcoholics. Problems in social functioning can lead to, as well as stem from, high levels of depression and anxiety. Each of the three therapeutic systems under discussion prescribes different interpersonal contexts and requirements, and each could conceivably be an effective treatment for some alcoholics with disturbed patterns of interpersonal behavior. For example, the AA regimen provides a mandate and a social context for developing social relationships; psychoanalytic treatment allows a relationship to develop between patient and therapist in a controlled, nonthreatening way; and behavioral treatment focuses on acquiring new social skills. Which of these treatment options is most effective with patients whose depression and anxiety stem at least in part from poor social functioning? For example, is the process of attending AA meetings for the first time too anxiety-provoking for the anxious alcoholic?

3.3.3. Summary

Psychiatric disorders and problem drinking coexist in a number of individuals. Frequently the psychiatric disorder can be shown to antedate the beginning of problem drinking. Data reported by Winokur *et al.* (1971) showed a sex difference in the prevalence of sociopathic and depressed subtypes, with female alcoholics more likely to be diagnosed as having an affective disorder and male alcoholics more likely to be sociopathic. The generality of this finding must be tempered somewhat by recent findings (Schuckit & Morrissey, 1979a) showing equal proportions of female alcoholic patients receiving diagnoses of antisocial personality and affective disorder. The prevalence of anxiety disorders in problem-drinking populations is not clear, since some researchers show surprisingly high rates (Mullaney & Trippett, 1979), while most investigators do not even mention this problem.

A number of biological and psychological treatments have been developed for use with depressed and anxious patients, but their effectiveness with alcoholic patients with these problems remain important questions. Several of the questions raised in this section include the following: Are psychoactive medications with abuse potential to be avoided with these patients? Is lithium a useful treatment with patients with affective disorder? Are behavioral and cognitive behavioral treatments that have been found useful in the treatment of anxiety and depression effective for alcoholics with these problems? Can the sociopath learn to modulate his or her arousal level in ways that do not lead to drug and alcohol abuse or other antisocial behavior? Are programs that have a strong focus on alcohol problems and "admitting alcoholism" acceptable or effective with patients whose alcoholism is secondary to a primary psychiatric disorder?

4. IMPLICATIONS

The general position being advocated here is that the traditional horserace approach be put aside in favor of patient–treatment matching. While a variety of writers have advocated similar positions in regard to the treatment of behavior disorders in general (e.g., Rachman & Wilson, 1980; Kiesler, 1971) and alcoholism treatment more specifically (Glaser, 1980; Institute of Medicine, 1980), little has been said about the implications of such an approach beyond the need for reducing heterogeneity of patients by examining treatment effects on relatively homogeneous subtypes. Furthermore, most authors have focused on strategies for optimally matching patients to established treatment modalities, sidestepping the question of how best to tailor interventions to specific subtypes of alcoholics. In the discussion to follow, several methodological issues deriving from the patient–treatment matching position will be explored.

4.1. Definition and Measurement of Problem Drinking for Specific Populations

The types of drinking problems occurring in different subtypes of alcoholics are not identical. Thus, measures of problem drinking that are suitable for some populations are not necessarily suitable for others. For example, an instrument such as the Michigan Alcoholism Screening Test (Selzer, 1971) may be more sensitive to male problem drinking than to problem drinking in females, elderly people, or adolescents simply because these other populations are less likely to encounter certain vocational and legal problems as consequences of their drinking. Measures of problem drinking relevant to each alcoholic subtype need to be developed, taking into account the specific psychological, social, and medical consequences that problem drinkers of a certain subtype are likely to develop. Even relatively universal measures such as quantity–frequency indexes of alcohol consumption, while often useful, must be interpreted cautiously at times, since factors such as body weight and alcohol metabolism rates can vary considerably across different subtypes.

The need to tailor assessment instruments to particular subtypes extends to general assessments of role functioning, psychological maladjustment, and adaptive coping. Greater precision in assessment should lead to stronger conclusions about the efficacy of our interventions.

4.2. Definition and Measurement of Mediating Variables for Specific Populations

Beside encountering different kinds of alcohol-related problems, subtypes of alcoholics can differ in the ways that various mediating variables are related to alcohol abuse. For example, decreased social opportunities, sex-role conflict, and depressed affect are each thought to be causally related to problem drinking in older people, women, and depressed individuals respectively. The clinical researcher, in designing or choosing a treatment strategy to employ with a subtype of alcoholic should first try identifying hypothesized mediating variables for alcohol abuse with this population. Once this is done, decisions can be made about how to measure these variables. Measurement of potential mediating variables permits a more detailed analysis of therapetic change than is possible if only outcome variables are assessed. This point is nicely illustrated in the study by Kline and Cooper (1979) reported above. In this study lithium was found to be effective at reducing alcohol abuse in chronic alcoholics. Somewhat surprisingly, subjective ratings of depression, the hypothesized mediating variable, were not related to treatment outcome. Kline and Cooper speculated that perhaps lithium mediated the therapeutic change by acting in such a way as to block alcohol's intoxicating effects. While these specific results must be considered tentative and Kline and Cooper's interpretation speculative, this example illustrates how measurement of potential mediator variables can permit evaluation of a treatment's anticipated mode of action.

The discussion so far has emphasized how different subtypes of alcoholics can have different factors mediating their alcohol abuse and that the clinical researcher should therefore attempt to assess the *specific* mediators thought to underly the problem drinking of a given population. It should probably be added that it may be helpful also to assess a potential mediator common to most problem drinking, namely beliefs about being able to abstain or drink in a controlled fashion (efficacy expectations). Bandura (1977) has argued that these beliefs are important mediators of therapeutic change.

4.3. Stages of Intervention

In studying the effect of treatment interventions, it may be helpful to discriminate four stages of intervention. These include (1) implementation of treatment, (2) changes in proposed mediators of problem drinking, (3) generalization of changes from treatment setting to the natural environment, and (4) maintenance of therapeutic gains over time. Although these four categories are not necessarily distinct, it may be helpful to use them as a conceptual framework for evaluating treatment effectiveness.

4.3.1. Implementation of Treatment

This refers to whether or not treatment was administered in the prescribed way. Factors such as patient dropout, noncompliance, incorrect or faulty treatment procedures, and so on can prevent a treatment from having significant effects. It is important for those concerned with patient-treatment matching to assess this variable since it is quite likely that certain treatment modalities will be compatible with the characteristics of certain subtypes and not others. Likewise, therapist variables such as sex of therapist, experience, orientation, and so on can have effects on treatment outcome and should at least be controlled and preferably systematically studied. An effective treatment program will have little practical utility if patients are not willing or able to meet the requirements or if it is extremely difficult for treatment staff to carry out the treatment properly.

4.3.2. Changes in Proposed Mediators

Therapeutic change does not occur by some magical connection between treatment variables and outcome variables. When change occurs, it is because some important attribute of the patient has changed, his or her environment has changed, or both. We feel it is important to attempt to measure these mediators of change so that they can be related to treatment outcome and the treatment process can be better understood. These hypothesized mediators can range from biological to individual to social factors.

4.3.3. Generalization of Change from Treatment Setting to the Natural Environment

Behavioral psychology has demonstrated how much of human behavior, including drinking behavior, is situationally specific (e.g., Mischel, 1968; Reid, 1978); thus behavior changes demonstrated in one setting will not necessarily generalize to others. It is always conceivable that newly acquired drinking skills, conditioned aversions, self-esteem, insights, faith in a higher power, and so on will not persist when the patient is confronted with situations that are dissimilar to the ones in which the new affects, cognitions, and behaviors were learned. Social reinforcement for sobriety or controlled drinking, which may be the norm of alcohol treatment programs, is not always the rule in the patient's natural social environment. In short, therapeutic changes observed in treatment might not be predictive of the patient's "real world" behavior. To accomplish this requires some form of *in vivo* assessment that could include objective assessment by trained observers or reports of significant others. While generalization is often thought to have greatest applicability to behavioral treatments, the same principles apply to psychoanalytic and AA approaches. For example, is the level of psychosexual development that characterizes the patient's relationship to the therapist representative of the patient's functioning with significant others? Do changes in the therapeutic relationship lead to changed interactions with the social network? Is the patient able to go beyond just attending meetings and apply AA principles to all aspects of his or her daily life? Treatments that show poor generalization may need to be refined or have specific components built in to transfer treatment effects across situations.

4.3.4. Maintenance of Therapeutic Gains

The significant proportion of treated problem drinkers who eventually relapse suggests that particular attention must be paid to the factors reponsible for the maintenance of treatment gains. Some writers (Moos, Finney, & Cronkite, 1980) discuss the need for a "paradigm shift" in alcohol treatment research where greater attention and effort are devoted to these factors. To date, maintenance strategies have included follow-up with AA, relapse-prevention training (Chaney, O'Leary, & Marlatt, 1978), booster sessions (Vogler, Compton, & Weissbach, 1975), and, although perhaps not intentionally, follow-up visits by clinical research staff. An obvious implication of the treatment–patient matching hypothesis is that specific maintenance strategies need to be devised with the specific needs, resources, and problems of each particular subtype in mind. Again, the factors felt to be important for treatment maintenance should be assessed by instruments sensitive to the uniqueness of the variables underlying successful maintenance for each group. Clinicians who base treatment efforts on attempting to bring about intrapsychic transformations and other internal changes may not see the need to address maintenance issues, since these internal changes are often thought to be durable and invariant across situations. However, empirically oriented clinicians of every persuasion probably acknowledge the reality of relapse and are interested in attempting to minimize this serious problem.

4.4. Other Implications for Treatment Research

The more we specify the characteristics of a patient population, the more difficult it is to constitute a reasonably sized sample for study which meets these characteristics. For this reason, "n of one" and small-sample studies are probably indicated in the beginning phases of treatment research programs focusing on patient subtypes. When larger group designs are required at later stages of research, the difficulty of obtaining large enough samples could be overcome to some degree by extending the time frame of the study or collaborating with other investigators at other sites. The treatment approach advocated here addresses what we have termed "mediator variables" underlying alcohol abuse. This emphasis readily lends itself to analog studies where the effectiveness of behavior change techniques at altering these hypothesized mediating variables can be evaluated in nonclinical samples. While not a substitute for clinical trials, analog research can be a proving ground where both techniques and assessment instruments are refined. The clinical value of analog studies is an empirical issue (Kazdin, 1978) and probably a function of the extent to which the type and intensity of the problems in the analog population resembles that of the clinical population (Rachman & Wilson, 1980).

4.5. A Brief Description of a Hypothetical Treatment Study with Women Alcoholics

Some of the above points on research implications of the patient–treatment matching approach will be illustrated in the following example, which is not meant to provide a model for treatment study but rather to illustrate how some of the issues discussed above can be applied.

In this study, the investigators will be interested in how a variety of treatment interventions can affect female alcoholics' level of self-esteem, a factor that has been related to problem drinking in this population (Beckman, 1978).

4.5.1. Treatment Variables

Three diverse techniques for altering self-esteem will be contrasted. These were chosen on the basis of their dissimilarity to each other and their possible relationship to levels of self-esteem.

1. *"External" behavioral approach.* Patients will contract with their therapists to perform a variety of tasks that are considered to be esteem-enhancing. Such tasks might include development of special recreational or athletic competencies, increasing vocational productivity, performing household tasks more efficiently, or taking on previously avoided responsibilities.
2. *Cognitive behavioral approach.* Patients will be taught to recognize "irrational" beliefs or thoughts related to low self-esteem. Generating more rational and positive thoughts will also be taught, and the patient will be given a system to use in practicing these positive thoughts and countering spontaneously occurring negative thoughts with more positive ones.
3. *Spiritual approach.* This approach, modeled after AA, will involve getting the patient to believe "she is powerless over alcohol" and that her life had become "unmanageable." The patient will be encouraged to adopt the position that she must turn her life over to a "higher power" if she is ever going to recover from her alcoholism.

Each of these treatment approaches will be implemented alone and in conjunction with a treatment package designed to help the patient maintain abstinence. Treatment components of this package will include learning to avoid high-risk drinking situations, learning drink refusal skills, learning about the harmful medical effects of alcohol, and leading discussions of alcohol-related problems that the patient has encountered in the past. Thus, in this study, there will be six treatment groups, as illustrated in Figure 1.

4.5.2. Outcome Variables

Measurements of problem drinking taken prior to, immediately after, and following treatment will be based on instruments that have been specifically derived for use with women problem drinkers. Similarly, more general outcome measures such as social functioning across a variety of important life roles (i.e., vocational, marital, recreational, parental) will be assessed by instruments clearly sensitive to each individual woman's life situation and problem areas.

	"External" behavior approach	Cognitive behavioral approach	Spiritual approach
Abstinence skills package			
No abstinence skills package			

Figure 1. Alcoholism treatment approaches and variables.

4.5.3. Mediating Variables

The following potential mediators of alcohol abuse with this population will be assessed:

1. Global measures of self-esteem
2. Specific self-efficacy expectations
   A. For dealing with important life roles
      (1) Vocational
      (2) Marital
      (3) Recreational
      (4) Parental
   B. For dealing with drinking situations
3. Measures of depression and hopelessness, since these may be important correlates of self-esteem

4.5.4. Assessment of Treatment Effects

Treatment will be evaluated using the stages of intervention framework outlined above to illustrate the application of this framework.

1. *Implementation of treatment.* The extent to which each treatment group received the specific treatment will be assessed. Issues to be answered include the following: Did the patient drop out of treatment? Was the patient compliant with assigned therapeutic tasks and/or the therapeutic process? Was treatment carried out by the therapist in accordance with the planned protocol?
2. *Mediating variables.* Differential effects of each treatment on the mediating variables described above will be assessed. These measures will be taken on subjects prior to, during, and following treatment.
3. *Generalization of treatment effects to the natural environment.* Are patients in the cognitive behavioral group able to employ newly learned cognitive strategies across a variety of settings? Are patients in the "external" behavioral group able to monitor and generate competency-enhancing activities independently, with no assistance from their therapist or others? Are patients in the "spiritual" group turning to their "higher power" for emotional strength and guidance when confronted by difficult life stresses?
4. *Maintenance of treatment gains.* The durability of treatment effects across the various treatment groups will be compared both on outcome variables and mediating variables. Since the variables that may mediate relapse or the reinitiation of problem drinking may be different from those that

maintain problem drinking, other relevant variables such as stressful life events and the presence of support systems compatible with sobriety will be assessed. As discussed above, longitudinal research on problem drinkers has shown that the course of their alcohol abuse can be quite varied over time, with many patients moving in and out of periods of problem drinking. To be sensitive to this fact, follow-up assessments will take place at six months, one year, two years, and, if possible, subsequent yearly intervals. It should be pointed out that most of the data on the natural history of problem drinking comes from men. It is conceivable that outcome research on women or other subtypes may permit shorter or dictate longer follow-up periods, depending on the natural course of drinking problems for that population.

4.5.5. Value of the Study

This study will evaluate the effect of three kinds of treatment intervention on problem drinking in women. The utility of including specialized alcohol treatment with this population will also be evaluated. Assessment of proposed mediators of problem drinking (and relapse) will permit analysis of the process of therapeutic change.

4.6. Concluding Remarks

In this chapter, we have explored similarities and differences among major treatment approaches to problem drinking, examined differences among subtypes of alcoholics, and attempted to integrate the areas of treatment variables and patient variables into a patient–treatment matching model. We believe there are several potential payoffs in adopting this model.

First, the shift in emphasis from contrasting different treatment approaches to contrasting treatment components possibly shared by different approaches provides a useful perspective. Working from this perspective, investigators with varying theoretical and practical emphases can join in the search for "effective ingredients" common to their approaches and move away from isolated research efforts each supporting a different camp. Effective treatment components can be added or subtracted in developing specific and efficient treatment packages for each subtype of alcoholic. Systematic evaluation of these packages will permit assessment of cost-effectiveness as well as therapeutic effectiveness.

By focusing attention on modifying postulated mediating variables of interest to investigators outside the alcoholism field (e.g., assertive behavior, efficacy expectations, self-esteem, ego strength, social isolation, sex-role conflict), the data generated by alcoholism treatment research might be more readily communicated to others outside of this field. Conversely, the results of more general investigations on behavior-change techniques might more readily be incorporated into alcohol treatment research endeavors.

While there are clear clinical differences between various subtypes of alcoholics that have obvious treatment implications from a therapeutic standpoint, there may be other important differences among these subtypes in terms of consumer satisfaction and treatment acceptibility (Kazdin & Wilson, 1978). Factors such as the length, cost, accessibility, and cultural acceptance of different kinds of treatment approaches might have differential impact on patient subtypes and ultimately be more important in determining the effectiveness of treatment in a natural clinical setting. While perhaps not the first dimension of treatment intervention that needs to be assessed in a research program, consumer variables represent an important domain of "real life" treatment impact and may be especially relevant to research on specific subpopulations that have traditionally underutilized mental health services (e.g., the elderly).

Implicit in the approach being advocated is that treatment research is not merely a simple evaluation of a behavior-change technology but a true scientific undertaking whereby the theoretical models and processes of therapeutic change can be studied. As Rachman and Wilson (1980) point out in their recent review of treatment outcome in regard to the behavioral treatment of fears, the question is no longer *whether* treatment works but *how* it works. Useful information from this approach is helpful not only to treatment reseachers but also to researchers interested in the etiology and prevention of alcohol problems. Furthermore, focusing attention on processes and techniques affecting hypothesized mediating variables can make the research endeavor more reinforcing for the investigator. Analyzing data on mediating variables and relating them to patient and treatment variables as well as short-term outcome could prove to be a particularly fruitful way to "pass the time" while waiting for long-term follow-up data to become available.

The ultimate utility of patient–treatment matching can only be determined by empirical research. However, even in the absence of definitive data, attention to patient–treatment matching issues can help clinicians formulate cases and devise and implement treatment plans. As treatment outcome research accrues, clinicians will be increasingly able to incorporate this knowledge into their practice. It is our hope that the matching model will facilitate this process.

ACKNOWLEDGMENTS

The authors are grateful to David Abrams and Nora Noel for their thorough and provocative reviews of an earlier draft of this chapter.

5. REFERENCES

Abbott, M. W., & Gregson, R. A. Cognitive dysfunction in the prediction of relapse in alcoholics. *Journal of Studies on Alcohol,* 1981, *42,* 230-243.

Abelsohn, D. S., & van der Spuy, H. I. J. The age variable in alcoholism. *Journal of Studies on Alcohol,* 1978, *39,* 800-808.

Alcoholics Anonymous. New York: Alcoholics Anonymous World Services, 1976.

Ashley, M. J., Olin, J. S., le Riche, W. H., Kornaczewski, A., Schmidt, W., & Rankin, J. G. Morbidity in alcoholics. *Archives of Internal Medicine,* 1977, *137,* 883-887.

Azrin, N. H. Improvements in the community-reinforcement approach to alcoholism. *Behavior Research and Therapy,* 1976, *14,* 339-348.

Bandura, A. Self-efficacy: Toward a unifying theory of behavioral change. *Psychological Review,* 1977, *84,* 191-215.

Beckman, L. J. Women alcoholics: A review of social and psychological studies, *Journal of Studies on Alcohol,* 1975, *36,* 799-823.

Beckman, L. J. Self-esteem of women alcoholics. *Journal of Studies on Alcohol,* 1978, *39*(3), 491-498.

Belfer, M. L., Shader, R. I., Carroll, M., & Harmatz, J. S. Alcoholism in women. *Archives of General Psychiatry,* 1971, *25,* 540-544.

Birnbaum, M., & Parker, E. S. *Alcohol and human memory.* Hillsdale, N.J.: Erlbaum, 1977.

Blakey, R., & Baker, R. An exposure approach to alcohol abuse. *Behavior Research and Therapy,* 1980, *18,* 319-326.

Blane, H. T. Psychotherapeutic approach. In B. Kissin & H. Begleiter, (Eds.). *The biology of alcoholism* (Vol. 5). New York: Plenum Press, 1977.

Blum, E. M. Psychoanalytic views of alcoholism. *Quarterly Journal of Studies on Alcohol,* 1966, *27,* 259-299.

Bourne, P. G., & Light, E. Alcohol problems in blacks and women. In J. H. Mendelson & N. K. Mello (Eds.), *The diagnosis and treatment of alcoholism.* New York: McGraw-Hill, 1979.

Bowman, K. M., & Jellinek, E. M. Alcoholic mental disorders. *Quarterly Journal of Studies on Alcohol,* 1941, *2,* 312-390.

Bromet, E., Moos, R., Bliss, F., & Wuthman, C. Posttreatment functioning of alcoholic patients: Its relation to program participation. *Journal of Consulting and Clinical Psychology,* 1977, *45,* 829-842.

Burtle, V., Whitlock, D., & Franks, V. Modification of low self-esteem in women alcoholics: A behavior treatment approach. *Psychotherapy: Theory, Research and Practice,* 1974, *11,* 35-40.

Cahalan, D. *Problem drinkers.* San Francisco: Jossey-Bass, 1970.

Cahalan, D., & Cisin, I. Epidemiological and social factors associated with drinking problems. In R. E. Tarter & A. A. Sugerman (Eds.), *Alcoholism: Interdisciplinary approaches to an enduring problem.* Reading, Mass.: Addison-Wesley, 1976.

Cahalan, D., Cisin, I. H., & Crossley, H. M. *American drinking practices: A national study of drinking behavior and attitudes, Monograph No. 6.* New Brunswick, N.J.: Rutgers Center of Alcohol Studies, 1969.

Cahn, S. *The treatment of alcoholics.* New York: Oxford University Press, 1970.

Cautela, J. R. Covert sensitization. *Psychological Reports,* 1967, *20,* 459-468.

Chafetz, M. E., Blane, H. T., Abram, H. S., Golner, J., Lacy, E., McCourt, W. F., Clark, E., & Meyers, W. Establishing treatment relations with alcoholics. *Journal of Nervous and Mental Diseases,* 1962, *134,* 395-409.

Chaney, E. F., O'Leary, M. R., & Marlatt, G. A. Skill training with alcoholics. *Journal of Consulting and Clinical Psychology,* 1978, *46,* 1092-1104.

Cohen, G. D. Perspectives on psychotherapy with the elderly. *American Journal of Psychiatry*, 1981, *138*, 347–350.

Corrigan. E. M. *Alcoholic women in treatment.* New York: Oxford University Press, 1980.

Coyne, J. Depression and the response of others. *Journal of Abnormal Psychology*, 1976, *85*, 186–193.

Curlee, J. A comparison of male and female patients at an alcoholism treatment center. *Journal of Psychology*, 1970, *74*, 239–247.

Diagnostic and statistical manual of mental disorders (3rd ed.) (DSM-III). Washington, D.C.: American Psychiatric Association, 1980.

Droller, H. Some aspects of alcoholism in the elderly. *Lancet,* 1964, *2*, 137–139.

Edwards, G., Orford, J., Egert, S., Guthrie, S., Hawker, A., Hensman, M., Mitcheson, M., Oppenheimer, E., & Taylor, C. Alcoholism: A controlled trial of "treatment" vs. "advice." *Journal of Studies on Alcohol,* 1977, *38*, 1004–1031.

Elkins, R. L. A note on aversion therapy for alcoholism. *Behavior Research and Therapy*, 1976, *14*, 159–160.

Emrick, C. D. A review of psychologically oriented treatment of alcoholism. I. The use and interrelationships of outcome criteria and drinking behavior following treatment. *Quarterly Journal of Studies on Alcohol,* 1974, *35*, 523–549.

Emrick, C. D. A review of psychologically oriented treatment of alcoholism. II. The relative effectiveness of different treatment approaches and the effectiveness of treatment versus no treatment. *Journal of Studies on Alcohol,* 1975, 36(1), 88–108.

Epstein, L. J., Mills, C., & Simon, A. Antisocial behavior of the elderly. *Comprehensive Psychiatry*, 1970, *11*, 36–42.

Ewing, J. A. Matching therapy and patients: The cafeteria plan. *British Journal of Addiction*, 1977, *72*, 13–18.

Ewing, J. A., & Rouse, B. A. Failure of an experimental treatment program to inculcate controlled drinking in alcoholics. *British Journal of Addiction*, 1976, *71*, 123–134.

Fozard, J. L. The time for remembering. In L. Poon (Ed.), *Aging in the 1980s: Psychological issues.* Washington, D.C.: American Psychological Association, 1980.

Freed, E. X. Alcoholism and manic-depressive disorders: Some perspectives. *Quarterly Journal of Studies on Alcohol,* 1970, *31*, 62–89.

Freud, S. On psychotherapy (1905). In J. Strachey (Ed. and trans.), *The standard edition of the complete psychological works of Sigmund Freud.* London: Hogarth Press, 1978.

Gatz, M., Snyder, M. A. & Lawton, M. P. The mental health system and the older adult. In L. Poon (Ed.), *Aging in the 1980s: Psychological issues.* Washington, D.C.: American Psychological Association, 1980.

Glaser, F. B. Selecting patients for treatment: An heuristic model. In *The phase zero report of the core-shell treatment system project: Early working papers.* Toronto: Addiction Research Foundation, 1978.

Glaser, F. B. Anybody got a match? Treatment research and the matching hypothesis. In G. Edwards & M. Grant (Eds.), *Alcoholism treatment in transition.* London: Croom Helm, 1980.

Goldman, M. S., Whitman, R. D., Rosenbaum, G., & Vandevusse, D. Recoverability of sensory and motor functioning following chronic alcohol abuse. In F. Seixas (Ed.), *Currents in alcoholism.* New York: Grune & Stratton, 1978.

Gomberg, E. S. The female alcoholic. In R. E. Tarter & A. A. Sugerman (Eds.), *Alcoholism: Interdisciplinary approaches to an enduring problem.* Reading, Mass.: Addison-Wesley, 1976.

Gomberg, E. S. Drinking and problem drinking among the elderly. In *Alcohol, drugs, and aging: Usage and problems* (No. 1). Ann Arbor, Mich.: The Institute of Gerontology, University of Michigan, 1980.

Goodwin, D. W., Schulsinger, F., Knop, J., Mednick S., & Guze, S. B. Alcoholism and depression in adopted-out daughters of alcoholics. *Archives of General Psychiatry*, 1977, *34*, 751–755.

Gorenstein, E. E., & Newman, J. P. Disinhibitory psychopathology: A new perspective and a model for research. *Psychological Review*, 1980, *87*, 301–315.

Gottesfeld, B. H., & Yager, H. L. Psychotherapy of the problem drinker. *Quarterly Journal of Studies on Alcohol*, 1950, *11*, 222–229.

Grant, I., Adams, K., Carlin, A., Rennick, P., Judd, L., Schooff, K., & Reed, R. Organic impairment in polydrug users: Risk factors. *American Journal of Psychiatry*, 1978, *135*, 178–184.

Gray, J. Drug effects on fear and frustration: Possible limbic site of action of minor tranquilizers. In L. L. Iverson, S. D. Iverson, & S. H. Snyder (Eds.), *Handbook of Psychopharmacology* (Vol. 8). New York: Plenum Press, 1977.

Gray, J. Anxiety and the brain: Not by neurochemistry alone. *British Journal of Psychology*, 1979, *9*, 605–609.

Hamburg, S. Behavior therapy in alcoholism: A critical review of broad spectrum approaches. *Journal of Studies on Alcohol*, 1975, *36*, 69–87.

Hare, R. D. *Psychopathy: Theory and research.* New York: Wiley, 1970.

Hay, W., & Nathan P. *Clinical case studies in the behavioral treatment of alcoholism.* New York: Plenum Press, 1982.

Haynes, S. N. Contingency management in a municipally aministered Antabuse program for alcoholics. *Journal of Behavior Therapy and Experimental Psychiatry*, 1973, *4*, 31–32.

Horowitz, M., Schaefer, C., Hiroto, D., Wilner, N., & Levin, B. Life event questionnaires for measuring presumptive stress. *Psychosomatic Medicine*, 1977, *39*, 413–431.

Hunt, G. M. & Azrin, N. H. A community-reinforcement approach to alcoholism. *Behavior Research and Therapy*, 1973, *11*, 91–104.

Institure of Medicine, *Alcoholism, alcohol abuse, and related problems: Opportunities for research.* Washington, D.C.: National Academy Press, 1980.

Jellinek, E. M. Current notes: Phases of alcohol addiction. *Quarterly Journal of Studies on Alcohol*, 1951, *12*, 673–684.

Kazdin, A. Evaluating the generality of findings in analogue therapy research. *Journal of Clinical and Consulting Psychology*, 1978, *46*, 673–686.

Kazdin, A. E., & Wilson, G. T. Criteria for evaluating psychotherapy. *Archives of General Psychiatry*, 1978, *35*, 407–416.

Keller, M., & Efron, V. Prevalence of alcoholism. *Quarterly Journal of Studies on Alcoholism*, 1955, *16*, 619–644.

Kiesler, D. J. Experimental designs in psychotherapy research. In A. E. Bergin & S. Garfield, (Eds.), *Handbook of psychotherapy and behavior change.* New York: Wiley, 1971.

Kissin, B. The pharmacodynamics and natural history of alcoholism. In B. Kissin & H. Begleiter, (Eds.), *The biology of alcoholism* (Vol. 3): *Clinical pathology.* New York: Plenum Press, 1974.

Klein, D. F. Delineation of two drug-responsive anxiety syndromes. *Psychopharmacologia*, 1964, *5*, 397–408.

Kline, N. S., & Cooper, T. B. Lithium therapy in alcoholism. In D. W. Goodwin & C. K. Erickson (Eds.), *Alcoholism and affective disorders.* New York: Spectrum, 1979.

Leach, B., & Norris, J. L. Factors in the development of Alcoholics Anonymous (A.A.). In B. Kissin & H. Begleiter (Eds.), *The biology of alcoholism* (Vol. 5). New York: Plenum Press, 1977.

Madill, M. F., Campbell, D., Laverty, S. G., Sanderson, S. E., & Vanderwater, S. L. Aversion treatment of alcoholics by succinylcholine-induced apneic paralysis. *Quarterly Journal of Studies on Alcohol*, 1966, *27*, 483–509.

Marks, I. M. *Living with fear: Understanding and coping with anxiety.* New York: McGraw-Hill, 1978. (a)

Marks, I. Behavioral psychotherapy of adult neurosis. In S. Garfield & A. E. Bergin (Eds.), *Handbook of psychotherapy and behavior change*. New York: Wiley, 1978 (b)

Marks, I. M., Birley, J. R., & Gelder, M. G. Modified leucotomy in servere agoraphobia, a controlled serial inquiry. *British Journal of Psychiatry*, 1966, *112*, 757–769.

Martensen-Larsen, O. Group psychotherapy with alcoholics in private practice. *International Journal of Group Psychotherapy*, 1956, *6*, 28–37.

Matarazzo, J. D. Behavioral health and behavioral medicine: Frontiers for a new health psychology. *American Psychologist*, 1980, *35*, 807–817.

McCrady, B. S. *Marital, spouse and self-control therapy of alcoholics.* NIAAA grant ROI AA 03984, 1978.

McCrady, B. S. Women, alcoholism and behavior therapy. In E. Blechman (Ed.), *Behavior modification with women*. New York: Guilford Press, in press.

McLachan, J. F. Benefit from group therapy as a function of patient–therapist match on conceptual level. *Psychotherapy: Theory, research and practice*, 1972, *9*, 317–323.

Meichenbaum, D. *Cognitive behavior modification*. New York: Plenum Press, 1977.

Miller, P. M. The use of behavioral contracting in the treatment of alcoholism: A case report. *Behavior Therapy*, 1972, *3*, 593–596.

Miller, W. Behavioral treatment of problem drinkers: A comparative outcome study of three controlled drinking therapies. *Journal of Consulting and Clinical Psychology*, 1978, *46*, 74–86.

Miller, W. R., Taylor, C. A., & West, J. C. Focused versus broad-spectrum behavior therapy for problem drinkers. *Journal of Consulting and Clinical Psychology*, 1980, *48*, 590–601.

Miller, W. R., & Muñoz, R. F. *How to control your drinking*. Englewood Cliffs. N.J.: Prentice-Hall, 1976.

Miller, W. R., Taylor, Ca. A., & West, J. C. Focused versus broad-spectrum behavior therapy for problem drinkers. *Journal of Consulting and Clinical Psychology*, 1980, *48*, 590–601.

Mindlin, D. The characteristics of alcoholics as related to prediction of therapeutic outcome. *Quarterly Journal of Studies on Alcohol*, 1959, *20*, 604–619.

Mischel, W. *Personality and assessment*. New York: Wiley, 1968.

Mishara, B. L., & Kastenbaum, R. K. *Alcohol and old age*. New York: Grune & Stratton, 1980.

Moore, R. A. Psychotherapeutics of alcoholism. *Proceedings of the Second Annual Conference of the NIAAA*, pp. 222–223, Washington, D.C.: June 1–2, 1972.

Moos, R. H., Finney, J. W., & Cronkite, R. C. The need for a paradigm shift in evaluations of treatment outcome: Extrapolations from the Rand research. *British Journal of Addiction*, 1980, *75*, 347–350.

Mulford, H. A. Women and men problem drinkers: Sex differences in patients served by Iowa's Community Alcoholism Centers. *Journal of Studies on Alcohol*, 1977, *38*, 1624–1639.

Mullaney, J. A., & Trippett, C. J. Alcohol dependence and phobias: Clinical descriptions and relevance. *British Journal of Psychiatry*, 1979, *135*, 565–573.

Nathan, P. Alcoholism. In H. Leithenberg (Ed.), *Handbook of behavior modification and behavior therapy*. Englewood Cliffs, N.J.: Prentice-Hall, 1976.

Nathan, P. E., & Briddell, D. W. Behavioral assessment and treatment of alcoholism. In B. Kissin & H. Begleiter (Eds.), *The biology of alcoholism* (Vol. 5). New York: Plenum Press, 1977.

Nestoros, J. M. Ethanol specifically potentiates GABA-mediated neurotransmisson in feline cerebral cortex. *Science*, 1980, *209*, 708–710.

Noble, E. P. (Eds.). *Third special report to the U.S. Congress on alcohol and health*. Washington, D.C.: U.S. Government Printing Office, 1978.

O'Farrell, T. J., & Cutter, H. S. G. A proposed behavioral couples group for male alcoholics and their wives. In D. Upper & S. M. Ross (Eds.), *Behavioral group therapy: An annual review*. Champaign, Ill. Research Press, 1979.

Ogborne, A. C., & Glaser, F. B. Characteristics of affiliates of Alcoholics Anonymous: A review of studies and speculations. *Journal of Studies on Alcohol,* 1981, *42,* 661–675.

O'Leary, M. R., Donovan, D. M., Chaney, E. F., & O'Leary, D. Relationship of alcoholic subtypes to treatment follow-up measures. *Journal of Nervous and Mental Disease,* 1980, *168,* 475–480.

Orford, J., Oppenheimer, E., & Edwards, G. Abstinence or control: The outcome for excessive drinkers two years after consultation. *Behavior Research and Therapy,* 1976, *14,* 409–418.

Paolino, T. J., Jr., & McCrady, B. S. *The alcoholic marriage: Alternative perspectives.* New York: Grune & Stratton, 1977.

Parsons, O. A. Neuropsychological deficits in alcoholics: Facts and fancies. *Alcoholism: Clinical and Experimental Research,* 1977, *1,* 51–56.

Parsons, O. A., & Farr, S. P. The neuropsychology of alcohol and drug use. In F. Filskov & T. Boll (Eds.), *Handbook of clinical neuropsychology.* New York: Wiley, 1981.

Paykel, E. S., Myers, J. K., Dienelt, M. N., Klerman, G. L., Lindenthal, J. J., Pepper, M. P. Life events and depression. *Archives of General Psychiatry,* 1969, *26,* 753–760.

Polich, J. M., Armor, D. J., & Braiker, H. B. *The course of alcoholism: Four years after treatment.* Santa Monica, Calif.: Rand, 1980.

Price, J. S. Chronic depressive illness. *British Medical Journal,* 1978, *1,* 1200–1201.

Price, R. H., & Curlee-Salisbury, J. Patient–treatment interactions among alcoholics. *Journal of Studies on Alcohol,* 1975, *36,* 659–669.

Quitkin, F. M., Rifkin, A., Kaplan, D., & Klein, D. F. Phobic anxiety syndrome complicated by drug dependence and addiction: A treatable form of drug abuse. *Archives of General Psychiatry,* 1972, *9,* 159–162.

Rachman, S. J., & Teasdale, J. Aversion therapy: An appraisal. In C. M. Franks (Ed.), *Behavior therapy: Appraisal and status.* New York: McGraw-Hill, 1969.

Rachman, S. J., & Wilson, G. T. *The effects of psychological therapy* (2nd ed.). Oxford, England, Pergamon, 1980.

Reich, L., Davies, R. K., &Himmelhoch, J. Excesive alcohol use in manic-depressive illness. *American Journal of Psychiatry,* 1974, *131,* 83–86.

Reid, J. B. Study of drinking in natural settings. In G. A. Marlatt & P. Nathan (Eds.), *Behavioral approaches to alcoholism.* New Brunswick., N. J.: Rutgers Center for Alcohol Studies, 1978.

Reynolds, C. M., Merry, J. & Coppen, A. Prophylactic treatment of alcoholism by lithium carbonate: An initial report. In D. W. Goodwin & C. K. Erickson (Eds.), *Alcoholism and affective disorders.* New York: Spectrum, 1979.

Rosin, A. J., & Glatt, M. M. Alcohol excess in the elderly. *Quarterly Journal of Studies on Alcohol,* 1971, *32,* 53–59.

Schmidt, W, & deLint, J. Mortality experiences of male and female alcoholic patients. *Quarterly Journal of Studies on Alcohol,* 1969, *30,* 112–118.

Schuckit, M. Alcoholism and sociopathy: Diagnostic confusion. *Quarterly Journal of Studies on Alcohol,* 1973, *34,* 157–164.

Schuckit, M. A. Inpatient and residential approaches to the treatment of alcoholism. In J. H. Mendelson & N. K. Mello (Eds.), *The diagnosis and treatment of alcoholism.* New York: McGraw-Hill, 1979.

Schuckit, M. A., & Morrissey, E. R. Psychatric problems in women admitted to an alcoholic detoxification center. *American Journal of Psychiatry,* 1979, *136,* 611–617.(a)

Schuckit, M. A., & Morrissey, E. R. Drug abuse among alcoholic women. *American Journal of Psychiatry,* 1979, *136,* 607–611.(b)

Scida, J., & Vanicelli, M. Sex-role conflict and women's drinking. *Journal of Studies on Alcohol,* 1979, *40,* 28–44.

Selzer, M. L. The Michigan alcoholism screening test: The quest for a new diagnostic instrument. *American Journal of Psychiatry,* 1971, *127,* 1653–1658.

Smith, C. G. Marital influences on treatment outcome in alcoholism. *Journal of the Irish Medical Association*, 1967, *15*, 433–434.

Sobell, L. Personal communication, October 1979.

Sobell, M. B., & Sobell, L. C. Alcoholics treated by individualized behavior therapy: One year treatment outcome. *Behavioral Research and Therapy*, 1973, *11*, 599–618.

Sobell, M. B., Sobell, L. C., & Sheahan, D.B. Functional analysis of drinking problems as an aid in developing individual treatment strategies. *Addictive Behaviors*, 1976, *1*, 127–132.

Tamerin, J. S. The psychotherapy of alcoholic women. In S. Zimberg, J. Wallace, & S. Blume (Eds.), *Practical approaches to alcoholism psychotherapy*. New York: Plenum Press, 1978.

Tarter, R. E. Etiology of alcoholism: Interdisciplinary integration. In P. Nathan, G. A. Marlatt, & T. Løberg (Eds.), *Alcoholism: New directions in behavioral research and treatment*. New York: Plenum Press, 1978.

Twelve Steps and Twelve Traditions. New York: Alcoholics Anonymous World Services, 1972.

Viamontes J. Review of drug effectiveness in the treatment of alcoholism. *American Journal of Psychiatry*, 1972, *128*, 120–121.

Virkkunen, M. Alcoholism and antisocial personality. *Acta Psychiatrica Scandinavica*, 1979, *59*, 493–501.

Volger, R. E., Compton, J. V., & Weissbach, T. A. Integrated behavior change techniques for alcoholics. *Journal of Consulting and Clinical Psychology*, 1975, *43*, 233–243.

Wallerstein, R. S. *Hospital treatment of alcoholism*. New York: Basic Books, 1957.

Willis, S. L. & Baltes, P. B. Intelligence in adulthood and aging: Contemporary issues. In L. Poon (Ed.), *Aging in the 1980s: Psychological issues*. Washington, D.C.: American Psychological Association, 1980.

Wilsnack, S. C. Sex role identity in female alcoholism. *Journal of Abnormal Psychology*, 1973, *82*, 253–261.

Wilsnack, S. C. The impact of sex roles on women's alcohol use and abuse. In M. Greenblatt & M. A. Schuckit (Eds.), *Alcoholism problems in women and children*. New York: Grune & Stratton, 1976.

Winokur, G., Reich, T., Rimmer, J., & Pitts, F. N. Alcoholism III. Diagnostic and familial psychiatric illness in 259 alcoholic probands. *Archives of General Psychiatry*, 1970, *23*, 104–111.

Winokur, G., Rimmer, J., & Reich, T. Alcoholism IV: Is there more than one type of alcoholism: *British Journal of Psychiatry*, 1971, *118*, 525–531.

Woodruff, R. A., Guze, S. B., & Clayton, P. J. Anxiety neurosis among psychiatric outpatients. *Comprehensive Psychiatry*, 1972, *13*, 165–170.

Woodruff, R. A., Guze, S. B., and Clayton, P. J. Alcoholics who see a psychiatrist compared with those who do not. *Quarterly Journal of Studies on Alcohol*, 1973, *34*, 1162–1173.

Zimberg, S. Psychosocial treatment of elderly alcoholics. In S. Zimberg, J. Wallace, & S. B. Blume, (Eds.), *Practical approaches to alcoholism psychotherapy*. New York: Plenum Press, 1978.

Zitrin, C., Klein, D. F., & Woerner, M. G. Treatment of agoraphobia with group exposure in vivo and imipramine. *Archives of General Psychiatry*, 1980, *37*, 63–72.

Prevention of Alcohol Abuse

PETER M. MILLER, TED D. NIRENBERG, AND GARY McCLURE

The abuse of alcohol presents a major, widespread health problem in the United States. Intervention aimed at modifying abusive drinking patterns has centered around treatment and rehabilitation programs, which have been developed primarily for middle-aged and older chronic alcoholics. For example, the median age of clients in treatment centers sponsored by the National Institute on Alcohol Abuse and Alcoholism is 45 years (Armor, Polich, & Stambul, 1976). More recently treatment has focused on younger and more diverse groups such as women, teenagers, and minority groups.

Historically, prevention has taken a back seat to treatment. Although priorities are gradually changing, prevention is still a "second-class citizen" in terms of federal funding and professional interest.

Alcoholism prevention is certainly not a simple concept. Exactly what are we trying to prevent? Basically, three types of prevention exist, each with a slightly different aim. Primary prevention attempts to prevent alcohol problems before they begin. Most alcohol education programs of this nature tend to target the junior high school student between the ages of 11 and 15. It is during these ages that initial experimentation with alcohol begins (Blane, 1976). Zucker and Barron (1973) and Jessor and Jessor (1977) argue that certain characteristics of youth in this age range, such as antisocial behavior, may assist in the early delineation of a high-risk population needing more intensive prevention efforts. Family history

PETER M. MILLER • Sea Pines Behavioral Institute, Sea Pines Plantation, Hilton Head Island, South Carolina 29928. TED D. NIRENBERG • Psychological Services, Veterans Administration Medical Center, Providence, Rhode Island 02908. GARY McCLURE • Department of Psychology, Georgia Southern College, Statesboro, Georgia 30458.

of alcoholism may also serve as a high-risk factor (Goodwin, Schulsinger, Hermansen, Guze, & Winokur, 1973). Other investigators indicate that primary prevention must begin at a much earlier age, since attitudes and concepts about alcohol and drinking begin even before school age. Jahoda and Gramond (1972) found that children as young as three years of age had developed established concepts of alcohol use and abuse. In fact, the Frederick County Council on Alcoholism in Maryland publishes a story coloring book dealing with attitudes toward alcoholism that is written for children as young as age four.

Secondary prevention is aimed at heavy drinkers who are just beginning to develop problems because of their drinking. Young adults between the ages of 18 and 25 tend to experience more significant life problems due to excessive alcohol consumption than any other group (USDHEW, 1974). Secondary prevention efforts have been primarily educational in nature and implemented through colleges and universities, the military, and driver safety programs.

Tertiary prevention actually refers to treatment. The goal is to prevent already diagnosed alcoholics from continuing their drinking. Chronicity and physical and psychological deterioration are the targets of the intervention.

This chapter will limit its focus to primary and secondary prevention efforts.

1. APPROACHES TO PREVENTION

Basically, three general approaches to prevention are currently in use. First, programs have been conducted to educate individuals regarding alcohol and to help them make informed decisions about their use of it. Second, the mass media influences have been analyzed as to their impact on drinking and their potential for modifying drinking attitudes and behaviors. Third, alcohol control policies and legal sanctions have been used to influence drinking among the young. This type of prevention effort includes minimum-drinking-age laws, pricing and taxation, situational controls, and criminalization.

The one characteristic shared by all preventive approaches is the marked paucity of systematic evaluations of their efficacy. The prevention field is years behind the treatment field in terms of outcome evaluation. This lack of research is due, to a great extent, to the myriad problems associated with the research. For example, a comprehensive evaluation of an alcoholism prevention project aimed at 12-year-olds necessitates a longitudinal study. Of course, attitudinal and short-term behavioral changes could be assessed. However, the most important question, "Does early intervention prevent later (adult) alcohol abuse?" must await an answer for several years.

In spite of these methodological and assessment problems, adequate evaluation of prevention programs is needed. Of all federally funded alcoholism prevention projects active in 1979, *none* used an experimental group design involving random assignment of individuals to prevention or control groups (Staulcup, Kenward, & Frigo, 1979). While most projects assessed knowledge, attitudes, and behavior toward alcohol, few used objective, observable measures, relying instead on self-reports.

2. ALCOHOL EDUCATION

Various alcohol education strategies and accompanying written and audiovisual materials have been developed over the years. While the overall goal of these programs is similar, content is often determined by the philosophy involved. Engs (1977) has identified five philosophical models upon which these materials and programs are based. The most common model of education is the *abstinence* model. This model is greatly influenced by the general orientation of Alcoholics Anonymous (AA) and stresses complete abstinence for health, moral, and religious reasons. The theme is simply that if you never begin to drink, you will never become an alcoholic. The *socioeconomic* model focuses on presenting statistics regarding potential problems resulting from drinking. These problems include automobile accidents, divorce, cost of treatment, and child abuse. The *alcoholism* approach emphasizes the disease of alcoholism and its related physical and psychological concomitants. Diagnostic criteria for alcoholism are often described in detail. The *alternatives* model proposes the notion that the development of behaviors such as sports and hobbies that are incompatible with excessive drinking will reduce alcohol consumption. Finally, the *responsible drinking* model assumes that those individuals who choose to drink should be taught methods of moderate, nonproblem drinking. Educational materials of this nature teach such techniques as pacing drinks, eating food while drinking, and avoiding alcohol under certain high-risk conditions (e.g., while depressed or upset). No comparisons among these differing philosophical approaches are as yet available, although an ongoing study by the present authors will be described later in this chapter.

In recent years the goal of alcohol education programs has shifted away from complete abstinence to prevention. The National Institute on Alcohol Abuse and Alcoholism (USDHEW, 1978) notes that the most recent projects attempt (1) to promote responsible decision making about drinking, (2) to reduce deviant or problem drinking, (3) to promote life values as guides to behavior, and (4) to improve psychological and social coping skills.

Although alcohol education programs of this nature are widely used, especially in school systems, their efficacy has yet to be demonstrated. In fact, after a comprehensive review of the literature, Braucht, Follinstad, Brakarsh, and Berry (1973) concluded that no form of alcohol or drug education has been shown to be effective in changing drinking or drug use patterns. Attitudes and knowledge are often improved without concomitant reductions in alcohol consumption. The fact that information alone does not significantly affect behavior should not be surprising news. Any physician will attest to the fact that people simply do not always do what they are told even if health or life itself is at stake. Milgram (1976) describes the past and current state of the art of alcohol education quite succinctly:

> In the 1940's alcohol education was characterized as weak and chaotic. . . . In the . . .
> 50's . . . the approach was hit-or-miss. . . . In the 60's alcohol education was described
> as being ineffective. . . . Alcohol education in the schools in the 70's can be character-
> ized as inadequate, ambivalent, and vague.

Others have raised fundamental questions regarding the appropriateness of including alcohol education in school curricula. Blane (1976) has questioned the use of the school system as a vehicle for moral training and the prevention of social problems. On the other hand, state legislators often consider alcohol and drug education a necessity in the school system and have passed legislation requiring its inclusion in public elementary and high schools.

In one of the few well-designed analyses using a matched control group, Engs (1977) evaluated an alcohol education program developed for students at Indiana University. The program was presented in small group meetings in residential units. The experimental group viewed a film entitled, *Booze and Yous,* which presents information about alcohol, common misconceptions about drinking, consequences of irresponsible drinking, and advice regarding responsible social drinking. In addition, five values-clarification exercises were used with trained peer counselors as facilitators. These exercises assisted students to examine values regarding drinking, to define responsible drinking behaviors for themselves, and to examine personal reasons for drinking. The control group viewed a film on human sexuality and used similar values-clarification exercises focusing on sexual behavior rather than drinking. Groups were initially equated on demographic variables and pretest mean alcohol knowledge and consumption. The Student Alcohol Questionnaire was administered to all subjects before and after the intervention and again at a three-month follow-up. The questionnaire included 36 items regarding alcohol knowledge and 23 items regarding alcohol behavior, such as quantity and frequency of alcohol consumption. Significant differences in posttest alcohol knowledge scores were found between the experimental and control groups immediately after and at three months after the educational program. Subjects in the experimental group had increased their knowledge of alcohol and its use. While knowledge was influenced, the program had little effect on behavior. No significant differences were noted in drinking behavior on the pre–post tests, either between or within the experimental and control groups. Thus, didactic education plus values clarification may influence knowledge and attitudes, but such changes may be unrelated to actual behavior change.

However, two other investigations were able to demonstrate behavioral changes as a function of educational technique. Williams, DiCicco, and Unterberger (1968) evaluated the effects of a series of five small group discussions on alcohol with high school students. Control groups were also included. Follow-up was conducted at 1 month and 12 months. While attitudes at 1 month were changed, frequency of drinking occasions did not differ between experimental and control groups. However, the experimental groups evidenced fewer episodes of intoxication. This is particularly noteworthy, since this is one of the few studies demonstrating actual changes in behavior. Unfortunately, at the one-year follow-up, none of these changes was maintained. Ongoing educational sessions or at least periodic booster sessions may be necessary to maintain these benefits.

Goodstadt, Sheppard, and Crawford (1978) evaluated the effects of an alcohol education program for Toronto school children in grades 7 through 10. A control group was included that received no alcohol education. A total of 1,351 students participated in the study. The educational package was presented by teachers and included (1) alcohol and myths, (2) drinking and driving, (3) media portrayal of alcohol, (4) alcohol and the family, and (5) alcohol and athletics. The curriculum resulted in a marked increase in knowledge in the experimental group but only mixed effects on atttidues. Alcohol use as well as expected future alcohol use also decreased in the experimental group.

2.1. Comprehensive Educational Programs

Several comprehensive, multimodal educational programs have been developed and implemented as demonstration projects. While most of these lack extensive evaluation and results from some are still pending, two of these projects deserve mention because of their scope. The CASPAR Alcohol Education Program and the University of Massachusetts Alcohol Education Project are noteworthy programs chosen by the National Institute on Alcohol Abuse and Alcoholism for replication and more detailed evaluation.

The Cambridge–Somerville Program for Alcoholism Rehabilitation (CASPAR) has been in existence since 1974 (Carifio, Biron, & Sullivan, 1978). Its overall goal has been to develop a responsible decision-making curriculum and to train teachers to implement the system in a densely populated city of 85,000 people. Comparative data were gathered on three separate groups. Group 1 consisted of 432 junior and senior high school students who received all elements of the CASPAR curriculum. Group 2 consisted of 192 students who received an incomplete and improper form of the CASPAR program. (That is, ratings of teacher instruction indicated that the program was not implemented as planned.) Group 3 consisted of 255 students from another community who were receiving a different, less comprehensive alcohol education program.

Pre- and posttest assessments indicated that the proper implementation of the CASPAR curriculum (Group 1) produced more positive gains in alcohol knowledge and attitude changes than did the other methods. Knowledge appeared to be more amenable to change than attitudes. The greatest gains in attitudes were found in younger students and those with fewer prior exposures to alcohol education. The investigators suggested that alcohol education may be maximally effective if initiated in lower grades. Jahoda's (1972) data, mentioned earlier, would tend to support this contention.

Replications of this project are currently in operation. Continued, longer-term changes in attitudes and knowledge and the effects of the CASPAR program on drinking behavior itself await further investigation. It is unfortunate that in a program of such magnitude no measures of behavior were included.

The University of Massachusetts Project, under the direction of Dr. David Kraft, is one of the most extensive alcohol education programs to date (Kraft, Duston, & Mellor, 1977). In fact, its impact was aimed at a total of 26,000 college students, faculty, and staff members. The educational program included training peer educators by conducting seminars and small group discussion meetings for residence hall staff and campus tavern bartenders. In addition, public discussions on alcohol use and abuse were held for students, emphasizing increased knowledge, improved attitudes and values clarification, and healthy alternatives to alcohol use.

The project was evaluated in a number of ways. First, a sample of 25,000 students were administered a survey regarding their knowledge, attitudes, and use of alcohol. Second, the number of students arrested for alcohol-related offenses was recorded. Third, the number of students treated for alcohol related medical problems at the University Helath Service was assessed. Fourth, on-campus property loss due to drinking was estimated. Results indicated that students demonstrated an increased level of awareness of alcohol use and misuse. However, as in other studies, no changes in alcohol consumption or patterns of drinking behavior were noted. The number of students arrested for alcohol-related offenses decreased and the percentage of students seeking medical help for alcohol-related problems increased. However, without a control group for comparison, such results are suspect. Such changes might have occurred without the alcohol education program and might be due to other, unknown causes.

Kraft (1979) indicates that the lack of documented changes in drinking behavior is particularly frustrating for all college projects of this nature. He notes that perhaps the measurement techniques being used are too crude to detect these changes. Indeed, more direct measures of consumption—such as behavioral observations in dormitories and customer counts in campus taverns—are being incorporated into these programs. It may be that changes in drinking behavior are so subtle that, while short-term consumption does not change, patterning does (e.g., drinking may become less likely under social pressure or stress). In addition, longitudinal studies are needed to determine whether such programs decrease the incidence of alcoholism and alcohol-related problems in given populations.

2.2. Behavioral Programs

Behavior modification techniques have been used primarily for the treatment of alcohol abuse, although there is a tendency for them to be used for secondary prevention. This trend is particularly noteworthy, since behavioral procedures are aimed more directly at modifying drinking behavior than at simply changing knowledge and attitudes (Miller, 1979). A responsible drinking-skills-oriented approach is usually used. Young adults are taught either alternatives to problem drinking (such as relaxation), methods of monitoring and controlling alcohol consumption via self-management, or a combination of both.

Marlatt, Pagano, Rose, and Marques (1976), for example, evaluated the effects of relaxation training on the drinking behavior of 44 young men whose mean age was 23 years. All subjects were heavy social drinkers. Participants were divided into four groups. Group 1 received meditational relaxation as developed by Benson (1975). This method emphasizes a passive attitude, muscle relaxation, and the subvocal repetition of a sound or word. Group 2 subjects were taught progressive muscle relaxation as developed by Jacobson (1938). Group 3 subjects, an attention–placebo control group, were told to rest every day. Group 4 subjects received no relaxation training and no specific instructions. Alcohol consumption decreased for Groups 1, 2, and 3 but not for Group 4. Consumption was reduced by as much as 50% in the meditation–relaxation group. The regular practice of relaxation was also associated with feelings of self-efficacy and self-control. Thus, some form of daily relaxation appears to decrease alcohol consumption in young adults.

While assertiveness training has been shown to influence drinking in alcholics (Foy, Miller, Eisler, & O'Toole, 1976), it has not been used in prevention. Certain forms of assertiveness training, such as drink-refusal training, would seem to be particularly useful in prevention packages aimed at adolescents. This training teaches individuals to cope with social pressure. Through role playing, rehearsal, instruction, and feedback, clients are taught ways of effectively dealing with such comments as "Oh, come on, one drink won't hurt you; don't you want to be one of the guys?"

Miller (1979) also describes the potential use of self-management training and physical-fitness programs for young adult drinkers. While total behavioral prevention programs including several of these elements are few, two recent projects are worthy of note.

Miller (1978) evaluated a multimodal behavioral intervention package for young problem drinkers—essentially a secondary prevention project. The program included alcohol education, blood alcohol discrimination training, drink refusal and assertiveness training, relaxation training, and self-management training. The following three treatment variations were assessed: (1) aversive conditioning in which electric shocks were associated with alcohol; (2) self-control training including self-monitoring, self-management, and training in behavioral alternatives to drinking; and (3) controlled-drinking training involving blood alcohol discrimination to teach the components of responsible drinking. The self-control and controlled-drinking training proved to be the most effective packages, reducing weekly alcohol consumption by more than half. The most cost-effective training in terms of time and money was the self-control package. The investigators also noted that some participants seemed to be able to modify their drinking habits simply through the use of a written manual describing self-control techniques. The manual differs from traditional alcohol education materials in that it provides very specific instructions on habit change.

Nirenberg, Miller, and McClure (1981) are currently evaluating different prevention strategies with moderate- and heavy-drinking college students. The study is unique in that it compares differing prevention philosophies (e.g., behavior modification versus AA) and because it utilizes an objective assessment of results. College students are exposed to one of four prevention programs, each requiring four 2-hour sessions. The programs include (1) behavioral self-control training using assertiveness, relaxation, problem solving, responsible drinking skills, and self-management training; (2) behavioral self-control training with actual experience at discrimination of different blood alcohol levels; (3) messages on alcohol education–information and attitude change based upon a responsible-drinking model; (4) AA-type alcohol education based upon an abstinence-oriented approach; and (5) a no-treatment control group. A comprehensive assessment will be conducted prior to training and at one-, three-, and five-year follow-ups. Assessment will include self-monitoring of alcohol-related behaviors, self-report measures of alcohol use and life functioning, health profile, biochemical determinants of alcohol misuse, and information from subject collaterals. One-year follow-up evaluation will be available in 1982.

3. MASS MEDIA

If one considers the consumption and abuse of alcohol as habitual behaviors detrimental to health, then strategies in the prevention of these behaviors would obviously do well to focus on how they first occur and by what processes they become habitual. The role of mass media effects, both programmed and incidental, is assumed to be significant. However, the literature provides very little empirical evidence to support the varied assumptions attributed to the effects of the mass media on alcohol-related behaviors. This is not to say that programmatic attempts to influence such behaviors have been lacking; just the opposite is true. The assumed cause–effect relationship in virtually all such efforts is at best equivocal. This is especially true regarding television, where "we are rich in opinions and poor in facts" (Comstock, 1976).

It is important to note that the effect of the media, especially television, on behavior other than alcohol consumption has received substantial attention in recent years. In a critical review of the overall influence of the media on attitude and behavior, Mischel (1971) concluded that:

> television, movies, books, and stories, and other symbolic media play an important part in the transmission of nformation about the probable response consequences of diverse behaviors and may influence people's preferences, values, and choices to a considerable degree.

Given the present absence of adequate research bearing directly on the effects of television on alcohol consumption, we may cautiously extrapolate from other data bases that are substantially more solid in their empirical foundations.

Certainly no media variable has been more thoroughly researched than the effect of televised aggression and the increased probability of subsequent viewer aggression. While there remains much debate about the social implication of such a relationship, the fact that it exists has been well documented (e.g., Surgeon General's Scientific Advisory Committee on Television and Social Behavior, 1972; Bandura, 1973; Comstock, 1972; Leifer & Roberts, 1972). Research in the area has moved on to more subtle variables, such as that of Drabman and Thomas (1974) investigating the relationship between desensitization to violence and exposure to aggressive programming. Liebet and Poulos (1974) have concluded that television can function as an adverse "moral teacher." These and other investigations, especially that leading to the Surgeon General's Report, have led professionals to lodge protests against televised violence (Ingelfinger, 1976; Somers, 1976) and have given rise to systematic efforts among lay groups such as parent–teacher organizations.

Interestingly, if television has the power to serve as the "adverse moral teacher" (Liebert & Poulos, 1974), it probably serves equally well as a nonadverse or "prosocial teacher." Researchers, however, have not addressed the potential impact of television on prosocial behaviors with the same zeal as that with which they have addressed other antisocial variables, especially aggression. Liebert and Schwartzenberg (1977), in their review of the published literature between 1970 and 1975 on mass media effects, noted that prosocial effects of television were gaining increased attention (cf. Sprafkin, Liebert, & Poulos, 1975; Stein & Bryan, 1972; and Friedrich & Stein, 1973).

Media campaigns designed to control alcohol consumption were implicitly intended to be prosocial messages. Research examining the relationship between television and alcohol consumption is, as noted earlier, very limited and has not addressed the more subtle aspects of the potential "incidental" influence of TV programming on such variables as the pattern and characteristic portrayals of alcohol consumption on television (Comstock, 1976). Although vast sums of time and money are expended to design media campaigns, clearly more research is needed to document empirically the relationship between alcohol consumption and the incidental and programmatic influence of television.

While the influence of television as a medium is ubiquitous in contemporary society, it is important to recognize the historical and continuing impact of the printed word. In fact, the campaigns that brought about both the adoption and repeal of prohibition were ambitious even by present marketing standards. The Women's Christian Temperance Union and the Association Against the Prohibition Amendment made great use of mass-distributed printed materials. Since the repeal of prohibition in 1934, a variety of mass-media efforts have addressed alcohol consumption and alcohol-related health problems.

The belief that any use of alcohol for some is by definition abuse became popular with the emergence of AA as a nationally viable organization in the early 1940s. This group made wide use of mass-media techniques, especially in communicating the "disease model" of alcoholism. Until 1972, mass-media communication emphasized the goal of abstinence. However, Seagram's Distributors, a notable exception, have for decades stressed moderation in the use of their product. Obviously the goal of a distillery could not be total abstinence.

In 1972 there was a significant shift in the media message on alcohol consumption. The National Institute on Alcohol Abuse and Alcoholism launched a three-stage program derived from a responsible-drinking model. A multimedia campaign which launched Stage 1 focused on the view that abuse of alcohol is inappropriate and unacceptable. It attempted to do so by alerting the public to various patterns of drinking that were potentially dangerous as well as to early symptoms and signs of alcoholism. The media message of Stage 1 was simply "If you need a drink to be social, that's not social drinking." Since it did not explicitly promote abstinence, it departed significantly from the "any use equals abuse" perspective. Although it emphasized what responsible drinking *is not*, little attention was given the task of clarifying what responsible drinking *is*. As Blane (1974) pointed out, "There is almost a total absence of messages having to do with positive clarification of responsible drinking or tolerance of responsible drinking and nondrinking." During the latter part of the same year, Stage 2 was initiated via a multimedia approach, including, for example, televised messages and open letters to physicians. These messages focused on the theme that alcohol is indeed a drug which, if abused, produces health hazards for the abuser and myriad other problems indirectly for family, friends, employers, and society. Phase 2 sought to encourage the recognition, diagnosis, and treatment of alcoholism. In 1973, Stage 3 was launched with a campaign openly contradicting the view that overconsumption of alcohol was a laughing matter and depicting the drunk as anything but humorous. Stage 3 further solidified the disease model of alcoholism.

In addition to focusing attention on direct health risks inherent in the abuse of alcohol, several prevention programs have focused on indirect or secondary problems associated with alcohol abuse and relevant to the general public welfare. Most notably, the problem of drunken driving as a public safety menace has historically received much attention. In fact, by far the largest part of the money and effort dedicated to media campaigns on alcohol abuse has served to focus on the drinking–driving problem.

The slogan "If you drink, don't drive—if you drive, don't drink" has become quite familiar. Introduced by the National Safety Council in the 1930s, this slogan as well as others (e.g., "The life you save may be your own") had been cooperatively supported by government, the liquor industry, and the insurance industry. This cooperation has resulted in a common media message with broader coverage than would have been the case if each source had gone its separate way with individual media campaign efforts. However, Donovan (1972) noted that this intuitively valid campaign has had no empirically demonstrable success in achieving its purpose. Nonetheless, these "scare tactics" messages continued until 1970, when both the tactics and the content of the media messages changed. During that year the "Scream Bloody Murder" media campaign was begun (Blane & Hewitt, 1977) and the National Safety Council coalesced with the insurance industry to "Get the drunk driver off the road" (Van Natta, 1972). The liquor industry, meanwhile, made a substantial departure from its historical position of separating drinking and driving by suggesting for the first time that one *could* drink and drive, but with the proscription to "Know your limits." That is, if one knows his or her limits, then one can reduce drunk-driving risks. For example, you may "Let someone else drive"; "Limit yourself to two drinks"; or "Take time to sober up." Clearly, the 1970s witnessed a marked change from previous decades in media campaigns relating to drinking and driving.

Media campaigns have obviously focused on systematic attempts to prevent alcohol abuse. Less obvious, perhaps, is the implicit influence the media may exert via the incidental programming of alcohol-related behaviors and attitudes. Curiously, the major problem is that there simply is little known about how this behavior is actually portrayed on television. The most relevant data available concern the frequency of references to or portrayals of alcohol consumption. Dillon (1975a,b,c) reports that 80% of all prime-time TV programs during two months in 1975 contained one or more such references or portrayals. In a more recent survey by Breed (1978), alcohol was found to be consumed more often on television than water, soft drinks, coffee, or tea.

The impact of beer and wine commercials on television and liquor advertisements in magazines and newspapers is also an important consideration. Professionals and government officials have expressed concern over the influence of such advertising on youth, since it often portrays drinking as exciting or "manly" behavior or as a self-reward for a "job well done." This is particularly significant in view of the fact that the overall advertising budget for beverage alcohol is approaching a *billion* dollars annually, with the individual budgets of the major breweries in excess of 100 million dollars each. Although "hard" alcohol commercials are not permitted on television, those for "soft" alcoholic beverages are. With respect to television as a media influence, the state of the art of research in this area is best summarized by George Comstock (1976) of the Rand Corporation. He says that there is no scientific evidence bearing directly on the question of television's contributions to alcohol consumption and abuse. He documents this statement as follows:

> (a) A recently published analysis of the 450 items judged to be most important in the scientific literature regarding television and human behavior includes *none* that deal with alcohol consumption or abuse. (Comstock, 1975)
>
> (b) A guide to the entire scientific literature on the topic that covers more than 2,300 items similarly includes *none* that deal with alcohol consumption or abuse. (Comstock & Fisher, 1975)
>
> (c) In addition, an account of research underway in mid-1975, covering about 50 projects in-progress, uncovered *no* projects focusing on alcohol consumption or abuse. (Comstock & Lindsey, 1975)

Since these observations were made, projects have been undertaken to assess the characteristic portrayals in media programming content and advertising of alcohol beverage consumption (e.g., Mosher & Wallack, 1979a). Such projects have focused on developing reliable and valid assessment instruments for monitoring and coding the pattern and character of alcohol use in audiovisual media materials. Utilization of these assessment tools in the analysis of actual media programs, especially television and the motion picture industry, can then be used in developing prevention strategies. Namely, prevention efforts can be addressed directly to the industry writers and producers responsible for alcohol-related program content, or, alternatively, education/prevention efforts can be directed to the viewing public.

4. ALCOHOL CONTROL LEGISLATION

Legislation concerning consumption of alcoholic beverages has been as abundant and varied as its aims. Legislation has attempted to protect society from the alcohol abuser, to protect alcohol abusers from themselves, as a source of revenue in the form of taxation, to influence social mores, and/or as a means of preventing alcohol abuse. Although legislation can achieve one or many of these objectives, this section will focus on whether legislation provides a viable strategy for the prevention of alcohol abuse.

Alcohol control legislation may be categorized into (1) efforts to limit the availability of alcohol and (2) criminalization and punishment of alcohol-related behaviors.

4.1. Efforts to Limit Availability of Alcohol

By far the most effective means of preventing alcohol abuse is to simply eliminate alcohol from society. Without alcohol, problems of abuse would be nonexistent. Attempts at prohibition, however, have been neither simple to enact nor a popular alternative to the problem of alcohol abuse. Current legislation regarding availability has evolved in the course of an essentially muddled attempt to placate the "drys," the "wets," and also the influential liquor industry.

The strategy of reducing the availability of alcohol is based on the distribution model of prevention (Bruun, Edwards, Lumio, Mäkelä, Pan, Popham, Room, Schmidt, Skog, Sulkunen, & Oesterberg, 1975; Popham, Schmidt, & De Lint, 1976). This model predicts a direct relationship between per capita consumption and alcohol abuse. Therefore, a reduction in per capita consumption by way of a reduction in availability will reduce the number of alcohol abusers as well as physical and social damage due to alcohol. The model has propagated significant amounts of international research and controversy (Bruun *et al.*, 1975; Schmidt & Popham, 1978; Schmidt, 1977; Parker & Harman, 1978). Although it has received only cursory empirical support, its tenets lie in the forefront of many alcohol abuse prevention strategies.

Regulation of consumption has been attempted by various agencies. At the federal level, for example, the U.S. Bureau of Alcohol, Tobacco, and Firearms establishes standards for the quality and content of alcoholic beverages and, along with the Federal Communications Commission, regulates alcohol advertising on television and radio. The Federal Civil Aviation Agency controls the sale and consumption of alcohol on airlines; the Internal Revenue Service governs how alcohol can be used as a business expense; and the National Park Service, Army Corps of Engineers, Bureau of Indian Affairs, and the Department of Defense regulate the availability and use of alcoholic beverages on federal reserves and lands. Equally as diverse are the state- and local-level agencies; these include, for example, departments of alcohol beverage control, liquor licensing boards, local zoning ordinances on the location of liquor establishments, and state legislature control over drinking-age restrictions.

Alcohol control legislation has primarily focused on (1) price setting and taxation, (2) setting legal drinking ages, and (3) situational controls. These last have included licensing of alcohol beverage businesses; guidelines on the location, number, and types of alcohol sale outlets; hours of liquor sales; availability of food in drinking establishments; alcohol content limits; and restrictions on the sale of alcoholic beverages to intoxicated patrons.

4.1.1. Price Setting and Taxation

A basic assumption of economic theory states that product demand is inversely related to price. Therefore, keeping other variables constant, an increase or decrease in the price of alcoholic beverages should lead to a respective decrease or increase in overall consumption. Although supported in part by a few reviews (Bruun *et al.*, 1975; Popham *et al.*, 1976; Ornstein, 1980), the relationship between the price of alcohol and per capita consumption remains unclear. Issues still unresolved include whether:

1. An individual's overall income rather than the price of alcoholic beverages is a significant determinant of demand (Parker & Harman, 1978).
2. Different types of drinkers (heavy versus moderate) respond differently to price manipulations. For example, Parker and Harman (1978) suggest that heavy drinkers probably are less apt to alter their drinking consumption in response to price manipulation than are moderate or light drinkers.
3. Different beverage types (beer, wine, distilled spirits) have different demand curves. Ornstein (1980), in his review of studies examining U.S. pricing manipulations, found that when all other variables are kept constant, an increase in the price of beer was followed by a significantly less than proportional decline in beer consumption, an increase in the price of distilled spirits led to an equally or slightly greater proportional decline in distilled spirits consumption, but an increase in the price of wine resulted in nonsignificant changes.
4. Different beverage types may serve as substitutes for one another as the price of one type is increased (Parker & Harman, 1978; Schmidt & Popham, 1978). For example, if the price of distilled spirits is increased, does it lead to a decline in consumption or lead to an increase in demand for wine and/or beer? If beverage type substitution occurs with price manipulations, then the price of all beverages must be increased simultaneously in order to achieve an overall decline in consumption.
5. Price manipulation effects may be significantly influenced by the nature of alcohol itself. Unlike many commodities, alcohol has a variety of uses (i.e., social, ritual, medical) and use patterns which may have quite different demand elasticities. Across cultural groups or even over time, changes in the type of needs for alcohol may influence demand to a far greater extent than price manipulations. For example, Brisbane (1976) found that black youths living in a poor socioeconomic community drank heavily in response to their disadvantaged environment. Even though the price of alcohol in all likelihood represented a very high cost relative to their income, they drank in an effort to cope with their present life situation. We may find that such drinking patterns may be less responsive to price manipulations.

4.1.2. Setting Legal Drinking Ages

The Twenty-First Amendment, signaling the end of Prohibition, gave the states the power to set alcohol distribution guidelines, including minimum age requirements for buyers of alcoholic beverages. Until 1970, most states had a legal drinking age of 21. However, during the early 1970s, many began passing legislation to reduce the legal drinking age (ages 18 to 20). The trend toward a lower drinking age was viewed as a progressive step, possibly instigated by a concurrent push for the enfranchisement of 18-year-olds. It was argued that if 18-year-olds could vote, engage in military service, marry, and pay taxes, they should certainly be able to purchase and consume alcohol. Also supporting the lower drinking age were those who espoused the "forbidden fruit" theory, indicating that young adults were attracted toward alcohol because they could not legally obtain it and that, if they could legally obtain it, they would consume less.

More recently drinking ages are again changing. Following the decline in minimum drinking ages, there have been several reports of increases in alcohol-related driving accidents, fatalities, and juvenile crime involving 18- to 20-year-olds (e.g., Douglass, Filkins, & Clark, 1974; Cucchiaro, Fereira, & Sicherman, 1974; Williams, Rich, Zador, & Robertson, 1974; Yoakum, 1979). In response, several states have raised their drinking ages (e.g., Minnesota in 1976 and Maine in 1977). Although it appears that jurisdictions that have lowered the legal drinking age produced a moderate increase in alcohol-related problems among the new drinking-age group, it is unclear whether or not these changes will maintain themselves over time. Recent investigations suggest that the long-term effects may be much less pronounced (Douglass & Freedman, 1977; Whitehead, 1977). The effects may be quite similar to the apparent short-term effects of other related legislation. For instance following the introduction of the 0.08 BAC legal limit law in Britain, there was an immediate reduction in the number of alcohol-related problems. However, within a few years the problem rate returned to normal. Similarly, the effects of the "Surgeon General's message" about the harmful effects of cigarette smoking was short-lived.

Finally, the increase in alcohol use among the young may be related to liberal changes in attitudes by parents and society rather than changes in the legal drinking ages. Since liberal attitudes toward drinking probably superseded the liberalized legislation, it is quite possible that a return to greater restriction (increases in drinking age) will not be an effective deterrent to alcohol abuse unless societal attitudes toward the use of alcohol are also modified.

4.1.3. Situational Controls

These controls attempt to regulate the environmental availability of alcohol—to change the drinking environment in a manner so as to reduce abusive drinking. Most of these controls are governed by state alcohol beverage control (ABC) boards. In 32 states and the District of Columbia, state ABC boards have created their control of alcohol sales by licensing private alcohol beverages businesses. The licensing procedures have served both the licensed establishment and the ABC agency. By limiting the number of available licenses, ABC agencies have created a monopoly and therefore restricted competition among licensed beverage concerns. However, by using the threat of license removal, ABC agencies are able to usurp regulatory controls. In the remaining 18 states, ABC boards have actually taken over the wholesale and retail sale of distilled spirits. Studies of the ABC agencies' direct involvement in sales versus licensing controls have thus far yielded only minor differences in consumption rates (Popham *et al.*, 1976).

State ABC agencies have also established guidelines regarding fixed hours for bars and liquor stores, type and location of outlets, the availability of food in drinking establishments, alcohol content levels, and restrictions of the sale of alcohol to intoxicated patrons. Investigations examining these control strategies, although frequently limited in scope and plagued with methodological problems, suggest that such strategies result in insignificant changes in overall consumption rates (Popham *et al.*, 1976; Blane & Hewitt, 1977; De Lint, 1976). These control strategies have traditionally served to meet the general purposes of the ABC agencies, which have been to maintain an orderly alcoholic beverage sales market, to control crime in the liquor trade, and to provide tax revenue (Room & Mosher, 1979; Medicine in the Public Interest, 1979; Driver, 1974). The use of ABC legislation to encourage prevention has been minimal.

A recent program conducted by the California ABC department serves as an exemplary model of fusing regulatory power with an educational program to produce a viable prevention program. Recent dram-shop laws and court decisions have produced considerable interest in the legal responsibility of serving alcoholic beverages to an intoxicated patron. In a two-year pilot study, the California ABC agency set up a program designed to locate and provide prevention training to licensees who had served patrons later arrested for driving under the influence (DUI) (Room & Mosher, 1979–80; Mosher & Wallack, 1979b). Licensees identified as serving a patron offender the last drink prior to the DUI arrest were informed by letter of their violation, reminded of the potential criminal and financial consequences, given some educational materials, and offered additional training for their staff. Licensees found guilty of a second violation were contacted personally and strongly encouraged (license was threatened) to undergo training. Most violators participated in the required training. Educational training, conducted by specially trained ABC personnel, focused on ways to cut off service to intoxicated customers. This included strategies to determine signs of intoxication, setting limits on the number of drinks served, talking with patrons to determine whether they could handle another drink, serving coffee to patrons when they reached their limit, and using public transportation for those patrons who were obviously intoxicated. Although the influence of the California program as a prevention strategy is not yet clear, the demand for the training aspect of the program has proliferated. The synthesis of regulatory power and educational programs may prove to be a more viable strategy than simply regulatory power alone. The utility of such programs awaits further investigation.

4.2. Criminalization and Punishment of Alcohol-Related Behaviors

Legislation has also been used to establish consequences for "problem drinking." Assuming that efforts to reduce availability are inadequate, the alcohol abuser is faced with the threat of negative consequences made contingent upon certain alcohol-related behaviors.

Many offenders guilty of serious crime are under the influence of alcohol at the time of their offense. Although alcohol has been reported to be used by 7% to 72% of robbery offenders, 13% to 50% of sex offenders, 24% to 72% of assault offenders, and 28% to 86% of homicide offenders, the use of alcohol in these and many other crimes does not have any legal bearing (USDHEW, 1978; Shupe, 1954; Amir, 1971; Pittman & Handy, 1964; Hollis, 1974). The role of alcohol in such crimes and its influence in the prevention (primary and secondary) of recidivism is scant and in need of further investigation.

Criminalization of alcohol abuse has focused primarily on drunken driving and public drunkeness. The extremely high incidence of such offenses, which have for several years overloaded the American justice system (Logan, 1978), coupled with judicial recognition that alcoholism is an "illness" (Daggett & Rolde, 1980), has led to decriminalization of public drunkeness and increased emphasis on education for drunk-driving offenders. In response to the Uniform Alcoholism and Intoxication Treatment Act in 1971, many states have abolished the crime of public drunkeness and have advocated increased treatment rather than imprisonment. The overall results of these changes are confusing. Arrests for public drunkeness, of course, declined, since it was no longer considered a crime. However, law enforcers in several states continued to arrest public drunks by using other criminal charges (e.g., Nimmer, 1971). For example, Daggett and Rolde (1980) found that following the decriminalization of public drunkeness in several suburban towns in Massachusetts, protective custody detention increased by 19% and disorderly conduct charges increased by 27%. The effectiveness of treatment or detoxification centers as a component of decriminalization has not been adequately evaluated. Although inherently it would appear that treatment would be more effective than detention alone, the rehabilitation now offered as an alternative to detention may be inadequate to prevent recidivism.

There have been numerous reports establishing a strong relationship between the level of intoxication of a driver and his or her auto accident potential. As the blood alcohol level of drivers increases, the probability of crash involvement and causation increases. For instance, drivers at a BAC of 0.10 are twice as likely to be involved in a crash and four times as likely to cause a crash than drivers at a BAC of 0.03 (USDHEW, 1978). It is also estimated that over one-third of the injuries and one-half of the fatalities from auto accidents are alcohol related.

Due to the tremendous incidence and negative impact of driving under the influence of alcohol, this offense has become a leading international concern. Initial legislation outlawing drunk driving has generally resulted in declines in the proportion of accidents and accident fatalities involving alcohol. In an effort to increase the benefit of early legislation, several countries have introduced more severe legislation (e.g., Germany in 1965 and Finland in 1963 and 1967). Although the harsher penalties produced a favorable decline in alcohol-related driving accidents and arrests, the change was effective for only a short time (Mäkelä, 1974). More recently, emphasis has been directed at educational programs for DUI offenders and the general public. The Alcohol Safety Action Project, for example, was established by the Department of Transportation to provide public education about drunken driving, driver education, and increased DUI law enforcement (Comptroller General of the United States, 1979). Overall, the project communities exhibited a decline in alcohol-related nighttime fatalities, an increase in the number of arrests and convictions of drunk drivers, and an increase in the number of problem drinkers referred to rehabilitation programs. Further evaluation of similar programs combining legislative controls with educational programs is essential.

The use of DUI legislation may be a very useful tool not only as a means of reducing the number of DUIs but also in the overall prevention of alcohol abuse. Evaluations of DUI offenders have revealed that between 11% and 48% have a serious drinking problem (e.g., Selzer, 1969; Minnesota Department of Public Safety, 1979). In addition, "alcoholics exhibit a significantly greater number of traffic accidents and violations than does the general driving population" (USDHEW, 1978). Utilization of legislation not only as a deterrent in terms of its negative consequences but as a means of identifying the problem drinker and as a source of leverage to get problem drinkers into treatment may prove quite useful.

5. CONCLUSIONS

Unfortunately, the most appropriate conclusion revolves around the fact that more controlled evaluations are necessary for all types of prevention approaches. Alcoholism prevention is still in its infancy. In spite of this, certain trends that may provide a basis for future intervention attempts are evident.

In terms of alcohol education, more information is needed on the efficacy of differing philosophies. While studies demonstrating chnges in knowledge and attitudes are available, the effect of alcohol education on drinking behavior *per se* is equivocal. More efforts aimed at children below high school age are needed. Some evidence exists that prevention programs for children below the eighth-grade level may be maximally effective. However, such programs are rare, with most targeting junior and senior high school students. One-shot programs are typical, even though there is evidence that the results of such programs are short-lived. Periodic booster training sessions may be needed. Finally, behavior modification techniques show promise for the prevention of alcoholism, but they require further evaluation. Such evaluations are currently under way.

The influence of mass media campaigns used alone or as part of comprehensive alcohol abuse prevention programs is unclear. While it has been assumed for many years that media influence has a significant effect, empirical support is lacking. Current research projects examining the incidental and programmatic influence of television on viewer behavior, including the use and abuse of alcohol, will be useful. It is also necessary to delineate the utility of the mass-media efforts that have frequently been incorporated into mutlifaceted prevention programs.

Alcohol control legislation includes the criminalization and punishment of alcohol-related behaviors as well as efforts to limit the availability of alcohol. The efficacy of such legislation in the prevention of alcohol abuse is mixed. For instance, although increasing the cost of alcohol by price setting and taxation appears to reduce per capita consumption, a number of unresolved issues still remain. These include the relationship between price manipulation and income, heavy versus moderate drinkers, different beverage types, beverage substitution, and the diversity of alcohol use patterns. The setting of legal drinking ages has led to much debate. Although investigations have reported a strong correlation between lowered drinking ages and an increase in alcohol-related problems among 18- to 20-year-olds, there has been some recent evidence that this relationship declines over time. Further investigations on the long-term effects of lowered drinking age are needed. Investigations examining situational controls have suggested that such strategies result in, at best, minimal changes in per capita consumption. Current attempts at combining regulatory power with educational programs seem promising. Attempts at criminalization and punishment have focused primarily upon drunk-driving offenses. Legislation outlawing drunk driving has generally resulted in a decline in alcohol-related car accidents. Such legislation may be useful not only as a deterrent but also as a means of identifying the problem drinker and as a source of leverage to get the problem drinker into treatment.

6. REFERENCES

Amir, M. *Patterns in forcible rape.* Chicago: University of Chicago Press, 1971.

Armor, D. J., Polich, J. M., & Stambul, H. B. *Alcoholism and treatment.* Santa Monica, Calif.: Rand Corporation, 1976.

Bandura, A. *Aggression: A social learning analysis.* Englewood Cliffs, N.J.: Prentice-Hall, 1973.

Benson, H. *The relaxation response*. New York: Morrow, 1975.

Blane, H. T. Education and mass persuasion as preventive strategies. In R. Room & S. Sheffield (Eds.), *The prevention of alcohol problems: Report of a conference*. Sacramento, Calif.: Office of Alcoholism Health and Welfare Agency, State of California, 1974.

Blane, H. T. Issues in preventing alcohol problems. *Preventive Medicine*, 1976, *5*, 176–186.

Blane, H. T., & Hewitt, L. E. *Mass media, public education and alcohol: A state of the art review*. Paper prepared for NIAAA, Contract NIA-76-12, 1977.

Braucht, G. N., Follinstad, D., Brakarsh, D., & Berry, K. L. Drug education: A review of goals, approaches and effectiveness, and a paradigm for evaluation. *Quarterly Journal of Studies on Alcohol*, 1973, *34*, 1279–1292.

Breed, W. *National Institute on Alcohol Abuse and Alcoholism: Information and Feature Services*, 1978, May 1–2.

Brisbane, F. The cause and consequences of alcohol abuse among black youth. *Journal of Afro-American Issues*, 1976, *4*, 241–254.

Bruun, K., Edwards, G., Lumio, M., Mäkelä, K., Pan, L., Popham, R. E., Room, R., Schmidt, W., Skog, O. J., Sulkunen, P., & Oesterberg, E. *Alcohol control policies in public health perspective*. Helsinki: Finnish Foundation for Alcohol Studies, 1975.

Carifo, J., Biron, R. M., & Sullivan, D. *Selected findings on the impact of the CASPAR alcohol education program on teacher training and curriculum implementation* (Evaluation report No. 8). Somerville, Mass: CASPAR, Inc., 1978.

Comptroller General of the United States. *The drinking-driver problem—What can be done aobut it?* (Report to Congress). Washington, D.C.: U.S. General Accounting Office, 1979.

Comstock, G. A. *Television violence: Where the Surgeon General's study leads*. Santa Monica, Calif.: The Rand Corporation, 1972.

Comstock, G. *Television and human behavior: The key studies*. Santa Monica, Calif.: The Rand Corporation, 1975.

Comstock, G. *Television and alcohol consumption and abuse*. Santa Monica, Calif.: The Rand Corporation, 1976.

Comstock, G., & Fisher, M. *Television and human behavior: A guide to the pertinent scientific literature*. Santa Monica, Calif.: The Rand Corporation, 1975.

Comstock, G., & Lindsey, G. *Television and human behavior: The research horizon, future and present*. Santa Monica, Calif.: The Rand Corporation, 1975.

Cucchiaro, S., Fereira, J., & Sicherman, A. *The effect of the 18-year-old drinking age on auto accidents*. Cambridge, Mass.: Massachusetts Institute of Technology Operation Research Center, 1974.

Daggett, L. R., & Rolde, E. J. Decriminalization of drunkenness: Effects on the work of suburban police. *Journal of Studies on Alcohol*, 1980, *41*, 819–828.

De Lint, J. *Alcohol control policies a strategy for prevention: A critical examination of the evidence*. Paper presented at the International Conference on Alcoholism and Drug Dependence, Liverpool, England, 1976.

Dillon, J. TV drinking: How networks pour liquor into your living room. *Christian Science Monitor*, June 30, 1975. (a)

Dillon, J. TV drinking: Do networks follow own code? *Christian Science Monitor*, July 1, 1975. (b)

Dillon, J. TV drinking does not mirror U.S. *Christian Science Monitor*, July 11, 1975. (c)

Donovan, T. J. (Untitled). In J. W. Swinehart & A. C. Grimm (Eds.), *Public information programs on alcohol and highway safety*. Ann Arbor, Mich.: University of Michigan Highway Safety Research Institute, 1972.

Douglass, R. L., Filkins, L. D., & Clark, F. A. *The effect of lower legal drinking age on youth crash involvement: Final report to U.S. Department of Transportation, National Highway Traffic*

Safety Administration. Ann Arbor, Mich.: Highway Safety Research Institute, The University of Michigan, 1974.

Douglass, R. L., & Freedman, J. A. *A study of alcohol-related casualties and alcohol beverage availability policies in Michigan.* Ann Arbor, Mich.: Highway Safety Research Institute, 1977.

Drabman, R. S., & Thomas, M. H. Does media violence increase children's toleration of real-life aggression? *Developmental Psychology,* 1974, *10,* 418–421.

Driver, R. J. *A survey of alcoholic beverage control in the U.S.* Unpublished report prepared for the National Institute of Alcohol Abuse and Alcoholism, March, 1974.

Engs, R. Let's look before we leap: The cognitive and behavioral evaluation of a university alcohol education program. *Journal of Alcohol and Drug Education,* 1977, *2,* 39–48.

Foy, D. W., Miller, P. M., Eisler, R. M., & O'Toole, D. H. Social skills training to teach alcoholics to refuse drinks effectively. *Journal of Studies on Alcohol,* 1976, *37,* 1340–1345.

Friedrich, L. K., & Stein, A. H. Aggressive and prosocial television programs and the natural behavior of preschool children. *Monographs of the Society for Research in Child Development,* 1973, *38,* 421–444.

Friedrich, L. K., & Stein, A. H. Prosocial television and young children: The effects of verbal labeling and role playing on lerning and behavior. *Child Development,* 1975, *22,* 1250–1262.

Goodstadt, M. S., Sheppard, M. A., & Crawford, S. H. *Development and evaluation of two alcohol education programs for the Toronto Board of Education.* Toronto: Addiction Research Foundation, 1978.

Goodwin, D. W., Schulsinger, F., Hermansen, L., Guze, S. B., & Winokin, G. Alcohol problems in adoptees raised apart from alcoholic biological parents. *Archives of General Psychiatry,* 1973, *28,* 238–243.

Hollis, W. S. On the etiology of criminal homicides—The alcohol factor. *Journal of Political Science Administration,* 1974, *2,* 50–53.

Ingelfinger, F. J. Violence on TV: An unchecked environmental hazard. *The New England Journal of Medicine,* 1976, *294,* 837–838.

Jacobson, E. *Progressive relaxation.* Chicago: University of Chicago Press, 1938.

Jahoda, G., & Gramond, J. *Children and alcohol.* London: HMSO, 1972.

Jessor, R., & Jessor, S. L. *Problem behavior and psychosocial development: A longitudinal study of youth.* New York: Academic Press, 1977.

Kraft, D. P. Strategies for reducing drinking problems among youth: College programs. In H. T. Blane & M. E. Chafetz (Eds.), *Youth, alcohol and social policy.* New York: Plenum Press, 1979.

Kraft, D. P., Duston, E., & Mellor, E. T. *Alcohol education programming at the University of Massachusetts and evaluation of results to date.* Amherst: University of Massachusetts Demonstration Alcohol Education Project, 1977.

Leifer, A. D., & Roberts, D. F. Children's responses to television violence. In J. P. Murray, E. A. Rubinstein & G. A. Comstock (Eds.), *Television and social behavior* (Vol. 2): *Television and social learning.* Washington, D.C.: U.S. Government Printing Office, 1972.

Liebert, R. M., & Poulos, R. W. Television as a moral teacher. In T. Lickona (Ed.), *Man and morality: Theory, research, and social issues.* New York: Holt, 1974.

Liebert, R. M., & Schwartzenberg, N. S. Effects of mass media. *Annual Review of Psychology,* 1977, *28,* 141–173.

Logan, A. B. Alcohol abuse: Overloading the American justice system. In *Alcohol and Drug Problems Association of North America.* Proceedings of the twenty-ninth annual meeting, Seattle, Washington, Washington, D.C., September 24–28, 1978.

Mäkelä, K. Criminalization and punishment in the prevention of alcohol problems. In R. Room & S. Sheffield (Eds.), *The prevention of alcohol problems: Report of a conference.* Sacramento, Calif.: Office of Alcoholism, Health, and Welfare Agency, State of California, 1974.

Marlatt, G. A., Pagano, R. R., Rose, R. M., & Marques, J. K. *The effects of meditation upon alcohol consumption in male social drinkers.* Unpublished research, University of Washington, 1976.

Medicine in the Public Interest, Inc. *The effects of alcoholic beverage control laws.* Washington, D.C.: MIPI, 1979.

Milgram, G. A. A historical review of alcohol education: Research and comments. *Journal of Alcohol and Drug Education,* 1976, *2,* 1–16.

Miller, P. M. Behavioral strategies for reducing drinking behavior. In H. T. Blane & M. E. Chafetz (Eds.), *Youth, alcohol, and social policy.* New York: Plenum Press, 1979.

Miller, W. R. Behavioral treatment of problem drinkers: A comparative outcome study of three controlled drinking therapies. *Journal of Consulting and Clinical Psychology,* 1978, *46,* 74–86.

Minnesota Department of Public Safety Study Shows Drunk Drivers Often Have Alcohol Problems. *Traffic Safety,* 1979, *79,* 19.

Mischel, W. *Introduction to personality,* New York: Holt, 1971.

Mosher, J. F., & Wallack, L. M. Proposed reforms in the regulation of alcoholic beverage advertising. *Contemporary Drug Problems,* 1979, *8,* 87–106. (a)

Mosher, J. F., & Wallack, L. M. The DUI project: *Description of an experimental program conducted by the California Department of Alcoholic Beverage Control.* Sacramento, Calif.: California Department of Alcoholic Beverage Control, June 1979. (b)

Nimmer, R. T. *Two million unnecessary arrests: Removing a social service concern from the criminal justice system.* Chicago: American Bar Foundation, 1971.

Nirenberg, T. D., Miller, P. M., & McClure, G. *Comparative efficacy of alcohol abuse prevention strategies.* Research in progress at Georgia Southern College, 1981.

Ornstein, S. I. Control of alcohol consumption through price increases. *Journal of Studies on Alcohol,* 1980, *41,* 807–817.

Parker, D. A., & Harman, M. S. The distribution of consumption model of prevention of alcohol problems: A critical assessment. *Journal of Studies on Alcohol,* 1978, *39,* 377–399.

Pittman, D., & Handy, W. Patterns in criminal aggravated assault. *Journal of Criminal Law and Criminal Police Science* 1964, *55,* 462–470.

Popham, R. E., Schmidt, W., & De Lint, J. The effects of legal restraint on drinking. In B. Kissin & H. Begleiter (Eds.), *The biology of alcoholism* (Vol. 4). New York: Plenum Press, 1976.

Room, R., & Mosher, J. F. Out of the shadow of treatment: A role of regulatory agencies in the prevention of alcohol problems. *Alcohol Health and Research World,* 1979, *4,* 11–17.

Schmidt, W. Cirrhosis and alcohol consumption: An epidemiological perspective. In G. Edwards & M. Grant (Eds.), *Alcoholism: New knowledge and new responses.* London: Croom Hall, 1977.

Schmidt, W., & Popham, R. E. The single distribution theory of alcohol consumption: A rejoinder to the critique of Parker and Harman. *Journal of Studies on Alcohol,* 1978, *39,* 400–419.

Selzer, M. L. Alcoholism, mental illness and stress in 96 drivers causing fatal accidents. *Behavioral Science,* 1969, *14,* 1–10.

Shupe, L. M. Alcohol and crime. *Journal of Criminal Law and Criminal Police Science* 1954, *44,* 661–664.

Somers, A. R. Violence, television and the health of American youth. *The New England Journal of Medicine,* 1976, *294,* 811–817.

Sprafkin, J. N., Liebert, R. M., & Poulos, R. W. Effects of a prosocial televised example on children's helping. *Journal of Experimental Child Psychology,* 1975, *3,* 248–254.

Staulcup, H., Kenward, K., & Frigo, D. A review of federal primary alcoholism prevention projects. *Journal of Studies on Alcohol,* 1979, *11,* 943–968.

Stein, G. M., & Bryan, J. H. The effect of a television model upon rule adoption behavior of children. *Child Development,* 1972, *43,* 268–273.

Surgeon General's Scientific Advisory Committee on Television and Social Behavior. *Television and growing up: The impact of televised violence.* Report to the Surgeon General, United States Public Health Service. Washington, D.C.: U.S. Government Printing Office, 1972.

U.S. Department of Health, Education, and Welfare. *Second Special Report to the U.S. Congress on Alcohol and Health.* DHEW Publ. No. HSM 72-9099. Washington, D.C.: U.S. Government Printing Office, 1974.

U.S. Department of Health, Education, and Welfare. *Third Special Report to the U.S. Congress on Alcohol and Health.* DHEW Publ. No. (ADM) 79-832. Washington, D.C.: U.S. Government Printing Office, 1978.

Van Natta, R. E. (Untitled). In J. W. Swinehart & A. C. Grimm (Eds.), *Public information programs on alcohol and highway safety.* Ann Arbor, Mich.: University of Michigan Highway Safety Research Institute, 1972.

Whitehead, P. C. *Alcohol and young drivers: Impact and implications of lowering the drinking age.* Department of National Health and Welfare, Monograph Series No. 1, Ottawa, 1977.

Williams, A. F., DiCicco, L. M., & Unterberger, M. Philosophy and evaluation of an alcohol education program. *Quarterly Journal of Studies on Alcohol,* 1968, *29,* 685-702.

Williams, A. F., Rich, R. F., Zador, P. L., & Robertson, L. S. *The legal minimum drinking age and fatal motor vehicle crashes.* Washington, D.C.: Insurance Institute for Highway Safety, 1974.

Yoakum, C. Many states reconsidering lowered drinking-age laws. *Traffic Safety* 1979, *79,* 24-28.

Zucker, R. A., & Barron, F. H. Parental behaviors associated with problem drinking and antisocial behavior among adolescent males. In M. E. Chafetz (Ed.), *Research on alcoholism I: Clinical problems and special populations.* Washington, D.C.: U.S. Government Printing Office, 1973.

Index